FREE WITH NEW COPIES OF THIS TEXTBOOK*

Scratch here for access code

Scratch here for access code

Start using myBusinessCourse Today: www.mybusinesscourse.com

myBusinessCourse is a web-based learning and assessment program intended to complement your textbook and faculty instruction.

Student Benefits

- **eLectures**: These videos review the key concepts of each Learning Objective in each chapter.
- **Guided examples**: These videos provide step-by-step solutions for select problems in each chapter.
- **Auto-graded assignments**: Provide students with immediate feedback on select assignments. **(with Instructor-Led course ONLY)**.
- **Quiz and Exam preparation**: myBusinessCourse provides students with additional practice and exam preparation materials to help students achieve better grades and content mastery.

You can access myBusinessCourse 24/7 from any web-enabled device, including iPads, smartphones, laptops, and tablets.

Interactive content that runs on any device.

Built for PCs, iPads, Laptops, Tablets, Smartphones

*****Each access code is good for one use only.** If the textbook is used for more than one course or term, students will have to purchase additional myBusinessCourse access codes. In addition, students who repeat a course for any reason will have to purchase a new access code. If you purchased a used book and the protective coating that covers the access code has been removed, your code may be invalid.

Access to myBusinessCourse is free ONLY with the purchase of a new textbook.

Computerized Accounting with
QuickBooks® Online
2023 Update

GAYLE WILLIAMS
Sacramento City College (Retired)

JENNIFER JOHNSON
The University of Texas at Dallas

Cambridge
BUSINESS PUBLISHERS

To my son, Marcus, who has inspired me and encouraged me and remains my biggest fan.
—Gayle Williams

To my husband, Brad, who helps me stay balanced.
—Jennifer Johnson

Photo Credit
Cover: © shutterstock

Cambridge Business Publishers

COMPUTERIZED ACCOUNTING WITH QUICKBOOKS ONLINE 2023 Update, by Gayle Williams and Jennifer Johnson

ISBN 978-1-61853-574-0

Bookstores & Faculty: to order this book, contact the company via email customerservice@cambridgepub.com or call 800-619-6473.

Students: to order this book, please visit the book's website and order directly online.

Printed in Canada.
10 9 8 7 6 5 4 3 2 1

About the Authors

Gayle Williams is a retired Professor of Accounting at Sacramento City College, where she still occasionally teaches accounting courses. She received a BA in Comparative Literature and an MBA with a concentration in Accounting from the University of Washington. Professor Williams, licensed as a CPA in Washington and California, was an audit partner in a CPA firm in Washington, the CFO for a national computer leasing company, and the financial manager for the Public Performing Arts department at the University of Washington.

Jennifer Johnson is Associate Professor of Instruction at the University of Texas at Dallas, where she teaches accounting information systems courses and related software courses, cost accounting, and seminars in Excel. She is a CPA licensed in the state of Texas. In 2020, she received the Outstanding Undergraduate Teaching Award—Jindal School. In 2017 she was named as an Outstanding Accounting Educator by the Texas Society of CPAs. Prior to joining UT Dallas in 2009, Professor Johnson spent time in both public accounting and industry as an auditor with PwC, an Assistant Controller at a regional financial services firm, and a Finance Manager at Dr Pepper Snapple Group. Professor Johnson holds both a BBA and MS in Accounting from Texas A&M University, is a Certified QuickBooks User, and is on the Board of Directors for the Dallas CPA Society and the Texas Society of CPAs. Professor Johnson has a passion for using systems and accounting to communicate the language of business.

Preface

Welcome to *Computerized Accounting with QuickBooks Online*. We wrote this book to give students an introduction to QuickBooks Online that focuses not only on the software mechanics, but also on the basic accounting concepts that underlie all accounting systems.

This book is not meant to be a user manual. It is our intention that students will come away from this book with an understanding that it is their knowledge of the principles of accounting, not their data-entry skills, that will contribute the most to their success in business.

TARGET AUDIENCE

This book is primarily intended for use in undergraduate accounting programs, although it could be used in business or computer information programs as well. It is expected that students taking this course have already successfully completed a course in financial accounting and have a firm understanding of the basic principles of accounting.

ACCESS TO QUICKBOOKS ONLINE PLUS

Intuit, the developer of QuickBooks Online Plus, provides students with a free one-year software subscription. Students should refer to the insert at the front of the book, which contains instructions on obtaining their software license and accessing the complimentary cloud-based software. With QuickBooks Online, students use their Internet browser to use the software—no installation required—and it can be used on any device with Internet access. Browsers supported by Intuit are: Google Chrome, Mozilla Firefox, Microsoft Edge, Safari, Opera, or Samsung. (A high-speed Internet connection is recommended, such as DSL or cable modem. For more information go to https://quickbooks.intuit.com/learn-support/en-us/help-article/product-system-requirements/system-requirements-quickbooks-online-accountant/L3nbfnOxn_US_en_US.)

NEW TO THIS EDITION

- **Road Maps** (reference tables identifying page numbers, practice exercises, and videos associated with each learning objective) have been added to the first page of each chapter.

- The test bank of questions related to the Accounting Refresher module has been expanded.

- PowerPoint presentations have been revised to work with the Chapter Outlines available to instructors.

- Coverage of artificial intelligence has been expanded in Chapter 13.

- Math Revealed! and Salish Software Solutions homework companies have both been updated with new transaction dates. Math Revealed! has also been updated with new transaction amounts.

- The book has been updated for changes to QBO software.

- A second set of midterm and final exams have been added.

OUTSTANDING FEATURES OF THIS BOOK

Structure

The book is designed in such a way that the accounting concepts, as well as the software mechanics, get more complex with each section. Other books focus primarily on software data entry. This book allows the students to see why events are recorded the way they are in a computerized accounting system while refreshing students' knowledge of accounting concepts and reinforcing the accounting and journal entries behind transactions.

- *Section One—Introduction*
    - Chapter 1 introduces students to the basic structure of QuickBooks Online Plus (QBO).
    - Chapter 2 covers the process of creating company files in QBO. Students create their homework company file in the chapter assignment.

- *Section Two—Service Companies*
    - The section introduction includes suggestions for finding errors in QBO.
    - Chapters 3, 4, and 5 cover basic transactions in the sales, purchase, and end-of-month cycles of a service company.

- *Section Three—Merchandising Companies*
    - The section introduction includes a description of internal controls in QBO.
    - Chapters 6, 7, and 8 cover more advanced transactions including those found in the sales, purchase, and end-of-month cycles of a merchandising company.

- *Section Four—Beyond the Basics*
    - Chapter 9 covers budgeting, segment reporting, and automated entries.
    - Chapter 10 covers tracking and billing for time and expenses.
    - Chapter 11 covers a number of special tools in QBO such as saving customized reports, customizing forms, managing attachments, exporting to Excel, and uploading receipts.

- *Section Five—Paying Employees*
    - Chapter 12 covers basic payroll functions.

- *Section Six—Artificial Technologies, Data Analysis, and QBO*
    - Chapter 13 covers big data, artificial intelligence, cognitive technologies, and QBO.
    - Chapter 14 covers data analysis and data visualization.

Clear Writing

The book is written clearly to aid student understanding of difficult concepts. Clear explanations of why certain procedures are used in QBO are supported by relevant examples and relatable end-of-chapter assignments, serving to bridge the gap between computerized accounting concepts and real-world application.

Real-World Scenarios

Most computerized accounting textbooks on the market approach the teaching of QuickBooks in a prescriptive manner, going through the procedures of the software while overlooking how an accountant would actually utilize the software in the real world. The book takes a practical approach and shows the student how the software is used in a business environment. In addition to the standard financial reports, students are exposed to job, segment, and variance reports.

Unique Pedagogy

The book's four-color format facilitates student understanding and draws attention to the key concepts and pedagogy. Ample screenshots provide students realistic snapshots of what they will see when working in the software. A host of pedagogical elements serve as helpful illustrations, providing additional context and further concept reinforcement.

HINT Boxes

HINT boxes appear throughout to provide helpful quick tips and tricks for working more efficiently in QBO.

> **HINT:** If a company has a lot of walk-in customers and it doesn't want to track each cash customer's name, it can set up a "Cash Customer" or "Walk-in" customer. Click **+ Add new** in the **Choose a customer** dropdown menu, enter a descriptive term in the **Company name** and **Customer display name** fields, and click **Save**. The name will appear in the customer list, but no additional detail will need to be added to the customer record unless any sales at the location are subject to sales tax. In that case, the physical address of the business would need to be added.

WARNING Boxes

WARNING boxes highlight common technical pitfalls to avoid.

> **WARNING:** Do not select **Finish Now** in the dropdown menu if you haven't finished the reconciliation (the **difference** isn't zero). QBO will give you a warning if you try but if you persist, it will allow you to "reconcile" without actually reconciling. That would leave what my former accounting professors would call a "dangling" credit or debit. Of course QBO won't actually allow you to create an unbalanced transaction so it will either debit (or credit) an account called **Reconciliation Discrepancies** for the **Difference** amount. You'd then have to fix that later.

BEHIND THE SCENES Boxes

BEHIND THE SCENES boxes provide additional context in support of the accounting that is going on inside the computer.

> **BEHIND THE SCENES** QuickBooks Online uses the original check date to record a voided check. This can create problems if financial reports have already been distributed for that accounting period. For example, let's say a $100 check was written in December to pay for some travel expenses. In the December income statement, net income would, of course, be decreased by the $100 travel expense. Now let's say that the $100 check was lost so a new check was issued and the original check was voided in QBO in February. The replacement check would have a February date, but the original check would be voided by QBO as of the original December check date. If you then prepared a new December income statement, net income would automatically be $100 higher than it was before due to the voided check. On the other hand, February's net income would be reduced by the $100 December travel expense. The expense is now reported in the wrong **accounting period**. If the amounts are significant or if tax reports have already been filed, journal entries should be made to correct the balances.

QuickChecks

When students are learning accounting application software, it's natural for them to focus on the software mechanics and forget that they're taking an accounting course. To help put some of their focus back on accounting, students are periodically asked a question related to material covered in the chapter. The questions are intended to remind them, either directly or indirectly, of underlying accounting concepts. The answers are included at the end of each chapter.

Why aren't purchase orders and estimates accounting transactions? (Answer at end of chapter.)	**Quick**Check **1-2**

Key Terms

Appearing in red, bold font in the first instance, key terms are defined for the student in the margins of the text for a quick refresher. A comprehensive glossary is included in the back of the book.

Recording Uncollectible Accounts

Unfortunately, companies don't always collect the balances owed to them by their customers. Merchandisers will often try to get the product back when the customer defaults, but, depending on the type and value of the products sold, that may not be feasible or even possible.

eLecture

If the company has exhausted all reasonable collection methods, the invoice must be written off. Deleting or voiding the invoice in QBO would not be good accounting. The company did make the sale and should show the revenue. They should also report that uncollectible sales (recorded as **bad debt expenses**) are a real cost of selling on credit.

There are two methods for accounting for uncollectible accounts: the **allowance method** and the **direct write-off method**. Only the allowance method is acceptable under generally accepted accounting principles.

Allowance Method Refresher

Under the allowance method, an estimate of the amount of uncollectible receivables is made at the end of an accounting period. The initial entry to establish an allowance for those amounts is:

	Bad debt expense		
	Allowance for bad debts		

Bad debt expense The expense stemming from the inability of a business to collect an amount previously recorded as receivable. It is normally classified as a selling or administrative expense.

Allowance method An accounting procedure whereby the amount of bad debts expense is estimated and recorded in the period in which the related credit sales occur.

Direct write-off method An accounting procedure whereby the amount of bad debts expense is not recorded until specific uncollectible customer accounts are identified.

Practice Exercises

Practice Exercises are included at the end of sections in the first eleven chapters. The exercises provide students an immediate opportunity to practice the material they just learned and prepare them for completing the chapter assignments. The exercises use the QBO test drive company, a fictional company called Craig's Landscaping and Design set up by Intuit.

The Practice Exercises can be done in class, with the instructor, or can be done by the students, on their own, as part of the lab component of a face-to-face course or in online courses. Check figures are included with the exercises to reassure students that they are recording the transactions accurately.

In many Practice Exercises, students are asked to make a note of certain information visible on the screen. A related test bank is available if instructors want to check that students have completed the exercises.

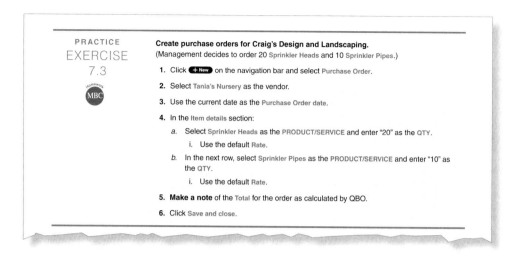

End-of-Chapter Material

End-of-chapter review material includes:

- Chapter shortcuts.
- Chapter review with **matching of terms** to definitions and **multiple-choice questions** related to chapter content.
- Essay questions focused on issues faced by accounting and information systems managers, related to chapter content.
- A choice of two end-of-chapter assignments featuring fictional companies that move from selling services exclusively in the early chapters to selling both services and products in the later chapters.

The assignments include transaction and end-of-assignment check numbers for students. This allows them to focus on the process and reduces student frustration.

Appendices

There are a number of additional topics that are helpful to students as they master QBO, and these have been included as end-of-chapter and end-of-book appendices. Instructors may wish to cover these topics in class or have students go over them on their own time. End-of-chapter appendices on special topics include:

Appendix	Title	Description
Appendix 1A	Customization of Certain Reports	Covers new report customization tools introduced by Intuit
Appendix 1B	Comparison of Old and New Account Setup Screens	Explains differences between old and new general ledger account setup process
Appendix 1C	Keyboard Shortcuts in QBO	Provides a list of keyboard shortcuts available in QBO
Appendix 2A	Which Accounts Get Debited and Credited When Lists Are Imported into QBO?	Explains the entries underlying imports of lists into QBO

(continued)

(continued from previous page)

Appendix	Title	Description
Appendix 2B	Setting Up a Google Gmail Account	Instructions for opening a separate Gmail account used in registering the student's company file
Appendix 4A	Reporting 1099 Vendor Activity	Covers 1099 setup and reporting tools available in QBO
Appendix 5A	Getting It Right	Suggestions to help students find errors in the month-end financial statements, mirroring what accountants in industry might look at before publishing financial statements
Appendix 5B	Understanding the Reconciliation Report	Provides a review of temporary and permanent differences and covers the sections in QBO's reconciliation report
Appendix 5C	Fixing Reconciliation Errors	Includes instructions for manually "undoing" a reconciliation
Appendix 7A	Identifying FIFO Layers in QBO	Covers FIFO valuation of inventory in QBO
Appendix 8A	Connecting QBO to Bank Accounts	Covers QBO features allowing the download of banking and credit card activity
Appendix 9A	Creating and Managing Tags	Covers new QBO transaction "tagging" feature
Appendix 10A	Working with Estimates	Covers creating and managing customer estimates

Students often have a difficult time seeing any similarities between computerized accounting systems and the more manual systems they saw in their introductory financial accounting classes (the journal entries, T-accounts, and general ledgers). To help students connect the two, **Appendix A (Is Computerized Accounting Really the Same as Manual Accounting?)** is an accounting refresher that compares manual and computerized accounting and provides examples of how journal entries, journals, T-accounts, and trial balances show up in QBO. It also covers cash versus accrual accounting.

Appendix	Title	Description
Appendix A	Is Computerized Accounting Really the Same as Manual Accounting?	Comparison of manual and computerized accounting
Appendix B	Account Types and Common Transaction Types Used in QBO	A summary of account types and transaction types in QuickBooks Online
Appendix C	Common Options Available on Various Forms	Common options available on various toolbars in QuickBooks Online

Certiport-Mapped

The book has been mapped to the five domains that comprise the exam objectives for the Intuit QuickBooks Online Certified User Exam. A map correlating the chapter content to the Certiport domains is available to students on the book's website so they can streamline their exam preparation. A practice exam question bank is included in myBusinessCourse.

What Is the Intuit QuickBooks Online Certified User Exam?

The Intuit® QuickBooks Online Certification exam is an online exam that is proctored at Certiport Authorized Testing Centers. The certification program validates QuickBooks Online accounting skills while providing students with credentials that demonstrate real-world abilities to prospective employers. Once passed, test takers receive an official digital certificate representing their skills in QuickBooks Online.

TECHNOLOGY THAT IMPROVES LEARNING AND COMPLEMENTS FACULTY INSTRUCTION

BusinessCourse is an online learning and assessment program intended to complement textbook and faculty instruction. Access to **myBusinessCourse** (MBC) is included with the purchase of a new textbook and can also be purchased separately.

MBC is ideal for faculty seeking opportunities to augment their course with an online component. MBC is also a turnkey solution for online courses. Following are some of the features of MBC.

Increase Student Readiness

95.5% of students who used MBC responded that MBC helped them learn accounting.*

- **Auto-graded question banks** comprised of practice exercises and assignment questions related to the end-of-chapter content provide immediate feedback to students. Assignments available in MBC are denoted by the (MBC).
- **Test Bank** questions can be incorporated into your assignments for additional quizzing and tests.
- **Instructor gradebook** with immediate grade results.
- **eLecture videos** created and narrated by the author provide extra coverage of essential topics and procedures (see the *For Students* section below for the full list of videos). eLecture videos available in MBC are denoted by the (eLecture).

Make Instruction Needs-Based

- Identify where your students are struggling and customize your instruction to address their needs.
- Gauge how your entire class or individual students are performing by viewing the easy-to-use gradebook.
- Ensure your students are getting the additional reinforcement and direction they need between class meetings.

Provide Instruction and Practice 24/7

- Assign homework from your textbook and have MBC grade it for you automatically. Assignments with the (MBC) logo in the margin are available in my BusinessCourse.
- With the author-created eLecture videos, your students can revisit accounting topics as often as they like or until they master the topic. Topics with the (eLecture) logo next to it in the margin are available as an eLecture video in myBusinessCourse.
- Offer students multiple homework attempts giving them valuable practice finding and fixing accounting errors.

Integrate with LMS

88.3% of students said they would encourage their professor to continue using MBC in future terms.*

BusinessCourse integrates with many learning management systems, including **Canvas**, **Blackboard**, **Moodle**, **D2L**, **Schoology**, and **Sakai**. Your gradebooks sync automatically.

Supplement Package

For Instructors

- **Solutions Manual** files prepared by the authors contain solutions to all the assignment material.
- **Test Bank** questions written by the authors include true/false, dropdown selection, drag and drop, matching, and multiple-choice questions. Test banks are available

---

*These statistics are based on the results of five surveys in which 4,195 students participated.

for homework assignments, practice exercises, chapter content, exams, end-of-chapter review, and certification practice.

- **Chapter Outlines** with student and instructor versions. Teaching notes included on instructor version.
- **PowerPoint** presentations that mirror the Chapter Outlines.
- **Extra credit** project suggestions including solutions. One business memo project, one "find and fix" project, and two financial analysis projects (one for each homework company).
- A **Midterm** and **Final Exam** are provided with solution files. The exams are designed to test students' understanding of the fundamentals of accounting and the mechanics of QBO. The exams can be completed in a two-hour class session using the test drive company available in QBO.
- **my BusinessCourse:** An online learning and assessment program intended to complement your textbook and classroom instruction (see previous section for more details). Access to myBusinessCourse is included with the purchase of a new textbook and can also be purchased separately. Detailed diagnostic tools assess class and individual performance. myBusinessCourse is ideal for online courses or traditional face-to-face courses for which you want to offer students more resources to succeed.
- **Teaching Tips** that include tools for helping students resolve common issues in QBO and instructions for dealing with QBO software changes.
- **Getting Started** videos and PDFs related to using the prebuilt course in myBusinessCourse and Intuit's Educator Portal.
- **Website:** All instructor materials are accessible via the book's website (password protected) along with other useful links and marketing information. www.mybusinesscourse.com.

For Students

- Access to QuickBooks Online software.
- **my BusinessCourse:** An online learning and assessment program intended to complement your textbook and faculty instruction (see previous section for more details). This easy-to-use program grades assignments automatically and provides you with additional help when your instructor is not available. Access is included with new copies of this textbook (look for the page containing the access code towards the front of the book).
- **Over 55 eLecture Presentations** created and narrated by the authors and available in myBusinessCourse cover essential topics and procedures in QuickBooks Online. Look for the ⬤ logo in the margins.

  - Moving Around in QuickBooks Online
  - Adding, Editing, and Deleting Accounts
  - Customizing QBO (multiple)
  - Setting Up Company Files
  - Setting Up Customers
  - Recording Sales Transactions (multiple)
  - Managing Sales Taxes
  - Managing Vendors
  - Recording Purchase Transactions (multiple)
  - Managing Employees
  - Recording Payroll Transactions
  - Tracking and Billing for Time in QBO (multiple)
  - Managing Product and Service Items (multiple)
  - Reconciling Bank and Credit Card Accounts (multiple)
  - Making Adjusting Journal Entries
  - Setting Up Recurring Transactions
  - Customizing Reports
  - Segment Tracking
  - Setting Up Budgets
  - Hints for Finding Errors (multiple)

- **Check Figures** are included for assignments, allowing students to focus on the process and reduce frustration.
- **Student Ancillaries** include spreadsheets uploaded as part of their homework company setup and tips for handling common issues in QBO and QBO software changes.
- **Accounting Refresher Module**, available in myBusinessCourse, includes review materials for basic accounting principles.

ACKNOWLEDGMENTS

We would like to thank the following people for their assistance and support.

Thank you also to the following accounting faculty from across the country who provided review feedback on the book:

Sara Adams	Jen Emerson	Mark Law
Dave Alldredge	Keith Engler	Theresa Laws-Dahl
Deepthi Amaradasa	Farima Fakoor	Gary Laycock
Kim Anderson	Thomas Francl	Miriam Lefkowitz
Richard Andrews	Rena Galloway	Heather Lynch
Ulises Arcos-Castrejon	Edie Gardner	Angela MacKenzi
Connie Augustine	Jessie George	DeAnna Martin
Felicia Baldwin	Yan Gibson	Kristy McAuliffe
Patricia Ball	Marianina Godinho	Molly McFadden-May
Sara Barritt	Patricia Goedl	Paul McLester
Erica Beam	Victoria Hall	Kristi Mendoza
Erick Bell	James Halstead	Karen Mills
Brenda Bindschatel	Margaret Hamza	Allen Montgomery
James Bird	Becky Hancock	Sheila Muller
Sean Bliley	Tracey Hartley	Arlene Murphy
Bryan Bouchard	Michelle Hayes	Carolyn Nelson
Jean Bradley	Merrily Hoffman	Brian Newman
Lisa Briggs	Janet Hosmer	Joseph Nicassio
Marilyn Brooks-Lewis	Zack Houk	Jeffrey Niccum
Regina Butts	Nancy Howard	Lisa Novak
Karlencia Calvin	James Human	Joanne Orabone
Amy Cesario	Neil S. Hwang	Denice Pardee
Amy Chataginer	Nelson Ildefonso	Tami Park
Jay Chittal	Paul Jaijairam	Paige Paulsen
Russell Ciokiewicz	Yan Jin	Lincoln Pinto
Howard Clampman	Bill Jefferson	Margaret Pond
Jay Cohen	Kathy Johnson	Abraham Posner
Renee Crawford	Ked Kederian	Mark Quinlan
Dana Cummings	Tynia Kessler	Kristen Quinn
Patricia Davis	Ethan Kinory	Carmen Quivran-Hazera
Wanda DeLeo	Angela Kirkendall	Michelle Randall
Tiffany DeLuze	Rebecca Kiser	Arwyna Randall-Gay
Suryakant Desai	Michael Klatchak	Napoleon Raymundo
Anne Diamond	Becky Knickel	Robin Reilly
Donna Dixon	Polly Knutson	Steven Rice
Candace Dobert	Harold Krul	Cecile Roberti
Doris Donovan	Christopher Kwak	Jennifer Robinson
Carol Dutchover	Scott Lail	Robert Rovegno
Pennie Eddy	Amber Lamadrid	Stephanie Anne Rowe

Dasha Russell   Stephanie Swaim   Vasseliki Vervilos
Joanne Salas   Jay Thibodeaux   Pamela Watkins
Perry Sellers   Ron Trucks   Kelly Williams
Vikram Sharma   Odemaris Valdivia   Lori Yecoshenko
Sherrie Slom   Christine VanNamee   Melissa Youngman
Dave Sobotka   Adria Vasquez   Ranae Ziwiski
Kortney Song

We would also like to thank George Werthman, Jocelyn Mousel, Karen Amundson, Nelson Connell, Cara Jacobsen, Lorraine Gleeson, Debbie McQuade, Terry McQuade, and everyone at Cambridge Business Publishers for their encouragement, guidance, and dedication to this book.

Finally, thank you to the instructors and students using this book.

Gayle Williams & Jennifer Johnson
May 2023

Brief Table of Contents

Contents

⑩ Project Tracking and Billing for Time and Expenses   *10-1*

⑪ Additional Tools   *11-1*

SECTION FIVE
Paying Employees   *12-1*

⑫ Payroll Activity   *12-3*

QuickBooks

SECTION ONE

Introduction

Before we go any further, let's be clear about two facts.

First, "computerized accounting" uses the same accounting principles and processes you're learning in your financial accounting courses.

- **Assets = Liabilities + Equity**.

- **Debits** are on the left; **credits** are on the right.

- Transactions are recorded through journal entries.

- Assets, liabilities, and equity accounts are reported on the balance sheet; revenue and expense accounts are reported on the income statement.

The advantage of using accounting software is that certain processes are automated, which makes the job of the accountant a little easier. For example, in QuickBooks Online (the software that you'll be using in this class), when you prepare an invoice for a customer:

- A journal entry will automatically be created,

- the entry will automatically be posted to the general ledger,

- and the balance sheet and income statement will automatically be adjusted to reflect the new account balances.

The second fact you should be clear about is this: A computer application only knows as much accounting as has been programmed into it. For example:

- QuickBooks Online (QBO) is programmed to know that an account that's been identified by the user as an asset should appear on the balance sheet. What QBO doesn't know is whether the account identified by the user as an asset IS actually an asset.

Assets The economic resources of a business that can be expressed in money terms.

Liabilities The obligations or debts that a business must pay in money or services at some time in the future as a consequence of past transactions or events.

Equity The residual interest in the assets of a business after all liabilities have been paid off; it is equal to a firm's net assets, or total assets less total liabilities.

Debit An entry on the left side (or in the debit column) of an account.

Credit An entry on the right side (or in the credit column) of an account.

- QuickBooks Online (QBO) is also programmed to know that a journal entry must balance (the sum of the debits must equal the sum of the credits), and it will not save an unbalanced entry. However, it doesn't know whether the specific accounts you just debited and credited in an adjusting journal entry are the appropriate accounts.

It's important that you remember these two facts as you're going through this book. The software is not the accountant; you are. You are the one who ultimately controls the accuracy of the financial data. You are the one who is ultimately responsible for providing meaningful information to users of the financial reports.

SECTION OVERVIEW

Chapter 1 covers:

- The general organization of QBO
- Navigating QBO
- Management of general ledger accounts in QBO
- Reporting using QBO

Chapter 2 covers setting up and customizing QBO company files.

Introduction to QuickBooks Online (QBO)

Road Map

A LITTLE BACKGROUND

LO 1-1 Recognize the various versions of QuickBooks

There are many, many different accounting software applications available for purchase. They range in price from under $1,000 to well over $1,000,000. In this book, we're going to look at QuickBooks Online Plus, an application developed and marketed by Intuit, Inc.

Intuit creates accounting software solutions for consumers and professionals. Intuit first came out with desktop accounting software for small businesses (QuickBooks) in 1992. QuickBooks Pro, Premier, and Enterprise (more robust versions of the software), were released over the next 10 years.

 HINT: The software for desktop versions is loaded on to your computer (either downloaded from Intuit's website or loaded using a disk). QuickBooks Desktop company files can be networked but each user must have the software loaded on his or her computer.

In 2001, Intuit introduced QuickBooks Online. The software was completely rebuilt in 2013. There are currently four primary versions of QuickBooks Online.

Table 1.1

QuickBooks Online versions

Version	Basic Features	Number of Users Allowed
Simple Start	Users can: ✓ Bill customers ✓ Track income and expenses ✓ Download banking and credit card transactions ✓ Import receipts ✓ Run basic reports ✓ Send estimates ✓ Track sales tax ✓ Manage 1099 vendors	1
Essentials	Includes all the features of Simple Start. In addition, users can: ✓ Enter vendor bills for payment later ✓ Track time ✓ Limit access by user	3
Plus	Includes all the features of Essentials. In addition, users can: ✓ Create purchase orders ✓ Track inventory ✓ Track revenue and costs by project ✓ Create budgets ✓ Categorize income and expenses by class and/or location	5
Advanced	Includes all the features of Plus. In addition, users can: ✓ Perform business analytics with Excel ✓ Backup and restore data ✓ Receive premium technical support from Intuit	25

There is also a QuickBooks Online Accountant version that includes additional features for those users who are working with multiple clients and a Self Employed version for independent contractors. Payroll is an add-on feature available to users of any of the QuickBooks Online products.

QuickBooks Online is a cloud-based system. This means that the software and the accounting data of all customers is stored (hosted) on a web server by Intuit. Users can access the software from any computer with Internet access. Although Intuit does back up company data, backups are not currently accessible to users in versions other than QuickBooks Online Advanced.

There are a variety of apps developed by other companies that work with QuickBooks Online. Although we will not be using any apps in this course, those of you who are interested can check them out at https://apps.intuit.com.

QuickBooks Online is a subscription service. Users pay a monthly fee based on the version of QuickBooks Online being used. The annual cost of QuickBooks Online Plus (the software you will be using) is normally around $1,000 per year, not including payroll. Fortunately, Intuit provides a free one-year subscription to QuickBooks Online Plus to students. You will be using your subscription to complete your homework assignments. Directions for obtaining your subscription license and setting up your homework company are included in Chapter 2.

In this textbook, the terms QuickBooks Online and QBO are used interchangeably to refer to the QuickBooks Online Plus version you will be using.

QUICKBOOKS ONLINE

QBO is a powerful tool for small businesses.

- It is flexible (can be used by most small businesses).
- It is intuitive (easy to understand).
- It is accessible from any computer with an Internet connection.
- It is accessible (through the QBO mobile app) from most smartphones and tablets.

 HINT: Supported browsers for QBO include Google Chrome, Microsoft Edge, Mozilla Firefox, Safari, Opera, and Samsung.

- It is updated regularly and automatically.

As noted in the Section One Introduction, these are some of the things that QBO automatically knows:

- It knows that behind every transaction is a **journal entry** and that each journal entry must balance. You will not be allowed to save an unbalanced journal entry.
- It knows that accounts identified as assets, liabilities, or equity appear on the **balance sheet** and accounts identified as income or expense accounts appear on the profit and loss statement (QBO's name for the **income statement**).

These are some of the things that QBO **doesn't** automatically know (so make sure you DO know):

- It doesn't know whether the account you just set up as an asset really does represent a resource owned or controlled by the company that is expected to provide future benefit.
- It doesn't know whether the amounts on the invoice you just created represent income the company has already earned or income that will be earned in the future.
- It doesn't know whether there are salaries that employees have earned but haven't been paid for.
- Etc., etc.

Journal entry An entry of accounting information into a journal (a tabular record in which business transactions are analyzed in debit and credit terms and recorded in chronological order).

Balance sheet A financial statement showing a business's assets, liabilities, and stockholders' equity as of a specific date.

Income statement A financial statement reporting a business's sales revenue and expenses for a given period of time.

BEFORE WE GO ANY FURTHER

Writing about QBO is a little like trying to throw a dart at a moving target. By the time the book gets written, the software has changed! So, fair warning: The information and screenshots in this book are based on QuickBooks Online Plus as it existed at the beginning of 2023. There will likely be changes to the software during the class term. A feature might have changed or your screen might look different than a screenshot in the book. We will provide information and instructions as new features roll out. If you're using myBusinessCourse, updates will be accessible to you in Student Ancillaries. If you're not using myBusinessCourse or you don't see relevant information in Ancillaries, talk to your instructor.

 HINT: Some updates to QBO are released in batches so you may see changes before or after your classmates or instructor.

Continuous updating, of course, is one of the benefits of QBO. Corrections can be made and new features can be added without users needing to download and install a new release. Given the popularity of cloud computing, Intuit is choosing to put a great deal of energy into developing its online accounting software products and that benefits all users.

 HINT: There may be times when a particular feature in QBO cannot be activated or is not working as you expected. Issues are often resolved by:
1. Refreshing your browser.
2. Switching browsers.
3. Opening QBO in a private (incognito) window in your browser.
4. Clearing your cache.

WHERE TO GO FOR HELP

Although QBO is a very intuitive program, there are a lot of "places to go and things to see" and that can be intimidating. It's also easy to forget what was covered in a previous chapter. Most of the time, you'll be able to find the answer to a QBO question by using the index for this book. If you can't, here are some options:

- Use the Help feature in QBO.
  - Help is accessed by clicking the **Help** icon in the icon bar at the top of the screen.

Figure 1.1

Help icon

 Help

 WARNING: QBO changes often, and information on the internet (even from the QuickBooks Community) may be out-of-date. Make sure you check the date the information was created or updated.

- Check the Tips and Updates folder in the Student Ancillaries module of myBusinessCourse for information about recent changes to the software.
  - If you're not using myBusinessCourse, your instructor will provide you with the updates.

- Ask for help from your instructor, from a student assistant (if there is one), or from your fellow students (if they're willing and you're not taking a test!).

- If you have a technical (software) question (not an accounting question), email Intuit's student support team at Education@intuit.com.

PRACTICE

Throughout this textbook, you will practice the steps necessary to record transactions and use the various tools available in QBO using an imaginary company set up by Intuit to allow users to sample the software. The test drive company (sample company), Craig's Design and Landscaping Services, provides landscaping services for individuals and small businesses.

LO 1-2 Access the test drive version of QuickBooks Online

Practice Exercises using Craig's Design and Landscaping will be located at the end of each section. Read through each section **before** you attempt the exercises. The explanations and screenshots provided in each section are meant to help you complete the Practice Exercises and your assignments.

Some Practice Exercises will include an instruction to **make a note** of certain information. Your instructor may ask you questions about the Practice Exercises in graded quizzes so it's a good idea to have a notebook handy where you can write down this information.

> **!** **WARNING:** Whenever you close out of the test drive website (or whenever you're automatically logged out for lack of activity), <u>nothing you previously entered will be saved</u>. The next time you access the site, the Intuit-developed transactions will stay the same in name and amount, but the dates will most likely differ. The Practice Exercises have been developed with that in mind.
>
> To save yourself time and minimize frustration, complete each Practice Exercise in one study session. If you log off in the middle of a Practice Exercise, you will need to start the exercise over from the beginning when you return.

Your homework will be done in a separate company file. The homework company will be introduced in Chapter 2.

Accessing the Test Drive Company

To access the practice company file, enter https://qbo.intuit.com/redir/testdrive as the URL in your browser.

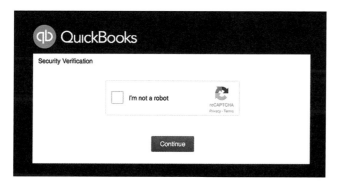

Figure 1.2

Security screen displayed when the test drive company is accessed

In the first screen, you'll be asked to check **I'm not a robot** before clicking **Continue**.

> **HINT:** You may get a message denying access because of privacy settings related to cookies. To enable cookies in Google Chrome, click **Settings** on the Chrome menu, select **Privacy and Security**, and click **Cookies and other site data**. If you don't want to allow all cookies, add the test drive URL in the **Sites that can always use cookies** section.
>
> Occasionally, QBO will ask you to identify pictures containing specific content (mountains, trains, etc.) after you've checked the **I'm not a robot** box. These are security measures so try to be patient.

The home screen (the **Dashboard** screen) will look something like Figure 1.3 when your identity as a human and not a robot has been confirmed!

Figure 1.3

The Dashboard (home page)

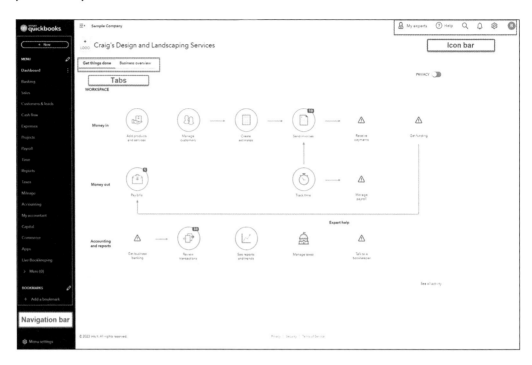

MOVING AROUND IN QUICKBOOKS ONLINE

LO 1-3 Identify and use the various access tools in QBO

You can access lists, forms, reports, and anything else you might need from a variety of locations in QBO.

Icon Bar

The icon bar is located at the top of the **Dashboard** screen.

Figure 1.4

The icon bar

Each icon on the icon bar has a purpose:

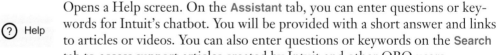

My Experts	Opens to a link for users looking to find an accounting professional or to add their accountant to their file.
Help	Opens a Help screen. On the **Assistant** tab, you can enter questions or keywords for Intuit's chatbot. You will be provided with a short answer and links to articles or videos. You can also enter questions or keywords on the **Search** tab to access support articles created by Intuit and other QBO users.
🔍	Opens to a search tool. Information about using the search tool is included in the **Finding transactions** section of this chapter.
🔔	Opens to notifications from Intuit related to software changes or upgrade offers. ■ A red dot next to the bell indicates a new notification.

Opens to a menu where company preferences can be set and other general operational tools can be accessed.

Opens to a sign out link. In your homework company, the first letter of your first name will appear here.

The icon you'll be accessing most often is the ⚙ icon.

The menu accessed through the ⚙ icon is shown in Figure 1.5:

YOUR COMPANY	LISTS	TOOLS	PROFILE
Account and settings	All lists	Order checks	Feedback
Manage users	Products and services	Import data	Privacy
Custom form styles	Recurring transactions	Import desktop data	
Chart of accounts	Attachments	Export data	
QuickBooks labs	Custom fields	Reconcile	
	Tags	Budgeting	
		Audit log	
		SmartLook	
		Resolution center	

You should be in Accountant view

You're viewing QuickBooks in **Accountant view**. Learn more   Switch to Business view

Figure 1.5

The gear icon menu

This menu is sometimes called the **Company** menu. The options here primarily relate to setting up and managing the overall structure of the company file.

> ✳ **HINT:** Intuit has been working on simplifying some of the terms and forms in QBO for non-accountant users. Those simplifications are included in the **Business view** version. All of the terms and screenshots in this book are from the **Accountant view.**

Navigation Bar

The navigation bar is located at the far left of the screen.

NOTE: Occasionally, Intuit changes the navigation bar. A new link may be added. An existing link may be removed. Sometimes the order or the terminology changes.

Stay flexible! You may need to click the links to find the feature you need.

Create menu

The button opens the following menu:

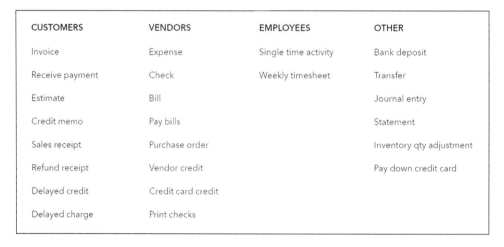

CUSTOMERS	VENDORS	EMPLOYEES	OTHER
Invoice	Expense	Single time activity	Bank deposit
Receive payment	Check	Weekly timesheet	Transfer
Estimate	Bill		Journal entry
Credit memo	Pay bills		Statement
Sales receipt	Purchase order		Inventory qty adjustment
Refund receipt	Vendor credit		Pay down credit card
Delayed credit	Credit card credit		
Delayed charge	Print checks		

This menu is sometimes referred to as the **Create** menu. All of the forms needed to record transactions in QBO can be accessed through this screen.

Dashboard

There are two tabs on the QBO **Dashboard**.

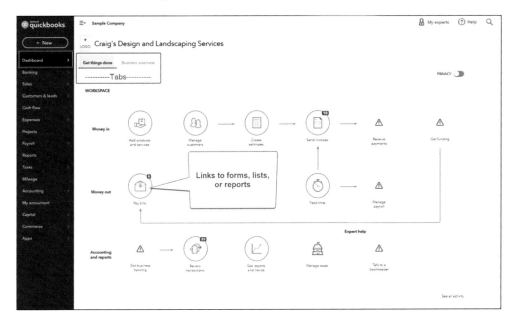

Figure 1.8

Getting things done tab
on the Dashboard

Shortcuts (links) to specific forms and lists are included on the **Get things done** tab shown in Figure 1.8.

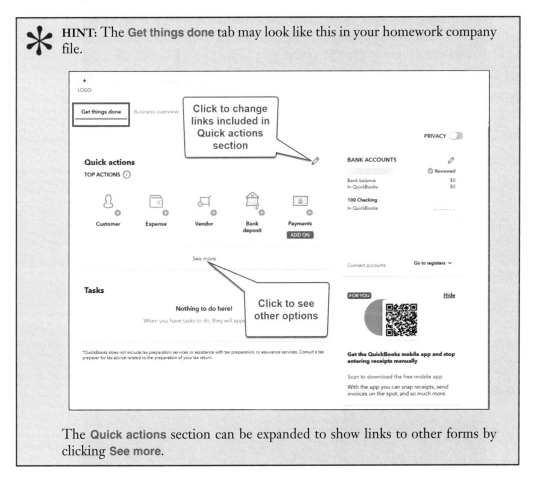

✱ **HINT:** The **Get things done** tab may look like this in your homework company file.

The **Quick actions** section can be expanded to show links to other forms by clicking **See more**.

Figure 1.9

Business overview tab
on the Dashboard

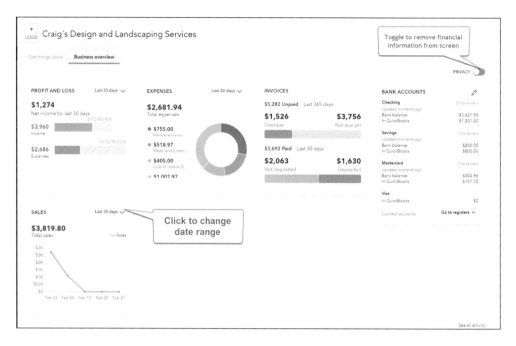

Financial information is included on the Business overview tab shown in Figure 1.9. The data is generally displayed graphically (charts and graphs). Clicking some, but not all, of the amounts allows you to drill down to more detail.

If users don't want financial information to be visible, they can toggle the Privacy button in the top right corner of the display area.

As discussed earlier, Intuit is constantly improving QBO in response to user needs and requests. The Dashboard page is one area that tends to change fairly frequently so if your screen doesn't look exactly like the screenshots above, don't be alarmed.

Other links in the navigation bar

There are subsections in most of the links on the navigation bar. The subsections (called drawers) are visible when you hover over a specific link. The drawers in the Expenses link are shown in Figure 1.10.

Figure 1.10

Drawers in the
Expense link on the
navigation bar

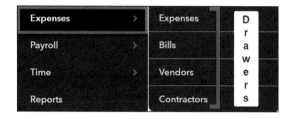

If you click a link on the navigation bar, drawers will appear as tabs on the display screen.

Figure 1.11

Tabs in Expenses

> ✳ **HINT:** In early 2023, Intuit tested a modified navigation bar. You may see that version in the test drive or your homework company. In the revised version, the navigation bar collapses when a link is clicked, and the **drawers** are displayed in a left panel.
>
> If **Banking** was clicked in the modified navigation bar, the left panel would look like this:
>
>
>
> To return to the main navigation bar, click anywhere in the **drawers** list and click **Dashboard**.

Table 1.2 summarizes some of the information and tools provided on screens opened from the **drawers** in navigation bar.

		Table 1.2
		Navigation bar screens

Link	Drawer/Tab	Overview
Banking		
	Banking	Where users who download (or upload) banking transactions directly into QBO can verify and accept those transactions.
	App transactions	Includes links to certain external applications that work with QBO. The Amazon Business App allows users to track purchases made on Amazon. Users can syn sales transactions from Square accounts on the Square App.
	Rules	Where users can specify accounts and names to be used with downloaded transactions that meet certain conditions.
	Tags	Where users can categorize information without using general ledger accounts or the various segment reporting features in QBO.
	Receipts	Where users can upload and manage vendor bills and receipts.
Sales		
	Overview	Includes links to activate features related to online customer payments and shortcut links to various sales forms.
	All Sales	Includes a list of all sales-related transactions: sales on account, cash sales, credit memos, and payments. Sales transactions can be created or edited using links on this screen.
	Invoices	Includes a list of invoices (sales on account) and their status (due, overdue, or paid). Invoices can be created or edited using links on this screen.
	Estimates	Includes list of all estimates and their status (pending, accepted, rejected, closed, or converted). Estimates can be created or edited on this screen.
	Payment links	Where the features for online customer payments can be set up.
	Customers	Includes a list of all customers. Customers can be added or edited using links on this screen.
	Products and services	Includes a list of all products held for sale and all services performed by the company. Products and services can be added or edited using links on this screen.

(continued)

(continued from previous page)

Link	Drawer/Tab	Overview
Customers & leads		
	Customers	Identical to the Customers drawer/tab in the Sales link.
	Marketing	Where users can sign up for Intuit's marketing platform (Mailchimp).
Cash flow		Where cash flow budgets can be created using receivable and payable information in the company file plus expected cash receipt and expenditure information added by users. Cash flow planning is not covered in this textbook.
Expenses		
	Expenses	Includes a list of all purchase-related transactions: checks, bill payments, vendor bills, etc. Purchase transactions can be created or edited using links on this screen.
	Bills	Includes a list of bills (purchases on account). Unpaid and paid invoices are listed on separate tabs. Transactions can be entered or edited using links on the screen.
	Vendors	Includes a list of all vendors. Vendors can be added or edited using links on this screen.
	Contractors	Includes a list of company's independent contractors. New contractors can be added using links on the screen.
Projects		Where customer projects (jobs) can be set up and managed. Link will only appear if project tracking is activated.
Payroll		
	Employees	Includes a list of all employees. Employees can be added or edited using links on this screen.
	Contractors	Includes a list of all independent contractors. Contractors can be added, and 1099 reporting features can be accessed using links on this screen.
	Workers' comp	The tab only appears in files for companies located in states that require employers to have workers' compensation insurance. Workers' comp will not be covered in this textbook.
Reports		
	Standard	Includes various reports developed by Intuit, by category.
	Custom reports	Includes reports customized by the user.
	Management reports	Includes report packages developed by Intuit.
Taxes	Sales tax	Includes information about sales taxes due and links to tax settings and sales tax reporting features.
	Payroll tax	The tab only appears if payroll has been activated.
	1099 filings	Where users can create, file, and deliver 1099 forms.
Mileage		Includes the QR code for downloading the QuickBooks Mobile App where employee or owner mileage can be tracked automatically and a link for tracking mileage manually. Mileage is not covered in this textbook.
Accounting		
	Chart of accounts	Includes a list of all general ledger accounts and links to each account register. Accounts can be added or edited using links on this screen.
	Reconcile	Includes access to the reconciliation feature in QBO.
My accountant		Includes a tool for providing administrative access to QBO files to outside accountants. Also where users can search for external accountants who have passed at least one of Intuit's QuickBooks proficiency exams.
Capital		Where users can get information about funding options offered by Intuit partners.
Commerce		Where users can get information about connecting sales channels (Shopify, Amazon, etc.) to QBO.
Apps		Where users can search for integrated apps and add-ons for QBO developed by Intuit and third-party vendors.

The navigation bar can be closed by clicking the triple lines at the far left edge of the icon bar, right above the navigation bar.

Figure 1.12

Tool to open or close the navigation bar.

Re-clicking the triple lines will reopen the navigation bar.

Customizing the navigation bar

In early 2023, QBO introduced a new navigation bar customization tool. If the tool is activated in your homework company file, you will be able to customize your navigation bar in two different ways:

● Add, delete, or change the order of links in the navigation **menu**

● Add, delete, or change the order of **bookmarks** (links to specific forms and pages)

Figure 1.13

Navigation bar
customization tool

To change the navigation bar links, click the pencil icon next to **MENU** on the navigation bar.

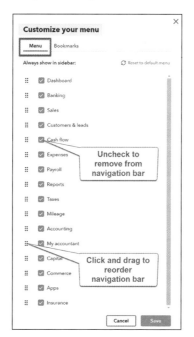

Figure 1.14

Menu customization
options

Uncheck the boxes next to links you do not want to be displayed.

To reorder the list, click and drag the item anywhere within the menu list.

The menu can be changed by clicking **More** or the pencil icon shown in Figure 1.13.

Bookmarks are links to specific forms or pages within QBO.

Click the pencil icon next to **BOOKMARKS** on the navigation bar shown in Figure 1.13 to add or change **bookmarks**.

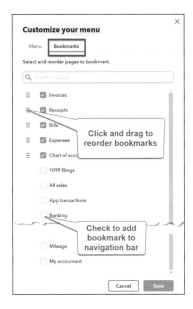

Check the boxes next to the forms or pages you want to add to the navigation bar. Click and drag to reorder the list.

Customizing the navigation bar is optional, of course. But as you progress through the homework, you may want to use the feature to streamline your workflow.

Multiple Open Screens

Most of the time, a user will only need one screen open at a time. Sometimes, though, it's convenient to have multiple screens open.

If you want to have a screen open in a new tab or in a new window, simply right-click a link and select the preferred option. You can right-click links in the ⊕ **New** or ⚙ menus or in the navigation bar.

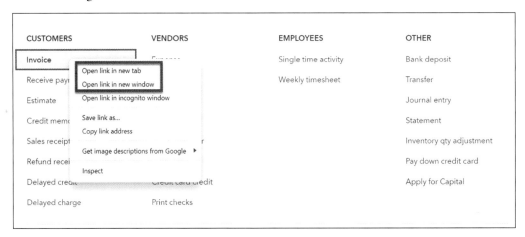

THE IMPORTANCE OF "LISTS"

QBO uses lists as part of the organizational structure of the software so it's important that you have a good understanding of the types and uses of the various lists.

LO 1-4 Explain the purpose of the various lists in QBO

Chart of Accounts List

The primary list in QBO is the **chart of accounts**. An **account type** and a **detail type** must be selected for each **account** used by an organization.

The **account type** chosen will determine:

- The financial statement on which an account will appear

- Where on that statement the account will be displayed

- Which QBO features are available for that account

QBO prepares **classified balance sheets** and **multi-step income statements**. There are lots of groupings and subtotals in those statements (as you might remember from your previous classes). To provide the necessary flexibility, QBO uses an expanded list of financial statement classifications and a set of **account types**. Here's a list of financial statement account classifications and the corresponding **account types** used by QBO:

Account A record of the additions, deductions, and balances of individual assets, liabilities, stockholders' equity, dividends, revenues, and expenses.

Classified balance sheet A balance sheet in which items are classified into subgroups to facilitate financial analysis and management decision making.

Financial Accounting Categories					
Assets		Liabilities		Equity	Revenues	Expenses

QBO Financial Statement Categories					
Banks	Assets	Credit Cards	Liabilities	Equity	Income	Expenses

QBO Account Types					
Bank accounts	Accounts Receivable Other Current Assets Fixed Assets Other Assets	Credit Cards	Accounts Payable Other Current Liabilities Long-Term Liabilities	Equity	Income Other Income	Cost of Goods Sold Expenses Other Expenses

You can have many different accounts with the same **account type** in your chart of accounts.

Here are some examples of the way **account type** determines placement in a financial statement: Let's say you are going to set up an account called Petty Cash. You would want to set the account up as type **Bank** so that it shows up at the top of the balance sheet along with any checking or savings accounts the company has. (Checking and savings accounts would also be set up with the **account type Bank**.) A Salaries Payable account would be set up as type **Other Current Liabilities**. That way it shows up on the balance sheet as a current liability along with accounts like Interest Payable and Payroll Taxes Payable.

Here are some examples of the way **account type** is associated with various features in QBO: If an account were set up as an **Accounts receivable (A/R)** type, you would be able to use that account when preparing customer invoices. You would also be able to pull an accounts receivable aging report for that account. You would not be able to do either of those things with an account set up as an **Other Current Assets** type. You will learn more about these features as you go through the textbook. For now, just be aware that selecting the appropriate **account type** is important for a variety of reasons.

Detail types are subsets of each **account type** and are used for tax reporting purposes. The options available for **account** and **detail types** are defined by QBO and cannot be modified. Although it should be easy for you to determine the correct **account type**, it can be difficult to find an appropriate **detail type**. If you don't find an exact match, select the available **detail type** that most closely matches the account you're setting up. In your homework, you will usually be given the appropriate **detail type**.

Multi-step income statement An income statement in which one or more intermediate performance measures, such as gross profit on sales, are derived before the continuing income is reported.

> **WARNING:** As you work through your homework assignments, you'll find that QBO occasionally adds an account to your chart of accounts without warning. This might happen if you add a new feature or if you initiate certain types of transactions. Make sure you closely follow the directions in your assignment to ensure that you're using the proper accounts.

Familiarize yourself with the chart of accounts used in Craig's Design and Landscaping.

1. Click Accounting in the navigation bar.

2. Open the Chart of accounts drawer (tab).

3. Click See your Chart of Accounts.

4. Find the Checking account information in the first row.

   a. **Make a note** of the amount listed in the QUICKBOOKS BALANCE column.

      i. Remember, **make a note** instructions may be used by your instructor in quizzes. It would be a good idea to keep a notebook handy.

   b. **Make a note** of the account type for the Checking account.

5. Looking in the TYPE column, scroll down to the first account with an Expenses account type. **TIP:** Don't click Type. (If you do, the list will re-sort.) Just scroll down.

   a. **Make a note** of the name of the account.

Instructions for adding and editing accounts are included in the **MANAGING THE CHART OF ACCOUNTS** section of this chapter.

Products and Services List

The Products and Services list contains sales and purchase information about every product sold and service provided by the organization. The individual items on the list are used when billing customers and when purchasing inventory in QBO.

The Products and Services list can be accessed by clicking the ⚙ on the icon bar (Figure 1.4).

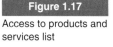

Figure 1.17

Access to products and services list

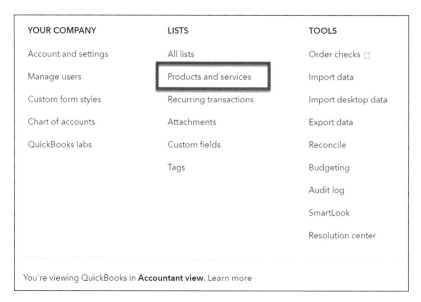

YOUR COMPANY	LISTS	TOOLS
Account and settings	All lists	Order checks
Manage users	Products and services	Import data
Custom form styles	Recurring transactions	Import desktop data
Chart of accounts	Attachments	Export data
QuickBooks labs	Custom fields	Reconcile
	Tags	Budgeting
		Audit log
		SmartLook
		Resolution center

You're viewing QuickBooks in **Accountant view**. Learn more

Click **Products and services** in the **Lists** column.

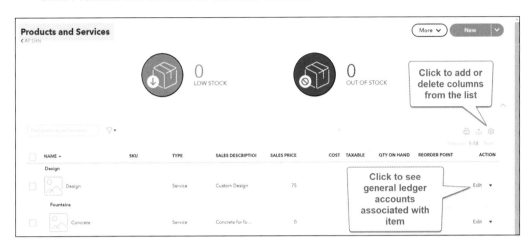

Figure 1.18

Products and services list

Columns displayed on the screen include default information about cost, price, and tax status for each product or service item. For **products**, quantity on hand is also displayed. Column settings can be changed by clicking the small above the **ACTION** column.

Click **Edit** in the **ACTION** column of each row to see the general ledger account(s) associated with the item.

Managing services items will be covered in Chapter 3, and products will be covered in Chapter 6.

Familiarize yourself with the products and services list in Craig's Design and Landscaping.

1. Click the ⚙ in the icon bar.

2. Click **Products and services**.

3. Scroll down to the **Pump** item.

   a. **Make a note** of the sales price.

   b. **Make a note** of the number of **pumps** on hand.

4. Scroll down to the **Gardening** item.

   a. Select **Edit** in the dropdown menu in the **ACTION** column.

   b. **Make a note** of the account selected in the **Income account** field.

PRACTICE EXERCISE 1.2

Homework MBC

Other Lists in QBO

There are lists of customers, vendors, and employees. There are also lists of options that might be used with customers or vendors. For example, there is a list of payment terms that can be used for entering credit terms offered to customers or entering credit terms set by vendors. These (and other) lists will be covered in detail in later chapters.

MANAGING THE CHART OF ACCOUNTS

A company can include up to 250 accounts in QBO Plus. To better organize the chart of accounts and improve the look of financial reports, users can create sub-accounts. There can be up to four levels of sub-accounts.

LO 1-5 Explain and demonstrate the QBO process for adding, editing, and inactivating general ledger accounts in QBO

eLecture

To open the chart of accounts, click the ⚙ on the icon bar.

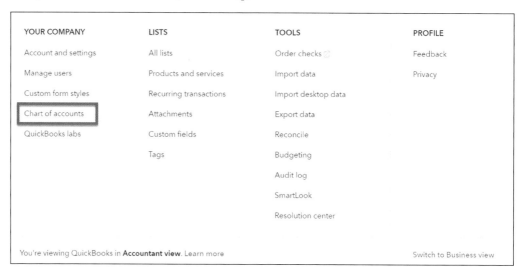

Click **Chart of Accounts**.

Click **See your Chart of Accounts**.

If account numbers are used, accounts will be listed in numeric order by **account type** in the chart of accounts. (Account numbers will be used in your homework company.) If account numbers aren't used, accounts will be listed alphabetically by **account type**.

HINT: The **Bank Balance** column displays the current bank (or credit card) balance for those users downloading transactions directly from financial institutions. You can ignore those balances.

Adding an Account

To add an account, click **New** in the account list window (Figure 1.22).

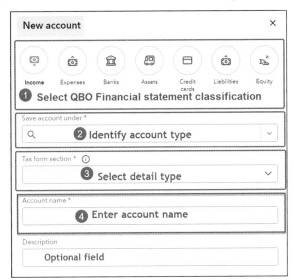

Figure 1.23

Account set up screen

Step 1—The appropriate QBO financial statement classification is selected first.

 HINT: Third-party bank and credit card accounts can be directly connected with QBO. For security purposes, they have their own financial statement categories.

Once the classification is selected, a **NEW ACCOUNT PREVIEW** section will appear in the panel. **All account types** in that classification will be displayed on the preview screen. The financial statement on which the account will appear will also be identified. For example, if **Assets** was selected as the QBO financial statement classification, the preview screen would look something like Figure 1.24.

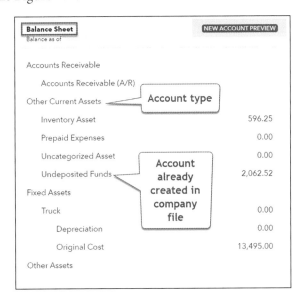

Figure 1.24

Example of the account preview screen

Step 2—The account type is identified next, in the Save account under field shown in Figure 1.23. The account type specified here will determine where the account appears on the financial statement and any available features. Available options in the dropdown menu will include all the QBO account types included in the financial statement classification selected, **plus** any accounts of that type that already exist in the chart of accounts. Sub-accounts are created by selecting an existing account in the Save account under field.

 HINT: Sub-accounts must have the same account type but can have different detail types. On financial statements, sub-accounts can be shown individually under the parent account, or all accounts can be summarized at the parent account level.

Step 3—Detail type is selected in the Tax form section field. The dropdown menu options vary based on the account type chosen in the Save account under field. For example, detail type options for accounts with a cost of goods sold account type are shown in Figure 1.25.

Figure 1.25

Example of detail type options

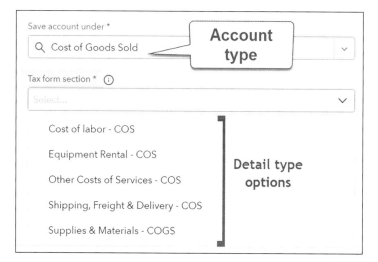

 HINT: Tax form section types (detail types) can be helpful when preparing a company's federal tax return, but they do not affect financial statement presentation and will not affect your homework. If you don't see a type that matches your account exactly, choose the most appropriate one.

Step 4—A name must be entered in the Account name field shown in Figure 1.23. An Account number field will be available if account numbers have been activated. Account numbers are not used in the test drive company but will be used in your homework company.

For new balance sheet accounts, Starting date and opening balance fields will appear below the Description field in Figure 1.23.

Figure 1.26

Opening balance options in new account setup

These fields can be used when users manually convert to QBO from another accounting system. You will NOT be entering opening balances utilizing this feature.

Your account will appear in the **NEW ACCOUNT PREVIEW** section as you enter data. The record for an account set up to track the cost of newspaper advertising, a sub-account of advertising, would look something like Figure 1.27.

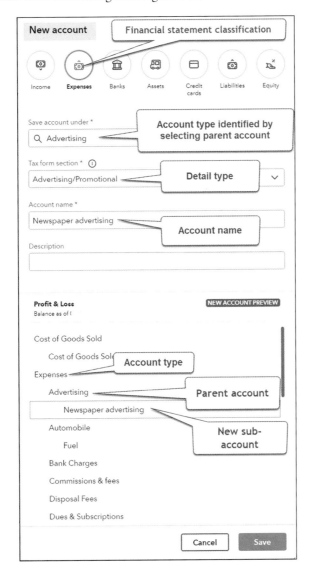

Figure 1.27

Example of a completed account record

Editing an Account

To edit an account in the chart of accounts list, open the dropdown menu in the **ACTION** column of the account you wish to edit.

Figure 1.28

Access to account editing

Click Edit to open the Account window.

You can change the account's name, number (if applicable), account type, or detail type. You can also make it a sub-account.

Inactivating an Account

Once created, an account cannot be deleted in QBO. It can, however, be inactivated.

To inactivate an account, follow the procedures listed above for editing an account but instead of clicking Edit, click Make inactive. (See Figure 1.28.)

If you click Make inactive on an account with activity, QBO will make the account inactive but the data is not deleted. An inactive account is not available in new transactions but the account would appear in any financial reports covering the period the account was used. Reactivating accounts is covered in Chapter 8.

Also in Chapter 8, we will cover how to manage accounts that are no longer useful but can't be deleted.

QuickCheck
1-1

> True or False? QBO will allow you to create an account with the name Salaries Payable with an Expenses account type. (Answer at end of chapter.)

PRACTICE
EXERCISE
1.3

Work with Craig's Design and Landscaping's chart of accounts.

(Craig needs an account to track interest payable and wants to change some existing accounts.)

1. Click ⚙ in the icon bar.

2. Click Chart of Accounts.

    a. If you get a screen that says "Take a peek under the hood," click See your Chart of Accounts.

3. To add a new account:

    a. Click New.

    b. Select Liabilities as the QBO financial statement classification.

    c. Interest payable is a liability due in less than 12 months, so select Other Current Liabilities as the account type in the Save account under field.

        i. **Make a note** of the number of existing accounts with an Other Current Liabilities account type.

    d. Select Other Current Liabilities as the detail type in the Tax form section field.

        i. No exact match exists, so "other" is the best choice.

    e. Enter Interest Payable as the Account name.

4. To edit an account:

    a. Select Edit in the ACTION column dropdown menu for the Travel Meals account.

    b. Change the Save account under field to Travel.

    c. Change the account name to "Hotel and meals."

    d. Click Yes if asked about changing types.

    e. Click Save.

(continued)

(continued from previous page)

5. To inactivate an account:

    a. Select Make inactive (won't reduce usage) in the ACTION column dropdown menu for Other Portfolio Income account.

    b. Click Yes when prompted.

6. **Make a note** of the number of sub-accounts under Legal & Professional Fees.

7. Click Dashboard to exit the chart of accounts list.

TRANSACTIONS IN QUICKBOOKS ONLINE

In a manual accounting system, the mechanics of accounting work something like this:

✓ Documentation (for transactions) is received from outside sources or prepared internally.

✓ Details from the documents are recorded in **journals**.

✓ Journal entries are posted (transferred) to the **general ledger** and, as appropriate, to **subsidiary ledgers**.

✓ A **trial balance** is prepared.

✓ Financial statements are prepared from the trial balance and subsidiary ledger reports are prepared from the subsidiary ledgers.

In QBO, the mechanics work like this:

✓ Certain documents (invoices and checks, for example) are prepared directly in QBO using specific forms.

✓ Documents received from outside sources (vendor invoices for example) are entered into QBO using other forms.

✓ That's all the user has to do (other than making those pesky adjusting journal entries!).

> **BEHIND THE SCENES** The journal entries related to transactions are automatically created by QBO and posted to the general ledger when the form is completed (saved). Subsidiary ledgers, trial balances, and financial statements are also automatically updated every time a transaction is entered.

There is a journal entry behind every completed form in QBO EXCEPT (there are always exceptions, right?):

● **Purchase orders** (not **accounting transactions**)

● **Estimates** (not accounting transactions)

● Timesheets

LO 1-6 Identify the various transaction types used to record transactions in QBO; Find and use search functions in QBO

Journal A tabular record in which business transactions are analyzed in debit and credit terms and recorded in chronological order.

General ledger An accounting record with enough flexibility so that any type of business transaction may be recorded in it; a diary of a business's accounting transactions.

Subsidiary ledger A ledger that provides detailed information about an account balance.

Trial balance A list of the account titles in the general ledger, their respective debit or credit balances, and the totals of the debit and credit balances.

Accounting transaction An economic event that requires accounting recognition; an event that effects any of the elements of the accounting equation—assets, liabilities, or stockholders' equity.

- Delayed charges and delayed credits
  - These transactions are unique to QBO and are covered in Chapter 6.

> **BEHIND THE SCENES** Timesheets are, strictly speaking, accounting transactions. (A liability is created as soon as employees work.) Wages are only recorded in QBO, however, when payroll checks are created or when general journal entries are made by the user to recognize earned but unpaid salaries.

QuickCheck
1-2

> Why aren't purchase orders and estimates accounting transactions? (Answer at end of chapter.)

Forms

Every transaction is recorded on a specific "form" in QBO.

> **WARNING:** In early 2023, Intuit started updating various QBO forms. Some of those forms may have been updated after your textbook was printed.
>
> If you see a form that doesn't match the screenshot in your book, start by looking for an option to return to a previous version. In most cases, you'll see a link that looks like one of the following:
>
> ⤢ Old layout   Switch to classic view
>
> If there is no link available, check the Student Ancillaries page in myBusiness-Course for information about the updated form or ask your instructor.

To open the **check** form, click ⊕ New on the navigation bar. The transaction menu will appear.

Figure 1.29

Access to the Check form

CUSTOMERS	VENDORS	EMPLOYEES	OTHER
Invoice	Expense	Single time activity	Bank deposit
Receive payment	Check	Weekly timesheet	Transfer
Estimate	Bill		Journal entry
Credit memo	Pay bills		Statement
Sales receipt	Purchase order		Inventory qty adjustment
Refund receipt	Vendor credit		Pay down credit card
Delayed credit	Credit card credit		
Delayed charge	Print checks		

Click **Check.** You are now in a new window.

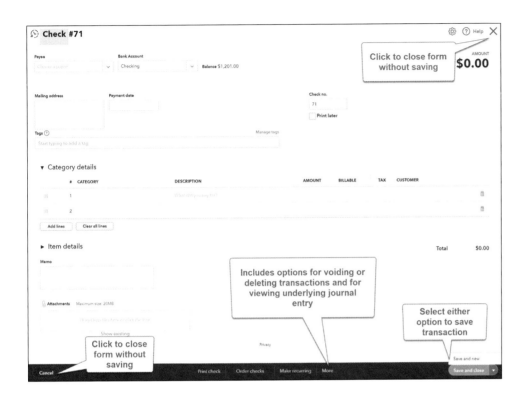

Figure 1.30

Check form

All information needed to create a journal entry and update any subsidiary ledgers is entered on the form.

All transaction forms will have a **Save and close** or **Save and new** button that is used to save the transaction and automatically exit the window. (In Figure 1.30 the dropdown menu has been opened so that both options are displayed.) If you want to close the form without saving, simply click the **X** at the top right of the window or the **Cancel** button in the lower left corner. Other **Save** options are available on some of the sales and purchase forms.

Options for voiding or deleting transactions, and reviewing underlying journal entries, for example, are available in the **More** dropdown menu in the black bar at the bottom of each saved form. The specific options available will depend on the type of transaction.

All transaction forms are accessible through the **Create** menu shown in Figure 1.29. Many of the forms are also accessible through other links in the navigation bar. The various alternatives will be covered in future chapters.

Transaction Types

Each form is identified as a specific **transaction type** in QBO. Knowing the various types allows you to easily find transactions or modify reports.

There are many **transaction types**. Here are a **few** of them (see Appendix B for a list of other types):

- **Sales receipt** (cash sales)
- **Invoice** (sales on account)
- **Payment** (collections from customer for sales on account)
- **Check** (payments by check NOT including payments on account or payroll checks)
- **Bill** (purchases from vendors on account)
- **Bill payment (Check)** (payments by check to vendors for purchases on account)
- **Journal entry** (adjusting entries)

Transaction type names in QBO are **very** specific.

In business, we might "bill" a customer OR we might receive a "bill" from a vendor. In QBO, we invoice customers for amounts we will be collecting later, and we record bills from vendors that we will be paying later. You cannot enter a sale to a customer, on account, using a bill.

In business, we write "checks" to pay for something on the spot. We write "checks" to pay the phone bill we recorded in the general ledger last month. We also write "checks" to pay our employees. In QBO there are three different transaction types for those activities. Check is the transaction type used when we pay for something on the spot. Checks written to vendors to pay account balances are bill payment transaction types. Paycheck is the transaction type for employee payroll checks.

> **BEHIND THE SCENES** You will be using various sales and purchase forms to enter transactions in QBO. You **could** enter these transactions as journal entries. However, it's important to use the appropriate form for a number of reasons.
> 1. Forms (transaction types) are connected to subsidiary ledgers in QBO. Not all ledgers can be updated using journal entries.
> 2. Companies often need to provide documentation to customers and vendors. QBO forms can be printed out or emailed.

Finding Transactions

You can find transactions and details about transactions in QBO in various ways:

- You can "drill down" (double-click) on a specific transaction in a report to see the transaction details.

- You can re-sort lists by name, amount, date, or account by clicking the title of the column you want to use as the sort criterion.

- You can find recent same-type transactions using the clock icon that appears in the top left corner of certain forms.

Figure 1.31

Clock icon

For example, if you opened a check form in QBO and clicked the clock icon, you would see the most recent check transactions:

Figure 1.32

Recent transactions displayed using the clock icon

- You can use the Search feature to look for transactions using one or more filters.

The Search tool has the most flexibility.

Figure 1.33

Icon bar access to
search feature

The **Search** tool is accessed by clicking the **magnifying glass** in the icon bar.

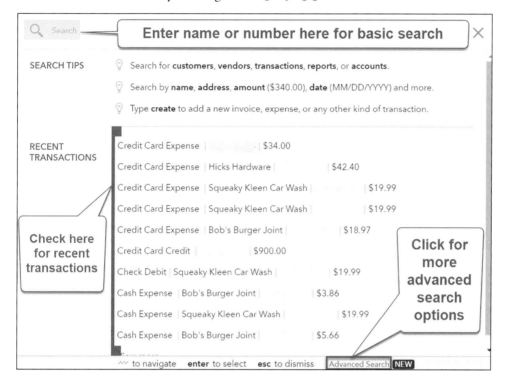

Figure 1.34

Basic search window

In the search bar at the top of the screen, you can enter a single detail about a transaction. Press **Enter** on your keyboard to open the form that matches your search.

Clicking **Advanced Search** under the list of recent transactions opens a new window:

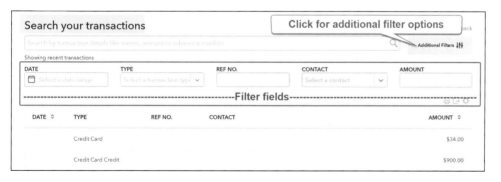

Figure 1.35

Filter fields in advanced
search

In the advanced screen, you can narrow the search using one or more filter fields. Field options include:

- **DATE** (single date or range of dates)
- **TYPE** (specific **transaction type**)
- **REF NO.** (form number, e.g., check number or invoice number)
- **CONTACT** (customer, vendor, or employee name)
- **AMOUNT** (specific dollar amount)

Filters by item (**product** or **service**) or general ledger account can be added by clicking **Additional Filters** (Figure 1.35).

A search for **Bills** received from **Cal Telephone** and charged to the **Telephone expense** account in the test drive company would return the following:

Figure 1.36

Results of advanced
search

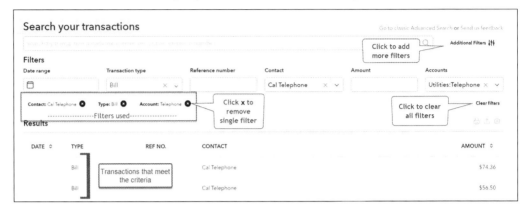

Access forms using the navigation bar and use the Search tool in Craig's Design and Landscaping to locate specific transactions.

1. To access a form using the navigation bar:

   a. Click **+ New** on the navigation bar.

   b. Click **Receive Payment**. **TIP:** This is the form used to record payments by customers on account balances.

   c. **Make a note** of the account displayed in the **Deposit to** field.

   d. Close the **Receive Payment** window by clicking **Cancel** (bottom left corner of the window).

2. To search using the **Search** feature:

   a. Click the **magnifying glass** on the icon bar.

   b. Click **Advanced Search**.

   c. Select **Bill** in the **Transaction type** field.

   d. Select **Norton Lumber and Building Materials** in the **Contact** field.

   e. Enter "205" in the **Amount** field.

   f. Click the $205.00 in the **AMOUNT** field to open the vendor bill.

   g. **Make a note** of the descriptions for the two items purchased from Norton Lumber.

   h. Close the window by clicking **Cancel** (bottom left corner of the window).

REPORTING

There are lots of reports already set up in QBO. You'll be using many of those reports during the class term.

Reports are accessed by clicking **Reports** on the navigation bar.

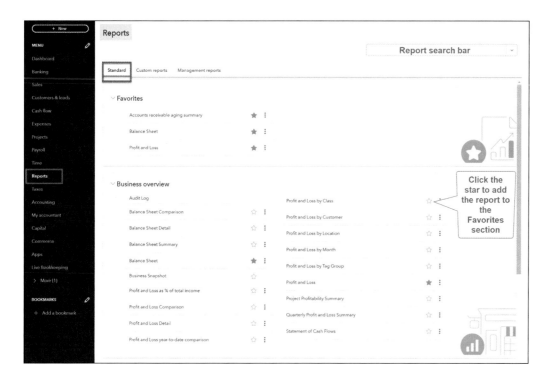

Figure 1.37

Report Center

The **Standard** tab includes the reports already set up in QBO. Figure 1.37 is a partial view of the **Standard** tab in the **Reports** window.

Reports on this tab are grouped by category. Some reports are included in multiple categories. The categories are:

Favorites—the most popular reports from all the categories. Reports can be added to or deleted from this list by clicking the star next to the report name. Reports added to **Favorites** will still be listed in the original category.

Business Overview—the typical accounting reports created at the end of each accounting period

Who Owes You—reports related to accounts receivable

Sales and Customers—reports related to sales and customer activity

What You Owe—reports related to accounts payable

Expenses and Vendors—reports related to purchase and vendor activity

Sales Tax—reports related to state and local sales taxes

Employees—reports related to employees and time tracking

For My Accountant—common accounting reports created at the end of each accounting period plus fairly detailed reports of financial activity. Journal reports are included in this category.

Payroll—reports related to employees, compensation, and time tracking. Certain reports will only be listed here if payroll is activated in QBO.

 HINT: There is a search box at the top of the screen to help you find specific reports. CTRL F (or ⌘ F) can also be used on the page.

Reports customized and saved by users are included on the **Custom Reports** tab. The **Management Reports** tab includes three report packages developed by Intuit.

Figure 1.38

Management Reports
tab in report center

> ✳ **HINT:** The management report options may differ slightly in your company
> file. **Management Reports** are covered in Chapter 11.

Customizing Reports

Most reports in QBO can be customized, and you'll likely need to be able to customize
reports to complete your homework assignments.

There are many ways you can customize reports:

- You can add or delete the types of information that appear on the report and/or the
  order in which the information is presented.
- You can specify which transactions are included in the report.
- You can modify the appearance of the reports (fonts, titles, etc.).

> ❗ **WARNING:** In early 2023, Intuit started updating the customization tools on
> QBO reports. **Modern View** refers to reports using the new tools. **Classic
> View** refers to reports using the former layout. Directions for customizing re-
> ports in **Classic View** are included in this section. Customization tools in **Mod-
> ern View** are covered in APPENDIX 1A New Report Customization Tools.
>
> If you see a report that does not match the screenshot in your book, start by
> looking for a link to **Switch to classic view**. If there is no link available, use
> the information in APPENDIX 1A to guide you, check the Student Ancillaries
> page in myBusinessCourse for updated information about report customiza-
> tion, or ask your instructor.

Simple Report Modification

Certain report modifications can easily be made on the face of most report screens.

For an example, click **Reports** on the navigation bar. On the **Standard** tab, click **Journal**
report in the **For My Accountant** section.

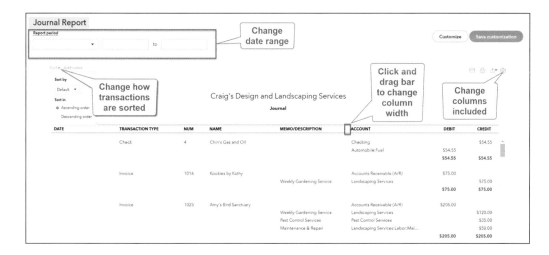

Figure 1.39

Simple report
modification options on
a Journal report

On the **Journal** report shown in Figure 1.39, simple modifications could include:

- Changing the date range of the report.
- Changing how the data in the report is sorted (under **Sort**).
- Changing the column widths (done by clicking the separator bar just to the right of the column name and dragging left to decrease the width and dragging right to increase the width).

Other reports, the Profit and Loss statement, for example, have many more modifications that can be made directly on the report screen.

Reports can be created with differing levels of detail for different users. For example, a creditor might need less detail on an income statement than an owner. If there are sub-accounts set up for income or expense accounts, the income statement can easily be modified to:

- Show all sub-accounts with subtotals by parent account.
- Show only parent accounts.

QBO calls changing this level of detail **expanding** or **collapsing** a report. This option, when available, is included on the face of the report screen.

When a report is initially opened, the report will show all detail. For example, Figure 1.40 shows a **profit and loss** report if **All Dates** was selected as the **Report period**.

Figure 1.40

Expanded profit and
loss report

Click **Collapse** to include only parent accounts.

Figure 1.41

Collapsed profit and loss report

To return to the more detailed report, click **Expand**.

Advanced Report Modification

Sometimes a company might want to limit the type of information included in a report or do more extensive modifications to the appearance of the report. For example, a company might want to limit a sales report to include only sales to certain customers. Or a company might want to show reports in whole dollars.

Modifying the type of information that is included in a report is done through a filtering process. Modifying the appearance of a report is done through a selection process. Both are done through a customization window.

To more extensively modify a **Journal** report, click **Customize** in the top right of the report screen.

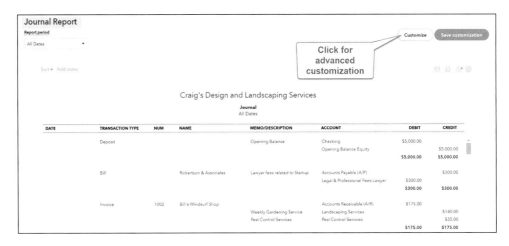

Figure 1.42

Access to report customization window

You'll see a window that looks something like Figure 1.43 (different reports have different customization options, so the screens will differ):

Figure 1.43

General section of report customization window

There are four customization sections: General, Rows/Columns, Filter, Header/Footer.

In the General section of the customization window, you can change dates and number formatting.

> **HINT:** The QBO default is to display negative numbers with a leading minus sign in reports. However, in financial reports, negative numbers are more commonly displayed using parentheses. To create more professional looking statements, the negative numbers formatting should be changed by customizing the report.

Click Change columns.

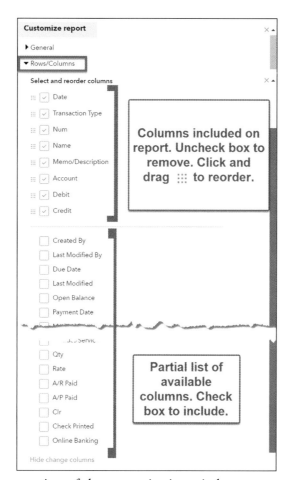

Figure 1.44

Example of Rows/
Columns section of
report customization

In the **Rows/Columns** section of the customization window, you can select and reorder
included fields.

Click the arrow next to **Filter**.

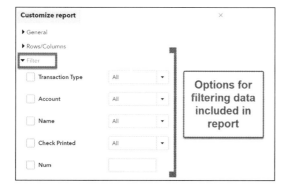

Figure 1.45

Example of Filter
section of report
customization

In the **Filter** section of the customization window, you can filter the data that's included in
the report. Figure 1.45 shows the filters available on a **Journal** report.

Click the arrow next to Header/Footer.

Figure 1.46

Example of Header/
Footer section of report
customization

Basic changes to report titles and footers are made in the Headers/Footers section of the customization window as shown in Figure 1.46.

Click Run Report in the bottom right corner of the customization window to apply the changes.

Figure 1.47

Link to save
customized report

Customized reports can be saved to the Custom Reports tab of the report center by clicking Save customization on the report screen.

Figure 1.48

Saved report options

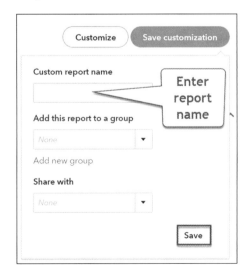

Reports can be saved in groups set up by the user. If there are multiple users of a company file, reports can be shared with some or all the other users. Report structures (no financial data) can be shared with the Intuit community.

Printing Reports

Reports can be printed, emailed, or exported (to Excel or PDF).

All of the options are accessible from the toolbar at the top of each report.

Figure 1.49

Report print and export options

The first two links (for emailing or printing) take you first to a new window where page orientation (portrait or landscape) is selected. Final links for printing or emailing appear in the new window.

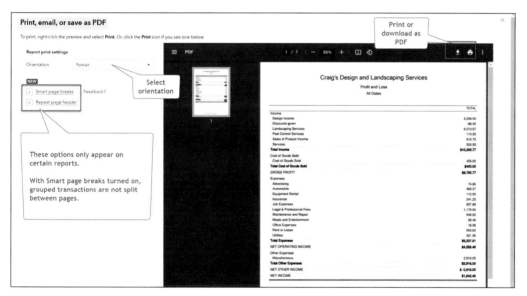

Figure 1.50

Print, email, or save as PDF options

The **Export** dropdown menu allows you to select **Export to Excel** or **Export to PDF**. Page orientation can be selected for an export to PDF but not for an export to Excel.

The options available by clicking ⚙ at the far right of the toolbar (Figure 1.49) vary depending on the report. For some reports, columns can be changed or reordered in the ⚙ window. In other reports, the only option included is to change the display density to compact.

Customize and print reports for Craig's Design and Landscaping.
(Craig's wants a hard copy of its chart of accounts and general journal.)

1. Modify and print a chart of accounts.

    a. Click **Reports** in the navigation bar.

    b. Scroll down to the **For My Accountant** section on the **Standard** tab.

PRACTICE

EXERCISE

1.5

(continued)

(continued from previous page)

    c. Click Account List.

    d. Click Customize.

    e. Click Change columns in the Rows/Columns section.

        i. Remove the checkmarks next to Description and Balance.

    f. Click Run report.

    g. Open the Sort dropdown menu.

    h. Select Type in the Sort by dropdown.

    i. Choose Descending order under Sort in.

    j. **Make a note** of the number of sub-accounts associated with Maintenance and Repair.

    k. Click the export link and select Export to PDF.

    l. Select Portrait as the orientation.

    m. Click Save as PDF.

    n Save to your desktop, laptop, or USB drive.

        i. Close out of Adobe Acrobat if needed.

    o. Click Close (bottom left corner of the report) to exit out of the report window.

    p. Click Back to report list (top left corner of the window).

2. Modify a Journal report.

    a. Click Journal in the For My Accountant section of Reports.

    b. Click Customize.

    c. In the General section, change Report period to All Dates.

    d. Click Change columns in the Rows/Columns section.

        i. Remove the checkmarks next to Num, Memo/Description.

    e. Open the Filter section.

        i. Check the box left of Transaction Type.

        ii. In the dropdown menu, check the box for Bill.

    f. Open the Header/Footer section.

        i. Change the Report Title to "Vendor Bills."

    g. Click Run report.

    h. Select Date in the Sort dropdown menu. Keep the sort in order as ascending.

    i. **Make a note** of the total (dollars) in the Debit column.

3. Click Dashboard to exit out of Reports.

ANSWER TO
QuickCheck
1-1

> Yes. The user creates the account name and chooses the account type. Be careful that the account type you select is correct.

ANSWER TO
QuickCheck
1-2

> Purchase orders and estimates are not considered accounting transactions because the **accounting equation** does not change as a result of those transactions.

Accounting equation An expression of the equivalency of the economic resources and the claims upon those resources of a business, often stated as Assets = Liabilities + Stockholders' Equity.

CHAPTER SHORTCUTS

Open the test drive company

1. Open your browser.
2. Enter https://qbo.intuit.com/redir/testdrive as the URL.
3. Check "I'm not a robot" and, if asked, select the correct images displayed on the screen.

Add an account

1. Click ⚙ on the icon bar.
2. Click **Chart of Accounts**.
3. Click **New**.

Edit an account

1. Click ⚙ on the icon bar.
2. Click **Chart of Accounts**.
3. In the **ACTION** column of the account you want to edit, select **Edit** from the dropdown menu.

Inactivate an account

1. Click ⚙ on the icon bar.
2. Click **Chart of Accounts**.
3. In the **ACTION** column of the account you want to inactivate, select **Make inactive** from the dropdown menu.

CHAPTER REVIEW

Matching

Match the term or phrase (as used in QuickBooks Online) to its definition.

Assignments with the MBC are available in myBusinessCourse.

1. products
2. transaction type
3. expand or collapse button
4. dashboard
5. icon bar
6. privacy
7. account type
8. navigation bar

_____ name given to a specific form

_____ toggle button used to remove all financial data from the display area of the Dashboard

_____ home screen

_____ items sold to customers

_____ tool for modifying the level of detail included on a report

_____ set of links to the left of the display area of the Dashboard

_____ type associated with each account to identify where it should appear in the financial statements

_____ set of links on the bar above the display area of the Dashboard

Multiple Choice

1. QuickBooks Online can be accessed through _____.

   a. Safari
   b. Edge
   c. Chrome
   d. Any of the above

2. Which QBO **account type** should be selected when setting up the general ledger account "Buildings"? (Assume the buildings are used as the corporate headquarters.)

   a. Other asset
   b. Property, plant & equipment
   c. Asset
   d. Fixed Asset

3. Invoice forms can be accessed _____.
    a. in the **+ New** menu
    b. on the **Customers** tab of **Sales**
    c. on the **Get things done** tab of the **Dashboard**
    d. **Invoice** forms can be accessed in all of the above locations.

4. Which of the following statements is false?
    a. General ledger accounts can be added to QBO by users.
    b. A company's checking account should have the **account type Bank** in QBO.
    c. You can make an account with an **expense account type**, a sub-account of an account with a **cost of goods sold account type**.
    d. The chart of accounts is considered a "list" in QBO.

5. In QBO, the **transaction type** for recording a cash sale is _____.
    a. Sale
    b. Sales receipt
    c. Bill
    d. Invoice

BEYOND THE CLICKS—THINKING LIKE A MANAGER

Accounting: Click **Reports** on the navigation bar and open the **Standard** tab. A balance sheet report, a profit and loss report, and an accounts receivable aging summary report are all, by default, included in the **Favorites** section. Look through the other report sections on that tab and pick three additional reports you would include as **Favorites** if you were the accounting manager for a large law firm. Explain why you picked those reports.

Information Systems: You're opening a small toy store. Identify three decisions about inventory you would need to make during your first year of operations. What type of information would you want or need to have available in your accounting information system to help you make each of those decisions?

ASSIGNMENT

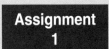

Assignment 1

Search and Find

Use the test drive company (Craig's Design and Landscaping Service) at https://qbo.intuit.com/redir/testdrive to answer the following questions.

1. Click **Expenses** on the navigation bar. Using the information on the **Expenses** and **Vendors** tabs, determine
    a. the **Total** amount for Check No. 75, Hicks Hardware payee
    b. the **Total** amount for Bill Payment (check) 6, PG&E payee
    c. the total amount due to Brosnahan Insurance Agency

2. Click **+ New** on the navigation bar, and select **Receive Payment**. Determine what must be selected in the first dropdown menu (top left):
    a. Date
    b. Customer name
    c. Vendor name
    d. Account name

3. Use the **Advanced search** function to determine how many transactions have occurred between Books by Bessie (a vendor) and Craig's Design and Landscaping Services. **HINT:** Books by Bessie is a **Display name**.

4. Customize a **Journal** report. Set the **report period** as **All Dates**. Filter the report to only include **Journal Entry transaction types** and run the report. What is the total in the debit column?

5. Identify whether the following can be found through links in the navigation bar, the icon bar, or both.
   a. Customer list
   b. QB Assistant (Intuit chatbot)
   c. Bank rules
   d. List of products and services

6. Which of the following is not a **detail type** option for the **Other current liabilities account type**? **TIP:** To see the options, click {⚙} on the icon bar and open the **Chart of accounts** list. Click **New**. Select **Other current liabilities** as the **Account Type** and open the dropdown menu under **Detail Type** to see the options.
   a. Federal Income Tax Payable
   b. Payroll Clearing
   c. Unearned Revenue
   d. Line of Credit

7. Click **Reports** on the navigation bar. Which of the following **standard** report sections includes the **Accounts Receivable Aging Summary** report? (Select all that apply.)
   a. **Favorites**
   b. **Business Overview**
   c. **Who owes you**
   d. **Sales and customers**
   e. **For my accountant**

8. Click **Dashboard** on the navigation bar. Which bank account listed on the **Business Overview** tab shows a zero balance?
   a. Checking
   b. Savings
   c. Mastercard
   d. Visa

9. Run a balance sheet report. Click **Customize** in the top right corner of the report. Which of the following does not appear as a **filter** option?
   a. Account
   b. Customer
   c. Vendor
   d. Product/Service

10. Run a Journal report (all dates). Determine the **transaction type** for the following:
   a. $300 debit to Legal & Professional Fees: Lawyer (Robertson & Associates)
   b. $140 credit to Landscaping Services (Bill's Windsurf Shop)

APPENDIX 1A CUSTOMIZATION OF CERTAIN REPORTS

LO 1-8 Use the new report customization tools

In early 2023, Intuit made changes to the customization tools on a few of the standard reports. **Modern View** refers to reports using the new tools. **Classic View** refers to reports using the former layout. As of March, 2023, **Modern View** was available in the following reports.

- Product/Service List
- Journal
- Transaction List By Vendor
- Transaction List By Customer
- Transaction List By Date
- Invoice List

Additional reports will likely have been changed by the time you're working in QBO. The new tools and features are essentially the same for all reports using the new view. We'll use the **Product/Service List** report to explain the changes.

Click **Reports** in the navigation bar.

In the **Sales and customers** section, select **Product/Service List**.

Figure 1A.1

Default Product/Service List report

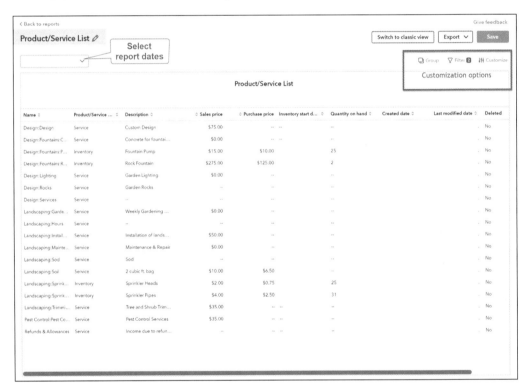

Report dates are changed using the dropdown menu at the top left of the screen.

Other customization options include the following

- **Group**
  - Provides options for grouping items by row
- **Filter**
  - Provides options for restricting the types of items included in the report
- **Customize**
  - Provides options for changing the layout (columns included) of the report

Grouping

Figure 1A.2

Report customization options

Click **Group**.

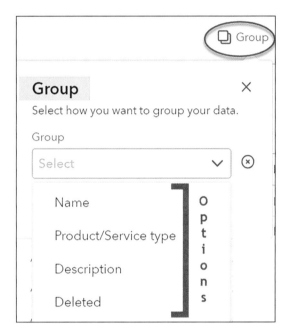

Figure 1A.3

Report grouping options

The options for grouping will depend on the report being customized.

 HINT: For a list of products and services offered for sale, the most common choice would be **Product/Service type. Deleted** means inactivated in QBO.

When a **group** is selected, the report will automatically condense the report. For example, if **Description** was selected, the **Product/Service List** report would look something like Figure 1A.4.

Figure 1A.4

Example of grouped report

Filtering

Filtering allows users to limit the report to display only those items that match one or more criteria.

A panel is displayed when **Filter** is selected in the top right section of the report screen, as shown in Figure 1A.5.

Report filtering criteria

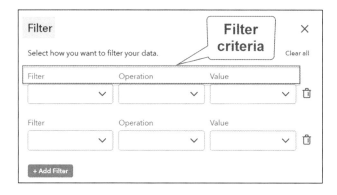

There are three choices made for each **filter**:

- **Filter**—which field should be filtered

- **Operation**—what criteria should be used
  - Operations for text fields would be limited to equals, not equals, is empty, is not empty.
  - Operations for numeric fields would include greater than, less than, equals, is empty, etc.

> ✳ **HINT:** In the **Operations** dropdown menu, **empty** refers to the content in a field. If a user wanted to see only the inventory items that didn't include a value in the **Sales price** field, **Sales price** would be selected in the **Filter** dropdown menu, and **Is empty** would be selected in the **Operations** dropdown menu.

- **Value**—what is the match value(s)
  - For text fields, the match would typically be a dropdown menu. Multiple values can not be selected.
  - For numeric fields, the match would be an amount.

The report itself changes as the various filters are identified.

The filter panel would look like Figure 1A.6 if a **Product/Service List** report was filtered to include only those **inventory** items that sell for more than $50 per unit.

Figure 1A.6

Example of filtering selections

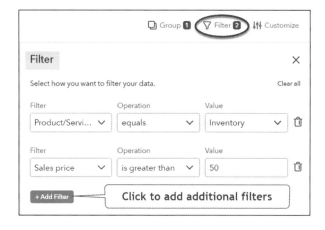

Customizing

The fields (columns) to be included in the report are selected by clicking **Customize** in the top right section of the report screen, as shown in Figure 1A.7.

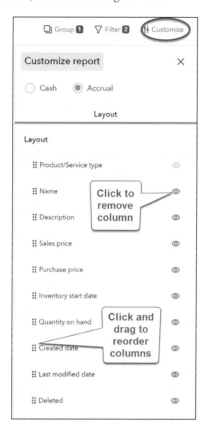

Figure 1A.7

Report customizing options

To remove a field (column), click the ⊚ (eye icon). To add a field back, click the ∅ . If the icon is grayed out, the field can not be removed. Icons for fields that have been selected for filtering would be grayed out.

Click and drag the ⠿ (double vertical ellipsis) to reorder the layout.

 HINT: The choice between **Cash** and **Accrual** would only be necessary on reports that include accounting transactions.

Saving and Exporting Customized Reports

Figure 1A.8

Save and export tools

Customized reports can be saved in QBO or exported as an Excel or CSV file.

Saved customized reports are accessible on the Custom tab in the Report Center.

Future of Report Customization in QBO

Certain tools available in the former customization panel (described in the Advanced Report Modification section in Chapter 1) were not yet available in the new panel when this book was printed. These include:

- Ability to change the formatting of numbers in reports
- Ability to modify the header and footer sections of reports

Intuit will likely add those features in the near future. If you are confused by new options, check Student Ancillaries in myBusinessCourse for updated information or check with your instructor.

APPENDIX 1B COMPARISON OF OLD AND NEW ACCOUNT SETUP SCREENS

LO 1-9 Set up a new account using the old system

In 2022, Intuit changed the new account setup screen. That screen, described in Chapter 1, is the one you'll see when setting up an account through the **Chart of Accounts** list.

You **may** see the old setup screen when you click + **Add new** in the **CATEGORY** (account) field of a form (e.g., bill, check, purchase order, etc.).

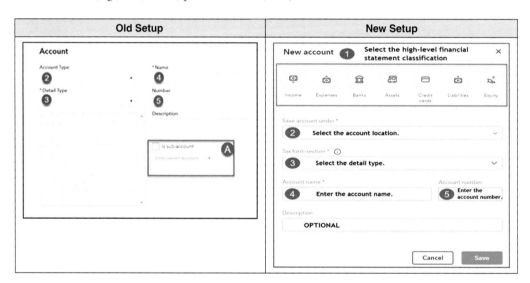

1. Selecting the high-level financial statement classification is only done in the new process.

2. The **Account type** field in the old setup is similar to the **Save account under** field. However, the dropdown menu in the old setup will only include the QBO **account types**. It will not include any accounts of that **type** that currently exist in the file.

3. The **detail type** field corresponds to the **Tax form section** field in the new screen.

4. The **Account name** field is the same. **TIP:** Names must be unique.

5. The **Account number** field is also the same. **TIP:** Numbers must be unique.

A: To create sub-accounts in the old setup screen, check the **Is sub-account** box and select the parent account in the dropdown menu. In the new system, sub-accounts are created by selecting the parent account in the **Save account under** field. **TIP:** The parent account must exist before a sub-account can be created.

APPENDIX 1C KEYBOARD SHORTCUTS IN QBO

There are many keyboard shortcuts available in QBO. These shortcuts work in Internet Explorer, Firefox, and Chrome. Most also work in Safari.

LO 1-10 Become familiar with various keyboard shortcuts in QBO

QBO Keyboard Shortcuts Available on the Dashboard or in Navigation Tab Windows

To take advantage of the shortcuts, press and hold Ctrl/control and Alt/option and then press one of the keys below. (Press and hold CMD and Alt first in Macs.)

Shortcut Key	Action
i	Opens an **Invoice** form
w	Opens a **Check** form
e	Opens an **Estimate** form
x	Opens an **Expense** form
r	Opens a **Receive payment** form
c	Opens the Customer center
v	Opens the Vendor center
a	Opens the Chart of Accounts
f	Opens the Find screen
l	Opens the List screen
h	Opens the Help screen

QBO Keyboard Shortcuts Available in Forms

To take advantage of the shortcuts, press and hold Ctrl/control and Alt/option and then press one of the keys below. (Press and hold CMD and Alt first in Macs.)

Shortcut Key	Action
x or c	Exits the transaction
s	Saves the transaction and opens a new form
d	Saves the transaction and closes the window
m	Saves the transaction and opens an email dialog box (not available on all forms)
p	Opens print preview screen (not available on all forms)

Useful Shortcuts in Date Fields

Enter	Action
+ / −	Next day / Previous day
t	Today
w / k	First day of the week / Last day of the week
m / h	First day of the month / Last day of the month
y / r	First day of the year / Last day of the year

2

Setting Up Company Files

Road Map

LO	Learning Objective	Topic	Subtopic	Page	Practice Exercises	Videos
LO 2-1	Describe the process for setting up a brand new company in QBO [p. 2-2]	Setting up a brand new company in QBO		2-2		
LO 2-2	Explain and demonstrate how existing companies can be converted to QBO [p. 2-4]	Converting an existing company to QBO	Purging a company file	2-4		Setting up your QBO company (multiple)
			Importing lists	2-5		
			Importing account balances	2-7		
			Fixing errors in company file setups	2-8		
LO 2-3	Explain and demonstrate how company files can be customized in QBO [p. 2-8]	Customizing QuickBooks Online	Customizing settings in a company file	2-8	2.1	Customizing settings in a company file
			Setting up credit terms	2-12	2.2	Setting up credit terms
			Setting up payment methods	2-15		Setting up payment methods
			Organizing the products and services list	2-17	2.3	Organizing the products and services list
LO 2-4	Understand how imported data is accounted for in QBO [p. 2-65]	APPENDIX 2A—Which accounts get debited and credited when lists are imported into QBO?				
LO 2-5	Understand how Gmail accounts are set up [p. 2-66]	APPENDIX 2B—Setting up your Google Gmail account				

INTRODUCTION

New company files can be created in QBO for:

- Newly formed companies.

- Existing companies that are converting from a manual system (or other accounting software system) to QBO.

- Existing companies that are converting from QuickBooks Desktop software to QBO. (Desktop conversions will not be covered in this textbook.)

In all of these cases, obtaining a clear understanding of business operations and the organization's informational needs is the best place to start. Some questions you might ask your client or yourself (if you're the accountant or the owner) include:

- Does the company currently sell or anticipate selling products, services, or both?
  - If products are currently being sold:
    - Does the company manufacture the products?
    - Is a product inventory maintained, or are products purchased to order?
    - Are products sold to consumers, to distributors, or to both?
  - Is the company responsible for collecting sales taxes from customers?

- Are there significant business segments within the company currently or expected in the future?

- Does the company have employees?

- Does the company have specific reporting needs (internal or external) currently, or does it expect to have such needs in the future?

There is a reason that "anticipated" operations are part of some of the questions. If you understand the direction of the company, you can design a system that will accommodate expected changes. For example, let's say you're opening a barbershop. You have some great ideas and expect that you will be able to open several more shops within the next year. When you have multiple shops, you're going to want to track operations by shop. QBO has features that can handle multiple locations.

If this is an existing company, management will need to decide the conversion date (start date). Although you can start recording transactions at any point in time, it is important to understand the implications of selecting various dates. For example, all federal and state payroll reporting is based on calendar quarters or calendar years, so companies often convert data as of the first day of a calendar quarter or calendar year.

In this chapter, we're going to go over the basics of setting up new companies in QBO. We'll also cover setting up files for existing companies and we'll use data imported from Excel and CSV files to create the company file you'll be using for your homework assignments.

SETTING UP A BRAND NEW COMPANY IN QBO

LO 2-1 Describe the process for setting up a brand new company in QBO

The initial setup of a new company in QBO is very straightforward. To start, a user only needs an email address and some general information about the company and about which QBO features the user expects to use.

Subscriptions to the various versions of QBO are purchased through the Intuit website: https://quickbooks.intuit.com/pricing/.

Once a QBO version is selected, users create an Intuit account and register for the software.

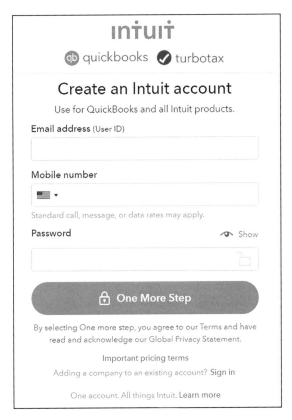

Figure 2.1

QBO sign up screen

Once they've registered, users are asked to enter the company name and answer a series of questions about their business. The answers are used by QBO to activate features in the software and develop a customized chart of accounts.

The questions cover:

- company business structure
- company industry
- expected business activities
- types of users that will be accessing the company file

Once all questions have been answered, the user clicks **All set** to create the new company file.

 HINT: Once the company file has been created, the new company's **Dashboard** will appear.

QBO automatically creates basic accounts and makes other certain selections based on the features selected as part of the setup. For example, QBO will assume the company uses accrual, not cash, as its basis of accounting. Standard date and number formatting conventions are automatically selected as well (MM/dd/yyyy for date; 123,456.00 for number).

If a company has just started business, the software is now ready for use. All users need to do is review and modify, if necessary, the settings, the chart of accounts, and the items created by QBO to match the needs of the company. Modifying settings is covered in the **CUSTOMIZING QUICKBOOKS ONLINE** section of this chapter. Modifying **accounts** was covered in Chapter 1.

> **BEHIND THE SCENES** Intuit automatically assigns a software license to each user when a company file is created. The license number (called **Company ID**) can be found on the **Billing and Subscription** tab of **Account and Settings**.

LO 2-2 Explain and demonstrate how existing companies can be converted to QBO

CONVERTING AN EXISTING COMPANY TO QBO

The initial setup outlined in the **SETTING UP BRAND NEW COMPANIES IN QBO** section of this chapter is also required for converting existing companies to QBO.

- Users register with an email address.
- Users enter the company name and describe the business industry.
- Users select the basic features needed.
- The users identify their role at the business.

 HINT: Your assignment for Chapter 2 consists of converting an existing company to QBO.

As part of the initial setup of a company file, QBO activates (or deactivates) various features based on the answers to the setup questions. Those features and settings may need to be changed to fit the company's needs. (Customizing QBO is covered in this chapter's **Customizing Settings in a Company File** section.)

QBO also automatically creates a chart of accounts based on the answers to the setup questions. It is unlikely that the default chart of accounts will exactly match a company's current chart of accounts. Instead of changing each account individually, best practice is to delete the default chart of accounts and import the company's current account list. Deleting the chart of accounts is done by purging the company file. Purging a company file deletes all transactions, any names (customers, vendors, and employees), and most accounts. (A few accounts cannot be deleted because they're connected to certain features.) Features and settings are not affected by a purge.

Purging a Company File

With QBO open and on the **Dashboard** screen, the user changes the URL by replacing 'homepage' with 'purgecompany' (app.qbo.intuit.com/purgecompany) and clicks **Enter**.

Figure 2.2

Purge warning message

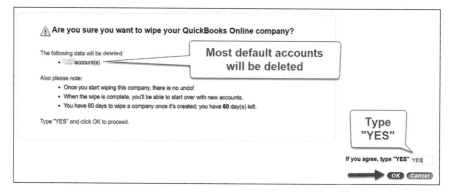

The user responds to the warning message question and clicks **OK**.

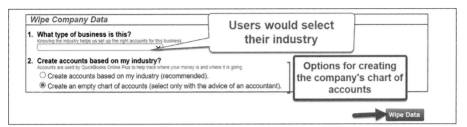

Figure 2.3

Final purge screen

The user answers two final questions (one about the business type and one about the chart of accounts) and clicks **Wipe Data**.

Importing Lists

The company's current chart of accounts, products and services, customers, vendors, and employees must also be entered. To make it easier, these lists and some of the account balances can be directly imported into QBO. The import feature is found on the ⚙ menu accessed from the icon bar.

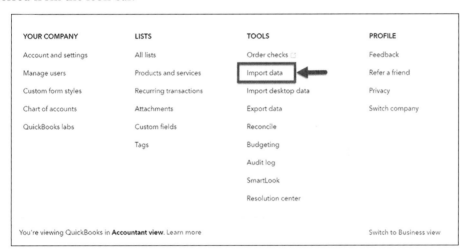

Figure 2.4

Link Access to the file import screen

A user would click **Import data**.

Figure 2.5

Data import window

Most imports are done from spreadsheets created in Microsoft Excel or Google Sheets. (Invoices are imported using CSV files. Bank transactions can be automatically downloaded from bank websites.)

The spreadsheets (or CSV files) must be formatted correctly. For example, the top row of each sheet must contain a title (a header) for each column of information. Sample files are available for each category (chart of accounts, customers, etc.) that show the types of information that can be imported. Not all possible information types need to be imported.

The list that would usually be imported first would be the chart of accounts. The screen that appears if **Chart of Accounts** is selected is shown in Figure 2.6:

Figure 2.6

Chart of accounts import window

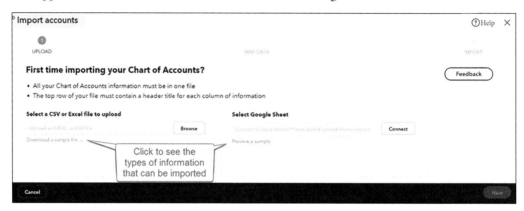

Once the Excel or Google Sheets file to be imported has been selected, the user must verify that QBO has accurately matched (mapped) the title fields in the spreadsheet to the fields in QBO. The mapping screen might look like Figure 2.7 if a user was importing a chart of accounts.

Figure 2.7

Mapping to be verified in a chart of accounts import

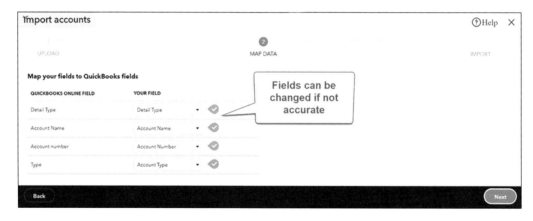

Once the user verifies the mapping, QBO verifies that all the data in the spreadsheet can be imported.

Figure 2.8

QBO verification of data included in import

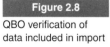
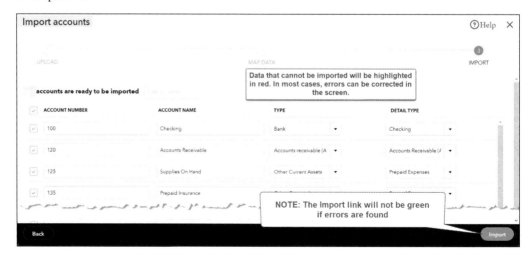

For example, if a user is importing a chart of accounts, QBO would verify that all names in the **TYPE** field are legitimate QBO **account types**. If a user were importing a list of customers, QBO would verify that addresses were included for all customers in the list. All errors must be corrected before any of the data can be imported.

> **HINT:** As noted, not all types of information need to be imported. For example, the mapping window for the import of the customer list for your homework company file will look something like this:

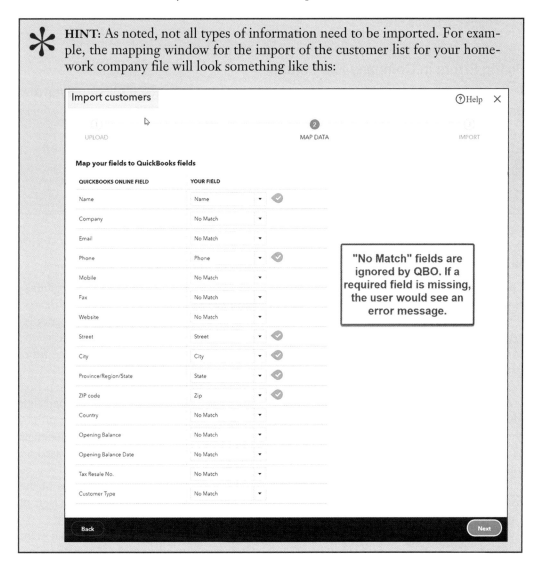

Importing Account Balances

To complete the conversion, account balances must be entered as of the conversion date. How that's done depends on the account type.

Accounts receivable balances can be imported in one of two ways:

- Total unpaid balances can be included in the Customer list import.

- Specific invoice balances can be included in the Invoice import.

Accounts payable balances are imported as totals in the Vendor list import (**Opening balance** column).

Inventory item quantities on hand are imported as part of the Products and Services import. The inventory account balance is then automatically calculated by multiplying each item's quantity on hand by the unit purchase price included in the import.

All other account balances are entered using journal entries.

> **BEHIND THE SCENES** A journal entry is automatically created whenever financial transaction amounts (from invoices, customer/vendor balances, or inventory values) are imported into QBO . Appendix 2A explains which accounts are debited and credited by QBO as part of the import process. We recommend that you read through the appendix.

Fixing Errors in Company File Setups

If a user imports the wrong chart of accounts or incorrect balances, it's best to purge the file, as explained in the *Purging a Company File* section of this chapter.

> **BEHIND THE SCENES** When a company file is purged, the chart of accounts, all names, and all transactions are permanently deleted. All of the settings remain intact.
> Purging a company can be done an unlimited number of times within the first 60 days of a new subscription.

CUSTOMIZING QUICKBOOKS ONLINE

LO 2-3 Explain and demonstrate how company files can be customized in QBO

One of the reasons QBO is so popular is that it can be used in different types of organizations and in many different industries. That flexibility, however, presents some challenges. The tools needed by a retail store (the ability to track inventory held for sale, for example) are not the same as the tools needed by a law firm (the ability to bill clients from timesheets, for example). If all the tools needed in all the different industries were visible all the time, users might justifiably complain that the menu options are a little TOO extensive.

Optional tools and features are known as settings in QBO. When a company file is first created, choices between settings are made automatically. For example, it's assumed that all US companies use the accrual method of accounting, have January as the first month of the fiscal year, show dates in the MM/dd/yyyy format, and use commas and two decimals as the number format. Other settings are automatically activated (or deactivated) based on answers to questions posed in the initial file setup process.

Some of the initial settings may need to be changed to better meet the needs of the user. Changing settings is covered in the Editing Settings in a Company File section of this chapter.

Users can also customize QBO by creating custom lists for credit terms and payment methods. Products and services can be organized into customized groups called categories. Setting up these lists is covered later in this chapter.

Customizing Settings In a Company File

Figure 2.9
Icon bar

 My Experts   Help

To edit settings, click the ⚙ in the icon bar.

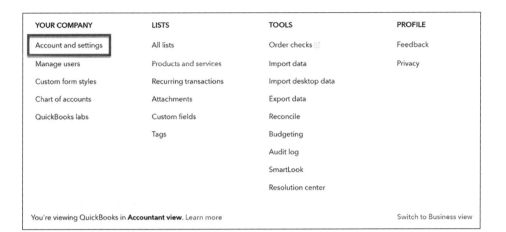

Figure 2.10

Link to company
settings

Click **Account and Settings** in the **YOUR COMPANY** column.

 HINT: You can also access **Account and Settings** by clicking your company name at the top of the **Dashboard** screen.

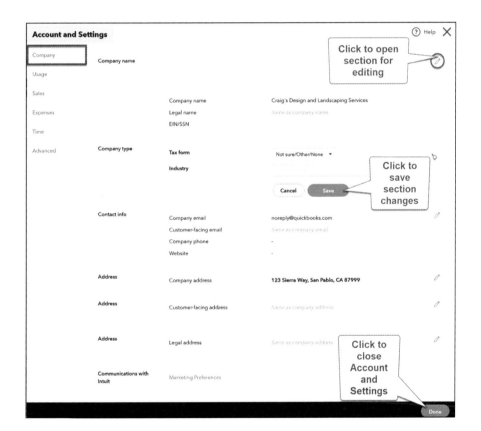

Figure 2.11

Company tab of
Account and Settings

There are six tabs on the left side of the page in the test drive company file. (You will see several additional tabs related to activating QuickBooks banking and user subscriptions in your homework company file.) On each tab, settings are grouped into sections. Sections can be opened for editing by clicking the pencil icon in the top right corner of the section or by clicking anywhere inside the section. Clicking **Save** in a modified section saves the changes. Clicking **Done** in the bottom right corner of the screen closes **Account and Settings**.

On the **Company** tab, basic information about the company is entered.

Information about usage and usage limits in the company file are included on the **Usage** tab.

> **BEHIND THE SCENES** Intuit has set limits to the number of accounts and users that can be used in a single company file. The limits depend on the QBO version being used.

Figure 2.12

Sales tab of Account and Settings

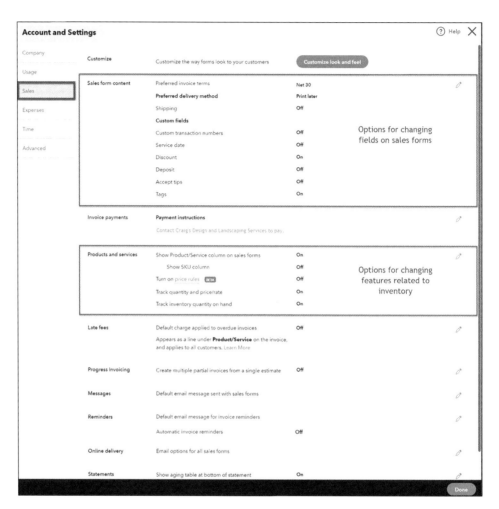

On the **Sales** tab, changes can be made to sales form content and inventory tracking options.

Figure 2.13

Expenses tab of Account and Settings

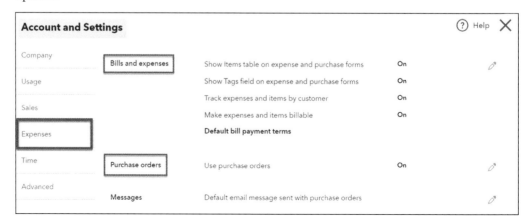

On the **Expenses** tab, features such as purchase orders and expense tracking by customer can be turned on and off.

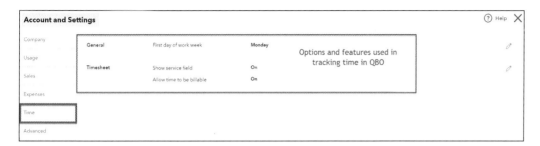

Figure 2.14

Time tab of Account and Settings

Companies that track employee or contractor time can customize timesheet forms on the **Time** tab.

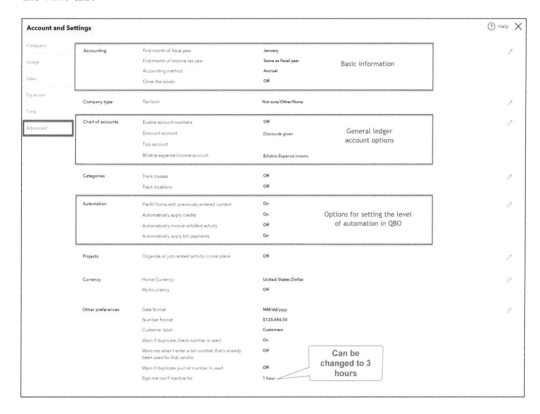

Figure 2.15

Advanced tab of Account and Settings

A significant number of settings are included on the **Advanced** tab. Choices related to accounting methods, the chart of accounts, and the level of automation are included here. Features for tracking projects or business segments are also activated on this tab.

One very helpful setting that can be changed in the **Advanced** tab relates to the amount of user inactivity (in hours) that the software will allow before automatically signing off. This is especially important for you to change in the test drive company because all your work is lost whenever the company file is closed. Users can extend the amount of time up to three hours.

Settings will be discussed in more detail in future chapters.

HINT: Remember—All of your settings and transactions are cleared/deleted whenever you log or time out of the test drive company. If you expect to be working on Practice Exercises for an extended period of time, you might want to edit the **Sign me out if inactive for** time range when you first open the test drive.

PRACTICE
EXERCISE
2.1

Customize QBO for Craig's Design and Landscaping.

(Craig's wants to increase the amount of allowed inactivity and set up a default message for invoices.)

1. Click the ⚙ on the icon bar.

2. Click **Account and Settings**.

3. Open the **Advanced** tab to change the amount of time of inactivity allowed.

    a. In the **Other preferences** section, click **Sign me out if inactive for**.

    b. Select **3 hours** on the dropdown menu.

    c. Click **Save**.

4. Open the **Sales** tab to set up a default message on sales forms.

    a. Click the **pencil** icon in the **Messages** section.

    b. Select **Invoices and other sales forms** from the **second** **Sales Form** dropdown menu (the one at the bottom of the **Messages** section just above the **SAVE** button).

    c. Type in "We appreciate your business."

    d. Click **Save**.

5. **Make a note of** the following:

    a. the company address on the **Company** tab.

    b. the **Preferred invoice terms** on the **Sales** tab.

    c. whether the **Purchase order** feature is activated on the **Expenses** tab.

    d. the **First month of fiscal year** on the **Advanced** tab

    e. the **Accounting method** selected on the **Advanced** tab.

6. Click **Done** (bottom right corner of screen) to exit the **Account and Settings** window.

Setting Up Credit Terms

Companies that sell on account set up payment terms for their customers to let them know when payment is due and whether there's a discount if they pay early. A company can, of course, have different terms for different customers.

Required payment dates are usually based on the invoice date. Payment would be due a certain number of days after the date of the invoice. Payment terms of 10, 15, and 30 days are common choices.

Some companies set a particular day of the month as the payment due date. A common date is the last day of the month. An invoice dated January 3rd would be due on January 31st. An invoice dated January 23rd would also be due on the 31st. Companies that use a date-driven payment term will usually give an extra month for invoices dated close to the payment date. For example, if the payment date were the last day of the month, an invoice dated January 29th would be due at the end of February instead of the end of January.

New credit terms can be created by clicking the ⚙ on the icon bar.

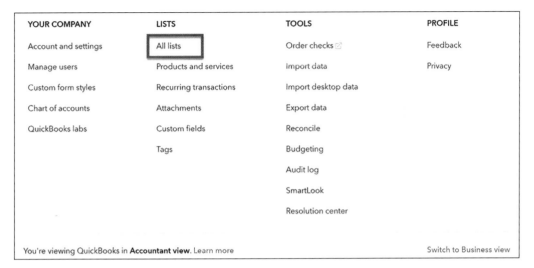

Figure 2.16
Access to Lists page

Click **All Lists.**

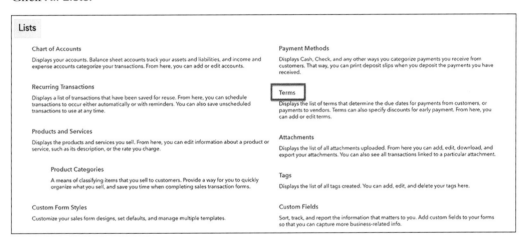

Figure 2.17
Lists page

Click **Terms.**

Figure 2.18
Terms list

Click **New.**

Figure 2.19

Figure 2.19

New credit term
window

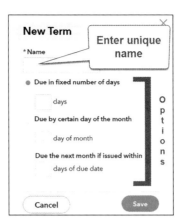

A **Name** for the new term must be entered. Users can either create a new term that is based on the invoice date (**Due in fixed number of days**) or a term that is based on a particular day (**Due by certain day of the month**). The window would look something like Figure 2.20 if a user created a new term called EOM that required payment by the last day of the month unless the bill was issued during the last five days of the month.

Figure 2.20

Example of new term
setup

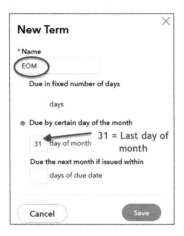

At the time this book was written, credit terms with early payment discounts (e.g., 2% 10, net 30) can be set up in QBO but there is no tracking or automatic calculation of those discounts built into the software. Options for recording early payment discounts taken by customers will be covered in Chapter 6.

> **BEHIND THE SCENES** The terms list is used for both customers and vendors. When a company enters a vendor bill (covered in Chapter 4), QBO will use the term selected on the form to determine the due date.

PRACTICE
EXERCISE
2.2

Set up a new credit term for Craig's Design and Landscaping.
(Craig's wants to add a new term (Net 45).)

1. Click the ⚙ on the icon bar.
2. Click **All Lists** in the **LISTS** column.
3. Click **Terms**.
   a. **Make a note** of the payment terms already set up for Craig's.

(continued)

(continued from previous page)

4. Click New.

5. Enter "Net 45" as the Name.

6. Click Due in fixed number of days and enter "45" in the days field.

7. Click Save.

8. Click Dashboard.

Setting Up Payment Methods

Companies may decide to accept a variety of customer payment methods, including:

- Cash
- Check
- MasterCard

- VISA
- Electronic funds transfer

When recording customer payments, the payment method should be identified to make it easier to group cash receipts when recording deposits.

Each payment method is included on the **Payment method** list. To set up (or edit) a payment method, click the ⚙ on the icon bar.

YOUR COMPANY	LISTS	TOOLS	PROFILE
Account and settings	All lists	Order checks ☑	Feedback
Manage users	Products and services	Import data	Privacy
Custom form styles	Recurring transactions	Import desktop data	
Chart of accounts	Attachments	Export data	
QuickBooks labs	Custom fields	Reconcile	
	Tags	Budgeting	
		Audit log	
		SmartLook	
		Resolution center	

You're viewing QuickBooks in **Accountant view**. Learn more   Switch to Business view

Figure 2.21

Access to Lists page

Click **All Lists**.

Lists

Chart of Accounts
Displays your accounts. Balance sheet accounts track your assets and liabilities, and income and expense accounts categorize your transactions. From here, you can add or edit accounts.

Payment Methods
Displays Cash, Check, and any other ways you categorize payments you receive from customers. That way, you can print deposit slips when you deposit the payments you have received.

Recurring Transactions
Displays a list of transactions that have been saved for reuse. From here, you can schedule transactions to occur either automatically or with reminders. You can also save unscheduled transactions to use at any time.

Terms
Displays the list of terms that determine the due dates for payments from customers, or payments to vendors. Terms can also specify discounts for early payment. From here, you can add or edit terms.

Products and Services
Displays the products and services you sell. From here, you can edit information about a product or service, such as its description, or the rate you charge.

Attachments
Displays the list of all attachments uploaded. From here you can add, edit, download, and export your attachments. You can also see all transactions linked to a particular attachment.

Product Categories
A means of classifying items that you sell to customers. Provide a way for you to quickly organize what you sell, and save you time when completing sales transaction forms.

Tags
Displays the list of all tags created. You can add, edit, and delete your tags here.

Custom Form Styles
Customize your sales form designs, set defaults, and manage multiple templates.

Custom Fields
Sort, track, and report the information that matters to you. Add custom fields to your forms so that you can capture more business-related info.

Figure 2.22

Access to payment method list

Click **Payment Methods**.

Figure 2.23

Payment method list

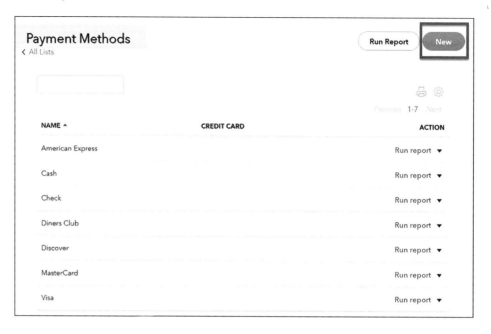

Click **New** to set up a new method.

Figure 2.24

Payment method record

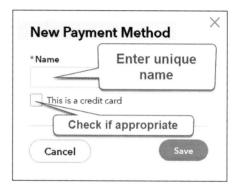

Enter a unique name. Check the **This is a credit card** box, if appropriate.

HINT: A payment method's name or credit card status can be changed by selecting **Edit** on the dropdown menu in the **ACTION** column of the **Payment method** list.

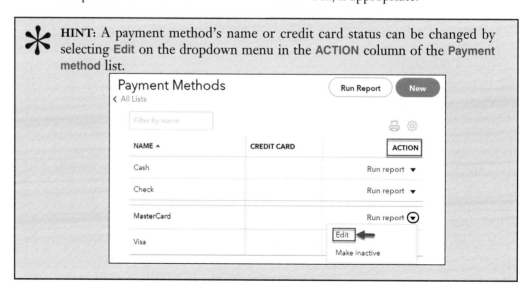

Organizing the Products and Services List

Products and **services** can be grouped into **categories** in QBO. Grouping items makes it easier for users to access (find) specific items when entering specific transactions. Grouping also makes it easier to create effective reports about company operations.

> **BEHIND THE SCENES** **Categories** are only used for organizing items. Assigning an item to a **category** does not determine the general ledger account debited or credited when the item is used in a transaction. See the **Adding a Service Item** section in Chapter 3 for information about assigning general ledger accounts to items.

To set up **categories**, click the ⚙ on the icon bar and select **Products and Services** under **Lists**.

Figure 2.25

"More" options on Products and Services page

Select **Manage categories** on the **More** dropdown menu.

Figure 2.26

Access to new category sidebar

To add a new **category**, click **New category**. A sidebar will open:

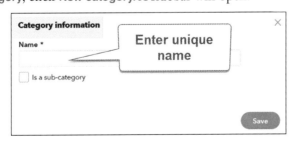

Figure 2.27

New category window

Enter a **category** name.

Users can group categories together by identifying **sub-categories**. Multiple **sub-categories** can be created for each parent **category**. Users can also create **sub-categories** of **sub-categories** (up to 4 levels).

Figure 2.28

Access to Category list

Categories can be changed or deleted. Open the Products and Services list.

Select Manage categories on the More dropdown menu.

Figure 2.29

Options to edit or remove categories

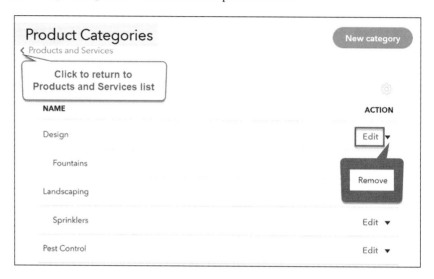

Click Edit to change the name or Remove to delete the category. If you delete a category, any related sub-categories will be moved up one level.

To return to the Products and Services list, click the back arrow under Product Categories.

Categories can be assigned to specific items when the item is initially set up or by editing existing items. To access the record for an existing item, click Edit in the ACTION column of the Products and Services list.

Figure 2.30

Category field in item record

The **category** field appears in the top section of the item record.

If a **category** needs to be added or changed for multiple **products or services**, a batch processing tool is available.

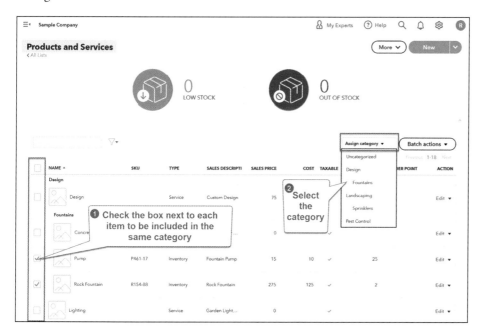

Figure 2.31

Batch tool for assigning categories

Check the boxes next to all the items to be included in a specific **category**.

Open the **Assign category** dropdown menu that appears next to **Batch actions** and select the appropriate **category**.

The item records will be automatically updated.

Set up categories for Craig's Design and Landscaping.

(Craig decides to add a new **category** to separate out services related to general gardening jobs.)

1. Set up the category.

   a. Click the ⚙ in the icon bar and select **Products and services** in the **LISTS** column.

   b. Click **Manage categories** in the **More** dropdown menu in the top right corner.

   c. Click **New category**.

   d. Enter "Gardening" as the name.

   e. Click **Save**.

   f. Click **Products and Services** under **Product Categories** to return to the Products and services list.

2. Assign the category to existing items.

   a. Check the boxes in the far left column of the rows for **Gardening** and **Trimming**.

   b. In the **Assign category** dropdown menu next to **Batch actions**, select **Gardening**.

3. **Make a note** of the **Sales price/rate** for Trimming.

PRACTICE
EXERCISE
2.3

Homework
MBC

CHAPTER SHORTCUTS

Change settings
1. Click ⚙ on the icon bar.
2. Click **Account and Settings**.

Purge the chart of accounts
1. Open your company file.
2. Enter http://qbo.intuit.com/app/purge-company as the URL.
3. Type YES in the **If you agree** field.
4. Click **OK**.
5. Choose a business similar to your home-work company in the **What type of business is this?** dropdown menu.
6. Select **Create an empty chart of accounts**.
7. Click **Wipe Data**.

Import data
1. Click ⚙ on the icon bar.
2. Click **Import Data**.
3. Select the type of list to be imported.
4. Upload the appropriate Excel or CSV file.

Add or edit credit terms
1. Click ⚙ on the icon bar.
2. Click **All lists**.
3. Click **Terms**.

Add or edit payment methods
1. Click ⚙ on the icon bar.
2. Click **All lists**.
3. Click **Payment Methods**.

Add or edit categories
1. Click ⚙ on the icon bar.
2. Click **Products and services**.
3. Select **Manage categories** in the **More** dropdown menu.

CHAPTER REVIEW

Assignments with the are available in myBusinessCourse.

Matching
Match the term or phrase (as used in QuickBooks Online) to its definition.

1. Settings
2. Importing
3. Categories
4. License number
5. Purge
6. Opening balance equity (Appendix 2A)

_____ the act of bringing external data into a company file

_____ default account used by QBO as part of the import process

_____ number used to identify a specific user of QBO

_____ removal of all data from a company file

_____ customizable features

_____ custom groups used to organize the products and services list

Multiple Choice

1. Which of the following cannot be imported into QBO?
   a. Sales and expense settings
   b. Inventory balances
   c. Accounts receivable balances
   d. Accounts payable balances

2. Which of the following is not deleted when a company file is purged?

    a. Transactions

    b. Most general ledger accounts

    c. Company settings

    d. None of the listed answers are correct. Transactions, accounts, and settings are all deleted.

3. A company file _____.

    a. can be purged an unlimited number of times as long as the user's subscription is active

    b. can be purged an unlimited number of times within the first 60 days of a new subscription

    c. can be purged up to 60 times

    d. cannot be purged

4. Which of the following statements is false?

    a. The **category** assigned to a product or service item identifies the general ledger account associated with that product or service item.

    b. **Categories** can be used to organize the products and services list.

    c. Specific **categories** are not automatically set up in QBO.

    d. There can be up to four levels of **categories** in QBO.

5. Which account might be credited when a **Product and Services List** is imported? (Refer to Appendix 2A for help answering this question.)

    a. Inventory

    b. Cost of goods sold

    c. Accounts payable

    d. Opening balance equity

BEYOND THE CLICKS—THINKING LIKE A MANAGER

Accounting: You're opening a restaurant and want to be able to analyze operations on a monthly basis. You can only add 10 revenue and expense accounts to your general ledger. Which accounts would you choose and why?

Information Systems: What are the pros and cons of a company using a cloud-based accounting software system like QuickBooks Online compared to a desktop accounting software system like QuickBooks Desktop?

ASSIGNMENTS

Check with your instructor before you move forward. This assignment should only be used if your instructor assigned Math Revealed! for homework.

In this assignment, you'll be setting up your homework company file. This is the QBO file you'll be using to complete your homework in Chapters 3 through 11.

The steps should be completed in order.

> ✳ **HINT:** There are multiple videos available in myBusinessCourse to help you with this assignment.

Assignment 2A

Math Revealed!

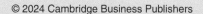

STEP 1—Review the following background information about your company.

Martin Smith, a college student and good friend of yours, has always wanted to be an entrepreneur. He is very good in math, so, to test his entrepreneurship skills, he has decided to set up a small math tutoring company serving local high school students who struggle in their math courses. He set up the company, Math Revealed!, as a corporation in 2023. Martin is the only owner. He has not taken any distributions from the company since it opened.

The business has been successful so far. In fact, it's been so successful he has decided to work in his business full time now that he's graduated from college with a degree in mathematics.

He has decided to start using QuickBooks Online to keep track of his business transactions. He likes the convenience of being able to access his information over the Internet. You have agreed to act as his accountant while you're finishing your own academic program.

Martin currently has a number of regular customers that he tutors in pre-algebra, algebra, and geometry. His customers pay his fees by cash or check after each tutoring session, but he does give terms of Net 15 to some of his customers. He has developed the following fee schedule:

Name	Description	Rate
Refresher	One-hour session	$ 55 per hour
Persistence program	Two one-hour sessions per week	$105 per week
Crisis program	Five one-hour sessions per week	$250 per week

The tutoring sessions usually take place at his students' homes, but he recently signed a two-year lease on a small office above a local coffee shop. The rent is only $850 per month starting in January 2024. A security deposit of $1,000 was paid in December 2023.

The following equipment is owned by the company:

Description	Date placed in service	Cost	Life	Salvage Value
Computer	7/1/23	$2,600	48 months	$200
Printer	7/1/23	$ 270	36 months	$ 0
Graphing Calculators (3)	7/1/23	$ 360	36 months	$ 90

All equipment is depreciated using the straight-line method.

As of 12/31/23, Martin owed $2,500 to his father (Richard Smith) who initially helped him get started. Richard is charging him interest at a 6% annual rate. Martin has been paying interest only on a monthly basis. His last payment of interest only was on 12/31/23.

Over the next month or so, he plans to expand his business by selling a few products he believes will help his students. He has already purchased a few items:

Category	Description	Vendor	Quantity on Hand	Cost per Unit	Sales Price
Books and Tools					
	Geometry in Sports	Books Galore	20	17	28
	Solving Puzzles: Fun with Algebra	Books Galore	20	15	25
	Getting Ready for Calculus	Books Galore	20	18	30
	Geometry Kit	Math Shack	10	10	15
	Handheld Dry-Erase Boards	Math Shack	25	15	25
	Notebooks (pack of 5)	Paper Bag Depot	10	8	14

STEP 2—Obtain your license and open your company file.

Your instructor will direct Intuit to provide you with a one-year free license to QuickBooks Online Plus. Intuit Education will then email you an invitation to set up your homework file.

 HINT: The email will likely be sent to the address on file for you at your school. Make sure that the email address is correct.

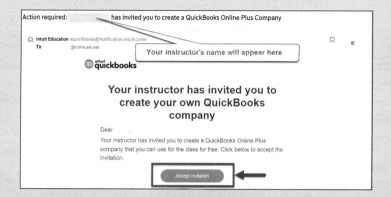

Figure 2.32

Email invitation to set up a company file

> **WARNING:** Make sure you have enough time to complete STEP 3 before you move forward. It could be difficult to get back into your QBO file if the initial setup process wasn't finished.

✓ When you're ready, click **Accept Invitation**.

> ✱ **HINT:** If you get an error message about the link not working, right-click the *Accept invitation* link, select *Copy link location*, open a new window in Incognito (private) mode, and paste the copied URL into the address bar. If that doesn't work, clear your cache and try again. If you're still having issues, contact your instructor.

Figure 2.33

Registration screen

✓ Create your Intuit account by entering an email address, your name, and creating a password. The email address (and the related password) will be used each time you log in to QBO.

> ✳ **HINT:** You can use your school email address, your own personal email address, or you can set up an email address specifically for this course. Setting up a separate email offers the most security. Instructions for setting up a Gmail account are provided in Appendix 2B if you want to use a unique email address.
>
> If you already have an Intuit account, simply sign in using the link under **Create your account** at the top of the screen shown in Figure 2.33.

- Intuit accepts passwords that have the following characteristics:
  1. It must be at least 8 characters long.
  2. It must include both lowercase and uppercase letters.
  3. It must include a number.
  4. It must include a symbol.

✓ Click **Create Account**. You will see a welcome message:

Figure 2.34

Welcome message

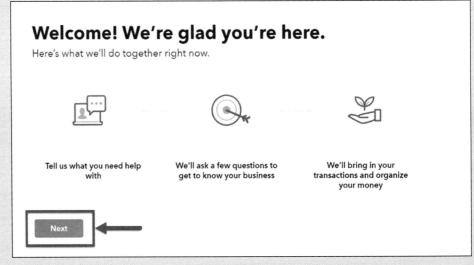

✓ Click **Next**.

STEP 3—Answer the informational questions that appear in the next set of screens.

General information is entered in the first screens you'll see in QBO. The company name is entered, and its legal structure and business activities are identified. Intuit uses this information to activate various features so users can get started.

Intuit occasionally changes the order and wording of the setup questions. The specific questions that appear in your homework company file setup may differ from those that appear for your fellow students or your instructor.

Table 2A.1 shows the most common question wording and the answers that you should answer or select. Your questions may be in a different order. Some of the questions may not appear as part of your setup. New questions may be added. Use your best judgement. If you don't know how to answer a question, reach out to your instructor.

Screen Heading	Answers
What do you call your business?	Your homework company name should be your name followed by Math Revealed! For example, if your name were John Smith, you would enter *John Smith Math Revealed!* as your business name. Check the box next to **This is my legal business name**, if necessary.
How have you been managing your finances?	Click **Spreadsheets or pen & paper**
How long has your company been in business?	Click **Under a year**
What kind of business is this?	Click **No** to **Is it an LLC**? Click **C Corp** or **Corporation**.
What's your industry?	Enter *Professional services* in the field. Select **All other professional, scientific, and technical services** from the displayed options.
How does your business make money?	Click **Provides services** and **Sells products**.
Do you track projects?	Click **Sometimes**
What's your main role at Your Name Math Revealed?	Click the option that includes the word **Accountant**.
Is Math Revealed! your main source of income?	Click **No** and select **I do freelance/contract work**.
Who works at this business?	Click **Only the owner** or **I fly solo**.
Does an expert help with your books?	Click **Yes**. **TIP:** You're the expert!
What apps do you use for your business?	Click **Skip for now** or **I don't use any apps**.
Link your accounts and see everything in one place.	Click **Skip for now**.
What is everything you want to set up?	Click all options **other than** those related to paying employees, accepting payments, tracking mileage, creating estimates, purchasing insurance, and getting a business bank account.
Want to add QuickBooks Online Payroll Premium?	Click **No, I don't want to add payroll**.
What should we do first?	Click **Track receipts and expenses**.
How do you track your receipts today?	Click **I save paper and digital receipts**.

> ✳ **HINT:** Don't be concerned if you didn't see all the questions or saw some new ones. You will be reviewing settings in STEP 4.

✓ Once the questions are answered, QBO will create your company file.

You're on your way!

Pooling your info ✓

Personalizing your setup ✓

Building your checklist ✓

Let's go

✓ Click **Let's go** in the final screen.

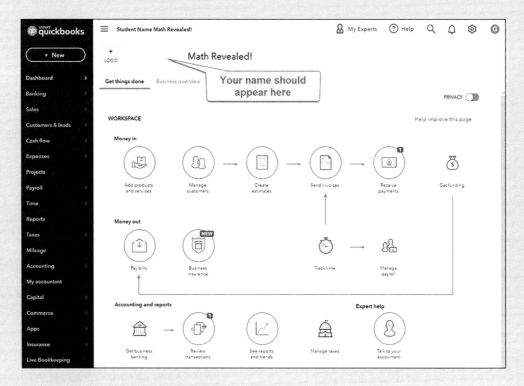

- You now have a company file!

> ✳ **HINT:** You may see a **SETUP CHECKLIST** at the top of the Dashboard.
> You will not need to complete the checklist, so go ahead and close it. You may
> also see an invitation to take a quick tour. You can accept that invitation or close
> the window and proceed to STEP 4.

eLecture

STEP 4—Change the settings.

✓ Now that you have a company file, it's time to change some of the settings.

> ✳ **HINT:** If you signed out or were logged out of QBO after setting up your
> new company, go to qbo.intuit.com to sign back in. You may be asked to add
> a company address before you can access the file. If so, enter "3835 Freeport
> Blvd, Sacramento, CA 95822."

✓ Click the on the icon bar.

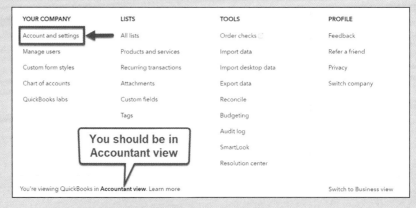

> **!** **WARNING:** If you inadvertently selected a role other than **Accountant** when answering the **What is your role?** question in STEP 3, you will be in **Business view** and certain tools and features may not be available to you. Click **Switch to Accountant view** at the bottom of the ⚙ menu before moving forward.

✓ Click **Account and settings.**

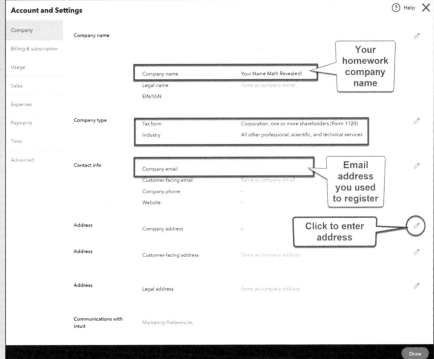

Figure 2.38

Company tab of Account and Settings

- On the **Company** tab, make sure the **Company name** includes your actual name and Math Revealed! Edit the field if necessary so your name comes first.

- Click the pencil icon in the **Address** section and enter "3835 Freeport Blvd, Sacramento, CA 95822." The same address is used for **customer-facing** and **legal** addresses.

> **✳ HINT:** Clicking the pencil icon will open the following box:
>
>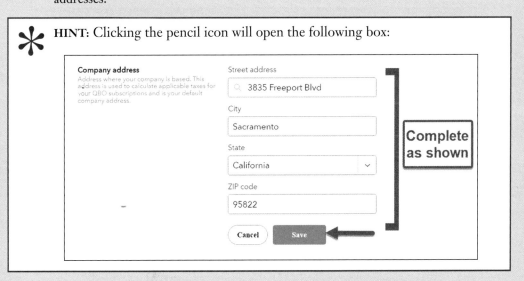

✓ **BEFORE YOU MOVE ON**, review your settings. Your screen should match the highlighted sections of Figure 2.38 and *Same as company address* should appear in the **customer-facing** and **legal** address fields.

✓ Open the **Sales** tab.

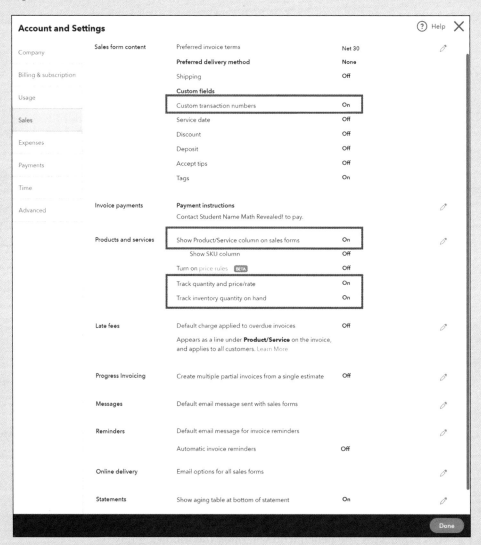

✓ Check to make sure the **Custom transaction numbers** setting is **On**. If not, click the pencil icon in the **Sales form content** section and check the **Custom transaction numbers** box. Click **Save**.

✓ Many of the sales settings were automatically changed when you selected the services needed. For example, when you checked **Manage your inventory** in the initial setup of your company file (STEP 3), QBO should have automatically made changes to the **Products and services** section.

✓ **BEFORE YOU MOVE ON**, review your settings. Your screen should match the highlighted sections of Figure 2.39.

✓ No changes need to be made on the **Expenses** or **Time** tabs at this point. You also can ignore the **Billing & subscription**, **Usage**, and **Payments** tabs.

✓ Open the **Advanced** tab and make the following changes. **TIP:** Click the pencil icon to open each section. You will need to click **Save** after making changes to a section.

- Company type—If necessary, select **Corporation, one or more shareholders (Form 1120)** in the **Tax form** dropdown menu.
- Chart of accounts—Toggle the box next to **Enable account numbers** to turn the feature on. Check the box next to **Show account numbers**.
- Automation—Toggle off all automation settings.
- Other preferences—Toggle all the warnings on. Warnings minimize the risk of duplicate entries!
    - You may also want to extend the amount of time QBO remains open when you're not actively working on your assignments. If so, make the change in the dropdown menu next to **Sign me out if inactive for**.

✓ **BEFORE YOU MOVE ON**, review your settings. Your screen should match the highlighted sections of Figure 2.40.

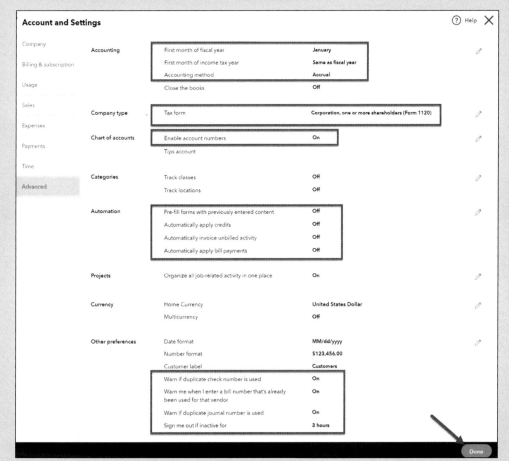

✓ Click **Done**.

STEP 5—Purge the chart of accounts.

QBO automatically created quite a few accounts for you when you set up your company in STEP 3. Unfortunately, many of the accounts that were set up are not needed in your homework company and many of the accounts you will need were not created by QBO.

 HINT: To see the chart of accounts set up by QBO, click the ⚙ on the icon bar and click **Chart of accounts**. Click **See your Chart of Accounts**.

Instead of adding and deleting these accounts (which is a tedious process), you will be purging the chart of accounts QBO set up and importing your own accounts into the company file.

✓ With QBO open to the **Dashboard**, change the URL by replacing 'homepage' with 'purgecompany' and click Enter. The URL will look something like app.qbo.intuit.com/app/purgecompany.

✓ You will get the following message:

Figure 2.41

Purge warning message

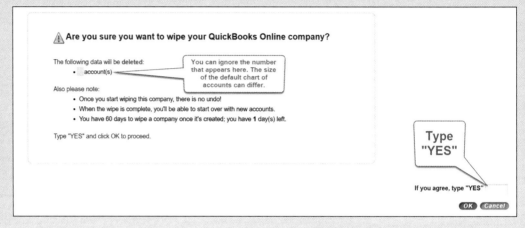

✓ Enter **YES** and click **OK**.

Figure 2.42

Final purge screen

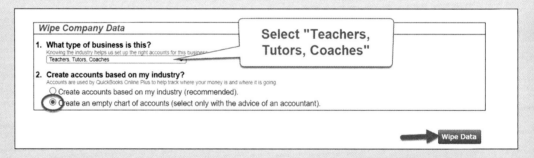

- Select "Teachers, Tutors, Coaches" in the dropdown menu for the first question. (It's in the **Educational Services** section.)
- Select **Create an empty chart of accounts** to answer the second question.
- Click **Wipe Data**. The chart of accounts has now been purged.

✓ Click on the icon bar and click **Chart of Accounts** in the **YOUR COMPANY** column.

✓ Click **See your Chart of Accounts**.

Figure 2.43

Purged chart of accounts

- The accounts remaining in the chart of accounts are default accounts that can't be deleted.

 HINT: Don't worry if you see several additional accounts listed in your **Chart of Accounts** or sightly different wording. You will be importing the accounts you need to get started.

BEHIND THE SCENES The chart of accounts and any recorded transactions are deleted when a company file is purged. All of the settings remain intact. Purging a company and importing data into a company can be done an unlimited number of times within the first 60 days of a new subscription.

✓ You are now ready to start importing data. If you are using myBusinessCourse, all of the files you will need for importing can be downloaded from the *Math Revealed! Import, Upload, and Dataset Files* folder in Student Ancillaries. You may want to download them all to your desktop, hard drive, or to a USB drive before you move forward. If you are not using myBusinessCourse, your instructor will provide the import files to you.

STEP 6—Import a new chart of accounts.

✓ In QBO, click the ⚙ on the icon bar.

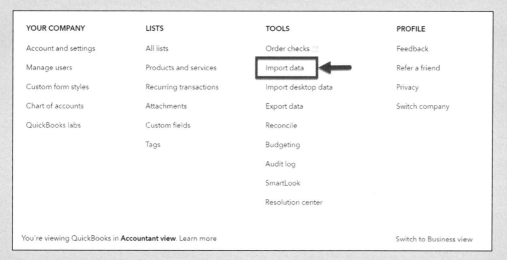

Figure 2.44

Access to import feature

✓ Click **Import data**.

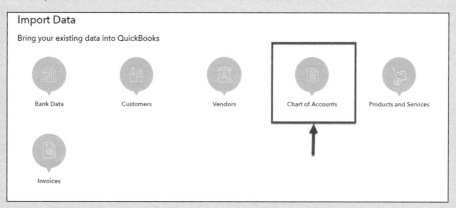

Figure 2.435

Import data selection

✓ Click **Chart of Accounts**.

Figure 2.46

File selection screen
for account import

✓ Upload your 7e Math Revealed Chart of Accounts for Importing .xlsx file into the **Select a CSV or Excel file to upload** field. The file name may be barely visible in the field. As long as you can see it, you'll be fine.

✓ Click **Next**.

BEHIND THE SCENES QBO automatically maps the fields on the Excel worksheet to the fields in the chart of accounts in QBO. Only certain data can be uploaded. Any fields that can't be imported, like account balances, will need to be entered manually.

Figure 2.47

Mapped fields for
account import

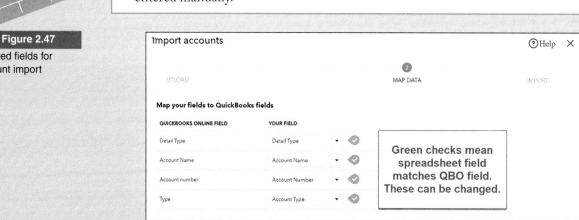

✓ Check to make sure the mapping of your fields to the QBO fields is accurate.

✓ Click **Next**.

Figure 2.48

Accounts to be
imported

● Scroll down through the screen. Any problems will be highlighted in red. If you have inadvertently changed a field, refer to the Excel spreadsheet and make the correction.

WARNING: If the **Import** light is not bright green, there is a problem with the data. Click **Back** to see if you uploaded the correct file. QBO is very sensitive to issues in import files. If changes have inadvertently been made to the Excel file, you will not be able to import the accounts. Download the correct Excel file from Student Ancillaries and try again.

✓ Click Import.

✓ **BEFORE YOU MOVE ON**, check your work. Click ⚙ on the icon bar. Click Chart of Accounts to see the new chart of accounts. It should include all of the accounts listed on the Excel spreadsheet with their account numbers.

STEP 7—Import the products and services list.

The process for importing products and services is similar to the process for importing the chart of accounts.

✓ Click the ⚙ on the icon bar.

✓ Click Import Data.

✓ Click Products and Services.

✓ Upload the **7e Math Revealed Products and Services List for Importing.xlsx** file.

✓ Click Next.

✓ Check to make sure the mapping of your fields to the QBO fields is accurate. **TIP:** Not all QBO fields need to be matched.

✓ Click Next.

✓ Correct any highlighted errors in fields. **TIP:** You will see red 0s in the QTY field in the first 3 rows. (These are service items so there are no quantities.) Click each 0 to remove the red. (Sometimes, the red can't be removed. If the Import link is bright green, you're fine!) If you see other errors, you may have inadvertently made changes to the Excel file. Download the correct file from Student Ancillaries and try again.

✓ Click Import.

✓ **BEFORE YOU MOVE ON**, check your work. Click the ⚙ on the icon bar and click Products and services. You should see all nine items from the Excel worksheet plus two items automatically set up by QBO (Hours and Services).

STEP 8—Clean up the chart of accounts and organize the products and services list.

A few changes need to be made to the chart of accounts. **TIP:** If you need help adding or editing accounts, refer back to the MANAGING THE CHART OF ACCOUNTS section of Chapter 1. To open the chart of accounts, click the ⚙ on the icon bar and click Chart of accounts.

✓ Change the Account name of the Services account to Tutoring Revenue and add 400 as the Account number. You don't have to change the detail type in the Tax form section field. **TIP:** To edit an account, click Edit in the ACTION column of the account row. You may need to scroll down the list to find the Services account.

✓ Several of the accounts don't have account numbers. Edit the accounts as follows:

Account Name	New Account Numbers
Inventory Asset	130
Retained Earnings	350
Sales of Product Income	420
Cost of Goods Sold	500

BEHIND THE SCENES All of the accounts listed in the table above (other than Retained Earnings) were automatically added to the chart of accounts when you imported the products and services.

✓ Advertising expense (Account 641) isn't showing as a sub-account of Marketing Costs. Edit the account to make Advertising expense (Account 641) a sub-account of Marketing Costs (Account 640). **TIP:** To make Advertising expense a sub-account, select Marketing Costs (the parent account) in the **Save account under** field.

✓ Add a new **expenses** account called Client relations expense (a sub-account of Marketing Costs). Select Marketing Costs in the **Save account under** field and **Entertainment** as the **detail type** in the **Tax form section** field. Use 645 as the account number. **TIP:** After saving this new account, you might want to review the chart of accounts list to make sure the account appears as a sub-account with the correct detail type and name.

✓ Organize the products and services list using **categories**. To open the list, click the ⚙ on the icon bar and click **Products and services**. On the **More** dropdown menu, select **Manage categories**. **TIP:** If you need help creating **categories**, refer back to the **Organizing the Products and Services List** section of this chapter.

✓ Set up the following **categories**:
- Books and Tools
- Tutoring
- Other

✓ Assign a **category** to each item on the **Products and Services** screen. **TIP:** To save time, use the shortcut for assigning **categories** to multiple items described in the **Organizing the Products and Services List** section of this chapter.

Item	Category
Crisis	Tutoring
Dry-Erase	Books and Tools
Hours (see HINT below)	Other
Kit	Books and Tools
Notebook	Books and Tools
Persistence	Tutoring
Puzzles	Books and Tools
Ready	Books and Tools
Refresher	Tutoring
Services (see HINT below)	Other
Sports	Books and Tools

✓ **BEFORE YOU MOVE ON**, check your work. Click **Reports** on the navigation bar. Open the **Product/Service List** report located in the **Sales and Customers** section of the **Standard** tab. Each item on the list above should appear as *Category:Item Name* in the **Name** column. For example, the first item on the list should appear as **Tutoring:Crisis**. If you find an error or forgot to assign a category, go back to your **Products and Services** list. Click **Edit** in the **ACTION** column of the item row to open the item record.

HINT: You may not see the Hours or Services items in your list. These are auto-generated by QBO and are not used in your homework so they can be ignored.

STEP 9—Import customers.

The process for importing customers is similar to the process for importing the chart of accounts.

✔ Click the ⚙ on the icon bar.

✔ Click **Import Data.**

✔ Click **Customers.**

✔ Upload the 7e Math Revealed Customer List for Importing.xlsx file.

✔ Click **Next.**

✔ Check to make sure the mapping of your fields to the QBO fields is accurate. **TIP:** Not all QBO fields need to be matched.

✔ Click **Next.**

✔ Correct any highlighted errors on the import list. **TIP:** If you inadvertently made changes to the Excel file, you may see errors. Download the correct file from Student Ancillaries and try again.

✔ Click **Import.**

✔ **BEFORE YOU MOVE ON,** check your work. Click **Sales** on the navigation bar and open the **Customers drawer** (tab). The customer list should include all of the customers included on the Excel spreadsheet.

STEP 10—Set up credit terms and payment methods

✔ Martin has decided to use "Net 15" as the default credit term for most customers. (Customers will be expected to pay within 15 days of the invoice date if they don't pay at the time of service.) He also wants to have the option of giving 30-day terms.

● Set up both Net 15 and Net 30 as credit terms. **TIP:** The **Terms** list is on the **All Lists** menu accessed through the ⚙ icon.

● You will be assigning terms to specific customers in Chapter 3.

 HINT: Credit terms may already be set up in your file. Check to make sure both Net 15 and Net 30 are listed. If additional terms are listed as well, you can leave them.

✔ Martin has also decided to accept Cash, Checks, VISA, or Mastercard as payment methods.

● Set up all four payment methods. **TIP:** The **Payment Methods** list is on the **All Lists** menu accessed through the ⚙ icon.

 HINT: Cash and Check may already be set up. You may also see a generic "Credit Card" listed as a payment method. You can leave the generic "credit card" method, but you'll need to create the two credit card methods (VISA and Mastercard).

STEP 11—Import vendors.

The process for importing vendors is similar to the process for importing the chart of accounts.

✓ Click the ⚙ on the icon bar.

✓ Click **Import Data**.

✓ Click **Vendors**.

✓ Upload the **7e Math Revealed Vendors List for Importing.xlsx** file.

✓ Click **Next**.

✓ Check to make sure the mapping of your fields to the QBO fields is accurate. **TIP:** Not all QBO fields need to be matched.

✓ Click **Next**.

✓ Correct any highlighted errors on the import list. **TIP:** If you inadvertently made changes to the Excel file, you may see errors. Download the correct file from Student Ancillaries and try again.

✓ Click **Import**.

✓ **BEFORE YOU MOVE ON**, check your work. Click **Expenses** on the navigation bar and select the **Vendors drawer** (tab). The vendor list should include all of the vendors and balances included on the Excel spreadsheet.

STEP 12—Import invoices.

There is a slightly different process for importing **invoices**.

✓ Click the ⚙ on the icon bar.

✓ Click **Import Data**.

✓ Click **Invoices**.

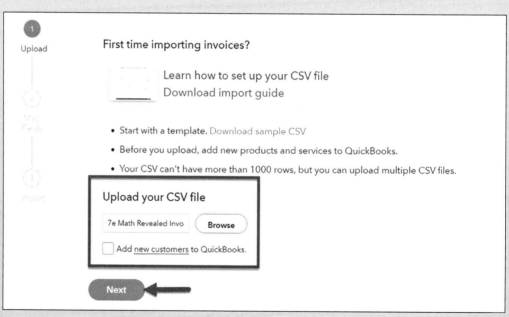

Upload

First time importing invoices?

Learn how to set up your CSV file
Download import guide

• Start with a template. Download sample CSV
• Before you upload, add new products and services to QuickBooks.
• Your CSV can't have more than 1000 rows, but you can upload multiple CSV files.

Upload your CSV file

| 7e Math Revealed Invo | Browse |

☐ Add new customers to QuickBooks.

Next

✓ Upload the 7e Math Revealed Invoices for Importing.csv file into the **Upload your CSV file** field and click **Next**.

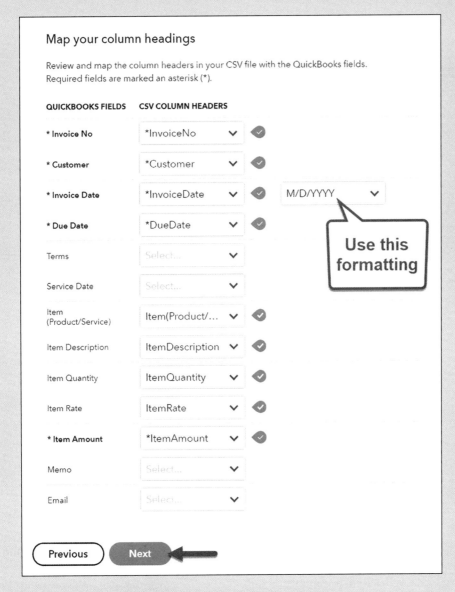

Figure 2.50

Mapped fields for
invoice import

✓   Check to make sure the mapping of your fields to the QBO fields is accurate. Select
    M/D/YYYY as the format for dates.

✓   Click **Next**.

Figure 2.51

Link to start invoice
import

✓   Click **Complete import.**

   •   When the import is complete, the following screen will appear:

Figure 2.52

Invoice import results
screen

✓ Click **OK**.

✓ **BEFORE YOU MOVE ON**, check your work. Click **Sales** on the navigation bar and select the **All Sales drawer** (tab). If the three invoices appear on the list, the import was successful.

✻ **HINT**: Occasionally, the invoice import tool appears to fail even though the import was successful. The screen looks something like this:

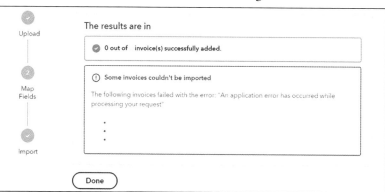

Click **Done**.

Click **Sales** on the navigation bar and select the **All Sales drawer** (tab). If the three invoices appear on the list, the import was successful.

Click to open one of the invoices on the list. If you get an **Error loading transaction** message, log out of QBO.

Log back in at qbo.intuit.com.

Click **Sales** on the navigation bar.

Click one of the invoices on the **All Sales drawer** (tab). You should now be able to open the transaction.

STEP 13—Check your balances.

This is still accounting so all the importing you just did should have resulted in a number of balanced journal entries, right? QBO creates entries for the accounts receivable, accounts payable, and inventory balances you imported using several different offset accounts. You will be adjusting those entries in STEP 14.

BEHIND THE SCENES One of the accounts used by QBO when importing data is **Opening balance equity**, an equity account. This account is unique to QBO and is used as a tool for balancing entries. There is no equivalent to this account in financial accounting. Any balance in **opening balance equity** should be cleared before financial reports are prepared. You will be clearing this account in STEP 14. Other offset accounts used by QBO are covered in Appendix 2A.

✓ To make sure you've got a good start, click **Reports** on the navigation bar.

✓ Click **Balance Sheet** in the **Favorites** section of the **Standard** tab. Change the date to 12/31/23 (in both date fields).

✓ Click **Run report**.

- Your balance sheet should look like Figure 2.53. If it doesn't, go back to STEP 5, purge the data, and start the import process over.

Figure 2.53

Starting balance sheet for Math Revealed!

Your Name Math Revealed!
Balance Sheet
As of December 31, 2023

	TOTAL
▾ ASSETS	
▾ Current Assets	
▾ Accounts Receivable	
120 Accounts Receivable	570.00
Total Accounts Receivable	**$570.00**
▾ Other Current Assets	
130 Inventory Asset	1,555.00
Total Other Current Assets	**$1,555.00**
Total Current Assets	**$2,125.00**
TOTAL ASSETS	**$2,125.00**
▾ LIABILITIES AND EQUITY	
▾ Liabilities	
▾ Current Liabilities	
▾ Accounts Payable	
200 Accounts Payable	381.00
Total Accounts Payable	**$381.00**
Total Current Liabilities	**$381.00**
Total Liabilities	**$381.00**
▾ Equity	
350 Retained Earnings	
Opening Balance Equity	1,555.00
Net Income	189.00
Total Equity	**$1,744.00**
TOTAL LIABILITIES AND EQUITY	**$2,125.00**

STEP 14—Enter the remaining account balances

The final step is to bring in the remaining **permanent account** balances as of December 31. There's more than one way to do this but the easiest way is to create a journal entry. You'll be learning more about journal entries in Chapter 5. For now, the basics are all you need.

✓ Click **+ New** on the navigation bar.

Permanent account An account used to prepare the balance sheet—that is, an asset, liability, or stockholders' equity account. Any balance in a permanent account at the end of an accounting period is carried forward to the following accounting period.

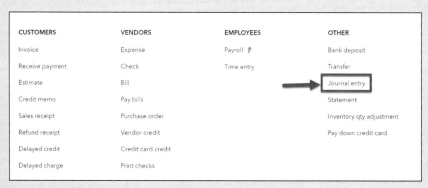

✓ Click **Journal Entry**.

- Change the **Journal date** to 12/31/23 and enter "Opening Entry" as the **Journal no.**
- Complete the entry exactly as it appears below:

Account	Debit	Credit	Description
100 Checking	3,620.00		Opening entry
125 Supplies On Hand	75.00		Opening entry
180 Computer & Office Equipment	3,230.00		Opening entry
189 Accumulated Depreciation		390.00	Opening entry
195 Security Deposit	1,000.00		Opening entry
280 Note Payable - Richard Smith		2,500.00	Opening entry
300 Common Stock		2,500.00	Opening entry
350 Retained Earnings		4,279.00	Opening entry
Opening Balance Equity	1,555.00		Opening entry
400 Tutoring Revenue	570.00		Opening entry
700 Interest expense		381.00	Opening entry
Total	**10,050.00**	**10,050.00**	

HINT: You can directly enter the accounts (using account names or numbers), or you can use the dropdown menu.

QBO will constantly try to "help" you by populating the debit or credit field with an amount that will balance the entry. Don't get distracted. Continue to enter the amounts as shown in Figure 2.56.

✓ Click **Save and close.**

✓ Click **Reports** on the navigation bar. Click **Balance Sheet.**
  - Change the dates to 12/31/23.
  - Click **Run report.** The report should look like Figure 2.57.

Figure 2.57

Opening balance sheet for Math Revealed!

Your Name Math Revealed!	
Balance Sheet	
As of December 31, 2023	
	TOTAL
▾ ASSETS	
▾ Current Assets	
▾ Bank Accounts	
100 Checking	3,620.00
Total Bank Accounts	**$3,620.00**
▾ Accounts Receivable	
120 Accounts Receivable	570.00
Total Accounts Receivable	**$570.00**
▾ Other Current Assets	
125 Supplies On Hand	75.00
130 Inventory Asset	1,555.00
Total Other Current Assets	**$1,630.00**
Total Current Assets	**$5,820.00**
▾ Fixed Assets	
180 Computer & Office Equipment	3,230.00
189 Accumulated Depreciation	-390.00
Total Fixed Assets	**$2,840.00**
▾ Other Assets	
195 Security Deposit	1,000.00
Total Other Assets	**$1,000.00**
TOTAL ASSETS	**$9,660.00**
▾ LIABILITIES AND EQUITY	
▾ Liabilities	
▾ Current Liabilities	
▾ Accounts Payable	
200 Accounts Payable	381.00
Total Accounts Payable	**$381.00**
Total Current Liabilities	**$381.00**
▾ Long-Term Liabilities	
280 Note Payable - Richard Smith	2,500.00
Total Long-Term Liabilities	**$2,500.00**
Total Liabilities	**$2,881.00**
▾ Equity	
300 Common Stock	2,500.00
350 Retained Earnings	4,279.00
Opening Balance Equity	0.00
Net Income	0.00
Total Equity	**$6,779.00**
TOTAL LIABILITIES AND EQUITY	**$9,660.00**

✓ If it does, you're ready to start entering January 2024 transactions for Math Revealed! in Chapter 3. If it doesn't, go back through the STEPs and see where you went wrong. Although QBO is a fairly easy system to use for day-to-day operations, it can be tough to get everything set up.

Suggested reports for Chapter 2 assignment

All reports can be found by clicking **Reports** on the navigation bar. All reports should be in portrait orientation. Customizing and exporting reports was covered in Chapter 1.

✓ Balance Sheet (in the **Favorites** section)
- Report date should be December 31, 2023.
- Customize the report as follows:
  - In the **General** section, select **(100)** in the **Negative Numbers** dropdown menu. This is a normal accounting convention for displaying negative numbers.
  - In the **Rows/Columns** section, select **Non-zero** for both rows and columns in the **Show non-zero or activity only** dropdown menu.

> **HINT:** You're going to be preparing balance sheet reports at the end of each chapter. You may want to save your customized report. Saving customized reports in QBO is covered in the *Advanced Report Modification* section of Chapter 1.

- Save as a PDF (export to PDF).

✓ Account List (in the **For My Accountant** section)
- Customize the report so just the **Account #**, **Account**, and **Type** columns appear.
- Save as PDF (export to PDF).
- **TIP:** There will be a few accounts without account numbers. These are default accounts that you will not be using.

✓ Product/Service List (in the **Sales and Customers** section)
- Click **Switch to classic view** if necessary and customize the report so that the following columns appear (in this order):
  - Product/Service
  - Type
  - Description
  - Qty On Hand
  - Price
  - Income Account
  - Cost
  - Expense Account
- Click **Run report**.
- In the **Sort** dropdown menu on the report toolbar (left edge), select **TYPE** and click **ascending order**.
- Save as a PDF (export to PDF).

✓ **Journal** report (in the **For my accountant** section)
- Enter 12/01/23 and 12/31/23 in the two **Report period** date fields.

✓ **Accounts receivable aging summary** report (in the **Who owes you** section)
- Enter 12/31/23 in the **As of** field

✓ **Accounts payable aging summary** report (in the **What you owe** section)
- Enter 12/31/23 in the **As of** field

Assignment 2B

Salish Software Solutions

Check with your instructor before you move forward. This assignment should only be used if your instructor assigned Salish Software Solutions for homework.

In this assignment, you'll be setting up your homework company file. This is the QBO file you'll be using to complete your homework in Chapters 3 through 11.

The steps should be completed in order.

 HINT: There are multiple videos available in myBusinessCourse to help you with this assignment.

STEP 1—Review the following background information about your company.

Background information: Sally Hanson, a good friend of yours, double majored in computer science and accounting in college. She worked for several years for a software company in Silicon Valley but the long hours started to take a toll on her personal life.

Last year she decided to open up her own company, Salish Software Solutions. Sally currently advises clients looking for new accounting software and assists them with software installation. She also provides training to client employees and occasionally troubleshoots software issues.

She has decided to start using QuickBooks Online to keep track of her business transactions. She likes the convenience of being able to access financial information over the Internet. You have agreed to act as her accountant while you're working on your accounting degree.

Sally has a number of clients that she is currently working with. She gives 15-day payment terms to her corporate clients but she asks for cash at time of service if she does work for individuals. She has developed the following fee schedule:

Name	Description	Rate
Select	Software selection	$500 flat fee
Set Up	Software installation	$ 75 per hour
Train	Software training	$ 50 per hour
Fix	File repair	$ 60 per hour

Sally rents office space from Alki Property Management for $650 per month.

The following furniture and equipment are owned by Salish:

Description	Date placed in service	Cost	Life	Salvage Value
Office furniture	6/1/23	$1,400	60 months	$200
Computer	7/1/23	$4,234	24 months	$250
Printer	7/1/23	$ 900	24 months	$ 0

All equipment is depreciated using the straight-line method.

As of 12/31/23, she owed $3,000 to Dell Finance. The monthly payment on that loan is $150 including interest at 5%. Sally's last payment to Dell was 12/31/23.

Over the next month or so, Sally plans to expand her business by selling some of her favorite accounting and personal software products directly to her clients. She has already purchased the following items:

Item Name	Description	Vendor	Quantity on Hand	Cost per Unit	Sales Price
Easy1	Easy Does It	Abacus Shop	15	$100	$200
Retailer	Simply Retail	Simply Accounting	2	$300	$600
Contractor	Simply Construction	Simply Accounting	2	$400	$800
Organizer	Organizer	Personal Software	20	$ 25	$ 50
Tracker	Investment Tracker	Personal Software	20	$ 30	$ 60

STEP 2—Obtain your license and open your company file.

Your instructor will direct Intuit to provide you with a one-year free license to QuickBooks Online Plus. Intuit Education will then email you an invitation to set up your homework file.

> **HINT:** The email will likely be sent to the address on file for you at your school. Make sure that the email address is correct.

Figure 2.58

Email invitation to set up a company file

> **WARNING:** Make sure you have enough time to complete STEP 3 before you move forward. It could be difficult to get back into your QBO file if the initial setup process wasn't finished.

✓ When you're ready, click **Accept Invitation**.

> **HINT:** If you get an error message about the link not working, right-click the *Accept invitation* link, select *Copy link location*, open a new window in Incognito (private) mode, and paste the copied URL into the address bar. If that doesn't work, clear your cache and try again. If you're still having issues, contact your instructor.

Figure 2.59

Registration screen

✓ Create your Intuit account by entering an email address, your name, and creating a password. The email address (and the related password) will be used each time you log in to QBO.

> **HINT:** You can use your school email address, your own personal email address, or you can set up an email address specifically for this course. Setting up a separate email offers the most security. Instructions for setting up a Gmail account are provided in Appendix 2B if you want to use a unique email address.
>
> If you already have an Intuit account, simply sign in using the link under **Create your account** at the top of the screen.

- Intuit accepts passwords that have the following characteristics:
  1. It must be at least 8 characters long.
  2. It must include both lowercase and uppercase letters.
  3. It must include a number.
  4. It must include a symbol.

✓ Click **Create Account**. You will see a welcome message:

Figure 2.60

Welcome message

✓ Click **Next**.

STEP 3—Answer the informational questions that appear in the next set of screens.

General information is entered in the first screens you'll see in QBO. The company name is entered, and its legal structure and business activities are identified. Intuit uses this information to activate various features so users can get started.

Intuit occasionally changes the order and wording of the setup questions. The specific questions that appear in your homework company file setup may differ from those that appear for your fellow students or your instructor.

Table 2B.1 shows the most common question wording and the answers that you should answer or select. Your questions may be in a different order. Some of the questions may not appear as part of your setup. New questions may be added. Use your best judgement. If you don't know how to answer a question, reach out to your instructor.

Table 2B.1

Company setup questions

Screen Heading	Answers
What do you call your business?	Your homework company name should be your name followed by Salish Software Solutions. For example, if your name were John Smith, you would enter *John Smith Salish Software Solutions* as your business name. Check the box next to **This is my legal business name**, if necessary.
How have you been managing your finances?	Click **Spreadsheets or pen & paper**
How long has your company been in business?	Click **Under a year**
What kind of business is this?	Click **No** to **Is it an LLC?** Click **C Corp** or **Corporation.** Click **C Corp** or **Corporation**.
What's your industry?	Enter *Professional services* in the field. Select **All other professional, scientific, and technical services** from the displayed options.
How does your business make money?	Click **Provides services** and **Sells products**.
Do you track projects?	Click **Sometimes**
What's your main role at Your Name Salish Software Solutions?	Click the option that includes the word **Accountant**.
Who works at this business?	Click **Only the owner** or **I fly solo**.
Is Salish Software Solutions your main source of income?	Click **No** and select **I do freelance/contract work**.
Does an expert help with your books?	Click **Yes**. **TIP:** You're the expert!
What apps do you use for your business?	Click **Skip for now** or **I don't use any apps**.
Link your accounts and see everything in one place.	Click **Skip for now**.
What is everything you want to set up?	Click all options **other than** those related to paying employees, accepting payments, tracking mileage, creating estimates, purchasing insurance, and getting a business bank account.
Want to add QuickBooks Online Payroll Premium?	Click **No, I don't want to add payroll**.
What should we do first?	Click **Track receipts and expenses**.
How do you track your receipts today?	Click **I save paper and digital receipts**.

 HINT: Don't be concerned if you didn't see all the questions or saw some new ones. You will be reviewing settings in STEP 4.

 Once the questions are answered, QBO will create your company file.

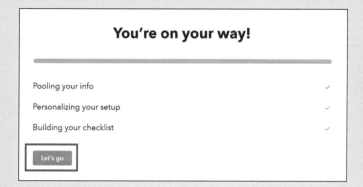

Figure 2.61

Final setup screen

✓ Click **Let's go** in the final screen.

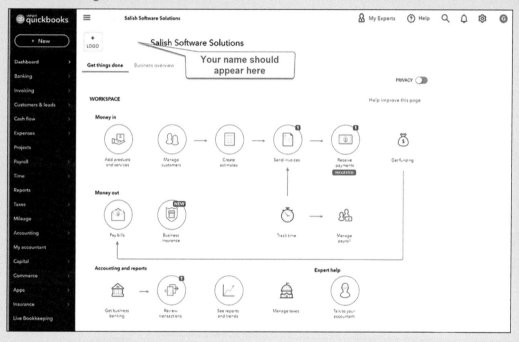

Figure 2.62

Dashboard

• You now have a company file!

✳ **HINT:** You may see a **SETUP CHECKLIST** at the top of the **Dashboard**. You will not need to complete the checklist, so go ahead and close it. You may also see an invitation to take a quick tour. You can accept that invitation or close the window and proceed to STEP 4.

STEP 4—Change the settings.

✓ Now that you have a company file, it's time to change some of the settings.

✳ **HINT:** If you signed out or were logged out of QBO after setting up your new company, go to qbo.intuit.com to sign back in. You may be asked to add a company address before you can access the file. If so, enter "3835 Freeport Blvd, Sacramento, CA 95822."

✓ Click the ⚙ on the icon bar.

eLecture

Figure 2.63

Gear menu

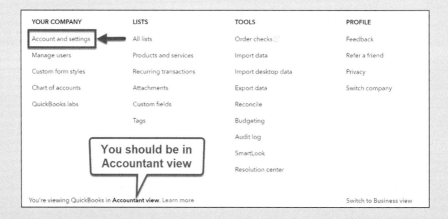

> **WARNING:** If you inadvertently selected a role other than **Accountant** when answering the **What is your role?** question in STEP 3, you will be in **Business view** and certain tools and features may not be available to you. Click **Switch to Accountant view** at the bottom of the ⚙ menu before moving forward.

✓ Click **Account and settings**.

Figure 2.64

Company tab of Account and Settings

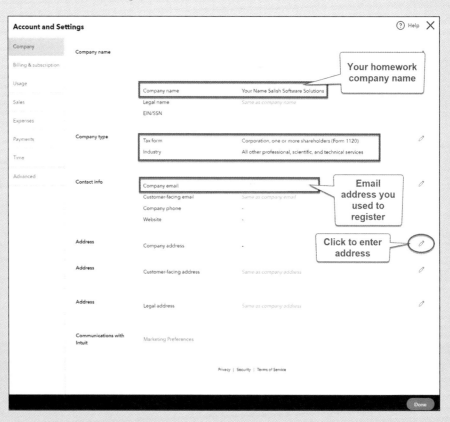

- On the **Company** tab, make sure the **Company name** includes your actual name and Salish Software Solutions. Edit the field if necessary so your name comes first.

- Click the pencil icon in the **Address** section and enter "3835 Freeport Blvd, Sacramento, CA 95822." The same address is used for **customer-facing** and **legal** addresses.

HINT: Clicking the pencil icon will open the following box:

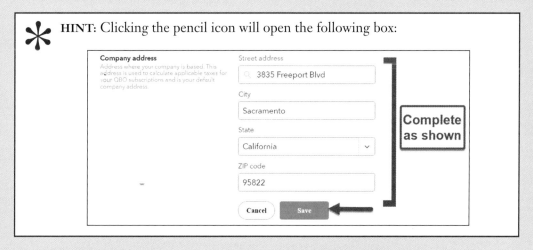

✓ **BEFORE YOU MOVE ON**, review your settings. Your screen should match the highlighted sections of Figure 2.64 and *Same as company address* should appear in the **customer-facing** and **legal** address fields.

✓ Open the **Sales** tab.

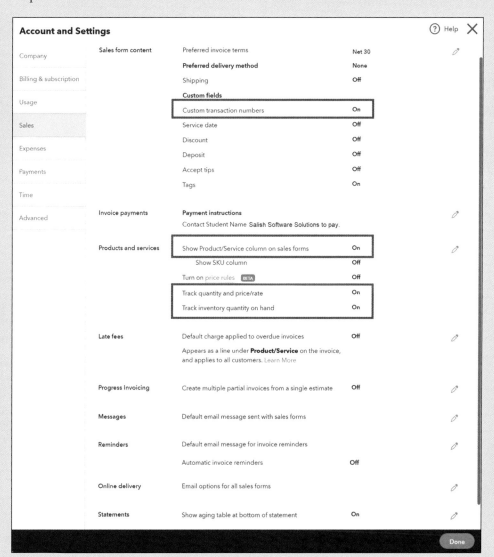

© 2024 Cambridge Business Publishers

Figure 2.65

Completed Sales tab in Account and Settings

✓ Check to make sure the **Custom transaction numbers** setting is **On**. If not, click the pencil icon in the **Sales form content** section and check the **Custom transaction numbers** box. Click **Save**.

✓ Many of the sales settings were automatically changed when you selected the services needed. For example, when you checked **Manage your inventory** in the initial setup of your company file (STEP 3), QBO should have automatically made changes to the **Products and services** section.

✓ **BEFORE YOU MOVE ON**, review your settings. Your screen should match the highlighted sections of Figure 2.65.

✓ No changes need to be made on the **Expenses** or **Time** tabs at this point. You can ignore the **Billing & subscription**, **Usage**, and **Payments** tabs.

✓ Open the **Advanced** tab and make the following changes. **TIP:** Click the pencil icon to open the section. You will need to click **Save** after making changes to a section.

- **Company type**—If necessary, select **Corporation, one or more shareholders (Form 1120)** in the **Tax form** dropdown menu.

- **Chart of accounts**—Toggle the box next to **Enable account numbers** to turn the feature on. Check the box next to **Show account numbers**.

- **Automation**—Toggle off all automation settings.

- **Other preferences**—Toggle all the warnings on. Warnings minimize the risk of duplicate entries!

  - You may also want to extend the amount of time QBO remains open when you're not actively working on your assignments. If so, make the change in the dropdown menu next to **Sign me out if inactive for**.

✓ **BEFORE YOU MOVE ON**, review your settings. Your screen should match the highlighted sections of Figure 2.66.

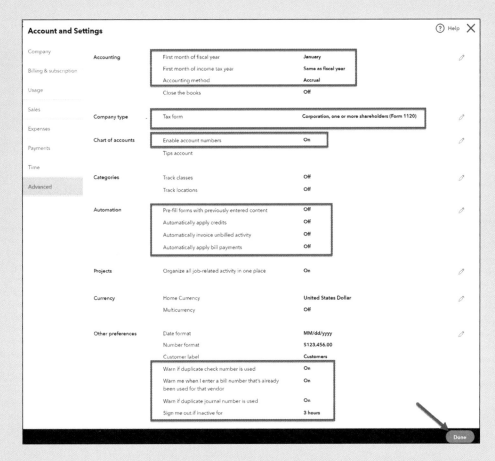

Figure 2.66

Completed Advanced tab of Account and Settings

✓ Click **Done**.

STEP 5—Purge the chart of accounts.

QBO automatically created quite a few accounts for you when you set up your company in STEP 3. Unfortunately, many of the accounts that were set up are not needed in your homework company and many of the accounts you will need were not created by QBO.

 HINT: To see the chart of accounts set up by QBO, click the ⚙ on the icon bar and click **Chart of accounts** in the **YOUR COMPANY** column. Click **See your Chart of Accounts**.

Instead of adding and deleting these accounts (which is a tedious process), you will be purging the chart of accounts QBO set up and importing your own accounts into the company file.

✓ With QBO open to the **Dashboard**, change the URL by replacing 'homepage' with 'purgecompany' and click Enter. The URL will look something like app.qbo.intuit.com/app/purgecompany.

✓ You will get the following message:

Figure 2.67

Purge warning
message

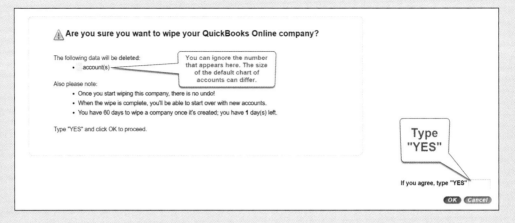

✓ Enter **YES** and click **OK**.

Figure 2.68

Final purge screen

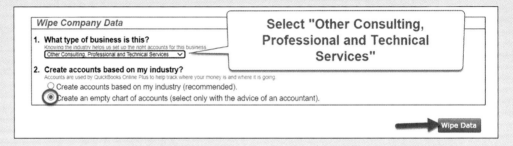

- Select "Other Consulting, Professional, and Technical Services." in the dropdown menu for the first question. (It's in the **Consulting, Professional, and Technical Services** section.)
- Select **Create an empty chart of accounts** to answer the second question.
- Click **Wipe Data**. The chart of accounts has now been purged.

✓ Click ⚙ on the icon bar and click **Chart of Accounts** in the **Your Company** column.

✓ Click **See your Chart of Accounts**.

Figure 2.69

Purged chart of
accounts

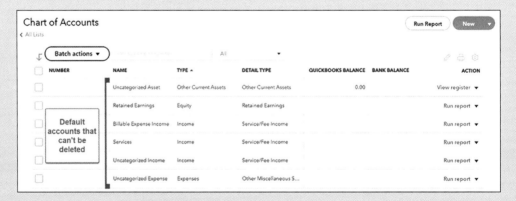

- The accounts remaining in the chart of accounts are default accounts that can't be deleted.

 HINT: Don't worry if you see several additional accounts listed in your **Chart of Accounts** or sightly different wording. You will be importing the accounts you need to get started.

> **BEHIND THE SCENES** The chart of accounts and any recorded transactions are deleted when a company file is purged. All of the settings remain intact. Purging a company and importing data into a company can be done an unlimited number of times within the first 60 days of a new subscription.

✓ You are now ready to start importing data. If you are using myBusinessCourse, all of the files you will need for importing can be downloaded from the *Salish Software Solutions Import, Upload, and Dataset Files* folder in Student Ancillaries. You may want to download them all to your desktop, hard drive, or to a USB drive before you move forward. If you are not using myBusinessCourse, your instructor will provide the import files to you.

STEP 6—Import a new chart of accounts.

✓ In QBO, click the ⚙ on the icon bar.

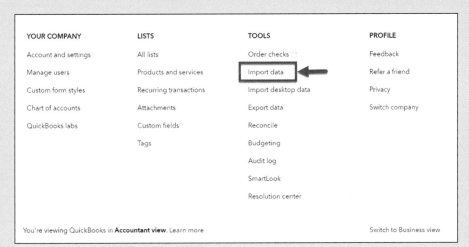

Figure 2.70

Access to import feature

✓ Click **Import data**.

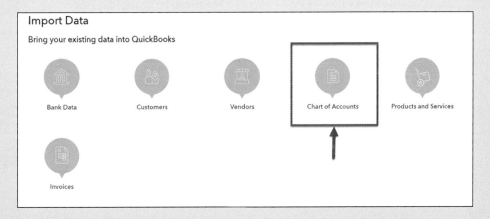

Figure 2.71

Import data selection

✓ Click **Chart of Accounts**.

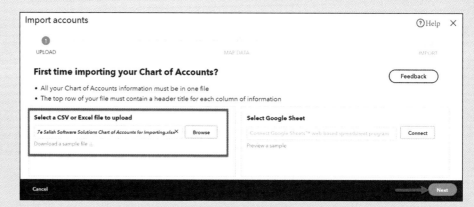

✓ Upload your 7e Salish Software Solutions Chart of Accounts for Importing .xlsx file into the **Select a CSV or Excel file to upload** field. The file name may be barely visible in the field. As long as you can see it, you're fine.

✓ Click **Next**.

> **BEHIND THE SCENES** QBO automatically maps the fields on the Excel worksheet to the fields in the chart of accounts in QBO. Only certain data can be uploaded. Any fields that can't be imported, like account balances, will need to be entered manually.

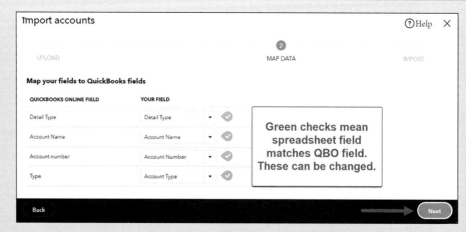

✓ Check to make sure the mapping of your fields to the QBO fields is accurate.

✓ Click **Next**.

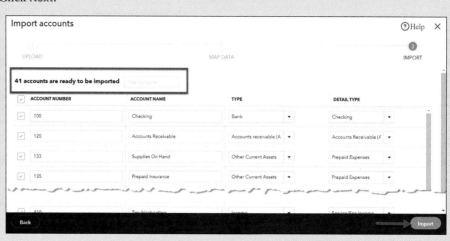

- Scroll down through the screen. Any problems will be highlighted in red. If you have inadvertently changed a field, refer to the Excel spreadsheet and make the correction.

> **!** **WARNING:** If the **Import** light is not bright green, there is a problem with the data. Click **Back** to see if you uploaded the correct file. QBO is very sensitive to issues in import files. If changes have inadvertently been made to the Excel file, you will not be able to import the accounts. Download the correct Excel file from Student Ancillaries and try again.

✓ Click **Import**.

✓ **BEFORE YOU MOVE ON**, check your work. Click ⚙ on the icon bar. Click **Chart of Accounts** to see the new chart of accounts. It should include all of the accounts listed on the Excel spreadsheet with their account numbers.

STEP 7—Import the products and services list.

The process for importing products and services is similar to the process for importing the chart of accounts.

✓ Click the ⚙ on the icon bar.

✓ Click **Import Data**.

✓ Click **Products and Services**.

✓ Upload the 7e Salish Software Solutions Products and Services List for Importing.xlsx file.

✓ Click **Next**.

✓ Check to make sure the mapping of your fields to the QBO fields is accurate. **TIP:** Not all QBO fields need to be matched.

✓ Click **Next**.

✓ Correct any highlighted errors in fields. **TIP:** You will see red 0s in the **QTY** field in the first 4 rows. (These are **service** items so there are no quantities.) Click each 0 to remove the red. (Sometimes, the red can't be removed. If the **Import** link is bright green, you're fine!) If you see other errors, you may have inadvertently made changes to the Excel file. Download the correct file from Student Ancillaries and try again.

✓ Click **Import**.

✓ **BEFORE YOU MOVE ON**, check your work. Click the ⚙ on the icon bar and click **Products and services**. You should see all nine items from the Excel worksheet plus two items automatically set up by QBO (**Hours** and **Services**).

STEP 8—Clean up the chart of accounts and organize the products and services list.

A few changes need to be made to the chart of accounts. **TIP:** If you need help adding or editing accounts, refer back to the **MANAGING THE CHART OF ACCOUNTS** section of Chapter 1. To open the chart of accounts, click the ⚙ on the icon bar and click **Chart of accounts**.

✓ Change the **Account name** of the Services account to Software Selection and Installation Revenue and add 400 as the **Account number**. You don't have to change the **detail type** in the **Tax form section** field. **TIP:** To edit an account, click **Edit** in the **ACTION** column of the account row. You may need to scroll down the list to find the **Services** account.

✓ Several of the accounts don't have account numbers. Edit the accounts as follows:

Account Name	New Account Numbers
Inventory Asset	130
Retained Earnings	350
Sales of Product Income	420
Cost of Goods Sold	500

BEHIND THE SCENES All of the accounts listed in the table above (other than Retained Earnings) were automatically added to the chart of accounts when you imported the products and services.

✓ Advertising expense isn't showing as a sub-account of Marketing Costs. Edit the account to make Advertising expense (Account 651) a sub-account of Marketing Costs (Account 650). **TIP:** To make Advertising expense a sub-account, select Marketing Costs (the parent account) in the **Save account under** field.

✓ Add a new account called Client relations expense. This is an **Expense** account and a sub-account under Marketing Costs. Select **Entertainment** as the **detail type** in the **Tax form section** and use 655 as the account number. **TIP:** After saving this new account, you might want to review the chart of accounts list to make sure the account appears as a sub-account with the correct detail type and name.

✓ Organize the products and services list using **categories**. To open the list, click the ⚙ on the icon bar, click **Products and services**, and select **Manage categories** from the **More** dropdown menu. **TIP:** If you need help creating or assigning **categories**, refer back to the **Organizing the Products and Services List** section of this chapter.

✓ Set up the following **categories**:
- Consulting and Installation
- Products
- Other

✓ Assign a **category** to each item on the Products and Services list. **TIP:** To save time, use the shortcut for assigning **categories** to multiple items described in the **Organizing the Products and Services List** section of this chapter.

Item	Category
Contractor	Products
Easy1	Products
Fix	Consulting and Installation
Hours (See HINT below)	Other
Organizer	Products
Retailer	Products
Select	Consulting and Installation
Services (See HINT below)	Other
Set Up	Consulting and Installation
Tracker	Products
Train	Consulting and Installation

✓ **BEFORE YOU MOVE ON**, check your work. Select **Reports** from your navigation bar. Locate and run the **Product/Service List** report located in the **Sales and Customers** section of the **Standard** tab. Each item on the list above should appear on the report as *Category:Item Name* in the **Name** column. For example, the first item in the list should appear as **Products:Contractor**. If you find an error or forgot to assign a **category**, go back to your **Products and Services** list to make a change.

HINT: You may not see the Hours or Services items in your list. These are auto-generated by QBO and are not used in your homework so they can be ignored.

STEP 9—Import customers.

The process for importing customers is similar to the process for importing the chart of accounts.

✓ Click the ⚙ on the icon bar.

✓ Click **Import Data**.

✓ Click **Customers**.

✓ Upload the 7e Salish Software Solutions Customer List for Importing.xlsx file.

✓ Click **Next**.

✓ Check to make sure the mapping of your fields to the QBO fields is accurate. **TIP:** Not all QBO fields need to be matched.

✓ Click **Next**.

✓ Correct any highlighted errors on the import list. **TIP:** If you inadvertently made changes to the Excel file, you may see errors. Download the correct file from Student Ancillaries and try again.

✓ Click **Import**.

✓ **BEFORE YOU MOVE ON**, check your work. Click **Sales** on the navigation bar and open the **Customers drawer** (tab). The customer list should include all of the customers included on the Excel spreadsheet.

STEP 10—Set up credit terms and payment methods

✓ Sally has decided to use "Net 15" as the default credit term for most customers. (Customers will be expected to pay within 15 days of the invoice date if they don't pay at the time of service.) She also wants to have the option of giving 30 day terms.

- Set up both Net 15 and Net 30 as credit terms. **TIP:** The **Terms** list is on the **All Lists** menu accessed through the ⚙ icon.
- You will be assigning terms to specific customers in Chapter 3.

 HINT: Credit terms may already be set up in your file. Check to make sure both Net 15 and Net 30 are listed.

✓ Sally has also decided to accept Cash, Checks, VISA, or Mastercard as payment methods.

- Set up all four payment methods. **TIP:** The **Payment Methods** list is on the **All Lists** menu accessed through the ⚙ icon.

 HINT: Cash and Check may already be set up. You may also see a generic "Credit Card" listed as a payment method. Make sure you set up the specific credit card types (VISA and Mastercard). If additional terms are listed as well, you can leave those there.

STEP 11—Import vendors.

The process for importing vendors is similar to the process for importing the chart of accounts.

✓ Click the ⚙ on the icon bar.

✓ Click **Import Data**.

✓ Click **Vendors**.

✓ Upload the **7e Salish Software Solutions Vendors List for Importing.xlsx** file.

✓ Click **Next**.

✓ Check to make sure the mapping of your fields to the QBO fields is accurate. **TIP:** Not all QBO fields need to be matched.

✓ Click **Next**.

✓ Correct any highlighted errors on the import list. **TIP:** If you inadvertently made changes to the Excel file, you may see errors. Download the correct file from Student Ancillaries and try again.

✓ Click **Import**.

✓ **BEFORE YOU MOVE ON**, check your work. Click **Expenses** on the navigation bar and select the **Vendors drawer** (tab). The vendor list should include all of the vendors and balances included on the Excel spreadsheet.

STEP 12—Import invoices.

There is a slightly different process for importing **invoices**.

✓ Click the ⚙ on the icon bar.

✓ Click **Import Data**.

✓ Click **Invoices**.

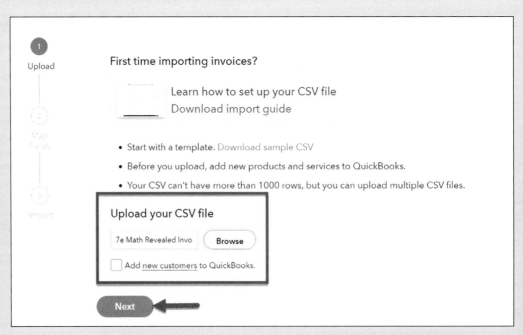

Figure 2.75

File selection screen for invoice import

✓ Upload the 7e Salish Software Solutions Invoices for Importing.csv file into the **Upload your CSV file** field and click **Next**.

Figure 2.76

Mapped fields for invoice import

✓ Check to make sure the mapping of your fields to the QBO fields is accurate. Select **M/D/YYYY** as the format for dates.

✓ Click **Next**.

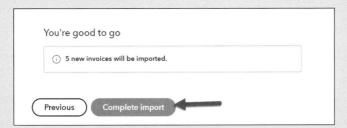

Figure 2.77

Link to start invoice import

✓ Click **Complete import**.

- When the import is complete, the following screen will appear:

Figure 2.78

Invoice import results screen

✓ Click **OK**.

✓ **BEFORE YOU MOVE ON**, check your work. Click Sales on the navigation bar and select the **All Sales drawer** (tab). If the five invoices appear on the list, the import was successful.

 HINT: Occasionally, the invoice import tool appears to fail even though the import was successful. The screen looks something like this:

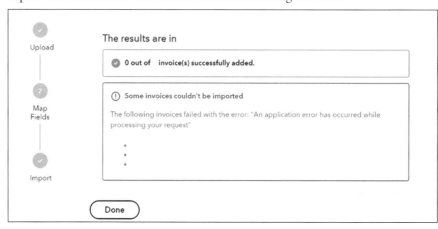

Click **Done**.

Click **Sales** on the navigation bar and select the **All Sales drawer** (tab). If the five invoices appear on the list, the import was successful.

Click to open one of the invoices on the list. If you get an **Error loading transaction** message, log out of QBO.

Log back in at qbo.intuit.com.

Click **Sales** on the navigation bar.

Click one of the invoices on the **All Sales drawer** (tab). You should now be able to open the transaction.

STEP 13—Check your balances.

This is still accounting so all the importing you just did should have resulted in a number of balanced journal entries, right? QBO creates entries for the accounts receivable, accounts payable, and inventory balances you imported using several different offset accounts. You will be adjusting those entries in STEP 14.

> **BEHIND THE SCENES** One of the accounts used by QBO when importing data is **Opening balance equity**, an equity account. This account is unique to QBO and is used as a tool for balancing entries. There is no equivalent to this account in financial accounting. Any balance in **opening balance equity** should be cleared before financial reports are prepared. You will be clearing this account in STEP 14. Other offset accounts used by QBO are covered in Appendix 2A.

✓ To make sure you've got a good start, click **Reports** on the navigation bar.

✓ Click **Balance Sheet** in the **Favorites** section of the **Standard** tab. Change the date to 12/31/23 (in both date fields).

✓ Click **Run report**.

● Your balance sheet should look like Figure 2.79. If it doesn't, go back to STEP 5, purge the data, and start the import process over.

Figure 2.79

Starting balance sheet for Salish Software Solutions

Your Name Salish Software Solutions

Balance Sheet
As of December 31, 2023

	TOTAL
▾ ASSETS	
▾ Current Assets	
▾ Accounts Receivable	
120 Accounts Receivable	1,380.00
Total Accounts Receivable	**$1,380.00**
▾ Other Current Assets	
130 Inventory Asset	4,000.00
Total Other Current Assets	**$4,000.00**
Total Current Assets	**$5,380.00**
TOTAL ASSETS	**$5,380.00**
▾ LIABILITIES AND EQUITY	
▾ Liabilities	
▾ Current Liabilities	
▾ Accounts Payable	
200 Accounts Payable	895.00
Total Accounts Payable	**$895.00**
Total Current Liabilities	**$895.00**
Total Liabilities	**$895.00**
▾ Equity	
350 Retained Earnings	
Opening Balance Equity	4,000.00
Net Income	485.00
Total Equity	**$4,485.00**
TOTAL LIABILITIES AND EQUITY	**$5,380.00**

Permanent account An account used to prepare the balance sheet—that is, an asset, liability, or stockholders' equity account. Any balance in a permanent account at the end of an accounting period is carried forward to the following accounting period.

STEP 14—Enter the remaining account balances

The final STEP is to bring in the remaining **permanent account** balances as of December 31. There's more than one way to do this but the easiest way is to create a journal entry. You'll be learning more about journal entries in Chapter 5. For now, the basics are all you need.

✓ Click **＋New** on the navigation bar.

Figure 2.80

Access to journal entry form

CUSTOMERS	VENDORS	EMPLOYEES	OTHER
Invoice	Expense	Payroll 🔾	Bank deposit
Receive payment	Check	Time entry	Transfer
Estimate	Bill		Journal entry
Credit memo	Pay bills		Statement
Sales receipt	Purchase order		Inventory qty adjustment
Refund receipt	Vendor credit		Pay down credit card
Delayed credit	Credit card credit		
Delayed charge	Print checks		

✓ Click **Journal Entry**.

Figure 2.81

Journal entry form

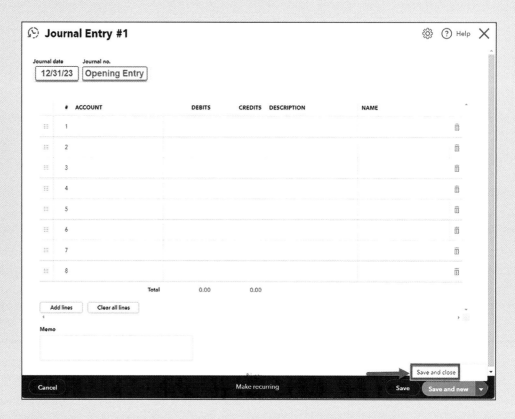

Figure 2.82

Journal entry for
recording balances
for Salish Software
Solutions

- Change the **Journal date** to 12/31/23 and enter "Opening Entry" as the **Journal no.**
- Complete the entry exactly as it appears below:

Account	Debit	Credit	Description
100 Checking	10,500.00		Opening entry
180 Computer & Office Equipment	5,134.00		Opening entry
182 Office Furniture & Equipment	1,400.00		Opening entry
189 Accumulated Depreciation		1,361.00	Opening entry
195 Security Deposit	1,000.00		Opening entry
280 Note Payable		3,000.00	Opening entry
300 Common Stock		2,000.00	Opening entry
350 Retained Earnings		16,158.00	Opening entry
Opening Balance Equity	4,000.00		Opening entry
400 Software Selection and Installati	1,200.00		Opening entry
410 Troubleshooting	180.00		Opening entry
700 Interest expense		895.00	Opening entry
Total	**23,414.00**	**23,414.00**	

> ✱ **HINT:** You can directly enter the accounts (using account names or numbers), or you can use the dropdown menu.
>   QBO will constantly try to "help" you by populating the debit or credit field with an amount that will balance the entry. Don't get distracted. Continue to enter the amounts as shown in Figure 2.82.

✓ Click **Save and close**.

✓ Click **Reports** on the navigation bar. Click **Balance Sheet**.

- Change the dates to 12/31/23.
- Click **Run report**. The report should look like Figure 2.83:

Figure 2.83

Opening balance sheet for Salish Software Solutions

Your Name Salish Software Solutions

Balance Sheet
As of December 31, 2023

	TOTAL
▾ ASSETS	
▾ Current Assets	
▾ Bank Accounts	
100 Checking	10,500.00
Total Bank Accounts	**$10,500.00**
▾ Accounts Receivable	
120 Accounts Receivable	1,380.00
Total Accounts Receivable	**$1,380.00**
▾ Other Current Assets	
130 Inventory Asset	4,000.00
Total Other Current Assets	**$4,000.00**
Total Current Assets	**$15,880.00**
▾ Fixed Assets	
180 Computer Equipment	5,134.00
182 Office Furniture & Equipment	1,400.00
189 Accumulated Depreciation	-1,361.00
Total Fixed Assets	**$5,173.00**
▾ Other Assets	
195 Security Deposit	1,000.00
Total Other Assets	**$1,000.00**
TOTAL ASSETS	**$22,053.00**
▾ LIABILITIES AND EQUITY	
▾ Liabilities	
▾ Current Liabilities	
▾ Accounts Payable	
200 Accounts Payable	895.00
Total Accounts Payable	**$895.00**
Total Current Liabilities	**$895.00**
▾ Long-Term Liabilities	
280 Note Payable	3,000.00
Total Long-Term Liabilities	**$3,000.00**
Total Liabilities	**$3,895.00**
▾ Equity	
300 Common Stock	2,000.00
350 Retained Earnings	16,158.00
Opening Balance Equity	0.00
Net Income	0.00
Total Equity	**$18,158.00**
TOTAL LIABILITIES AND EQUITY	**$22,053.00**

✓ If it does, you're ready to start entering January 2024 transactions for Salish Software Solutions in Chapter 3. If it doesn't, go back through the STEPs and see where you went wrong. Although QBO is a fairly easy system to use for day-to-day operations, it can be tough to get everything set up.

Suggested reports for Chapter 2 assignment

All reports can be found by clicking **Reports** on the navigation bar. All reports should be in portrait orientation. Customizing and exporting reports was covered in Chapter 1.

✓ Balance Sheet (in the **Favorites** section)
- Report date should be December 31, 2023.
- Customize the report as follows:
  - In the **General** section, select **(100)** in the **Negative Numbers** dropdown menu. This is a normal accounting convention for displaying negative numbers.
  - In the **Rows/Columns** section, select **Non-zero** for both rows and columns in the **Show non-zero or activity only** dropdown menu.
- Save as a PDF (export to PDF).

> ✳ **HINT:** You're going to be preparing balance sheet reports at the end of each chapter. You may want to save your customized balance sheet. Saving customized reports in QBO is covered in the *Advanced Report Modification* section of Chapter 1.

✓ Account List (in the **For My Accountant** section)
- Customize the report so just the **Account #**, **Account**, and **Type** columns appear.
- Save as PDF (export to PDF).
- **TIP:** There will be a few accounts without account numbers. These are default accounts that you will not be using.

✓ Product/Service List (in the **Sales and Customers** section)
- Click **Switch to classic view** if necessary and customize the report so that the following columns appear (in this order):
  - Product/Service
  - Type
  - Description
  - Qty On Hand
  - Price
  - Income Account
  - Cost
  - Expense Account
- Click **Run report**.
- In the **Sort** dropdown menu on the report toolbar (left edge), select **TYPE** and click **ascending order**.
- Save as a PDF (export to PDF).

✓ **Journal** report (in the **For my accountant** section)
- Enter 12/01/23 and 12/31/23 in the two **Report period** date fields.

✓ **Accounts receivable aging summary** report (in the **Who owes you** section)
- Enter 12/31/23 in the **As of** field

✓ **Accounts payable aging summary** report (in the **What you owe** section)
- Enter 12/31/23 in the **As of** field

APPENDIX 2A WHICH ACCOUNTS GET DEBITED AND CREDITED WHEN LISTS ARE IMPORTED INTO QBO?

When users convert existing companies to QBO, they often bring in lists and beginning account balances using the Import data feature. Information typically imported includes:

LO 2-4 Understand how imported data is accounted for in QBO

Import Option	What information typically gets imported?	What doesn't get imported
Chart of accounts	Account names, numbers, type (account and detail)	Account balances
Products and Services	Name and description, type, default sales and purchase prices, associated general ledger accounts, quantity on hand, and tax status	
Customers	Name and contact information	Terms
Vendors	Name and contact information, any unpaid vendor balance	Terms
Invoices	Details of unpaid invoices (invoice number and date, due date, product or service item, quantity, and rate and tax status and rate)	

 HINT: Although accounts receivable balances (totals by customer) can be included in the customer list import, most companies choose instead to import individual invoices. The invoice detail allows the company to better communicate with customers and monitor past due accounts.

When account balances are included in the imports, a journal entry is automatically created by QBO.

Import Option	Transaction Type	Account Debited	Account Credited
Products	Inventory Starting Value	Default inventory asset account	Opening balance equity
Vendors	Bill	An expense account	Accounts Payable (A/P)
Invoices	Invoice	Accounts Receivable (A/R)	An income account

The account credited in the import of products (opening balance equity) is a default account (equity account type) used by QBO to keep entries in balance. This same account is used when opening balances are entered in an account record. Any balances in opening balance equity must be transferred out before financial statements are prepared. In your homework assignment, you zero out the account balance as part of STEP 14.

QBO debits an expense account (expense account type) when unpaid balances are included in the import of vendors. There is no standard expense account used. For example, the Miscellaneous account is debited if vendor balances are imported into the test drive company. When vendor balances are imported into your homework company file, the Interest expense account will likely be debited.

An income account (income account type) is credited when invoices are imported into QBO. Typically, the account used is the default Services account. You edited the Services account as part of your Chapter 2 assignment, so that will be the account credited in the underlying journal entry.

You can check which accounts have been debited or credited in your homework company file by creating a Journal report for the period 12/1 to 12/31/23.

APPENDIX 2B SETTING UP YOUR GOOGLE GMAIL ACCOU

If This Is Your First Gmail Account

Open your Internet browser and enter https://accounts.google.com/signup as the URL. You should see the following screen.

Figure 2B.1

Google account setup screen

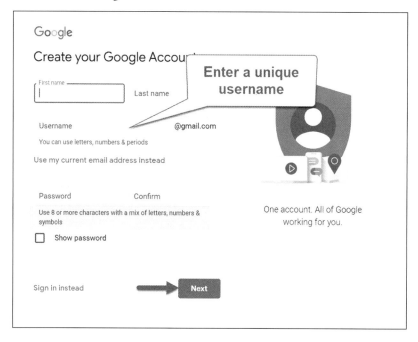

You may want to use your own name followed by your homework company name or your accounting course number as your username.

The password you create should be unique and include 8 or more characters (letters, numbers, and symbols). Click Next.

Figure 2B.2

Security information for Google account

To increase your security, enter your phone number and an alternate email address. You are not required to provide that information, but it can be helpful for keeping your account secure. You will be required to enter your birth date and gender.

Click **Next**.

You may be asked about using your phone number for various Google services. Click **Skip** or **I'm in**.

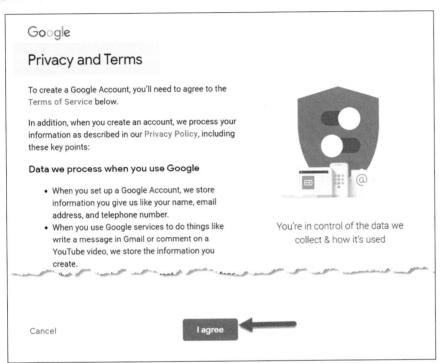

Figure 2B.3

Google account privacy and terms information

You will need to read and agree to Google's **Terms of Service**. Click **I agree** when you've completed your review.

If You Already Have a Gmail Account

It's probably best to set up a new Gmail account for use with your homework assignments but it's not required.

To set up a new Gmail account, open your Internet browser and enter www.google.com as the URL.

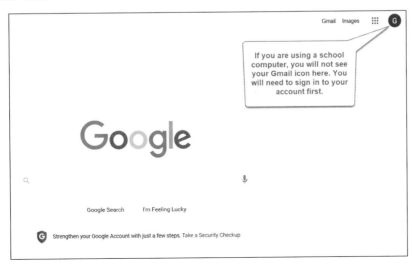

Figure 2B.4

Google sign-in screen

Click your account icon at the top right corner of the page.

Figure 2B.5

Access to new Gmail
account setup

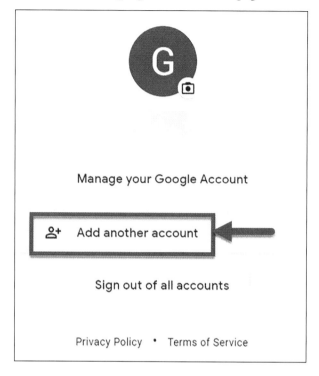

Click **Add another account** to progress to the next screen.

Figure 2B.6

Access to create
account

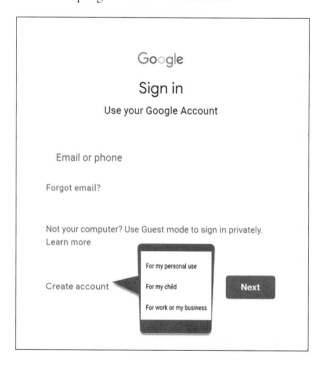

Click **Create account** and choose **For my personal use**.

 HINT: If you see a **Choose an account** screen instead of the one shown above, click **Use another account**, click **More options**, and then click **Create account**.

Figure 2B.7
Google account setup
screen

You may want to use your own name followed by your homework company name or your accounting course number as your username.

The password you create next should be unique and include 8 or more characters (letters, numbers, and symbols). Click **Next**.

If you already have security features activated with Google, you will get a screen asking for your phone number. An activation code will be texted to you. You will need to enter the code to move forward.

Figure 2B.8
Security information for
Google account

To increase your security, enter your phone number and an alternate email address. You are not required to provide that information, but it can be helpful for keeping your account secure. You will be required to enter your birth date and gender.

Click Next.

You may be asked about using your phone number for various Google services. Once you've verified your number, click Skip or Yes, I'm in.

Figure 2B.9

Google account privacy and terms information

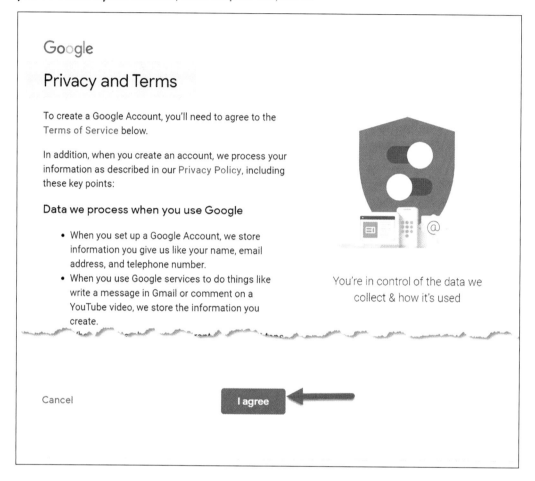

You will need to read and agree to Google's Terms of Service. Click I agree when you've completed your review.

QuickBooks

SECTION TWO

Service Companies

Businesses are frequently classified by primary source of revenue.

* Service companies earn revenue by charging a fee for services they perform.
* Merchandising companies earn revenue by buying products from one company and selling those products to consumers (or to distributors).
* Manufacturing companies earn revenue by making products and selling them to consumers (or to merchandisers).

In this textbook, we'll be looking at how QuickBooks Online can be used by service and merchandising companies.

> **BEHIND THE SCENES** Currently, the features needed for managing inventory in a manufacturing company are not available in QBO. There are, however, a few apps (add-on products) that can be purchased by manufacturing companies interested in using QBO.

We'll look at service companies first because the accounting for them is, in general, the least complex.

WHEN YOU MAKE MISTAKES

QBO is very forgiving. You can change, void, or delete most transactions pretty much at will.

Just remember, in a regular company transactions would not be changed or deleted if the transaction has been completed. (For example, the invoice has been sent out or a check has been sent to the vendor.) Why? Because the transaction has already occurred. (The customer has the invoice. The vendor has the check.) Instead, errors are corrected by creating a new transaction. (A credit memo or additional invoice is sent to the customer. A new check or a request for credit is sent to the vendor.) If the transaction has not been completed, it could be changed or voided. For example, if an invoice was created but not sent to the customer, it could be changed. If a check was printed but not mailed, it could be voided.

That being said, we're not in a real business, so you will probably want to edit or delete transactions that you enter incorrectly in your homework assignments.

> **BEHIND THE SCENES** In QBO, deleted transactions don't appear on reports. Voided transactions do appear but with zero dollar amounts. (Keeping a record of voided transactions is a good internal control policy.)

There is one thing you need to know before you start changing or deleting transactions in QBO. Oftentimes, transactions are related. For example, you record a customer invoice. You record the customer payment of that invoice. You record the deposit of the customer payment. Those are three transactions that are linked in QBO.

Certain linked transactions cannot be changed. For instance, QBO will not allow you to change a customer payment that's already been deposited. You would need to delete the deposit of that check, make any necessary changes to the payment, and then re-record the deposit. If a linked transaction **can** be changed or deleted, QBO will give you a warning first.

Figure S3.1

Warning message when editing linked transactions

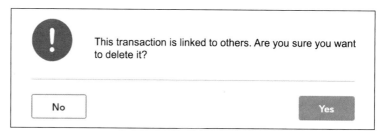

This transaction is linked to others. Are you sure you want to delete it?

No   Yes

Although QBO will allow you to make the change, related transactions will likely be affected. Make sure you consider the full impact of your changes.

Suggestions for Finding Mistakes

You will be given check figures to help you as you complete your homework assignments. If all your numbers agree to the check figures, you have a reasonably good chance of having completed the assignment correctly. (Agreeing to check figures is not a **guarantee** that all the entries are recorded correctly, but it's certainly a comfort!)

What if you don't agree? Where do you start looking? Here are some suggestions.

- **CHECK DATES.** Entering an incorrect date is the single most common cause of student errors—and student headaches! QBO enters default dates when you first open a form. It defaults to the current date when you start entering transactions during a work session. If you change the date on the first invoice, it will default to that new date when you enter the second invoice. If you open a new form, however, it will default back to the current date. Accounting is date driven, so your financial statements won't match the check figures if you enter a transaction in the wrong month. First thing to do? Pull a report of transactions dated BEFORE the first transaction date in the assignment (a **journal**) and then one of the transactions dated AFTER the last transaction date of the assignment.

- **There are always two sides to every story.** This is **double-entry accounting**, so if one account is wrong, then at least one other account is also wrong. It's hard to find errors in cash, accounts receivable, and accounts payable due to the sheer volume of transactions that affect these accounts. So, if your numbers don't match the check figures, see if you can find the other account(s) that is (are) also off. If you can find the error(s), you can fix all the affected accounts.

- **Debits on the left, credits on the right.** QBO gets the debit and credit part down really well when it comes to standard transactions (invoices, checks, etc.). However, when it comes to journal entries, QBO relies completely on you. It will debit (credit) whatever you tell it to debit (credit). We're all human. Sometimes we get our journal entries reversed. You can often fairly quickly spot those errors by looking at the balance sheet. Does Accumulated Depreciation show a debit balance? That's a problem. Look at supplies accounts, prepaid accounts, and accrued expense accounts and see if the balances look reasonable. Adjusting journal entries are frequently made to those accounts.

- **Math hints.** Errors can also be found, sometimes, by checking the difference between the check figure and your total. Is the number divisible by nine? You may have a transposition error. (For example, you entered 18 instead of 81.) All differences due to transposition errors are divisible by nine. Is the difference equal to the amount of a transaction? Maybe you forgot to enter it (or entered it on the wrong date). Is the difference equal to twice one of your transactions? You may have entered in a journal entry backward. (Watch those debits and credits!)

SECTION OVERVIEW

Chapter 3 will cover the sales cycle in a service company.
Chapter 4 will cover the purchase cycle in a service company.
Chapter 5 will cover end-of-period accounting in a service company.

Double-entry accounting A method of accounting that results in the recording of equal amounts of debits and credits.

Debit An entry on the left side (or in the debit column) of an account.

Credit An entry on the right side (or in the credit column) of an account.

3 Sales Activity
(Service Company)

Road Map

LO	Learning Objective	Topic	Subtopic	Page	Practice Exercises	Videos
LO 3-1	Describe and demonstrate the process for modifying sales settings in QBO [p. 3-6]	Modifying standard sales settings		3-6	3.1	Modifying standard sales settings
LO 3-2	Explain and demonstrate the QBO process for adding, editing, and inactivating customers in QBO [p. 3-7]	Managing customers	Customer center display	3-8	3.2	Managing customers
			Adding a customer	3-9		
			Viewing customer information	3-12		
			Editing customer information	3-14		
			Inactivating or merging customers	3-14		
LO 3-3	Demonstrate an understanding of the purpose and use of service items in QBO [p. 3-17]	Managing service items	Adding a service item	3-18	3.3	Managing service items
			Editing, duplicating, and inactivating services	3-20		
LO 3-4	Describe and demonstrate the process for recording sales revenue in QBO [p. 3-23]	Recording sales revenue	Recording sales on account	3-24	3.4	Recording sales revenue
			Recording cash sales	3-29		
LO 3-5	Describe and demonstrate the process for recording payments on account made by customers [p. 3-33]	Recording payments from customers	Payments on account	3-33	3.5	Recording payments from customers
LO 3-6	Demonstrate an understanding of the process for depositing customer payments in QBO [p. 3-36]	Making deposits		3-36	3.6	Making deposits
LO 3-7	Describe and demonstrate the process for recording credits and refunds to customers in QBO [p. 3-38]	Recording customer credits and refunds	Creating credit memos	3-39	3.7	Recording customer credits and refunds
			Applying credit memos	3-41		
			Issuing refunds to customers	3-46		
LO 3-8	Recognize and prepare common reports used in the sales cycle [p. 3-50]	Preparing sales and customer reports		3-50	3.8	

WHAT IS THE SALES CYCLE IN A SERVICE COMPANY?

The sales cycle in a service company normally follows these steps:

- Get the job (client).
- Provide the service.
- Bill for the service.
- Collect the fee.

Getting the job (or the client) is outside the accounting function, but the accounting system does need to maintain records related to the transactions with every customer.

At the very least, the following information must be maintained for each customer:

- Contact information
- Terms of payment
- Record of past transactions
- Record of any unpaid invoices

MODIFYING STANDARD SALES SETTINGS

LO 3-1 Describe and demonstrate the process for modifying sales settings in QBO

eLecture

When a company file is first created, certain sales settings are automatically selected in QBO. You made changes to some of those settings when you set up your company file in Chapter 2. Other changes may be made as the company grows and changes.

For example, a company might decide to send out bills in batches. An invoice might be created when work is performed, but instead of printing the invoice immediately, it is batched with other invoices and printed later. Other companies might want to customize messages added to sales forms.

To modify default sales settings, click the ⚙ in the icon bar. Click **Account and Settings**. Open the **Sales** tab.

Settings are changed by toggling features on or off. Features with multiple options use dropdown menus. To get more information about the feature, click the **?** next to the option.

The **Sales form content** section of the **Sales** tab would look like Figure 3.1 for a company that:

- has standard payment terms of Net 10
- does not do batch processing
- uses custom transaction numbers
- gives discounts to customers on occasion

Figure 3.1

Sales form content section of Account and Settings

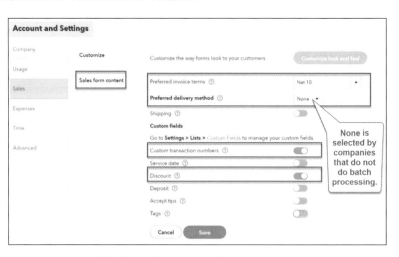

> **BEHIND THE SCENES** The settings selected are defaults. Many defaults can be changed when specific transactions are entered.

PRACTICE
EXERCISE
3.1

Make some changes to the sales settings for Craig's Design and Landscaping.
(Craig has decided that most customers will be given terms of Net 15.)

1. Click the ⚙ on the icon bar.
2. Click **Account and Settings**.
3. Open the **Sales** tab.
4. **Make a note** of the **Preferred delivery method** for Craig's Design and Landscaping as identified in the **Sales form content** section.
5. Click **Preferred invoice terms**.
6. Select **Net 15** as the preferred terms in the dropdown menu.
7. Click **Save**.
8. Click **Done** to close **Account and Settings**.

MANAGING CUSTOMERS

Customers are managed in the Customer Center. The Customer Center is accessed through the **Sales** link on the navigation bar. (It can also be accessed through the **Customers & leads** link.)

LO 3-2 Explain and demonstrate the QBO process for adding, editing, and inactivating customers in QBO

eLecture

| Figure 3.2 |

Drawers on Sales link in navigation bar

> **HINT:** A description of what's included in the various **drawers** (tabs) in the **Sales** link is included in Chapter 1 (Table 1.2).

Select the **Customers drawer** (tab).

The Customer Center screen is shown in Figure 3.3.

In the Customer Center, you can:

- access the new customer setup window.

- access forms necessary to record activity with existing customers.

- access existing customer data for editing.

Customer Center Display

Selected information about sales activity is highlighted in the **Money bar** at the top of the Customer Center screen.

Click on any of the amounts to bring up a list of the transactions included in the total.

Just above the **ACTION** column in the list of customers are three small icons.

The **printer** icon (far left) allows users to print a list of all vendors. The list includes all customer information included on the screen.

Clicking the **export** icon (the middle icon) automatically downloads the list as an Excel file.

Clicking the third icon (the ⚙) allows users to customize the fields displayed in the Customer Center.

Display columns can include any of the following:

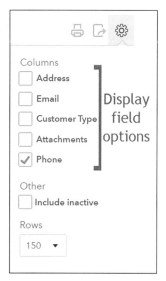

Figure 3.6

Column options for Customer Center screen

If other features were activated in QBO, other options would be available.

> **BEHIND THE SCENES** Having the phone number or the email address displayed can be time-saving for users working directly with customers on a regular basis.

Adding a Customer

To add a new customer, open the Customer Center by clicking **Sales** in the navigation bar and selecting the **Customers drawer** (tab).

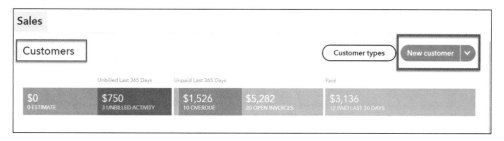

Figure 3.7

Link to add customer

Click **New customer** to open a sidebar.

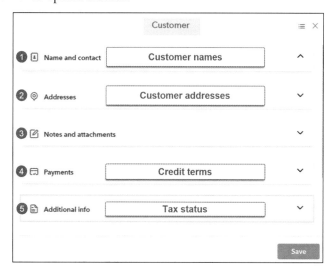

Figure 3.8

Customer record

There are five sections in the customer record.

Figure 3.9

Name and contact
section of customer
record

Basic contact information is entered in the **Name and contact** section. The name entered in the **Company name** field is the name used in any correspondence with businesses' customers (on invoices for example). If the customer was an individual, the name would be entered in the row above (**First name** and **Last name**, for example). In most cases, the company name or individual's name would be entered in the **Name to print on checks** field.

The **Customer display name** is used as a customer identifier. It could be a number or a shortened version of the name. This is the primary name used to organize the customer list. It's also the name used in any search functions. The **Customer display name** is primarily used for internal purposes. In the homework, you'll use the **Company name** as the **Customer display name**.

 HINT: **Customer display names** must be unique. An entity that is both a customer and a vendor can use the same **Customer name** but must have two different **Customer display names**. One option would be to add a C (customer) or a V (vendor) to the end in the **Customer display name** fields.

Phone and other contact information is also entered in the **Name and contact** section.

Figure 3.10

Addresses section of
customer record

Billing and shipping addresses are included in the **Addresses** section.

If shipping and billing addresses differ, both must be entered. The shipping address generally determines the sales tax rate used. Sales taxes are covered in detail in Chapter 6.

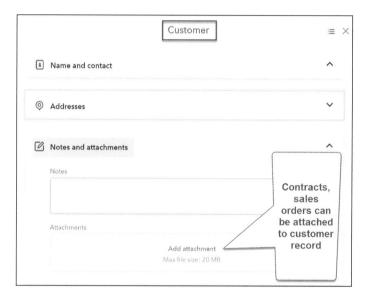

Figure 3.11

Notes and attachments section of customer record

The **Notes and attachments** section is used for adding information about the customer. For example, if companies have documents that apply specifically to the customer, they can be uploaded here.

Figure 3.12

Payments section of customer record

Default credit terms for the customer are noted on the **Payments** section. This is an important field. Payment terms need to be communicated to customers, and payment status needs to be tracked by companies. Users can also indicate information about the customer's preferred payment method (check, cash, credit card, etc.). If the user normally prints or emails invoices in batches, that would be noted in the **Sales form delivery options** field. If **Use company default** is selected in that field, the option selected on the **Sales** tab of **Account and settings** will be used. These are all defaults. Terms and payment methods can be changed when a specific sales transaction is entered.

Users can elect to send **invoices** to companies in a specific language. The language is identified in the **Language to use when you send invoices** field in the **Payments** section.

English is the default. Other options are French, Spanish, Italian, Chinese, and Portuguese. Only the basic field titles are translated. The language used in setting up item names and messages is used in the body of the invoice.

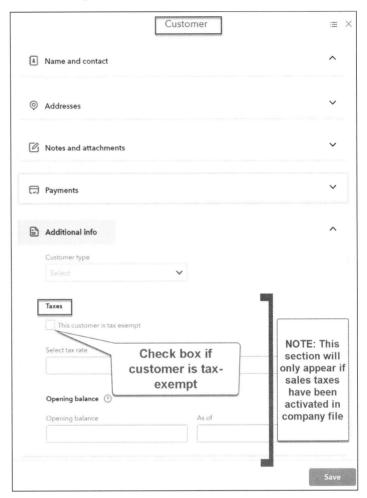

The tax status of a customer is identified in the Additional info section of the customer record. The screenshot in Figure 3.13 is what will you see in your homework company file once sales tax is activated. New customers are automatically identified as taxable and the rate is determined by QBO based on the location of the sale. If the This customer is tax exempt box is checked, the user would need to identify the reason for the exemption. (The section in the test drive company looks slightly different, but the basic information is the same.) Sales taxes will be covered in detail in Chapter 6.

Companies can also identify a Customer type in the Additional info section. This feature might be useful to companies that want to track revenues by customer size or industry. Customer types are set up by the user. There are no default types set up in QBO.

Viewing Customer Information

To view information about a specific customer, click the customer's name in the Customer Center. The Customer Details tab in the customer record would look something like Figure 3.14 for Craig's customer, Cool Cars.

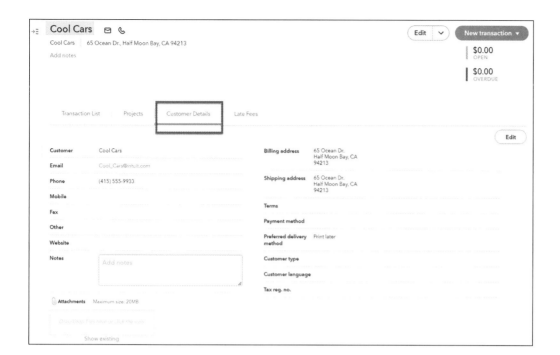

Figure 3.14

Customer Details tab in customer record

Contact information for the customer is included on the **Customer Details** tab.

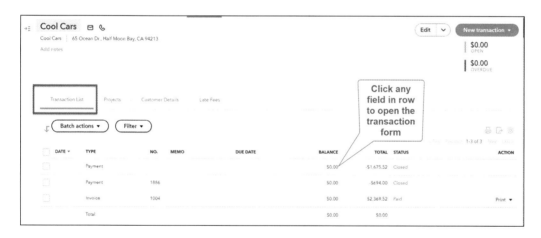

Figure 3.15

Transaction List tab in customer record

On the **Transaction List** tab, prior transactions are listed. Click anywhere on a transaction row to open the appropriate form.

Projects can be set up for customers on the **Projects** tab. (The **Projects** tab will only appear if project tracking has been activated in the company file.) Projects will be covered in Chapter 10. We will not cover late fees (the final tab) in this course.

 HINT: For access to the full list of customers when you're in a specific customer record, click the three parallel lines to the left of the customer name. A sidebar will open.

(continued)

(continued from previous page)

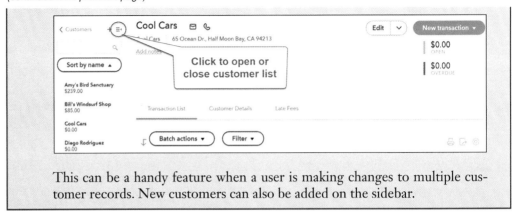

This can be a handy feature when a user is making changes to multiple customer records. New customers can also be added on the sidebar.

Editing Customer Information

Customer information can be changed at any time. To edit an existing customer, open the Customer Center by selecting **Sales** on the navigation bar and opening the **Customers drawer** (tab).

Click the name of the company you wish to edit.

Customer record window

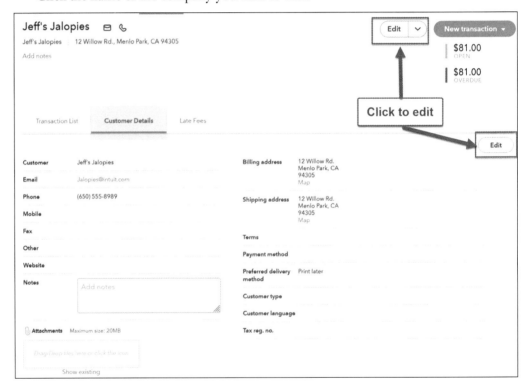

Click the **Edit** link at the top of the screen or the **Edit** link on the **Customer Details** tab to open the customer record sidebar. Changes can be made in any field.

Inactivating or Merging Customers

Inactivating a customer

Although customers cannot be deleted in QBO, customers with no open balance can be identified as inactive.

HINT: If customers with open balances are inactivated, a journal entry or credit memo is automatically created. Accounts receivable is credited and a revenue account is debited. Open balances should be cleared before customers are inactivated.

Companies might inactivate customers that are no longer in business or that have not purchased products or services in the past year.

To inactivate a customer, open the Customer Center by clicking **Sales** in the navigation bar and selecting the **Customers drawer** (tab).

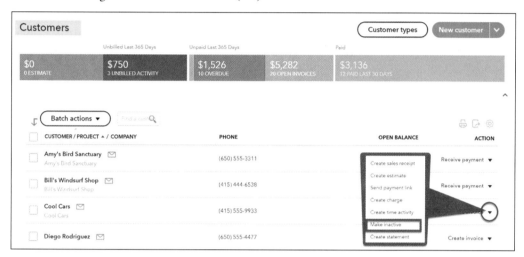

Figure 3.17

Make inactive option on Action dropdown menu

On the dropdown menu in the far-right column of the customer name, select **Make inactive**.

Inactive customers can't be used in transactions and aren't available in search functions, although they will show up on appropriate reports.

To reactivate a customer, all inactive customers must be visible in the Customer Center. Click the ⚙ icon right above the **ACTION** column in the Customer Center.

Figure 3.18

Option to include inactive customers in Customer Center display

Check the **Include inactive** box to make inactive customers visible.

Figure 3.19

Option to reactivate customer

An option to reactivate the customer will now appear in the **ACTION** column next to the inactivated customer name.

> **BEHIND THE SCENES** Although the customer shows as "deleted" in Figure 3.19, the customer has been inactivated.

Merging customers

Customers can be merged together in QBO. When two customers are **merged**, all transactions with one customer are "transferred" to the other customer (i.e., the customer name fields are changed on all transactions). **Merging** might be necessary if a duplicate customer was set up by mistake or if a customer combined multiple stores or locations.

As an example, let's say a single customer was inadvertently set up as two separate customers in the test drive company in QBO (Dylan Sollfrank and Dylan Sollfranks). Transactions were entered under both customer names.

Assuming the correct spelling of the customer's name was Dylan Sollfrank, the company would want to **merge** Dylan Sollfranks **into** Dylan Sollfrank.

To combine (**merge**) two companies, open the Customer Center by clicking **Sales** on the navigation bar and opening the **Customers drawer** (tab).

Click the name of the customer to be merged.

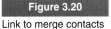

Figure 3.20

Link to merge contacts

Select **Merge contacts** on the **Edit** dropdown menu.

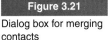

Figure 3.21

Dialog box for merging contacts

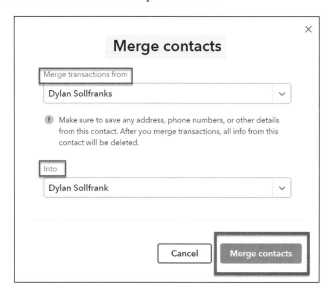

Select the name of the customer with transactions to be merged in the **Merge transactions from** dropdown menu. Select the name of the customer to be retained in the **Into** dropdown menu.

Click **Merge contacts**.

HINT: Only the **transactions** for the customer being **merged** are transferred. Addresses, sales tax status, terms, etc., are not. Important notes, contact information, or attachments should be added to the record of the customer to be retained before starting the **merge** process.

Add and edit customers for Craig's Design and Landscaping.
(Craig's gets a new client and receives an address change for an existing client.)

1. Click **Sales** (navigation bar).

2. Open the **Customers drawer** (tab).

3. Click **New Customer** and set up Barrio Café as a new customer:

   a. Enter "Barrio Cafe" in the **Company name** field. The **Customer display name** and **Name to print on checks** fields should autofill.

   b. Tab to the **Phone number** field and enter "415-199-2222."

   c. Open the **Addresses** section.

      i. Enter "1515 Oceanspray Drive; Sausalito, CA 94965" as the **Billing address**.

      ii. Check the box next to **Same as billing address** in the **Shipping address** section.

   d. Open the **Payments** section.

      i. Select **Net 15** in the **Terms** dropdown menu.

   e. Click **Save**.

4. Click **Sales** (navigation bar).

5. Click the **Customers drawer** (tab).

   a. Verify that the new customer (Barrio Cafe) appears on the list.

6. Edit a customer. (Change the billing address for Jeff's Jalopies.)

   a. Click the name **Jeff's Jalopies** in the Customer Center.

   b. Click **Edit** to open the customer record.

   c. **Make a note** of Jeff's last name.

   d. In the **Addresses** section change the billing street address to "4848 Dragrace Road."

   e. Open the **Payments** section and select **Net 15** as the **Terms**.

   f. Click **Save**.

7. Click **Dashboard**.

PRACTICE EXERCISE 3.2

MANAGING SERVICE ITEMS

There are various types of **product** and **service** items in QBO. In this chapter, we are concerned only with **service** items. **Inventory** and **non-inventory products** are covered in Chapter 6.

Service items represent charges for the various services performed by a company as part of its regular operations and are used when entering sales transactions and when reporting sales activity.

The following information is included in the setup of a **service** item:

• The standard rate (price) to be charged to the customer.

LO 3-3 Demonstrate an understanding of the purpose and use of service items in QBO

- The description that should appear on sales transaction forms.
- The income account that should be credited when the customer is charged and debited when a credit memo is issued.

> **BEHIND THE SCENES** Each **service** item can be associated with only one income account, but one income account can be associated with many items. This allows the company to keep considerable detail in subsidiary ledgers but keep the general ledger (and the financial statements) relatively simple. For example, a law firm might have one income account called Client Fees but could have separate service items to track the various types of fees (meetings, research, courtroom time, etc.).

All **products** and **services** appear on the **Products and Services** list. The list page is often referred to as the Products and Services Center.

Adding a Service Item

To add a new **service** item, click the ⚙ on the icon bar and select **Products and services** under **Lists**.

Figure 3.22

Access to new item sidebar

Click **New**. A sidebar will appear (Figure 3.23).

Figure 3.23

New item sidebar

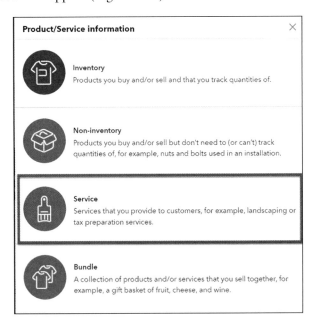

Click **Service** to open the **service** item setup window:

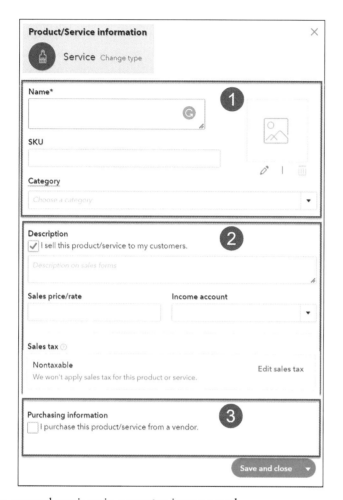

Figure 3.24

New service item screen

There are three general sections in a **service** item record.

	Service Item Record	
Section	**Purpose**	**Fields**
1	Naming details	Name, SKU, Category
2	Details for sales transaction forms	Description, Sales price/rate, Income account, Tax status
3	Details for purchase transaction forms, **if applicable**	Description, Cost, Expense account, Preferred vendor

The only required fields are **Name**, **Income account**, and **Sales tax** (if sales taxes have been activated in the company file).

- **Name**—item identifier
  - Must be unique
  - Could be a word, number, or combination
- **Income account**—account that will be credited when a customer sale is recorded; debited when a customer credit is recorded
- **Sales tax**—identifies the tax status of the item (taxable or nontaxable)
  - Most service fees are nontaxable

> **HINT:** The **Sales tax** field (visible in Figure 3.24) is not included on the item setup screen if sales tax is not activated. In your homework company, you will activate sales tax as part of your homework in Chapter 6, so you will not see it until then.

The following fields are also available in the top two sections of the item record:

- **SKU**—stock keeping unit, or a product or service identification code assigned by the company
  - A SKU is similar to the UPCs (Universal Product Codes) used by most retailers. Both are codes used for tracking purposes. The difference is that a SKU is unique to a particular company. UPCs are standardized for all businesses.
- **Category**—group assigned for tracking purposes
  - **Categories** were covered in the **Organizing the Products and Services List** section of Chapter 2.
- **Description**—the default description that will appear on all sales forms
- **Sales price/rate**—the default selling price

If a service may be performed by an outside vendor (an independent contractor for example), **I purchase this product/service from a vendor** should be checked. If the box is checked, the record will expand to show the the third section.

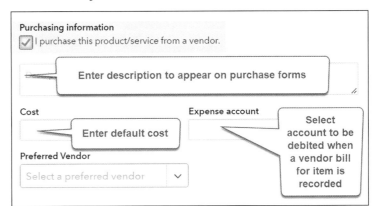

Default descriptions and costs (rates) can be entered. The general ledger account to be debited when the purchase of the service is recorded (credited if the item is returned) is identified in the **Expense account** field.

> **HINT:** Descriptions and rates entered in item records are defaults. They can be changed on forms.

Editing, Duplicating, and Inactivating Services

Editing services

To edit **products** and **services**, click the ⚙ on the icon bar and select **Products and services**.

	NAME ▲	SKU	TYPE	SALES DESCRIP	SALES PRICE	COST		ACTION
	Design							
	Design		Service	Custom De...	75			Edit ▼

Click **Edit** in the **ACTION** column of the appropriate item. You can edit the item name or description, the default rate, the general ledger account associated with the item, and any other fields.

Figure 3.27

Option to update prior transactions when distribution account is changed

If you edit the general ledger account associated with an item that has already been used in a transaction, you have the option of updating existing transactions (called historical transactions in QBO) in addition to changing the account for future transactions.

Duplicating services

Items can also be duplicated.

Figure 3.28

Option to create a duplicate item

A user might choose to duplicate an item instead of creating a new item from scratch to save time. Only the name would need to be changed if all other selections (rates, categories, etc.) were the same.

> **BEHIND THE SCENES** If the duplicated item **name** isn't changed by the user, QBO will save the new item using the original **name** and adding—**copy** at the end. For example, if the Deck Design item was duplicated and the **name** wasn't changed, the new item would be saved with the **name** Deck Design—copy.

Inactivating and reactivating services

Items can be made inactive but cannot be deleted. Historical activity would be retained for an inactive item, but you would no longer be able to use the item in future sales transactions.

Figure 3.29

Option to inactivate an item

Inactive items can be reactivated. To display inactive items, select **inactive** in the **status** field of the **Filter** dropdown menu (above the **NAME** column). A **Make active** option will then be available in the **ACTION** column.

PRACTICE
EXERCISE
3.3

Add and edit items for Craig's Design and Landscaping.

(Craig's Design & Landscaping has decided to offer deck design and construction services. Since the company wants to track the income from each type of service in separate accounts, two service items are needed. Information for gardening services also needs to be adjusted.)

1. Set the new service items.
   a. Click the ⚙ icon in the icon bar.
   b. Click **Products and services** in the **Lists** column to open the Products and Services Center.
   c. Click **New**.
   d. Click **Service**.
   e. Enter "Deck Design" as the **Name**.
   f. Select **+ Add new** in the **Category** dropdown menu.
      i. Enter "Decks" as the new **category** name.
      ii. Click **Save**. **Tip:** You should still be in the new item setup screen.
   g. Enter "Deck design work" as the **Description**.
   h. Enter "75" as the **Sales price/rate**.
   i. Select **Design income** as the **Income account**.
   j. You can ignore the **Sales tax** section for this exercise. Sales tax will not be activated in your homework company file until Chapter 6.
   k. Click **Save and new**.
      i. A new **service** item record should open.

(continued)

(continued from previous page)

     l.   Enter "Deck Construction" as the **Name** for the second item.

     m. Select **Decks** as the **category** name.

     n.   Enter "Supervision of deck construction" as the **Description**.

     o.   Enter "40" as the **Sales price/rate**.

     p.   Select **Services** as the **Income account**.

     q.   Click **Save and close**.

         i.   You should be back in the Products and Services Center.

2. Review the **Categories** list.

     a.   Click **More**.

     b.   Select **Manage categories**.

     c.   **Make a note** of the number of **sub-categories** on the list.

     d.   Click **Products and Services** (under **Product Categories** at the top of the page) to return to the Products and Services Center.

3. Change information in the Gardening item.

     a.   Click **Edit** in the **ACTION** column in the **Gardening** row.

     b.   Enter "35" as the **Sales price/rate**.

     c.   Check the box next to **I purchase this product/service from a vendor**.

     d.   Enter "Gardening" in the description field.

     e.   Enter "25" as the **Cost**.

     f.   Select **Cost of Labor** (a sub-account of **Job Expenses**) as the **Expense account**.

     g.   Click **Save and close** to return to the Products and Services Center.

4. **Make a note** of the amount listed in the **COST** column for **Rock Fountains** on the **Products and Services** list.

5. Click **Dashboard** to exit the Products and Services Center.

RECORDING SALES REVENUE

In a manual accounting system:

- An invoice is created.

- The invoice is recorded in the sales journal if sales are made on account and in the cash receipts journal for cash sales.

- The journals are posted, in total, to the general ledger.

- Each transaction in the sales journal is posted to the appropriate customer's subsidiary ledger.

In QBO:

- A form is completed for each sale.

    ▪ Each **transaction type** has its own form.

- When the form is saved, QBO automatically records the transaction in the sales journal and automatically posts the transaction to the general ledger and to the appropriate subsidiary ledger.

LO 3-4 Describe and demonstrate the process for recording sales revenue in QBO

eLecture

Because everything is done automatically, the form must include all the relevant information needed.

- Who is the customer? (The customer name is needed for posting to the subsidiary ledger.)
- What are we charging them for? (What general ledger account should QBO credit?)
- Have they paid already, or will they pay later? (What general ledger account should QBO debit?)

We've already got the customers and the **product** and **service** items set up, so QBO knows which subsidiary ledger should be updated and which income accounts should be credited when the sales form is completed. But how does QBO know which account to debit in a sale? Should it be Cash or Accounts Receivable? QBO solves that problem by setting up two different forms (two separate **transaction types**).

> **BEHIND THE SCENES** For processing purposes, QBO assigns certain default accounts for common transactions. For example, the default debit account for recording a sale on account is Accounts Receivable (A/R). The default credit account for recording a bill from a vendor is Accounts Payable (A/P). These accounts are automatically set up (categorized with the proper account type) by QBO. The user can change the name of the account but not the type.

Recording Sales on Account

The form (**transaction type**) used to record sales on account is the **Invoice**. The default debit account for **invoices** is Accounts Receivable (A/R).

> **WARNING:** Although multiple accounts can be set up in QBO using the **Accounts Receivable account type**, only the default **Accounts Receivable (A/R)** account is associated with sales transactions in the current version of QBO. If a company wanted to track accounts receivable in multiple accounts, it would need to be done through journal entries.

The credit account(s) in the journal entry underlying an invoice transaction will depend, of course, on the items included on the invoice. As explained earlier in this chapter, the general ledger account associated with a specific item is identified in the item record as shown in Figure 3.24.

QBO provides many opportunities for users to record sales on account. The **invoice** form can be accessed:

- by clicking on the navigation bar and selecting **Invoice** in the **CUSTOMERS** column.
- by clicking **Sales** on the navigation bar and selecting **Invoice** in the **New transaction** dropdown menu in the **All Sales drawer** (tab).
- by clicking **Sales** on the navigation bar and clicking **New invoice** in the **SHORTCUTS** section of the **Overview drawer** (tab).
- by clicking **Sales** on the navigation bar and clicking **Create invoice** in the **Invoices drawer** (tab).
- by clicking **Sales** on the navigation bar, opening the **Customer drawer** (tab), and selecting **Create invoice** in the **ACTION** column dropdown menu for the customer.

Intuit started releasing a new **invoice** form in early 2023. The new layout is shown in Figure 3.30.

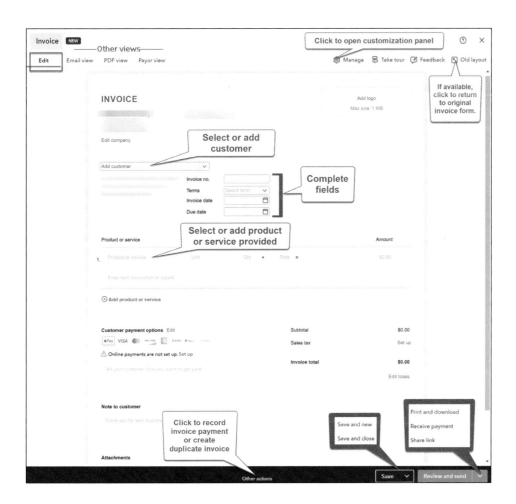

Figure 3.30
Invoice form

 HINT: A customization panel (Figure 3.32) will open automatically when an invoice form is first opened. (The panel is closed in Figure 3.30 for better visibility of the fields.) To close (or open) the panel, click **Manage** (the gear icon in the menu bar at the top of the screen).

To complete an **invoice**, you must enter the customer name, the invoice date, the terms, and the **services** or **products** being charged to the customer.

If the **custom transaction number** feature is activated on the **Sales** tab of **Accounts and Settings**, an invoice number can be entered in the **Invoice No.** field. QBO will automatically generate an invoice number if the feature is not activated.

Default credit terms accessible in the **Terms** dropdown menu include:

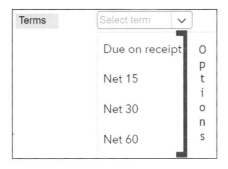

Figure 3.31
Default credit terms

Adding additional credit terms is covered in the **Setting Up Credit Terms** section of Chapter 2.

If an existing customer is selected, the customer address and the terms field will autofill using information from the customer record, and an Edit customer link will appear under the customer address. Clicking that link opens the customer record, where changes can be made.

The charges to the customer are entered in the middle section of the form. There are five fields.

- The type of charge is selected in the Product or service field.
    - If + Add new is selected, a condensed version of an item record will open as a side panel. Currently, only service and non-inventory items can be added.

 HINT: The condensed version does not include many of the fields needed to properly account for sales and purchases. To avoid having to go back and edit items later, we recommend that you set up new products and services before adding them to a sales transaction form.

- The measure used in calculating charges is selected in the Unit field.
    - Options include Unit, Hour, or Flat rate. The choice can be saved by clicking the vertical ellipsis at the far right end of the row, so the measure field will auto-fill when that item is selected on a future invoice. In your homework company, you can use any of the options.
- The number of hours or units is entered in the Qty field.
    - The Qty field disappears if Flat rate is selected in the Unit field.
- Once the service or product is selected, the Rate field will autofill with the Sales price/rate identified in the item record.
    - The amount can be changed if needed. Changing the **rate** on the form does not update the sales price/rate in the item record.
- The Amount field is automatically calculated.
    - If the amount is changed (the field is edited), QBO will automatically recalculate the rate.

If a default message has been set up on the Sales tab of Account and Settings, it will appear in the Note to customer field. The message can be modified or deleted for a specific invoice.

 HINT: Documents related to the charges can be uploaded to QBO by clicking Attachments in the bottom-left corner of the invoice. Documents related to the customer (price lists, contracts, etc.) that are not unique to the invoice would normally be uploaded to the customer record. Attachments are covered in Chapter 11.

To customize an invoice, click Manage at the top of the form shown in Figure 3.30. A side panel will appear.

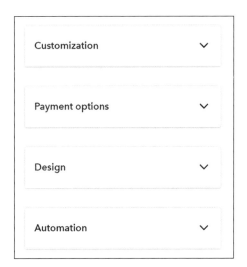

Figure 3.32

Invoice customization sidebar

The customization side panel has four sections (**Customization**, **Payment options**, **Design**, and **Automation**).

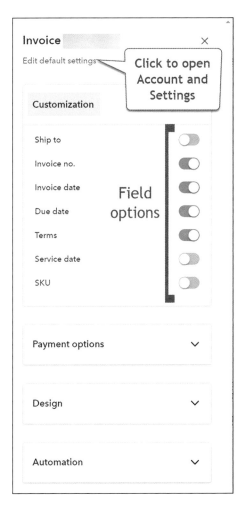

Figure 3.33

Options for adding fields to invoice

In the **Customization** section, fields can be added to or removed from the form. In your homework assignments, the **Ship to** field would need to be added when the company starts selling products (Chapter 6).

Options for setting up online payment of invoices

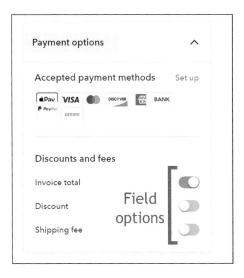

In the **Payment options** section, users can set up online payment methods. Online payments are not covered in this book.

Additional fields can also be added in the section. The **Discount** field will be added to the **invoice** form in Chapter 6.

Options for changing look of invoices

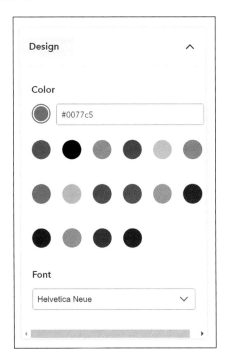

Invoice fonts and colors can be customized in the **Design** section.

Invoice automation options

The **Automation** section includes a link to the setup page for recurring invoices. **Recurring transactions** are covered in Chapter 9.

> ✳ **HINT:** As of early 2023, customization choices made on a specific invoice are automatically applied to both past and future invoices.

There are a number of options for saving (recording) an **invoice**. All are located in the bottom-right corner of the form (Figure 3.30).

- **Save** records the transaction but leaves the form open.
  - If you click **Save**, options to delete or void the transaction will appear in a new **Other actions** link in the black bar at the bottom of the page.
- **Save and close** records the transaction and closes the window.
- **Save and new** records the transaction and opens a new **invoice** form.
- **Review and send** opens a new window where email addresses can be entered and an email message can be added. The **invoice** is saved when **Send invoice** is clicked.
- **Share link** records the transaction and emails a link to the customer for online payment.
  - This is only available to companies that have linked bank accounts in QBO.

The form for recording customer payments can be directly accessed from the **invoice** by selecting **Receive payment** in the far right dropdown menu on the black bar at the bottom of the form (Figure 3.30).

BEHIND THE SCENES Remember: As soon as you save a transaction, a journal entry is created and posted to the general ledger, and the subsidiary ledgers and financial statements are updated.

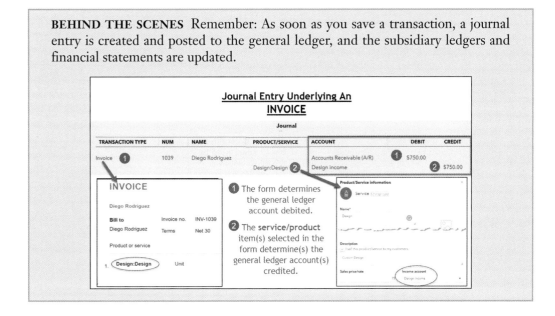

Recording Cash Sales

The **transaction type** (form) used to record cash sales is the **Sales Receipt**. The default debit account for **sales receipts** in the test-drive company is an asset account called Undeposited Funds. (The Undeposited Funds account is covered later in this chapter under the section **MAKING DEPOSITS**.) Users can also elect to record the debit directly to a **Bank** account. The credit accounts for **sales receipts** depend on the **product** and **service** items included in the sale.

The **Sales Receipt** form can be accessed in four ways:

- by clicking **+ New** on the navigation bar and selecting **Sales Receipt** in the **CUSTOMERS** column.

- by clicking **Sales** on the navigation bar and selecting **Sales Receipt** in the **New transaction** dropdown menu on the **All Sales drawer** (tab)

- by clicking **Sales** on the navigation bar and clicking **New sale** in the **SHORTCUTS** section of the **Overview drawer** (tab).

- by clicking **Sales** on the navigation bar, opening the **Customer drawer** (tab), and selecting
Create Sales Receipt in the **ACTION** column dropdown menu for the customer.

The **Sale Receipt** form is shown in Figure 3.37.

> **!** **WARNING:** In early 2023, Intuit started updating various QBO forms. Some of those forms may have been updated after your textbook was printed. If you see a form that doesn't match the screenshot in your book, start by looking for an option to return to a previous version. In most cases, you'll see a link to **Old layout** or **Switch to classic view**. If there is no link available, check the Student Ancillaries page in myBusinessCourse for information about the updated form or ask your instructor.

Figure 3.37

Sales Receipt form

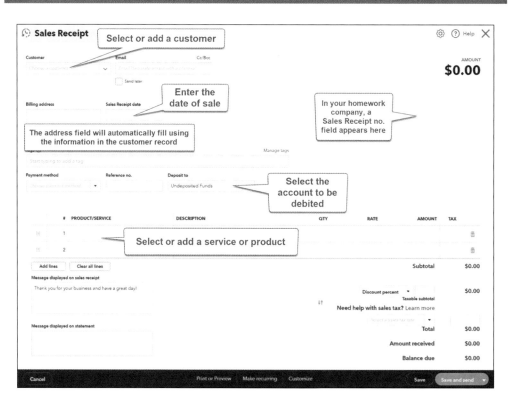

To complete a **sales receipt**, enter the customer name, the receipt date, and the items to be charged. You also select the **Payment method** (cash, check, or credit card).

If the customer is paying with a check, the customer's check number can be entered in the **Reference no.** field. For security reasons, full credit card numbers would normally not be included in the **Reference no.**

> **HINT:** If a company has a lot of walk-in customers and it doesn't want to track each cash customer's name, it can set up a "Cash Customer" or "Walk-in" customer. Click **+ Add new** in the **Choose a customer** dropdown menu, enter a descriptive term in the **Company name** and **Customer display name** fields, and click **Save**. The name will appear in the customer list, but no additional detail will need to be added to the customer record unless any sales at the location are subject to sales tax. In that case, the physical address of the business would need to be added.

You can also add a customer message at the bottom of sales receipts or use the default message set up on the **Sales** tab in **Account and settings**.

To record the transaction and view the underlying journal entry, click **Save** in the bottom-right corner of the form (Figure 3.37). A new link (**More**) will appear in the black bar at the bottom of the page. Click the link and select **Transaction journal**. Additional options for recording the transactions are:

● **Save and close**—the transaction is recorded and the form is closed

● **Save and new**—the transaction is recorded and a new form is opened

● **Save and send**—the transaction is recorded and emailed to the customer

BEHIND THE SCENES Remember: As soon as you save a transaction, a journal entry is created and posted to the general ledger, and the subsidiary ledgers and financial statements are updated.

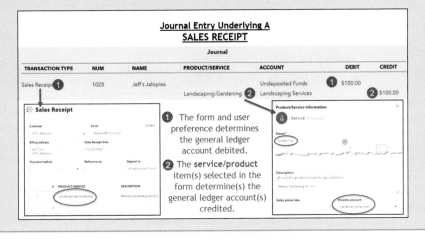

Record cash and credit sales for Craig's Design and Landscaping.
(Craig's Design and Landscaping prepares invoices for some work it did for Kookies by Kathy and Video Games by Dan. It also records the cash collected at time of service for some repair work it did for Red Rock Diner.)

PRACTICE
EXERCISE
3.4

> **HINT:** The new invoice form was not active in the test drive company when the book was published. The following steps are for the old layout. If you see the new layout, refer to the instructions in the **RECORDING REVENUE** section of this chapter.

(continued)

(continued from previous page)

1. Create invoices.

   a. Click (**+ New**) on the navigation bar.

   b. Click **Invoice** in the **CUSTOMERS** column.

   c. Invoice Kookies by Kathy for 3 hours of design work.

      i. Select **Kookies by Kathy** in the **Select a customer** field.

      ii. Select **Net 30** for the **Terms**.

      iii. Use the current date for the **Invoice date**.

      iv. Select **Design** as the Item in the **PRODUCT/SERVICE** field.

      v. Enter "3" as the **QTY** (hours in this case).

      vi. The default rate of 75 should appear in the **RATE** field.

      vii. Total invoice balance should be $225.

      viii. Click **Save and new**.

   d. Invoice Video Games by Dan for some gardening and pest control work.

      i. Select **Video Games by Dan** in the **Select a customer** field.

         1. Ignore any charges that appear in a sidebar.

      ii. Select **Net 30** as the **Terms**.

      iii. Use the current date for the **Invoice date**.

      iv. Select **Gardening** in the **PRODUCT/SERVICE** field with a **QTY** of "5" (hours) and a **RATE** of "$30." **NOTE:** Adding or editing rates (or descriptions) on a form does not update the item record.

      v. On the second line select **Pest Control** as the **PRODUCT/SERVICE**. Enter "2" as the **QTY** (hours). Leave the **RATE** at $35.

      vi. Total invoice balance should be $220.

      vii. Click **Save and close**.

2. Record a cash sale. (Red Rock Diner paid $180 (by check #6789) for some maintenance work.)

   a. Click (**+ New**) on the navigation bar.

   b. Select **Sales Receipt** in the **CUSTOMERS** column.

   c. Select **Red Rock Diner** in the **Choose a customer** field.

   d. Enter the current date for the **Sales Receipt date**.

   e. Select **Check** as the **Payment method**.

   f. Enter "6789" as the **Reference no**.

   g. Leave **Undeposited Funds** in the **Deposit to** field.

   h. Select **Maintenance & Repair** in the **PRODUCT/SERVICE** field.

   i. Enter a **QTY** of "3" (hours) and a **RATE** of "60."

   j. The total should be $180.

   k. Click **Save**.

   l. Click **More** in the black bar at the bottom of the page.

   m. Select **Transaction Journal**.

   n. **Make a note** of the accounts that were debited and credited for the sales receipt you created for Red Rock Diner.

| What's the underlying journal entry for Invoice 1038 to Kookies by Kathy in Practice Exercise 3.4? (Answer at end of chapter.) | **Quick**Check **3-1** |

RECORDING PAYMENTS FROM CUSTOMERS

Companies generally give customers or clients a number of payment options.

- Customers can pay with check, cash, or credit card at the time of service.
  - Recorded as **sales receipts** (covered earlier in this chapter).
- Customers can buy on account and pay later.
  - Recorded as **payments**.

LO 3-5 Describe and demonstrate the process for recording payments on account made by customers

eLecture

Most companies that sell to individuals would generally only accept cash/check or major credit cards. An exception would be retail outlets that have their own credit cards. (Target and Lowe's are two examples.)

Most companies that sell to other companies sell primarily on account. It would simply be impractical for their customers to pay cash or have checks or credit cards ready whenever goods or services are delivered.

In a manual accounting system, customer payments are recorded through the Cash Receipts Journal. The journal is posted, in total, to the general ledger, and each transaction is posted to the appropriate customer's subsidiary ledger (if paying on account). In QBO, all of the steps are done when the form recording the payment transaction is saved.

Payments on Account

Customer payments on account balances are recorded using the **Receive Payment** form (**Payment transaction type**).

To access the form, click **+ New** on the navigation bar.

CUSTOMERS	VENDORS	EMPLOYEES	OTHER
Invoice	Expense	Single time activity	Bank deposit
Receive payment	Check	Weekly timesheet	Transfer
Estimate	Bill		Journal entry
Credit memo	Pay bills		Statement
Sales receipt	Purchase order		Inventory qty adjustment
Refund receipt	Vendor credit		Pay down credit card
Delayed credit	Credit card credit		
Delayed charge	Print checks		

Figure 3.38

Access to customer payment form

Select **Receive Payment** in the **CUSTOMERS** column. The **payment** form is shown in Figure 3.39.

> **!** **WARNING:** In early 2023, Intuit started updating various QBO forms. Some of those forms may have been updated after your textbook was printed. If you see a form that doesn't match the screenshot in your book, start by looking for an option to return to a previous version. In most cases, you'll see a link to **Old layout** or **Switch to classic view**. If there is no link available, check the Student Ancillaries page in myBusinessCourse for information about the updated form or ask your instructor.

Figure 3.39

Customer payment form

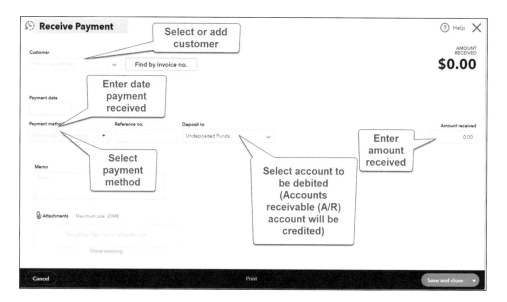

To enter a customer payment, you need to know the customer name, the payment amount, the date received, and the payment method. If payment is made by check, the check number would normally be entered in the **Reference no.** field.

Once the customer is selected, all outstanding invoices from that customer will be displayed. The screen would look something like Figure 3.40.

Figure 3.40

Example of customer payment screen

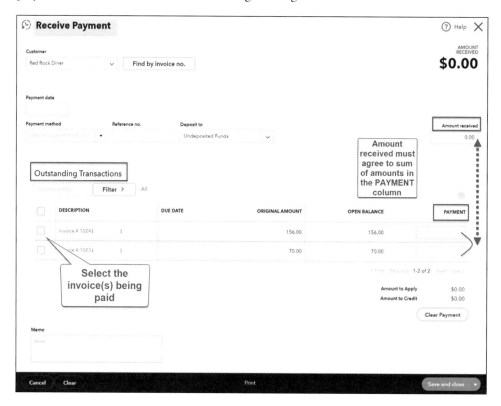

Once the payment amount is entered, QBO automatically applies the amount in this order:

- It will be applied first to an invoice of the **exact** same dollar amount as the payment.

- If there's no exact match, QBO will apply the payment in due date order (oldest invoice first).

You can change how payments are applied if needed.

Full or partial payments can be entered. If a partial payment is received, you should make sure that the amount(s) entered in the **PAYMENT** field(s) agree(s) with the payment amount that should be applied to the specific invoice.

If a partial payment is entered, QBO will leave the unpaid balance for the invoice in Accounts Receivable.

If there are unapplied credits available to the customer, they will appear when the **Receive Payment** form is opened. The user has the option of applying the credit or leaving it as an open credit that would be available at a later date.

> **BEHIND THE SCENES** Users can elect to have credit memos applied automatically. If that election is made, only open balances would appear in the **Receive payment** form. Credit memo application options are covered in the **Recording Customer Credits and Refunds** section of this chapter.

The default journal entry underlying a **payment** transaction in the test-drive company includes a debit to **Undeposited Funds** and a credit to Accounts Receivable. The **Undeposited Funds** account is discussed in the **MAKING DEPOSITS** section of this chapter.

Record customer payments on account for Craig's Design and Landscaping.
(Craig's Design and Landscaping received payments from two of its customers.)

PRACTICE
EXERCISE
3.5

1. Record customer payment in full. (Check #5865 for $160 received from Sushi by Katsuyuki in payment of invoices 1018 and 1019)

   a. Click **+ New** on the navigation bar.

   b. Click **Receive Payment** in the **CUSTOMERS** column.

   c. Select **Sushi by Katsuyuki** as the customer.

   d. Enter the current date as the **Payment date**.

   e. Select **Check** as the **Payment method**.

   f. Enter "5865" as the **Reference no.**

   g. Leave **Undeposited Funds** as the **Deposit to** account.

   h. Enter "$160" as the **Amount received**.

   i. Make sure that QBO automatically:

      i. placed a checkmark next to both **invoices** in the **Outstanding Transactions** section.

      ii. entered $80 in both **PAYMENT** fields.

   j. The total **Amount to Apply** should be $160.00.

   k. Click **Save and new**.

2. Record customer partial payment. (Check #6899 for $40 received from Bill's Windsurf Shop in partial payment of invoice 1027)

   a. Select **Bill's Windsurf Shop** as the customer.

   b. Enter the current date as the **Payment date**.

   c. Select **Check** as the **Payment method**.

   d. Enter "6899" as the **Reference no.**

(continued)

(continued from previous page)

> e.   Leave **Undeposited Funds** as the **Deposit to** account.
>
> f.   Enter "$40" as the **Amount** received.
>
> g.   Make sure that QBO automatically:
>
>   i.   placed a checkmark next to Invoice #1027 under **Outstanding Transactions**.
>
>   ii.   entered $40 in the **PAYMENT** field.
>
> h.   The total **Amount to Apply** should be $40.00.
>
> i.   Click **Save and close**.

3. **Make a note** of the outstanding balance owed by Bill's Windsurf Shop after check #6899 was posted. **TIP:** Open balances are shown on the **Customers drawer** (tab) of the **Sales** link on the navigation bar.

MAKING DEPOSITS

LO 3-6 Demonstrate an understanding of the process for depositing customer payments in QBO

eLecture

Before you learn how to record bank deposits, you need to understand how QBO handles cash receipts. As you know, there's a journal entry behind every sales receipt (cash sale) and every customer payment on account. Based on your knowledge of accounting, you would probably expect that the debit account for each of the transactions would be Cash, right? (Debit Cash, Credit Revenue for cash sales and Debit Cash, Credit Accounts Receivable for customer payments on account.)

Since QBO updates the general ledger automatically and immediately for every transaction, that would mean there would be a debit entry to the cash account for every check and cash payment received. Why is that a problem? Well, it's not if you're depositing every payment separately. But most companies group checks when they're making deposits. On the bank statement, the total deposit amount is shown (not each check that makes up the deposit). It would be difficult (not impossible, but difficult) to reconcile the bank account every month if QBO didn't group the payments together to correspond to the actual deposit amount.

So, here's what QBO does. Instead of debiting Cash for every customer payment, an account called "Undeposited Funds" is debited. **Undeposited Funds** is an **Other Current Asset account type** (not a **Bank account type**). You can think of it as a temporary holding account.

When the actual deposit is later recorded, QBO credits **Undeposited Funds** and debits the **bank** (Checking) account for the total of the funds deposited. Now the entries in the Checking account agree (hopefully!) with the entries on the bank statement.

Deposits are recorded using the **Bank Deposit** form. (The **transaction type** is **Deposit**.) This form is accessed by clicking **+ New** on the navigation bar.

Figure 3.41

Access to deposit form

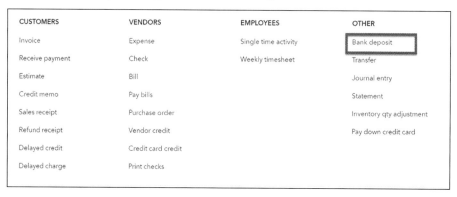

Click **Bank Deposit** in the **OTHER** column. The form will look like Figure 3.42 if there are undeposited funds.

> ! **WARNING:** In early 2023, Intuit started updating various QBO forms. Some of those forms may have been updated after your textbook was printed. If you see a form that doesn't match the screenshot in your book, start by looking for an option to return to a previous version. In most cases, you'll see a link to **Old layout** or **Switch to classic view**. If there is no link available, check the Student Ancillaries page in myBusinessCourse for information about the updated form or ask your instructor.

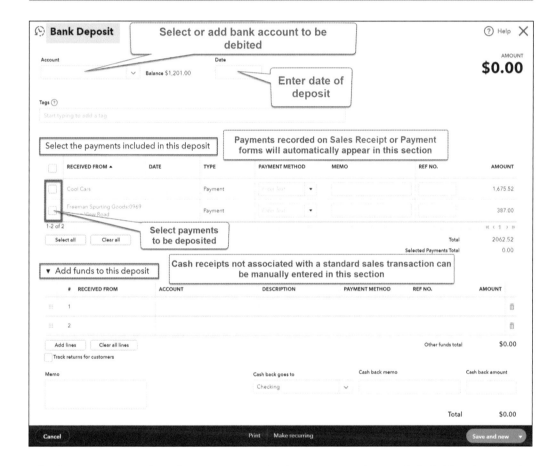

Figure 3.42

Example of deposit form

The first step is to select the appropriate bank account in the top-left field and enter the deposit date. This tells QBO which account to debit.

Customer payments (receipts) that are being included in the day's bank deposit are selected by placing a checkmark next to the payor's name in the **Select the payments included in this deposit** section. (The names are in the **RECEIVED FROM** column.) You can select all the payments or just some of them. Any customer payments selected will create a credit to Undeposited Funds. The amount is debited to the cash (checking) account.

You can also add cash receipts directly into this form. For example, if a company received a tax refund, the amount would be entered in the **Add funds to this deposit** section in the lower half of the form. Cash received from lenders (loan processed) and owner contributions would also be entered in the **Add funds to this deposit** section. Additional cash receipts are covered in more detail in Chapter 8.

HINT: When a customer is paying an account balance, the best practice is to enter it through the **Payment** form. Although QBO does allow direct entry of customer payments on account into the **Bank Deposit** form, the payment would then have to be linked to the appropriate invoice at a later date. This adds another step to the process.

The **cash back** fields at the bottom-right corner of the window are used to record cash withdrawals taken directly from a deposit amount.

Figure 3.43

Cash back section of deposit form

This would rarely be done in a business organization.

 HINT: If there are **no** undeposited receipts in the Undeposited Funds account, only the **Add funds to this deposit** section will appear when you open the **Bank Deposit** form.

PRACTICE
EXERCISE
3.6

Make a deposit for Craig's Design and Landscaping.
(Craig's Design and Landscaping deposits checks received from customers.)

1. Click **+ New** on the navigation bar.

2. Click **Bank Deposit** in the **OTHER** column.

3. Select **Checking** as the account.

4. Enter the current date as the **Date**.

5. Check the boxes next to Cool Cars and Freeman Sporting Goods.

6. **Make a note** of the amount received from Cool Cars.

7. The **Selected Payments Total** should be $2,062.52.

8. Click **Save and close**.

RECORDING CUSTOMER CREDITS AND REFUNDS

LO 3-7 Describe and demonstrate the process for recording credits and refunds to customers in QBO

Stuff happens! A client is mistakenly overbilled, or maybe the work isn't done to the satisfaction of the client. In either case, a company will probably decide to either credit the customer's account by issuing a **credit memo** or issue a refund to the client.

  If the client has unpaid invoices, the company will normally decide to credit the client's account using the **transaction type Credit Memo**. The credit account underlying a **credit memo** is Accounts Receivable (A/R). The debit account(s) underlying the transaction depend(s) on the **product** and **service** item(s) selected in the form.

Depending on the **settings** in the company file, **credit memos** are either:

- automatically applied by QBO or
- manually applied by the user.

Automatic application of **credit memos** is the default **setting**. To change the **setting**, click the ⚙ on the icon bar. Click **Account and settings** in the **YOUR COMPANY** column.
   On the **Advanced** tab, click the **pencil** icon in the **Automation** section.

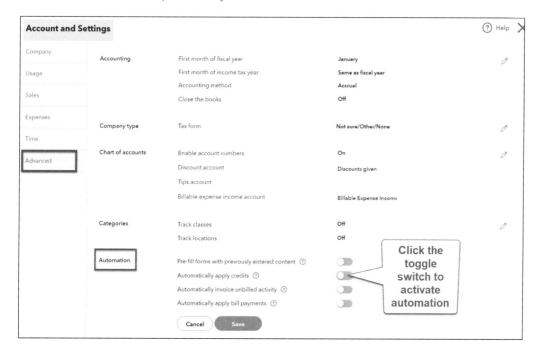

Figure 3.44

Automation section of the Advanced tab in Account and Settings

The toggle switch next to **Automatically apply credits** turns the feature on or off. If the switch is turned off, the user can manually select the specific **invoice** to be credited. Automatic application saves time; manual selection gives the user better control. You turned off the automatic application in your homework company as part of your assignment in Chapter 2.

Creating Credit Memos

Click **+ New** on the navigation bar.

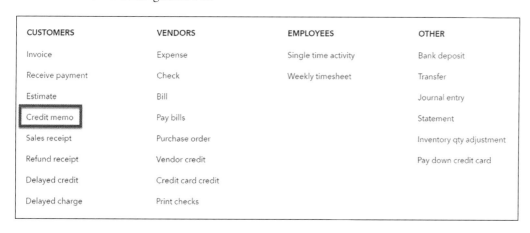

Figure 3.45

Access to credit memo form

Click **Credit Memo**.
   The form will look something like Figure 3.46.

> **WARNING:** In early 2023, Intuit started updating various QBO forms. Some of those forms may have been updated after your textbook was printed. If you see a form that doesn't match the screenshot in your book, start by looking for an option to return to a previous version. In most cases, you'll see a link to **Old layout** or **Switch to classic view**. If there is no link available, check the Student Ancillaries page in myBusinessCourse for information about the updated form or ask your instructor.

Figure 3.46

Credit memo form

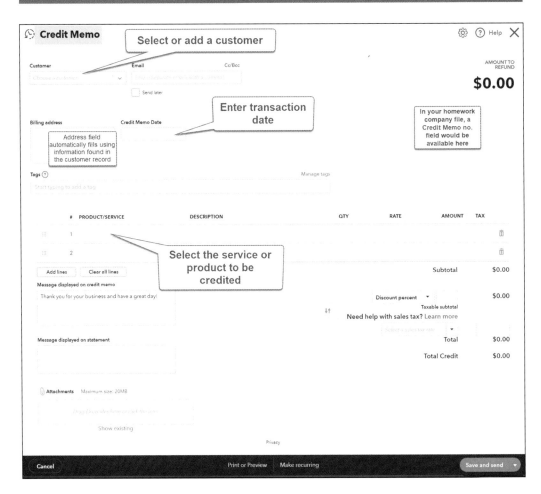

The customer account to be credited must be selected. The credit memo date and number must be entered.

The item selected in the **PRODUCT/SERVICE** column represents the service (or product) for which the credit memo is being issued. For example, if the client is being issued a credit for two hours of gardening services, then the item associated with gardening would be selected.

> **BEHIND THE SCENES** Remember: As soon as you save a transaction, a journal entry is created and posted to the general ledger, and the subsidiary ledgers and financial statements are updated.

(continued)

(continued from previous page)

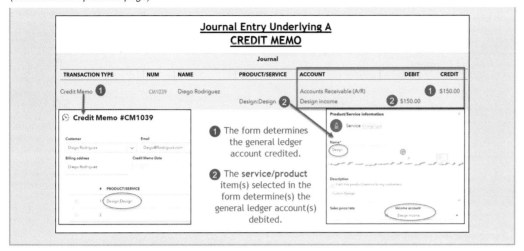

Applying Credit Memos

Applying credit memos with automatic application set as the preference

credit memos are automatically applied once the credit memo is saved if automatic application is activated on the **Sales** tab of **Account and Settings**.

If the customer has open invoices, QBO applies the credit in this order:

- Oldest open invoice first.

- If the credit is greater than the oldest invoice, the balance is credited to the second oldest.

    - QBO will continue to apply any balances (in reverse chronological order) until the credit is fully applied.

If the client has no open invoices, the credit will be automatically applied to the next invoice recorded.

A completed **credit memo** might look something like Figure 3.47 after it was saved.

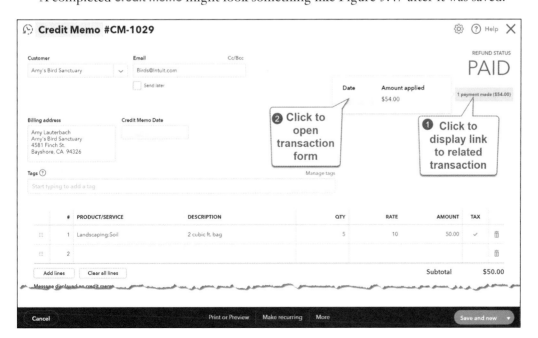

Figure 3.47

Example of an applied credit memo

QBO applied the credit by creating a customer **payment** transaction. The **payment** transaction can be viewed by clicking the link to the payment that appears directly under **PAID** in the top-right corner of the form.

Figure 3.48

Example of automatic application of credit memo

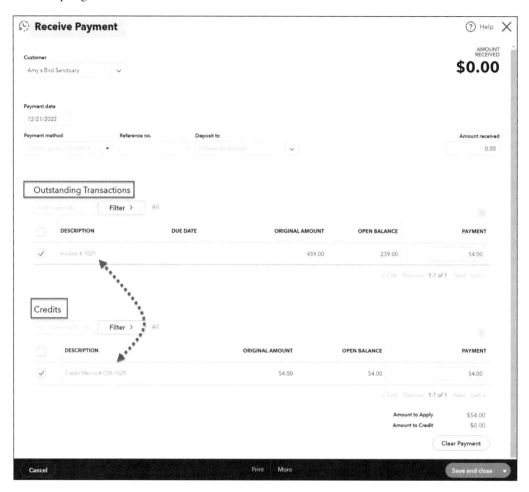

Users could change the application of the **credit memo** in this window if there were other open **invoices** available.

> **BEHIND THE SCENES** In Figure 3.48, the customer (Amy's Bird Sanctuary) had an unpaid balance (**OPEN BALANCE**) of $239 on Inv #1021. A $54 credit was automatically applied. The remaining amount due on the invoice would now be $185.

Applying credit memos with manual application (automatic application preference turned off)

When automatic application of customer credits is turned off, **credit memos** are stored in the customer record with a status of **Unapplied**.

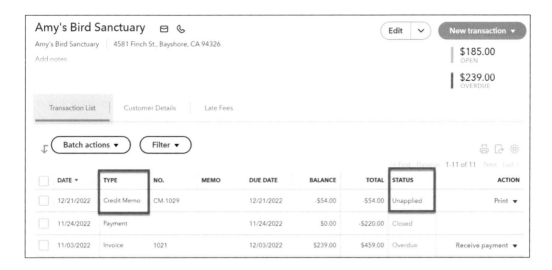

Figure 3.49

Customer transaction list screen

Credits are then applied using the **Receive Payment** form.

Applying credit memos with automation turned off can be confusing. Using examples in the next few sections should help.

APPLYING CREDIT MEMOS TO OPEN INVOICES WHEN NO PAYMENT IS RECEIVED

Let's say a $45 credit memo has been created for Bill's Windsurf (a customer of Craig's). We want to apply it to Invoice #1027. No payment has been received. The application process would go as follows.

Click **+ New** on the navigation bar and select **Receive payment**.

Select Bill's Windsurf as the **customer**.

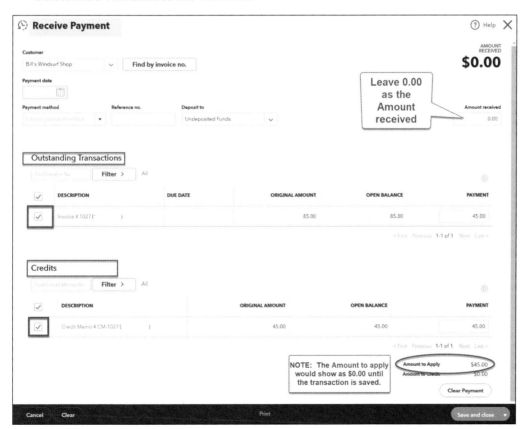

Figure 3.50

Example of manual application of credit memo

QBO has automatically applied the credit to the open invoice. The **Amount received** shows as $0.00, and the **PAYMENT** fields in the invoice and credit memo rows equal the credit amount. Once the **credit memo** is saved, the **Amount to Apply** amount at the bottom of the page will change to the amount of the credit memo ($45 in our example).

APPLYING CREDIT MEMOS TO OPEN INVOICES WHEN CUSTOMER PAYMENTS ARE RECORDED

We'll use the same example as we used in the previous section. Bill's Windsurf has an $85 outstanding invoice (#1027) and an unapplied credit of $45. This time, though, Bill's has made a payment. Instead of opening the **Payment** form through the ⊕ New menu, we'll use features in the Customer Center to make it a little easier.

Click **Sales** on the navigation bar.

Open the **Customers drawer** (tab) and click the name of the customer. (Bill's Windsurf in our example.)

On the **Transaction List** tab, click **Receive payment** in the **ACTION** column of the **invoice** being paid by the customer. (Bill's Windsurf is paying Invoice #1027)

The **Receive Payment** form will look like Figure 3.51.

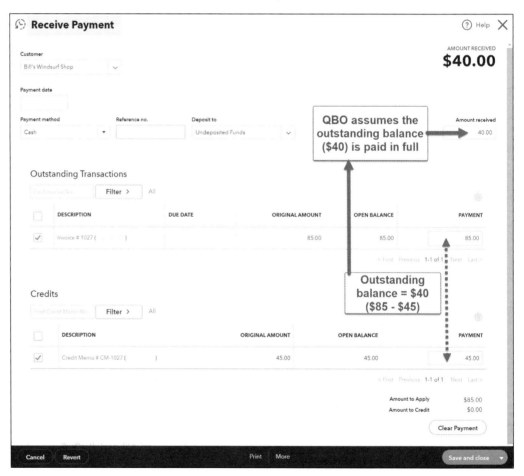

When the **receive payment** form is opened from the **Transaction List** in the customer record, QBO autofills the form assuming the customer has paid any outstanding balance. In Figure 3.51, **Amount received** shows as $40 and the **Amount to apply** shows as $85 (the $40 payment plus the $45 credit). As long as Bill actually paid the full balance (the $40), the transaction can be saved, and the credit will be applied appropriately.

But what if Bill only pays $20? If the **Amount received** is changed to $20, the form will automatically adjust to this:

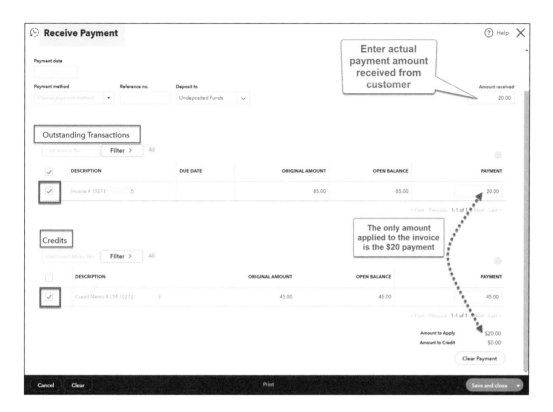

Figure 3.52

Example of credit memo application when invoice balance is partially paid

Now, only the payment amount was applied to Invoice #1027, which is inaccurate. If the form is saved at this point, the customer balance in the **A/R Aging Summary** report would look like this:

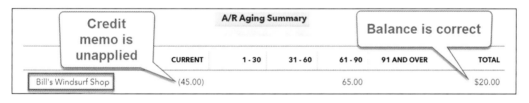

Figure 3.53

Accounts receivable aging report with misapplied credit

The customer account balance is correct, but the credit memo has not been applied to the invoice.

Correcting the misapplication can be tricky. You may need to work with the fields on the **payment** form a few times. We've found that this process usually works:

- Leave the **Amount received** field as is. ($20 in our example)
- Uncheck the box next to the **credit memo**.
- Uncheck the box next to the **invoice**.
- Recheck the box next to the **invoice**.
- Recheck the box next to the **credit memo**.
- Enter the sum of the payment and credit amounts in the **PAYMENT** field in the invoice row. ($65 in our example)

If done correctly, the form would now look like this:

Figure 3.54

Example of improper application of credit memo

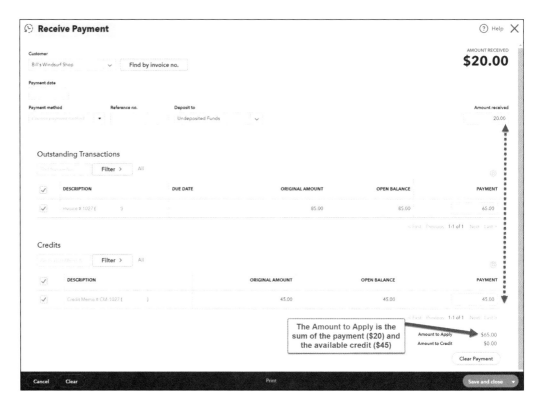

Figure 3.54

Example of improper application of credit memo

The **A/R Aging Summary** report will look like this:

Figure 3.55

Accounts receivable aging report with properly applied credit

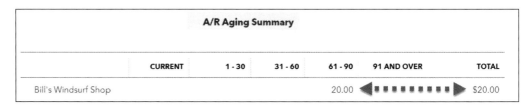

 HINT: If you access the **Receive payment** form through the ➕**New** menu, QBO does not auto-fill the payment amount. The credit amount is fully applied to the invoice, but no payment amount is entered. Once you add an amount in the **Amount received** field (full or partial payment), the **payment** field in the **Invoice** row will be updated with that amount. This will again result in a misapplication of the credit memo (see Figure 3.52). Use the steps outlined above to make the correction.

BEHIND THE SCENES Although automatic application of credit memos in QBO is easier, most companies would choose manual application in order to control how and when customer credits are applied.

Issuing Refunds to Customers

Instead of issuing a credit memo, companies may choose to issue a refund directly to the client. This would most likely occur when the company wants to give a credit to a client with no open (unpaid) invoices.

Refunds to clients are entered as **transaction type Refund Receipt**. The underlying credit in the transaction is to the **Bank** account. The underlying debit depends on the **product** or **service** item selected in the form.

To access the form, click **+ New** on the navigation bar.

Figure 3.56

Access to Refund Receipt form

Select **Refund receipt**. The form is shown in Figure 3.57.

> **WARNING:** In early 2023, Intuit started updating various QBO forms. Some of those forms may have been updated after your textbook was printed. If you see a form that doesn't match the screenshot in your book, start by looking for an option to return to a previous version. In most cases, you'll see a link to **Old layout** or **Switch to classic view**. If there is no link available, check the Student Ancillaries page in myBusinessCourse for information about the updated form or ask your instructor.

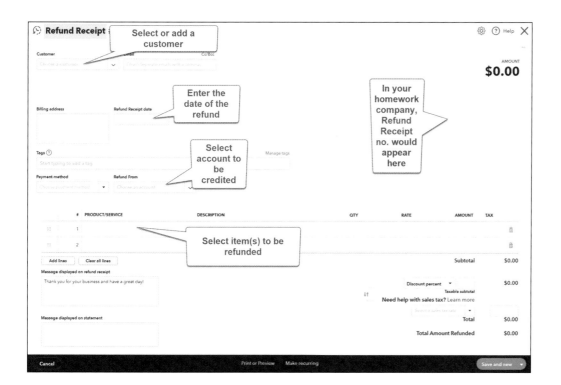

Figure 3.57

Refund Receipt form

The form must include the customer name, the date of the refund, and **product** or **service** items refunded. The **Payment method** used (usually cash or check) and the bank account to be credited must also be selected. If the refund is being made using a check, a **Check No.** field must be completed.

A completed **refund receipt** might look something like Figure 3.58 if a check was issued for the refund.

Figure 3.58

Example of completed refund receipt

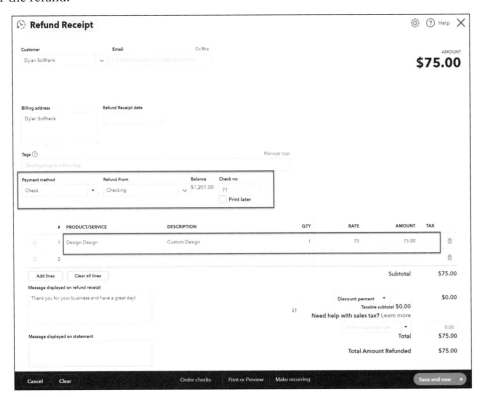

> ✳ **HINT:** The **Check no.** field and the bank balance appeared when the Checking account was selected in the **Refund From** dropdown menu.

The following message will appear after a **refund receipt** is saved:

Figure 3.59

Refund receipt message

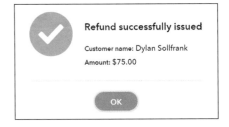

PRACTICE
EXERCISE
3.7

MBC

Record a credit memo and a refund for Craig's Design and Landscaping.
(Amy's Bird Sanctuary complained about the amount of its recent bill. Craig's Design and Landscaping decides to give Amy's Bird Sanctuary a $150 credit toward that invoice. Dylan Sollfrank paid $337.50 for a custom landscape design. Dylan was happy with the design but has decided to postpone the project. To maintain good client relations, Craig decides to issue Dylan a $75 refund.)

(continued)

(continued from previous page)

1. Change settings to allow for manual application of credit memos and custom transaction numbers.
   a. Click the ⚙ in the icon bar.
   b. Click **Account and settings**.
   c. Open the **Advanced** tab.
   d. Click the **pencil** icon in the **Automation** section.
   e. Toggle **Automatically apply credits** to turn the feature off.
   f. Click **Save**.
   g. Open the **Sales** tab.
   h. Click the **pencil** icon in the **Sales form content** section.
   i. If necessary, toggle **Custom transaction numbers** box to turn the feature on.
   j. Click **Save**.
   k. Click **Done**.

2. Create a credit memo.
   a. Click ⬤ **＋New** on the navigation bar.
   b. Click **Credit memo** in the **CUSTOMERS** column.
   c. Select **Amy's Bird Sanctuary** as the customer.
   d. Enter the current date as the **Credit Memo Date**.
   e. Enter CM1011 as the **Credit Memo no.**
   f. Select **Design** as the **PRODUCT/SERVICE** and enter "2" as the **QTY**.
   g. The total credit amount should be $150.00.
   h. Click **Save and close**.
   i. **Make a note** of the open balance for Amy's Bird Sanctuary as displayed in the Customer Center.

3. Apply the credit. (No payment was received from Amy's.)
   a. Click **Sales** in the navigation bar and select the **Customer drawer** (tab).
   b. Click **Amy's Bird Sanctuary**.
   c. Click **New transaction** and select **Payment**.
   d. Enter $0 as the **Amount received**.
   e. Place checkmarks in the boxes next to Credit Memo #CM1011 and Invoice #1021.
      i. Verify **Amount to apply** is $150.
   f. Click **Save and close**.

4. Record a refund.
   a. Click ⬤ **＋New** on the navigation bar.
   b. Click **Refund receipt** in the **CUSTOMERS** column.
   c. Select **Dylan Sollfrank** as the customer.
   d. Enter the current date as the **Refund Receipt date**.
   e. Enter "1045" as the **Refund Receipt no.**
   f. Select **Check** as the **Payment method**.

(continued)

(continued from previous page)

> g.   Select **Checking** in the **Refund From** field and enter "1002" as the **Check no.**
>
> h.   Select **Design** as the **PRODUCT/SERVICE** and enter "1" as the **QTY.**
>
> i.   The **Total Amount Refunded** should be $75.00.
>
> j.   Click **Save and close.**
>
> k.   Click **OK** on the **Refund successfully issued** message.
>
> l.   Click **Dashboard.**

PREPARING SALES AND CUSTOMER REPORTS

LO 3-8 Recognize and prepare common reports used in the sales cycle

Sales and customer reports can be accessed through **Reports** on the navigation bar.

Figure 3.60

Sales and customer reports section

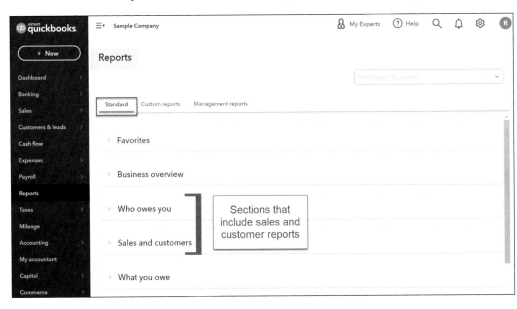

Most of the sales and customer reports are included in the **Who owes you** and **Sales and customers** sections. Some of the most commonly used sales reports in service companies are highlighted in Figure 3.61:

Figure 3.61

Common sales reports for service companies

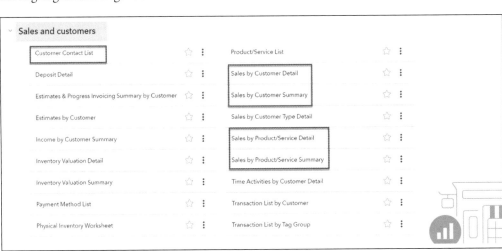

The **Who owes you** group includes reports on uncollected invoices as seen in Figure 3.62:

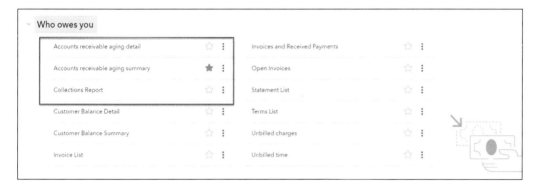

Figure 3.62

Common customer reports for service companies

As discussed in Chapter 1, reports can be modified as needed. (Refer to the **REPORTING** section of Chapter 1 for a refresher on report customization.)

For example, the **A/R Aging Summary** default report is shown in Figure 3.63.

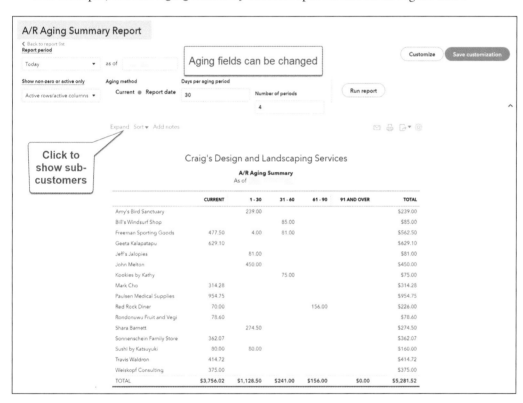

Figure 3.63

A/R Aging Summary Report

> **HINT:** Your report will show different balances if you haven't logged out since completing Practice Exercise 3.7.

The same report modified to show eight 15-day aging periods is shown in Figure 3.64.

Figure 3.64

Customized A/R Aging Summary Report

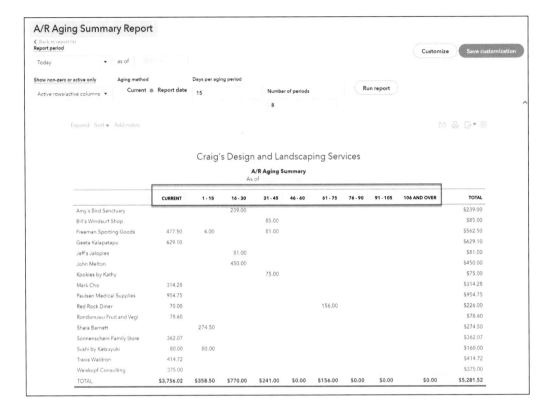

PRACTICE

EXERCISE

3.8

Prepare sales and receivable reports.

(Craig's Design and Landscaping needs an A/R aging and a revenue by type of service report.)

1. Prepare an accounts receivable aging report.

   a. Click **Reports** on the navigation bar.

   b. Open the **Standard** tab.

   c. Click **Accounts receivable aging summary** in the **Who owes you** section.

   d. Drill down (click) on the **TOTAL** column for Sonnenschein Family Store.

      i. **Make a note** of the invoice number for the $362.07 charge to Sonnenschein.

   e. Click **Dashboard**.

2. Prepare a sales report by service item.

   a. Click **Reports** on the navigation bar.

   b. Open the **Standard** tab.

   c. Click **Sales by Product/Service Detail** in the **Sales and customers** section.

   d. Change **report period** to **All Dates**.

   e. Click **Customize**.

   f. Open the **Filter** dropdown section.

   g. Check **Product/Service** and select **Design:Design** and **Design:Lighting**.

   h. Open the **Rows/Columns** section.

   i. Click **Change columns**.

   j. Check **Product/Service** to add the column to the report.

(continued)

(continued from previous page)

k. Uncheck **Balance**.

l. Click **Run Report**.

m. **Make a note** of the **AMOUNT** included in the report for **Design:Lighting**.

n. Click **Dashboard**.

SALES CYCLE SUMMARY

Let's summarize the sales steps we have learned and their related journal entries. First let's review the difference between a cash sale and a sale on account.

Cash sales are recorded on Sales receipts. The customer is buying something now and paying for it now.	**Sales on account are recorded on Invoices. The customer is buying something now and will pay for it at a later date.**

2-step process:
  1. Create a **Sales receipt** for each sale.
  2. Record a **Deposit** when receipts are deposited into the bank account.
	3-step process:
	  1. Create an **Invoice** for each sale.
	  2. **Receive payments** from customers.
	  3. Record a **Bank deposit** when customer payments are deposited into the bank account.

Let's also review the basic sales journal entries that are created in service companies based on the above transactions.

Cash Sales—Journal Entry	**Sales on Account—Journal Entry**

• Journal entry underlying a **Sales receipt**
  – Dr: Undeposited Funds
  – Cr: Revenue
• Journal entry underlying a **Deposit**
  – Dr: Checking
  – Cr: Undeposited Funds
NOTE: Multiple payments can be grouped
	• Journal entry underlying an **Invoice**
	  – Dr: A/R
	  – Cr: Revenue
	• Journal entry underlying a **Payment** from customer
	  – Dr: Undeposited Funds
	  – Cr: A/R
	• Journal entry underlying a **Deposit**
	  – Dr: Checking
	  – Cr: Undeposited Funds
	NOTE: Multiple payments can be grouped

 HINT: Journal entries for sales of products (covered in Chapter 6) would include additional debits and credits to accounts such as Cost of Goods Sold, Inventory, and Sales Taxes Payable.

	Accounts receivable (A/R)	$225	
	Design income		$225

ANSWER TO

QuickCheck

3-1

CHAPTER SHORTCUTS

Add a customer
1. Click Sales on the navigation bar.
2. Open the Customers drawer (tab).
3. Click New Customer.

Edit a customer
1. Click Sales on the navigation bar.
2. Open the Customers drawer (tab).
3. Click customer name.
4. Click Edit.

Inactivate a customer
1. Click Sales on the navigation bar.
2. Open the Customers drawer (tab).
3. Open the dropdown menu in the AC-TION column for the customer to be inactivated.
4. Select Make inactive .

Add service item
1. Click the ⚙ in the icon bar.
2. Click Products and services.
3. Click New.
4. Click Service.

Edit item
1. Click the ⚙ in the icon bar.
2. Click Products and services.
3. Click Edit in the ACTION column for the item to be edited.

Inactivate an item
1. Click the ⚙ in the icon bar.
2. Click Products and services.
3. Open the dropdown menu in the ACTION column for the item to be inactivated.
4. Select Make inactive.

Record cash sale
1. Click ＋New on the navigation bar.
2. Click Sales Receipt in the CUSTOMERS column.

Record sale on account
1. Click ＋New on the navigation bar.
2. Click Invoice in the CUSTOMERS column.

Record credit memo
1. Click ＋New on the navigation bar.
2. Click Credit Memo in the CUSTOMERS column.

Record customer payments on account balances
1. Click ＋New on the navigation bar.
2. Click Receive Payment in the CUSTOMERS column.

Record deposits
1. Click ＋New on the navigation bar.
2. Click Bank Deposit in the OTHER column.

CHAPTER REVIEW

Matching

Match the term or phrase (as used in QuickBooks Online) to its definition.

1. company name
2. customer display name
3. sales receipt
4. invoice
5. deposit
6. credit memo
7. undeposited funds
8. payment

_____ transaction type used for recording cash sales

_____ specific customer identifier

_____ transaction type used to record money taken to the bank

_____ account debited for customer cash receipts not yet deposited

_____ transaction type used for recording customer payments on account

_____ transaction type used to record sales on account

_____ transaction type used to record credit given to customer

_____ customer name appearing on invoices, sales receipts, or credit memos

Multiple Choice

1. A **service** item in QBO

   a. can be linked to more than one general ledger account.
   b. must be linked to one, and only one, general ledger account.
   c. can only be linked to an accounts receivable type account.
   d. can be, but doesn't need to be, linked to an account.

2. The general ledger account Undeposited Funds in QBO represents _____.

   a. all cash sales
   b. the balance in accounts receivable
   c. amount of cash, checks, or credit card payments received and recorded but not yet deposited
   d. None of the above

3. The account that is credited when a credit memo is completed in QBO has the **account type** _____.

   a. Bank
   b. Accounts Receivable
   c. Accounts Payable
   d. Other Current Assets
   e. Other Current Liabilities

4. The default account Undeposited Funds has the **account type** _____.

   a. Bank
   b. Other Current Assets
   c. Other Assets
   d. Other Current Liabilities
   e. Accounts Receivable

5. There is an underlying journal entry behind every completed form listed below **except** _____.

   a. Invoice
   b. Credit memo
   c. Bank deposit
   d. Sales receipt
   e. None of the above answers is correct.

BEYOND THE CLICKS—THINKING LIKE A MANAGER

Accounting: What factors are important to consider when setting credit terms for your customers?

Information Systems: Customer payments are sometimes received one day and deposited into the company's bank one or two days later. What are some internal control processes that could be used to safeguard the payments until they are deposited?

ASSIGNMENTS

Assignment 3A

Math Revealed!

1/2/24

✓ You're ready to start recording some transactions for Martin, but first you want to set some preferences in **Account and Settings** that you think will be helpful.

- In the **Sales form content** section of the **Sales** tab:
  - ▪ You select **Net 15** as the **Preferred invoice terms**.
  - ▪ You choose **None** as the **Preferred delivery method** since you intend to print out invoices or receipts to customers when the services are completed.
  - ▪ **TIP:** **Custom transaction numbers** should have been turned **On** as part of the homework in Chapter 2. If you missed that, make sure you turn it on now. Also make sure all **Automation** features are turned off on the **Advanced** tab.

✓ Martin has let you know that he will be giving payment terms of Net 15 to all existing customers. You edit all customers to add the Net 15 payment terms in the **Payments** section of the customer record.

TIPS: To speed up the process, use the sidebar described in the HINT on page 3-13. Terms are added in the **Payments** section of the customer record.

1/5/24

✓ Martin gives you a check from a new customer for $110 for two tutoring sessions.

- You set up the new customer.
  - ▪ The customer is Alonso Luna. You use Luna, Alonso as the **customer display name**.
    4755 Hastings Road, Sacramento, CA 95822
    916-118-8111
    You set the payment terms at Net 15.
- You create a sales receipt (SR-101) for the two **Refresher** sessions. **TIP:** You can select **Unit** in the unit of measure field. Alonso paid the $110 with a check (#56772) dated 1/5.
  - ▪ You make sure to use 150 Undeposited Funds as the **Deposit to** account. You'll be depositing checks in batches.

✓ Martin also gives you a list of all sessions held this past week. He did not collect payment for any of these sessions, so you prepare invoices dated 1/5, with credit terms of Net 15, for the following customers. **TIP:** If you are asked to set up payment instructions and methods, select **Other ways to get paid** in the **Payment methods box**. Click **Done**.

- Debbie Han—**Crisis** $250, INV-1004
- Marcus Reymundo—**Refresher** $55, INV-1005
- Eliot Williams—**Persistence** $105, INV-1006

TIP: You are starting the invoices at INV-1004 because Invoices 1001-1003 were imported in Chapter 2.

✓ Several customers have also set up tutoring sessions for the next few weeks. Now that Martin has decided to offer payment terms to his customers, you will be invoicing them in advance. All customers have Net 15 terms. You use 1/5/24 as the invoice date.

- Jon Savidge—Three weeks of the **Persistence** program, starting 1/8. $315, INV-1007
- Paul Richard—Two weeks of the **Crisis** program, starting 1/15. $500, INV-1008
  - ▪ Paul is totally focused on an upcoming Algebra exam. He intends to get an A.

1/9/24

✓ Martin is always looking for ways to expand his services. He decides to offer a walk-in tutoring clinic on January 13. It will be open to all high school students. He's going to charge each student $25 for the afternoon. A couple of his college friends have agreed to help out.

- You set up the new **service** item you'll use to record Saturday's fees. Martin is calling the clinic "Mathmagic" so that's what you decide to name the item. You add the new item to the **Tutoring category**. You select Tutoring Revenue as the **Income account**. You use "Mathmagic Clinic" as the description.

1/10/24

✓ You receive two checks in the mail from customers. **TIP:** Make sure you use 150 Undeposited Funds for the **Deposit to** account for both. You are receiving payments on invoices you imported in the Chapter 2 assignment.

- Check #189 from Kim Kowalski, dated 1/10, for $105 on INV-1001.
  - ■ You give Kim a call and remind her that the total amount due was $210. She apologizes and promises to pay the balance before the end of the month.
- Check #2840 from Annie Wang, dated 1/10, for $250 in full payment of INV-1003.

✓ You deposit the checks received today with the check received last week into the Checking account. The total deposit is $465.

1/12/24

✓ Annie Wang's mother calls. She is so happy with the progress Annie is making in her Advanced Algebra course that she sets up appointments for the next four weeks (1/17/24–2/14/24) under the **Persistence** package. You invoice Annie $420, net 15. (INV-1009, dated 1/12).

- You realize that some of the revenue just invoiced to Annie will not be earned until February. (The four weeks will be up on February 13.) You decide to wait until the end of the month to make any necessary adjustments to the income statement. **TIP:** You'll do this as part of the homework for Chapter 5, so don't worry about it now.

1/15/24

✓ Thirty high school students showed up for the Mathmagic Clinic. All of them paid cash ($750 in total). You create one **sales receipt** (SR-102) to record all the payments instead of creating a receipt for each student.

- You decide to create a "Drop-In" customer for this purpose. You select **+ Add new** in the **Customer** dropdown menu. You enter "Drop-In" in the **Company name** and **Customer display name** fields. In the **Addresses** section, you enter 3835 Freeport Blvd, Sacramento, CA 95822 as the billing address.

  TIP: Enter the number of students in the **QTY** field on the **Sales Receipt**. Check to make sure Undeposited funds shows in the **Deposit to** field.

✓ One of the students, Navi Patel, decides to also sign up for two **Refresher** sessions. She pays the $110 in cash. Martin schedules the service for 1/17 and 1/24.

- Since she may be an ongoing customer, you decide to set her up as a customer and prepare a separate receipt for the future tutoring sessions (SR-103).
- Navi's address is 2525 Fractal Drive, Sacramento, CA 95822. Her phone number is 916-121-8282. Credit terms (for future invoices) are Net 15. You use Patel, Navi as the **customer display name**.

1/17/24

✓ You receive the following checks in the morning mail all dated 1/17:

- $425 from Jon Savidge, check #3334, in payment of INV-1002 and INV-1007.
- $105 from Eliot Williams, check #8114 in payment of INV-1006.
- $250 from Debbie Han, check #4499 in payment of INV-1004.

✓ You deposit all checks and cash received since 1/10. The total deposit is $1,640.

1/19/24

✓ Martin gives you a list of the sessions for the past two weeks. (He's gotten a little behind on his paperwork, and you remind him that his business needs cash to grow!)

- Some of the students paid for the sessions. You use 1/19 as the date on the **sales receipts**.
  - Marley Roberts paid $210 for two weeks of **Persistence** with check #1701. (SR-104)
  - Alonso Luna paid $110 for two **Refresher** sessions with check #56792. (SR-105)
- Jon Savidge came in with four of his friends. All of them chose the **Crisis** package. Jon's father agreed to pay for all five of them. You bill Jon for $1,250. (INV-1010, **net 30**). Martin rewarded Jon's generosity by giving him longer terms!

✓ Martin lets you know that he closed the office on January 15 for Martin Luther King Day. As a result, Paul Richard missed one of his **Crisis** sessions. You create a **credit memo** (CM-1008) for $50, dated 1/19. You use **Crisis** as the **PRODUCT/SERVICE**, enter 0 in the **QTY** field, and change the **AMOUNT** to 50. You enter "Credit for missed session due to holiday" in the **Message displayed on credit memo** field. Since Paul has an outstanding invoice, you'll apply the credit when he pays the balance due. All other students scheduled make-up sessions and did not miss any tutoring.

✓ The father of one of Martin's Mathmagic students storms into the office right before closing. Gus Ranting is very upset that Math Revealed! did not get his consent before tutoring his son. Martin talks to the father and explains that the tutoring clinic was voluntary and that there was no pressure on any of the students to sign up for more sessions. Nonetheless, Martin agrees to refund the $25, and that seems to calm Gus down.

- You add Gus Ranting as a customer when you create **refund receipt** (RR-100). You enter Ranting, Gus as the **customer display name**. You don't enter any contact information.
  - You issue the $25 refund from the Checking account. The Math Revealed! check number is 1100.
  - You use Mathmagic as the **PRODUCT/SERVICE**.

✓ You deposit the two checks received. The total deposit is $320.

1/22/24

✓ Martin gets a call from Teacher's College. Mr. Learn, the college president, has heard that Martin has developed some innovative techniques for helping students develop strong math skills. Mr. Learn asks Martin whether he's ever considered training other educators in his techniques. Martin is always up for new challenges and agrees to develop a workshop for the college for $3,000. Mr. Learn expects that there will be at least 50 math teachers from around the area in attendance. The workshop will be held February 9-10.

- You decide to set up a new **income** account called Workshop Revenue to track this new source of revenue. You select **Income** as the **account type** (**Save account under** field) and **Service/Fee Income** as the **detail type** (**Tax form section** field). You assign 405 as the account number.
- Martin thinks there may be opportunities for other types of workshops in the future, so you decide to set up a new **category** named "Workshops."
- You also create a new **service** item called "Educator Workshop."
  - You use "Tips for Teaching Math Workshop" as the item description and link the item to the Workshops **category**.
  - You enter a rate of "$3,000" as the default **sales price/rate** and select account 405 Workshops as the **Income account**.
- And you set up Teacher's College as a customer.
  - 21 Academy Avenue, Sacramento, CA 95822.
  - 916-443-3334.
  - Terms are Net 30.

✓ Teacher's College asks you to prepare an **invoice** for them now so that they can start processing the paperwork. You prepare INV-1011, dated 1/22, for the $3,000.

  ■ **TIP:** You will make an adjustment for unearned income as part of the homework for Chapter 5, so don't worry about it now.

1/25/24

✓ You receive two checks from customers.

  ● Check #7788090, dated 1/25, from Teacher's College for $3,000, in payment of INV-1011.

  ■ Martin was very surprised but very grateful for the prompt payment.

  ● Check #45678, dated 1/25 from Paul Richard for $450 in full payment of INV-1008.

  ■ **TIP:** Before you close the transaction, make sure that the **PAYMENT** field for the **Invoice** row shows the full amount (the original amount of the invoice), the **Amount received** is accurate, and the **Credit memo** box is checked. If you're having trouble, review the *Applying Credit Memos to Open Invoices When Customer Payments Are Recorded* section of this chapter.

  ● Martin was really impressed by Jon Savidge's father's willingness to pay for tutoring sessions for his son's friends. He decided to help out by crediting Jon's bill $250. You prepare a credit memo (CM-1010) and date it 1/25. **TIP:** The original invoice was for **Crisis** tutoring packages. The $250 is a small adjustment of the price. You enter "Credit for multiple students" in the **Message displayed on credit memo** field. **TIP:** Enter 0 in the **QTY** field and change the **AMOUNT** field to 150.

1/26/24

✓ Martin gives a list of tutoring sessions held since 1/19.

  ● You prepare an invoice for:

  ■ Marley Roberts, one **Persistence** package $105, INV-1012, Net 15

  ● One student paid by check so you created a sales receipt for:

  ■ Eliot Williams, one **Persistence** package $105 (Check # 8144, SR-106)

✓ Martin lets you know that he won't be setting up any additional sessions for the first three days of next week (January 29–31). He's going to use that time to prepare the workshop for Teacher's College.

✓ You deposit all the checks received this week. The deposit totals $3,555.

Check numbers 1/31

  Checking account balance: $9,575
  January Sales Revenue: $7,070

Suggested reports for Chapter 3:

All reports should be in portrait orientation.

● Journal—1/01 through 1/31 transactions only **TIP:** The **Journal** report is in the **For my accountant** section of **Reports**. Click **Switch to classic view**.

● Sales by Product/Service Summary (January sales only)

  ■ Customize (filter) the report to only show items in the Tutoring or Workshops **categories**.

● Accounts receivable aging summary dated 1/31

● Balance Sheet as of 1/31

● Profit and Loss for January

● Product/Service List (in the **Sales and Customers** section). Click **Switch to class view** and customize the report so that the following columns appear (in this order):

  ■ Product/Service

  ■ Type

- Description
- Qty On Hand
- Price
- Income Account
- Cost
- Expense Account

● Customer Contact List

- Customize the report to show Customer, Billing Address, and Terms columns only.

Assignment 3B

Salish Software Solutions

1/2/24

✓ You are ready to start recording some transactions, but first you want to set some preferences in the Sales tab of Account and Settings that you think will be helpful.

● In the Sales form content section of the Sales tab:

- You select Net 15 as the Preferred invoice terms.
- You choose None as the Preferred delivery method since you intend to print out invoices or receipts for customers when the services are completed.
- **TIP:** Custom transaction numbers should have been turned On as part of the homework in Chapter 2. If you missed that, make sure you turn it on now.

● In the Advanced tab you double-check that all of the Automation features are turned off.

✓ Martin has let you know that he will be giving payment terms of Net 15 to all existing customers. You edit all customers to add the Net 15 payment terms in the Payments section of the customer record.

● **TIPS:** To speed up the process, use the sidebar described in the Hint on page 3-13. Terms are added in the Payments section of the customer record.

1/5/24

✓ Sally did some work for Dew Drop Inn today. There were some software issues and Sally spent three hours fixing the file. Dew Drop Inn gave Sally a check (#8134), dated 1/5, for $180. The check (#8134) is dated 1/5.

● You create a sales receipt (SR-101) for the three hours of file repair (Fix). **TIP:** You can select Unit or Hour in the unit of measure field.

- You make sure to use 150 Undeposited Funds as the Deposit to account. You'll be depositing checks in batches.

✓ Sally also gives you a list of all of her other hours from the week. She did not collect payment from any of these customers so you prepare invoices dated 1/5, with credit terms of Net 15, as follows. **TIP:** If you are asked to set up payment instructions and methods, select Other ways to get paid in the Payment methods box. Click Done.

● Lou's Barber Shop—Set Up—10 hours ($750, INV-1006)
● Alki Deli—Set Up—6 hours ($450, INV-1007)
● Uptown Espresso—Train 6 hours ($300, INV-1008)

TIP: You are starting the invoices at INV-1006 because Invoices 1001-1005 were imported in Chapter 2.

1/8/24

✓ Sally is always looking for ways to grow her business. She decides to offer a Software Workshop on January 19th. She will be offering tips on software selection and will be demonstrating some of the software products she expects to start selling in February. She's going to charge participants $75 for the afternoon. A couple of her college friends have agreed to help out with what she hopes is a large crowd. You decide to go ahead and set up the new revenue account, new category, and the new service item you'll need to record the workshop revenue on the 19th.

- You decide to track the revenue from the workshop in a new **income** account (Workshop Revenue).
    - You select **Income** as the **account type** in the **Save account under** field and **Service/Fee Income** as the **detail type** in the **Tax form section** field. You use 415 as the account number.
- You set up a new **category** called "Workshops and Seminars."
- You also set up a new **service** item. Sally is calling the workshop "Picking the Right Software" so you decide to name the item "Picks." You set it up in the Workshops and Seminars category.
    - You enter "Picking the Right Software Workshop" as the description and 75 as the **sales price/rate**.
    - You select 415 Workshop Revenue as the **income account**.

1/10/24

✓ You receive two checks in the mail. **TIP:** Make sure you use 150 Undeposited Funds as the **Deposit to** account for both. You are receiving payments on invoices you imported in the Chapter 2 assignment.

- Check #1998 from Champion Law, dated 1/10, for $150 on INV-1003.
    - You call Lawrence (the accountant at the law firm) and remind him that the total amount due was $200. He apologizes and promises to pay the balance before the end of the month.
- Check #3751 from Lou's Barber Shop, dated 1/10, for $200 full payment of INV-1004.

✓ You deposit the checks received today with the check received last week into the checking account. The total deposit is $530.

1/12/24

✓ The Operations Manager at Butter and Beans calls. The software Sally helped to select is ready for installation. The company would prefer to be billed for the entire cost in one invoice. Sally estimates that the **Set up** work will take 40 hours. (It's a complicated system to set up.) You invoice Butter and Beans for the $3,000 and give them 30-day terms as agreed to by Sally. (INV-1009).

- You realize that some of the revenue just invoiced to Butter and Beans may not be earned until February. You decide to wait until the end of the month to make any necessary adjustments to the income statement. **TIP:** You'll do this as part of the homework for Chapter 5 so don't worry about it now.

1/16/24

✓ Sally gives you a breakdown for her hours since 1/5. (She's gotten a little behind on her paperwork and you remind her that her business needs cash to grow!) You use 1/16 as the date for each transaction.

- Two of her customers paid her when she completed the work. You record both on **sales receipts**.
    - Dew Drop Inn paid for 4 more hours of file repair (**Fix**) work with check #8144. ($240, SR-102)
    - Lou's Barber Shop paid for 8 more hours of training (**Train**) with check #3767. ($400, SR-103)
- Sally also did software research work for a new client (Fabulous Fifties).
    - You set them up as a new customer using the following information:
        834 Fashion Boulevard
        Sacramento, CA 95822
        916-555-5555
        Terms: Net 15
    - You invoice Fabulous Fifties the $500 **Select** fee on INV-1010.

1/19/24

✓ Twenty-five people showed up for the "Picking the Right Software" (**Picks**) workshop. All of them paid with cash ($1,875 in total), which was convenient but very surprising. You decide to create one sales receipt (SR-104) to record all the payments instead of creating a receipt for each participant.

- You select **+ Add new** in the **Customer** dropdown menu. You enter "Cash Customer" in the **Company name** and **Customer display name** fields. You enter 3835 Freeport Blvd, Sacramento, CA 95822 as the billing address in the **Addresses** section.
- **TIP:** On the **sales receipt** use 25 as the quantity sold.

✓ One of the participants, Leah Rasual, asks Sally to come to her home to do some trouble-shooting on her personal computer. She's using QuickBooks to track the fees she gets from her singing engagements and she's having some issues. Since Sally hasn't worked with Leah before she asks for payment in advance for the first two hours. She pays the $120 by check (#241). Sally schedules the appointment with Leah for Monday 1/22.

- Since Leah may be an ongoing customer, you decide to set her up as a customer and prepare a separate **sales receipt** for the **Fix** work. (**Sales Receipt** SR-105).
- You use **Rasual, Leah** as the **customer display name** and enter her first and last name in the appropriate boxes. Leah's address is 3131 Tyson Avenue, Sacramento, CA 95822. Her phone number is 916-281-2086. Credit terms (for future invoices) are Net 15.

✓ With all that cash, you head straight to the bank and make a deposit into the checking account. The total (including the checks received last week) is $2,635.

1/23/24

✓ Sally met with Leah Rasual and the work only took 2 hours. No additional billing is necessary.

✓ Sally lets you know that she made an error on the **Set Up** hours for Lou's Barber Shop included on INV-1006. She actually worked 8 hours not the 10 hours Lou's was billed for. You create a **credit memo** (CM-1006) for $150, dated 1/23. Since Lou's has an outstanding invoice, you'll apply the credit when he pays the balance due.

- You enter "Sorry for the overbilling." in the **Message displayed on credit memo** box.

✓ You receive the following checks, all dated 1/24, in the morning mail:

- $750 from Alki Deli, check #3334, in payment of INV-1001 and INV-1007.
- $50 from Champion Law, check #2001 for the remaining balance due on INV-1003.
- $500 from Butter and Beans, check #9191 in payment of INV-1002.

✓ One of the participants at Saturday's workshop (Marie Elle) stops by the office. She explains that she was only able to stay for the first 30 minutes of the workshop and would like to request a refund. She had to leave right after she got a call from her office letting her know that the pipes had burst in the warehouse basement. Sally agrees to refund the $75 **Picks** fee and promises to let her know about any future workshops.

- You add Marie Elle when you create **refund receipt** (RR-104). You enter her first and last name and you enter Elle, Marie in the **Customer display name** field. You don't need any other details. You pay the refund out of your Checking Account. The Salish Software check number is 1100.

✓ You deposit the 3 checks into the checking account. The total deposit is $1,300.

1/25/24

✓ Sally gets a call from Albus Software. Mr. Deposit, the CEO, has heard from several people that Sally does an exceptional job troubleshooting software problems. Mr. Deposit asks Sally whether she would be willing to share some tips and techniques with Albus' technical support staff. Sally thinks this might be an interesting project and agrees to develop a workshop for the company for $2,500. Mr. Deposit expects that there will be around 20 Albus employees in attendance. The workshop will be held in mid-February.

- You set up a new **service** item called "Tips." You include it in the **Workshops and Seminars category**.
  - You enter "Effective Troubleshooting" as the description and select 415 Workshop Revenue as the **Income Account**.
  - You set the default **sales price/rate** as $2,500.
- You also set up Albus Software as a customer.

  > 11 Potter Road, Sacramento, CA 95822.
  > 916-443-3334.
  > Terms are Net 30.

✓ The accountant for Albus Software asks you to create an **invoice** for the workshop now so that they can start processing the paperwork. You prepare INV-1011, dated 1/25, for the $2,500.
  - **TIP:** You won't earn the $2,500 until you present the workshop in February. You will make an adjustment for unearned income as part of the homework for Chapter 5 so don't worry about it now.

1/26/24

✓ Dew Drop Inn decided they need to install a new accounting software system after paying Sally for multiple hours spent trying to repair their current system. They asked Sally to help them select an appropriate program. She reviewed the company's needs this week and put together a proposal for them that spelled out her recommendation. You prepare the invoice for that service. (**Select**, $500, INV-1012, Net 15).

✓ Sally lets you know that she won't be doing any consulting during the last few days of January. She's going to use that time to prepare training materials for the Effective Troubleshooting workshop at Albus Software.

1/30/24

✓ You receive two checks from customers. Both checks are dated 1/30.
- Check #5333 from Uptown Espresso ($480) in payment of INV-1005 and INV-1008.
- Check #3790 from Lou's Barber Shop ($600) in full payment of INV-1006.
  - You apply CM-1006 to the balance when you enter the payment.
  - **TIP:** This can be tricky. Before you close the transaction, make sure that the **PAYMENT** field for the **Invoice** shows the full amount (the original amount of the invoice), the **Amount received** is accurate, and the **Credit memo** box is checked. If you're having trouble, review the *Applying Credit Memos to Open Invoices When Customer Payments Are Recorded* section of this chapter.

✓ You deposit both checks in the bank. The deposit should total $1,080.

Check numbers 1/31

Checking account balance:. . . .$15,970
January Sales Revenue:. $10,590

Reports to create for Chapter 3:

- Journal—1/01 through 1/31 **TIP:** The **Journal** report is in the **For my accountant** section of **Reports**. Click **Switch to classic view**.
- Accounts receivable aging summary dated 1/31
- Sales by Product/Service Summary (January sales only)
  - Customize (filter) the report to only show items in the Consulting and Installation and Workshops and Seminars **categories**.
- Balance Sheet as of 1/31
- Profit and Loss for January

- Product/Service List (in the **Sales and Customers** section). Click **Switch to classic view** and customize the report so that the following columns appear (in this order):
    - Product/Service
    - Type
    - Description
    - Qty On Hand
    - Price
    - Income Account
    - Cost
    - Expense Account
- Customer Contact List
    - Customize the report to show Customer, Billing Address and Terms columns only.

4 Purchasing Activity
(Service Company)

Road Map

LO	Learning Objective	Topic	Subtopic	Page	Practice Exercises	Videos
LO4-1	Set up and edit vendors in QBO [p. 4-2]	Managing vendors	Vendor center display	4-3	4.1	Managing vendors
			Adding a vendor	4-4		
			Viewing vendor information	4-6		
			Editing vendor information	4-7		
			Inactivating or merging vendors	4-8		
LO4-2	Identify and use QBO forms to record purchase transactions [p. 4-10]	Recording purchases	Purchasing on account	4-11	4.2	Recording purchases (on account)
			Purchasing with cash, check, electronic transfer, or debit card	4-15	4.3	Recording purchases (with cash or credit card)
			Voiding checks	4-17	4.4	
			Purchasing with a credit card	4-19	4.5	
LO4-3	Explain and use various methods for paying vendor balances [p. 4-23]	Paying vendor balances	Paying multiple vendor bills	4-24	4.6	Paying vendor balances
			Paying one or more bills from a single vendor	4-26		
LO4-4	Recognize and prepare common reports used in the purchase cycle [p. 4-27]	Preparing purchase and vendor reports		4-27	4.7	
LO4-5	Describe the QBO process for reporting 1099 vendor activity [p. 4-38]	APPENDIX 4A— Reporting 1099 activity (Appendix 4A)		4-38		

WHAT IS THE PURCHASE CYCLE IN A SERVICE COMPANY?

The purchase cycle in a service company, like the sales cycle, is fairly straightforward. A company

- Incurs the cost.
- Receives a bill from the vendor.
- Pays the vendor.

Service companies can

- Pay at the time of purchase of goods or services.
- Pay later (buy "on account" or "on credit").

Before any purchases can be recorded in QuickBooks Online, a vendor must be set up.

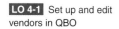 **LO 4-1** Set up and edit vendors in QBO

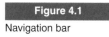

MANAGING VENDORS

Vendors are managed in the Vendor Center.

> **BEHIND THE SCENES** In business, a vendor is an individual or company from whom a company purchases products or services. The phone company, the landlord, and the local newspaper are all vendors. In QBO, a **vendor** is set up for any individual (other than an employee) or company that the user expects to pay. Vendors might include owners, lenders, and tax authorities.

The Vendor Center is accessed through the **Expenses** link on the navigation bar.

Figure 4.1

Navigation bar

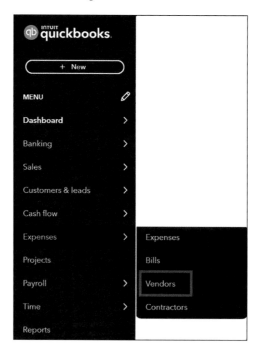

 HINT: A description of what's included in the various **drawers** (tabs) in the **Expenses** link is included in Chapter 1 (Table 1.2).

Select the **Vendors drawer** (tab) to open the Vendor Center.

Figure 4.2

Vendor Center

In the Vendor Center, you can:

1. Access the new vendor setup sidebar.
2. Access forms necessary to record activity with existing vendors.
3. Access existing vendor data for editing.

Vendor Center Display

Selected information about vendor activity is highlighted in the **Money Bar** at the top of the Vendor Center screen.

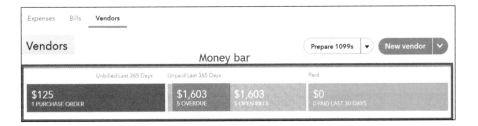

Figure 4.3

Money Bar in Vendor Center

Clicking any of the amounts brings up a list of the transactions included in the total.

 HINT: The amounts displayed in your **Money Bar** may differ slightly from those shown in Figure 4.3.

On the right side of the Vendor Center screen, just above the list of vendors, are three small icons.

Figure 4.4

Icons on Vendor Center screen

The **printer** icon (far left) allows the user to print a list of all vendors. The list includes all vendor information currently displayed on the screen (including **OPEN BALANCE**).

Clicking the **export** icon (the middle icon) automatically downloads the list as an Excel file.

Clicking the third icon (the ⚙) allows users to customize the fields displayed in the Vendor Center.

Display columns can include any of the following:

Figure 4.5

Column options for
Vendor Center screen

Adding a Vendor

To add a new vendor, open the Vendor Center by clicking **Expenses** in the navigation bar
and opening the **Vendors drawer** (tab).

Figure 4.6

Link to add vendor

Click **New Vendor**. A side panel will open.

Figure 4.7

Vendor record

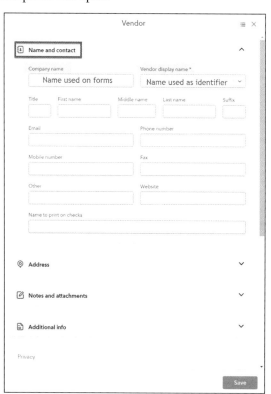

There are four sections in the vendor record. The top section is open in Figure 4.7.

Basic contact information is entered in the **Name and contact** section. The name entered in the **Company name** field is the name used in any correspondence with the vendor. This would normally be the business name used by the vendor. If the vendor is an individual, their name would be entered in the **First name**, **Last name** fields directly below the **Company name** field.

The **Vendor display name** is used as a vendor identifier. It could be a number or a shortened version of the vendor name. This is the primary name used to organize the vendor list. It's also the name used in any search functions. The **Vendor display name** is primarily used for internal purposes.

In this class, we'll use the **Company name** name (or individual name) as the **Vendor display name**.

> **HINT:** **Vendor display names** must be unique. An entity that is both a customer and a vendor can use the same **Company name** but must have two different **Vendor display names**. One option would be to add a C (customer) or a V (vendor) to the end in the **Vendor display name** fields.

QBO will automatically add the **vendor display name** to the **Name to print on checks** field. That field would need to be edited if the **display name** is a number or abbreviation.

The vendor address is entered in the second section of the vendor record, the **Address** section (Figure 4.7).

Figure 4.8

Additional information section of the vendor record

Other important information is entered in the **Additional info** section (Figure 4.8). This includes the vendor terms and any account number assigned to the company by the vendor.

Companies are required to report payments of more than $600 during the year to certain types of vendors to the Internal Revenue Service. Payments to independent contractors are reported on Form 1099-NEC. Payments to attorneys and landlords are reported on Form 1099-MISC.

Required tax information for 1099 vendors (including their federal tax identification number) is entered in the fields at the top of the section. (Reporting payments to 1099 vendors is covered in the Appendix to this chapter.)

> **BEHIND THE SCENES** Using QBO, users can obtain 1099 information directly from vendors through email. The setup is done by clicking **Payroll** on the navigation bar and selecting **Add a contractor** in the **Contractors drawer** (tab). Any vendor set up as a **Contractor** will appear in the Vendor Center. Independent contractors are covered in more detail in Chapter 10.

If a general ledger account is selected in the **Default expense category** field in the **Additional info** section, QBO will use that account in all transactions with that vendor. It can be changed when a purchase form (**bill**, **expense**, **check**, etc.) is completed.

Documents can be uploaded to the vendor record for easy access in the **Notes and attachments** section of the vendor record. **Attachments** will be discussed further in Chapter 11.

Viewing Vendor Information

To view information about a specific vendor, click the vendor's name in the Vendor Center. The vendor screen has two tabs.

Figure 4.9

Transaction List tab in vendor record

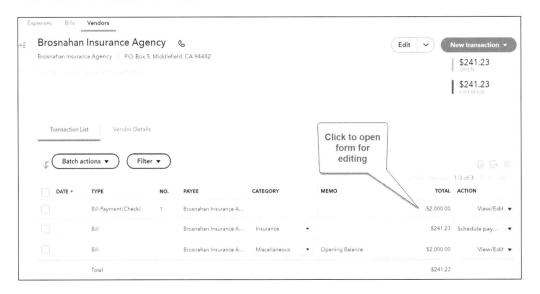

Prior transactions are listed on the **Transaction List** tab. Clicking any of the transactions listed will open the original form. Once in the form, details can be edited (dates, amounts, distribution accounts, etc.).

 HINT: Distribution accounts can also be changed directly on the **Transaction List** tab for **bill** transactions as long as the original transaction was not split into multiple accounts.

Basic contact information is displayed in the **Vendor Details** tab shown in Figure 4.10.

Figure 4.10

Vendor Details tab in vendor record

> ✳ **HINT:** For access to the full list of vendors when you're in a specific vendor record, click the three parallel lines to the left of the vendor name (top left corner in Figure 4.10). A sidebar will open.

Editing Vendor Information

Vendor information can be changed at any time. To edit an existing vendor, open the Vendor Center by clicking **Expenses** on the navigation bar and opening the **Vendors drawer** (tab).

Click the name of the vendor you wish to edit and open the **Vendor Details** tab.

Figure 4.11

Access to edit vendor record

Click either **Edit** link to open the vendor record. Make the desired changes and click **Save**.

Inactivating or Merging Vendors

Inactivating a vendor

Vendors cannot be deleted in QBO. Vendors can, however, be inactivated. Most companies would choose to inactivate vendors they don't expect to use in the future to minimize the size of the vendor list.

To inactivate a vendor with no open balance, open the Vendor Center.

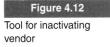

Figure 4.12

Tool for inactivating vendor

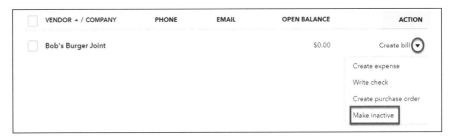

On the dropdown menu in the far right column of the vendor row, select **Make inactive**.

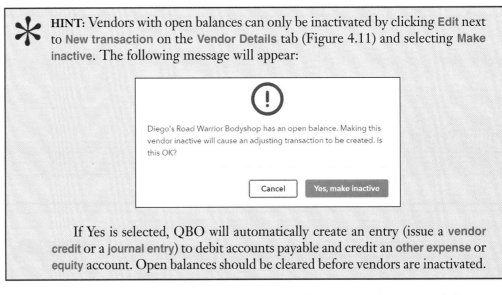

HINT: Vendors with open balances can only be inactivated by clicking **Edit** next to **New transaction** on the **Vendor Details** tab (Figure 4.11) and selecting **Make inactive**. The following message will appear:

Diego's Road Warrior Bodyshop has an open balance. Making this vendor inactive will cause an adjusting transaction to be created. Is this OK?

Cancel   Yes, make inactive

If Yes is selected, QBO will automatically create an entry (issue a **vendor credit** or a **journal entry**) to debit accounts payable and credit an **other expense** or **equity** account. Open balances should be cleared before vendors are inactivated.

Inactive vendors can't be used in transactions and aren't available in search functions, although they will show up on the appropriate reports.

To reactivate a vendor, inactive vendors must be visible in the Vendor Center.

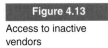

Figure 4.13

Access to inactive vendors

Click the ⚙ icon right above the **ACTION** column in the Vendor Center to make inactive vendors visible.

VENDOR ▲ / COMPANY	PHONE	EMAIL	OPEN BALANCE	ACTION
☐ Bob's Burger Joint (deleted)			$0.00	Make active

Figure 4.14

Tool to reactivate an inactive vendor

An option to reactivate a vendor will now automatically appear in the **ACTION** column next to the vendor name.

> **BEHIND THE SCENES** Although the vendor shows as "deleted" in Figure 4.14 above, the vendor had been inactivated.

Merging vendors

Vendors can be combined in QBO. When two vendors are **merged**, all transactions with one vendor are "transferred" to the other vendor (i.e., the vendor name fields are changed on all transactions). **Merging** might be necessary to correct duplicate records or if multiple locations of a vendor are combined.

To combine (**merge**) two vendors, open the Vendor Center by clicking **Expenses** on the navigation bar and opening the **Vendors drawer** (tab). Click the name of the vendor to be merged and select **Merge contacts** in the **Edit** dropdown menu in the top right section of the page.

Figure 4.15

Dialog box for merging contacts

Select the name of the vendor with transactions to be merged in the **Merge transactions from** dropdown menu. Select the name of the vendor to be retained in the **Into** dropdown menu.
Click **Merge contacts**.

Set up and edit vendors for Craig's Design and Landscaping.
(Craig's Design adds two new vendors and edits an existing vendor's record.)

1. Enter a new vendor: Office Supplies Shop.

   a. Click **Expenses** in the navigation bar.

   b. Open the **Vendors drawer** (tab).

   c. Click **New Vendor** (top right of screen).

PRACTICE
EXERCISE
4.1

Homework
MBC

(continued)

(continued from previous page)

     d. In the Name and contact sections of the vendor record, enter "Office Supplies Shop" in the Company name and Vendor display name fields.

     e. Open the Address section and enter the following:

          2121 Capital Avenue

          West Sacramento, CA 95691

     f. Open the Additional info section and select Net 30 in the Terms dropdown menu.

     g. Click Save.

2. Enter a new 1099 vendor: Beverly Okimoto (accountant who may be hired as contract labor to assist with consulting work).

     a. Click New Vendor in the Vendor Center (top right of screen).

     b. Open the Name and contact section of the sidebar and enter the following:

         i. "Beverly" in the First name field and "Okimoto" in the Last name field

         ii. Use Beverly Okimoto as the Vendor display name.

     c. Open the Address section and enter the following:

          2525 Paradise Road

          Suite 2502

          Sacramento, CA 95822

     d. Open the Additional info section.

         i. Check the box next to Track payments for 1099 and enter "444-22-9898" in the Business ID No. field.

         ii. Select Net 15 in the Terms dropdown menu.

     e. Click Save.

3. Edit a vendor.

     a. Click Computers by Jenni in the Vendor Center.

     b. Click Edit to open the vendor record.

     c. Change the Mobile number to "916-375-5511" in the Name and contact section.

     d. Open the Additional info section.

         i. Enter Business ID No. as "91-1112222."

         ii. Check the box next to Track payments for 1099.

     e. **Make a note** of Jenni's last name.

     f. Click Save.

4. Click Dashboard.

RECORDING PURCHASES

LO 4-2 Identify and use QBO forms to record purchase transactions

In a service company, most purchases are made "on account." It's just an easier, more efficient way to do business. There are times, however, when payment is made at the time of purchase (by cash/check or by credit card). As you can probably guess by now, QBO has a separate form for each alternative. The **transaction types** are:

- Bill—used for purchases on account.
- Check—used when payment is made with a check, automatic transfer, or debit card at the time of purchase or when the bill wasn't entered into QBO before payment was made.
    - A different transaction type (**Bill payment**) is used when **bills** previously entered in QBO are paid. **Bill payments** are covered in the **PAYING VENDOR BALANCES** section of this chapter.
- Expense—generally used when payment is made at the time of purchase with a credit card although the form can also be used with other payment methods.

> **BEHIND THE SCENES** QBO gives users many options for accomplishing the same task. As you continue to work with the software, you'll find yourself developing personal preferences. In your homework, you will only be using **Expense** transaction types for purchases with a credit card.

eLecture

Purchasing on Account

In a manual accounting system, a bill is received from the vendor. The bill is recorded in the purchases journal. The purchases journal is posted, in total, to the general ledger, and each transaction in the purchases journal is posted to the appropriate vendor's subsidiary ledger.

In QBO, the form for entering a purchase on account is called a **bill**. (Remember, the vendor might call it an invoice but QBO calls it a **bill**. Only charges to customers are called invoices in QBO.) All accounts, ledgers, and statements are updated automatically when the **bill** is saved, so the form must include answers to the following questions:

- Who's the vendor? (This is needed for posting to the subsidiary ledger.)
- What are we buying? (What account should QBO debit?)
    - The credit account for **bills** is Accounts payable.
- When do we have to pay for it? (What are the vendor's credit terms?)

> **WARNING:** Although users can set up multiple accounts payable accounts in the chart of accounts. **Bills** are automatically credited to the default Accounts Payable (A/P) account set up by Intuit. As of early 2023, this cannot be changed.

The **bill** form can be accessed:

- by clicking **+ New** on the navigation bar and selecting **Bill** in the Vendors column
- by clicking **Expenses** on the navigation bar, opening the **Expenses drawer** (tab), and selecting **Bill** in the **New transaction** dropdown menu
- by clicking **Expenses** on the navigation bar, opening the **Bills drawer** (tab), and clicking **Create bill** in the **Add bill** dropdown menu.
- by clicking **Expenses** on the navigation bar, opening the **Vendors drawer** (tab), and selecting **Create bill** in the **Action** column dropdown menu for the vendor
- by clicking **Expenses** on the navigation bar, opening the **Vendors drawer** (tab), clicking the vendor name, and selecting **Bill** in the **New transaction** dropdown menu

Using the first option, click + New on the navigation bar and select **Bill**.

Figure 4.16

Bill form

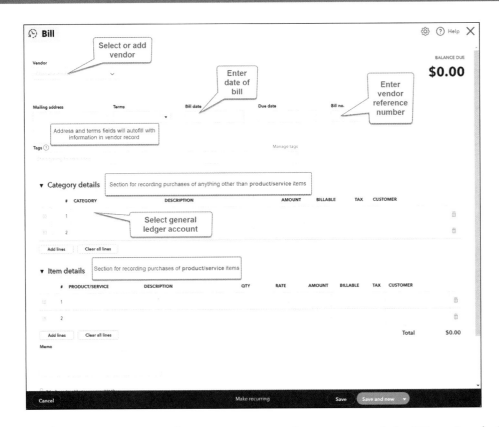

To complete a **bill**, you must select a **Vendor**, enter the **Bill date**, and the **Bill no.** (vendor's reference number) in the top section of the form.

HINT: If the vendor hasn't been previously entered, you can click **+ Add new** at the top of the **Choose a vendor** dropdown menu. A new vendor record panel will open. If you don't need to enter details, simply enter the **Company name** and **Vendor display name** and click **Save**.

You also need to enter the vendor's credit terms. If you've already set up the credit terms for the vendor, these will show up automatically in the **Terms** field. If you haven't, you can select a term from the dropdown menu or create a new one by clicking **+ Add new** in the **Terms** dropdown menu. QBO can be used to keep track of any available early payment discounts so it's important to make sure the date and the terms are entered correctly.

> **BEHIND THE SCENES** The same **terms** are used for both vendors and customers. You can see the full **Terms** list by selecting the ⚙ icon and selecting **All Lists** from the **List** menu.

Amounts and the accounts to be debited (the distribution accounts) are entered in the lower section of the form. As you can see in Figure 4.16, there are two sections in the bottom half of the form (**Category details** and **Item details**). Clicking the triangle just to the left of the name opens or closes the section.

Both sections are used to specify the account(s) to be debited.

- **Category details**
  - ▪ Used to record all purchases other than **product/service** items. Most likely you would be debiting an asset or expense account in this section, but you could debit any type of account.
- **Item details**
  - ▪ Used to record purchases of **product/service** items. The general ledger account debited depends on the account identified in the record of **service** or **product** item selected. Inventory (**product**) purchases will be covered in Chapter 7.

You can enter multiple accounts in the account distribution section of the form. You can even enter negative amounts, which would, of course, appear as credits in the underlying journal entry. A negative amount would be entered if, for example, the vendor gives you a discount and you decide to track discounts in a separate account. The sum of all the distributions must equal the total amount of the bill. (This is, after all, still accounting! The underlying journal entry must balance.)

> What's the default credit account for a bill? (Answer at end of chapter.)

QuickCheck
4-1

You can enter additional information about the nature of each charge in the **Description** field. You can also enter general information about the bill in the **Memo** field at the bottom left of the form. Anything included in either the **Description** or **Memo** fields will appear in **Journal** reports.

The bill itself or other documents related to the charge can be uploaded to QBO by clicking **Attachments** in the bottom left corner of the **bill**. (The **Attachments** link would appear under the **Memo** field in Figure 4.16.) Documents related to the vendor (price lists, contracts, etc.) that are not unique to the bill would normally be uploaded to the vendor record. **Attachments** will be covered in greater depth in Chapter 11.

Click **Save and close** in the bottom right corner of the window to exit the form. Click **Save and new** to open a new blank **bill** form. **Save and schedule** is used to set up automatic payments. A company must have set up a bank connection in QBO in order to use the payment scheduling feature.

Enter bills for Craig's Design and Landscaping.

(Craig's Design enters several bills received in the mail.)

1. Click **+ New** on the navigation bar.

2. Click **Bill** in the **Vendors** column.

PRACTICE
EXERCISE
4.2

(continued)

(continued from previous page)

3. Enter the telephone bill for the current month. (The total bill was $285: $35 for the phone and a $250 charge for a repair.)

   a. Select Cal Telephone as the Vendor.

   b. Select Net 30 for Terms.

   c. Enter the current date as the Bill date.

   d. Enter "118-1119" as the Bill No.

   e. In the Category details section, select Telephone as the ACCOUNT and enter "35" as the AMOUNT. **TIP:** The CATEGORY and AMOUNT fields autofilled because automation is turned on in the test drive company.

      i. **Make a note** of the parent account for Telephone.

   f. On the second line, select Equipment repairs as the ACCOUNT and enter "250" as the AMOUNT.

   g. Click Save and new.

4. Enter a $450 bill for an ad placed in the Business Weekly.

   a. Select + Add new in the Choose a vendor dropdown menu.

      i. Enter "Business Weekly" in the Company name and Vendor display name fields of the Name and contact section.

      ii. Open the Additional info section and select Net 15 in the Terms dropdown menu.

      iii. Click Save.

   b. Enter the current date as the Date.

   c. Enter "121520" as the Bill no.

   d. In the Category details section, select Advertising as the CATEGORY.

   e. Enter "Ad in the Weekly" in the DESCRIPTION field.

   f. Enter "450" as the AMOUNT.

   g. Click Save and new.

5. Enter a $720 bill from Tania's Nursery for the purchase of a new lawn mower ($650) and 10 boxes of trash bags ($70).

   a. Select Tania's Nursery as the Vendor.

   b. Select Net 15 for the Terms.

   c. Enter the current date as the Bill date.

   d. Enter "67-1313" as the Bill no.

   e. The lawn mower is expected to last for more than one year so it should be recorded in a fixed asset account. In the Category details section, select + Add new in the CATEGORY dropdown menu to set up a new account.

      i. Select Assets. **TIP:** You may not see the financial statement classification menu option on your screen.

      ii. Account Type (Save account under field)—Fixed Assets

      iii. Detail Type (Tax form section field)—Machinery & Equipment

      iv. Name—Mowing equipment

         • Do **not** check Track depreciation of this asset. **TIP:** When this box is checked, QBO automatically creates two sub-accounts. One called "Orig-

(continued)

(continued from previous page)

inal cost" and one called "Depreciation." Both sub-accounts have the fixed assets account type. This option would not be used by companies that do not create individual accumulated depreciation accounts for each property, plant, or equipment account. This option may not appear on your screen.

    v. Click Save and Close.

  f. Enter "$650" as the AMOUNT for the mower in the category details section of the bill.

  g. The trash bags are expected to be used in the current month so the cost is debited to an Expense account type. Select Supplies as the CATEGORY and use "$70" for the AMOUNT.

  h. Click Save and close.

6. Review the accounts set up for the lawn mower.

  a. Click the ⚙ on the icon bar.

  b. Click Chart of Accounts.

  c. Click See your Chart of Accounts, if necessary.

  d. **Make a note** of how many accounts have an account type of Fixed Assets.

  e. Click Dashboard to close the window.

Purchasing with Cash, Check, Electronic Transfer, or Debit Card

In a manual system, cash payments are recorded in the cash disbursements journal. The journal is recorded, in total, to the general ledger.

In QBO, cash payments (payments made by check, currency, electronic transfer, or debit card) made at the time of purchase or when a vendor bill was not previously entered into QBO can be entered through the form (transaction type) Check.

  HINT: Cash payments can also be entered using the form Expense. In this course, Expense forms are exclusively used for credit card transactions.

You can easily access the form by clicking **＋New** on the navigation bar and clicking Check in the Vendor column. You can also access the Check form through Expenses on the navigation bar (in both the Expenses and Vendor drawers (tabs).

The form will look something like Figure 4.17.

  WARNING: In early 2023, Intuit started updating various QBO forms. Some of those forms may have been updated after your textbook was printed. If you see a form that doesn't match the screenshot in your book, start by looking for an option to return to a previous version. In most cases, you'll see a link to **Old layout** or **Switch to classic view**. If there is no link available, check the Student Ancillaries page in myBusinessCourse for information about the updated form or ask your instructor.

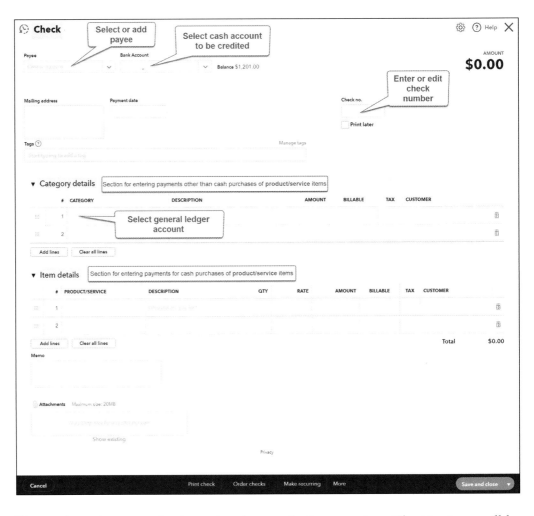

You need to select a vendor (**Payee**) and enter the **Payment date**. The **Check no.** will be automatically updated by QBO but you can change the number if necessary.

The **Bank Account** you want to be credited for the check amount also needs to be selected. Users can track multiple bank accounts in QBO.

You'll notice the form has the same two distribution sections as the **Bill** form (**Category details** and **Item details**). Both sections are used for identifying the general ledger accounts to be debited (or credited if a negative is entered) and the amounts.

> **BEHIND THE SCENES** Users can add information about the payment in the **Description** field and/or the **Memo** field. If the user prints the check from QBO, anything included in the **Memo** field will appear on the face of the check; anything included in the **Description** field will appear on the voucher copy of the check.

PRACTICE
EXERCISE
4.3

Enter checks for Craig's Design and Landscaping.

(Craig's Design pays its rent, makes a loan payment, and pays a retainer fee to a consultant.)

1. Record $900 rent payment for the current month.

   a. Click ➕ New on the navigation bar.

(continued)

(continued from previous page)

    b. Click Check.

    c. Select Hall Properties as the vendor.

    d. **Make a note** of the contact name for Hall Properties. **TIP:** The name is included in the Mailing address box.

    e. Leave Checking as the Bank Account.

    f. Enter the current date as the Payment date.

    g. Use "71" as the Check no.

    h. In the Category details section, select Rent or Lease as the CATEGORY.

    i. Enter "900" as the AMOUNT.

    j. Click Save and new.

2. Record a $120 check for the loan payment ($100 of principal; $20 of interest for the current month).

    a. Select Fidelity as the vendor.

    b. Leave Checking as the bank account.

    c. Enter the current date as the Payment date.

    d. Use "72" as the Check no.

    e. There are two distributions in the Category details section.

        i. On the first line, select Notes Payable as the CATEGORY and enter "100" as the AMOUNT (principal).

        ii. On the second line, select + Add new in the CATEGORY field, choose Other expense as the account type (Save account under field), Vehicle loan interest as the detail type (Tax form section field), and enter "Interest Expense" as the Name. Click Save and close.

        iii. Enter "20" as the AMOUNT.

        iv. The check total should be $120.

    f. Click Save and new.

3. Record check to Computers by Jenni for a retainer fee. (You're giving her an advance for future computer work.)

    a. Select Computers by Jenni as the vendor.

    b. Leave Checking as the bank account.

    c. Enter the current date as the Payment date.

    d. Use "73" as the Check no.

    e. In the Category details section, select Prepaid Expenses as the CATEGORY.

    f. Enter "400" as the AMOUNT.

    g. Click Save and close.

Voiding Checks

If a check is printed but contains an error and won't be distributed, it should be voided (not deleted) in QBO. This ensures that all check numbers are properly accounted for.

> **BEHIND THE SCENES** Information about **checks** that have been voided is retained in QBO (payee, check number, date, and distribution accounts). No information is retained for **deleted** checks.

To void a check in QBO (**Check** and **bill payment (check) transaction types**), click **Expenses** on the navigation bar.

Open the **Expenses drawer** (tab).

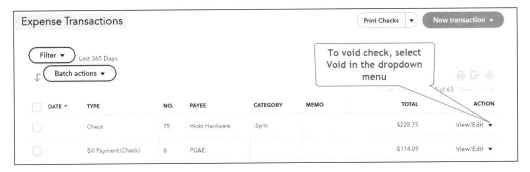

Select **Void** in the dropdown menu in the **ACTION** column of the check to be voided.

Checks can also be voided by opening the check form, clicking **More** in the black bar at the bottom of the form, and selecting **Void**.

You will have an opportunity to cancel the transaction before QBO completes the voiding process and will get an additional message when void is successful.

Voided checks do appear on journal reports (0.00 dollar amounts) and are accessible using the **Search** feature. A voided check would look something like Figure 4.19.

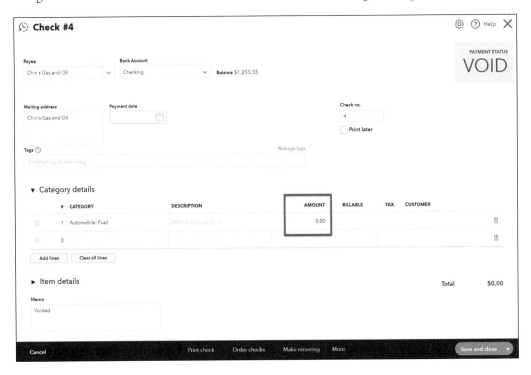

BEHIND THE SCENES QuickBooks Online uses the original check date to record a voided check. This can create problems if financial reports have already been distributed for that accounting period. For example, let's say a $100 check was written in December to pay for some travel expenses. In the December income statement, net income would, of course, be decreased by the $100 travel expense. Now let's say that the $100 check was lost so a new check was issued and the original check was voided in QBO in February. The replacement check would have a February date, but the original check would be voided by QBO as of the original December check date. If you then prepared a new December income statement, net income would automatically be $100 higher than it was before due to the voided check. On the other hand, February's net income would be reduced by the $100 December travel expense. The expense is now reported in the wrong **accounting period**. If the amounts are significant or if tax reports have already been filed, journal entries should be made to correct the balances.

Void a check for Craig's Design and Landscaping.

(Craig's Design voids a check prepared in error.)

1. Void the check to Books by Bessie. Craig used a company check instead of his own personal check when he had his personal taxes done.

   a. Click the **magnifying glass** icon in the icon bar.

   b. Click **Advanced Search**.

   c. Select **Check** in the **TYPE** dropdown menu.

   d. Select **Books by Bessie** in the **CONTACT** dropdown menu.

      i. QBO will automatically display transactions that match the filters.

   e. Click Check #12. The original check form should appear.

   f. **Make a note** of the amount of the check being voided.

   g. Click **More** at the bottom of the screen.

   h. Click **Void**.

   i. Click **Yes** when asked about voiding the check.

   j. Click **OK**.

      i. You should be back in the **Search** screen.

   k. Click Check #12 again to verify that the check has been voided.

   l. Click **Cancel**.

   m. Click **Dashboard**.

Purchasing with a Credit Card

Some companies obtain corporate credit cards. Owners or employees who need to be able to purchase items when they're traveling are the typical users of these cards.

Although the seller might see a payment by credit card as the same as cash, the purchaser is really buying on credit. The company that issued the card is the creditor.

In QBO, credit cards are set up as a separate liability **account type (Credit Card)**. When individual credit card charges are entered, the amounts are credited to the credit card account and debited to the appropriate expense or asset account. This allows the user to track the details of all purchases.

When the credit card statement is received, the user reconciles the amounts recorded in QBO to the statement and processes the credit card bill for payment. (Credit card reconciliations are covered in Chapter 5.)

Before you can enter credit card charges, the general ledger account must be set up. This is done through the Chart of Accounts list. Remember, the account must be set up as a **Credit Card account type.**

Users would normally use the **Expense** form (transaction type) for entering credit card charges.

You can easily access the form by clicking ⊕ **New** on the navigation bar and clicking **Expense** in the **Vendor** column. **Expense** forms can also be accessed through **Expenses** on the navigation bar (in both the **Expenses** and **Vendor drawers** (tabs)).

The form will look something like Figure 4.20.

> ! **WARNING:** In early 2023, Intuit started updating various QBO forms. Some of those forms may have been updated after your textbook was printed. If you see a form that doesn't match the screenshot in your book, start by looking for an option to return to a previous version. In most cases, you'll see a link to **Old layout** or **Switch to classic view**. If there is no link available, check the Student Ancillaries page in myBusinessCourse for information about the updated form or ask your instructor.

Figure 4.20

Expense form

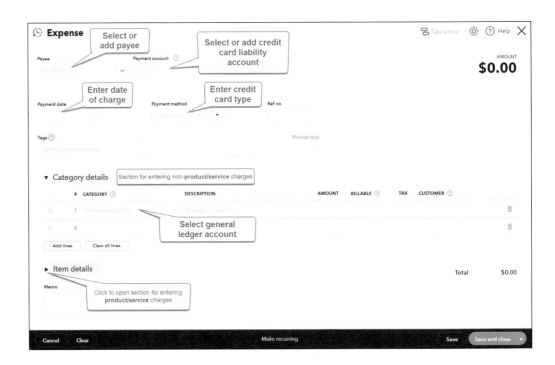

The **Expense** form is similar to the **Bill** and **Check** forms. You need to enter the name of the business where the credit card was used in the **Payee** field and the date of the charge in the **Payment date** field.

BEHIND THE SCENES Remember, you will be paying the entity that issued the card, not the business where you used the card. The business name is entered for informational purposes only. Many companies will add the vendor name for credit card transactions but will not add much vendor detail (address, etc.).

The account credited (**credit card account type**) is selected in the **Bank/Credit account** field.

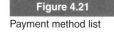

Figure 4.21
Payment method list

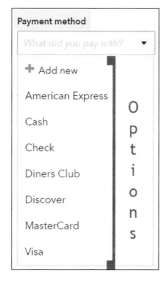

The type of credit used can be selected in the **Payment method** dropdown menu.

 HINT: Payment methods were covered in Chapter 2.

The accounts debited will be identified in the **Category details** section, the **Item details** section, or both.

Expenses charged to credit card liability accounts are not automatically available to pay through the bill payment feature in QBO. Instead, credit card balances are transferred to accounts payable when the card is reconciled. (Credit card reconciliations are covered in Chapter 5.)

Below is a summary of how the various transactions and journal entries occur for purchases made with a credit card.

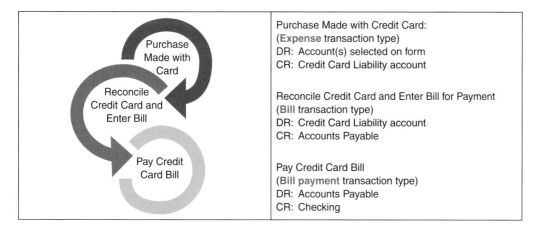

Purchase Made with Credit Card:
(**Expense** transaction type)
DR: Account(s) selected on form
CR: Credit Card Liability account

Reconcile Credit Card and Enter Bill for Payment
(**Bill** transaction type)
DR: Credit Card Liability account
CR: Accounts Payable

Pay Credit Card Bill
(**Bill payment** transaction type)
DR: Accounts Payable
CR: Checking

BEHIND THE SCENES Users can record payments on a credit card balance without reconciling the statement first.

CUSTOMERS	VENDORS	EMPLOYEES	OTHER
Invoice	Expense	Single time activity	Bank deposit
Receive payment	Check	Weekly timesheet	Transfer
Estimate	Bill		Journal entry
Credit memo	Pay bills		Statement
Sales receipt	Purchase order		Inventory qty adjustment
Refund receipt	Vendor credit		Pay down credit card
Delayed credit	Credit card credit		
Delayed charge	Print checks		

Click **+ New** on the navigation bar and select **Pay down credit card**.

The credit card being paid and the bank account used to make the payment would need to be selected. A payment, by check, of $500 toward the Mastercard balance would look something like this:

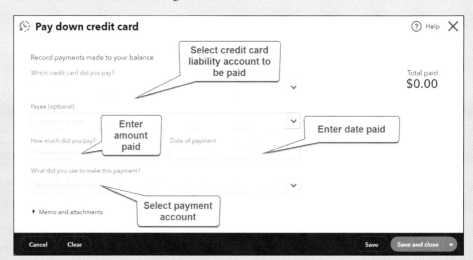

Credit card payment is the form's **transaction type**. The underlying entry would be a debit to the credit card liability account and a credit to the checking account.

PRACTICE
EXERCISE
4.5

MBC

Set up and use a credit card in Craig's Design and Landscaping.
(Craig's Design uses its corporate credit card to make several purchases.)

1. Set up a credit card account.
   a. Click the ⚙ on the icon bar.
   b. Click **Chart of Accounts**.
   c. Click **See your Chart of Accounts**, if necessary.

(continued)

(continued from previous page)

    d.   Click New.

    e.   Select Credit Cards as the financial statement classification.

    f.   Select Credit Card in the Save account under and Tax form section fields.

    g.   Enter "Global Credit Card" as the Account name.

    h.   Click Save.

2.   To record a client lunch (paid with credit card):

    a.   Click ➕ New on the navigation bar.

    b.   Click Expense.

    c.   Select + Add new in the Who did you pay? dropdown menu.

        i.   Enter "Fancy Restaurant" in the Company name and Vendor display name fields.

        ii.   Click Save.

    d.   Select Global Credit Card as the Payment account (the account to be credited).

    e.   Enter the current date as Payment date.

    f.   Select MasterCard as the Payment method.

    g.   Leave Ref. No. blank.

    h.   In the Category details section, select Meals and Entertainment as the CATEGORY.

    i.   Enter "94.10" as the AMOUNT.

    j.   Enter "Lunch with July Summers" in the DESCRIPTION field.

    k.   Click Save to record the transaction without leaving the form.

    l.   Select Transaction journal on the More dropdown menu.

    m.   **Make a note** of the transaction type and the account that was credited.

    n.   Click Dashboard.

PAYING VENDOR BALANCES

Eventually vendors must be paid! Most companies pay vendors in batches. A check run might be processed twice a month in a smaller company. Check runs would likely be processed more frequently in larger companies.

    In a manual system, checks are prepared and then entered in the cash disbursements journal. The totals of the journal are posted to the general ledger and each transaction is posted to the appropriate vendor's subsidiary ledger.

    In QBO, bill payment transactions are automatically posted to the general ledger and the vendor subsidiary ledger when the transaction is saved.

    Companies can pay bills using cash, checks, or credit cards. Paying vendor balances by check is the most common payment method in small- to medium-sized companies.

    There are two methods for recording payments of vendor balances in QBO. Payments to more than one vendor can be batch processed through the **Pay Bills** window. Payment of one or more **bills** to a single vendor can be processed through the Vendor Center. The **transaction type** under either method is **bill payment**.

LO 4-3 Explain and use various methods for paying vendor balances

eLecture

Paying Multiple Vendor Bills

Click ⊕ New on the navigation bar.

Figure 4.22

Access to bill payment screen

Click **Pay Bills** to open the **Pay Bills** window (Figure 4.23).

 WARNING: In early 2023, Intuit started updating various QBO forms. Some of those forms may have been updated after your textbook was printed. If you see a form that doesn't match the screenshot in your book, start by looking for an option to return to a previous version. In most cases, you'll see a link to **Old layout** or **Switch to classic view**. If there is no link available, check the Student Ancillaries page in myBusinessCourse for information about the updated form or ask your instructor.

Figure 4.23

Bill payment screen

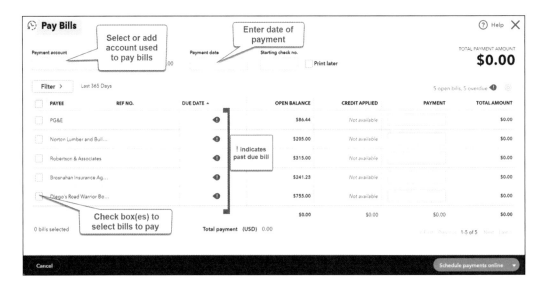

There is a lot to do on this screen so take your time!

You must identify the **Payment account** being used (checking, credit card, etc.) and the **Payment date**. If you choose to pay by check, QBO will display a **Starting check no.** That can be changed, if needed.

You can limit the number of items displayed by opening the **Filter** dropdown menu.

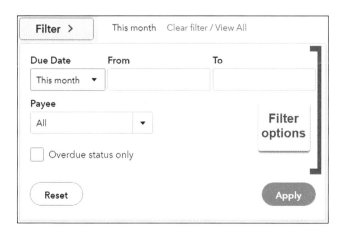

Figure 4.24

Filtering options in bill payment screen

Filtering is available by due date or by vendor (**payee**) name. For vendor names, your choice is limited, however, to either all vendors or one specific vendor.

Overdue bills are highlighted (with an exclamation point!) in the **DUE DATE** column. If there are any available credits, the amounts will be displayed in the **CREDIT APPLIED** field when the vendor is selected for payment. Vendor credits are covered in Chapter 7.

Bills to be paid are selected by checking the box to the left of the specific **bill**. If you want to see more details, click the **PAYEE** name to access the original **bill**.

The total amount to be paid is displayed on the screen. The balance remaining in the account used to pay the **bill** is also displayed. The window might look something like this if two bills were paid:

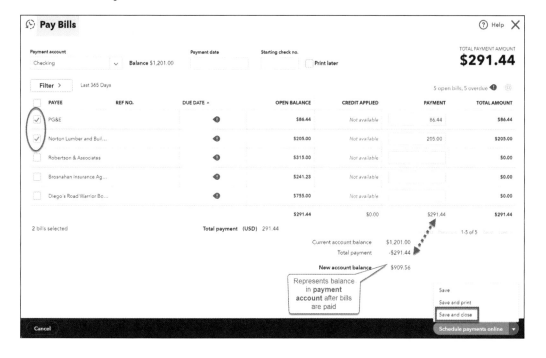

Figure 4.25

Example of completed bill payment screen

> **BEHIND THE SCENES** If multiple bills from the same vendor have been selected for payment, QuickBooks Online will automatically combine the amounts and create a single check for that particular vendor.

Click **Save and close** to record the payments without printing physical checks. **Schedule payments online** is available to users who have connected a bank account to QBO.

> **BEHIND THE SCENES** If **bill payments** are printed from QBO, the **Account no.** identified in the vendor record will appear on the face of the check. Information entered in the **Description** or **Memo** fields of the **bill** will not be printed.

Paying One or More Bills from a Single Vendor

Payment of one or more **bills** from a single vendor can be processed through the Vendor Center.

Click **Expenses** on the navigation bar and open the **Vendors drawer** (tab).

Figure 4.26

Access to vendor bill payment form

Select **Make payment** in the **ACTION** column of the vendor row.

> ✳ **HINT: Schedule payment** is used by companies using QBO's online bill payment service.

The form will look something like Figure 4.27.

> ! **WARNING:** In early 2023, Intuit started updating various QBO forms. Some of those forms may have been updated after your textbook was printed. If you see a form that doesn't match the screenshot in your book, start by looking for an option to return to a previous version. In most cases, you'll see a link to **Old layout** or **Switch to classic view**. If there is no link available, check the Student Ancillaries page in myBusinessCourse for information about the updated form or ask your instructor.

Figure 4.27

Example of a sidebar on a bill payment form

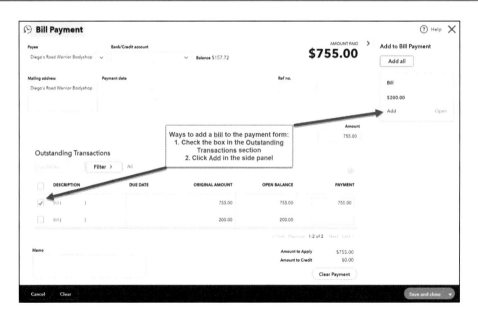

QBO automatically assumes all outstanding bills are being paid. Users can make partial payments by removing the checkmarks next to one or more bills. Any unselected bills will appear in a side panel. Partial payments on a single bill can be made by changing the **PAYMENT** amount.

QBO automatically creates a **Bill Payment** transaction when the form is saved.

HINT: Payments to specific vendors can also be recorded by selecting **Mark as paid** in the **ACTION** column dropdown menu on the **Transaction List** tab of the Vendor record.

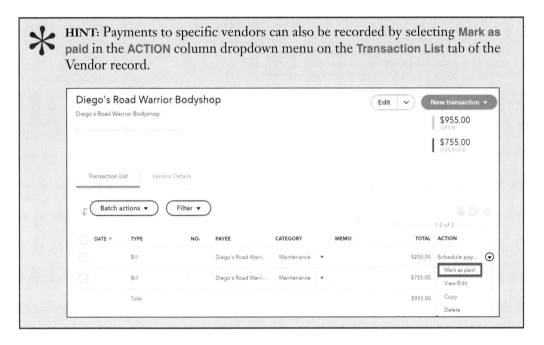

Record payment of bills for Craig's Design and Landscaping.
(Craig's Design pays several vendor balances.)

1. Click **+ New** on the navigation bar.

2. Click **Pay Bills**.

3. **Make a note** of the balance due to **Robertson & Associates**.

4. Select **Checking** as the **Payment account** and enter the current date as the **Payment date**.

5. Leave the **Starting check no.** as 71.

    a.   **TIP:** If you haven't logged out recently, use 77 as the **Starting check no.**

6. Place a checkmark next to **Norton Lumber** and **Robertson & Associates**.

7. **Make a note** of the total amount paid.

8. Click **Save and close**.

PRACTICE
EXERCISE
4.6

MBC

Assume you selected 5 bills to be paid in a single run. Three of the bills were to the same vendor. How many checks would QBO create? (Answer at end of chapter.)

QuickCheck
4-2

PREPARING PURCHASE AND VENDOR REPORTS

Reports related to vendors and purchases can be accessed by clicking **Reports** on the navigation bar and opening the **Standard** tab.

Common reports used by service companies are highlighted in Figure 4.28.

LO 4-4 Recognize and prepare common reports used in the purchase cycle

Standard vendor
reports menu

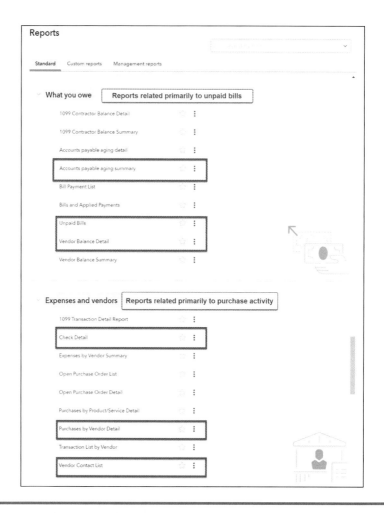

EXERCISE

4.7

Prepare reports on payables for Craig's Design and Landscaping.

(Craig's Design needs an A/P Aging and wants a report of all check and bill payment (check) transactions. You decide to customize the Check Detail report.)

1. Prepare an A/P Aging.

   a. Click Reports.

   b. Open the Standard tab.

   c. Click Accounts payable aging summary in the What you owe section.

   d. Change date to the current date and click Run report.

   e. **Make a note** of the amount due to PG&E.

   f. Click Back to report list. (The link is directly below A/P Aging Summary Report.)

2. Prepare the transaction report.

   a. Click Check Detail in the Expenses and vendors section.

   b. Change Report period to All Dates.

   c. Click Customize.

   d. Open the Rows/Columns section.

      i. Click Change columns.

      ii. Remove the check next to Clr.

      iii. NOTE: Checks not marked as Clr are still outstanding (haven't cleared the bank).

(continued)

(continued from previous page)

  e. Open the **Filter** section.
    i. Check the box next to **Transaction Type**.
    ii. Select **Check** and **Bill Payment (Check)**.
  f. Click **Run report**.
  g. **Make a note** of the account debited in the journal entry underlying the $250 check to Hicks Hardware (**Bill Payment (Check) transaction type**). **Tip:** Click on the transaction in the report to open up the form. Select **Transaction journal** in the **More dropdown** menu to view the underlying entry. Click **Cancel** to return to the report.
 3. Click **Dashboard** to exit the window.

PURCHASES CYCLE SUMMARY

Let's summarize the purchasing steps we have learned and their related journal entries. First let's review the difference between a purchase now (with a check) and a purchase on account.

Cash purchases mean that the company paid up front (right away) for the purchase of an item or service, usually with a check.	Purchases on account mean that the company purchased an item or received a service which it will pay for at a future date. A bill documents the purchase if the company will pay the vendor. A credit card receipt documents the purchase if the company used a credit card and will pay the credit card company at a later date.
1-step process: 1. Write a **Check** for each purchase.	2-step process 1. Enter each **Bill** (or **Expense**). 2. **Pay bills** when due.

Let's also review the basic purchase and cash disbursement journal entries that are created based on the above transactions.

Purchase with cash or check—Journal Entry	Purchase on Account—Journal Entry
• Journal Entry to record **Check** – Dr: Asset/Expense/Inventory – Cr: Checking	• Journal Entry to record **Bill** or **Expense** – Dr: Asset/Expense/Inventory – Cr: Accounts Payable (or Credit Card Payable) • Journal Entry to record transfer of credit card balance to accounts payable – Dr: Credit Card Payable – Cr: Accounts Payable • Journal Entry to pay vendor or credit card company – Dr: Accounts Payable – Cr: Checking

NOTE: The transfer from the credit card liability to accounts payable is covered in Chapter 5.

Accounts Payable (A/P)

ANSWER TO
QuickCheck
4-1

Three checks would be created.

ANSWER TO
QuickCheck
4-2

CHAPTER SHORTCUTS

Add a vendor

1. Click **Expenses** on the navigation bar.
2. Open the **Vendors drawer** (tab) to open the Vendor Center.
3. Click **New Vendor**.

Edit a vendor

1. Open Vendor Center.
2. Click vendor name.
3. Click **Edit**.

Inactivate a vendor

1. Open Vendor Center.
2. Open the dropdown menu in the **ACTION** column for the vendor to be inactivated.
3. Select **Make inactive**.

Record a check

1. Click **+ New** on the navigation bar.
2. Click **Check** in the **Vendors** column.

Enter a bill

1. Click **+ New** on the navigation bar.
2. Click **Bill** in the **Vendors** column.

Record a credit card charge

1. Click **+ New** on the navigation bar.
2. Click **Expense** in the **Vendors** column.

Record payments to vendors on account balances

1. Click **+ New** on the navigation bar.
2. Click **Pay Bills** in the **Vendors** column.

CHAPTER REVIEW

Assignments with the
MBC are available in
myBusinessCourse.

Matching

Match the term or phrase (as used in QuickBooks Online) to its definition.

1. Bill
2. 1099 vendor
3. Bill Payment
4. Vendor display name

5. Vendor
6. Expense
7. Bill No.
8. Void

_____   transaction type used to record invoices received from vendors

_____   vendor invoice number

_____   transaction type used to record payments to vendors on account

_____   individual or company from whom goods or services are purchased

_____   an individual or company that receives payments that must be reported to the IRS

_____   transaction type often used to record credit card charges

_____   command used to remove dollar amounts from a transaction without deleting the transaction

_____   vendor identifier

Multiple Choice

1. A purchase of a computer, on account, would be recorded in the _____ section of a **bill** in QBO.
   a. Item details
   b. Fixed assets
   c. Category details
   d. Computer Equipment

2. Vendors
   a. can be **deleted** as long as there are no outstanding amounts due to the vendor.
   b. can be **deleted** at any time.
   c. can be **deleted** if there has never been any activity with that vendor.
   d. cannot be **deleted**.

3. When a purchase made with a credit card is recorded in QBO,
   a. cash is credited.
   b. a liability account is credited (**Account Payable (A/P) account type**).
   c. a liability account is credited (**Credit Card account type**).
   d. a liability account is credited (**Other Current Liabilities account type**).

4. Payments to vendors can be entered _____.
   a. using the **Check transaction type** only
   b. using the **Bill Payment transaction type** only
   c. using the **Expense transaction type** only
   d. using **Check, Bill Payment, or Expense transaction types**

5. Which of the following statements is true?
   a. You can only have one account with an **Accounts Payable account type** in QBO.
   b. You can have multiple accounts payable accounts for use in recording vendor bills and tracking vendor balances in QBO but they must each have a different name.
   c. You can have multiple accounts payable accounts in QBO but only the default **Accounts Payable (A/P)** account created by Intuit is used when entering bills.
   d. Vendor balances cannot be tracked in QBO.

BEYOND THE CLICKS—THINKING LIKE A MANAGER

Accounting: Your company uses the accrual method of accounting. List three types of purchase transactions you would want to review at the end of each month to determine if an accrual adjustment needs to be made. Explain your choices.

Information Systems: Many companies give credit cards to multiple employees in a business. List three good practices around the use of company credit cards.

ASSIGNMENTS

1/2/24

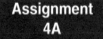

✓ Since Martin is expanding his business, he decides to purchase a general liability insurance policy from Protector Insurance Company. The annual premium is $480. It covers the period 1/1–12/31/24. You write a check (#1101) to pay the full year premium amount. (You add Protector Insurance as a vendor without adding any detail information.) You will make an adjustment to recognize insurance expense for January at the end of the month. **TIP:** Enter the policy period in the description or memo field. This will help when you make the adjustment as part of Chapter 5's assignment.

✓ Martin is moving into his new space today. The furniture arrives in the morning. The total cost of the desk, large study table, and eight chairs Martin ordered from Frank's Furniture is $1,690. A bill, dated 1/2 (#ST8990) for the total amount, is included with the shipment. The terms are Net 30.

Assignment 4A

Math Revealed!

- You set up a new **asset** account called Office Furniture first. You use 185 as the account number. **TIP:** In the **Save account under** field, select **Fixed Assets**. (This is the **account type**.) In the **Tax form section** field, select **Furniture & Fixtures**. (This is the **detail type**.)
- You also set up the new vendor:

  Frank's Furniture
  2174 Hardwood Street
  Sacramento, CA 95822
  Terms: Net 30
- Martin expects the furniture to last four years.

✓ Martin also purchases two more computers and six more calculators since he's doing more tutoring at his new location. The equipment, purchased from Paper Bag Depot, costs $1,572 in total ($312 for the six calculators and $1,260 for the two computers). Martin expects the computers to last three years and the calculators to last four years. Martin uses a new credit card to make the purchase.

- You set up the credit card general ledger account for the VISA credit card first. You use Prime Visa Payable as the account name and 220 as the account number. **TIP:** In the **Save account under** field, select **Credit Cards**. (This is the **account type**.) In the **Tax form section** field, select **Credit Card**. (This is the **detail type**.)
- You enter the credit card charge using 1/2 as the date. You select Computer & Office Equipment (#180) as the distribution account for the calculators and the computers. **TIP:** Use the **Expense** form to record credit card charges. Paper Bag Depot is the **payee**. Select the new credit card account as the **Payment account**. Select VISA as the **payment method** and leave the **Ref no.** blank.
- **TIP:** Ignore the sidebar that appears on the right-hand side of the screen. You are not paying the outstanding bill from Paper Bag Depot as part of this transaction.

✓ You know you will have to pay the credit card company eventually so you go ahead and set them up as a vendor.

- Prime Visa Company
  55 Wall Street
  New York, NY 10005
  Terms: Net 15

✓ You pay January's rent ($850) with check #1102. The landlord is Pro Spaces.

1/3/24

✓ Martin purchases some graphing paper, lined paper, markers, and pencils from Math Shack for $240.82, on account (Vendor Invoice #3659). He is tracking all tutoring supplies as an asset Account #125. At the end of the month, he'll determine the value of the supplies on hand and you'll make any necessary adjustments. The terms are Net 15.

1/5/24

✓ Martin hands you the receipt for the $35 of gas he purchased at Cardinal Gas & Snacks using his VISA credit card and you enter the credit card expense in QBO.

- You select **+ Add new** in the **Payee** dropdown and add the new vendor without adding any additional vendor details.

✓ You take a look at the **Unpaid Bills** report in the **What You Owe** section of **Reports**. It looks like some of the bills were due last month! You know that can't be true so you look through the unpaid bill file. You correct the terms on each of the bills as follows:

- Kathy's Coffee ($32)—Net 15
- Math Shack ($255)—Net 15
- Paper Bag Depot ($94)—Net 30

TIP: Click on the appropriate bills in the **Unpaid Bills** report, enter the terms, and click **Save and close**. You don't need to update reference numbers or change account distributions.

✓ Since these are the normal terms for these three vendors, you also change the terms in the vendor records. **TIP:** Open the Vendor Center and click the vendor name to open the vendor record. Use the Edit link. Terms are entered in the Additional info section of the vendor record.

✓ While you're in the Vendor Center, you go ahead and add Net 30 terms to Sacramento Utilities, Books Galore, and Horizon Phone Inc. and Net 15 terms to Parent's Survival Weekly.

✓ You pay all bills due on or before 1/24/24 from the Checking account.

- **TIP:** There should be four bills totaling $621.82. Start with check #1103. (There will be three checks.) Make sure the date is correct.

1/9/24

✓ You use the credit card to purchase a few general supplies (hand sanitizer, hand towels, etc.) from Math Shack. The cost ($31.52) is insignificant so you decide to expense the entire amount to the Office supplies expense account.

1/15/24

✓ You receive two bills in the mail, which you record in QBO.

- One of the bills, dated 1/15, is from Sacramento Utilities. The January bill (#01-59974) total is $161.34. The bill is due in 30 days.

- The other bill is from Parent's Survival Weekly, a parenting magazine targeting parents with teenage children. Martin had placed an ad for the Mathmagic clinic in this week's issue. The total advertisingcost is $112 (vendor invoice #12213, dated 1/15). The payment terms are Net 15.

✓ Although the Mathmagic Clinic was a success overall, there was one small incident. One of the friends of Martin who helped with the tutoring tripped over the feet of one of the students and fell into the study table. She ended up with a gash on her left hand. She went to the 24 Hour Quick Stitch Clinic and had her hand bandaged up. Luckily, she didn't require any stitches. The cost of the visit was $180 and the clinic gave Martin a bill, dated 1/13 (#121521). The Clinic's payment terms are Net 10. **TIP:** You'll need to set up a new term. Setting up credit terms is covered in Chapter 2.

- The 24 Hour Quick Stitch Clinic's address is 7500 Medical Boulevard, Sacramento, CA 95822. The phone number is 916-222-9999. The terms are Net 10.

- You decide to expense the cost to Miscellaneous expense (Account 699).

1/17/24

✓ Martin asks you to contact Frank's Furniture and order some shelving for the new space. He wants a unit that includes open shelves and some drawers. You call and talk to the representative who gives you an estimate of $820. That sounds reasonable to you and you place the order. The furniture should arrive by the end of the month.

1/22/24

✓ Your friend Samantha Levin helped Martin out at the clinic last Saturday by checking students in and out. Martin doesn't expect to hire her as an employee, but if you pay her more than $600 during the year, you'll need to file a 1099 for her at year-end. You decide to get everything set up just in case she's paid over the threshold.

- You set up a new general ledger expense account. You decide to name the account "Contract labor" and use account #625. You make it a sub-account of Labor costs and you use Cost of labor as the detail type (Tax form section field). **TIP:** To make Contract labor a subaccount, select 620 Labor Costs in the Save account under field.

- You also set Samantha up as a vendor. Her address is 901 Angles Lane, Sacramento, CA 95822. Her phone number is 916-654-4321. Terms are Net 10.

  - You set her up as a 1099 vendor. Her social security number (Business ID number) is 222-33-6666.

✓ Samantha had agreed to a $25 per hour pay rate. She helped out for five hours so you write her a check (#1106) for $125.

1/25/24

✓ Martin hands you another gas receipt for $34. He purchased the gas at Cardinal Gas & Snacks using his credit card today. You record the charge in QBO.

✓ You pay all bills due on or before 2/5/24.

  ● **TIP:** There should be three bills totaling $1,982. Start with check #1107.

1/30/24

✓ Martin brings in coffee drinks from Kathy's Coffee as a treat for getting through the first month in the new space. He hands you the receipt for $7.50. (He used the credit card to buy the coffee.) You decide to charge the coffee to a new expense account called "Staff relations" (a sub-account of Labor Costs). You select "Labor Costs" in the Save account under field and "Other Business Expense" as the detail type in the Tax form section field. You use 628 as the account number. **TIP:** If you set up the new account within the form by clicking + Add new in the CATEGORY dropdown menu, you may see an older version of the account record screen. The account type should be Expense and the detail type should be Other Business Expenses. Check the box next to Is sub-account and select "Labor Costs." Refer to **APPENDIX 1B** if you need help.

✓ The shelving unit is delivered and installed by Frank's Furniture. Martin is impressed by the quality of the product. He thinks it will last for two years. The actual price is the $820 you were originally quoted. The invoice number is ST9998, dated 1/30, and the terms are Net 30.

✓ Martin has been working hard and asks you to write him a check for $2,500. (Use check #1110.)

  ● **TIP:** This is a corporation so a payment to Martin (other than salary or reimbursement) is a dividend, an equity account. Use 345 as the account number and "Dividends" as the account name. QBO doesn't have a detail type for dividends so select Partner Distributions as the detail type in the Tax form section field as a substitute.

Check numbers as of 1/31

Checking account balance:. $3,016.18
Accounts Payable:. . . . . $ 981.34
Net income (January only):. $5,533.64

Suggested reports for Chapter 4:

All reports should be in portrait orientation.

● Journal—1/01 through 1/31.

  ● Using Classic View, customize the report to include only these transaction types: Check, Bill, Bill Payment (Check), Expense. **TIP:** You'll need to scroll down the list in the Filter section to find the Expense transaction type.

● Vendor Balance Detail (as of 1/31)

  ▪ **TIP:** You'll need to change the report period to Custom before you can enter a date.

● Vendor Contact List

  ▪ Customize the report to show Vendor, Address, and Terms columns only.

● Balance Sheet as of January 31

● Profit and loss statement (January only)

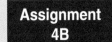

Assignment 4B

Salish Software Solutions

1/2/24

✓ You pay January's rent ($650) to Alki Property Management with check #1101.

✓ Sally recently decided to purchase business insurance from Albright Insurance Company. The policy was effective as of 1/1/24. You write a check (#1102) to pay the full year premium amount ($780).

- You add Albright Insurance as a vendor without adding any detail information.

- You will make an adjustment to recognize insurance expense for January at the end of the month. **TIP:** Enter the policy period in the description or memo field. This will help when you make the adjustment as part of Chapter 5's assignment.

✓ You notice that payment terms aren't set up for many of Salish's vendors. You change the vendor records as follows:

- Abacus Shop—Net 15
- Paper Bag Depot—Net 30
- Personal Software—Net 30
- Sacramento Light & Power—Net 30
- Simply Accounting—Net 15
- Western Phone Company—Net 30

TIP: Open the Vendor Center and click the vendor name to open the vendor record. Use the Edit link. Terms are entered in the Additional info section.

1/3/24

✓ Sally receives the credit card she applied for last month.

- You set up the credit card general ledger account for the new credit card. You use Capital Three Visa Payable as the account name and 220 as the account number. (**TIP:** In the Save account under field, select Credit Cards. (This is the account type.) In the Tax form section field, select Credit Card. (This is the detail type.)

- You also set up a new vendor for the card using the following information:

  > Capital Three
  > 58 Wall Street
  > New York, NY 10005
  > Terms: Net 15

✓ Sally had completely run out of office supplies at the end of December so she uses her new Capital Three VISA card to purchase paper, pens, and file folders at Paper Bag Depot. You enter the credit card purchase of $500 using the Expense form. You select the new credit card account you just set up as the Payment account. You select VISA as the payment method and leave the Ref no. blank. You're not sure how long the supplies will last but you're sure they won't all be used in January so you select the Supplies on Hand account in the category field (Account 133). You will take an inventory to see how many supplies are on hand at the end of the month. **TIP:** You will do this in the homework for Chapter 5.

✓ Sally purchases some new computer software today from Abacus Shop. The software costs $1,200 and will help Sally track her installation projects. She expects it to last 2 years (no salvage value). Abacus gives you a bill (#8944-11) with 15-day payment terms.

- You set up a new asset account called Computer Software first. You use 184 as the account number. **TIP:** In the Save account under field, select Fixed Assets. (This is the account type.) In the Tax form section field, select Fixed Asset Software. (This is the detail type.)

- You record the bill from Abacus.

1/9/24

✓ You receive two bills in the mail, which you record in QBO.

- One of the bills (#01-59974), dated 1/9, is from Sacramento Light & Power. The bill total is $95 and is due in 30 days. The bill is for January utilities.
- The other bill (#8911-63) is from Western Phone Company for Sally's January cell phone service. The $103.95 bill, dated 1/9, has payment terms of Net 30.

You record the bill from Abacus.

1/11/24

✓ You take a look at the Unpaid Bills report in the What You Owe section of Reports. It looks like some of the bills were due last month! You know that can't be true so you look through the unpaid bill file. You correct the payment terms on each of the bills with a December date as follows:

- Abacus Shop—Net 15
- Personal Software—Net 30
- Simply Accounting—Net 15
- **TIP:** Click each invoice on the Unpaid Bills report to open the bill form. Enter the terms and save.

✓ You pay all bills due on or before January 20 from the Checking account using 1/11 as the payment date.

- **TIP:** There should be four bills totaling $2,095. Start with check 1103. Make sure the date is correct.

1/15/24

✓ You receive a bill from Entrepreneur, a local magazine targeting small business owners. Sally had placed an ad in January's magazine for the upcoming workshop. The total cost is $120 (vendor invoice #12213, dated 1/15). The payment terms are Net 10. **TIP:** You'll need to create a new payment term before you set up the vendor.

- Entrepreneur Magazine
  534 American River Drive
  Sacramento, CA 95822
  Terms: Net 10

✓ Sally asks you to order a large storage cabinet from Rikea. She needs to have a storage area for the inventory she plans to sell starting in February. You call and talk to a sales representative who gives you an estimate of $1,500. That sounds reasonable to you and you place the order. The expected arrival date is 1/30.

- You go ahead and set up the vendor anticipating the future bill.
- Rikea
  25 Bigbox Lane
  Sacramento, CA 95822
  Terms: Net 30

✓ Sally uses her credit card to pay for the space she rented at Hacker Spaces (a new vendor) for next week's workshop. You don't add any address or other details to the vendor record. This is a new type of expense for Salish Software so you set up two new expense accounts.

- You add a parent account "Workshop Costs" with 660 as the account number and Expenses as the account type (Save account under field). You use Other Miscellaneous Service Cost as the detail type (Tax form section field).
- You add a sub-account "Space rental expense" (account #661). You use the parent account 660 Workshop Costs in the Save account under field and Other Miscellaneous Service Cost as the detail type (Tax form section field).
- You charge the $400 credit card charge to Account 661.

✓ Sally brings you a credit card receipt from Fast Copy, a new vendor, for $150. She had some materials copied to give the attendees at the workshop coming up on the 20th. You don't add any detail information to the vendor record. You set up another sub-account to record this.

- You call the new sub-account "Workshop supplies expense" and use 662 as the account number. You select Workshop Costs (Account 660) as the parent account in the **Save account under** field. You use **Other Miscellaneous Service Cost** as the **detail type** (**Tax form section** field). **TIP:** If you set up the new account within the form by clicking **+ Add new** in the **CATEGORY** dropdown menu, you may see an older version of the account record screen. The **account type** should be **Expense** and the **detail type** should be **Miscellaneous Service Cost**. Check the box next to **Is sub-account** and select "Workshop Costs." Refer to **APPENDIX 1B** if you need help.
- You record the credit card purchase of $150 using account 662.

1/22/24

✓ Although the Picking the Right Software workshop was a great success overall, there was an unexpected additional expense. Sally ended up breaking one of Hacker Spaces' tables when she was trying to get the room set up. You write Hacker Spaces a check for $200 to cover the cost of replacing the table. Check #1106 was damaged so you used #1107.

- You decide to expense the cost to Space rental expense.

✓ While you are writing the check to Hacker, you realize that there is one other bill due soon. You pay the $120 bill from Entrepreneur Magazine with check number #1108.

1/24/24

✓ Your friend Oscar Torres helped Sally out at the workshop last week. Sally doesn't expect to hire him as an employee, but you know that if you pay him more than $600 during the year, you'll need to file a 1099-NEC for him at the end of the year. You decide to get everything set up just in case he's paid over the threshold.

- You set up a new general ledger account. You decide to name the account "Workshop helper expense" with 665 as the account number. You make it a sub-account of Workshop Costs by selecting Workshop Costs in the **Save account under** field. You select **Cost of Labor** as the **detail type** in the **Tax form section** field.
- You also set Oscar up as a vendor. His address is 901 Luna Drive, Sacramento, CA 95822. His phone number is 916-654-4321.
    - You select Net 10 as the **terms**.
    - You set him up as a 1099 vendor in the **Additional info** section. His social security number (**Business ID number**) is 222-33-4444.

✓ Oscar had agreed to work for $20 per hour pay rate. He helped out for five hours so you write him a check (#1109) for $100.

1/26/24

✓ Sally has lunch with the IT director for Metro Markets, a large grocery chain. She is hoping to do some work for the company in the future. She uses her credit card to pay for the $89, very nice, lunch at The Blue Door (a new vendor). You record the charge to Client relations expense.

- Nothing is decided at the lunch so you don't set up Metro Markets as a customer.

1/30/24

✓ The storage cabinets are delivered and installed by Rikea. The final price is the $1,500 you were originally quoted. The invoice number is RK65541, dated 1/30, and the terms are Net 30. You expect the cabinets to last for 5 years.

✓ Sally has been working hard and asks you for a $2,000 check. (Check #1110.)

- You set Sally Hanson up as a vendor first.
  14 Technology Drive
  Sacramento, CA 95822
  916-346-9258
  Net 10

- **TIP:** This is a corporation so a payment to Sally (other than salary or reimbursement) is a dividend, an equity account. Use 345 as the account number and "Dividends" as the account name. QBO doesn't have a **detail type** for dividends, so select **Partner Distributions** in the **Tax form section** field as a substitute.

Check numbers as of 1/31

Checking account balance:. . . . $10,025.00
Accounts Payable:. $1,698.95
Net income (January only):. $8,682.05

Suggested reports for Chapter 4:

All reports should be in portrait orientation; fit to one page wide

- Journal—1/01 through 1/31.
  - Using **Classic View**, customize the report to include only these transaction types: Check, Bill, Bill Payment (Check), Expense.
  - **TIP:** You'll need to scroll down the list in the **Filter** section to see the **Expense transaction type**.
- Vendor Balance Detail (as of 1/31)
  - **TIP:** You'll need to change the report period to **Custom** before you can enter a date.
- Vendor Contact List
  - Customize the report to show Vendor, Address, and Terms columns only.
- Profit and loss statement (January only)
- Balance Sheet as of January 31

APPENDIX 4A REPORTING 1099 VENDOR ACTIVITY

LO 4-5 Describe the QBO process for reporting 1099 vendor activity

Companies are required to report certain types of payments of more than $600 during the year. Payments to independent contractors are reported on Form 1099-NEC to the Internal Revenue Service annually. Independent contractors are, in general, individuals who provide services to the general public through an independent business.

Payments to landlords and attorneys are reported on Form 1099-MISC.

As noted in the **Adding a Vendor** section of this chapter, 1099 vendors can be identified, along with the required tax information, in the **Additional Info** section of the vendor record. Users can update 1099 information about existing vendors by clicking **Vendors** on the navigation bar, clicking the vendor name, and clicking **Edit**.

To prepare 1099s, click **Expenses** on the navigation bar and open the **Vendors drawer** (tab).

Figure 4A.1

Access to 1099 reporting

Click **Prepare 1099s**.

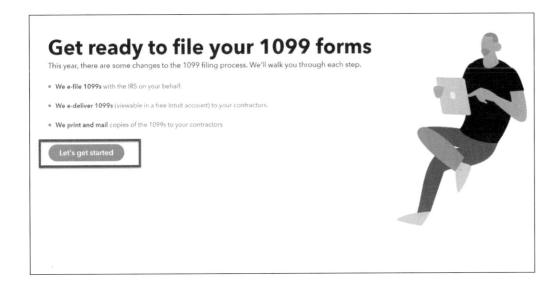

Click **Let's get started**.

The address, tax identification number, and phone number of the company filing the 1099s are reviewed and edited if necessary. Click **Next** after updating any information.

Screen for mapping general ledger accounts to 1099-Misc form

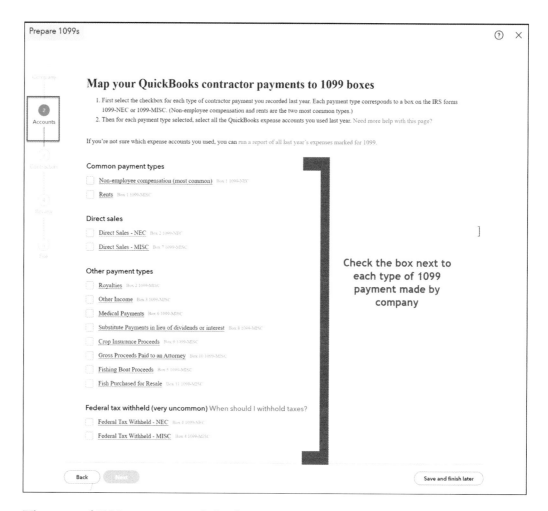

The types of 1099 payments made by the company (1099-NEC and 1099-MISC) are identified first. If any federal taxes have been withheld from any 1099 vendors, that is identified as well.

For each payment type identified, the user is also required to indicate the account used to record the payments. The screen might look something like this for the test drive company.

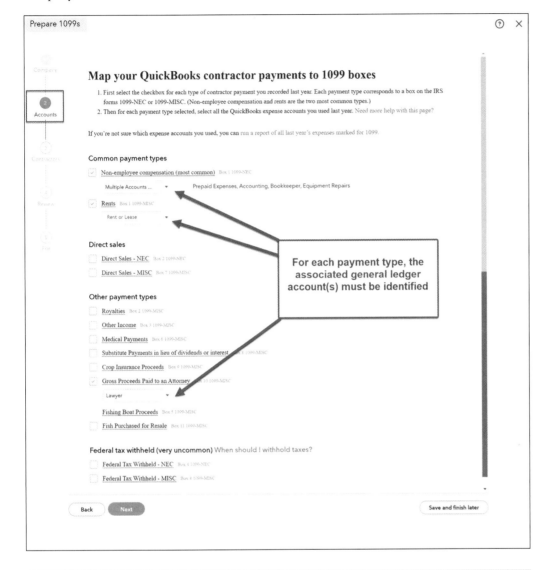

Figure 4A.5

Example of completed account mapping

> **BEHIND THE SCENES** Any account that **could** include payments to independent contractors should be included when mapping accounts to payment types. QBO would only include payments made to identified 1099 vendors and charged to the listed accounts when preparing the forms.

Click **Next** to review 1099 vendor details (address, tax identification number).

Figure 4A.6

1099 Vendor
information screen

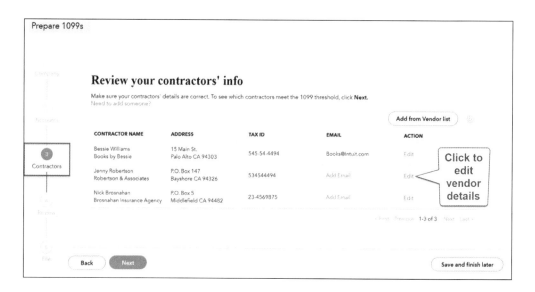

Computers by Jenni and Robertson & Associates will not appear in your test drive company. Certain changes were made to the file for illustration purposes.

Edits can be made to vendor information on this screen. Any edits here will also update the vendor record.

Click Next to review vendors who were paid amounts over the IRS threshold during the calendar year.

Figure 4A.7

Review of 1099
amounts by vendor

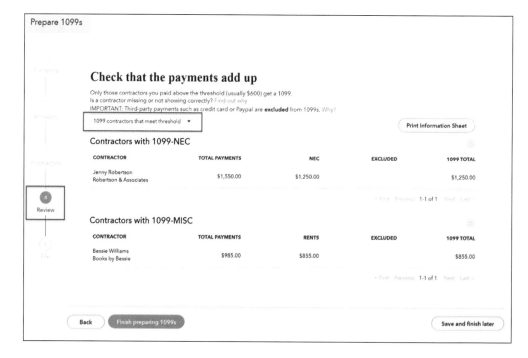

BEHIND THE SCENES Any amounts paid to 1099 vendors using a credit card would not be included on 1099-MISC forms. Reporting credit card payments is the responsibility of the credit card company.

Click Finish preparing 1099s to review options for filing. Intuit provides filing services for a fee or users can prepare the forms independently.

End-of-Period Activity
(Service Company)

Road Map

LO	Learning Objective	Topic	Subtopic	Page	Practice Exercises	Videos
LO5-1	Complete bank and credit card reconciliations in QBO [p. 5-3]	Reconciling bank and credit card accounts	Bank reconciliations	5-3	5.1	Reconciling bank accounts
			Credit card reconciliations	5-8	5.2	Reconciling credit card accounts
LO5-2	Prepare entries for adjusting accounts in QBO [p. 5-12]	Making adjusting journal entries		5-12	5.3	Making adjusting journal entries
LO5-3	Describe and prepare financial reports available in QBO [p. 5-15]	Preparing financial statements		5-15	5.4	
LO5-4	Describe the method for closing accounting periods in QBO [p. 5-19]	Closing the books	Closing an accounting period	5-20	5.5	Closing an accounting period
			Year-end closing	5-21		
LO5-5	Understand common causes of errors in QBO [p. 5-29]	APPENDIX 5A—Getting it right		5-29		Getting it right
LO5-6	Describe the elements in QBO reconciliation reports [p. 5-30]	APPENDIX 5B—Understanding the reconciliation report		5-30		Understanding the reconciliation report
LO5-7	Explain how to manually undo a bank reconciliation in QBO [p. 5-33]	APPENDIX 5C—Fixing reconciliation errors		5-33		

BEFORE ISSUING FINANCIAL STATEMENTS

Sales, purchases, cash receipts, and cash payments make up the vast majority of transactions in a company. You've already learned how most of those standard transactions are entered in QBO and you've seen how QBO does a lot of the work related to posting and tracking those transactions for you. As we discussed in Chapter 1, though, the accuracy and the usefulness of all that data are still dependent on the operator(s) of QBO.

For most companies, the primary financial reports (such as the profit and loss statement and the balance sheet) are prepared monthly. It's at the end of the month, then, that the accountant needs to make sure that:

- All accounting transactions have been recorded.

- No accounting transactions have been duplicated.

- All accounting transactions have been recorded in the proper accounts at the appropriate amounts.

- All accounting transactions are recognized in the proper accounting period.

There is, unfortunately, no foolproof method for ensuring the accuracy of the financial statements. There are some tools, though. They include:

- Reconciling account balances to external sources
  - Cash accounts to bank statements
  - Vendor payable balances to vendor statements
  - Debt balances to lender reports

- Reconciling account balances to internal sources
  - Physical count of supplies on hand costed and agreed to supplies account balance
  - Physical count of inventory costed and agreed to inventory account balance
  - Timesheets for the last period of the month agreed to salaries payable account if all salaries have not been paid as of the end of a period

- Reviewing accounts for reasonableness

  Normal balance The side (debit or credit) on which increases to the account are recorded

  Contra account An account with the opposite normal balance as other accounts of the same type

  - Most account balances should reflect their **normal** balance (assets should have debit balances, **contra** assets should have credit balances, expenses should have debit balances, etc.).
  - Relationships between accounts should make sense. For example, payroll tax expense wouldn't normally be higher than salaries expense!
  - Account balances that are significantly higher or lower than the prior month should be investigated.

As a result of all this reconciliation and review, we can virtually **guarantee** you that adjustments will need to be made! Without even thinking very hard, we know you can come up with a few examples.

They might include:

- Recording bank charges that you weren't aware of until you saw the bank statement

- Adjusting the Supplies on Hand account to record supplies used during the period

- Adjusting revenue accounts to ensure that all revenue reported is earned revenue and all earned revenue is recognized

- Recording depreciation expense for the period

- Accruing expenses that weren't recorded through the normal payable process (interest for example)

- Amortizing prepaid expenses for amounts expiring in the period (insurance for example)

RECONCILING BANK AND CREDIT CARD ACCOUNTS

LO 5-1 Complete bank and credit card reconciliations in QBO

Bank Reconciliations

QBO has an account reconciliation tool that can actually be used for any balance sheet account other than Accounts Receivable, Accounts Payable, Undeposited Funds, and Retained Earnings. That's a useful tool for companies that take advance deposits, for example. In this textbook, we'll only be using the tool for bank and credit card reconciliations.

To access the reconciliation tool, click the ⚙ on the icon bar.

YOUR COMPANY	LISTS	TOOLS
Account and settings	All lists	Order checks ⬀
Manage users	Products and services	Import data
Custom form styles	Recurring transactions	Import desktop data
Chart of accounts	Attachments	Export data
QuickBooks labs	Custom fields	Reconcile
	Tags	Budgeting
		Audit log
		SmartLook
		Resolution center

Figure 5.1

Access to reconciliation tool

Click **Reconcile**.

  HINT: You can also access the reconciliation tool by clicking **Accounting** on the navigation bar and opening the **Reconcile drawer** (tab).

The first time you use the reconciliation function, you'll need to move through a few informational screens.

Chart of accounts   **Reconcile**

Match the books to the bank records

Connected accounts are easier to reconcile. Connect now

▶ See how it works (1:53)

- Keep yourself on track
- Find holes in your accounting
- Get things tidy for tax time

Get started

Figure 5.2

Link to reconciliation tool

Click **Get started**.

Figure 5.3

Informational screen for reconciliations

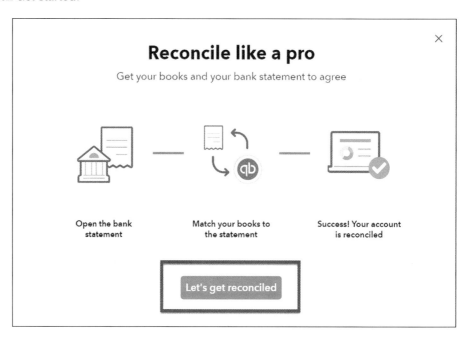

Click **Let's get reconciled**.

Figure 5.4

Initial data screen for account reconciliations

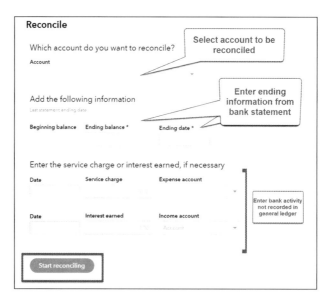

Select the account to be reconciled.

The date and balance fields must agree to the bank statement you're reconciling.

- The **Ending balance** would be the ending **bank** balance listed on the bank statement you're reconciling.

- The **Ending date** would be the ending date listed on the bank statement.

In your homework company file, you will also be able to enter bank charges or interest income amounts that appear on the bank statement. (The **Service charge** and **Interest earned** fields will not appear in the test drive company.) You can use the dropdown menus to select the general ledger account you want debited for service charges or credited for interest income. If you had already entered these transactions, you would leave the fields blank.

Click **Start reconciling.**

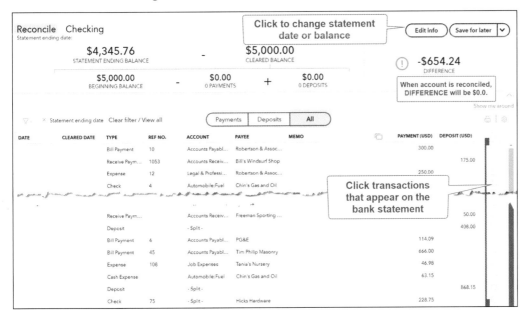

Figure 5.5
Account reconciliation screen

There are three tabs on the screen (**Payments, Deposits,** and **All**). All transactions in the account being reconciled that have **not** been cleared in a prior reconciliation are listed on the **All** tab.

 HINT: Transactions appearing in the reconciliation screens can be filtered using the funnel icon above the **DATE** column. Options include filtering by date, payee, and transaction type.

The **Payments** tab includes only those transactions (**checks, bill payments, transfers,** or **journal entries**) that credit the cash account. The **Deposits** tab includes the transactions (**deposits, transfers,** or **journal entries**) that debit the cash account.

BEHIND THE SCENES Take a look at the column titles on the right side of the **All** tab. These are set up from the bank's point of view. You'll notice that the far right column (the credit column to accountants) is titled **DEPOSIT.** A debit to cash to record a bank deposit on the company's books is a credit (liability) on the bank's books since they now owe you that amount. The transactions in the **PAYMENT** column to the left of the **DEPOSIT** column are credits to cash on the company's books but represent debits to cash on the bank's books (reductions of the bank's liability to the company).

To reconcile the account, click the circle next to any transaction on this screen that also appears on the bank statement. These are the transactions that "cleared" the bank. Any unclicked transactions represent outstanding checks or deposits in transit.

 HINT: It's sometimes easier to use the **Payments** and **Deposits** tabs (instead of the **All** tab) when reconciling.

A few hints that might help with the reconciliation process:

- If you can't complete the reconciliation in one sitting, you can:

▪ click the **Save for later** button in the dropdown menu at the top right corner of the screen. QBO will save all your work until you return to complete the reconciliation. When you open the **Reconcile** function again, QBO will ask if you want to **Resume reconciling** the account that was in process.

▪ select **Close without saving** in the same dropdown menu. The reconciliation process could then be restarted at a later date.

● Click **Edit Info** in the top right corner of the screen to make changes to the **Ending balance** or **Ending date**.

● You can leave the reconciliation window open and create (or edit) a transaction if you need to. QBO will automatically refresh the screen for any changes. To add a new transaction, click **+ New** on the navigation bar.

● If you click any of the listed transactions, the row will expand, and you will be able to change data fields that are not grayed out.

Figure 5.6

Expanded transaction on reconciliation screen

▪ To make more substantial changes to the transaction, click **Edit**.

● QBO automatically filters the list to only include those uncleared transactions dated prior to the statement ending date (the only transactions that **could** have cleared the bank assuming all transactions are dated correctly).

▪ If you only want to display certain types of transactions, click the funnel above the far left column.

● You can change the sort order of the listed transactions by clicking any of the column headings.

When you've reconciled the account, the **Difference** field in the top right section of the screen will equal zero and **Finish Now** will be the default option in the dropdown menu in the top right corner of the reconciliation screen.

> **!** **WARNING:** Do not select **Finish Now** in the dropdown menu if you haven't finished the reconciliation (the **difference** isn't zero). QBO will give you a warning if you try but if you persist, it will allow you to "reconcile" without actually reconciling. That would leave what my former accounting professors would call a "dangling" credit or debit. Of course QBO won't actually allow you to create an unbalanced transaction so it will either debit (or credit) an account called **Reconciliation Discrepancies** for the **Difference** amount. You'd then have to fix that later.

Once you've reconciled the account and clicked **Finish now**, the following screen will appear:

Figure 5.7

Message when reconciliation is complete

To view the reconciliation report immediately, click **View report**. The report includes lists (by type) of all cleared transactions and all uncleared transactions. Appendix 5B goes over the reconciliation report in detail.

Reconciliation reports are also accessible in the **For My Accountant** section of **Reports**.

Reconcile the bank account for Craig's Design and Landscaping.

(Craig's Design receives its bank statement. The ending balance is $4,345.76. There were no bank service charges included on the statement.)

1. Click the ⚙ on the icon bar.

2. Click **Reconcile**.

3. Click **Get started**.

4. Click **Let's get reconciled**.

5. Select **Checking** as the **Account**.

6. Enter the current date as the **Ending Date** and "4,345.76" as the **Ending Balance**.

   a. Since you're working in the test drive company and dates in that company are constantly being updated, you need to enter the date you're actually doing the reconciliation.

7. Click **Start reconciling**.

8. Click the **Payments** tab and check the circles next to the first ten amounts.

   a. The ten payments you're marking as cleared should start with a $300 check and end with a $250 check for a total of $1,245.64.

9. Click the **Deposits** tab and check the circles next to the first four amounts.

   a. The first amount you check as cleared should be for $175. The last one should be for $105 for a total of $591.40.

10. **Difference** should be 0.00.

11. Click **Finish Now**.

12. Click **View reconciliation report**. **TIP:** Don't click **Done**.

13. **Make a note** of the total for **Uncleared checks and payments**.

14. Click **Dashboard** to close the window.

PRACTICE
EXERCISE
5.1

Reviewing the Reconciliation Status of Transactions in the Register

In QBO, each account on the balance sheet has a **register**. A **register** is a listing of the activity in the account along with the **reconciliation status** of each item. As you reconcile items in the account, the reconciliation status of an account is updated.

• Click the ⚙ on the icon bar and select **Chart of Accounts**.

Figure 5.8

Access to account register

- Click View Register in the ACTION column for the Checking account.

Figure 5.9

Reconciliation status
column in account
register

- The column to the left of the BALANCE column shows the reconciliation status of each transaction. The status field for every bank account transaction listed will either be R, C, or blank.
  - R means that the transaction has been reconciled.
  - C means that the transaction has been identified as "cleared" in a reconciliation that's open (in process).
  - Blank means that the transaction is outstanding and has not yet been reconciled.

> **BEHIND THE SCENES** Transactions that are downloaded directly from bank accounts are automatically assigned a C (cleared) status in the register.

Fixing Bank Reconciliation Errors

It can be quite difficult to correct a bank reconciliation. Best practice, by far, is to make sure the reconciliation is completed correctly before moving forward.

That being said, one option for correcting reconciliation errors is outlined in Appendix 5C.

> **HINT:** There is an "Undo Reconciliation" feature available to users of the QBO Accountant edition of the software. You may want to check with your instructor to see if they might be able to assist you.

Credit Card Reconciliations

You learned in Chapter 4 how company credit cards are handled in QBO. A separate account is set up (Credit Card account type), and individual card transactions are posted to the account as they occur. There are a number of credit card forms (transaction types). One thing they all have in common though is that because they are not bills or vendor credits they do not show up in the Pay Bills screen. That's a good thing since companies would rarely pay individual credit card charges; they would, instead, pay the credit card statement balance or make a partial payment against the balance.

At some point, though, the balance of all credit card activity must be paid to the credit card company. QBO provides a few options.

- The statement balance can be paid after the reconciliation is complete.

- A partial payment can be made after the reconciliation is complete.

- A payment can be made against the credit card balance without reconciling the credit card by clicking Pay down credit card on the (+ New) menu.

The first two options are covered in this section. The third option was covered in the Purchasing with a Credit Card section of Chapter 4.

BEHIND THE SCENES It's important to reconcile credit card account activity to the credit card statement because there aren't a lot of controls on credit cards. Whoever holds the card can generally use the card and companies need to make sure that all charges are legitimate. Companies would normally require employees with access to credit cards to submit original receipts for all purchases.

The process for reconciling a credit card account is very similar to the bank reconciliation process.

The reconciliation tool is easily accessed by clicking the ⚙ on the icon bar and choosing **Reconcile**.

In the **Reconcile an account** window, the credit card account should be selected.

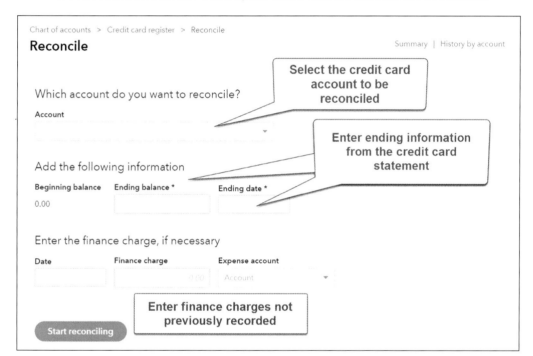

Figure 5.10

Initial data screen for credit card reconciliations

The dates and amounts entered on the initial screen are from the statement being reconciled. Interest or late fee charges can be entered in this window if they haven't been previously recorded.

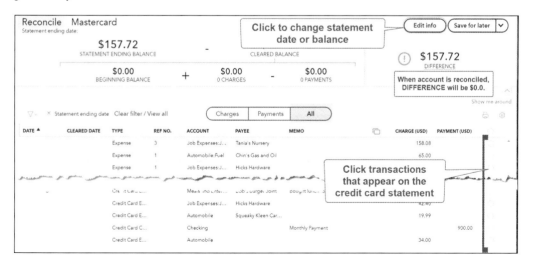

Figure 5.11

Credit card reconciliation screen

You will notice a change in column titles when reconciling a credit card compared to reconciling a bank account.

- The PAYMENT column is now CHARGE.
    - The CHARGE column includes the credit card Expenses that have been recorded.
- The DEPOSIT column is now PAYMENT.
    - The PAYMENT column includes payments made to the credit card company as well as any Credit Card Credits.

All displayed transactions that agree to items listed on the credit card statement should be checked (marked).

 HINT: If you discover that there's an error on one of the recorded Charges or Payments while you're in the reconciliation process, you can click the transaction to edit the form. You can also leave the reconciliation screen open while you create a new transaction. The new transaction will automatically appear in the reconciliation screen once it's saved.

Once the statement is reconciled, the following screen will appear:

Figure 5.12

Successful reconciliation message with payment options

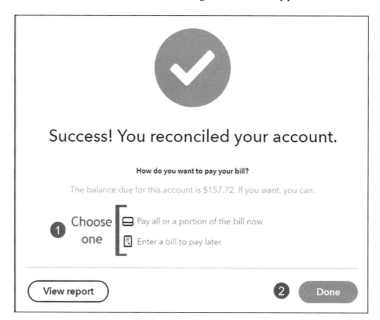

 WARNING: If you click **Done** on the screen in Figure 5.12 before selecting one of the two options, the credit card balance will remain in the credit card account. The amount would not be available in the **Pay Bills** screen. A **Bill** would have to be manually entered after the fact, or the account would need to be re-reconciled.

Users have two options on this screen.

1. If the Pay all or a portion of the bill now option is selected, a Check form will automatically appear. The credit card company name would be selected in the payee field.
2. If Enter a bill to pay later is selected, a Bill form will automatically appear. The appropriate vendor (the credit card company) would need to be selected. QBO will automatically enter the credit card liability account in the distribution section of the form (in

the **Category details** section). The amount entered should be the total amount of the credit card bill.

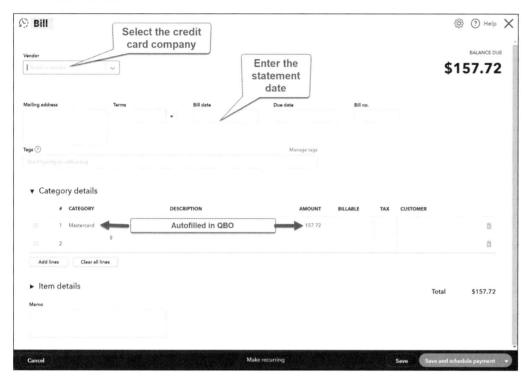

Figure 5.13

Bill for credit card statement balance

 HINT: Remember, credit cards are issued either by banks (VISA or Master-Card credit cards for example) or by companies (like Macy's or Union 76 credit cards). You will need to set up the company that issued the credit card as a vendor in QBO.

Once the **Bill** is completed and saved, it would appear on the **Pay Bills** screen and would be included in the Accounts Payable account.

Figure 5.14

Bill payment screen including a credit card bill

What journal entry does QBO make if you select the **Enter a bill for payment later** option after reconciling a credit card?

QuickCheck
5-1

PRACTICE
EXERCISE
5.2

Reconcile Craig's Design and Landscaping's credit card statement.
(Craig's Design received its statement from Global Credit. The ending statement balance is $157.72. There were no service charges.)

1. Click the ⚙ on the icon bar.

2. Click Reconcile.

     a. If you exited Craig's Design and Landscaping after the previous exercise, then do the following:

         i. Click Reconcile an account.

         ii. Click Get started.

3. Select Mastercard as the Account.

4. Enter the current date as the Statement Ending Date and "157.72" as the Ending Balance.

5. Click Start reconciling.

6. Check the circles next to all charge and all payment transactions. **TIP:** Checking the circle at the top of the far right column will mark all circles.

7. Difference should be 0.00.

8. **Make a note** of the amount of the transaction on the Payments tab.

9. Click Finish Now.

10. Select Enter a bill to pay later. **TIP:** Don't click Done.

     a. Set up a vendor for the bank that issued the card.

         i. Click + Add New in the Vendor dropdown menu.

         ii. Vendor name is "Global Credit, Inc." (Company and Vendor display names)

                 1000 Wall Street

                 New York, NY 10000

         iii. Terms are Net 15.

         iv. Click Save. You should be back on the bill form.

11. Enter "CC Stmt" as the Bill No.

12. Make sure Mastercard shows as the CATEGORY in the Bill.

13. Make sure "157.72" shows as the AMOUNT.

14. Click Save and close to return to the reconciliation screen.

15. Click Done.

16. Click Dashboard to close the window.

LO 5-2 Prepare entries for adjusting accounts in QBO

Journal entry An entry of accounting information into a journal.

MAKING ADJUSTING JOURNAL ENTRIES

All transactions are recorded as journal entries, right? You only have to look at a Journal report in QBO to see that all the Invoices, Checks, Bills, Bill Payments, etc. are listed (and they're in journal entry form, too).

Adjusting **journal entries** are simply journal entries that are made to adjust account balances. Although they can be made at any time during an accounting period, the majority of them are made at the end of an accounting period.

In a manual system, adjusting journal entries are created in the general journal. The entries are then posted to the general ledger.

In QBO, adjusting journal entries are created in an electronic version of the general journal. They are posted automatically to the general ledger.

The form used to create an adjusting entry (**Journal Entry** transaction type) is accessed by clicking **+ New** on the navigation bar.

Figure 5.15

Link to journal entry form

Select **Journal Entry** in the **Other** column. The form is shown in Figure 5.16.

> **WARNING:** In early 2023, Intuit started updating various QBO forms. Some of those forms may have been updated after your textbook was printed. If you see a form that doesn't match the screenshot in your book, start by looking for an option to return to a previous version. In most cases, you'll see a link to **Old layout** or **Switch to classic view**. If there is no link available, check the Student Ancillaries page in myBusinessCourse for information about the updated form or ask your instructor.

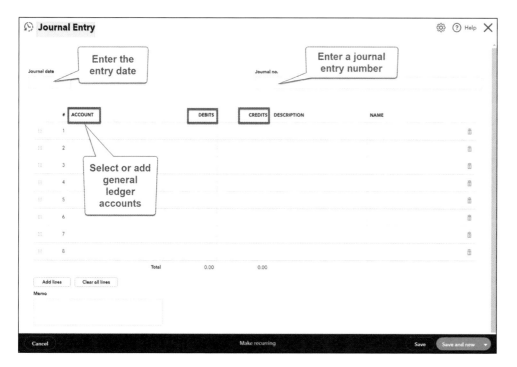

Figure 5.16

Journal entry form

To complete the form, you need to enter the date, the accounts (selected in the **ACCOUNT** field), and the amounts (entered in the **DEBITS** and **CREDITS** columns).

> **BEHIND THE SCENES** Although you **can** use the **Journal Entry** form to create entries in accounts receivable, accounts payable, and cash accounts, it's generally better to use the standard forms for transactions that affect those accounts. If you do make an adjusting journal entry to accounts receivable (or payable), you would need to enter the name of the customer (vendor) in the **NAME** field so that the subsidiary ledger is updated.

Here are some "good practice" points for working with adjusting entries:

- Include a brief description of the transaction in the **Description** field of the form.
    - It's easy to forget the source of an adjusting journal entry.
    - Information included in the **Description** field will appear on journal reports.
- Make one entry per type of adjustment. In other words, don't make one big entry with lots of different types of transactions on it. Companies should keep documentation to support adjusting journal entries, and it's easier to match the entry to the documentation if you keep the entries simple.
- Journal entries are numbered in the **Journal no.** field. QBO will number these automatically, or you can create your own numbering pattern such as Jan24.1, Jan24.2 to clearly identify the accounting period.

The mechanics of recording adjusting journal entries in QBO are very simple. To help with the hardest part (knowing what adjustments need to be made), here's a list of common monthly entries for service companies:

- Depreciation
- Accrual of:
    - Unpaid salaries
    - Interest or other charges for which a vendor bill has not yet been received
    - Unbilled revenue
- Expiration (consumption) of
    - Prepaid expenses
    - Supplies on hand
- Recognition of deferred revenue as earned

PRACTICE
EXERCISE
5.3

Record some adjusting journal entries for Craig's Design and Landscaping.
(Craig's Design records month-end adjustments for depreciation on the truck and prepaid rent.)

1. Click **+ New** on the navigation bar.

2. Click **Journal entry** (in the **OTHER** column).

3. Record depreciation expense of $225 for the current month.

    a. Enter the current date as the **Date**. You can leave the **Journal no.** as 1.

    b. In the first row, select **Depreciation** (the one with the **Other Expense account type**) in the **ACCOUNT** field and enter "225" in the **DEBITS** column.

        i. Enter "Current month depreciation" in the **DESCRIPTION** field.

(continued)

(continued from previous page)

c. In the second row, select **Depreciation** (the one listed as a **sub-account** of **Truck**) in the **ACCOUNT** field and enter "225" in the **CREDITS** column. **TIP:** This account has a **Fixed Assets account type**. This account would normally be named "Accumulated Depreciation."

  i. The **Description** field should have autofilled.

d. Click **Save and next**.

4. Craig originally expensed $900 to rent expense. Half of that amount is rent for next month. You reclassify the $450 paid in advance.

a. Enter the current date as the **Date**. Leave the **Journal no.** as 2.

b. In the first row, select **Prepaid Expenses** in the **ACCOUNT** field and enter "450" in the **DEBITS** column.

  i. Enter "Rent paid in advance" in the **DESCRIPTION** field.

c. In the second row, select **Rent or Lease** in the **ACCOUNT** field and enter "450" in the **CREDITS** column.

d. Click **Save and close**.

Balance sheet A financial statement showing a business's assets, liabilities, and stockholders' equity as of a specific date

Income statement A financial statement reporting a business's sales revenue and expenses for a given period of time

Statement of stockholders' equity A financial statement presenting information regarding the events that cause a change in stockholders' equity during a period. The statement presents the beginning balance, additions to, deductions from, and the ending balance of stockholders' equity for the period.

PREPARING FINANCIAL STATEMENTS

LO 5-3 Describe and prepare financial reports available in QBO

As you know, there are four basic financial statements:

- **Balance sheet**
- Profit and loss statement (**Income statement**)
- Statement of retained earnings (or **Statement of stockholders' equity**)
- **Statement of cash flows**

You can prepare a balance sheet, profit and loss statement, and statement of cash flows automatically in QBO. In this course, we'll only be looking at the balance sheet and profit and loss statement.

Statement of cash flows A financial statement showing a firm's cash inflows and cash outflows for a specific period, classified into operating, investing, and financing activity categories

> **BEHIND THE SCENES** QBO's statement of cash flows can contain some inaccuracies. For example, activity in short-term loans is classified in the operating activity section instead of the financing activity section. Although it's still a useful tool for management, it's generally better to prepare the cash flow statement manually.

The financial statements are accessed by clicking **Reports** on the navigation bar. The most common reports are found in the **Business Overview** section.

Figure 5.17
Business Overview
section of Reports

BEHIND THE SCENES The **Business Snapshot** report included in the **Business Overview** section is a great report for owners and managers. It includes six focus boxes.

- Pie chart of income accounts during any selected period
- Pie chart of expense accounts during any selected period
- Bar chart comparing current and prior period revenues
- Bar chart comparing current and prior period expenses
- List of customer balances
- List of vendor balances

The four charts can be filtered in a variety of ways by the user.

Statements can be prepared on the accrual or the cash basis. QBO allows for a number of simple modifications to be made on the face of reports.

Figure 5.18

Modification options on face of balance sheet report

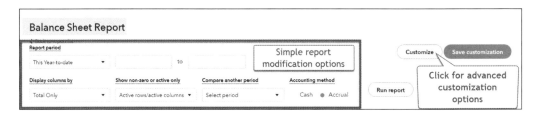

The modification bar for a **Balance Sheet** report is shown in Figure 5.18.

HINT: The purpose of start and end dates on a QBO balance sheet report is to provide users with access to all the activity in the listed accounts over the period of time selected in the date range. The amounts showing on the report will **always** represent the balance as of the last date of the identified date range (the balance sheet "as of" date). When you click (drill-down) on an account balance, a **transaction report** listing the activity over the date range will be displayed. Specific forms can be accessed by clicking any amount in the **transaction report**.

Figure 5.19

Column display options for balance sheet report

In the **Display columns by** field, the **Balance Sheet** report can be modified to show balances by month, by quarter, even by customer (Figure 5.19).

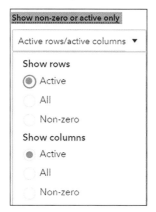

Figure 5.20

Account display options for balance sheet report

Accounts displayed can be limited to accounts with activity (**Active**) or to accounts with balances (**Non-zero**) in the **Show non-zero or active only** modification dropdown. Activity options can be used for rows or columns (Figure 5.20).

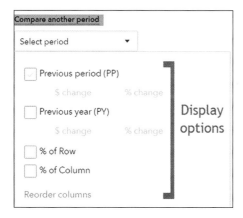

Figure 5.21

Comparative statement options for balance sheet report

Comparative statements can be created using the **Compare another period** options (Figure 5.21).

Other modifications can be made by clicking **Customize** in the top right corner of the report screen shown in Figure 5.18.

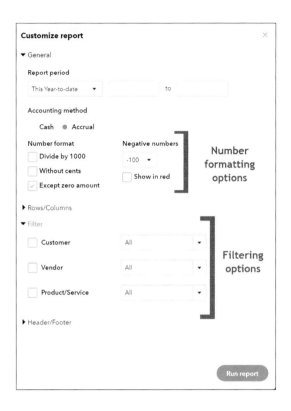

> **WARNING:** In early 2023, Intuit started updating various QBO forms. Some of those forms may have been updated after your textbook was printed. If you see a form that doesn't match the screenshot in your book, start by looking for an option to return to a previous version. In most cases, you'll see a link to **Old layout** or **Switch to classic view**. If there is no link available, check the Student Ancillaries page in myBusinessCourse for information about the updated form or ask your instructor.

In the Customize report sidebar (Figure 5.22), the format of numbers can be changed and data included can be filtered.

Profit and Loss reports have similar modification and customization options.

Keep in mind that financial statements may be distributed to:

- Owners
- Management
- Lenders
- Potential investors
- Regulatory agencies

They should be clear and professional in appearance. There are a few standard reporting conventions to consider:

- Assets are generally reported in descending order of liquidity (how quickly or easily they can be converted to cash).
- Liabilities are generally reported in descending order of their priority for payment.
- Revenue and expense sections of the income statement are generally reported in order of dollar amount (highest to lowest).
  - Categories are sorted first; then individual accounts within each category.

> **BEHIND THE SCENES** There are no absolute rules for presentation, particularly in the order of accounts on the profit and loss statement. For instance, there are some accounts that are frequently reported last (like depreciation expense and miscellaneous expense) regardless of the dollar amount. As the accountant, your responsibility is to organize the information in the clearest and most meaningful manner possible.

QBO doesn't have an easy way to change the account order. In your homework assignment, you'll be using account numbers. Account numbers can be changed to reorder the accounts. Another option for companies using QBO is to export the statements to Excel and reorder the accounts there. Exporting reports to Excel will be covered in Chapter 11.

Prepare year-end financial statements for Craig's Design and Landscaping.
(Craig's Design needs a balance sheet and profit and loss statement.)

1. If you didn't log out of QBO after the last practice exercise, you'll need to sign out now to clear your previous transactions. Log back in to continue.

2. Review balance sheet.
    a. Click Reports on the navigation bar.
    b. Open the Standard tab.
    c. Click Balance Sheet in the Favorites section.
    d. Select Today in the Report period dropdown menu.
    e. Click Customize.
    f. In the General section, select (100) in the dropdown for Negative numbers.
    g. In the Rows/Columns section, select Non-zero for both rows and columns in the Show non-zero or active only dropdown menu.
    h. Click Run Report.
    i. **Make a note** of the balance in Accounts Receivable.
    j. Click Back to report list. **TIP:** It's in blue right above the Report period field in the top left corner.

3. Review the income statement.
    a. Click Profit and Loss in the Favorites section.
    b. Select All Dates in the report period dropdown menu.
    c. Click Run report.
    d. **Make a note** of the total for NET INCOME.
    e. Select Cash as the Accounting method.
    f. Click Run report.
    g. **Make a note** of the total for NET INCOME on the cash basis.
    h. Click Dashboard to close the report window.

PRACTICE
EXERCISE
5.4

CLOSING THE BOOKS

There are really two types of period closings:

- Closing a period after financial statements are prepared and distributed (generally every month).

- Year-end closing (closing the books at the end of the company's legal year [fiscal year]).

LO 5-4 Describe the method for closing accounting periods in QBO

Closing an Accounting Period

When we talk about closing an accounting period, we are usually simply talking about not making any additional entries to that accounting period. An additional small bill might come in that relates to the period, or we might discover that we made a small error in a reconciliation affecting the closed period, but, once financial statements have been prepared and distributed, we generally don't want to go back and make changes. Instead, we simply record those transactions in the subsequent period.

> **BEHIND THE SCENES** The constraint of **materiality** applies here. If the dollar amount of a potential adjustment is significant (would influence decisions made by users of the financial statements), the entry should be made and the statements reissued.

Materiality An accounting guideline that states that insignificant data that would not affect a financial statement user's decisions may be recorded in the most expedient manner

So what does all this have to do with QBO? QBO gives us a tool that's useful here.

As I'm sure you've noticed by now, QBO will let you enter any date you want for transactions. Many of our students (and clients) have spent hours trying to reconcile their financial statements, and it turns out they simply entered a wrong date on a transaction or two.

QBO allows you to set a **Closing Date** in your company file. When a closing date is set, QBO will warn you if you try to enter a transaction dated prior to that date. You can override the warning but at least it's there.

Closing dates are set in **Account and Settings**.

Click the ⚙ on the icon bar and select **Account and Settings**.

On the **Advanced** tab, click the **pencil** icon in the top right corner of the **Accounting** section.

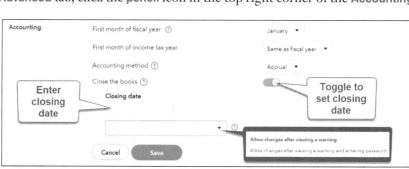

Toggle the **Close the books** button to activate the feature. Enter a **Closing date**. You then select one of two options.

- You can require a password to make changes.
  - ▪ Changes to transactions in the closed period could only be made after the correct password is entered.

- You can allow changes after viewing a warning.
  - ▪ Changes to transactions in the closed period could be made once the user clicks **Yes** on the warning screen.

PRACTICE
EXERCISE
5.5

Homework
MBC

Set a closing date for Craig's Design and Landscaping.
(Craig's Design sets a closing date in QBO.)

1. Click the ⚙ on the icon bar.
2. Click **Account and Settings**.
3. Open the **Advanced** tab.
4. Click the **pencil** icon to edit the **Accounting** section.
5. **Make a note** of the month displayed in the **First month of fiscal year** field.
6. Toggle the button next to **Close the books**.
7. Enter the last day of the current month as the **Closing date**.
8. Select **Allow changes after viewing a warning** in the dropdown menu.
9. Click **Save**.
10. Click **Done**.
11. Enter a transaction dated prior to the closing date to verify.
    a. Click **+ New** on the navigation bar.
    b. Click **Check**.
    c. Select **Cal Telephone** as the **payee**.
    d. Enter a date prior to the closing date (the date you set in Step 7) as the **Payment date**.
    e. Select **Telephone** as the **CATEGORY**.
    f. Enter $200 as the **AMOUNT**.
    g. Click **Save and close**.
    h. **Make a note** of the second sentence in the **Double-check the transaction date** message.
    i. Click **No**.
    j. Click **Cancel**.
12. Click **Yes** to close the window.

Year-end Closing

When a company file is originally set up, you must enter the first month of the fiscal (legal) year. QBO uses that date in reporting and budgeting. It also uses that date to automatically close (clear) all revenue and expense account types (Income, Cost of Goods Sold, Expense, Other Income, and Other Expense) to an equity account at the end of the year. The **closing process** is done automatically by QBO. QBO does **not** automatically close any temporary equity accounts.

Closing process A step in the accounting cycle in which the balances of all temporary accounts are transferred to the Retained Earnings account, leaving the temporary accounts with zero balances

> **BEHIND THE SCENES** To close revenue and expense accounts, QBO doesn't create an entry that's visible in the Journal. It does, however, change the reports. For example, let's say a company started business on 3/1/X1 and its year-end was 12/31/X1. For all reports dated between 3/1/X1 and 12/31/X1, revenues and expenses for the period would be reported on the profit and loss statement. A total for net income or loss for the year would show as a single line item on the balance sheet in the equity section.
>
> On 1/1/X2, the reports would automatically change. None of the 20X1 revenue and expense activity would appear on the profit and loss statement. Unless there were already some entries posted on 1/1/X2, the profit and loss statement would show net income of $0.00. On the balance sheet, the net income (or loss) line (related to 20X1 transactions) would also no longer appear. Instead, Retained Earnings would have been credited (or debited) for the 20X1 operating results.

Although QBO appropriately closes out revenue and expense accounts at year-end, there would be some final housekeeping entries that need to be made to close out any temporary equity accounts. These entries vary depending on the type of entity.

- For proprietorships: Most proprietorships set up separate capital investment and draw accounts (equity accounts) so that activity for the year is visible on the balance sheet. If so, those accounts should be closed out to an Owner's Equity at the beginning of a new year. Retained Earnings should also be closed out to Owner's Equity.

- For partnerships: Most small partnerships set up separate capital investment, draw, and capital balance accounts (equity accounts) for each partner. If so, the capital investment, draw, and Retained Earnings accounts should be closed out to each partner's capital balance account at the beginning of a new year.

- For corporations: Most corporations set up a dividends account (equity account) so that current-year distributions to shareholders are visible on the balance sheet. If so, the dividend account should be cleared out to Retained Earnings at the beginning of a new year.

ANSWER TO
QuickCheck
5-1

	Credit Card Payable	XXX	
	Accounts Payable		XXX

CHAPTER SHORTCUTS

Reconcile an account
1. Click ⚙ on the icon bar.
2. Click **Reconcile**.

Record adjusting journal entries
1. Click **+ New** on the navigation bar.
2. Click **Journal Entry**.

CHAPTER REVIEW

Assignments with the MBC are available in myBusinessCourse.

Matching

Match the term or phrase (as used in QuickBooks Online) to its definition.

1. journal entry
2. statement ending date
3. reconciled
4. charges

5. cleared
6. payments
7. fiscal year
8. closing date

_____ company's legal year

_____ status of a bank transaction marked as cleared **during** the reconciliation process

_____ date set by user; used to limit entry of transactions dated prior to that date

_____ date of statement received from bank

_____ title of column in the credit card reconciliation screen listing all debits to the account being reconciled

_____ status of bank transaction that has been marked as cleared as part of a **completed** reconciliation

_____ transaction type used for recording an adjusting entry

_____ title of column in the credit card reconciliation screen listing all credits to the account being reconciled

Multiple Choice

1. All transactions posted to an account being reconciled will appear on the bank reconciliation screen in QBO EXCEPT
   a. reconciled transactions and uncleared transactions recorded through a general journal entry.
   b. reconciled transactions.
   c. uncleared transactions.
   d. uncleared **bill payment** transactions.

2. Which of the following accounts **could** be reconciled using the reconciliation tool in QBO? (Select all that apply. Assume all of the accounts listed were in the company's chart of accounts.)
   a. Cash (**Bank account type**)
   b. Prepaid Expenses (**Other Current Assets account type**)
   c. Accounts Payable (**Accounts Payable account type**)
   d. Unearned Revenue (**Other Current Liabilities account type**)

3. The **Journal** report includes _____.
   a. all accounting transactions no matter where (how) they were recorded
   b. only those accounting transactions recorded using the **Journal Entry** form
   c. only accounting transactions recorded through certain forms
   d. only accounting transactions NOT recorded in the **Journal Entry** form

4. When a credit card statement is reconciled,
   a. the user can elect to create a **bill** for the statement balance.
   b. the user can elect to write a **check** for the statement balance.
   c. the user can elect to retain the balance in the credit card liability account.
   d. the user can elect any of the three options listed.

5. On the first day of a new fiscal year, QBO automatically closes
   a. all temporary accounts.
   b. all revenue and expense accounts.
   c. all revenue, expense, and equity accounts.
   d. all revenue, expense, and dividend accounts.

BEYOND THE CLICKS—THINKING LIKE A MANAGER

Accounting: A company issued inaccurate financial statements at the end of the year. There was no fraud involved, and the accounting staff was competent. What might have caused the error(s)?

Information Systems: How do closing dates work in a computerized system? How does setting a closing date prevent or reduce errors in the company's records?

ASSIGNMENTS

Assignment 5A

Math Revealed!

1/31/24

✓ Martin asks you to give him a summary of the hours you worked in January. He agrees to pay you $30 per hour for the 10 hours you worked on his accounting. You are only doing this temporarily since you have some extra time so you set yourself up as a 1099 vendor and write yourself a check for the $300. The check number is 1111. You consider this a professional service expense. **TIP:** Select the appropriate sub-account.

● You use 333-44-5555 as your **Business ID number** and 2119 Abacus Drive as your address. Use your home city, state. and zip code to complete the address. You select Net 10 in **Terms**.

✓ You reconcile the bank statement for January. You get the following information from the bank's website. **TIP:** Since this is the first time the checking account has been reconciled in QBO, the 12/31 balance will show as a deposit. Make sure you mark that deposit as cleared.

CITY BANK OF SACRAMENTO
51 Capital Avenue
Sacramento, CA 95822 (916) 585-2120

Student Name Math Revealed!
3835 Freeport Blvd
Sacramento, CA 95822
Account # 1616479   **January 31, 2024**

	CREDITS	CHARGES	BALANCE
Beginning Balance, January 1			$3,620.00
1/6, Check 1102—Pro Spaces		$ 850.00	2,770.00
1/10, Check 1101—Protector Insurance		480.00	2,290.00
1/10, Deposit	$ 465.00		2,755.00
1/13, Check 1103—Kathy's Coffee		32.00	2,723.00
1/17, Check 1104—Math Shack		495.82	2,227.18
1/17, Deposit	1,640.00		3,867.18
1/19, Check 1105—Paper Bag Depot		94.00	3,773.18
1/19, Deposit	320.00		4,093.18
1/23, Check 1100—Gus Ranting		25.00	4,068.18
1/24, Check 1106—Samantha Levin		125.00	3,943.18
1/26, Deposit	3,555.00		7,498.18
Ending Balance, January 31			$7,498.18

HINT: Your check numbers on **bill payments** may differ slightly from above. Pay attention to the payee and amount.

Also, note that the dates showing on the bank statement are the dates checks and deposits were received by the bank. They will not always be the same as the dates transactions were recorded in your company file.

✓ You also receive the credit card statement in the mail. You reconcile the statement to the credit card liability account and set up the balance for payment later to **Prime Visa**

Company. Use JanCC as the Bill no. **TIP:** Make sure you click Enter a bill to pay later before you click Done.

PRIME VISA COMPANY
55 Wall Street
New York, NY 10005

Student Name Math Revealed!
3835 Freeport Blvd
Sacramento, CA 95822
Account # 212456770439   **January 31, 2024**

	PAYMENTS	CHARGES	BALANCE
Beginning Balance, January 1			$ 0.00
1/02—Paper Bag Depot		$1,572.00	1,572.00
1/05—Cardinal Gas & Snacks		35.00	1,607.00
1/09—Math Shack		31.52	1,638.52
1/25—Cardinal Gas & Snacks		34.00	1,672.52
1/30—Kathy's Coffee		7.50	1,680.02
Ending Balance, January 31			**$1,680.02**

Minimum Payment Due: $10   **Payment Due Date: February 15**

✓ You make adjusting journal entries for the month of January as needed. (Start with Journal no. Jan24.1.) You carefully consider the following:

- Math Revealed! used the straight-line method to determine depreciation expense for all fixed assets.

  - Monthly depreciation expense for the equipment purchased prior to 12/31 is $65.00. (Computer $50; Printer $7.50; Calculators $7.50)

  - Math Revealed! purchased $1,690 of furniture on 1/2. You expect the furniture to last 8 years, with a $250 salvage value. You take a full month depreciation on the furniture.

  - Two computers ($1,260) and six calculators ($312) were also purchased on 1/2. You expect the computers to have a 3-year life (no salvage value) and the calculators to have a 4-year life (no salvage value). You take a full month depreciation on the equipment.

  - On 1/30, shelving was installed. The cost of the shelving was $820. You expect the shelving to last for the term of the lease (24 months). You estimate the salvage value at $100 at the end of the 2 years. You started using the shelving on February 1.

- You check the supplies on hand. You estimate that $185 of tutoring supplies were used during January.

  - You charge the amount to a new account (Tutoring supplies expense, a sub-account of Office and Tutoring Costs). You use 632 as the account number and Other Business Expenses as the detail type in the Tax form section field.

- The insurance policy premium paid in January was $480. The policy term is 1/1–12/31/24.

- You check to make sure that all the revenue recorded in January was earned during the month.

  - You realize that the $3,000 paid by Teacher's College on 1/27 (INV-1011) was for a workshop to be held in February.

  - You ask Martin about the Marley's two weeks of Persistence sessions paid for on 1/19 (SR-104). Martin says she actually finished all the sessions by the end of January.

  - You also take a look at INV-1009 to Annie Wang. Martin says half of the $420 billed on 1/12 was for February tutoring.

  - **TIP:** Consider whether you need a new account here. Choose an account number that fits with the account numbering scheme (assets are 100s; liabilities are 200s; revenues are 400s; expenses are 600s).

- Martin has agreed to pay his father interest on the $2,500 loan to help get the business started. The last payment was made on 12/31/23. The annual interest rate (simple interest) on the loan is 6%. You forgot to pay him in January. You call and let him know that the check will come in February.

- ■ **TIP:** Just because you didn't pay it in January doesn't mean you don't owe it in January. Consider whether you need a new account here.

Check numbers as of 1/31

Checking account balance: $ 2,716.18
Total assets: $14,327.50
Total current liabilities: . . . $ 5,883.86
Net income (January only): $ 1,664.64

TIP: If you are having a hard time getting to these check numbers, try some of the hints for finding errors and getting it right in Appendix 5A.

Suggested reports for Chapter 5:

All reports should be in portrait orientation.

- Journal—1/31 transactions only
- Balance Sheet (as of 1/31)
- Profit and loss statement (January)
- January bank reconciliation report
  - ■ **TIP:** To open the report, click the gear icon on the icon bar and select **Reconcile**. Click **History by account** for the appropriate bank account and **View report**. Select **Save as PDF** in the Print dropdown menu.
- January credit card reconciliation report
  - ■ **TIP:** To access the report, follow the instructions included in the tip for the bank reconciliation report.

Assignment 5B

Salish Software Solutions

Homework
MBC

1/31/24

✓ You talk to Sally about getting paid for the work you're doing. You suggest $25 an hour, and she agrees. You are only doing this temporarily since you have some extra time so you set yourself up as a 1099-NEC vendor and write yourself a check for the 12 hours you worked in January ($300). The check number is 1111. You consider this a type of professional fees expense. **TIP:** Select the appropriate sub-account.

- You use 999-88-7777 as your Business ID number and 3056 Abacus Drive as your address. Use your home city, state, and zip to complete the address. You select Net 10 in **Terms**.

✓ You decide to reconcile the bank statement for January. You get the following information from the bank's website:

- **TIP:** Since this is the first time the checking account has been reconciled, the beginning balance in QBO will be $0. That is ok. Once you start the reconciliation the opening balance per the bank statement will appear as a deposit. Select that as an amount that has cleared.

SACRAMENTO CITY BANK
1822 Capital Avenue
Sacramento, CA 95822 (916) 585-2120

Student Name Salish Software Solutions
3835 Freeport Blvd
Sacramento, CA 95822
Account # 855922   **January 31, 2024**

	CREDITS	CHARGES	BALANCE
Beginning Balance, January 1			**$10,500.00**
1/5, Check 1102—Albright Insurance		$ 780.00	9,720.00
1/7, Check 1101—Alki Property Management		650.00	9,070.00
1/10, Deposit	$ 530.00		9,600.00
1/14, Check 1103—Personal Software		120.00	9,480.00
1/15, Check 1104—Abacus Shop		1,375.00	8,105.00
1/15, Check 1105—Simply Accounting		600.00	7,505.00
1/19, Deposit	2,635.00		10,140.00
1/21, Check 1108—Entrepreneur Magazine		120.00	10,020.00
1/23, Deposit	1,300.00		11,320.00
1/30, Deposit	$1,080.00		12,400.00
1/31, Bank service charge		$ 15.00	12,385.00
Ending Balance, January 31			**$12,385.00**

 HINT: Your check numbers on **bill payments** may differ slightly from above. Pay attention to the payee and amount.

Also, note that the dates showing on the bank statement are the dates checks and deposits were received by the bank. They will not always be the same as the dates transactions were recorded in your company file.

✓ You also receive the credit card statement in the mail. You reconcile the card and set up the balance for payment later to Capital Three. Use JanCC as the Bill no. **TIP:** Make sure you click Enter a bill to pay later before you click Done.

CAPITAL THREE
58 Wall Street
New York, NY 10005

Student Name Salish Software Solutions
3835 Freeport Blvd
Sacramento, CA 95822
Account # 646630813344   **January 31, 2024**

	PAYMENTS	CHARGES	BALANCE
Beginning Balance, January 1			$ 0.00
1/3—Paper Bag Depot		$500.00	500.00
1/15—Hacker Spaces		400.00	900.00
1/15—Fast Copy		150.00	1,050.00
1/26—The Blue Door		89.00	1,139.00
Ending Balance, 1/31			**$1,139.00**
Minimum Payment Due: $10.00		**Payment Due Date: February 15**	

✓ You make adjusting journal entries for the month of January as needed. (Start with Journal no. Jan24.1.) You carefully consider the following:

● Salish Software Solutions used the straight-line method to determine depreciation expense for all fixed assets.

■ None of the assets purchased prior to 12/31 were fully depreciated. Monthly depreciation expense for the assets purchased prior to 12/31 is $223.50 (Computer $166.00, Printer $37.50, and furniture $20).

■ Sally paid $1,200 for software on 1/3. She expected the software to last two years, with no salvage value. Since the software was placed into service close to the beginning of the month, you decide to go ahead and take a full month of depreciation for January.

- ■ The storage cabinets were installed on 1/30. The cost was $1,500. Sally expects the cabinets to last for five years. You don't think the cabinets will have any resale value at the end of the five years. Sally started using the cabinets on February 1.

- You check the supplies on hand. You estimate that $175 of office supplies were used during January.

- The insurance policy premium paid in January was $780. The policy term is 1/1–12/31/24.

- You check to make sure that all the revenue recorded in January was earned during the month.

  - ■ You ask Sally about the Butter and Beans installation work. She says that she has completed about half the work (20 of the 40 hours billed on INV-1009 for $3,000).

  - ■ You also take a look at INV-1011 to Albus Software. The workshop will be held in mid-February.

  - ■ **TIP:** Consider whether you need to create a new account here. Choose an account number that fits with the account numbering scheme (assets are 100s; liabilities are 200s; revenues are 400s; expenses are 600s).

- Sally's last payment to Dell Finance was 12/31/23. That payment included interest through 12/31. The next payment of $150 is due on February 1. The annual interest rate (simple interest) on the loan is 5%. The unpaid balance on the note is $3,000.

  - ■ **TIP:** Think about what that February 1st payment will cover. Does any of the amount relate to January activity? You may need to create a new account.

Check numbers as of 1/31

Checking account balance:. $ 9,710.00
Total assets:. $29,849.50
Total current liabilities: . . . $ 6,850.45
Net income (January):. . . . . $ 3,841.05

TIP: If you are having a hard time getting to these check numbers, try some of the hints for finding errors and getting it right in Appendix 5A.

Suggested reports for Chapter 5:

All reports should be in portrait orientation; fit to one page wide

- Journal—1/31/23 transactions only

- Balance Sheet (as of 1/31)

- Profit and loss statement (January only)

- January bank reconciliation report
  - ■ **TIP:** To open the report, click the gear icon on the icon bar and select **Reconcile**. Click **History by account** for the appropriate bank account and **View report**. Select **Save as PDF** in the Print dropdown menu.

- January credit card reconciliation report
  - ■ **TIP:** To access the report, follow the instructions included in the tip for the bank reconciliation report.

APPENDIX 5A GETTING IT RIGHT

Most accountants work the hardest (use their brains the most!) at the end of an accounting period. They know the income statement for the period should accurately reflect the earnings (or loss) for the period. They know the balance sheet as of the period end should accurately reflect the assets owned and the liabilities owed by the company. The difficulty doesn't lie in knowing the basic concepts. The difficulty lies in knowing what the "accurate" amounts are.

LO 5-5 Understand common causes of errors in QBO

Most students have the most difficulty with the assignments for Chapter 5 and Chapter 8. You have check numbers to refer to, which will hopefully help, but if your numbers don't match those numbers, how do you figure out where you went wrong?

Here are some suggestions for finding your mistakes:

- Start by checking dates.
  - Entering an incorrect date is the **single most common** cause of student errors (and student headaches!). QBO enters default dates when you first open a form. It defaults to the current date when you start entering transactions during a work session. If you change the date on the first invoice, it will default to that new date when you enter the second invoice. If you open a new form, however, it will default back to the current date. Accounting is date driven, so your financial statements won't match the check figures if you enter a transaction in the wrong month. First thing to do? Pull a report of transactions dated BEFORE the first transaction date in the assignment and then one of transactions dated AFTER the last transaction date of the assignment. Transaction List by Date is a great report for this. Make sure you're only checking for transactions that **you** entered. (There were some transactions entered in the initial setup of the company file you are using for your homework. Those should **not** be changed.)

- Really **LOOK** at the balance sheet.
  - The account balances will be positive if they reflect the normal balance for that type of account. Are any of the amounts on your balance sheet negative numbers? If so, should they be negative? If they are contra accounts, the answer would be yes. If there are no negative amounts on your balance sheet, should there be? Again, if you have any contra accounts, the answer would be yes. Accumulated depreciation is a contra account so, if entries were made correctly, it would show as a negative number on the balance sheet. If accumulated depreciation isn't negative, you might have mixed up your debits and credits when making an entry. That's easy to do. Double-click on the amount, and then double-click on the underlying entry(ies) and make the necessary corrections.
  - Don't worry about errors in Cash, A/R, or A/P until you are comfortable with the other balances. This is double-entry bookkeeping so if one account is wrong, then at least one other account is also wrong. It's hard to find errors in Cash, A/R, and A/P due to the sheer volume of transactions that affect these accounts. SO: if you don't match the check figures, see if you can find the other account(s) that is (are) also off. If you can find and correct the other error(s), these accounts will, of course, fix themselves!
  - Pay particular attention to other current assets and to liabilities other than accounts payable. Are they adjusted properly? Does the supplies on hand account equal the check number given to you? Does the balance in prepaid insurance represent the cost of future (unused) insurance coverage? Should there be any interest accrued on debt? Keep asking questions.

- Really **LOOK** at the profit and loss statement.
  - Again, look for negative amounts that shouldn't be negative. There are some contra revenue and expenses accounts, of course. Sales discounts and purchase discount accounts are two examples of contra accounts that you'll be working with in future chapters.
  - Look at the detail for accounts that just look "odd." Is rent expense higher than income? That could happen, of course, but probably not in this class!
- If you're still off, you're going to have to do some detective work. Try to narrow down the possible errors first.
  - For example, let's say your A/R number is **higher** than the check figure given for A/R. You wouldn't start by looking for unrecorded invoices or cash sales. Why? Because missing invoices or cash sales wouldn't overstate A/R. You **would** start by looking for unrecorded customer payments or customer credits. Look through the assignment (day by day) and agree any customer payments or credits described to the payment and credit memo transaction types listed in your journal.
  - Another example—Let's say your cash number is **lower** than the check number given for cash. You might start by looking for undeposited checks by making sure there isn't a balance in the undeposited funds account. You might also look for duplicated customer payments. Then look through the assignment (day by day) and agree any payment transactions to check, expense, and bill payment transaction types listed in your journal.
  - Don't give up. Keep checking transactions. You'll find the error.
- I have one other suggestion. It's listed last here only because students tend to waste a lot of time looking for a specific amount when the difference is often the sum of several errors. That being said, sometimes you just get lucky! So, determine the difference between the check figure and your total. Is the number divisible by 9? You may have a transposition error (for example, you entered 18 instead of 81). Is the difference equal to the amount of a transaction? Maybe you forgot to enter it (or entered it on the wrong date). Is the difference equal to twice one of your transactions? You may have entered a journal entry backwards (watch those debits and credits!).

APPENDIX 5B UNDERSTANDING THE RECONCILIATION REPORT

LO 5-6 Describe the elements in QBO reconciliation reports

eLecture

The purpose of a bank reconciliation is to make sure the amount reported as cash in the balance sheet is accurate. Reconciliations are performed by comparing activity reported on statements received from the bank (an external source of information) to activity recorded internally in the cash general ledger account. Because internal information is being reconciled to external information, bank reconciliations are considered part of a company's internal control system.

There will be differences between what's recorded in the general ledger and what's reported on the bank statement.

Differences that represent **errors** are considered permanent differences. Permanent differences must be corrected before the reconciliation process is considered complete. If the error was made by the company, an adjusting entry would be made. If the error was made by the bank, the correction would be in the bank's records. Permanent differences are relatively uncommon.

Temporary differences, on the other hand, are very common. Temporary differences occur when a transaction is recorded by the company **before or after** that transaction is recorded by the bank.

Here are some examples:

- A check to a vendor is recorded by the company (cash is credited) when the check is issued. The check is sent to the vendor; the vendor records receipt of the check; and the vendor deposits the amount in its bank account. In the final step, the vendor's bank requests and receives the cash from the company's bank to cover the check. This process can occur over several days or even weeks.

- A check from a customer is received by the company. The customer payment is recorded (cash is debited) immediately but the checks are not deposited with the bank until a later date.

- The bank charges a monthly service fee to the company's account. The company isn't aware of the fee until the bank statement is received.

Most temporary (timing) differences are resolved before the bank statement is reconciled. As long as a transaction is recorded in the same accounting period (usually a month), any timing difference won't be an issue. Issues arise when the transactions are recorded by the bank and the company in two different accounting periods.

The two most common types of temporary differences are:

- Outstanding checks—Checks that were recorded by the company but had not been presented to the company's bank for payment as of the statement date.

- Deposits in transit—Deposits that were recorded by the company but had not yet been deposited at the bank as of the statement date.

The reconciliation report in QBO provides information about the differences that remain as of the statement date.

The top section of a reconciliation report is shown in Figure 5B.1.

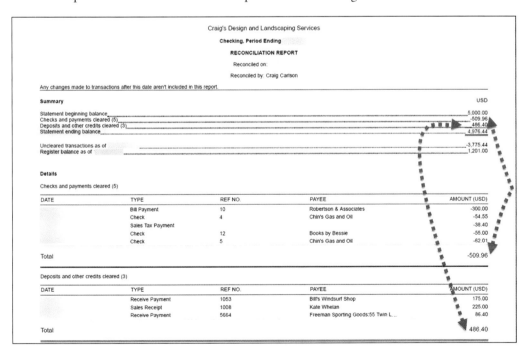

Figure 5B.1

Details of bank activity during the statement period

This section includes all of the transactions that were "matched" during the period. Although all of the transactions listed here were recorded in the bank's records during the current period, they could have been recorded in the company's records during the current period or in a prior period. If they were recorded in the company's books during a prior period, they would have been listed as outstanding checks in the prior reconciliation.

The balance in the company's cash account as of the statement date is also listed in this section.

The bottom section of a reconciliation report is shown in Figure 5B.2.

Additional Information

Uncleared checks and payments as of

DATE	TYPE	REF NO.	PAYEE	AMOUNT (USD)
	Expense	12	Robertson & Associates	-250.00
	Sales Tax Payment			-38.50
	Expense	9	Tania's Nursery	-89.09
	Expense	15	Tania's Nursery	-108.09
	Bill Payment	7	Hicks Hardware	-250.00
	Expense	8	Hicks Hardware	-24.36
	Check		Tony Rondonuwu	-100.00
	Cash Expense		Bob's Burger Joint	-5.66
	Cash Expense		Squeaky Kleen Car Wash	-19.99
	Check	70	Chin's Gas and Oil	-185.00
	Cash Expense		Chin's Gas and Oil	-52.14
	Bill Payment	11	Hall Properties	-900.00
	Expense	13	Hicks Hardware	-215.66
	Check	2	Mahoney Mugs	-18.08
	Cash Expense		Bob's Burger Joint	-3.86
	Bill Payment	1	Brosnahan Insurance Agency	-2,000.00
	Bill Payment	3	Books by Bessie	-75.00
	Refund	1020	Pye's Cakes	-87.50
	Check	Debit	Squeaky Kleen Car Wash	-19.99
	Expense	108	Tania's Nursery	-46.98
	Bill Payment	45	Tim Philip Masonry	-666.00
	Bill Payment	6	PG&E	-114.09
	Cash Expense		Chin's Gas and Oil	-63.15
	Check	75	Hicks Hardware	-228.75
	Expense	76	Pam Seitz	-75.00
	Cash Expense		Tania's Nursery	-23.50
	Credit Card Credit			-900.00
Total			**Outstanding checks**	-6,560.39

Uncleared deposits and other credits as of

DATE	TYPE	REF NO.	PAYEE	AMOUNT (USD)
	Receive Payment		Amy's Bird Sanctuary	105.00
	Receive Payment	1886	Cool Cars	694.00
	Sales Receipt	10264	Dylan Sollfrank	337.50
	Receive Payment		Freeman Sporting Goods:55 Twin Lane	50.00
	Deposit			218.75
	Receive Payment	2064	Travis Waldron	103.55
	Deposit			408.00
	Deposit			868.15
Total			**Deposits in transit**	2,784.95

All of the timing differences are listed in this section—outstanding checks and deposits in transit. This list includes all the transactions that had been recorded in the company's books but had not been recorded by the bank as of the statement date. Some of the transactions were recorded by the company during the statement period. Others were recorded by the company during a prior period. These would have been timing differences in the prior reconciliation as well.

The final step is to reconcile the bank statement balance to the book balance.

Although QBO doesn't include this in the report, the reconciliation summary you learned in your introduction to financial accounting course can be created using the data in the reconciliation report. It would look something like this given the information in Figures 5B.1 and 5B.2.

Balance per bank as of the statement date	$4,976.44
Add: Deposits in Transit	2,784.95
Less: Outstanding Checks	6,560.39
Balance per book as of the statement date	$1,201.00

APPENDIX 5C FIXING RECONCILIATION ERRORS

Although the process is time-consuming, the safest way to fix reconciliation errors is to manually unreconcile all the transactions and then start over.

LO 5-7   Explain how to manually undo a bank reconciliation in QBO

 HINT: Users with the QBO Accountant version of the software can **undo** a bank reconciliation. Check with your instructor to see if they might be able to use that feature.

- Print out the reconciliation report for the period that was reconciled incorrectly. This will give you a list of all transactions cleared during the period.
  - ▪ Click the ⚙ on the icon bar.
  - ▪ Click **Reconcile**.

Figure 5C.1

Access to reconciliation history

  - ▪ Click **History by account**.

Figure 5C.2

Link to reconciliation report

  - ▪ Click **View report**.
  - ▪ Print or save a PDF of the report.
- Find and delete the reconciliation discrepancy entry, if any. This is the entry QBO would have made if you clicked **Finish Now** before the difference between the book balance and the bank balance was zero.
  - ▪ Click **Reports** on the navigation bar.
  - ▪ Click **Profit and Loss**.
  - ▪ Change the dates to include the bank statement ending date.
  - ▪ Click the Reconciliation Discrepancies account to open the account **Transaction Report**.
  - ▪ Click the entry amount to open the form.
  - ▪ Click **More** on the black bar at the bottom of the form and select **Delete**.
- Open the **check register** and sort the list by cleared status.
  - ▪ Click the ⚙ on the icon bar and select **Chart of Accounts**.

- Click **View Register** in the **ACTION** column for the account being corrected.

- Change the order of transactions by clicking the checkmark at the top of the column between **DEPOSIT** and **BALANCE** (the status field). The list is now sorted by status.

BEHIND THE SCENES The status field for every **bank** account transaction listed in a register will either be R, C, or blank.

- **R** means that the transaction has been reconciled. The reconciliation has been closed.
- **C** means that the transaction has been identified as 'cleared,' but the reconciliation is still open.
- Blank means that the transaction is outstanding.

- Unreconcile the transactions cleared as part of the inaccurate reconciliation.
    - Every transaction listed on the reconciliation report as cleared will have an **R** in the status field. Click in the box until the status field is blank.
    - If the transaction is linked to another transaction, you will get the following warning message:

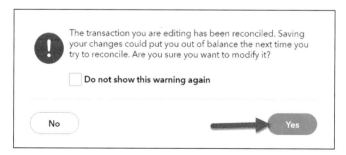

▪ Click Yes.

▪ You will get the following message each time you clear a status field.

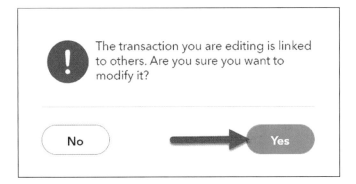

▪ Click Yes.

▪ Depending on the closing date set in your company file, you may also get this message:

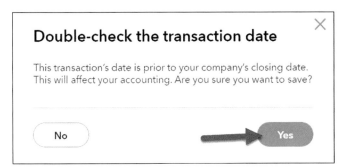

▪ Click Yes.

▪ Do **not** change the status of any transaction that does not appear as 'cleared' in the reconciliation report you printed out in the first step of the process.

● Re-reconcile the account.

▪ Click the ⚙ on the icon bar.

▪ Click Reconcile.

▪ Select the account to be re-reconciled.

▪ The beginning balance should now equal the ending balance from the prior month's reconciliation (the last correct reconciliation).

▪ Enter the ending date and the ending balance from the bank statement.

> **!** **WARNING:** An offer to "help you fix" the reconciliation will likely be available in QBO. If you accept the offer, a **Reconciliation Discrepancy Report** window will be displayed. In the window you can change the status of any unreconciled transaction. This would not solve the problem of missing transactions or transaction errors. It's best to ignore the offer.

▪ Proceed with the reconciliation.

QuickBooks

SECTION THREE

Merchandising Companies

In this section, we'll primarily be looking at how QuickBooks Online handles the unique needs of merchandising companies. However, some of the new processes and procedures you will learn can also be, and are, used by service companies.

Accounting in a merchandising company is a little more complex. For example, inventory purchases and sales need to be accounted for and sales tax may need to be collected and remitted.

Merchandising companies are also, generally, larger than service companies. That means more employees, including more employees involved in accounting functions. Although **internal controls** are important in **any** company, the complexity and size of merchandising companies make the review and development of internal control systems even more important.

Two of the primary purposes of a good internal control system are:

- To safeguard assets.
- To ensure the accuracy of financial records.

QBO has some features that can be part of a good internal control system.

CONTROLS IN QUICKBOOKS ONLINE

Managing Users

Many merchandising companies have multiple employees involved in the record-keeping functions. Those employees must, of course, have access to the accounting software. Allowing every employee **full** access to the software, however, presents opportunities for **fraud**.

QBO allows individual users to be limited in access to particular areas of the program and even to functions within those areas. QBO requires that at least one user, the administrator, have access to all functions. The administrator sets up the other users.

Internal controls Policies and procedures implemented by an organization to safeguard its assets, ensure integrity of its accounting records, ensure its compliance with laws and regulations, and monitor effectiveness and efficiency of its operations.

Fraud Any act by the management or employees of a business involving an intentional deception for personal gain.

> **BEHIND THE SCENES** The person who created the company file is automatically set up as the administrator. Because you created the homework company file, you are the administrator.

To manage users, click the ⚙ on the icon bar.

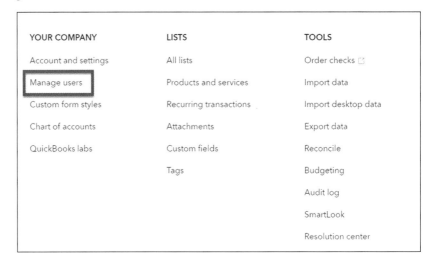

Click **Manage users**.

There are two tabs in the User Center. Owners and employees with accounting responsibilities are added on the **User** tab. In QuickBooks Online Plus (the version provided to you), a company can add up to 5 **Users**. (Employees with access only to reports or timesheets are not included in the **user** limit.)

External accountants are normally added on the **Accountants** tab. Up to 2 **Accountants** can be added.

Adding Users

Adding Standard Users with Full Access

Click the ⚙ on the icon bar and select **Manage Users** to open the User Center.

Click **Add user.**

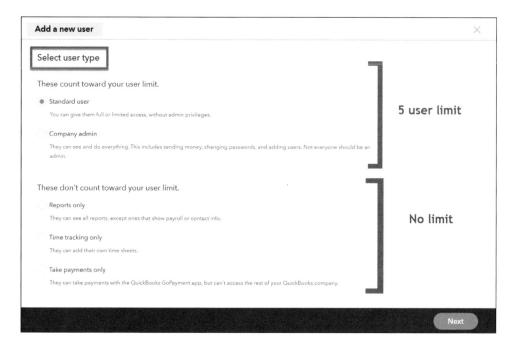

Figure S3.4

User type selection screen

Employees with accounting responsibilities would normally be set up as **standard users**.

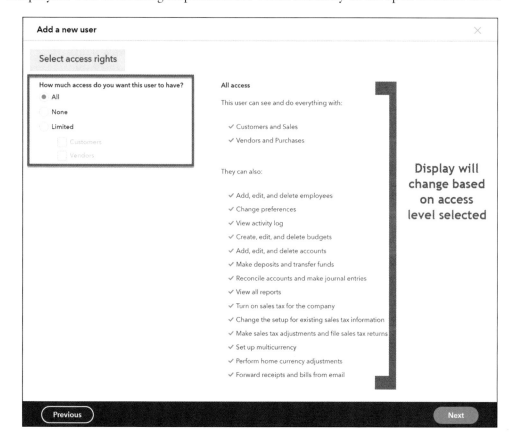

Figure S3.5

Access rights selection screen

Users can be given access to all features or access can be limited. In a small company, for example, the accountant might be given access to all the accounting functions listed on the screen shown in Figure S3.5. Click **Next** to identify access rights to administrative functions.

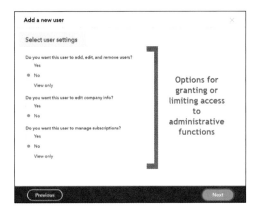

Administrative features include managing users and QBO subscriptions and editing information on the Company tab in Account and Settings (company contact details and tax structure).

Click Next.

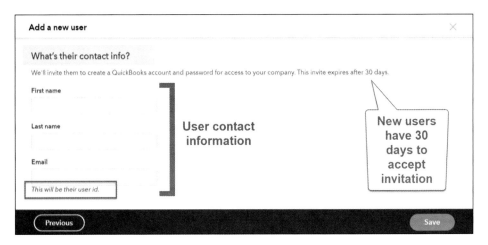

In the final screen, the new user's name and email address are entered. The email address becomes their user name. Once the information is saved, an email is automatically sent to the new user. The setup is completed when the new user logs in and accepts the invitation.

Adding Standard Users with Limited Access

Click the ⚙ on the icon bar and select Manage users to open the User Center.

On the Users tab, click Add user and click Next. Toggle Standard user as the user type and click Next.

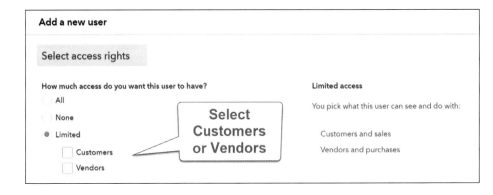

To limit access, toggle **Limited**. **Users** can be limited to sales cycle functions by checking the box next to **Customers**. **Users** can be limited to purchase cycle functions by checking the box next to **Vendors**. Click **Next** once the selection has been made.

The allowed (and disallowed) functions are displayed on the next screen. Figure S3.9 shows the functions for users with limited access rights to customer and sales activities.

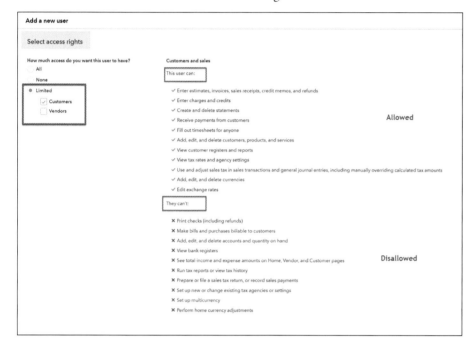

Figure S3.10 shows the functions for users with limited access rights to vendor and purchase activities.

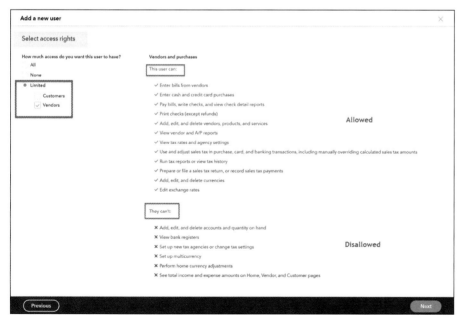

If both **Customers** and **Vendors** are checked, the user would be able to do all functions other than:

- Add or edit general ledger accounts
- Adjust inventory quantities

- View bank registers

- View total income and expense amounts on the Business overview tab of the Dashboard.

Click Next.

The final two screens for entering users with sales or purchase cycle responsibilities include setting administrative access rights (see Figure S3.6) and entering user contact information (see Figure S3.7). An invitation is automatically emailed to the employee once the information is saved.

Adding Users With Time Tracking Or Report Only Access

Companies can also add an unlimited number of users who only need access to either time tracking or reports.

If an employee only needs to enter their own time, select Time tracking only on the screen in Figure S3.4.

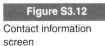

Figure S3.11

Employee selection for time-tracking only

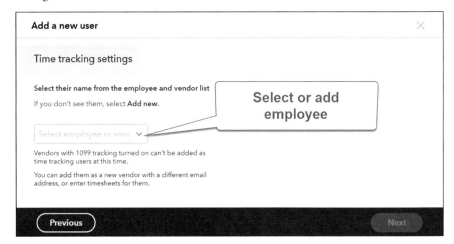

Select employee name and click Next.

Figure S3.12

Contact information screen

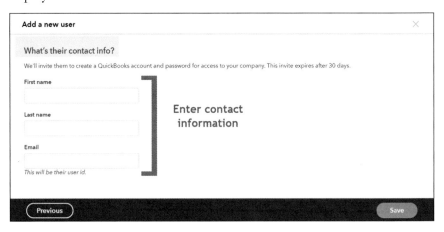

In the final screen, contact information is added.

Click Save. An email invitation to the employee is automatically generated.

To add owners or managers who only need access to reports, select Reports only on the screen shown in S3.4. An email invitation is automatically generated after contact information is entered. Reports only users have access to all reports other than payroll and contact information reports. They can create custom reports (and report groups) but they cannot view transactions included on the reports. They also can't open the audit log.

Adding Accountant Users

Companies can give company file access to two external accountants by setting them up as **accountant users**. This allows the accountant(s) to easily make any necessary adjustments. **Accountant** users have full administrative rights.

Click the ⚙ on the icon bar and select **Manage users**.

Accounting firms tab in user management screen

Click the **Accounting firms** tab.

Enter the external accountant's email address and click **Invite**.

An email to the accountant is automatically generated by QBO. Once the accountant accepts the invitation, the process is complete.

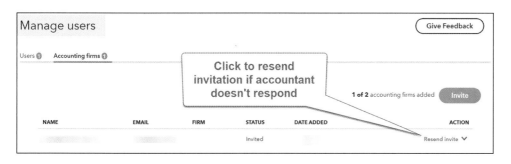

Accountant user setup screen

Users can resend an invitation if necessary. Accountant access can also be deleted by selecting **Delete** in the **ACTION** column dropdown menu.

BEHIND THE SCENES   There are no screens for limiting access and rights for **Accountants**. Accountant users will have administrator rights.

Editing, Monitoring, and Deleting Users

To edit, monitor, or delete a user, open the **Manage Users** screen. (Click the ⚙ icon to access the link.)

Figure S3.15

User Center actions

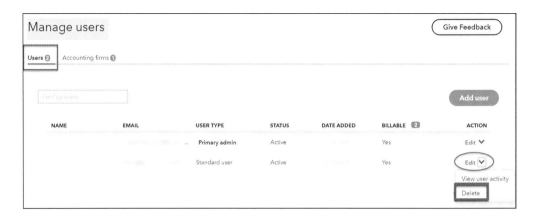

Select **Edit** in the **ACTION** dropdown menu to change access rights for a **user**. Select **Delete** to remove a **user**. The **Primary admin** user cannot be deleted.

Clicking **View user activity** allows the administrator to view all user activity in chronological order. Activity would include logins, transactions added or edited, setting changes, etc. Activity can also be accessed using the reports introduced in the next section (**Reporting on Transaction History**).

Reporting on Transaction History

QBO tracks all significant changes to transactions including the name of the user entering or modifying the transaction. Several reports are available.

The **Audit Log** is accessed by clicking the ⚙ icon in the icon bar and selecting **Audit Log** in the **Tools** column.

Figure S3.16

Audit log

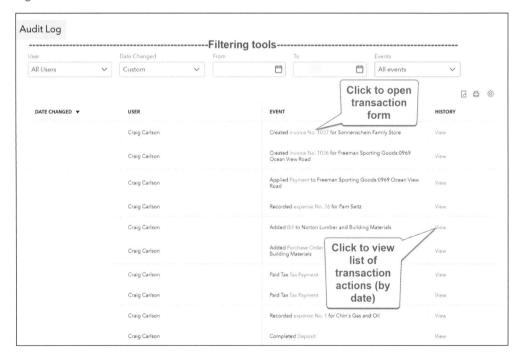

On the main page, transactions are listed in chronological order. Certain information is listed for every transaction (name of user initiating transaction, entry date, amounts, etc.). An initial entry is identified as **Added**. Any revisions are flagged as **Edited**. Links to the changes (to transactions, accounts, or items) are provided in the **Event** column. Further details about each transaction can be obtained by clicking the **View** link.

The **Audit Log** can be filtered by user, date changed, and activity using the dropdown menus at the top of the log.

> **HINT:** The **Audit Log** can be filtered by user, date, and activity type using the **Filter** menus.

If a closing date has been set in a company file, an **Exceptions to Closing Date** report can be created. The report lists only those prior period transactions that were changed after the closing date and includes the name of the user making the change. The **Exceptions to Closing Date** report, if available, is located in the **For My Accountant** section of **Reports**.

Reports, obviously, can't prevent fraud. However, the fact that these reports are available acts as a fraud deterrent because employees know they are identified (by user name) with all transactions they enter (or change).

SECTION OVERVIEW

Chapter 6 will cover the sales cycle in a merchandising company.
Chapter 7 will cover the purchase cycle in a merchandising company.
Chapter 8 will cover end-of-period accounting in a merchandising company.

6

Sales Activity
(Merchandising Company)

Road Map

LO	Learning Objective	Topic	Subtopic	Page	Practice Exercises	Videos
LO 6-1	Explain and demonstrate the process for managing sub-customers and multiple shipping addresses [p. 6-12]	Managing customers	Setting up sub-customers	6-12	6.1	
			Managing multiple shipping addresses	6-13	6.2	
LO 6-2	Describe and use QBO's automated sales tax system [p. 6-15]	Managing sales taxes	Setting up sales taxes	6-15		Setting up sales taxes
			Managing the tax status of customers	6-21		
			Editing sales taxes on sales transactions	6-22		
LO 6-3	Demonstrate an understanding of the purpose and use of product items in QBO [p. 6-27]	Managing products	Adding a product	6-27	6.3	Managing product items
			Editing, duplicating, and inactivating products	6-33		
LO 6-4	Describe and demonstrate the process for recording customer discounts, pending sales transactions, and uncollectible accounts [p. 6-34]	Recording sales revenue	Recording customer discounts	6-34	6.4	Recording sales revenue (customer discounts); Recording sales revenue (pending transactions); Recording uncollectible accounts
			Recording delayed charges and delayed credits	6-38	6.5	
			Recording uncollectible accounts	6-43	6.6	
LO 6-5	Demonstrate an understanding of the process for recording customer credit card payments, early payment discounts taken by customers, and NSF checks [p. 6-47]	Recording payments from customers	Recording customer payments by credit card	6-47	6.7, 6.8	Recording customer payments by credit card; Recording early payment discounts by customers; Recording NSF checks
			Recording early payment discounts taken by customers	6-50	6.9	
			Recording customer checks returned by bank due to insufficient funds	6-53	6.10	
LO 6-6	Recognize and prepare common sales and receivable reports used in merchandising companies [p. 6-56]	Preparing sales and collection reports		6-56	6.11	
LO 6-7	Describe the process for preparing customer statements [p. 6-58]	Preparing customer statements		6-58	6.12	

WHAT IS THE SALES CYCLE IN A MERCHANDISING COMPANY?

- Get orders.
- Fill orders.
- Bill for the products.
- Collect the sales price.

The sales cycle in a merchandising company is similar to that of a service company and many of the accounting functions are the same. There are some differences, though. In this chapter, we'll cover those differences. We'll also cover some more advanced topics that apply to both service and merchandising companies.

MANAGING CUSTOMERS

LO 6-1 Explain and demonstrate the process for managing sub-customers and multiple shipping addresses

The process for setting up and editing customers is covered in Chapter 3. This section covers:

- Setting up sub-customers.
- Entering shipping information for customers.

Entering sales tax information for customers is covered in the Managing Sales Taxes section of this chapter.

Setting Up Sub-Customers

Customers may have multiple locations or subsidiaries and they may want invoices to reflect the specific location or subsidiary being charged.

This can be accommodated by setting up a parent customer first. Separate locations or subsidiaries are set up as sub-customers next. The relationship between the two is identified in the Name and contact section of the sub-customer's record.

Figure 6.1

Sub-customer setup

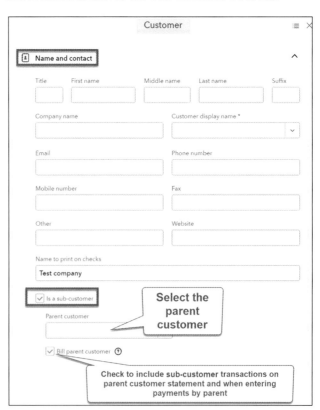

There are two billing options available when setting up **sub-customers** related to future billings.

- If the Bill parent customer box is checked, invoices created for the sub-customer will be included on statements created for the parent customer. In addition, when recording payments received directly from the parent, any outstanding invoices for the sub-customer will appear in the receive payment window.

- If the Bill parent customer box is **not** checked, invoices created for the sub-customer will not be included on statements created for the parent customer. In addition, any outstanding invoices for the sub-customer would not appear in the receive payment window if the payment was received from the parent customer.

Set up a sub-customer for Craig's Design and Landscaping.
(Craig gets a call from the owner of Pye's Cakes. She just opened a new location in California and wants Craig's Design to do some landscaping work in the future. She wants services for the new location billed on separate invoices, but she wants to pay for all services at the same time.)

1. Set up a sub-customer.
   a. Click Sales on the navigation bar.
   b. Open the Customers drawer (tab).
   c. Click New customer.
   d. In the Name and contact section:
      i. Check the box next to Is a sub-customer and check the Bill with parent box.
      ii. Select Pye's Cakes in the Parent customer dropdown menu.
      iii. Enter "West Sac Pye's" in the Customer display name field and "Pye's Cakes" in the Company name and Name to print on checks fields.
   e. Open the Addresses section.
      i. Verify that the billing address shows as 350 Mountain View Dr.
      ii. **Make a note** of the zip code in the Billing address.
   f. Click Save.

PRACTICE
EXERCISE
6.1

Managing Multiple Shipping Addresses

Merchandising companies often ship products to locations with addresses different from the customer's billing address. Billing **and** shipping addresses can be maintained in QBO.

Both addresses are entered in the **Addresses** section of the customer record.

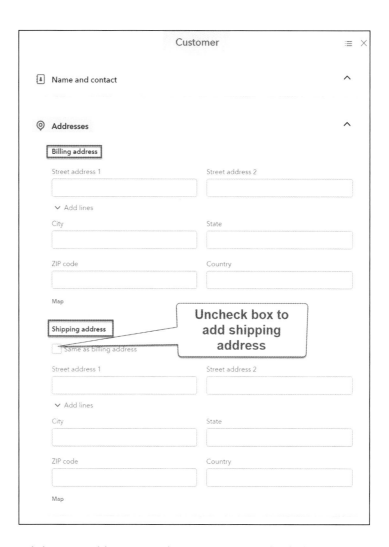

If the billing and shipping addresses are the same, you can check the Same as billing address field in the Shipping address section of the window. (The shipping address fields will be grayed out if Same as billing address is checked.)

Uncheck the Same as billing address field to add a shipping address. The shipping address would then be available on sales transaction forms.

> **BEHIND THE SCENES** In the current version of QBO, a single customer can only have one shipping address. If a customer had multiple shipping addresses, sub-customers could be set up.

PRACTICE
EXERCISE
6.2

Manage shipping addresses for customers of Craig's Design and Landscaping.
(Craig's Design needs to enter a shipping address for Amy's Bird Sanctuary.)

1. Click Sales on the navigation bar.
2. Open the Customers drawer (tab).
3. Click Amy's Bird Sanctuary.
4. Click Edit.

(continued)

(continued from previous page)

5. In the Addresses section, uncheck the Same as billing address box.

6. Enter the shipping address as:

   2580 Bluebird St.

   Bayshore, CA 94326

7. **Make a note** of the street name for Amy's billing address.

8. Click Save.

MANAGING SALES TAXES

Many states levy a tax on purchases of tangible products by consumers (users) of those products. The tax is called a "sales" tax because it is charged to the customer at the point of sale.

Unless a merchandising company is selling to a tax-exempt entity or to a reseller (a company that will, in turn, sell to consumers), the seller is responsible for collecting the tax from their customers and remitting the taxes to the taxing authorities.

The sales tax feature in QBO is highly automated. QBO updates rates and agency information for every sales tax authority as needed and automatically calculates sales taxes on all sales transactions.

Whether or not QBO calculates tax on a **particular** charge depends on the following:

- First, is the customer a consumer, a reseller, or a tax-exempt entity? If the customer is a reseller or tax-exempt entity, no sales tax is added.
  - QBO relies on the tax information included in the Additional info section of the customer record.
- Second, if the customer is a consumer, does the charge represent a sale of a taxable item? If the item is taxable, sales tax is added to the sales transaction.
  - QBO relies on the information included in the product or service item record.

In most states, the **amount** of tax, if any, QBO charges on a taxable item is determined by either the company's address (address where sale was made or where the product was shipped from) or the customer's address (address where taxable goods or services were received).

> **BEHIND THE SCENES** Almost all states (currently 45 of them) impose a tax (either state or local or both) on sales. In most cases, all sales of taxable products or services to non-exempt customers located in the same state as the company are subject to tax. Determining when a company must collect sales taxes on taxable sales to customers in **other** states can be difficult. The basic rule is this: If the company has a **presence** (called economic nexus) in the state (people, property, and/or significant sales), the company must collect sales taxes on sales to non-tax-exempt customers in that state. The actual rules about how many people, how much property, or how much in sales dollars is enough to establish nexus (and which products and services are taxable) vary from state to state. QBO users are responsible for knowing the rules.

LO 6-2 Describe and use QBO's automated sales tax system

Setting Up Sales Taxes

Overall management of sales taxes is done through the Sales Tax Center.

Click Taxes on the navigation bar to get started. In your homework company, the screen will look something like Figure 6.3.

eLecture

Access to sales tax
activation screens

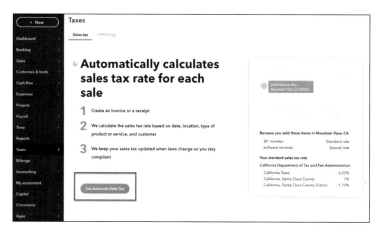

Click **Use Automatic Sales Tax**.

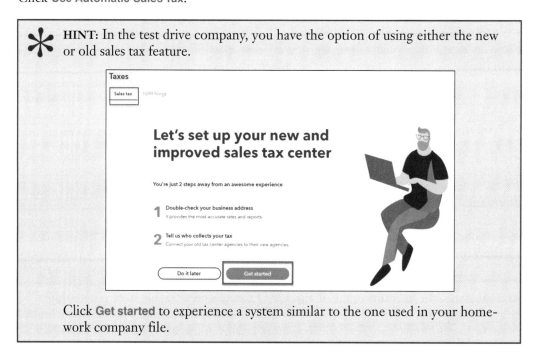

✳ **HINT:** In the test drive company, you have the option of using either the new
or old sales tax feature.

Click **Get started** to experience a system similar to the one used in your homework company file.

Confirmation of
company address
screen

QBO autofills the address information using information from the **Company** tab in **Account and Settings**. Click the **pencil** icon if the information is incorrect.

Click **Next**.

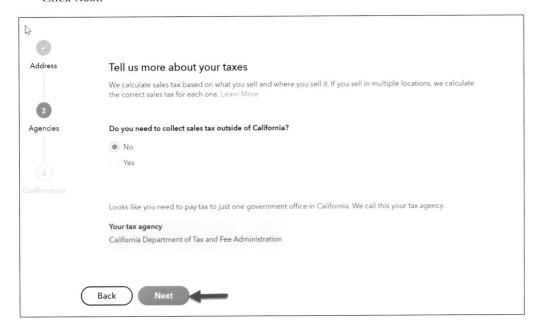

Figure 6.5

Interstate sales
information screen

If **Yes** is selected as the answer to the question about out-of-state sales, the user will be able to select additional tax jurisdictions from a list of tax authorities. QBO updates the list regularly. In this course, you will only be selling in California, so select **No**. QBO will display the name of the appropriate sales tax agency based on the company address.

Click **Next**.

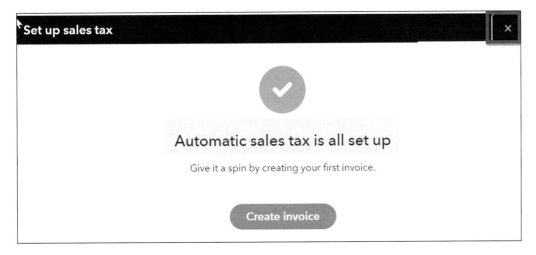

Figure 6.6

Successful sales tax
activation message

Since you are not entering invoices yet, click the small **X** in the top right corner of the window to escape.

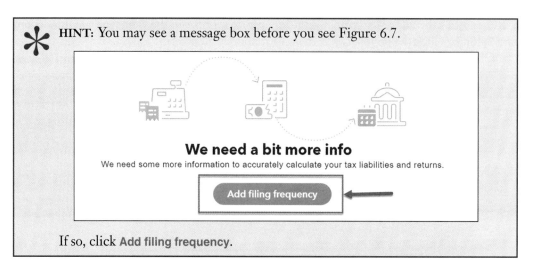

HINT: You may see a message box before you see Figure 6.7.

We need a bit more info

We need some more information to accurately calculate your tax liabilities and returns.

Add filing frequency

If so, click **Add filing frequency**.

The following screen should appear.

Figure 6.7

Filing frequency
options

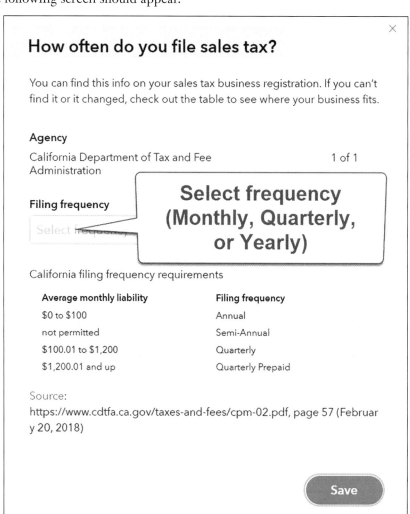

How often do you file sales tax?

You can find this info on your sales tax business registration. If you can't find it or it changed, check out the table to see where your business fits.

Agency

California Department of Tax and Fee Administration   1 of 1

Filing frequency

Select frequency

Select frequency (Monthly, Quarterly, or Yearly)

California filing frequency requirements

Average monthly liability	Filing frequency
$0 to $100	Annual
not permitted	Semi-Annual
$100.01 to $1,200	Quarterly
$1,200.01 and up	Quarterly Prepaid

Source:
https://www.cdtfa.ca.gov/taxes-and-fees/cpm-02.pdf, page 57 (February 20, 2018)

Save

Select **Monthly**.

BEHIND THE SCENES Filing frequencies are set by the state. They are normally based either on the average tax amounts collected or the average sales revenues.

Figure 6.8

Assignment of default start month for sales tax collection

QBO automatically assigns January as the start date for sales tax collection. That date can be changed later. Click **Save** to move to the Sales Tax Center.

Figure 6.9

Access to sales tax settings

Depending on the date on which you are setting up sales taxes, the next screen may show a number of overdue filings! To correct this, QBO must be updated with the actual start date (the date the company began selling taxable items).

> **BEHIND THE SCENES** Clicking **Economic Nexus** on the screen displayed in Figure 6.9 opens a tool for determining whether a company meets any of the criteria for economic nexus in a particular state. If met, companies can use QBO to file taxes in those states.

Click **Sales Tax Settings**.

Figure 6.10

Edit sales tax settings screen

> **HINT:** Once activated, the sales tax feature can't be turned off in QBO. It can, however, be inactivated. Tax amounts are no longer calculated if sales tax is inactivated.

Click **Edit**.

Figure 6.11

Sales tax filing information screen

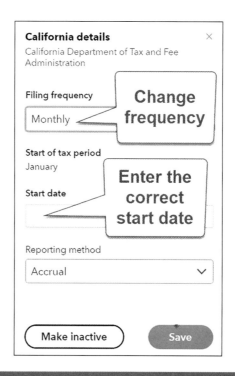

> **WARNING:** It's important to enter the correct starting date. QBO will not calculate tax on a sales form dated prior to the date entered here.

Enter the correct date in the sidebar and click **Save**. The correct date for your homework company will be given to you in your assignment.

> **BEHIND THE SCENES** QBO automatically sets up separate liability accounts (**Other current liability account type**) for all taxing authorities. When sales taxes are paid, QBO automatically debits the appropriate liability account. These accounts cannot be deleted.

Managing the Tax Status of Customers

When sales tax is activated in a company file, QBO will assume all new and existing customers are taxable.

Depending on state laws, QBO will either use the company location or the customer location in determining the appropriate tax rate. The shipping address entered in the customer record is considered the customer's physical location. If no shipping address is entered, QBO will use the billing address. If no address is entered in the customer record, QBO will use the company's physical address (the rate that would be charged on in-store sales). If necessary, a different sales location can be entered on sales transaction forms.

For nontaxable customers (for example resellers of products) the tax status must be set as tax exempt in the customer record.

Click **Sales** on the navigation bar and open the **Customers drawer** (tab).

Figure 6.12

Link to new customer setup

Click **New customer**.

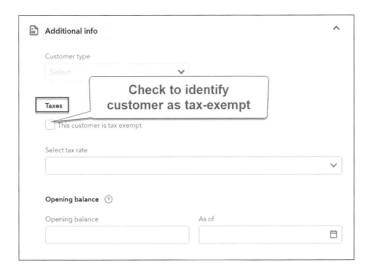

Figure 6.13

Tax status on customer record

Open the **Additional info** section. The default for new customers in QBO is taxable.

 HINT: For taxable customers, the tax rate used on sales transactions will automatically default to the rate in effect in the location of the sale. The **Location of sale** is identified on sales transaction forms and would normally be the company's retail or "ship from" address or the customer's "ship to" address.

To identify a customer as tax-exempt, check the This customer is tax exempt box in the Additional info section.

Figure 6.14

Tax exempt status
options

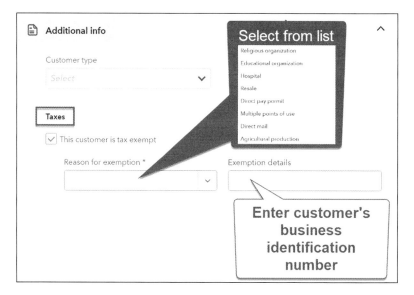

A reason for the tax exemption must be selected in the Reason for exemption dropdown menu. (A partial list is shown in Figure 6.14.) The customer's taxpayer identification number is entered in the Exemption details field.

> **BEHIND THE SCENES** Individual states set the rules for taxability of organizations and taxability of transactions with those organizations. Users would need to know those state rules in order to select an appropriate reason for not collecting sales tax.

Since the sales tax feature in the test drive company is not the same as the sales tax feature in your homework company, there is no Practice Exercise for this section.

Editing Sales Taxes on Sales Transactions

There may be times when sales tax amounts need to be changed on a specific sales transaction. For example, this might occur if:

- a customer that usually purchases products for resale purchases a product for internal use

- a customer that usually purchases products for internal use occasionally purchases products for resale

- the tax status of a product or service item is incorrect

- the tax location needs to be changed

- a tax rate is incorrect

Certain changes can be made directly on the sales form.

- The tax status of a product or service item can be changed in the TAX column by checking or unchecking the box.

- A new location can be entered in the Location of sale field.

All changes can be made by clicking Edit tax in the lower right corner of the form (Figure 6.15) to open a sidebar.

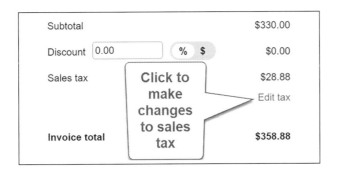

Figure 6.15

Access to sidebar for making sales tax changes

Editing Sales Taxes on Transactions with Taxable Customers

If the customer tax status was set as taxable in the customer record, the sidebar would look like Figure 6.16.

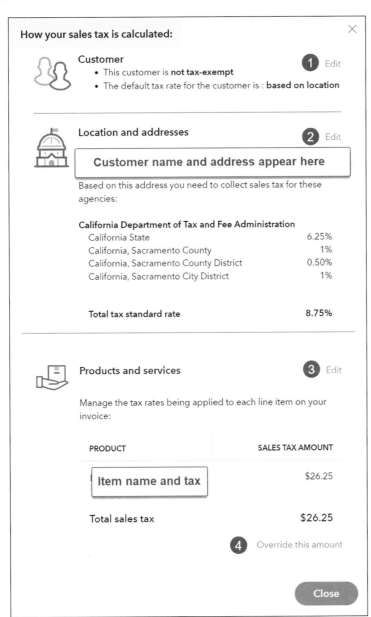

Figure 6.16

Sidebar for taxable customer

There are four ways to edit the sales tax amount on the sidebar.

To change the customer's tax status to tax-exempt, click Edit in the top section (❶ in Figure 6.16).

Figure 6.17

Option for editing
customer tax status

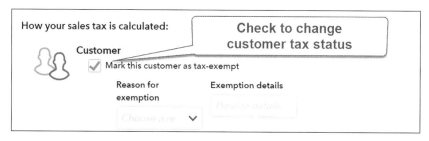

Check the Mark this customer as tax-exempt, enter Exemption details (business identification number), and select Reason for exemption. Changing the tax status here will change the customer record.

If a tax rate is incorrect because the product was shipped to or from a different location, click Edit in the Location and addresses section (❷ in Figure 6.16).

Figure 6.18

Options for changing
address for tax
calculation

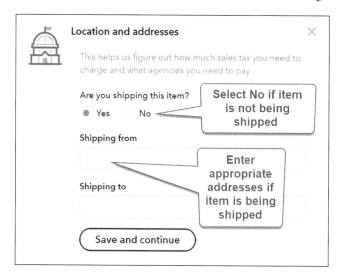

The Shipping from or Shipping to fields can be changed. If the item is not being shipped, a field for identifying where the location was sold would appear.

If the tax status of the service or product item sold is incorrect, click Edit in the Products and services section (❸ in Figure 6.16).

Figure 6.19

Link to change service
or product tax status

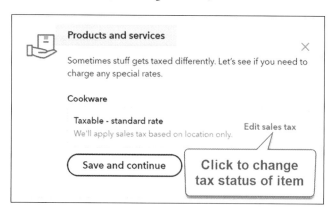

Click Edit sales tax.

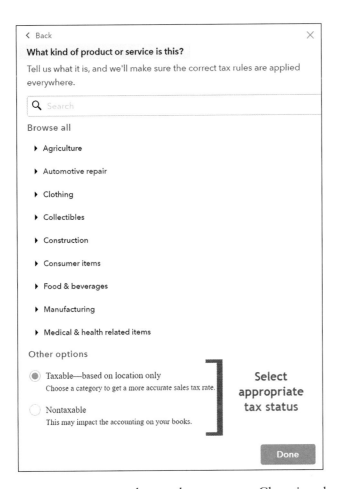

Figure 6.20

Options for changing
tax status of product or
service

Toggle **Taxable** or **Nontaxable** to change the tax status. Changing the tax status here will change the item record.

 HINT: When you change the tax status from **Taxable—Standard Rate** to **Non-taxable**, you **may** still see **Taxable—Standard Rate** displayed in the **Sales tax** field on the item record. As long as there is no checkmark in the **TAXABLE** column on the **Products and Services** list, QBO will not include sales tax on a sales transaction.

If the calculated tax amount is incorrect, click **Override this amount** in the **Products and services** section (❹ in Figure 6.16).

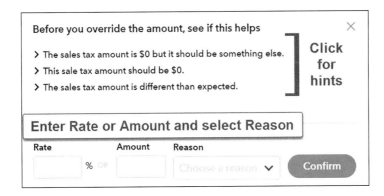

Figure 6.21

Options for changing
tax rate or amount
on specific sales
transaction

Enter either a new rate or a flat dollar amount, and select the **Reason** for the tax change.

Editing Sales Taxes on Transactions with Tax-exempt Customers

If sales taxes need to be charged on a transaction with a customer that has been identified as tax-exempt in the customer record, click **Edit tax** in the bottom right corner of the sales form screen (Figure 6.15) to open the sidebar.

Figure 6.22

Sidebar for tax-exempt customer

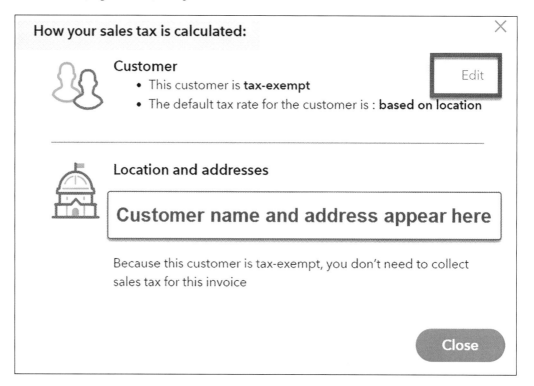

Click **Edit** in the **Customer** section.

Figure 6.23

Option to remove tax-exempt status

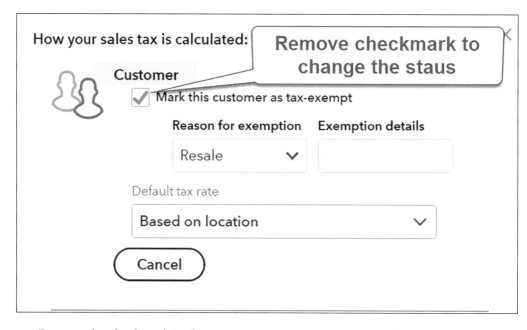

Remove the checkmark in the **Mark this customer as tax-exempt** box.

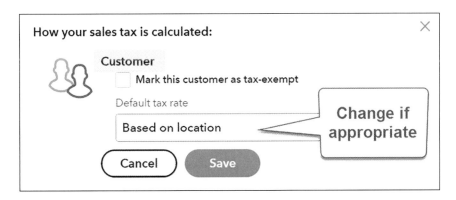

Figure 6.24
Final step to change tax-exempt status.

Click **Save**. The sidebar will expand to allow you to include the options shown in Figure 6.16.

Changing the tax status of a customer on a sales transaction changes the customer record. If the change is temporary, the customer record would need to be edited after the transaction is saved.

MANAGING PRODUCTS (MERCHANDISING COMPANY)

The single biggest difference between service and merchandising companies is, of course, inventory. There are several systems used by merchandising companies to track inventory (**periodic** and **perpetual**) and a number of acceptable methods used to value inventory (**FIFO, LIFO,** etc.).

Merchandising companies can use QBO whether they choose to use periodic or perpetual inventory systems. However, the program is most effectively used as a perpetual tracking system. QBO values inventory using the FIFO method.

A company will need to set up an item for each and every product that it sells. There are two **item types** that can be used for inventory:

- Inventory
  - Used for products that a company sells, maintains in inventory, **and** tracks using a perpetual inventory system.

- Non-inventory
  - Used for products that a company sells, maintains in inventory, but doesn't track.
    - Generally insignificant items.
    - More frequently used by manufacturing companies.
  - Used for products that a company purchases to order and doesn't maintain in inventory.
  - Used in a periodic tracking system.

> **BEHIND THE SCENES** There is a third **product/service type** called **Bundle** in QBO. **Bundles** are used when a company sells multiple products or services as a package. **Service, inventory,** and **non-inventory** items can be included in a **bundle.** You will not be working with **bundles** in this course.

LO 6-3 Demonstrate an understanding of the purpose and use of product items in QBO

Periodic inventory A system in which cost of goods sold is determined and recorded when a physical count of inventory is taken.

Perpetual inventory A system in which cost of goods sold is determined and recorded when products are sold.

First-in, first-out (FIFO) method An inventory costing method that assumes that the oldest (earliest purchased) goods are sold first.

Last-in, first-out (LIFO) method An inventory costing method that assumes that the newest (most recently purchased) goods are sold first.

Adding a Product

The process for setting up **products** is similar to the process for setting up **services**. Click the ⚙ on the icon bar.

Link to Products and
Services Center

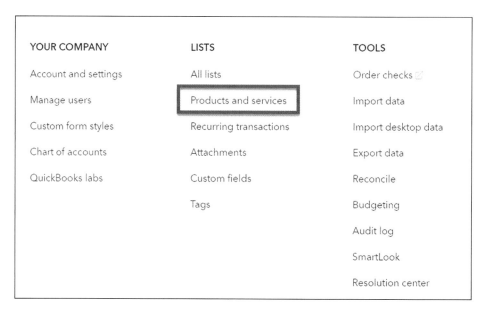

Click **Products and services**.

Link to set up new item

Click **New** to add a **product**.

New item sidebar

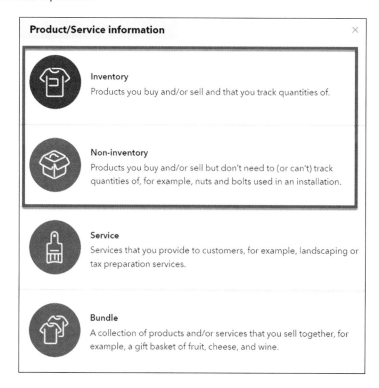

Select the type of product (**inventory** or **non-inventory**).

Setting Up Non-inventory Items

Click **Non-inventory** to set up a product that will not be tracked in QBO's perpetual inventory tracking system.

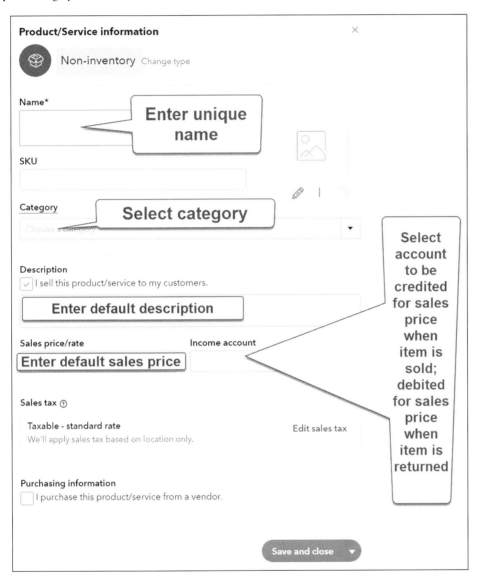

Figure 6.28

Non-inventory setup screen

A **name** must be assigned. Items can be identified using names or numbers. SKUs (identifier codes) are optional.

Users can elect to attach **products** to a **category**. (See Chapter 2 for help with **categories**.)

If the **product** is sold to customers (the most likely scenario in service and merchandising companies), additional information is needed.

A check in the box next to **I sell this product/service to my customers** opens the necessary additional fields for entering:

- A description of the item to appear on sales forms

- A default sales price/rate

- The general ledger revenue account to be credited in a sales transaction (debited if a credit memo is issued)

All **non-inventory** products are set as taxable by default.

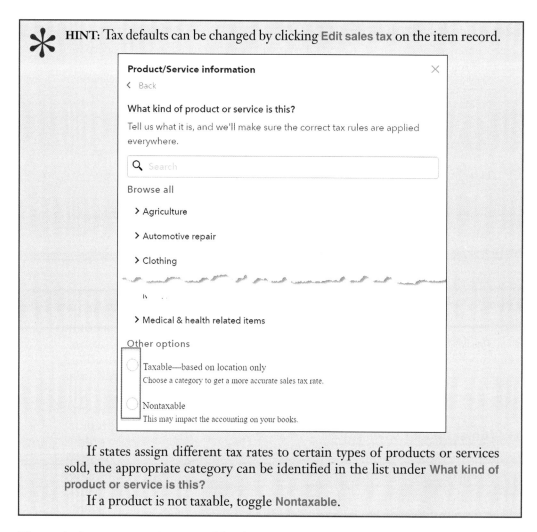

HINT: Tax defaults can be changed by clicking Edit sales tax on the item record.

If states assign different tax rates to certain types of products or services sold, the appropriate category can be identified in the list under What kind of product or service is this?

If a product is not taxable, toggle Nontaxable.

If a particular **customer** is nontaxable, the customer tax status will automatically override the product tax status when an invoice or sales receipt is created. You can also manually override the default item tax status, if needed, when preparing invoices or sales receipts.

In most merchandising companies, non-inventory items are purchased from vendors.

Check the box next to I purchase this product/service from a vendor to display additional fields related to purchase transactions.

Figure 6.29

Purchase information section of non-inventory item record

A default cost and description can be entered when the item is set up. The amount in the Cost field will automatically appear when a product is added to a purchase transaction. The actual cost, if different, would be entered before saving the transaction.

The account selected in the **Expense account** field will be debited for the purchase price when **non-inventory** items are purchased (and credited if items are returned).

> **BEHIND THE SCENES** Companies using a periodic inventory system would most likely select an account with a **cost of goods sold account type** in the **Expense account** field especially if the items are purchased to order (for specific customers). The company could also select an inventory account or, if **non-inventory item** costs are insignificant, might record the purchases in a parts expense account.

A **preferred vendor** can also be entered in the item record. The benefit of entering a **preferred vendor** will be covered in Chapter 7.

Setting Up Inventory Items

Inventory items (products tracked in QBO's perpetual inventory system) are set up by clicking **New** in the **Products and Services** list and selecting **Inventory** as the type.

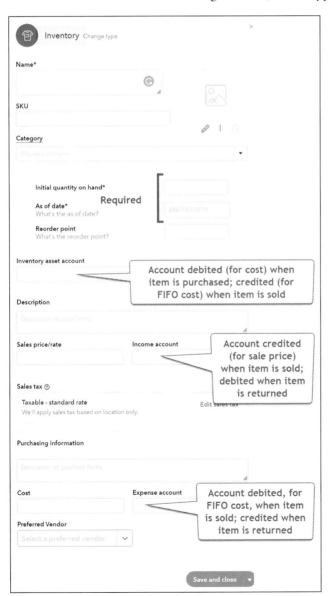

Figure 6.30

Inventory item setup screen

The **inventory** item name is entered in the top section along with the **category** (if used). Important, required information is included in the next section.

- **Initial quantity on hand**, required
  - When setting up a **new** **inventory** item, the **initial quantity on hand must** be set at 0. Inventory purchases are then recorded through **bills**, **checks**, or **expenses**.

> **WARNING:** If you do not set the starting quantity at 0, QBO will debit the inventory account for an amount equal to the quantity entered times the default cost listed.

- **As of date**, required
  - When setting up a new **inventory** item, the **as of date** represents the first date the item would be available for sale.

> **BEHIND THE SCENES** When a company is converted to QBO from the desktop version or when inventory data is imported into QBO, the **as of date** would be the conversion date. The **initial quantity on hand** would represent the amount of inventory on hand as of the conversion date.

- **Inventory asset account**
  - The account selected here will be debited, for cost, when **inventory** items are purchased or when a customer return is recorded. The account will be credited, for FIFO cost, when **inventory** items are sold or when the company returns an item to the vendor. The account selected would be an asset account (**current asset account type**) because **inventory** items are tracked using a perpetual tracking system in QBO.

You can also set a reorder point for **inventory** items. A reorder point indicates the lowest level of inventory the company wants to have on hand at any point in time. Reorder points will be discussed further in Chapter 7.

The next three fields include information used in recording sales transactions.

- The standard (default) description to appear on sales forms is entered in the **Description** field.

- The standard price charged for the item is entered in the **Sales price/rate** field.

- The **revenue** account to be credited when the item is sold (or debited if the customer returns the item) is selected in the **Income account** field.

All **inventory** products are set as taxable by default. For information about changing the tax status, see the **HINT** box in the *Setting Up Non-inventory Items* section of this chapter.

The **Purchasing information** section is identical to the purchasing section for **non-inventory** items. The description used in purchase transactions and the default **cost** is entered. The **Expense account** selected here, however, will be debited for the FIFO cost of the **inventory** item when it's sold, not when it's purchased. (The account selected would be credited if a customer return is recorded.) The **Expense account** selected for **inventory** items would normally have a **cost of goods sold account type**.

> **BEHIND THE SCENES** Most merchandising companies prepare multi-step income statements. QBO reports all **cost of goods sold** accounts directly below **income** accounts on the **profit and loss** report and appropriately includes a **gross profit** subtotal so the **account type** is important.
>
> QBO creates the following journal entry when an **inventory** item is purchased:
>   Inventory (using the account specified in the **Inventory asset account** field)
>   Accounts payable (or cash)
>
> QBO creates the following journal entry when an **inventory** item is sold:
>   Accounts Receivable (or Undeposited Funds if cash sale)
>   Cost of goods sold (using the account specified in the **Expense account** field)
>   Revenue (using the account specified in the **Income account** field)
>   Inventory (using the account specified in the **Inventory asset account** field)
>   Sales tax payable (if sale was subject to sales tax)
>
> QBO uses FIFO as the inventory valuation method. The debit to Cost of Goods sold and the credit to Inventory in an **inventory** item sales transaction are at the FIFO cost, not the purchase or default cost.

A **preferred vendor** can also be entered in the inventory item record. The benefit of entering a **preferred vendor** will be covered in Chapter 7.

Editing, Duplicating, and Inactivating Products

Like **service** items, most of the fields in **Inventory** and **non-inventory product** records can be edited. The process for editing names, categories, descriptions, default rates, and general ledger accounts (and for duplicating and inactivating items) is covered in detail in the **Editing, Duplicating, and Inactivating Services** section of Chapter 3.

The **As of date** and **Initial quantity on hand** fields in **inventory** item records cannot be edited. (Those fields disappear once the item is saved.) Although there is a **Quantity on hand** field in existing **inventory** item records that can be edited, inventory adjustments are best handled through the inventory adjustment process in QBO. That process is covered in Chapter 8.

> **HINT:** Once an **inventory product** is set up, its **item type** cannot be changed. If you inadvertently set up an inventory item with a **service** or **non-inventory item type**, you'll need to inactivate that item and create a new record. **Service** and **non-inventory item types** can be changed at will.

Add a new inventory item for Craig's Design and Landscaping.
(Craig's Design has decided to sell small planter boxes. It expects to purchase the items from Glorious Growers for $30 and sell them for $75. The company will be selling the product to consumers.)

1. Click the ⚙ on the icon bar.

2. Click **Products and Services**.

**PRACTICE
EXERCISE
6.3**

(continued)

(continued from previous page)

3. Click **New**.

4. Click **Inventory**.

5. Enter "Small planter box" as item **name**.

6. Select **+ Add new** in the **Category** dropdown menu.

7. Enter "Garden products" as the **category name**.

8. Click **Save**.

9. Enter "0" as the **Initial quantity on hand** and the current date as the **As of Date**.

10. Select **Inventory Asset** as the **inventory asset account**.

11. Enter "Small planter box" in the **Description** field.

12. Enter "75" as **Sales price/rate**.

13. Select **Sales of Product Income** as the **income account**.

14. Select **Taxable—standard rate** in the **Sales tax category** field.

15. Enter "Small planter box" in the **Purchasing information** field.

16. Enter "30" as the **cost**.

17. Select **Cost of Goods Sold** as the **Expense account**.

18. **Make a note** of the profit Craig's Design will make on each small planter box it sells, assuming the cost and sales price remain unchanged. **TIP:** You'll need to make a calculation to determine the profit.

19. Click **Save and close**.

RECORDING SALES REVENUE

LO 6-4 Describe and demonstrate the process for recording customer discounts, pending sales transactions, and uncollectible accounts

Merchandising companies, like service companies, make cash and credit sales. Recording **invoices** and **sales receipts** is covered in Chapter 3. In this chapter, we're going to cover:

- Customer discounts
- Delayed charges and credits
- Uncollectible accounts

None of the above are unique to merchandising companies. The processes outlined below would be used in service companies as well.

Recording Customer Discounts

Companies often give discounts to customers. They might include:

- Price breaks for large orders
- Discounts for nonprofits, senior citizens, students

Customer-specific discounts can be entered directly on sales forms (**Invoices** and **sales receipts**) if the **Discount** feature is activated.

Activating Sales Discounts

Activating sales discounts is a two-step process. You have to turn on the feature and then identify what account to use to capture the discount.

To activate **discounts**, click the ⚙ on the icon bar and click **Account and Settings**.

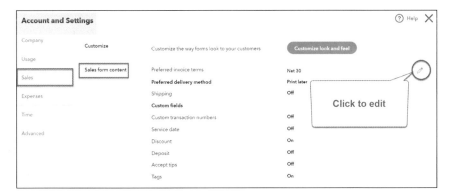

Figure 6.31

Access to edit sales
form content features

On the **Sales** tab, click the **pencil** icon in the **Sales form content** section.

Figure 6.32

Discount activation box

Use the toggle button next to **Discount** to turn the feature on and click **Save**. A discount field will now be available on all sales forms.

Users must then identify the account to be debited for the amount of the discount. This is done on the **Advanced** tab of **Account and Settings**.

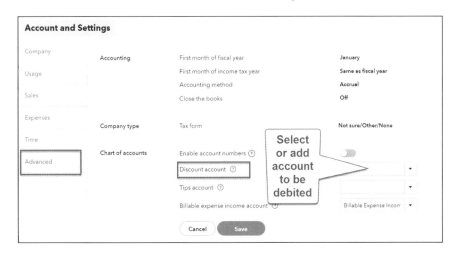

Figure 6.33

Selection of account
for recording customer
discounts

Click the **pencil** icon in the **Chart of accounts** section and change the **Discount account** as needed. (QBO uses a default account (**Discounts given**) in the test drive company.)

> **BEHIND THE SCENES** Sales discounts are normally reported as contra revenue accounts. For proper reporting, the account linked to **Discounts** should have an **Income account type.**

Recording Sales Discounts

> ✳ **HINT:** The instructions below use an **invoice** form as an example. The process would be the same for **sales receipts.** However, the wording and field placement will be slightly different if the **sales receipt** form has not been updated by the time you're taking this course. See the HINT box on page 6-37.

To include a discount on an **invoice**, click ⊕ **New** on the navigation bar and select **Invoice.**

Either a discount percent or amount can be given to a customer. Use the dropdown menu in the lower right section of the form to make the selection. In Figure 6.34, a customer was given a 10% discount on the purchase of taxable products. The discount is always calculated on the **Subtotal** amount ($200 in Figure 6.34) so the discount is 10% of $200 ($20).

Figure 6.34

Example of tax calculated on total before discount

Subtotal		$200.00
Sales tax	$200 X 8.75%	$17.50
Click % or $		Edit tax
Discount 10.00%	% $	-$20.00
Enter amount		
Invoice total		**$197.50**

By default, taxes are calculated on the **Subtotal**, the amount before any discount.

If the discount should be applied **before** tax is calculated, click **Manage** at the top of the **invoice** form (Figure 3.30) to open the customization panel.

Figure 6.35

Tax calculation option

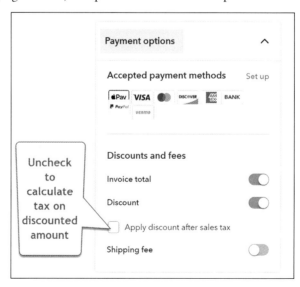

In the **Payment options** section, uncheck the box next to **Apply discount after sales tax.**

Figure 6.36

Example of tax calculated on total after discount.

The discount amount is now subtracted before sales tax is applied.

 HINT: A change in the tax calculation order on an invoice becomes the default order on future invoices. Previously saved invoices will not be affected.

 HINT: If the **sales receipt** form has not been updated, the **discount** fields will look like this:

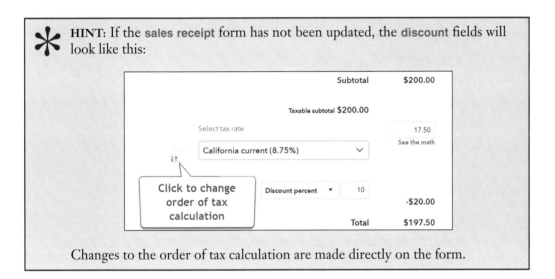

Changes to the order of tax calculation are made directly on the form.

Set up and give sales discounts in Craig's Design and Landscaping.
(Craig's Design has decided to give 10% sales discount on pumps sold to Dukes Basketball Camp.)
NOTE: For this practice exercise, you must use the old sales tax system. If you have activated the newer automated sales tax feature, log out and then log back in.

1. Activate sales discounts. (The feature should already be activated in your test drive company. Go through Steps 1*a* to 1*g* to make sure.)

   a. Click the ⚙ on the icon bar.

   b. Click **Account and Settings**.

   c. Open the **Sales** tab.

   d. Click the **pencil** icon in the **Sales form content** section.

   e. **Make a note** of the features included in the **Sales form content** section that have been activated (toggled on).

   f. Toggle the button next to **Discount** to activate the feature, if necessary.

   g. Click **Save**.

**PRACTICE
EXERCISE
6.4**

(continued)

(continued from previous page)

  2. Link the discount to a general ledger account.
     a. Click the **Advanced** tab. (You should still be in the **Account and Settings** screen.)
     b. Click the **pencil** icon in the **Chart of accounts** section.
     c. Open the **Discount account** dropdown menu.
     d. Select **+ Add new**.
     e. Select **Income** as the **account type** (**Save account under** field) and **Discounts/Refunds Given** as the **detail type** (**Tax form section** field).
     f. Use "Sales Discounts" as the **Name**.
     g. Click **Save and close**.
     h. Click **Save**.
     i. Click **Done**.

  3. Create an invoice for Dukes Basketball Camp (40 pumps with a 10% discount applied before tax).
     a. Click **+ New** on the navigation bar.
     b. Click **Invoice**.
     c. Select **Dukes Basketball Camp** as the customer.
     d. Select **Net 30** as the **Terms** and enter the current date as the **Invoice date**.
     e. Select **Pump** as the **PRODUCT/SERVICE** and enter "40" as the **QTY**.
     f. Leave the rate at 15.
     g. Enter "10" in the **Discount percent** field. **TIP:** The discount amount should automatically appear above the tax amount.
     h. **Make a note** of the balance due.
     i. **Make a note** of what the balance due would be if the discount was applied after tax.
        i. If the test drive company has been updated with the new **invoice** form, check the box next to **Apply discount after tax** in the **Payment options** section of the customization side panel (Figure 6.35).
        ii. If the test drive company has not been updated, the order is changed by clicking the arrows to the left of the discount field as shown in the HINT box directly above this Practice Exercise.
     j. Click **Save and close**.

Recording Delayed Charges and Delayed Credits

There are times when a company wants to be able to track a sales transaction that is in process but not yet completed. Here are two examples:

- A customer places an order for some products to be shipped or picked up later.

- A customer requests a credit for damaged or unwanted merchandise but the merchandise has not yet been returned.

Neither of these is an accounting transaction because the accounting equation hasn't changed yet. The customer order won't be an accounting transaction until the product is shipped or delivered. The customer credit won't be an accounting transaction until the company actually receives the damaged merchandise.

The company could, of course, track pending transactions outside of their accounting system but it's most efficient to be able to have information available in the system.

Delayed charges (for pending sales) and delayed credits (for pending customer returns or allowances) are options available in QBO for tracking these types of transactions. Both of these are non-posting transactions. A non-posting transaction does not create a journal entry and with pending transactions, we don't want a journal entry. The information is available in the system but account balances are not affected.

Delayed charge or delayed credit forms are accessed by clicking ⊕ New on the navigation bar.

CUSTOMERS	VENDORS	EMPLOYEES	OTHER
Invoice	Expense	Single time activity	Bank deposit
Receive payment	Check	Weekly timesheet	Transfer
Estimate	Bill		Journal entry
Credit memo	Pay bills		Statement
Sales receipt	Purchase order		Inventory qty adjustment
Refund receipt	Vendor credit		Pay down credit card
Delayed credit	Credit card credit		
Delayed charge	Print checks		

Figure 6.37

Access to delayed credit and delayed charge forms

Recording and Processing Delayed Charges

> **WARNING:** In early 2023, Intuit started updating various QBO forms. Some of those forms may have been updated after your textbook was printed. The instructions for **delayed charges** and **delayed credits** are for the original format. If your forms don't look the same, start by looking for an option to return to a previous version. In most cases, you'll see a link to **Old layout** or **Switch to classic view**. If there is no link, check the Student Ancillaries page in myBusinessCourse for information about the updated forms or ask your instructor.

When a customer places an order that will not be fulfilled immediately, a delayed charge can be created. A delayed charge might look something like Figure 6.38.

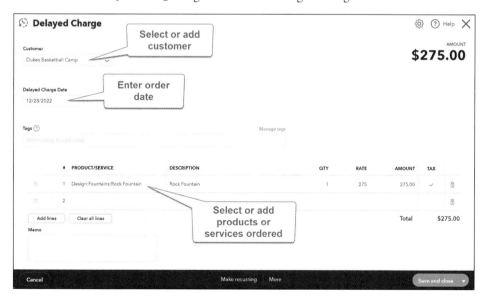

Figure 6.38

Delayed charge forms

Remember, a **delayed charge** does not create a journal entry so it does not affect account balances. A **delayed charge** would show up as a transaction in the customer record but it would not be included in the customer balance. For example, Figure 6.39 shows the account balance for a customer with a **delayed charge**.

Figure 6.39

Example of customer balance with delayed charge

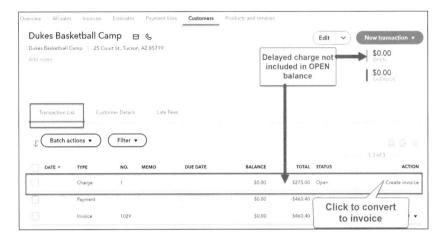

> **BEHIND THE SCENES** Sales tax and sales discount fields are not available on **delayed charge** forms although estimated taxes, if any, are included in the delayed charge balance showing in the customer record. Both fields are available when the **delayed charge** is converted to an **invoice**.

When the product is shipped or the work completed, the user clicks **Create invoice** to convert the **delayed charge** into an **invoice**.

Recording and Processing Delayed Credits

A **delayed credit** is created if a user wants to track a credit that will be available to a customer at some future date. For example, if a company promised a customer $75 off if the customer provided two referrals within a two-week period, that could be set up as a **delayed credit**. If and when the customer provided the referrals, the credit would be applied to the customer's account.

A **delayed credit** might look something like Figure 6.40.

Figure 6.40

Delayed credit form

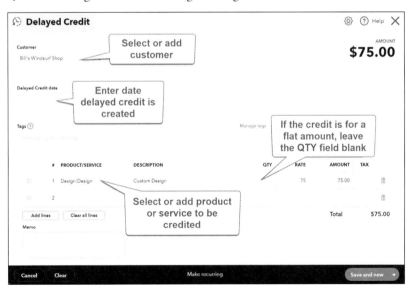

HINT: Leave the **QTY** field blank if the credit is for a set amount.

Delayed credits, like **delayed charges**, are **non-posting** transactions so account balances are not affected. The balance of a customer with a **delayed credit** would look something like Figure 6.41.

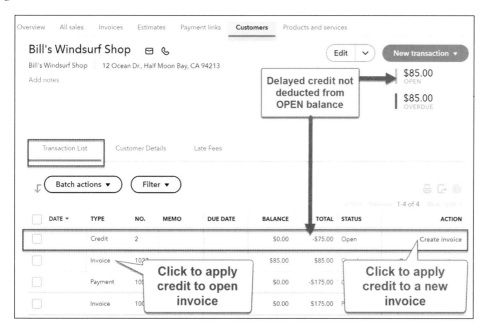

Figure 6.41

Example of customer balance with delayed credit

When the event that triggered the credit is completed, the **delayed credit** would be applied to a new or an open **invoice** by the user.

If a **delayed credit** is being applied to an open **invoice**, the unpaid **invoice** form is opened. To display the **delayed credit**, the small < icon in the top right corner of the **invoice** is clicked to open the sidebar. (The < changes to > when the sidebar is open.)

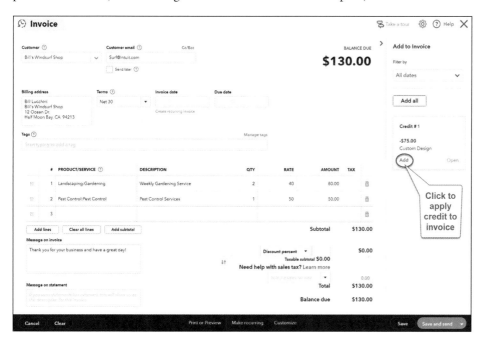

Figure 6.42

Application of delayed credit to invoice

Clicking **Add** applies the credit to the **invoice**. After application, the **invoice** would look something like Figure 6.43.

Figure 6.43

Invoice with delayed credit added

Managing Non-posting Transactions

Non-posting transactions like **delayed credits** and **delayed charges** can be deleted by opening the form, clicking **More** at the bottom of the screen, and selecting **Delete**.

For a list of all **delayed credit** and **delayed charge** transactions, click **Reports** on the navigation bar.

Select **Transaction List by Date** in the **For My Accountant** section.

Open the **Filter** section on the **Customize** sidebar.

Put a checkmark by **Transaction Type** and select **non-posting**.

Click **Run report**.

PRACTICE

EXERCISE

6.5

Set up a delayed charge for Craig's Design and Landscaping.

(Craig's Design has agreed to a fee of $420 for some gardening work to be done next month and wants to get the invoice set up in QBO. The work will be invoiced when the work is performed.)

1. Create the **delayed charge**.

   a. Click **+ New** on the navigation bar.

   b. Click **Delayed Charge**.

   c. Click **Wedding Planning by Whitney** as the **Customer**.

   d. Enter the current date as the **Delayed Charge Date**.

   e. Select **Trimming** as the **PRODUCT/SERVICE**.

(continued)

(continued from previous page)

    f.   Enter "12" as the QTY.

    g.   **Make a note** of the Total amount.

    h.   Click Save and close.

2. Create the invoice from the delayed charge.

    a.   Click Sales on the navigation bar.

    b.   Open the Customers drawer (tab).

    c.   In the dropdown menu in the ACTION column for Wedding Planning by Whitney, click Create Invoice.

    d.   Click Add in the Charge box in the sidebar.

    e.   Leave the terms as Net 30.

    f.   Enter the 1st day of next month as the Invoice date.

    g.   Click Save and close.

Recording Uncollectible Accounts

Unfortunately, companies don't always collect the balances owed to them by their customers. Merchandisers will often try to get the product back when the customer defaults, but, depending on the type and value of the products sold, that may not be feasible or even possible.

    If the company has exhausted all reasonable collection methods, the invoice must be written off. Deleting or voiding the invoice in QBO would not be good accounting. The company did make the sale and should show the revenue. They should also report that uncollectible sales (recorded as **bad debt expenses**) are a real cost of selling on credit.

    There are two methods for accounting for uncollectible accounts: the **allowance method** and the **direct write-off method**. Only the allowance method is acceptable under generally accepted accounting principles.

Bad debt expense The expense stemming from the inability of a business to collect an amount previously recorded as receivable. It is normally classified as a selling or administrative expense.

Allowance method An accounting procedure whereby the amount of bad debts expense is estimated and recorded in the period in which the related credit sales occur.

Allowance Method Refresher

Under the allowance method, an estimate of the amount of uncollectible receivables is made at the end of an accounting period. The initial entry to establish an allowance for those amounts is:

Direct write-off method An accounting procedure whereby the amount of bad debts expense is not recorded until specific uncollectible customer accounts are identified.

	Bad debt expense		
	Allowance for bad debts		

> **BEHIND THE SCENES** The allowance account is a contra asset account (contra to accounts receivable). Accounts receivable net of the allowance is referred to as the net realizable value of receivables (amount that the company actually expects to collect or "realize").

When a **specific** customer account is determined to be uncollectible, the account is written off. The entry is:

	Allowance for bad debts		
	Accounts receivable		

If a previously written off amount is subsequently received, the entry is:

	Cash		
	Allowance for bad debts		

At the end of each accounting period, the allowance account is adjusted to reflect the amount that is currently considered uncollectible. For example, if the end-of-period balance in the allowance account is estimated to be too low, the entry is:

	Bad debt expense		
	Allowance for bad debts		

Direct Write-off Method Refresher

Companies that historically do not have many uncollectible accounts often use the direct write-off method. Under this method, bad debt expense is only recognized when a specific customer account is determined to be uncollectible. This method violates generally accepted accounting principles but is often used when the amount of bad debts is insignificant.

The entry is:

	Bad debt expense		
	Accounts receivable		

QuickCheck
6-1

> Which accounting principle is violated under the direct write-off method?

Recording Bad Debts

Either the allowance or the direct write-off method can be used in QBO.

> ✳ **HINT:** There are several ways uncollectible accounts can be written off in QBO. The method described below uses **service** items to record write-offs and recoveries. Using **service** items allows users to easily apply write-offs to specific invoices. Journal entries can also be used.

If the allowance method is used, the entry to set up or adjust the allowance account should be made as a general journal entry (**Journal entry transaction type**). See Chapter 5 if you need help with making adjusting journal entries.

The actual write-off of an invoice (under either the allowance or direct write-off method) can be done by creating a **credit memo** recognizing the bad debt and then applying the **credit memo** to the uncollectible **invoice**.

The first step is to set up the necessary general ledger accounts. Under either method, a Bad Debt Expense account is necessary. Under the allowance method, an Allowance for Bad Debts account is also necessary. Remember, the Allowance account is a contra asset account.

- For the bad debt expense account, the **account type** (**Save account under** field) would be **Expenses**, and the **detail type** would be **Bad Debts** (**Tax form section** field).

- For the Allowance account, the **account type** (**Save account under** field) would be **Other Current Assets**, and the **detail type** would be **Allowance for Bad Debts** (**Tax form section** field).

The second step is to set up a new **service** item.

The item might be set up something like Figure 6.44 if the company uses the direct write-off method of recording uncollectible accounts.

Figure 6.44

Bad debt write-off setup screen

If the allowance method is used, the account selected in the **Income account** field should be Allowance for Doubtful Accounts. Bad debt expense would be the account selected if the direct method is used.

> **BEHIND THE SCENES** It might seem counterintuitive to select an asset or expense account in the **income** field of the **service** item setup. QBO automatically credits the account selected here when an **invoice** or **sales receipt** is created. QBO automatically debits the account selected here when a **credit memo** is created. Because write-offs are entered through **credit memos**, you're identifying the account to be debited when the **credit memo** is prepared. For uncollectible accounts, the debit account should be either bad debt expense or the allowance account, depending on the method used.

Whether sales tax should be recorded on the credit memo depends on the sale items included on the **invoice** being credited. That tax status, of course, is not known when the item is set up.

It's most efficient, then, to select the most likely status. That can always be changed when the credit memo is created. If the sale items **were** taxable and sales tax was included on the credit memo, the sales tax liability account would be debited appropriately.

Once the service item is created and the appropriate general ledger accounts are set up, the user creates a credit memo to record the write-off. The credit memo is then applied to the uncollectible invoice. (The application is automatic if the automation feature is turned on in Account and Settings. The credit memo must be manually applied if automation is turned off.)

The process is demonstrated in the next practice exercise.

PRACTICE

EXERCISE

6.6

Record an uncollectible account at Craig's Design and Landscaping.

(Jeff's Jalopies has gone bankrupt. There is an $81 balance due on his account. The original charge was for taxable services. Craig's Design and Landscaping has very few uncollectible accounts and has elected to use the direct write-off method to account for bad debts.)

1. Set up the appropriate account.
   a. Click the ⚙ on the icon bar.
   b. Click Chart of Accounts.
   c. Click See your Chart of Accounts, if necessary.
   d. Click New.
   e. Select Expenses as the financial statement classification, Expenses in the Save account under field, and Bad Debts in the Tax form section field.
   f. Enter "Bad Debt Expense" as the name.
   g. Click Save.

2. Set up the new service item.
   a. Click the ⚙ on the icon bar.
   b. Click Products and Services.
   c. Click New.
   d. Select Service.
   e. Enter "Write off" as the name.
   f. Select + Add new in the Category dropdown menu.
      i. Enter "Other Charges" as the Name and click Save.
   g. Enter "Write off of uncollectible account" in the description field.
   h. Select Bad Debt Expense as the Income Account.
   i. Leave Taxable—Standard rate in the Sales tax field. (For this practice exercise, we'll assume that most of Craig's revenue is subject to tax.)
   j. Click Save and close.

3. Change an automation setting.
   a. Click the ⚙ icon.
   b. Click Account and Settings.
   c. Click the Advanced tab.
   d. Click the pencil icon in the Automation section.
   e. Toggle the button next to Automatically apply credits to turn the feature off.

(continued)

(continued from previous page)

  f. Click **Save**.

  g. Click **Done**.

4. Create a credit memo.

  a. Click **+ New** on the navigation bar.

  b. Select **Credit Memo**.

  c. Select **Jeff's Jalopies** as the **name**.

  d. Use the current date.

  e. Select **Write off** as the **PRODUCT/SERVICE** and enter "75" in the **AMOUNT** field.

    i. Leave the **QTY** field blank.

  f. Select **California** in the **Select a sales tax rate** dropdown menu.

  g. Click **Save and close**.

5. Apply the credit memo.

  a. Click **Sales** on the navigation bar.

  b. Open the **Customers** tab.

  c. Click **Jeff's Jalopies**.

  d. In the dropdown menu in the **ACTION** column for Invoice 1022, select **Receive payment**.

  e. Check the box next to Invoice 1022 and the box next to the credit memo.

  f. The **Amount received** should show as 0.00. The **Amount to apply** should show as $81.00.

  g. Click **Save and close**.

RECORDING PAYMENTS FROM CUSTOMERS

Chapter 3 outlines the process for recording cash (or check) payments from customers. This chapter covers:

- Customer payments by credit card

- Customer checks returned by the bank due to insufficient funds (NSF checks)

- Early payment discounts

LO 6-5 Demonstrate an understanding of the process for recording customer credit card payments, early payment discounts taken by customers, and NSF checks

eLecture

Recording Customer Payments by Credit Card

Most retail stores accept credit cards as a form of payment. Credit card payments are considered **almost** the equivalent of cash. "Almost" because:

- The company pays a fee to the financial institution processing credit card receipts for the company (commonly called the merchant bank) on all credit card receipts.

- The merchant bank generally makes the deposits directly to the merchandiser's account (net of any fees) within a few days, in batches that correspond to the credit card type (VISA, MasterCard, etc.).

Credit card payments can be received at the time of sale or as payment on an account balance.

> ✱ **HINT:** Users can purchase a credit card processing service through QBO. Credit card receipts are processed automatically when entered. The processes described below assume that the company does **not** have that service.

Recording Receipt of Customer Credit Card Payment

Most companies receive credit card receipts from the merchant bank within a few days so sales paid by credit card, at point of sale, are normally recorded as Sales Receipts (similar to cash sales covered in Chapter 3). The type of credit card used (VISA, MasterCard, etc.) is selected as the payment method.

When customers use credit cards to pay account balances, the payment is recorded through the Receive Payment window (similar to payments of account balances by cash or check covered in Chapter 3). The type of credit card used (VISA, MasterCard, etc.) is selected as the payment method.

PRACTICE EXERCISE 6.7

Record customer credit card transactions for Craig's Design and Landscaping.

(The merchant bank is America's Bank. The transaction fee is 3% of credit card receipts.)

1. Record cash sale using a credit card. (Cool Cars pays $108 to purchase some garden lights.)
   a. Click **+ New** on the navigation bar.
   b. Click Sales Receipt.
   c. Select Cool Cars as the customer.
   d. Use the current date.
   e. Select Visa as the Payment method.
   f. Make sure Undeposited Funds appears in the Deposit to field.
   g. Select Lighting as the Product/Service.
   h. Enter a QTY of "5" and a RATE of "20."
   i. Select California in the Select a sales tax rate dropdown menu.
   j. **Make a note** of the tax rate listed for California.
   k. Click Save and close.

2. Record customer payment of an account balance with a credit card. (Mark Cho pays his $314.28 invoice balance with a credit card.)
   a. Click **+ New** on the navigation bar.
   b. Click Receive Payments.
   c. Select Mark Cho as the customer.
   d. Use the current date.
   e. Select Visa as the Payment method.
   f. Make sure Undeposited Funds appears in the Deposit to field.
   g. Enter "314.28" as the Amount received. The box next to Invoice #1035 should be checked automatically.
   h. Click Save and close.

> **WARNING:** The next practice exercise uses the transactions just entered. You'll save yourself some time if you continue through to the next exercise.

Depositing Credit Card Receipts

As you learned in Chapter 3, unless the default preference is changed, QBO debits **Undeposited Funds** for all payments received from customers through **Sales Receipt** or **Payment** forms. The receipts are transferred, in batches that correspond to the actual deposit amounts, from the **Undeposited Funds** account to the cash account through the **Bank Deposit** form.

The same considerations must be made for credit card receipts. The merchant bank makes deposits to the merchandiser's bank account in batches (grouped by credit card type), net of any transaction fees charged. The deposit in QBO for credit card receipts should be made in corresponding batches, net of the fees. Checks and cash receipts should not be included on the same deposit form in QBO as credit card receipts because they would show as separate transactions on bank statements.

Recording a deposit of credit card receipts is done using the **Bank Deposit** form accessed by clicking **+ New** on the navigation bar.

The user should mark (check) all receipts of the same credit card type for deposit.

Credit card fees are entered in the **Add funds to this deposit** section. To record the fee, the merchant bank is entered in the **RECEIVED FROM** field. The account used to record merchant bank fees should be selected in the **ACCOUNT** field. The fee is entered as a negative number in the **AMOUNT** field.

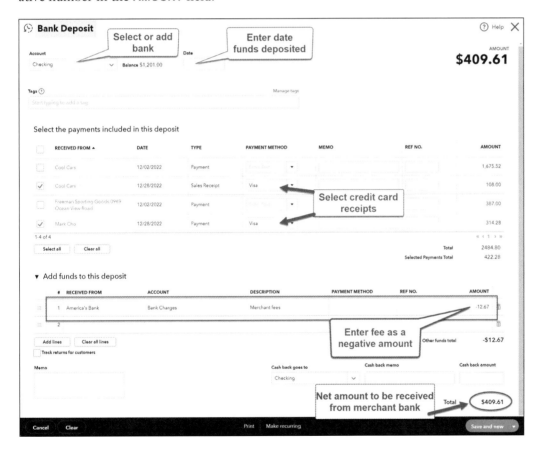

Figure 6.45

Example of deposit of credit card receipts

BEHIND THE SCENES Remember, the default journal entry underlying a deposit transaction includes a debit to the Bank account indicated for the total deposit amount and a credit to the Account(s) indicated on the deposit form. Credit card processing fees are expenses. Entering the amount as a negative tells QBO to debit, not credit, the **ACCOUNT** for the merchant fees.

> **HINT:** QBO has a built-in calculator feature that can be useful here. The feature is activated by entering a number and then a mathematical operator (+, −, *, or /). Ignore the **This value is out of range** warning that appears when you enter the operator. The message will disappear when you enter the next number. When you're done entering numbers, click the Tab key, not the Enter key.

If the transaction fee amount is not known when the deposit is initially recorded in QBO, the deposit form can be edited later (fees added) so that the net amount agrees to the amount actually received from the merchant bank.

Merchant fees can also be entered as journal entries.

PRACTICE
EXERCISE
6.8

Make a deposit of credit card receipts for Craig's Design and Landscaping.
(Craig's Design processes its VISA credit card receipts.)

> ! **WARNING:** This practice exercise uses transactions entered in the last exercise. If you logged out or timed out after the last practice exercise, you'll need to complete that exercise again before moving forward.

1. Click **+ New** on the navigation bar.

2. Click **Bank Deposit**.

3. Select **Checking** as the bank account, if necessary.

4. Use the current date.

5. Check all VISA transactions displayed in the **Select Existing Payments** section.
   a. **Selected Payments Total** should be $422.28.

6. Enter the credit card fees in the **Add funds to this deposit** section.
   a. Enter "America's Bank" as a vendor in the **RECEIVED FROM** field.
      i. Add without additional detail.
   b. Select **Bank Charges** as the **ACCOUNT**.
   c. Enter "Credit card fees" in the **DESCRIPTION** field.
   d. Enter the 3% transaction fee ($12.67) as a negative in the **AMOUNT** field.

7. **Total** should be $409.61.

8. Click **Save and close**.

Recording Early Payment Discounts Taken by Customers

Companies often give customers discounts if credit sales are paid before the due date. Any available early payment discounts are included as part of the credit terms listed on the invoice.

Examples of credit terms with early payment discounts include:

- 2/10, Net 30
  - Discount of 2% of the invoice total if paid within 10 days of the due date. Balance is due in full 30 days from the invoice date.

- 1/15, Net 45
  - Discount of 1% of the invoice total if paid within 15 days of the due date. Balance is due in full 45 days from the invoice date.

In QBO, all credit terms used by the company (for customers OR vendors) are included in the **Terms** lists accessed by clicking the ⚙ on the icon bar and selecting **All Lists**. Setting up **terms** was covered in Chapter 3.

The credit terms granted to a **specific** customer are entered in the **Payments** section of the customer record. These credit terms are automatically included on invoices prepared for the customer. They can be changed on a specific invoice if necessary.

HINT: There are currently no options for creating credit terms in QBO that trigger automatic calculations of early payment discounts.

Users can, however, create a **term** that references a discount in the term name. The term name can then be used to identify **invoices** with available discounts.

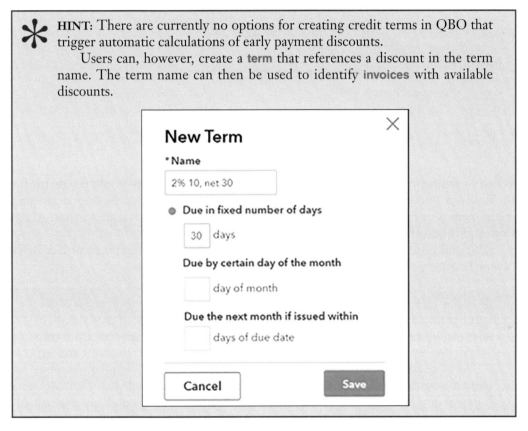

To record an early payment discount taken by a customer, a **credit memo** for the amount of the discount taken by the customer is created and applied when the customer's payment is recorded.

BEHIND THE SCENES Because early payment discounts should not be recognized until the customer actually takes the discount, the user would not enter the discount that **might** be taken on the original invoice.

A user could possibly edit the original invoice when the payment is received. However, this would not be an acceptable choice if the original invoice was recognized in a prior period. (Editing the invoice would automatically change the prior period's financial statements.)

The first step is to create a new **service** item.

Click the ⚙ on the icon bar and select **Products and Services**. Click **New** and select **Service**.

The early payment discount item might be set up something like Figure 6.46.

Figure 6.46

Figure 6.46

Setup of early payment
discount item

When a customer takes an early payment discount, the **credit memo** should be created for the discount amount before the payment is recorded. (This assumes the user is applying credit memos manually. If the **automation** feature is turned on, it shouldn't matter which step is done first.)

The credit memo is then applied to the **invoice** when the payment is recorded. Refer back to Chapter 3 for help with applying credits to customer balances.

> **BEHIND THE SCENES** The tax status of early payment discounts depends on the type of charge and state tax rules. Sales of service items are normally not subject to sales tax, so the tax status of early payment discounts would be **nontaxable**. States vary in how early payment discounts taken on sales of taxable products are treated.
>
> Most companies would set the default tax status for early payment discount items as **nontaxable**. If state law allows tax reductions for product sales when early payment discounts are taken, the **TAX** field on the **credit memo** should be adjusted.

PRACTICE

EXERCISE

6.9

Record an early payment discount taken by a customer of Craig's Design and Landscaping.

(Geeta Kalapatapu took a 2% early payment discount ($12.58) when she paid Invoice #1033 ($629.10 with check #2121.)

    1. Turn off the **automation** feature to allow for manual application of credit memos.

        a. Click the ⚙ on the icon bar.

        b. Click **Account and Settings** screen.

        c. Click the **Advanced** tab.

        d. Click the **pencil** icon in the **Automation** section.

        e. Toggle the button next to **Automatically apply credits** to deactivate the feature.

        f. Click **Save**.

        g. Click **Done**.

(continued)

(continued from previous page)

2. Set up a **service** item for early payment discounts.

   a. Click the ⚙ on the icon bar.

   b. Select **Products and Services**.

   c. Click **New**.

   d. Select **Service**.

   e. Enter "Early Payment Discount" as the **Name**.

   f. Select **+ Add new** in the **Category** dropdown menu.

   g. Enter "Other Charges" as the **Name**. **Note:** If you haven't logged out since completing Practice Exercise 6.6, the **category** will already exist.

   h. Click **Save**.

   i. Enter "Early payment discount" as the **Description**.

   j. Select **Discounts given** as the **Income account**. **TIP:** If you haven't logged out since completing Practice Exercise 6.4, the account name will be Sales Discounts.

   k. The tax field should be **Nontaxable**. Click **Edit sales tax** to make the change to the tax status.

   l. Click **Save and close**.

3. Create a **credit memo** for Geeta Kalapatapu in the amount of $12.58 for the early payment discount taken on Invoice 1033.

   a. Click **+ New** on the navigation bar.

   b. Select **Credit Memo**.

   c. Select **Geeta Kalapatapu** as the customer.

   d. Use the current date.

   e. Select **Early Payment Discount** as the **PRODUCT/SERVICE**.

   f. Enter "12.58" in the **AMOUNT** field.

   g. Click **Save and close**.

4. Record Geeta's check for $616.52.

   a. Click **Sales** on the navigation bar.

   b. Open the **Customers drawer** (tab).

   c. Click **Receive payment** in the **ACTION** column for Geeta Kalapatapu.

   d. Use the current date.

   e. Select **Check** as the **Payment method**.

   f. Use 2121 as the **Reference no.**

   g. Select **Undeposited Funds** as the **Deposit to** account.

   h. Make sure $616.52 appears in the **Amount received** field and the **Amount to Apply** shows $629.10.

   i. Click **Save and close**.

Recording Customer Checks Returned by Bank Due to Insufficient Funds (NSF Checks)

eLecture

Every company that accepts checks from customers accepts a risk that the customer does not have sufficient funds in the bank to cover the check.

When customer checks are returned NSF (non-sufficient funds), the companies will normally either:

- Attempt to redeposit the check OR
- Write off the invoice as a bad debt OR
- Re-invoice the customer (for the amount of the check plus processing fees).

Regardless of the choice made, an NSF check must be recorded in the accounting records along with any fees associated with the NSF check.

Remember, when the customer check was originally recorded in QBO, the entry was:

	Undeposited Funds		
	Accounts receivable (or income)		

When the check was deposited, the amount was transferred from Undeposited Funds to the Cash account.

	Cash		
	Undeposited Funds		

Cash is now overstated by the amount of the NSF check. The entry underlying the invoice created will need to reduce (credit) the Cash account, not an income account.

> **BEHIND THE SCENES** The process for handling NSF checks described below assumes that the company will attempt to collect the full amount. A new invoice is created for the amount of the NSF check and any processing fees the company might decide to charge the customer. If the company later decides that the amount is uncollectible, the following procedures should still be followed so that there is a record of the NSF check associated with the customer. The new invoice should then be written off as described earlier in the **Recording Uncollectible Accounts** section of this chapter.

Recording a Customer NSF (Bounced) Check and Associated Fees

The most efficient process in QBO is to set up two new **service** items that can be used to record an **invoice** charging the customer for the bounced check amount and any fees.

- **Bounced Check Amount**—used to invoice the customer for the check amount. The appropriate bank account would be selected as the income account associated with this item.

Figure 6.47

Setup of bounced check item

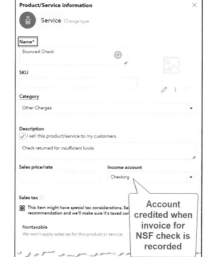

- **Processing Fee**—used to invoice the customer for any processing fees charged by the company. Most companies would select the Bank Service Charges expense account as the associated **income** account for this item to offset the fee charged to them by their bank.

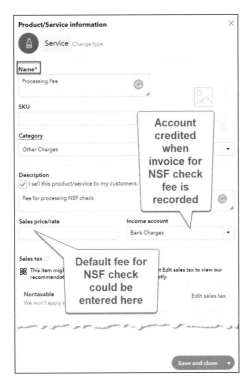

Figure 6.48

Setup of processing fee item

BEHIND THE SCENES   The underlying entry for the **invoice** created to record the NSF check would be:

	Accounts Receivable		
	Checking		
	Bank Service Charges		

The credit to cash offsets the original deposit amount—the amount that didn't clear the bank. The credit to Bank Service Charges offsets any fees charged by the company's bank. Fees charged by the bank would normally be entered through the bank reconciliation process or by journal entry.

Record a bounced check and related fees for Craig's Design and Landscaping.
(The check received from Travis Waldron for $81 was returned marked NSF. Craig's Design charges its customers $25 for processing bounced checks. Craig's Design intends to pursue collection of the $81.)

1. Set up the new **service** items.
   a. Click the ⚙ on the icon bar.
   b. Click **Products and Services**.
   c. Click **New**.
   d. Select **Service**.

PRACTICE
EXERCISE
6.10

(continued)

(continued from previous page)

  e. Enter "Bounced Check" as the name.

  f. Select Other Charges as the category.

    i. If you've logged out since completing Practice Exercise 6.6, you'll need to create the category.

  g. Enter "Check returned for insufficient funds" in the Description field.

  h. Select Checking as the Income Account.

  i. The tax field should be Nontaxable. Click Edit sales tax to make the change to the tax status.

  j. Click Save and new.

  k. Enter "Processing Fee" as the name.

  l. Select Other Charges as the category.

  m. Enter "Fee for processing NSF check" in the Description field.

  n. Select Bank Charges as the Income Account.

  o. The tax field should be Nontaxable. Click Edit sales tax to make the change to the tax status.

  p. Click Save and close.

2. Create an invoice.

  a. Click **+ New** on the navigation bar.

  b. Select Invoice.

  c. Select Travis Waldron as the name.

  d. Use the current date.

  e. Select Bounced Check as the PRODUCT/SERVICE and enter "81" as the AMOUNT.

  f. On the next line, select Processing fee as the PRODUCT/SERVICE and enter "25" as the AMOUNT.

  g. The Balance due should show as $106.

  h. Click Save.

  i. Open the More dropdown menu in the black bar at the bottom of the window.

  j. Select Transaction Journal.

  k. **Make a note** of the number of accounts included in the underlying journal entry,

  l. Click Dashboard to exit the screen.

PREPARING SALES AND COLLECTION REPORTS

LO 6-6 Recognize and prepare common sales and receivable reports used in merchandising companies

The sales and receivables reports in QBO used by merchandising companies are generally the same as those used by service companies (introduced in Chapter 3). However, the Sales by Product/Service Summary report used by a merchandising company would normally include cost of goods sold and gross margin (gross profit) fields for inventory items. A report of inventory item sales (included in the Sales and Customers section of Reports and customized to include inventory items only) would look something like Figure 6.49.

Figure 6.49
Report of sales of inventory items

Craig's Design and Landscaping Services

Sales by Product/Service Summary
All Dates

Columns specific to products

	TOTAL						
	QUANTITY	**AMOUNT**	**% OF SALES**	**AVG PRICE**	**COGS**	**GROSS MARGIN**	**GROSS MARGIN %**
▾ Design							
▾ Fountains							
Pump	4.00	72.75	2.65 %	18.1875	20.00	52.75	72.51 %
Rock Fountain	9.00	2,475.00	90.14 %	275.00	375.00	2,100.00	84.85 %
Total Fountains		**2,547.75**	**92.79 %**		**395.00**		
Total Design		**2,547.75**	**92.79 %**		**395.00**		
▾ Landscaping							
▾ Sprinklers							
Sprinkler Heads	25.00	50.00	1.82 %	2.00			
Sprinkler Pipes	37.00	148.00	5.39 %	4.00	10.00	138.00	93.24 %
Total Sprinklers		**198.00**	**7.21 %**		**10.00**		
Total Landscaping		**198.00**	**7.21 %**		**10.00**		
TOTAL		**$2,745.75**	**100.00 %**		**$405.00**		

One useful report that we haven't looked at yet is the **Collections Report**. The default report, available in the **Who Owes You** section of **Reports**, includes only those invoices that are at least one day past due. (The minimum number of days past due can be changed in the **Customize** sidebar.) The customer's phone number is included which comes in handy when making collection calls to tardy customers!

The report, customized to remove dates, looks something like Figure 6.50.

Figure 6.50
Customized collections report

Craig's Design and Landscaping Services

Collections Report
As of

Represents number of days past due

TRANSACTION TYPE	**NUM**	**PAST DUE**		
▾ Amy's Bird Sanctuary (650) 555-3311				
Invoice	1021	18	459.00	239.00
Total for Amy's Bird Sanctuary			**$459.00**	**$239.00**
▾ Bill's Windsurf Shop (415) 444-6538				
Invoice	1027	44	85.00	85.00
Total for Bill's Windsurf Shop			**$85.00**	**$85.00**
▾ Freeman Sporting Goods:55 Twin Lane (650) 555-0987				
Invoice	1028	44	81.00	81.00
Invoice	1005	5	54.00	4.00
Total for Freeman Sporting Goods:55 Twin Lane			**$135.00**	**$85.00**
▾ Jeff's Jalopies (650) 555-8989				
Invoice	1022	18	81.00	81.00
Total for Jeff's Jalopies			**$81.00**	**$81.00**
▾ John Melton (650) 555-5879				
Invoice	1007	21	750.00	450.00
Total for John Melton			**$750.00**	**$450.00**
▾ Kookies by Kathy (650) 555-7896				
Invoice	1016	45	75.00	75.00
Total for Kookies by Kathy			**$75.00**	**$75.00**
▾ Red Rock Diner (650) 555-4973				
Invoice	1024	65	156.00	156.00
Total for Red Rock Diner			**$156.00**	**$156.00**
▾ Shara Barnett:Barnett Design (650) 557-1289				
Invoice	1012	10	274.50	274.50
Total for Shara Barnett:Barnett Design			**$274.50**	**$274.50**
▾ Sushi by Katsuyuki (505) 570-0147				
Invoice	1018	5	80.00	80.00
Total for Sushi by Katsuyuki			**$80.00**	**$80.00**
TOTAL			**$2,095.50**	**$1,525.50**

**PRACTICE
EXERCISE
6.11**

Prepare various sales and receivable reports for Craig's Design and Landscaping.
(Craig asks for information about sales over the last two months. He also wants to see which customers have unpaid balances.)

1. Click Reports on the navigation bar.

2. Click Sales by Product/Service Summary in the Sales and Customers section.
    a. Select All Dates in the Report period dropdown menu.
    b. Click Run report.
    c. **Make a note** of the AVG PRICE amount for Concrete.
    d. Click Customize.
    e. Open the Filter section.
    f. Check the box next to Product/Service and select Pump and Rock Fountain.
    g. Click Run report.
    h. **Make a note** of the Gross Margin % for Rock Fountain.
    i. Click Back to report list.

3. Click Collections Report in the Who owes you section.
    a. Select All Dates in the Report period dropdown menu.
    b. Click Customize.
    c. Open the Filter section.
    d. Check the box next to Customer.
    e. In the Customer dropdown menu, select Sushi by Katsuyuki and the two sub-customers of Freeman Sporting Goods.
    f. Click Run report.
    g. **Make a note** of the OPEN BALANCE total.

4. Click Dashboard to close the window.

PREPARING CUSTOMER STATEMENTS

LO 6-7 Describe the process for preparing customer statements

Companies will often send statements to customers on a monthly basis. Statements, for the most part, are simply summaries of activity over some period of time. They generally include a beginning balance, a list of all invoices and payments during the period, and an ending balance. Statements can be an effective way of communicating with customers.

For internal control purposes, most companies will not pay from a statement. (Companies choose to only pay from original invoices to avoid the risk of making duplicate payments.) For that reason, statements rarely include new charges (amounts not previously billed using an invoice). The most common exception would be finance charges assessed on past-due balances.

Statements can be prepared in QBO and are easily accessed by clicking ⬤+New on the navigation bar.

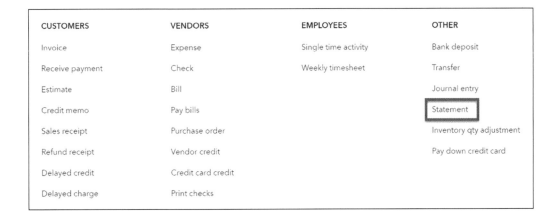

Figure 6.51

Access to statement feature

Click **Statement** in the **OTHER** column.

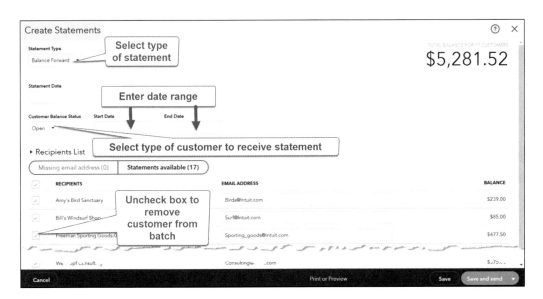

Figure 6.52

Statement options

A statement date is entered. A company can choose the data that will appear on the statements by selecting one of the options in the **Statement Type** dropdown menu.

- **Balance forward**—The ending balance from the prior period and all current period transactions are displayed. An aging of the current balance is included at the bottom of the statement.

- **Open item (last 365 days)**—All open transactions are displayed. An aging of the current balance is included at the bottom of the statement.

- **Transaction Statement**—Transactions during the period are listed in two columns. The **Amount** column includes any **invoices**, **credit memos**, or **sales receipts**. The **Received** column includes payments received. No ending balance is included.

The company can also choose which customers will receive statements. In the **Customer Balance Status** dropdown menu, options are available to select only customers with balances, only customers with overdue balances, or all customers.

Customers displayed in the **Recipients List** will change depending on options selected. Statements can be printed or emailed directly to customers. Unchecking the box in the far left column for a specific customer removes the customer from the batch.

PRACTICE
EXERCISE
6.12

MBC

Prepare statements for Craig's Design and Landscaping.
(Craig's Design decides to send statements to all customers with unpaid balances.)

1. Click **+ New** on the navigation bar.
2. Click Statement.
3. Select Balance Forward as the Statement type.
4. Use the current date.
5. Select Overdue in the Customer Balance Status dropdown menu.
6. Leave default dates.
7. Click Apply.
8. Click Print or Preview at the bottom of the screen to view statements.
9. Click Close (bottom left corner).
10. Click Cancel (bottom left corner of the window).

ANSWER TO
QuickCheck
6-1

> The matching (expense recognition) principle.

CHAPTER SHORTCUTS

Activate sales tax
1. Click Taxes in the navigation bar.
2. Click Use automatic sales tax.

Add item (inventory, non-inventory, service)
1. Click the ⚙ on the icon bar.
2. Click Product and Services.
3. Click New.

Create a delayed charge
1. Click **+ New** on the navigation bar.
2. Click Delayed Charge.

Create a delayed credit
1. Click **+ New** on the navigation bar.
2. Click Delayed Credit.

Create statements
1. Click **+ New** on the navigation bar.
2. Click Statement.

CHAPTER REVIEW

Assignments with the
MBC are available in
myBusinessCourse.

Matching

Match the term or phrase (as understood in QuickBooks Online) to its definition.

1. inventory item
2. statement
3. discount
4. delayed charge

5. bounced check
6. non-inventory item
7. delayed credit
8. economic nexus

_____ transaction type used for recording a pending sale

_____ product available for sale that is not being tracked in a perpetual tracking system

_____ sufficient presence used in determining seller sales tax requirements

_____ percentage or dollar amount reduction in charge to customer

_____   transaction type used for recording a pending customer credit
_____   report sent to customer to summarize activity for a period
_____   product available for sale that is being tracked in a perpetual tracking system
_____   customer check returned by bank due to insufficient funds in account

Multiple Choice

1. When a **customer** makes a purchase using his or her credit card, it would normally be recorded as a(n):
   - a. invoice.
   - b. bill.
   - c. sales receipt.
   - d. credit card charge.

2. When a bounced customer check is recorded, which account should QBO credit for the amount of the customer check?
   - a. Cash (or Checking)
   - b. Bad debt expense
   - c. Accounts payable
   - d. Unearned revenue
   - e. Undeposited funds

3. The inventory valuation method used by QBO is:
   - a. FIFO.
   - b. LIFO.
   - c. Specific identification.
   - d. Weighted average.
   - e. Any of the above can be selected by the user.

4. Which form might be used to record a customer order before the items are shipped?
   - a. Delayed Charge
   - b. Delayed Credit
   - c. Invoice
   - d. Sales Receipt

5. Credit card processing fees charged by merchant banks _____.
   - a. can be recorded when the deposit is recorded
   - b. can be recorded using a journal entry
   - c. can be recorded when the fee is known by editing the deposit transaction
   - d. All of the above are options for recording credit card fees.

BEYOND THE CLICKS—THINKING LIKE A MANAGER

Accounting: Identify and explain three things that a company should consider when determining the selling price of a new inventory item.

Information Systems: Review the steps taken to process the bounced check received from a customer in your homework company. Why is this method preferable to simply creating a journal entry to record the bad check?

ASSIGNMENTS

**Assignment
6A**

**Math
Revealed!**

MBC

2/1/24

✓ Now that Martin is selling more products, you know that Math Revealed! will need to start collecting sales taxes so you click Taxes on the navigation bar and set up the sales taxes feature.

● You use 3835 Freeport Blvd, Sacramento, CA 95822 as the address.

● You do not expect to sell any products to out-of-state customers.

● You confirm that the tax agency is the California Department of Tax and Fee Administration (CDTFA).

  ■ **TIP:** Don't click the Create invoice link. Exit out of the screen. You should then see the final setup screen. If not, click Taxes on the navigation bar.

● You know that you will be required to file monthly.

● You change the tax collection start date to 2/1/24. **TIP:** You will need to edit the sales tax settings to change the starting date. You must enter as 02/01/2024. Leave the reporting method as accrual.

✓ You review the records of all items in the Product and Services list, making sure that all inventory items are identified as Taxable-standard rate and all service items as Nontaxable. **TIP:** Click Edit for **every item** to review the settings. If a service shows as taxable, you'll need to change the status. Click Edit sales tax and toggle to Nontaxable. You will need to save and close whether you change the tax status or not. To make sure every item's tax status is correct, run a Product/Service List report. Customize the report by adding the Taxable field. Only inventory items should be identified as taxable.

✓ Martin comes in early with some great news. A new Center for High Academic Achievement has just opened in downtown Sacramento with a satellite campus in Elk Grove, CA. The space is supported and staffed by the local high schools. The director of the new program, Michelle Farman, has contacted Martin and asked him to provide materials that could be purchased by students enrolled in their program.

● You first set the Center up as a customer. **TIP:** This will be considered the parent customer.

> Center for High Academic Achievement
> 3635 Freeport Blvd
> Sacramento, CA 95822
> (916) 855-5558
> Terms are Net 30

  ■ You check This customer is tax exempt in the Additional Info section. The Center is a reseller of the materials and isn't subject to tax. You select Resale in the Reason for exemption dropdown menu and you enter the Center's resale number (SRY-333-444444) in the Exemption details field.

● Next you set up both locations as sub-customers and select the Bill customer parent option. You use the same company name, billing address, terms, and reseller number as the parent customer for both locations. You use "Downtown" and "Elk Grove" as the Customer display names. For the company names, you use Center for High Academic Achievement-Downtown (or Elk Grove). **TIP:** If you check Is a sub-customer first and select Center for High Academic Achievement as the parent, the address fields will be automatically filled. You will need to check the Terms and enter the tax information in the Additional info section.

  ■ For the Downtown location, the shipping address is the same as the billing address.

  ■ For the Elk Grove location, the shipping address is 445 Forest Drive, Elk Grove, CA 95624.

2/5/24

✓ Martin delivers the materials as promised to both locations of the Center for High Academic Achievement. You prepare separate invoices for:

- Downtown shipment
  - 5 each of the following books:
    - ◆ Geometry in Sports (**Sports**)
    - ◆ Solving Puzzles: Fun with Algebra (**Puzzles**)
    - ◆ Getting Ready for Calculus (**Ready**)
  - INV-1013 totals $415.
  - **TIP:** Depending on when you're doing your assignment, you may get a message about taxes not being set up yet. Make sure you've entered the correct start date for taxes and that you're entering the correct **invoice** date.
- Elk Grove shipment
  - 3 each of the following books:
    - ◆ Geometry in Sports (**Sports**)
    - ◆ Solving Puzzles: Fun with Algebra (**Puzzles**)
  - INV-1014 totals $159.
- **TIP:** The Center is a reseller of books (tax-exempt) so there should be no sales tax on either **invoice** even if the **Tax** field is checked in the **product/service** row.

✓ You receive a check in the mail from Jon Savidge for $1,000 in payment of INV-1010. (Check #3359, dated 2/5). Jon took the discount issued on the CM-1010 credit memo. **TIP:** This can be tricky. Before you close the transaction, make sure that the **PAYMENT** field in the **Invoice** row shows the full amount (the original amount of the invoice), the **Amount received** is accurate, and the **Credit memo** box is checked. Review the *Applying Credit Memos To Open Invoices When Payments Are Recorded* section of Chapter 3 if you need help.

✓ You realize that Kim Kowalski still hasn't paid the remaining $105 due on INV-1002. You had called her a month ago and she had promised to pay the balance by the end of January. You give her a call. She apologizes and drives over with a check for $105 (Check #198, dated 2/5). You record this payment in QBO.

2/7/24

✓ Martin gives you the detail for the tutoring sessions scheduled during the first week of February.

- Two customers paid using their VISA card. You complete **sales receipts** (dated 2/7) for both (starting with SR-107).
  - Alonso Luna—5 **Refresher** sessions and one **Puzzles** book to help him with Algebra— $302.19 (tax included). **TIP:** You may need to click down to another row or into the **QTY** or **RATE** field before the tax field is updated.
  - Marcus Reymundo—2 **Refresher** sessions—$110
- You complete invoices (dated 2/7) for the following customers:
  - Paul Richard—3 weeks of the **Crisis** program starting 2/5—$750 (INV-1015)
  - Debbie Han—4 weeks of the **Crisis** program starting 2/1—$1,000 (INV-1016)

✓ You deposit the credit card receipts received today and the two checks received on 2/5. **TIP:** You'll be making one deposit for the credit card receipts and another for the checks.

- The check deposit totals $1,105.
- The bank charges a 2% fee on all credit card sales. You record the fee and charge it to the **Bank Service Charges** account. You select **City Bank of Sacramento** in the **RECEIVED FROM** field.
- The credit card deposit totals $403.95 (after the fee).

2/9/24

✓ Martin delivers another order to the Downtown location of the Center for High Academic Achievement.

- You prepare INV-1017 for $705.
    - ■ 10 Geometry in Sports (**Sports**)
    - ■ 8 Solving Puzzles: Fun with Algebra (**Puzzles**)
    - ■ 5 Getting Ready for Calculus (**Ready**)
    - ■ 5 Geometry Kits (**Kit**)

✓ You receive checks in the mail from:

- Center for High Academic Achievement—$574 in payment of INV-1013 and INV-1014. Check #9758844, dated 2/9. **TIP:** You only need to select the parent customer (**Center for High Academic Achievement**) when you receive the payment since the **bill parent customer** option was selected in the customer setup for the locations.
- Marley Roberts—$105, Check #1731, dated 2/9, in payment of INV-1012

✓ You deposit the two checks received in the bank. Total deposit is $679.

2/12/24

✓ The Teacher's College workshop was a huge success. One of the teachers Martin met there asked him whether he'd be willing to put on a similar workshop this Friday (2/16). The teacher explains that this is for an independent group of educators and asks Martin if he'd consider discounting the Educator Workshop fee. Martin agrees to give the group a 10% discount on the $3,000 fee.

- The new customer is:

    Dynamic Teaching
        2121 Parallel Street
        Sacramento, CA 95822
        Dynamic Teaching is subject to sales taxes.
        Terms Net 30

- You set up a new account (Sales Discounts) to track discounts given to customers. You use #490 as the account number. **TIP:** Discounts are contra revenue accounts. Make sure you pick the correct **account type** in the **Save account under** field. Use **Discounts/Refunds Given** as the detail type (**Tax form section** field).
- You turn on the **Discount** feature on the **Sales** tab of **Account and Settings**.
- You select the new **Sales discount** account in the **Chart of accounts** section on the **Advanced** tab of **Account and Settings**.
- You don't want to forget to send the invoice next week so you create a **Delayed Charge** (DC-1000) for the $3,000 fee. **TIP:** You won't be able to add the discount directly on the **Delayed Charge** form. You'll do that when you convert it to an **invoice**.

2/15/24

✓ The Downtown location of the Center for High Academic Achievement returns two of the geometry kits (**Kit**). Both sets had broken compasses! Martin will be returning the compasses to Math Shack later.

- You create a $30 credit memo (CM-1017) for the Downtown location.

2/16/24

✓ You receive notice from the bank that the $105 check from Kim Kowalski that was recorded on 2/5 (deposited on 2/7) was returned for insufficient funds. You call Kim and she lets you know that she closed her bank account. She agrees to pay the $25 processing fee and the $105 owed to you with her VISA card.

- You set up two **service** items. You classify them both in a new **category** called Other Charges.

- For the first **service** item (Bounced Check) you use "Check returned for insufficient funds" as the **description**. You wouldn't need a default price here. You identify the item as **nontaxable**. **TIP:** Think about the account you want credited for the check amount.
  - For the second **service** item (Processing Fee), you use "Processing fee on NSF check" as the **description** and you select **Bank service charges** as the **income account**. You enter $25 as the default **sales price/rate** for the processing fee. This item is also **nontaxable**.
- You record her $130 payment using SR-109. **TIP:** The only items on the sales receipt will be the **Bounced check** and **Processing fee** items.

> **BEHIND THE SCENES**   This transaction can seem complicated. It might help to remember that the journal entry underlying this **sales receipt** is DR Undeposited Funds; CR Checking; CR Bank Service Charges.

✓ You process the credit card receipt right away. The deposit amount (after the 2% fee) is $127.40.

✓ You create the invoice for the workshop Martin put on for the Dynamic Teaching group from the **delayed charge** you created on the 12th. You remember to give the customer the promised discount of 10%. INV-1018 totals $2,700. **TIP:** The **delayed charge** will show up in the sidebar when you start the **invoice**.

2/17/24

✓ Martin holds another Mathmagic Clinic. This time 40 students show up, a 25% increase over last month's attendance! Luckily, Samantha is able to help out with the tutoring clinic again. You tell Martin he might want to think about hiring an assistant on a regular basis. Martin says he might think about doing that in the fall.

- All the students pay in cash—$25 each for the tutoring.
- Some of the students also purchase some supplies, with cash. You sell:
  - 10 Handheld dry-erase boards (**Dry Erase**)
  - 5 Notebook packs (**Notebook**)
  - 3 Geometry Kits (**Kit**)
- You create one **sales receipt** (SR-110), using Drop-In as the customer.
  - The **sales receipt** total is $1,396.94 (including sales tax).

2/20/24

✓ One of the students from the Mathmagic Clinic on the 17th (Isla Parker) returns the **Kit** she purchased. The compass broke the first time she used it! You write her a check (#1112) for the full $16.31 cost of the set plus sales tax. **TIP:** Refunds are recorded on **refund receipts**. Use RR-101.

- Her address is 1164 Rosa Drive, Sacramento, CA 95822.
- Martin is definitely going to talk to Math Shack about the quality of the sets. If they can't find a better substitute, he may need to find another supplier.

✓ Martin gives you the details for tutoring sessions held in the past week and a half.

- You create invoices (starting with INV-1019 and dated 2/20) for:
  - Navi Patel—Two weeks of **Crisis** starting 2/5—$500. Net 15
  - Eliot Williams—One week of **Persistence** starting 2/19—$105.

✓ You go to the bank and deposit the cash from Saturday's Mathmagic Clinic. The total deposit is $1,396.94

✓ Martin lets you know that he's going to take a few days off.

2/26/24

✓ You receive a check in the mail (# 9759115) from the Center for High Academic Achievement for $675 in payment of INV-1017. They took the credit for the returned Geometry Kits. **TIP:** Before you close, make sure the **Amount to Apply** shows as $705.

✓ You deposit the check right away.

✓ You review the A/R Aging Summary report (as of 2/26/24). INV-1005 to Marcus Reymundo was due over a month ago. You try calling him but discover that his phone has been disconnected. You decide to write off the balance of $55 to bad debt expense. Math Revealed uses the direct method because it has historically had very few uncollectible accounts.

● **TIP:** You'll need to set up a new account and a new nontaxable **service** item.

  ■ Set up the bad debt expense account as a **sub-account** of **Marketing Costs** (in the **Save account under** field). Select **Bad debts** as the **detail type** (**Tax form section** field). Use 648 as the account number.

  ■ Include the new **service** item in the **Other Charges category**. Use "Write off of uncollectible account" as the **description** and "Write off" as the **name**. Set the sales tax status as nontaxable. Remember, you will be recording write-offs using credit memos. The account selected in the **income account** field will be debited.

● You create a **credit memo** (WO-1005) for the $55 write-off.

● You apply the credit to INV-1005 through the **receive payment** form. **TIP:** There is no payment method or amount received. You are simply applying the credit memo to clear the account balance.

Check numbers 2/29

Checking account balance: $6,982.16
Accounts receivable: $5,475.00
Total cost of goods sold (February): . . . . $ 981.00
Net income (February) $7,042.16

Suggested reports for Chapter 6:

All reports should be in portrait orientation.

● Journal—February transactions only

● Sales by Product/Service Summary (February)

● A/R Aging Detail (2/29)

● Balance Sheet as of 2/29

● Profit and Loss (February)

  ■ Add a **Year-to-date** column to the report

Assignment 6B

Salish Software Solutions

Homework
MBC

2/1/24

✓ Now that Sally is ready to start selling products, you realize that you'll need to set up automatic sales taxes in QBO so you click **Taxes** on the navigation bar to set up the sales tax feature.

● You use 3835 Freeport Blvd, Sacramento, CA 95822 as the company address.

● You do not expect to sell any products to out-of-state customers.

● You confirm that the tax agency is the California Department of Tax and Fee Administration (CDTFA).

  ■ **TIP:** Don't click the **Create invoice** link. Exit out of the screen. You should then see the final setup screen. If not, click **Taxes** on the navigation bar.

● You contact the CDTFA and find out Salish Software will need to report monthly.

● You change the tax collection start date to 2/1/24. **TIP:** You will need to edit the **sales tax settings** to change the starting date. You must enter as 02/01/2024. Leave the reporting method as accrual.

✓ You review the records of all items in the **Product and Services** list, making sure that all **inventory** items are identified as **Taxable-standard rate** and all **service** items as **Nontaxable. TIP:**

Click **Edit** for **every item** to review the settings. If a **service** item shows as taxable, you'll need to change the status. Click **Edit sales tax** and toggle to **Nontaxable**. (You may need to click **Still don't see what you're looking for?** before you see the **Nontaxable** option.) You will need to **save and close** whether you change the tax status or not. To make sure every item's tax status is correct, run a **Product/Service List** report. Customize the report by adding the **Taxable** field.

2/2/24

✓ A friend of Sally's, Rey Butler, has been doing very well in his financial management firm Reyelle Consulting. He has an office in Sacramento and a recently opened office in Davis. He gives Sally a call to ask about purchasing some electronic tools to sell to his customers. Sally suggests that he try the **Organizers** and **Investment Trackers**.

- You first set Reyelle up as a **customer**. This will be the **parent customer**.

    Reyelle Consulting
    3200 Bullish Lane
    Sacramento, CA 95822
    (916) 558-4499
    Terms are Net 30

    - You check the **This customer is tax exempt** field in the **Additional info** section because Reyelle is a reseller of the materials and isn't subject to tax. You select **Resale** in the **Reason for exemption** dropdown menu and you enter the company's resale number (SRY-424-424242) in the **Exemption details** field.

- You also set up both locations as **sub-customers** and select the **Bill parent customer** option. You use the same company name, billing address, terms, and reseller number as the **parent customer** for both locations. You use "Sacramento" and "Davis" as the **customer display names**. For the **company names**, you use Reyelle Consutling-Sacramento (or Davis). **TIP:** If you check **Is a sub-customer** and select Reyelle Consulting as the **parent**, the address fields will be automatically filled. You will need to enter the **customer display** and **company names**. You will also need to check the **Terms** and enter the tax information in the **Additional info** section.

    - For the Sacramento location, the shipping address is the same as the billing address.
    - For the Davis location, the shipping address is 2911 Equity Street, Davis, CA 95616.

2/5/24

✓ Sally delivers the software CDs to both Reyelle locations. You prepare separate **invoices** for:
- Sacramento shipment
    - 6 each of the following:
        - Organizer
        - Tracker
    - INV-1013 totals $660.
    - **TIP:** Depending on when you're doing your assignment, you may get a message about taxes not being set up yet. Make sure you've entered the correct start date for taxes and that you're entering the correct **invoice** date.
- Davis shipment
    - 3 each of the following:
        - Organizer
        - Tracker
    - INV-1014 totals $330
- **TIP:** Reyelle Consulting is a reseller (tax-exempt) so there should be no sales tax on either invoice even if the **Tax** field is checked on the **product/service**.

✓ You receive two checks in the mail. Both are dated 2/5.
- Check # 9210 from Butter and Beans for $3,000. (INV-1009).
- Check #86115 from Fabulous Fifties for $500. (INV-1010).

2/7/24

✓ Sally gives you her client work hours for the past week and you prepare the invoices as follows:
- Fabulous Fifties—10 hours of **Set Up**—$750. INV-1015
- Alki Deli—8 hours of **Set Up** and 4 hours of **Train**—$800. INV-1016

✓ One of the owners of mSquared Enterprises (a local general contractor) stops in to ask about construction accounting software. Sally gives her a demonstration of **Contractor** and she's impressed. She uses her VISA card to purchase the software.
- You set the company up with the following address:

  595 Newbuild Avenue
  Sacramento, CA 95822
  Net 30 terms

- You complete a **sales receipt** (SR-106) to record the $870 purchase (tax included). **TIP:** You may need to click down to another row or into the **QTY** or **RATE** field before the tax field is updated.

✓ You deposit the credit card receipts received today and the two checks received on 2/5. **TIP:** You'll be making one deposit for the credit card receipts and another for the checks.
- The check deposit totals $3,500.
- The credit card deposit totals $852.60 (after the fee).
  - The bank charges a 2% fee on all card sales. You charge the fee to the **Bank Service Charges** account. You select **Sacramento City Bank** in the **RECEIVED FROM** field.

2/9/24

✓ Sally delivers another order to the Davis location of Reyelle Consulting. The **Trackers** are selling quickly. Reyelle also decides to purchase a few of the **Easy Does It** programs for its Davis location. It has a few clients that own very small businesses and the **Easy Does It** program would be sufficient for their needs.
- You prepare the invoice (INV-1017) for $1,200.
  - 10 **Tracker**
  - 3 **Easy1**

✓ You receive a $350 check, dated 2/9, in the mail from Dew Drop Inn (Check 8160). (INV-1012)
- You call Harry over at Dew Drop to ask about the $150 balance. He says they've had some issues recently. A guest at the hotel got stuck in the elevator for 16 hours and is now suing for emotional distress. He'll try to get the balance to you by the end of February.
- You deposit the check right away into the checking account.

✓ Sally tells you that she was talking to the staff at Fabulous Fifties. They mentioned that they knew some people who might be interested in getting some help picking out new accounting software. Sally offers them a $50 referral fee for any new software selection clients that they steer her way. You go ahead and set up a **delayed credit** (DCR-1000). You use **Select** as the service item. You enter 0 as the **QTY** so the quantity sold on reports isn't affected. **TIP:** You don't need to adjust the **RATE** field. Enter the $50 directly in the **AMOUNT** field.

2/15/24

✓ The Effective Troubleshooting (**TIPS**) workshop was a huge success. At the end of the workshop, Albus' CEO (Anatoly Deposit) tells Sally that he mentioned the workshop to James Gooden, a business acquaintance from Cezar Software who is very interested in presenting a similar workshop. Anatoly suggests giving James a call. **TIP:** The workshop at Albus was already invoiced in January.

✓ Sally calls James Gooden right away. James would like to host the workshop at their facility later the following week. James explains that Cezar Software creates software programs used by nonprofit organizations. He's hoping that there might be some kind of nonprofit discount available. Sally agrees to offer a 20% discount on the $2,500 fee.

- The new customer is:

  Cezar Software
  8644 Technology Avenue
  Sacramento, CA 95822
  Terms Net 30

- You set up a new account (Sales Discounts) to track discounts given to customers. You use #490 as the account number. **TIP:** Discounts are contra revenue accounts. Make sure you pick the correct **account type** in the **Save account under** field. Use **Discounts/Refunds Given** as the **detail type** (**Tax form section** field).

- You turn on the **Discount** feature on the **Sales** tab of **Account and Settings**.

- You select the new **sales discount** account in the **Chart of accounts** section in the **Advanced** tab of **Account and Settings**.

- You don't want to forget to send the invoice for the **Tips** workshop so you create a **Delayed Charge** (DC-1000) for the full $2,500. **TIP:** You won't be able to add the discount directly on the **Delayed Charge** form. You'll do that when you convert it to an **invoice**.

2/19/24

✓ The Sacramento location of Reyelle's returns one of the **Organizer** CDs because it was damaged. Sally will return it to the vendor (Personal Software) sometime next week.

- You create a $50 credit memo (CM-1013) for the Sacramento location of Reyelle.

✓ You get a call from the bank. Dew Drop Inn's check for $350 was returned for insufficient funds. You call Harry. He apologizes and agrees to pay a $20 processing fee. He uses his VISA credit card to cover the $370 total.

- You set up two **service** items. You classify them both in a new **category** called Other Charges.

  - For the first **service** item (Bounced Check), you use "Check returned for insufficient funds" as the **description**. You don't need to set a sales price. You identify the item as **nontaxable**. **TIP:** Think about the account you want credited for the check amount.

  - For the second **service** item (Processing Fee) you use "Processing fee on NSF check" as the **description** and you select **Bank service charges** as the **Income account**. This item is also **nontaxable**. You enter $20 as the default **sales price/rate** for the processing fee.

- You record Dew Drop Inn's credit card payment using **sales receipt** SR-107. **TIP:** The only items on the sales form will be the **Bounced Check** and **Processing Fee**.

BEHIND THE SCENES This transaction can seem complicated. It might help to remember that the journal entry underlying this **sales receipt** is DR Undeposited Funds; CR Checking; CR Bank Service Charges.

✓ You process the credit card payment right away. The deposit amount (after the 2% fee) is $362.60.

2/21/24

✓ You receive checks in the mail from the following customers, all dated 2/21

- Albus Software—Check 755566, $2,500 for INV-1011
- Fabulous Fifties—Check 415161, $750 for INV-1015
- Alki Deli—Check 71144, $800 for INV-1016

✓ You record the checks and take them down to the bank. The deposit totals $4,050.

2/23/24

✓ Sally gives you her work schedule for the past two weeks. You create the following invoices using 2/23 as the date.

- You create invoices (starting with INV-1018) for:
    - Metro Market—**Select**—$500
        - Metro Market is a new client. It was referred to Salish by Fabulous Fifties.
            - ▼ Metro Market
              210 Admiral Way
              Sacramento, CA 95822
              Net 15
    - Alki Deli—5 hours of **Train**—$250
    - Butter and Beans—11 hours of **Train**—$550
    - Fabulous Fifties—6 hours of **Fix** and 4 hours of **Train**
        - You remember to apply the $50 referral credit. The **Balance due** shows as $510.00. **TIP:** When the delayed credit is applied, the **QTY** field in that row may show a negative 1. If it does, remove the quantity so that reports of units sold remain accurate. Make sure the **AMT** field in that row shows a negative $50 and the total is $510. You may need to expand the sidebar on the right side of the window in order to see the **delayed credit**.

✓ Sally tells you she's taking a few days off (2/26 to 2/29) to visit family in Chicago.

2/26/24

✓ You create the **invoice** for the Effective Troubleshooting (**TIPS**) workshop Sally put on for Cezar Software from the **delayed charge** you created on the 15th. You remember to give the customer the promised discount of 20%. INV-1022 totals $2,000. **TIP:** The **delayed charge** will show up in the sidebar when you start the **invoice**.

✓ You receive a check (# 9759115) in the mail from Reyelle Consulting-Sacramento for $610 in payment of INV-1013. The check was dated 2/26. Reyelle took the credit for the returned **Tracker** disk. **TIP:** Before you close the payment, make sure the **Amount to Apply** shows as $660 and $660 shows in the **PAYMENT** column of the **invoice** row.

✓ You deposit the check right away.

✓ You get a call from Harry at Dew Drop Inn. The lawsuit has bankrupted his company. He apologizes but lets you know there are no assets remaining to cover the balance owed to Salish. You decide to write off the $150 to bad debt expense. Salish Software uses the direct write-off method because it has historically had very few uncollectible accounts.

- You set up a bad debt expense account as a **sub-account** of Marketing Costs (in the **Save account under** field). Select **Bad debts** as the **detail type** (**Tax form section** field). You use account #658.
- You create a new **service** item (Write off) and include it in the **Other Charges** category. You enter "Write off of uncollectible account" as the **description**. The new **service** item is not taxable. (You're writing off a nontaxable service (tutoring).)
    - **TIP:** Remember, you will be creating **credit memos** to record write-offs. The account selected in the **Income account** will be debited.
- You create a **credit memo** for the $150 write off. (You use WO-1012 as the **Credit Memo no.**)

BEHIND THE SCENES This transaction can seem complicated. It might help to remember that the journal entry underlying the **credit memo** is DR Bad Debt Expense; CR Accounts Receivable.

- You apply the credit to INV-1012 through the **receive payment** form. **TIP:** There is no payment method or amount received. You are simply applying the credit memo to clear the account balance.

Check numbers 2/29

Checking account balance: **$19,085.20**
Account receivable: . . . . **$ 5,340.00**
Total cost of goods sold (February): . . . . **$ 1,470.00**
Net income (February) . . . . **$ 6,675.20**

Suggested reports for Chapter 6:

All reports should be in portrait orientation

- Journal—February transactions only

- Sales by Product/Service Summary (February)

- A/R Aging Detail (2/29)

- Balance Sheet as of 2/29

- Profit and Loss (February)

  - Add a **Year-to-date** column to the report

7 Purchasing Activity
(Merchandising Company)

Road Map

LO	Learning Objective	Topic	Subtopic	Page	Practice Exercises	Videos
LO 7-1	Explain and demonstrate various methods for recording orders and receipts of inventory in QBO; explain the use of reorder points in QBO [p. 7-2]	Purchasing inventory	Paying at time of purchase	7-3	7.1	Paying for inventory at time of purchase
			Ordering inventory	7-5	7.2, 7.3	Ordering inventory - setting reorder points; Creating purchase orders
			Receiving ordered inventory	7-13	7.4, 7.5	Receiving ordered inventory (full and partial shipments)
			Managing purchase orders	7-18	7.6	Managing purchase orders
			Ordering inventory without using the purchase order system	7-19		
LO 7-2	Describe and demonstrate the method for recording and applying credits received from vendors in QBO [p. 7-19]	Managing vendor credits	Entering credits from vendors	7-20	7.7	Recording vendor credits
			Applying credits from vendors	7-20		
			Special considerations for returns of inventory	7-23	7.8	
LO 7-3	Explain and demonstrate how early payment discounts are recorded in QBO [p. 7-25]	Paying vendor balances	Taking early payment discounts	7-25	7.9	Taking early payment discounts
LO 7-4	Identify and prepare common inventory reports in QBO [p. 7-29]	Preparing vendor reports		7-29	7.10	
LO 7-5	Understand the use of FIFO as the inventory valuation method used in QBO [p. 7-39]	APPENDIX 7A— Identifying FIFO Layers		7-39		

WHAT IS THE PURCHASE CYCLE IN A MERCHANDISING COMPANY?

- Place an order for products.

- Receive the products.

- Receive a bill for the products.

- Pay the vendor.

The single biggest cost in service companies is usually labor. The single biggest cost in merchandising companies is usually inventory.

Proper inventory management is critical to the success of a merchandising company because:

- It costs money to store inventory.

  - Costs include warehouse rent, insurance, utilities, security, interest, etc.

- Inventory held too long can become obsolete.

  - It's hard to charge full price (or sometimes any price!) for last year's model.

- You can't sell what you don't have.

  - Customers who can't find what they want to buy are not happy customers!

To determine the optimal level of product inventory, management needs information about sales volume, accessibility of products, product returns, gross margins, etc. That information frequently comes from the accounting system.

In this chapter, we will cover transactions related to the purchase and management of inventory. We'll also add some purchase cycle topics that apply to both service and merchandising companies.

PURCHASING INVENTORY

LO 7-1 Explain and demonstrate various methods for recording orders and receipts of inventory in QBO; explain the use of reorder points in QBO

In Chapter 3 and again in Chapter 6, we covered how the various QBO items (**service**, **inventory** and **non-inventory** items) are used in sales cycle transactions. In this chapter, we look at how inventory items are used in purchase cycle transactions.

In summary, inventory items (**inventory** or **non-inventory** items) represent products purchased and sold by the merchandising company. **Inventory** items are tracked in QBO using a perpetual inventory system and are valued using the FIFO method.

Non-inventory items are often used for:

- Products that are purchased directly for customers (not stocked by the company)

- Very low-cost items that are not stocked in high volumes

- Parts used in assembly or manufacturing operations (not covered in this textbook)

Non-inventory items are not tracked in QBO. If the total value is significant, a periodic tracking system would be used.

General information about each product is stored in the inventory item record. That information includes:

- The standard sales price

- The expected unit cost

- The asset account (normally the inventory account) that should be debited when the product is purchased (**Inventory** items only)

- The income account that should be credited if the item is sold
- The expense account that should be debited when an inventory item is sold or when a non-inventory item is purchased

In addition, information about inventory quantities and values is maintained by QBO for each inventory item including the quantity and value of units ordered, received, sold, and on hand.

Using items allows a company to maintain considerable detail without creating a gigantic chart of accounts. For example, a retail store might have only one income account called "Sales Revenue" but it can still generate a report that lists sales quantities and dollars for each and every product sold in the store. A retail store might also have only one inventory (asset) account, but it can still track how many units are on hand at any point in time for each individual product.

In order to maintain that detail, of course, all transactions related to products must be recorded using items. That includes purchase and adjustment transactions as well as sales transactions.

 WARNING: Bill, Check, Expense Purchase Order, Vendor Credit and **Credit Card Credit** forms all have two distribution sections. One section is labeled **Category details** and one is labeled **Item details**. In order to properly adjust the subsidiary ledgers, the **Item details** section must always be used when entering inventory transactions. Charging a purchase to the "Inventory" account in the **Category details** section will result in a debit to the asset but will not properly adjust the inventory quantity in the subsidiary ledgers.

Paying at Time of Purchase

In most cases, merchandise inventory is **not** purchased by going directly to the supplier's location and paying at time of purchase BUT it could be. This might happen if the company needs to ship an order to a customer right away and it doesn't have sufficient products on hand to fill the order.

A company might pay for inventory at time of purchase using a check or credit card. The only difference between entering checks or credit card charges for inventory purchases and entering checks and credit charges for other purchases is the section used to identify the account distribution. We'll use a purchase by check to demonstrate using the appropriate section. (Refer to Chapter 4 for a refresher on entering credit card charges.)

If a company writes a check for the purchase, the check form is accessed by clicking 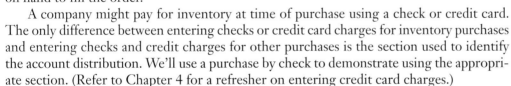 + New on the navigation bar and selecting **Check** in the **Vendors** column.

BEHIND THE SCENES Remember:
- The vendor name, date, and amount of purchase are all used by QBO to credit the bank account and to prepare the check (if checks are printed directly from QBO).
- The distribution section of the form is used to identify the debit account(s) in the underlying journal entry.

Purchases of inventory must be entered on the **Item details** section.

Figure 7.1

Check form

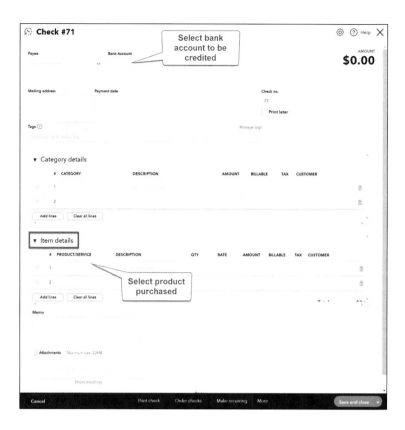

✳ HINT: Remember, forms (like the **check** shown in Figure 7.1) may have been updated. If possible, click **Old layout** or **Switch to classic view**. If that's not possible, check the Student Ancillaries page in myBusinessCourse for updated information or check with your instructor.

If an item is being purchased for a specific customer, the customer name can be included in the item row. Billing customers for costs is covered in Chapter 10.

When distributions are entered on the **Item details** section (and the form is saved), QBO automatically:

- Debits the account specified in the item setup for the amount of the purchase.
  - This would be an asset account if an **inventory** item was purchased; an expense account if a **non-inventory** item is purchased.
- Updates the quantity records if an **inventory** item is purchased.

BEHIND THE SCENES If **service** items are contracted out, checks to or bills from those vendors are also entered in the **Item details** section.

PRACTICE
EXERCISE
7.1

MBC

Purchase inventory for Craig's Design and Landscaping with a check.
(Purchased five **Fountain Pumps** for $65 to have on hand.)

1. Click **+ New** on the navigation bar and select **Check**.

2. Select **Norton Lumber and Building Materials** as the vendor.

(continued)

(continued from previous page)

    a. You may have to close the sidebar to access the full form. Click the > on the top left edge of the sidebar to close it.

3. Select Checking as the Bank Account and enter "71" as the check number.

4. Use the current date as the Payment date.

5. Open the Item details section (lower half of the screen) by clicking the triangle next to Item details.

6. Select Pump as the PRODUCT/SERVICE and enter "5" as the QTY.

7. Enter "65" as the AMOUNT.

8. **Make a note** of the new RATE calculated by QBO.

9. Click Save and close.

Ordering Inventory

Setting Reorder Points

eLecture

At the beginning of this chapter, we reviewed some important considerations in inventory management.

- Inventory levels should be high enough that customer orders can be promptly filled.

- Inventory levels should be low enough that costs and the risks of obsolescence are minimized.

Management generally puts considerable effort into determining what inventory level is appropriate for each product. As part of that process, they determine the **minimum** amount of product they should have on hand at any point in time to safely meet customer demand. When the quantity on hand reaches that minimum level, an order for more inventory is placed with the vendor. The minimum level is called the reorder point.

    A reorder point can be set for every inventory item in QBO. Reports can then be generated that list products that should be ordered based on current inventory levels.

    The reorder point is set in the inventory item record. (As a reminder, the item records are accessed by clicking the ⚙ on the icon bar and selecting Products and Services.)

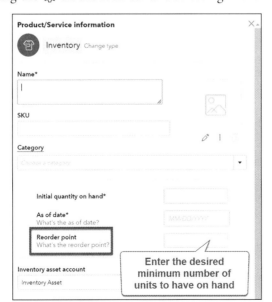

Figure 7.2

Inventory item record

The reorder point is entered in the **Reorder Point** field in the middle of the screen.

> **BEHIND THE SCENES** Reorder points are used by management to determine **when** to place orders. Setting a **reorder point** in QBO does not generate a transaction. QBO does not automatically generate a purchase order when the reorder point is reached.

Inventory items that have quantities on hand less than the reorder point (or have quantities of 0) are highlighted at the top of the Products and Services Center.

Figure 7.3

Stock status indicator

Click the quantity of low stock or out of stock items to display the item details.

Figure 7.4

List of items that are out of stock

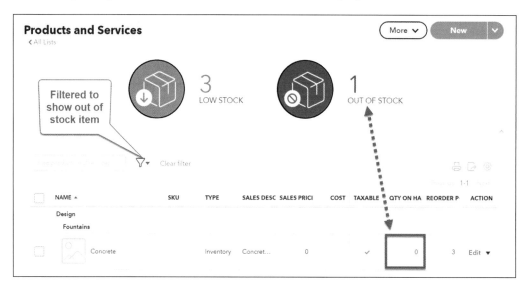

> **BEHIND THE SCENES** In manufacturing companies, the word "stock" is sometimes used to refer specifically to finished goods held for sale. The word "inventory" is generally used to refer either to finished goods held for sale or any of the materials used to manufacture those goods. QBO uses the terms "stock" and "inventory" interchangeably.

Reports can be created to assist employees responsible for ordering inventory.

To create a stock status report, select **Run report** in the **More** dropdown menu on the Products and Services Center screen. Customize the report by adding **Reorder Point** as a **Rows/Columns** field and removing **Price** as a **Rows/Columns** field. **Filter** the report by including only **inventory** items (**Fountains** and **Sprinklers**).

The customized report should look like Figure 7.5 after you complete Practice Exercise 7.2.

Craig's Design and Landscaping Services

Stock Status Report

PRODUCT/SERVICE	TYPE	DESCRIPTION	COST	QTY ON HAND	REORDER POINT
Design:Fountains:Pump	Inventory	Fountain Pump	10.00	25.00	50.00
Design:Fountains:Rock Fountain	Inventory	Rock Fountain	125.00	2.00	8.00
Landscaping:Sprinklers:Sprinkler ...	Inventory	Sprinkler Heads	0.75		25.00
Landscaping:Sprinklers:Sprinkler ...	Inventory	Sprinkler Pipes	2.50	31.00	25.00

Figure 7.5

Customized Product/Service list report

Adding **Preferred Vendor** and **Qty On PO** fields to the report would further improve the usefulness of the report.

Edit inventory items to include reorder points for Craig's Design and Landscaping.
(Craig's Design wants to set reorder points for pumps and rock fountains.)

1. Edit inventory items.
   a. Click the ⚙ on the icon bar.
   b. Select **Products and Services**.
   c. In the **Pump** row, click **Edit** in the **ACTION** column.
      i. Enter "50" as the **Reorder point**.
      ii. Click **Save and close**.
   d. In the **Rock Fountain** row, click **Edit** in the **ACTION** column.
      i. Enter "8" as the **Reorder point**.
      ii. Click **Save and close**.
   e. In the **Sprinkler Heads** and **Sprinkler Pipes** rows, click **Edit** in the **ACTION** column.
      i. Enter "25" as the **reorder point** for both.
      ii. Click **Save and close**.
2. Prepare a custom Stock Status report.
   a. Click **Run report** in the **More** dropdown menu on the **Products and Services** screen.
   b. Click **Customize**.
   c. Open the **Rows/Columns** section.
      i. Click **Change Columns**.
      ii. Check the **Reorder Point** field and uncheck the **Price** field.
   d. Open the **Filter** section.
      i. Check **Product/Service**.
      ii. In the **Product/Service** dropdown menu, check:
         1. **Design:Fountains:Pump**
         2. **Design:Fountains:Rock Fountain**
         3. **Landscaping:Sprinklers:Sprinkler Heads**
         4. **Landscaping:Sprinklers:Sprinkler Pipes**
   e. Open the **Header/Footer** section.
      i. Change the **Report title** to "Stock Status Report."
   f. Click **Run Report**.
   g. **Make a note** of the **QTY ON HAND** for **Sprinkler Heads**.
3. Click **Dashboard** on the navigation bar to exit the screen.

PRACTICE EXERCISE 7.2

MBC

QuickCheck
7-1

Creating Purchase Orders

Once the company decides how many of each item need to be purchased, the suppliers are contacted. Many suppliers will not fill an order without written documentation (a purchase order) from their customer. Even when the supplier doesn't require written documentation, most companies create purchase orders as part of their internal control system.

Although ordering inventory is not an accounting transaction, a good accounting software program will include a purchase order tracking system so that management knows, at all times, how many units are on their way.

> **BEHIND THE SCENES** Purchase orders are tracked in QBO for informational purposes only. No journal entry is recorded in QBO when a purchase order is created.

> Why isn't ordering inventory an accounting transaction?

The use of purchase orders is a **setting** (preference) in QBO. In the test drive company, the setting is turned on. To verify, click the ⚙ on the icon bar and select **Account and Settings**. Open the **Expenses** tab.

Figure 7.6

Purchase order feature activation

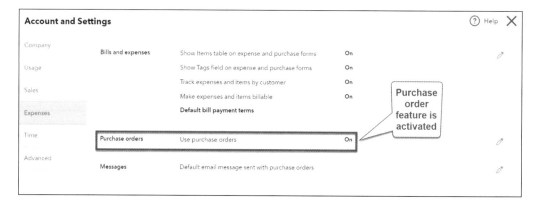

Figure 7.6 — Purchase order feature activation

Use purchase orders must be set to **On** for the feature to be available to use.

The **purchase order** form is accessed by clicking **+New** on the navigation bar and selecting **Purchase Order** in the **Vendors** column.

Figure 7.7

Link to purchase order form

The form is shown in Figure 7.8.

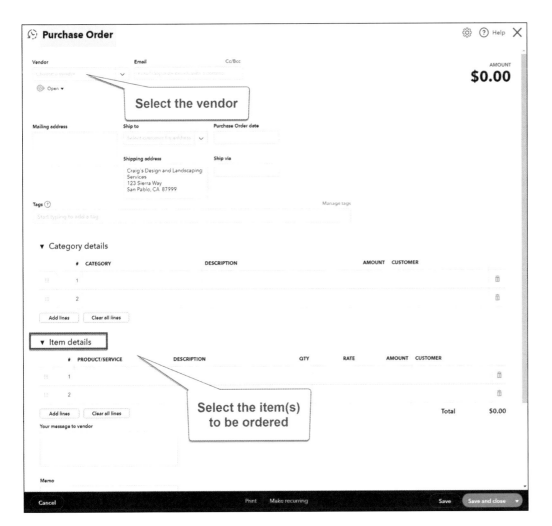

Figure 7.8

Purchase order form

 HINT: Remember, forms (like the **purchase order** shown in Figure 7.8) may have been updated. If possible, click **Old layout** or **Switch to classic view**. If that's not possible, check the Student Ancillaries page in myBusinessCourse for updated information or check with your instructor.

You need to enter the vendor name, the date, and the **products** being ordered to complete the form.

BEHIND THE SCENES QBO will automatically enter the default cost when an **inventory** item is selected. The unit cost can be changed at this point, if appropriate. The cost can also be changed later when the vendor bill is received.

If a **product** is being purchased for a specific customer, the customer name can be included in the product row (**item details** section). If a product will be shipped directly to the customer, the customer name should also be selected in the **Ship to** field.

Once a **purchase order** has been created, **product** records are automatically updated to show the number of items on open orders. Figure 7.9 shows the item record for Sprinkler Heads after a purchase order for 20 units was recorded.

Figure 7.9

Inventory item with
units on order

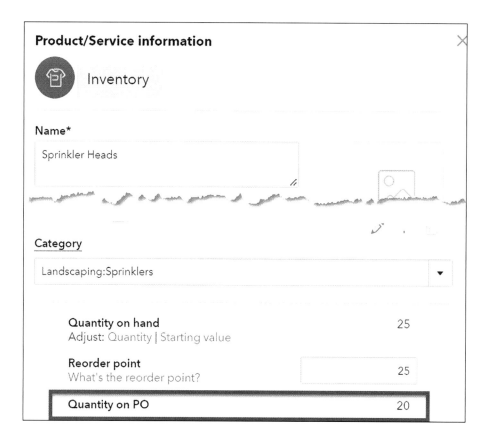

**PRACTICE
EXERCISE
7.3**

Create purchase orders for Craig's Design and Landscaping.

(Management decides to order 20 Sprinkler Heads and 10 Sprinkler Pipes.)

1. Click **+ New** on the navigation bar and select Purchase Order.

2. Select Tania's Nursery as the vendor.

3. Use the current date as the Purchase Order date.

4. In the Item details section:

   a. Select Sprinkler Heads as the PRODUCT/SERVICE and enter "20" as the QTY.

      i. Use the default Rate.

   b. In the next row, select Sprinkler Pipes as the PRODUCT/SERVICE and enter "10" as the QTY.

      i. Use the default Rate.

5. **Make a note** of the Total for the order as calculated by QBO.

6. Click Save and close.

Batching Multiple Items Ordered from the Same Vendor

Companies often purchase multiple inventory items from the same vendor.

Instead of adding each item individually to the purchase order form, you can streamline the process by creating a batch from the Products and Services list.

Click Sales on the navigation bar and open the Products and services tab.

Figure 7.10

Selection of items for reorder

Check the box in the far left column of each item to be ordered (❶ in Figure 7.10).

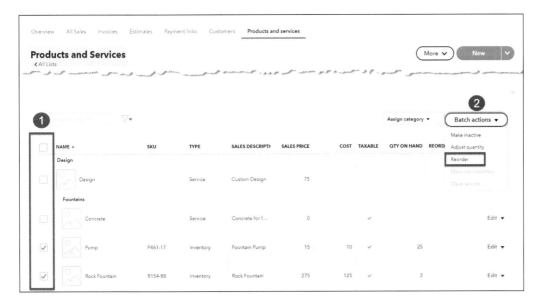

Figure 7.11

Batching inventory items

A new **Batch actions** dropdown menu will appear above the **ACTION** column. Select **Reorder** (❷ in Figure 7.11).

BEHIND THE SCENES As of early 2023, only **inventory** items could be batched for reordering.

A **purchase order** form will automatically open.

The vendor name and the order quantity would be added to the form. (The **QTY** field will default to 1.)

Adding a Preferred Vendor to an Item Record

Identifying a **preferred vendor** in the item record can be helpful if items are always (or almost always) ordered from the same supplier.

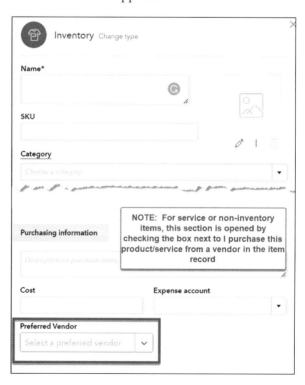

Preferred vendors are added in the **Purchasing information** section of the item record.

Figure 7.14 shows a **Product/Service List** report sorted by preferred vendor and customized to show quantity on hand, quantity on order, and reorder point. (The report was filtered to include only **inventory** items.)

Author developed report					
Craig's Design and Landscaping Services ✎					
Inventory Products by Vendor					
PREFERRED VENDOR	**DESCRIPTION**	**COST**	**QTY ON HAND**	**QTY ON PO**	**REORDER POINT**
Hicks Hardware	Fountain Pump	10.00	25.00	Order needed	30.00
Norton Lumber and Building Mat...	Sprinkler Heads	0.75	25.00		20.00
Norton Lumber and Building Mat...	Sprinkler Pipes	2.50	31.00		20.00
Tania's Nursery	Rock Fountain	125.00	2.00	3.00	4.00

Figure 7.14

Customized report of products by preferred vendor

This report could be a helpful tool in determining **if** any items should be ordered from the various vendors.

Receiving Ordered Inventory

Receiving Ordered Inventory with a Bill

When a vendor bill is received with the inventory shipment, click **+ New** on the navigation bar and select **Bill**.

Select the vendor name.

Figure 7.15 is an example of a **bill** entered for a vendor with an open purchase order.

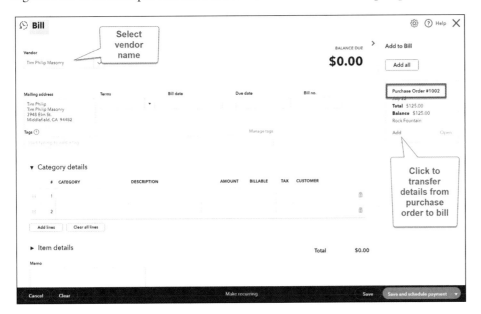

Figure 7.15

Link to add purchase order information to bill form

In the sidebar on the right side of the screen, click **Add** to transfer the information from the **purchase order** to the **bill**.

 HINT: The **purchase order** can be opened by clicking **Open** in the sidebar to make changes before the information is transferred.

Figure 7.16 shows the **bill** after the information is transferred over.

Figure 7.16

Bill form created from
purchase order

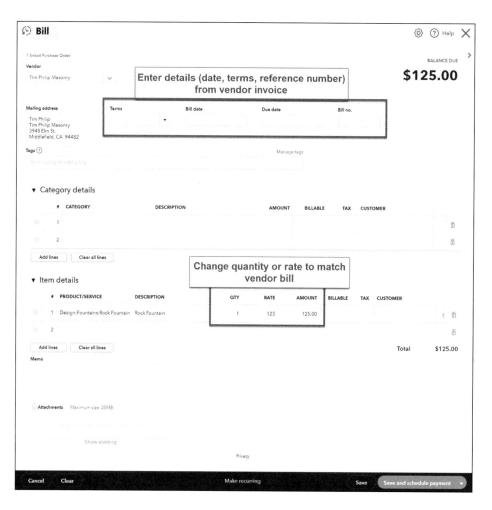

The Bill no., Bill date, and Terms should be added. RATE or AMOUNT fields can be changed. Additional charges can also be added. The final bill should match the vendor invoice.

To view or remove the purchase order, click linked transaction in the top left corner of the bill.

Figure 7.17

Options to open
or remove a linked
purchase order in a bill

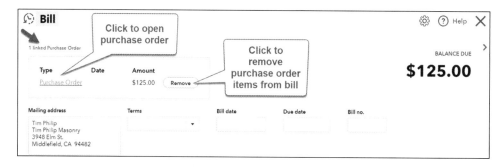

Click Purchase Order to view the original form.
To remove the purchase order (unlink it) from the bill, click Remove.

 HINT: A purchase order can be removed after the bill is saved. However, there must be some purchase information remaining or the bill can't be saved. (QBO will not save blank transactions.) If there is no other purchase information, the best practice is to delete the bill. The status of the purchase order will change to open if the linked bill is deleted.

Receive ordered inventory with a bill for Craig's Design and Landscaping.
(Items ordered on PO #1002 from Tim Philip Masonry received in full with a bill (#5011-33) for $130.00—slightly higher than expected.)

PRACTICE
EXERCISE
7.4

1. Click **Expenses** on the navigation bar.

2. Select the **Vendors drawer** (tab) to open the Vendor Center.

3. In the **ACTION** column in the row for **Tim Philip Masonry**, select **Create Bill**.

4. Select **Net 30** in the **Terms** field.

5. Use the current date as the **Bill date**.

6. Enter "5011-33" as the **Bill no.**

7. Click **Add** in the sidebar on the right side of the screen to transfer the **purchase order** information to the **bill** form.

8. **Make a note** of the **product** (description) transferred to the **bill**.

9. In the **Item details** section, change the **AMOUNT** to "130."

10. Click **Save and close**.

Receiving Partial Shipments

It's not unusual for a vendor to fill an order in multiple shipments. This would happen when:

- Ordered materials are coming from different locations.

- Vendors are out of stock of a particular item when the first shipment is sent but are able to send the backordered items at a later date.

QBO will track partially filled orders so that users can properly record inventory purchases as they're received.

To record a partial shipment of ordered items, click **+ New** on the navigation bar and select **Bill**.

Select the vendor's name and click **Add** in the sidebar to transfer information from the **purchase order** to the **bill**.

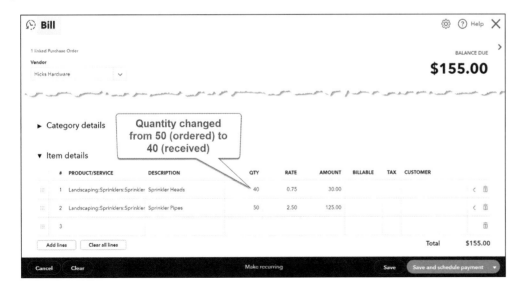

Figure 7.18

Example of purchase order modified for partial receipt

Enter the actual quantity received in the **QTY** field and save the **bill**.

To view the automatic changes to the purchase order, open the form. (To find the form, use the Advanced Search feature and filter the search to Purchase Orders and select the vendor name in the CONTACT dropdown menu.)

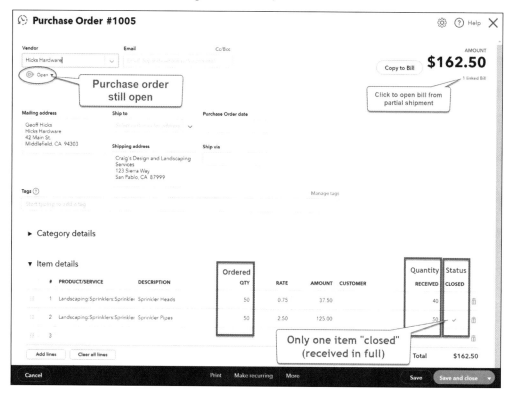

The purchase order will now display a RECEIVED quantity column and the purchase order will remain open.

When the remaining items are received, a new bill would be created from the updated purchase order.

PRACTICE
EXERCISE
7.5

MBC

Receive a partial shipment of ordered inventory for Craig's Design and Landscaping.
(Five of the eight fountain pumps ordered on PO #1005 from Norton Lumber and Building Materials received with a bill (#46464).)

1. Create a purchase order for eight fountain pumps and three rock fountains.

    a. Click ➕ New on the navigation bar.

    b. Click Purchase order.

    c. Select Norton Lumber and Building Materials as the Vendor.

    d. Use the current date as the Purchase Order date.

        i. QBO may have automatically added items and quantities in the Items detail section based on previous transactions with the vendor. (This happens when automation is not turned off in Account and Settings.) Click the trash icon in the far right of each row to remove them.

    e. Select Pump as the PRODUCT/SERVICE and enter "8" as the QTY.

    f. On the next line, select Rock Fountain as the PRODUCT/SERVICE and enter "3" as the QTY.

(continued)

(continued from previous page)

    g. Click **Save and close**.

2. Enter the bill for the items received:

    a. Click **+ New** on the navigation bar.

    b. Click **Bill**.

    c. Select **Norton Lumber and Building Materials** as the **Vendor**.

    d. Select **Net 30** in the **Terms** field.

    e. Use the current date as the **Bill date**.

    f. Enter "46464" as the **Bill no.**

    g. Click the **trash** icon in the far right column of the **item details** section for any rows automatically added by QBO.

    h. Click **Add** in the sidebar on the right side of the screen to transfer the **purchase order** information to the **bill** form.

    i. In the **Item details** section, change the **QTY** for **Fountain Pumps** from 8 to 5.

    j. Change the **QTY** for **Rock Fountains** from 3 to 0.

    k. **Make a note** of the new **Total**.

    l. Click **Save and close**.

3. Receive the backordered items.

    a. Click **+ New** on the navigation bar.

    b. Click **Bill**.

    c. Select **Norton Lumber and Building Materials** as the **Vendor**.

    d. Select **Net 30** in the **Terms** field.

    e. Use the current date as the **Bill date**.

    f. Enter "46468" as the **Bill no.**

    g. Click the **trash** icon in the far right column for any rows automatically added by QBO.

    h. Click **Add** in the sidebar on the right side of the screen to transfer the remaining items to the **bill**.

    i. **Make a note** of the **Total** amount.

    j. Click **Save**.

    k. Click **1 linked Purchase Order**. **TIP:** This should in the upper left corner of the form.

    l. Click **Purchase Order**.

    m. Each item should have a checkmark in the **Closed** column.

    n. Click **Save and close**.

Receiving Ordered Inventory without a Bill

Merchandising companies need to update their inventory records as soon as purchased goods arrive so that their inventory on hand quantities are accurate. However, many suppliers include a packing slip (detailing the products and quantities included in the carton) with their shipments but no bill. The vendor's invoice (detailing costs) frequently arrives after the shipment. This might be done:

- As part of a supplier's internal control system.

- Because a supplier's warehouse or store is physically separate from the supplier's accounting office.

QBO does not currently have a feature that allows the company to record an increase in inventory and the creation of a related liability in the accounting records without a **bill** being created.

To keep inventory quantities updated, the company would normally create a **bill** using the anticipated costs. The **bill** would then be updated (with actual costs and vendor reference numbers) when the vendor invoice was finally received.

It would be good practice to make a note of the packing slip number in the **Memo** box of the **bill**. This should make it easier to match the final bill to the draft bill created in QBO from the packing slip.

Managing Purchase Orders

QBO automatically "closes" purchase orders when all of the items have been received.

Sometimes a company might need to manually close a purchase order (or a single item on a purchase order). This might happen when:

* The supplier is unable to ship the item(s).

* The company decides to order from a different supplier.

Closing a purchase order is a housekeeping task. There are no underlying journal entries!

To manually close a purchase order, the **Purchase Order** form must be open. **Purchase orders** can be found by selecting **Open Purchase Orders Detail** report in the **Expenses and Vendors** section of **Reports**.

Figure 7.20

Access to open purchase order

Click the purchase order number of the **purchase order** you want to manually close to open the form.

Figure 7.21

Option to manually close purchase order

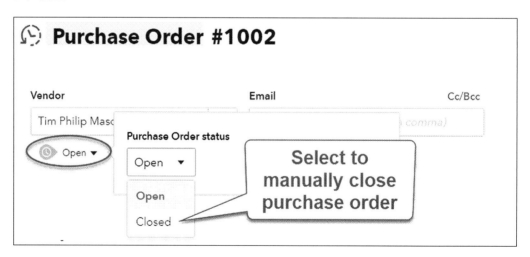

Select **Closed** on the purchase order status dropdown menu to close the entire order. (The purchase order status menu is directly below the vendor name field.)

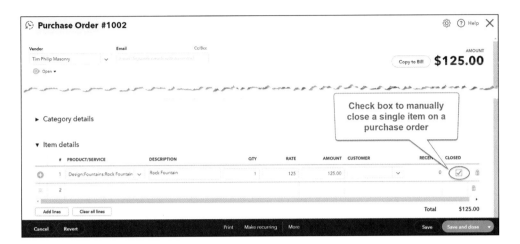

To close a single item on a purchase order, check the box in the **Closed** column.

Manually close a purchase order for Craig's Design and Landscaping.
(Craig's Design decides it doesn't need the Rock Fountain ordered from Tim Philip Masonry on PO #1002.)

1. **TIP:** If you didn't log out of the test drive company after completing Practice Exercise 7.4, log out to clear out previous transactions. Log back in to continue.

2. Click **Reports** on the navigation bar.

3. Click **Open Purchase Order List** in the **Expenses and Vendors** section.

4. Click PO #1002.

5. Click **Open** (directly under the vendor name field) to access the **Purchase Order status** dropdown menu.

6. Select **Closed**.

7. Click **Save**.

   a.   Verify that there's a check in the **CLOSED** column for the **Rock Fountain** row.

8. Click **Save and close**.

**PRACTICE
EXERCISE
7.6**

Homework
MBC

Ordering Inventory Without Using the Purchase Order System

Given the importance of maintaining proper inventory levels, most companies want to track the status of orders they've placed with suppliers (purchase orders) and choose to use the purchase order system outlined above.

Companies that do not use purchase orders can still, of course, use QBO!

MANAGING VENDOR CREDITS

Vendors issue credit memos for a variety of reasons. Those reasons might include the following:

- Goods were returned.

- There was an error on a previously issued bill.

- To give a "good faith" allowance when a customer isn't satisfied with goods or service.

LO 7-2 Describe and demonstrate the method for recording and applying credits received from vendors in QBO

eLecture

Vendor credits aren't unique to merchandising companies. Service and manufacturing companies would also use the procedures outlined here.

Entering Credits from Vendors

Credit memos from vendors are recorded in QBO as **transaction type Vendor Credit**. (Remember: a credit issued to a customer is **transaction type Credit Memo**.)

To access the vendor credit form, click **+ New** on the navigation bar and select **Vendor Credit** in the **Vendors** column.

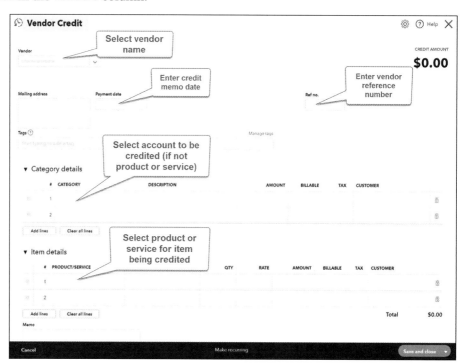

> **HINT:** Remember, forms (like the **vendor credit** shown in Figure 7.23) may have been updated. If possible, click **Old layout** or **Switch to classic view**. If that's not possible, check the Student Ancillaries page in myBusinessCourse for updated information or check with your instructor.

You'll need to enter the vendor name, date of the credit memo (identified as **Payment date** in QBO), vendor reference number, and the account (or items) that should be credited. The form includes some familiar sections (**Category details** and **Item details**).

Vendor credits received for returned inventory items or overbillings on inventory items would be entered in the **Item details** section. All other vendor credits would be entered in the **Category details** section.

Vendor credits are tracked in the vendor subsidiary ledger. All recorded credits are displayed on the **transaction list** tab in the vendor record.

Applying Credits from Vendors

To apply a **vendor credit** when a payment is made, click **Expenses** on the navigation bar.

Select the **Vendors drawer** (tab) to open the Vendor Center. Click the **vendor** to be paid to open the vendor record.

Open the **Transaction List** tab.

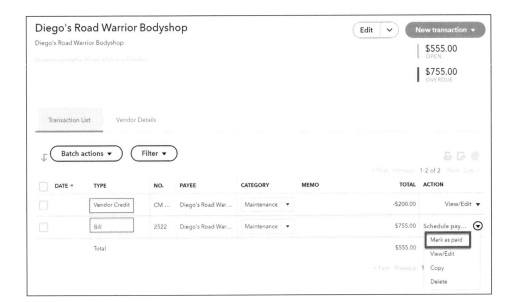

Figure 7.24

Access to vendor payment

Click **Mark as paid** in the **ACTION** column of an open **bill**.

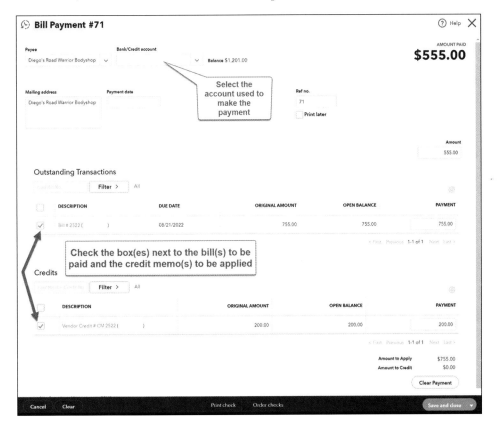

Figure 7.25

Example of credit applied on payment to a vendor

If there are available credits, QBO will automatically apply them. The **credit** can be deselected if the user elects to retain the credit for future use.

 HINT: Vendor credits can be applied to bills before payment is made. In the **bill payment** screen, enter 0 as the **Amount** and enter the credit amount in both **PAYMENT** fields.

Vendor credits can also be applied through the pay bills screen.
Click **+ New** on the navigation bar.
Select Pay bills.

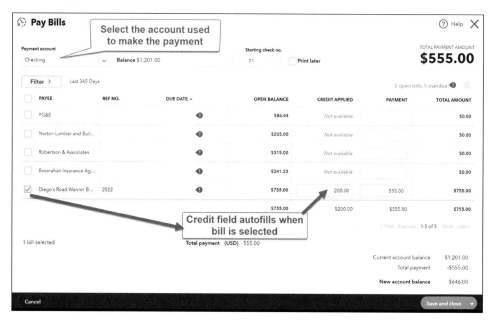

Available credits will be displayed for all vendors selected (checked).
If any of the available credit amount is manually entered in the CREDIT APPLIED field,
the PAYMENT amount will automatically adjust.

PRACTICE

EXERCISE

7.7

Enter a vendor credit for Craig's Design and Landscaping.

(Craig's Design receives a credit memo from Diego's Road Warrior Bodyshop. They had
been overcharged for some repair work done by Diego's.)

1. Record the vendor credit.

   a. Click **+ New** on the navigation bar and select Vendor Credit.

   b. Select Diego's Road Warrior Bodyshop as the Vendor.

   c. Use the current date as the Payment date.

   d. On the Category details section, select Equipment Repairs as the CATEGORY.

   e. Enter "Overcharge" in the DESCRIPTION field.

   f. Enter "200" as the AMOUNT.

   g. Click Save and close.

2. Apply the vendor credit.

   a. Click Expenses on the navigation bar.

   b. Select the Vendors drawer (tab) to open the Vendor Center.

   c. Select Make Payment in the ACTION column dropdown menu of Diego's Road
      Warrior Bodyshop.

   d. Select Checking as the payment method in the Bank/Credit account field.

   e. Use the current date as the payment date.

(continued)

(continued from previous page)

      f. Use "71" as the check number in the **Ref no.** field.

      g. Make sure that both the **credit** and the **bill** are checked.

      h. **Make a note** of the check amount.

      i. Click **Save and close**.

Special Considerations for Returns of Inventory

QBO uses the FIFO method for valuing inventory. When an item is returned (through a **vendor credit**), QBO credits the inventory account for the cost in the oldest FIFO layer. That may or may not agree to the amount on the vendor credit. If it doesn't agree, QBO will automatically debit (or credit) the difference to the **Expense account** identified in the item record (normally a cost of goods sold account).

    To illustrate, let's assume we return one Fountain Pump to Norton Lumber and Building Material. The pumps had cost us $10 each to purchase. The **vendor credit** would look like Figure 7.27 if Norton only gave us a $9 credit for the return.

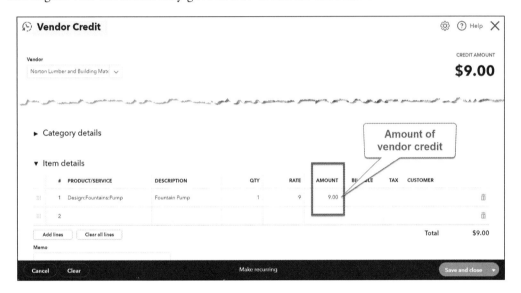

Figure 7.27

Example vendor credit for inventory item

To see how the inventory valuation is impacted, click **Reports** on the navigation bar. Select **Inventory Valuation Detail** in the **Sales and Customers** section. Change the dates to see transactions over the last thirty days. Click **Run report**.

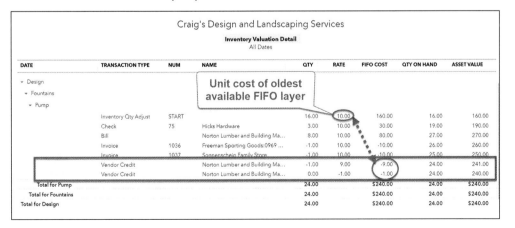

Figure 7.28

Illustration of inventory account detail

Two lines appear for the transaction. The first line shows a reduction of 1 unit at a FIFO cost of $9 (the amount of the credit). The second line shows an adjustment to the FIFO cost of an additional $1. This represents the difference between the credit of $9 and the oldest FIFO layer cost of $10 per unit.

To see the underlying journal entry, click the **Vendor Credit** transaction in the report.

Figure 7.29

Access to journal entry underlying form

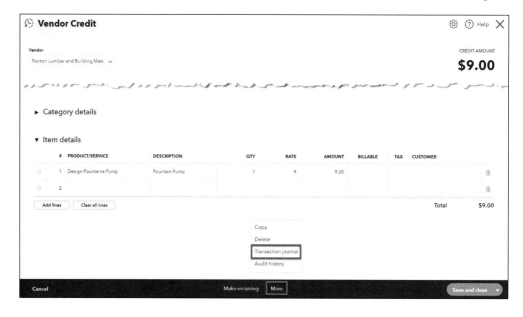

Click **More** and select **Transaction Journal**.

Figure 7.30

Example of a journal entry underlying vendor credit

In the entry (Figure 7.30), Inventory Asset has been credited for $10, Accounts Payable has been debited for $9, and the $1 difference has been debited to Cost of Goods Sold.

PRACTICE EXERCISE 7.8

MBC

Enter a vendor credit for return of inventory for Craig's Design and Landscaping.
(One damaged Fountain Pump was returned to Norton Lumber.)

1. Record the vendor credit for return of inventory.

   a. Click **+ New** on the navigation bar and select **Vendor Credit**.

   b. Select **Hicks Hardware** as the **Vendor**.

   c. Use the current date as the **Payment date**.

   d. In the **Item details** section, select **Rock Fountain** as the **PRODUCT/SERVICE**. **TIP:** You may need to click the triangle next to **Item details** to open the section.

   e. Enter "1" as the **QTY** and "110" as the **AMOUNT**.

(continued)

(continued from previous page)

     f. Click **Save**.

 HINT: If **Save** does not appear on the **vendor credit** form (Step 1(f)), click **Save and new**. Click the clock icon to the left of **Vendor Credit** (top left corner) and select the $110 credit for **Hicks Hardware**. You should now be able to complete Step 2.

2. Review the underlying entry for the **vendor credit**.
    a. Select **Transaction journal** in the **More** dropdown menu (bottom of page).
    b. **Make a note** of the account debited for $15.

PAYING VENDOR BALANCES

LO 7-3 Explain and demonstrate how early payment discounts are recorded in QBO

We covered the basics of paying vendor account balances in Chapter 4.

In this chapter, we'll look at reducing payments to vendors by taking available early payment discounts.

Although early payment discounts can be small in dollar amount, the return is quite high. For example, a common payment term is 2%/10, net 30. The customer gets a reduction of 2% off the bill just for paying 20 days early. The effective interest rate earned on that discount is almost 37%! Most companies want to take those discounts whenever possible.

Although vendor payment terms are set in the vendor record, QBO does not currently have a feature that allows users to track **bills** by discount date or to automatically apply any allowable early payment discounts when a **bill** is paid. There are some tools that can be used, though, as a substitute for automatic tracking.

Taking Early Payment Discounts
Setting Up Early Payment Discount Terms

Before we start, let's review the process for setting up payment terms initially covered in Chapter 3.

Click the ⚙ on the icon bar and select **All Lists**.

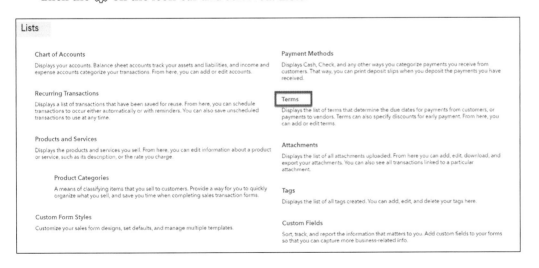

Figure 7.31

Access to credit terms list

Click **Terms** and click **New**.

Although QBO currently doesn't include automatic early payment discount feature options, you can create a **term** that identifies the available discount in the **name**. This would then appear on vendor **bills** and on customer **invoices**.

Figure 7.32

Credit term setup
screen

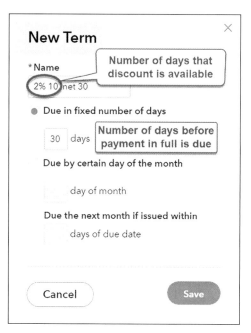

A payment term of 2% 10, net 30 means that the bill is due in full in 30 days. However, if you pay within 10 days you get a discount of 2%. Figure 7.32 shows how that payment term would be set up in QBO.

Tracking Bills with Early Payment Discounts

For tracking early payment discounts, it's fairly easy to create a custom report that can be used to identify discount opportunities.

Click **Reports** on the navigation bar. Select **Unpaid Bills** in the **What You Owe** section.

Click **Customize**. Open **Rows/Columns** and click **Change columns**. Check **Terms** to add that column to the report. **Past Due** and **Due Date** columns could be removed. The order of the columns could also be rearranged.

Figure 7.33

Illustration of
customization for
report of available early
payment discounts

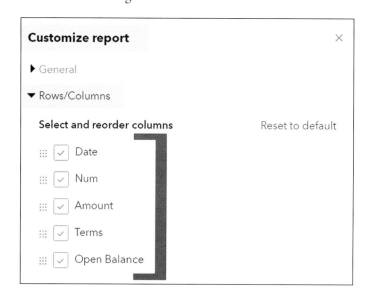

Open **Filter** on the **Customization** sidebar.

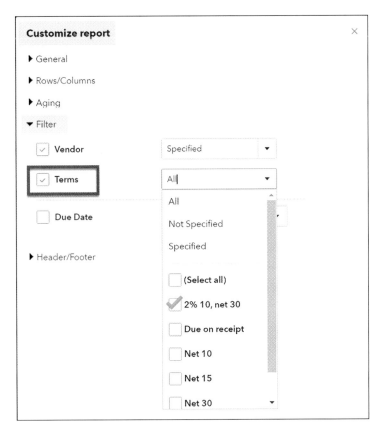

Figure 7.34
Illustration of filters for report of available early payment discounts

Check **Terms** and select all terms that include early payment discounts.
The report title could be changed in **Header/Footer**.

Click **Run Report**. The report might look something like Figure 7.35.

Figure 7.35
Example of customized unpaid bills report

The report can then be scanned for available discounts.

Taking Available Early Payment Discounts

As noted earlier, QBO does not currently have a feature that allows users to automatically apply available early payment discounts when a **bill** is paid.

> **BEHIND THE SCENES** Although it would be possible to enter the amount of the early payment discount as a line item in the **bill**, early payment discounts should not be recognized until it is certain that payment will be made within the payment terms.

What users can do is create a **vendor credit** in the amount of the discount just before the payment is processed.

The **vendor credit** would then be applied to the **bill** when the payment is recorded.

> **BEHIND THE SCENES** Under GAAP, discounts related to the purchase of inventory are properly accounted for as a reduction of the cost in inventory. QBO does not have the capacity to handle that level of complexity. As long as the error in inventory values (due to these discounts) is not material (not significant), crediting cost of goods sold for early payment discounts on inventory items is acceptable.

PRACTICE
EXERCISE
7.9

Record payment of a bill with an early payment discount for Craig's Design and Landscaping.

(Robertson & Associates has changed its credit terms to 2%/10, net 30. Craig's intends to take the discount as allowed on the $315 bill currently due to Robertson.)

1. Set up the new terms.
   a. Click the ⚙ on the icon bar.
   b. Click **All Lists**.
   c. Click **Terms**.
   d. Click **New**.
   e. Enter "2% 10, net 30" as the **Name**.
   f. Toggle **Due in Fixed number of days**.
   g. Enter "30" in the **days** field.
   h. Click **Save**.

2. Add the new terms to Robertson & Associates' vendor record.
   a. Click **Expenses** on the navigation bar.
   b. Select the **Vendors drawer** (tab) to open the Vendor Center.
   c. Click **Robertson & Associates**.
   d. Click **Edit** to open the vendor record.
   e. In the **Additional info** section, select **2%/10, net 30** in the **Terms** dropdown menu.
   f. **Make a note** of the **Account no.**
   g. Click **Save**.
   h. Open the **Transaction List** tab. (You should still be in the vendor record.)
   i. Click the $315 open bill.
   j. Select **2% 10, net 30** in the **Terms** field.
   k. Click **Save and close**.

3. Create a **vendor credit** to record the early payment discount.
   a. Click **+ New** on the navigation bar and select **Vendor Credit**.

(continued)

(continued from previous page)

   b.   Select Robertson & Associates as the Vendor.

   c.   Use the current date as the Payment date and enter "2533" as the Ref no.

   d.   In the Category details section, select Miscellaneous as the ACCOUNT.

       i.   If the discount was related to a purchase of inventory, a cost of goods sold
            account would be more appropriate.

   e.   Enter "2% early payment discount on $315 bill" in the DESCRIPTION field.

   f.   Enter "6.30" as the AMOUNT.

   g.   Click Save and close.

4. Pay the discounted bill.

   a.   Click Expenses on the navigation bar.

   b.   Select the Vendors drawer (tab) to open the Vendor Center.

   c.   Click Make Payment in the ACTION column for Robertson & Associates.

   d.   Select Checking as the payment method.

   e.   Use the current date as the payment date.

       i.   In this example, it is possible that the payment date is more than 10 days
            past the invoice date. Since the test drive company dates are constantly
            changing, we'll have to accept some departures from reality!

   f.   Use "72" as the check number in the Ref no. field.

   g.   Make sure that both the credit and the bill are checked.

   h.   **Make a note** of the amount of the check.

   i.   Click Save and close.

PREPARING VENDOR REPORTS

We reviewed some of the standard vendor and payables reports in Chapter 4. For this
chapter, we're most interested in inventory and purchase reports.

LO 7-4 Identify and prepare common inventory reports in QBO

   Inventory valuation reports are accessed through the Sales and Customers section of
Reports. A commonly used inventory report is:

● **Inventory Valuation Summary**

   ▪   A report of quantity, average cost, and total cost of units on hand, by item.

Inventory purchase reports are accessed through the Expenses and Vendors section of Reports. Commonly used reports include:

● **Open Purchase Order List**

   ▪   List of all unfilled purchase orders.

● **Purchases by Product/Service Detail**

   ▪   A report of purchases, by item, including information about quantity, unit cost,
       and vendor.

● **Purchases by Vendor Detail**

   ▪   A report of purchases, by vendor, including information about items, quantity,
       and unit cost.

<table>
<tr>
<td>

PRACTICE
EXERCISE
7.10

</td>
<td>

Prepare reports on inventory for Craig's Design and Landscaping.
(Craig's Design wants an inventory valuation report.)

1. Click Reports on the navigation bar.

    a. Click Inventory Valuation Summary in the Sales and Customers section.

    b. **Make a note** of the four columns included in the report other than the column including the product name.

    c. Click Dashboard to close the report screen.

</td>
</tr>
</table>

ANSWER TO
QuickCheck
7-1

> Because there is no change in the accounting equation when an order is placed.

CHAPTER SHORTCUTS

Record vendor credit memos
1. Click **+ New** on the navigation bar.
2. Click Vendor Credit.

Record purchase orders
1. Click **+ New** on the navigation bar.
2. Click Purchase Order.

CHAPTER REVIEW

Assignments with the MBC **are available in myBusinessCourse.**

Matching

Match the term or phrase (as used in QuickBooks Online) to its definition.

1. vendor credit
2. item details
3. make payment
4. open purchase orders list

5. reorder point
6. purchase order
7. stock
8. inventory valuation summary

_____ inventory
_____ dropdown option in vendor center used to open a bill payment form
_____ section of a form used to identify distribution of inventory charges or credits
_____ transaction type used to record credit memos received from vendors
_____ report summarizing the quantity and value of inventory items
_____ report of all unfilled purchase orders
_____ order for goods sent to vendor
_____ minimum desired quantity of inventory to have on hand

Multiple Choice

1. **Accounts Payable (A/P)** is credited in QBO when:
   a. inventory is ordered from the supplier.
   b. a vendor bill for inventory is paid.
   c. a bill for inventory is received from a supplier
   d. inventory purchases are made by check.

2. Recorded **vendor credits** _____.

   a. result in credits to the accounts payable account
   b. automatically appear in the **CREDIT APPLIED** field on the **pay bills** screen when a bill from the vendor is selected for payment
   c. must be applied when a payment is made to a vendor with open credits
   d. can not be created for inventory items

3. If some but not all of the items on a purchase order have been received, and the **bill** has been created,

   a. the purchase order is automatically marked as "closed" by QBO.
   b. the purchase order must be manually updated by checking the **CLOSED** column for each item received.
   c. the purchase order remains open until the bill has been paid.
   d. the purchase order remains open until all items have been received or the user manually closes the purchase order.

4. The reorder point for an **inventory** item represents:

   a. the minimum number of units that should be maintained in inventory.
   b. the minimum number of units that should included in a single order.
   c. the maximum number of units that should be maintained in inventory.
   d. the average number of units that should included in a single order.

5. To take an early payment discount on a vendor bill, _____.

   a. a **vendor credit** for the amount of the discount can be created and applied to the bill when paid
   b. the potential discount can be recorded when the **bill** is initially entered
   c. a **term** which includes the early payment discount rate can be created in QBO. The discount amount would be automatically applied by QBO when the **bill** is paid.
   d. Both *a* and *b* are possible in QBO although *a* would be considered best practice in accounting.

BEYOND THE CLICKS—THINKING LIKE A MANAGER

Accounting: You opened an office supply store several years ago. Business is picking up, and you realize you're going to need to delegate some of your duties in order to continue growing. You will continue to decide which products to sell, but you want one of your managers to take on the responsibility for determining when and how much of each item to order. Do you choose the accounting manager, the sales manager, or the warehouse manager on staff? Explain your choice.

Information Systems: The owner of the company has asked you to create a detailed report of vendor activity over the last 60 days. Look through the standard QBO reports. Which QBO report do you think would be the most useful to the owner? What modifications (customizations), if any, would you make to the report?

ASSIGNMENTS

2/1/24

✓ You pay the February rent ($850) to your landlord, Pro Spaces, (Check #1113).

✓ You also mail a check to Martin's dad (Richard Smith) for the interest owed to him for January (Check #1114). **TIP:** Look at the balance sheet if you've forgotten the interest amount due.

  ● You write the check to Richard Smith (Martin's dad). The address is 5406 Hawthorne Ave, Seattle, WA 98107. You set the terms at Net 30.

2/6/24

✓ Martin went to a Math Educators Conference in Los Angeles last weekend (2/3–2/4). You charge all his expenses to 624 Professional development expense in QBO, a new sub-account of **Labor Costs**. (You select **620 Labor Costs** in the **Save account under** field.) You use **Office/ General Administrative Expenses** as the **Detail Type** (**Tax form section** field). He used the VISA credit card to pay for the following:

  ● Gas for the trip $45 (LA Gasoline Stop)

  ● Hotel room (2 nights) $280 (Good Sleep Inn)

  ● Meals $125 (Good Sleep Inn)

  ● **TIP:** You **must** create a **separate** Expense transaction for each charge. The reason will become clear in the homework for Chapter 8. Use 2/4 as the date of the transactions.

2/9/24

✓ Since Martin has started selling products, you decide to enter reorder points for the items currently in QBO to help manage inventory levels. You enter reorder points of 15 for the books (**Puzzles**, **Sports**, and **Ready**), 15 for the geometry kits and dry-erase boards (**Kit** and **Dry-Erase**), and 8 for the notebooks (**Notebook**).

✓ You want to keep track of any orders you place so you turn on the purchase order feature in the **Expense** tab of **Account and Settings**. You also toggle **Custom transaction numbers** On. **TIP:** You need to open the **Purchase orders** section to see the **Custom transaction numbers** toggle button. Even if the **Purchase order** feature is on, **Custom transaction numbers** may not be activated.

✓ You look at the inventory items on hand and see that many of the items are below the reorder point.

✓ You prepare a **purchase order** (PO-100) and order the following from Books Galore:

  ● 15 each of **Puzzles** and **Sports**

  ● 10 **Ready**

  ● The PO total is $660.

✓ You also place an order with Math Shack (PO-101 for $100) for 10 of the geometry kits (**Kit**). You decide to wait and order more **Notebooks** later.

2/12/24

✓ You pay all bills due on or before 2/20.

  ● There are two bills to be paid. The total amount is $1,841.36. The first check number is 1115.

2/14/24

✓ Martin learned about a new product at the Math Educators Conference he attended in Los Angeles. It's a low-cost handheld game console that can be loaded with a variety of educational math games. His plan is to sell the consoles and the software packs to local math tutoring centers for elementary school children. He has found the following supplier that you go ahead and add.

- Cartables, Inc.
  1390 Freestone Road
  San Diego, CA 92104
  Main Phone: (619) 378-5432

- You see that Cartables allows a 2% discount if the payment is made within 10 days. You set up the new **term** and name it "2% 10, net 30." You add the term to Cartable's vendor record. **TIP:** Since the bill is due in 30 days if you do not pay it early, you use 30 as the **fixed number of days** in the term.

- You decide to set up a new category called "Math Games" for the new product line. **TIP:** Select **Manage categories** in the **More** dropdown menu in the **Products and Services** center to create a new **category**.

- You talk with Martin and decide that each new **inventory** item:
  - Will have a reorder point of 3.
  - Will be recorded in the **130 Inventory Asset** account.
  - Will use account **420 Sales of Product Income** and **500 Cost of Goods Sold** as the **Income** and **Expense** accounts, respectively.
  - Is taxable. **TIP:** If QBO suggests a tax status (Instructional materials), you can go ahead and click **Confirm**.
  - Has Cartables as the **preferred vendor**.
  - **TIP:** Enter 0 as the **initial quantity on hand** and 02/01/2024 as the **As of date**. You'll be entering purchases of the items when they are received.

- You set up all the new **inventory** items **TIP:** Once you create one new item, you can select **Duplicate** the item on the **ACTION** menu for that item and edit the copy for each additional item.
  - Console (Description—Game Console)—Expected cost $245; Selling price $375
  - Fractions (Description—Parts of a Whole)—Expected cost $40; Selling price $60
  - Equations (Description—Equal or Not?)—Expected cost $50; Selling price $70
  - Ratios (Description—Ratios and Proportions)—Expected cost $45; Selling price $65

- You prepare PO-102 for the first Cartables order—5 consoles and 5 each of the three game packs. The PO totals $1,900.

✓ You receive the 10 **Kits** from Math Shack ordered on PO-101. There was no bill included in the shipment. You go ahead and enter a **bill** dated 2/14 using the expected costs and terms (Net 15). The total is $100.

2/16/24

✓ You receive the following bills in the mail:
- Sacramento Utilities February bill (for heat and light) #01-77135 for $185.75 dated 2/16. The terms are Net 30.
- Horizon Phone February bill #121–775 for $41.58 dated 2/16. This is the first bill for the landline recently installed in the tutoring room. You charge the amount to the Utilities Expense account. The terms are Net 30.

2/19/24

✓ You receive the books ordered from Books Galore on PO-100. All items were received except for the 15 **Puzzles** books. Bill # 2117 for $435 was included. The terms are Net 30. **TIP:** You're just removing the one line from the bill.

2/21/24

✓ The order from Cartables (PO-102) comes in today. All items are received. A bill (#949444-55) for $1,900 is included with the shipment. You make a note to yourself to remember to pay the amount by 3/2 so that you can take advantage of the 2% discount.

✓ You receive a bill dated 2/21 from Math Shack for the 10 **Kits** received on 2/14. The bill (#M58822) is for $110, which is a little higher than expected. You call Math Shack and they let you know that they had to find a new supplier for the **Kits** and the price went up to $11 per kit. You adjust the bill you already recorded in QBO accordingly (**date** and **amount**). The terms are Net 15. **TIP:** You **must** change the date on the **bill** to 2/21 to keep the FIFO layers accurate. Consider using the search feature to find the Math Shack bill. You can ignore any message about linked transactions.

> **BEHIND THE SCENES** Most users prefer to enter the bill date, rather than the receive date, when recording vendor invoices so that the payable records are more accurate. (Due dates are generally based on the invoice date.) The difference in dates may affect the FIFO layer(s). However, this would normally be an insignificant amount.

✓ You edit the **Kit** item in **Products and Services** to reflect the new default cost ($11). Martin decides that the sales price shouldn't be adjusted. He'll absorb the small decrease in gross profit.

2/22/24

✓ Martin sees a great new book when he stops by Books Galore. The book is called "Making Sense with Statistics." He purchases 10 of them to hold for resale, using check #1117. The total cost is $190. **TIP:** Ignore any charges that appear in the sidebar. Make sure you're in the **Item details** section of the form.

● You set up the new **inventory** item using "Statistics" as the item name and "Making Sense with Statistics" as the description. The cost is $19 each. You set the sales price at $29 after discussing it with Martin and the reorder point at 5. **TIP:** Make sure you link the new item to a **category** and set the item as taxable. (You can use QBO's tax suggestion.) You can use 2/01/2024 as the **As of date** and 0 as the **Initial quantity on hand**.

✓ Samantha Levin stops by. She worked at the Mathmagic clinic for 5 hours last Saturday so you write her a check (#1118) for $125. **TIP:** Use the same labor cost account you did in the Chapter 4 payment to Samantha.

2/23/24

✓ Martin returns the 3 broken **Kits** to Math Shack. They prepare a credit memo, which he brings back to the office. You record the credit (#R2525-8) for $30. **TIP:** The rate on the returned **kits** is $10.

✓ You and Martin meet at Dick's Diner for lunch and a short meeting. You decide to bring him an $1,000 dividend check (Check # 1119). It's less than last month because you're a bit concerned about the big bill from Cartables. You want to take advantage of the discount, and plan to pay the bill early next week.

✓ The lunch at Dick's Diner comes to $22.60. You use the VISA card to pay the bill.

● You charge the lunch to **628 Staff Relations**.

✓ Martin reviews the inventory on hand when he gets back from the meeting.

● He places an order with Books Galore (PO-103) for the following:

▪ 10 each **Sports** and **Ready**

▪ He decides not to order **Puzzles** yet. He's still waiting for the backordered shipment from PO-100.

● He places an order with Math Shack (PO-104) for 8 **Kits**. You use the new $11 unit price.

✓ You enter both purchase orders in QBO. The total for PO-103 is $350. The total for PO-104 is $88.

2/27/24

✓ You receive a bill (#3330) for $875 in the mail from a consulting firm, Les & Schmidt, LLC. Martin had hired the company to create a marketing plan for him. Les & Schmidt completed the work in February. The bill is dated 2/28. The bill is due in 30 days. **TIP:** This is a consulting service.

- The address for Les & Schmidt is 25 Norton Way, Sacramento, CA 95822.

✓ You pay the Cartables bill, taking advantage of the early payment discount.

- You start by creating a **vendor credit** to record the early payment discount you will be taking on the Cartables bill. The discount is 2% of the total $1,900 due. You use "DISC" as the **Ref no.**

    ■ Since the early payment discount applies to inventory purchases, you charge the amount to a new **Cost of Goods Sold** account. You name the account "Purchase Discounts" and use 510 as the account number and **Supplies & Materials—COGS** as the detail type (**Tax form section** field). **TIP:** You identify the **account type** by selecting **Cost of Goods Sold** in the **Save account under** field. **Cost of Goods Sold** here does not have an account number because it represents an **account type**, not an actual account. Purchase discounts is not a sub-account.

- You then pay the Cartables bill with check #1120. The check totals $1,862. **TIP:** If you're using the **Pay bills** screen, available credits are displayed when you check the box next to the **bill**. The check total shows up in the **PAYMENT** column.

✓ You write a check (#1121) to Martin's father (Richard Smith) for February interest. Martin also asks you to include a $100 principal payment in the check. He wants to start paying his father back. **TIP:** Interest was paid through 1/31 on 2/1. Ignore the number of days in February. Apply the 6% annual rate to the principal balance and calculate one month's interest (1/12th of the annual amount).

✓ You plan to take a few days off so you prepare and mail the $850 March rent check (#1122) to your landlord (Pro Spaces).

- **TIP:** The matching (expense recognition) principle applies here.

Check numbers 2/29

Checking account balance:.....$ 138.80
Inventory: $3,179.00
Accounts Payable: $2,437.33
Net income (February): $4,517.73

Suggested reports for Chapter 7:

All reports should be in portrait orientation.

- Journal—2/01 through 2/29.
    ■ Transaction types: Check, Bill, Vendor Credit, Bill Payment (check), Expense
- Inventory Valuation Summary as of 2/29
- Open Purchase Order Detail
    ■ Change **Report period** to **All Dates**
- A/P Aging Summary as of 2/29
- Balance sheet as of 2/29
- Profit and Loss for February
    ■ Add a **Year-to-date** column to the report

Assignment 7B

Salish Software Solutions

2/1/24

✓ You pay the February rent ($650) to your landlord, Alki Property Management (Check #1112).

✓ You review unpaid bills and pay all bills that are due on or before February 10th. You pay two bills totaling $198.95 starting with check number 1113.

✓ You also write a check (Check # 1115) for the $150 monthly loan payment to Dell Finance.

  ● **TIP:** Think about what the payment is covering. Look at the balance sheet if you have forgotten how much interest is due. The monthly payment covers both principal and interest.

2/2/24

✓ Sally has decided to go to a seminar on new accounting software being held in San Francisco on Friday and Saturday of this week. She asks you to use the credit card to pay the $195 registration fee to the AAASP (American Association of Accounting Software Providers). You enter the credit card expense in QBO. **TIP:** This is a type of professional development seminar.

✓ Now that Sally has started selling products, you decide to enter reorder points for the items currently in QBO to help manage inventory levels. You enter reorder points of 20 for **Tracker** and **Organizer**; 15 for **Easy1**; and 2 for **Contractor** and **Retailer**. (**Contractor** and **Retailer** are expensive so Sally doesn't want too many of those on the shelf!)

✓ You want to keep track of any orders you place so you turn on the purchase order feature in the **Expense** tab of **Account and Settings**. You toggle **Custom transaction numbers** on. **TIP:** You need to open the **Purchase orders** section to see the **Custom transaction numbers** toggle button. Even if the **Purchase order** feature is on, **Custom transaction numbers** may not be activated.

2/5/24

✓ You receive the following bills in the mail:

  ● Sacramento Light and Power's February bill (for heat and light) #01-84443—$112 dated 2/5. The terms are Net 30.

  ● Western Phone February bill #8911-64 for $105.75 dated 2/5. The terms are Net 30.

2/8/24

✓ You look at the **inventory** on hand and see that some of the items are below the reorder point.

✓ You prepare PO-100 and order 10 **Organizers** and 20 **Trackers** from Personal Software. The PO total is $850.

✓ You see that there are a few other items you might need to order but you want to talk with Sally first.

2/9/24

✓ Sally had a great time at the software seminar last weekend. You record the credit card receipts she brings in for her travel expenses using 2/4 as the date:

  ● Hotel and Saturday breakfast—The Franciscan—$227.15

  ● Gas—Bell Gas—$35

  ● Friday Dinner—Top Of The Hill—$53.77

  ● You consider all the travel costs to be part of the cost of attending the seminar.

  ● **TIP:** You **must** create a **separate** **Expense** transaction for each charge. The reason will become clear in the homework for Chapter 8.

✓ You pay the balance due to Capital Three ($1,139) with check #1116.

✓ Sally places an order for two **Contractor** packages and one **Retailer** package from Simply Accounting. You create PO-101 for the $1,100 purchase.

✓ You decide to give Simply Accounting a call about their payment terms. The item costs are high and you're hoping to get some kind of early payment discount. Simply Accounting agrees to give Salish terms of 2% 10, net 30 so you set up a new **term**. You name the new term "2% 10, net 30."

You edit Simply Accounting's vendor record to add the new term. **TIP:** Since the bill is due in 30 days if you do not pay it early, you use 30 as the **fixed number of days** in the term.

2/12/24

✓ Sally was very impressed with a couple of the new products demonstrated by Abacus Shop at the AAASP Conference in San Francisco. The company has created appointment and client management systems for various types of professional firms. Sally decides to offer the products to her Sacramento clients.

- Since the product line is expanding, you decide to reorganize the product **categories** a bit.
  - ■ You decide to set up a **category** called "Management Products." You also change the name of the **Products category** to "Accounting Products."
  - ■ You edit the **Organizer** and **Tracker** items to include them in the new Management Products **category**.
- You talk with Sally and decide that each new **inventory** item:
  - ■ Will be included in the Management Products **category**.
  - ■ Will have a reorder point of 1.
  - ■ Will be recorded in the **130 Inventory Asset** account.
  - ■ Will use account **420 Sales of Product Income** and **500 Cost of Goods Sold** as the **Income** and **Expense** accounts, respectively.
  - ■ Will be taxable at the standard rate.
  - ■ Will use Abacus Shop as the preferred vendor.
  - ■ **TIP:** You **must** enter 0 as the **initial quantity on hand** and 02/12/2024 as the **As of date**. You'll be entering purchases of the items when they are received.
- The new **inventory products** are:
  - ■ Legal (Description—Manage Your Law Firm)—Expected cost $350; Selling price $500
  - ■ Medical (Description—Manage Your Medical Practice)—Expected cost $350; Selling price $500
  - ■ Engineering (Description—Manage Your Engineering Firm)—Expected cost $350; Selling price $500
  - ■ **TIP:** Once you create one new item, you can **Duplicate** the item from the **ACTION** menu and edit the copy for each additional item.

✓ You prepare a purchase order (PO-102) to Abacus to buy 2 of each of the new items. The PO totals $2,100.

2/14/24

✓ You receive the shipment from Personal Software for items ordered on PO-100. All items were received except for 2 of the **Organizers**. No bill was included with the shipment. You go ahead and create a **bill** using the expected costs and terms. The total is $800. **TIP:** Don't forget to **Add** the purchase order information from the sidebar of the **bill**.

2/16/24

✓ The order from Simply Accounting (PO-101) comes in today. All items are received. A bill (#65411-8) for $1,100 is included with the shipment. You make a note to yourself to remember to pay the amount within the discount period so that you can take advantage of the 2% discount.

✓ You receive the bill from Personal Software for the **Organizers** and **Trackers** received this week. The bill (#744466) for $820 is dated 2/16 (the date the bill was received). The terms are Net 30. The **Trackers** were slightly more than expected ($31.00 per unit instead of $30). You call Personal Software and they apologize for not letting you know about the price change sooner. They are looking for a new supplier and expect the cost to revert to $30 so you don't change the default cost in the item record. You open the **bill** to make the edits (**date** and **amounts**). **TIP:** You **must** change the date on the **bill** to 2/16 keep the FIFO layers accurate. Consider using the Find feature to locate the bill.

> **BEHIND THE SCENES** Most users prefer to enter the bill date, rather than the receive date, when recording vendor invoices so that the payable records are more accurate. (Due dates are generally based on the invoice date.) The difference in dates may affect the FIFO layer(s). However, this would normally be an insignificant amount.

2/21/24

✓ You receive the shipment from Abacus Shop for all items ordered on PO-102. The bill (TAS 25344) for $2,100 has terms of Net 15.

✓ You ask Sally whether she wants you to follow up on the 2 **Organizers** that weren't received in the Personal Software shipment on 2/14. She says she'll go ahead and call Personal Software to cancel the backorder. You close PO-100 in QBO.

2/26/24

✓ Sally returns one damaged **Organizer** CD to Personal Software and picks up a credit memo (RR744466) for $25, which you record. **TIP:** This is a vendor credit. Make sure you enter the item in the correct **details** section.

✓ You and Sally meet at Roscoe's for lunch and a short meeting before she takes off for Chicago.

- The lunch at Roscoe's comes to $28.50. You use the credit card to pay the bill.
- You decide to set up a new account, **Staff meetings expense**, a subaccount of **Labor Costs** to track the cost of staff meetings. You select **600 Labor Costs** in the **Save account under** field. You use **Office/General Administrative Expenses** as the detail type (**Tax form section** field) and 678 as the account number.

✓ At the end of lunch you give Sally her $2,500 dividend check (Check # 1117).

✓ Sally takes a few minutes to review the inventory on hand and asks you to order 5 **Easy1s** from Abacus Shop. When you get back to the office you create PO-103 for $500 and send it to the vendor.

✓ You receive a bill (#3330) dated 2/26 for $575 from an accounting firm, Dovalina & Diamond, LLC. Sally hired the company to do a two-year financial projection. She thinks she may need to either borrow some money from a bank or attract investors in order to grow as quickly as she'd like. The work was completed in February. **TIP:** This is a consulting fee.

- The vendor address is 419 Upstart Drive, Sacramento, CA 95822. Terms are Net 30.

✓ The early payment discount on the Simply Accounting bill is going to expire soon so you do a few things to be able to take advantage of the discount.

- Since the early payment discount applies to inventory purchases, you charge the amount to a new **Cost of Goods Sold** account—"Purchase discounts." You use 510 as the account number and **Other Costs of Services—COS** as the **detail type** in the **Tax form section** field. **TIP:** You set the **account type** by selecting **Cost of Goods Sold** in the **Save account under** field. **Cost of Goods Sold** here does not have an account number because it represents an **account type**, not an actual account. Purchase discounts is not a sub-account.
- You create a **vendor credit** to record the early payment discount you will be taking on the Simply Accounting bill. You use 65411-8D as the **ref no**. The discount is 2% of the total $1,100 due. **TIP:** Use the new account you just created in the **category details** section of the **vendor credit**.

✓ You pay all bills due on or before 3/6 PLUS the bill with the early payment discount using the vendor credit. The first check number is 1118. The total of the four checks is $2,795.75. **TIP:** The check total shows up in the **PAYMENT** column.

2/27/24

✓   You plan to take a few days off so you prepare and mail the $650 March rent check (#1122) to your landlord (Alki Property Management).

  ● **TIP:** The matching (expense recognition) principle applies here.

Check numbers 2/29

Checking account balance:. **$11,001.50**
Inventory: . . . . **$ 6,525.00**
Account payable:. . . . . **$ 3,470.00**
Net income (February): . . . **$ 4,715.03**

Suggested reports for Chapter 7:

All reports should be in portrait orientation.

● Journal (2/1-2/29)
  ▪ Transaction types: Check, Bill, Vendor Credit, Bill Payment (check), Expense

● Inventory Valuation Summary as of 2/29

● Open Purchase Orders List
  ▪ Remove Memo/Description and Ship Via columns

● A/P Aging Summary as of 2/29

● Balance sheet as of 2/29

● Profit and Loss for February
  ▪ Add a Year-to-date column

APPENDIX 7A IDENTIFYING FIFO LAYERS IN QBO

An important concept in many inventory valuation methods is that of **inventory layers**. Layers represent the quantity and unit cost of any addition to the inventory account. A separate layer is created:

LO 7-5 Understand the use of FIFO as the inventory valuation method used in QBO

● every time inventory items are received from vendors.

● every time inventory items are returned by customers.

Layers are reduced:

● whenever inventory items are sold.

● whenever inventory items are returned to vendors.

Under FIFO, the oldest layer is reduced first. In a sales transaction, the unit cost in the oldest layer is what is used to calculate the debit to Cost of Goods Sold and the credit to inventory. In a return of items to vendors, the unit cost in the oldest layer is what is used to calculate the credit to inventory. The debit would most likely either go to accounts payable (to reduce any balance owing to the vendor) or accounts receivable (to record the amount due from the vendor).

Here's an example of how FIFO layers work using the test drive company and a new product (Wheelbarrows):

1. On 1/15, Craig purchases 3 new Wheelbarrow products ($50 per unit).

2. On 1/18, Craig sells 2 of the Wheelbarrows for $75 each.

3. On 1/20, the customer returns one of the Wheelbarrows they purchased on 9/22. Craig reduces the customer's account balance by $75.

4. On 1/22, Craig returns a Wheelbarrow to the vendor for a $50 refund.

5. On 1/23, Craig purchases 4 more Wheelbarrows ($55 per unit).

6. On 1/26, Craig sells 3 Wheelbarrows for $75 each.

Here's how the inventory cost layers work given those transactions:

Transactions	Layer 1	Layer 2	Layer 3	Quantity on Hand
1/15 purchase	3 @ $50 each			3
1/18 sale	(2 @ $50 each)			1
1/20 customer return		1 @ $50		2
1/22 return to vendor	(1 @ $50)			1
1/23 purchase			4 @ $55 each	5
1/26 sale		(1 @ $50)	(2 @ $55)	2
Balance	0	0	2 @ $55	

At 1/26, Inventory equals $110 (2 @ $55 each).

In QBO, the FIFO layer activity can be seen in the **Inventory Valuation Detail** report:

Craig's Design and Landscaping Services
Inventory Valuation Detail

DATE		TRANSACTION TYPE		NUM	NAME	QTY	RATE	FIFO COST	QTY ON HAND	ASSET VALUE
▾ Landscaping										
▾ Wheelbarrow										
01/01		Inventory Starting Value		START		0.00	50.00	0.00	0.00	0.00
01/15	Layer 1	Bill		456-7	Hicks Hardware	3.00	50.00	150.00	3.00	150.00
01/18		Invoice	From Layer 1	1038	Amy's Bird Sanctuary	(2.00)	50.00	(100.00)	1.00	50.00
01/20	Layer 2	Credit Memo		CM1038	Amy's Bird Sanctuary	1.00	50.00	50.00	2.00	100.00
01/22		Vendor Credit	From Layer 1	CM456-7	Hicks Hardware	(1.00)	50.00	(50.00)	1.00	50.00
01/23	Layer 3	Bill		567-8	Hicks Hardware	4.00	55.00	220.00	5.00	270.00
01/26		Invoice	From Layer 2	1039	Diego Rodriguez	(1.00)	50.00	(50.00)	4.00	220.00
01/26		Invoice	From Layer 3	1039	Diego Rodriguez	(2.00)	55.00	(110.00)	2.00	110.00
Total for Wheelbarrow						**2.00**		**$110.00**	**2.00**	**$110.00**
Total for Landscaping						**2.00**		**$110.00**	**2.00**	**$110.00**

The valuations of the inventory layers in QBO correspond to our table.

> **HINT:** Check your dates if your inventory values are incorrect. QBO uses a perpetual inventory tracking system. If layers are created in the wrong order (incorrect dates are entered) and purchase costs are increasing or decreasing, unit costs used for reducing inventory balances and calculating cost of goods sold can be affected. You may need to delete and reenter transactions. Changing the date on a recorded transaction may not correct your error.

8

End-of-Period and Other Activity

(Merchandising Company)

Road Map

	Learning Objective	Topic	Subtopic	Page	Practice Exercises	Videos
LO 8-1	Describe and use the inventory adjustment tool in QBO [p. 8-2]	Adjusting inventory		8-2	8.1	Adjusting inventory quantities
LO 8-2	Explain the QBO process for adjusting and remitting sales taxes in QBO [p. 8-7]	Managing sales taxes	Remitting sales tax	8-9		Managing sales tax
			Adjusting sales tax liabilities	8-13		
			Deleting sales tax payments	8-16		
LO 8-3	Describe and demonstrate the process for recording miscellaneous cash receipts in QBO [p. 8-17]	Entering cash receipts from non-customers		8-17	8.2	Recording non-customer cash receipts
LO 8-4	Describe the process for recording bank transfers in QBO [p. 8-19]	Recording bank transfers		8-19	8.3	
LO 8-5	Understand and demonstrate the QBO process for uploading credit card transactions [p. 8-20]	Uploading credit card transactions into QBO		8-20		
LO 8-6	Understand how to inactivate or merge general ledger accounts in QBO [p. 8-27]	Inactivating and merging general ledger accounts	Inactivating an account	8-27	8.4	Inactivating and merging accounts
			Merging accounts	8-29		
LO 8-7	Describe how to add commentary to QBO reports [p. 8-31]	Adding notes to reports		8-31	8.5	
LO 8-8	Understand how transactions directly downloaded from bank are processed in QBO [p. 8-44]	Appendix 8A - Connecting QBO to bank accounts	Downloading transactions from bank accounts	8-44		
			Setting banking rules	8-47		

All of the "end-of-period" procedures we covered in Chapter 5 apply to merchandising companies as well as service companies. Bank accounts must be reconciled. Adjusting journal entries must be made. Remember: End-of-period procedures are focused on making sure the financial records are as accurate as possible. The financial statements should give internal and external users a fair picture of

- The operations of the company for the period (profit and loss statement).
- The financial position of the company at the end of the period (balance sheet).

There are a few additional procedures unique to merchandising companies that we'll cover in this chapter.

- Inventory adjustments
- Managing sales taxes

We'll also look at a few procedures and QBO features not covered in previous chapters:

- Recording non-customer cash receipts
- Recording bank transfers
- Inactivating and merging accounts
- Adding comments to reports

ADJUSTING INVENTORY

As you know, QBO features a perpetual inventory tracking system for **inventory** items so quantities are automatically updated when goods are received, sold, or returned.

If life were perfect, the inventory quantities in QBO would **always** equal inventory quantities on hand (physically in the store or warehouse). Unfortunately, we know that that isn't always the case. Differences can occur because of:

- Theft
- Unrecorded transactions (sales, item receipts, returns by customers, or returns to vendors)
- Damaged goods with little or no value

In addition to needing to know the quantity on hand for valuing inventory, companies must have an accurate record of how many of each of their products they have available to sell. That's part of a good inventory management system. A few of you have probably asked a clerk about a book you can't find on the shelf at your favorite bookstore. The clerk looks the book up in the store's computer system, and it says that they should have two in stock. You go back to the shelves with the clerk and neither of you can find the book. It may just be misplaced or it may have been stolen, but both you and the clerk have wasted time looking for it and you're a disappointed customer. The more accurate the inventory records, the smoother the operation and the more accurate the financial statements. So, periodically, the inventory on hand is physically counted, and the inventory records are adjusted as necessary.

Counts can be taken at any point during a year but are usually taken, at a minimum, at the end of the year. (Merchandising and manufacturing companies that need audited financial statements **must** take a count, with auditors present, at the end of the year.) Counts are frequently taken more often (quarterly, for example). If there hasn't been a history of significant inventory adjustments, taking an annual physical inventory count is probably sufficient. (If you're in the bookstore business and you have lots of books on shelves, you might want to consider more frequent counts!)

To get a good inventory count, it's usually best to take the count when products aren't moving (aren't being sold or received). Many companies take inventory counts after closing

The margin note for LO 8-1: **LO 8-1** Describe and use the inventory adjustment tool in QBO

eLecture

or on weekends. Counters are given a list of products and the unit of measure that should be used to count the products (units, cartons, pounds, etc.). As a control, the count sheets should not list the expected quantity. Why? For one thing, it's just too easy to see what you think you **should** see (i.e., what the count sheet says)!

Once the physical inventory count is taken, the count sheets are compared to the accounting records. Significant variations should be investigated. Documentation (particularly packing slips) related to transactions occurring close to the count date can often provide useful information. Goods might have been received or shipped out earlier or later than the customer invoice or vendor bill dates used in the accounting system. In practice, physical inventory counts usually involve a lot of recounts.

Once the company is confident that it has gotten a good count and all known transactions have been recorded, the accounting records are adjusted to the count.

In QBO, count sheets are available in the **Sales and Customers** section of **Reports**.

Figure 8.1

Access to inventory count sheet

The **Physical Inventory Worksheet** looks something like this:

Figure 8.2

Physical inventory count sheet

 HINT: Remember, report customization tools in reports (like the **Physical Inventory Worksheet** shown in Figure 8.2) may have been updated. If possible, click **Old layout** or **Switch to classic view**. If that's not possible, check the Student Ancillaries page in myBusinessCourse for updated information or check with your instructor.

The worksheet can easily be modified by clicking **Customize**. For example, a company that uses SKU numbers would likely want those included on the count sheet. The **QTY ON HAND** column should be removed. **REORDER POINT** and **QTY ON PO** information isn't necessary for a count and could be removed.

 HINT: You might have noticed that the date for the worksheet can't be changed. The count sheets must be printed on the day the count is taken.

After the count sheets are completed, the listed counts are compared to the inventory quantities in QBO. As noted earlier, recounts are normally requested if the counts vary significantly from the perpetual records.

Once the company determines that the count is accurate, any necessary inventory adjustments are recorded through the **Inventory Qty Adjustment** form accessed by clicking **+ New** in the navigation bar.

Figure 8.3

Access to inventory quantity adjustment

The form looks like this:

Figure 8.4

Inventory adjustment form

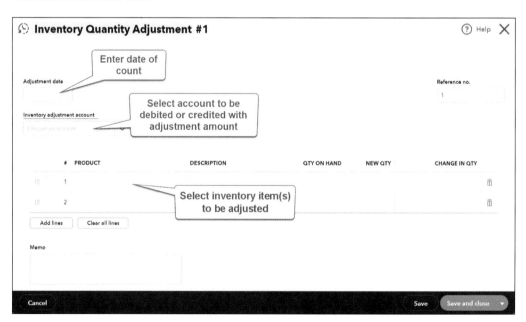

> **HINT**: Remember, forms (like the **Inventory Quantity Adjustment** shown in Figure 8.4) may have been updated. If possible, click **Old layout** or **Switch to classic view**. If that's not possible, check the Student Ancillaries page in myBusinessCourse for updated information or check with your instructor.

The **Adjustment date** would be the date of the inventory count. The **Inventory adjustment account** is the choice of management. Most companies debit or credit inventory adjustments to an account with a **cost of goods sold account type**. The offset account is, of course, the inventory (asset) account.

The **inventory** items to be adjusted are selected in the **PRODUCT** column.

> **WARNING**: Occasionally, QBO will not allow users to select a product in the **Inventory Quantity Adjustment** screen. In that case, use the following workaround:
>
> 1. Exit out of the **Inventory Quantity Adjustment** screen.
> 2. Click the ⚙ on the icon bar.
> 3. Click **Products and Services**.
> 4. In the far left column, check the box next to each item to be adjusted.
> 5. Select **Adjust Quantity** in the **Batch actions** dropdown menu. (The menu is on the right side of the list near the top.)

The form will look something like this when items have been selected:

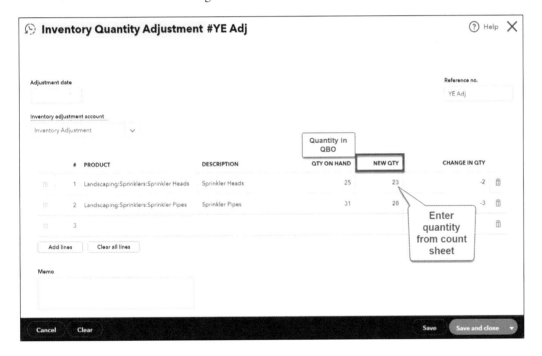

Figure 8.5

Example of inventory item adjustment

QBO autofills the **QTY ON HAND** column field with the current quantity in the item record. Users enter the quantity from the count sheet as the **NEW QTY**.

Once the **Inventory Qty Adjustment** form is saved, QBO adjusts both the quantity and the value of items selected in the form. The oldest FIFO layer is used to determine the amount of the value adjustment.

An **Inventory Valuation Detail** report customized to show only the items adjusted in Figure 8.5 would look something like this:

Figure 8.6

Inventory transaction
report after quantity
adjustment

> **BEHIND THE SCENES** Under GAAP, FIFO inventory values must be adjusted when the reported cost is less than the estimated selling price (net of any reasonably predictable selling costs). This is known as the "lower of cost or net realizable value" rule. Currently, QBO does not have a feature allowing users to change values for inventory to comply with the rule. As an alternative, companies could create a contra asset account and record an allowance to cover any difference.
>
> Inventory **starting** values (values entered when an existing company is initially set up in QBO) **can** be adjusted with or without changing quantities. This is done by selecting **Adjust starting value** in the **ACTION** column for the specific item in the **Products and Services** list.

PRACTICE

EXERCISE

8.1

MBC

Adjust inventory for Craig's Design and Landscaping.

(Inventory was counted today. All of the counts agreed to the QBO records except for Fountain Pumps (there were only 23 pumps) and Sprinkler Heads (there were only 24).)

1. Click **+ New** on the navigation bar.

2. Click **Inventory Qty Adjustment**.

3. Enter the current date as the **Adjustment date**.

4. Select **+ Add new** in the **Inventory adjustment account** field.

    a. Select **Expenses**.

        i. **TIP:** You may not see the financial statement classification menu option on your screen.

    b. Select **Cost of Goods Sold** as the **Account Type** (**Save account under** field).

    c. Select **Supplies & Materials—COGS** as the **Detail Type** (**Tax form section** field).

    d. Enter "Inventory adjustments" as the **Name**.

    e. Click **Save and close**. You should be back in the **Inventory Quantity Adjustment** form.

5. Enter "YE Adj" as the **Reference no.**

6. In the first row, select **Pump** in the **PRODUCT** field and enter "23" as the **NEW QTY**.

(continued)

(continued from previous page)

    a. **TIP:** If you are unable to select a product in the field, use the workaround described in the WARNING box in this section.

7. In the second row, select **Sprinkler Heads** in the **PRODUCT** field and enter "24" as the **NEW QTY**.

8. Click **Save**.

    a. Select **Transaction Journal** on the **More** dropdown menu.

    b. **Make a note** of the **total** debit to the Inventory Adjustments account. **TIP:** There's more than one debit to that account.

    c. Click **Back to report list** (top left corner of **Journal Report**.)

9. Open the **Standard** tab in the Report Center.

10. Click **Physical Inventory Worksheet** in the **Sales and Customers** section. **TIP:** The quantities for **Pump** and **Sprinkler Heads** should match the quantities you entered in Steps 6 and 7.

11. **Make a note** of the **QTY ON HAND** for **Rock Fountains** and **Sprinkler Pipes**.

12. Click **Dashboard** to exit the screen.

MANAGING SALES TAXES

Sales taxes are remitted to taxing authorities on a periodic basis—generally annually, quarterly, or monthly, depending on the size of the company. Remember, the responsibility to pay the tax is on the consumer but the responsibility to collect and remit the tax is on the seller. In most states, sellers are responsible for remitting to the tax authorities the tax amount they **should** have charged (which hopefully agrees with the amount they actually **did** charge!).

> **BEHIND THE SCENES** In most cases, a company is required to report and remit sales taxes when the tax is **charged** to the customer (accrual method). Some states also allow a company to remit the tax when it's **collected** from the customer (cash method). The default in QBO is the "charged" date (the date of the **invoice** or **sales receipt**). In the example below, and in the homework assignments, the default (charged) date will be used.

At the end of a tax-reporting period, a report should be prepared detailing sales and sales taxes charged, by taxing jurisdiction, and reviewed.

The **Sales Tax Liability**, **Taxable Sales Summary**, and **Taxable Sales Detail** reports are accessible in the **Sales tax** section of **Reports**.

LO 8-2 Explain the QBO process for adjusting and remitting sales taxes in QBO

eLecture

Figure 8.7

Available sales tax reports

The **Sales Tax Liability** report will look something like this if **All Dates** is selected in the **Report period** field:

Figure 8.8

Report of total taxable sales and tax charged to customers by jurisdiction

This report lists taxable sales by jurisdiction. This report would be used to prepare the various tax reports that are filed with the state and local tax agencies.

> **BEHIND THE SCENES** For control purposes, the company should carefully re-view its tax reports. Remember, QBO is reporting what **did** happen, not what **should** have happened.

The **Taxable Sales Summary** report lists taxable sales by product. Drilling down on any of the items listed allows you to see the specific sales included in the total. The report would look something like this if **All dates** was selected as the **Report period**.

Figure 8.9

Report of total taxable sales by item

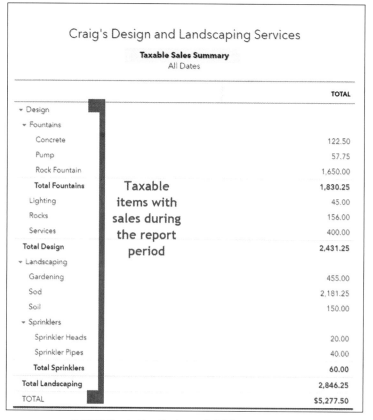

In the **Taxable Sales Detail** report, taxable sales are listed by sales transaction, grouped by customer.

Remitting Sales Tax

 WARNING: Your homework company includes the current, fully automated sales tax feature covered in Chapter 6. Although the automated system can be activated in Craig's Design and Landscaping Service (the test drive company), students have experienced a number of technical issues when using that system. As a result, there will be no Practice Exercise for this section. To help you with your homework, the processes and procedures described below are from the automated version.

Sales tax functions (like tax payments and adjustments) are accessed through the Sales Tax Center.

Click **Taxes** on the navigation bar in your homework company to open the Sales Tax Center.

If you're working on your homework prior to February 1, 2024, the screen should look something like Figure 8.10.

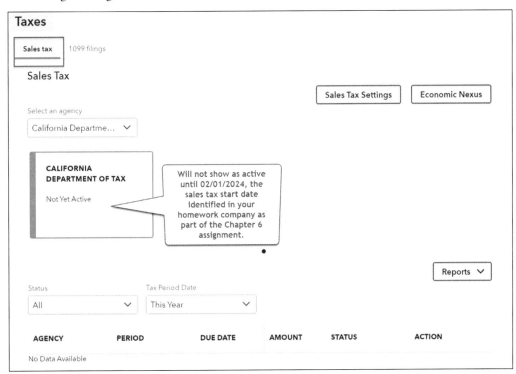

Figure 8.10

Possible Sales Tax Center display

If you're completing the homework in February 2024, the screen should look something like Figure 8.11.

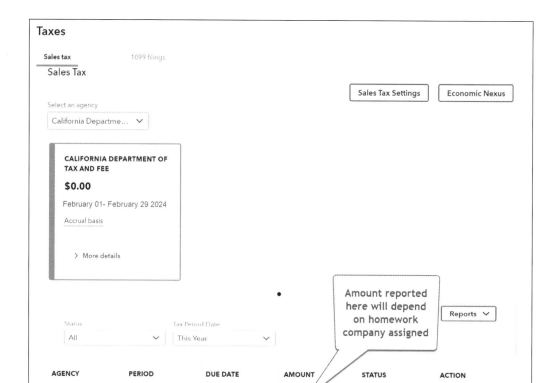

If you're completing the homework after February 2024, you will see also a row for March and, if you're working in Chapter 10, a row for April.

> **BEHIND THE SCENES** The difference in screen displays is related to sales tax filing periods. In QBO, no amounts are displayed in the Sales Tax Center if the sales tax **start date** is in a period (month) subsequent to the date QBO is accessed. (The **start date** was identified as the date sales taxes were first collected by the company as part of the sales tax feature activation process.) Since sales taxes were activated in your homework company as of 2/1/24, you would not see tax information displayed if you opened the Sales Tax Center prior to that date.

Each row (each tax period) will have a **STATUS** of either **Open**, **Due**, **Overdue**, or **Paid**.

- **Open**
  - Taxes charged to customers **during the current month**
  - The tax agency, tax period, tax due date, and amount are displayed
- **Due**
  - Taxes that are currently due for the reporting period just ended
  - The tax agency, tax period, tax due date, and amount are displayed
- **Overdue**
  - Taxes that are past due
  - The tax agency, tax period, tax due date, and amount are displayed
- **Paid**
  - Taxes that have been remitted to tax agency
  - The tax agency, tax period, and tax due date are displayed

0.00 is displayed in the amount field

> ! **WARNING:** If you're completing your homework prior to March 2024, you will not be able to complete the remittance process in your homework company. (Tax on February 2024 sales would not be due until March 2024.) Directions for recording the payment are included in the assignments.

To illustrate the material covered in the remaining sales tax sections, screenshots from a demonstration company (Sofie's Shop) are used. The Sales Tax Center for Sofie's Shop looked like this in December 2022:

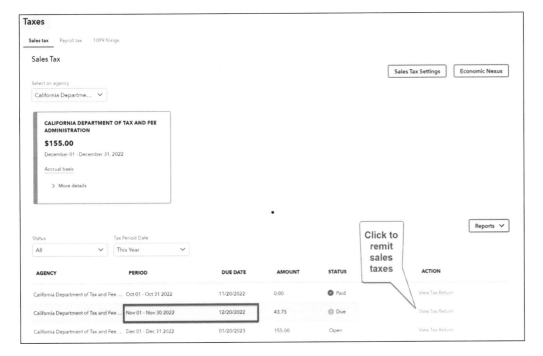

Figure 8.12

Sales Tax Center in demonstration company for this section

Click **View Return** to start the tax payment (remittance) process for any tax amounts with a status of **Due** or **Overdue**.

> **BEHIND THE SCENES** If **View Tax Return** is clicked for an **Open** period (current month), the user can see tax details and can make adjustments, but tax payments cannot be processed until the tax period has ended.

Sales tax review screen

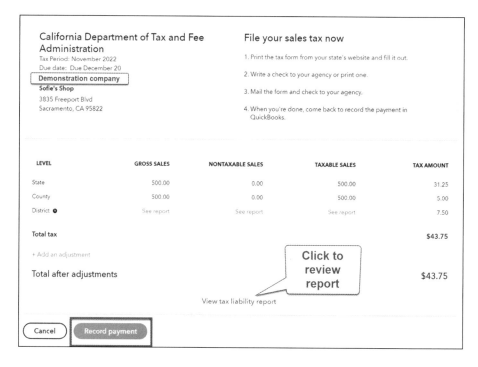

Users have a chance to review tax reports or adjust tax amounts on this screen. Click **Record payment**.

Figure 8.14

Sales tax filing method option screen

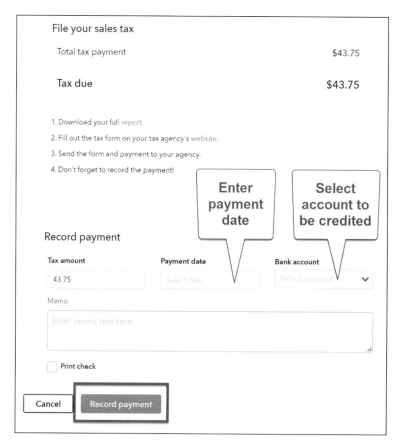

Enter the date and bank account to be charged. Click **Record payment** to enter the transaction. (The **transaction type** for sales tax remittances is **Sales Tax Payment**.)

BEHIND THE SCENES Transaction numbers (a check number for example) cannot be added to sales tax payments in QBO. (There is no **sales tax payment** form that can be edited.) Users should add payment information in the **Memo** field shown in Figure 8.14.

> ✓ **Return paid**
> It's marked as paid and saved in your History
>
> Back to sales tax center
>
> California Department of Tax and Fee Administration
> Tax Period: November 2022
> Demonstration company
> **Sofie's Shop**
> 3835 Freeport Blvd
> Sacramento, CA 95822
>
> Click to view a summary of the transaction
>
> Payment details
> Number of payments: 1
>
> | Payments | Amount paid |
> |---|---|
> | 12/20/2022 | $43.75 |
> | Total paid: | $43.75 |
> | Total due | $0.00 |
>
> | LEVEL | GROSS SALES | NONTAXABLE SALES | TAXABLE SALES | TAX AMOUNT |
> |---|---|---|---|---|
> | State | 500.00 | 0.00 | 500.00 | 31.25 |
> | County | 500.00 | 0.00 | 500.00 | 5.00 |
> | District ⓘ | See report | See report | See report | 7.50 |
> | **Total tax** | | | | **$43.75** |
> | **Total after adjustments** | | | | **$43.75** |
>
> View tax liability report
>
> Cancel

Click the payment date to see a summary of the transaction.

Once a **Sales Tax Payment** has been recorded, it can be deleted but not adjusted.

BEHIND THE SCENES QBO automatically sets up a separate liability account (**Other Current Liabilities account type**) for each sales tax agency. When sales taxes are paid, QBO automatically debits the appropriate liability account. These accounts cannot be changed in any way or deleted.

Adjusting Sales Tax Liabilities

Sales tax liabilities might need to be adjusted because:

- QBO wasn't yet updated for a recent rate change.

- A specific customer was inadvertently overcharged or undercharged for sales tax.

- The company is located in a state that levies an additional tax (called an excise tax) on the **seller**.

BEHIND THE SCENES Excise taxes are generally based on gross sales revenue. Excise taxes cannot be entered as a sales tax item because they are not charged to the customer. They are an expense of the seller.

Although sales tax payments can't be adjusted after they are recorded, adjustments **can** be made on the **Review your sales tax** screen before the payment is processed.

Access to sales tax adjustment screen

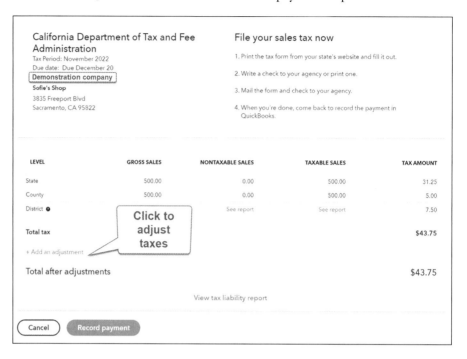

Click ✚ **Add an adjustment**

Sales tax adjustment screen

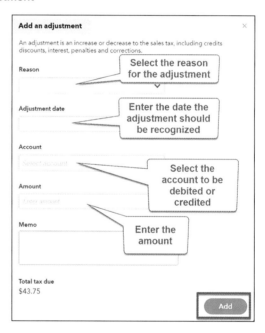

A reason for the adjustment must be selected from one of the following options.

Sales tax adjustment options

The account to be charged for the amount of the adjustment is entered in the **Account** field.

Adjustments due to corrections of errors would normally be charged to a miscellaneous expense or income account. Rounding errors, penalties, and adjustments for excise taxes would normally be charged to a business tax expense account.

The **Amount** is entered as a positive number if the user wants to increase the tax payment. If the payment amount should be decreased, the **Amount** is entered as a negative number.

An adjustment to increase the amount to be paid by $15.00 (penalty) would look something like Figure 8.19.

Figure 8.19

Example of sales tax adjustment

Click **Add** to adjust the tax amount to be paid.

Users have a chance to review the payment amount on the next screen.

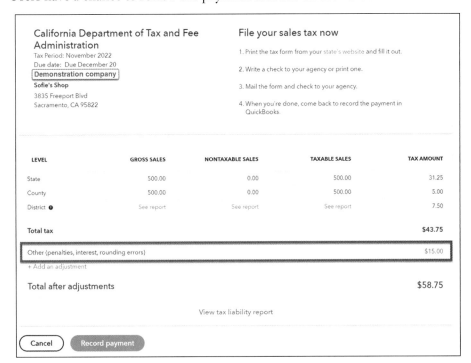

Figure 8.20

Example of sales tax review screen with tax adjustment

Click **Record payment**. Enter the payment date and select the bank account on the next screen (Figure 8.14) and click **Record payment**.

> **BEHIND THE SCENES** If a customer was overcharged, the company would generally want to reimburse the customer, if possible, by issuing a check or credit memo. If a customer was undercharged, the company might choose to invoice the customer for the tax. In that case, the company would need to set up a **service** item for uncollected tax. That item would, of course, be non-taxable.

Deleting Sales Tax Payments

Although **sales tax payments** can't be edited once they've been recorded, they can be deleted.

> **HINT:** The sales tax liability is automatically restored when **sales tax payments** are deleted. The user can then record the correct payment.

To delete the payment, click **Taxes** on the navigation bar and open the **Sales tax drawer** (tab).

Figure 8.21

Access to prior sales tax payment information

Click **View Tax Return** for the payment to be deleted.

Figure 8.22

Access to sales tax payment screen

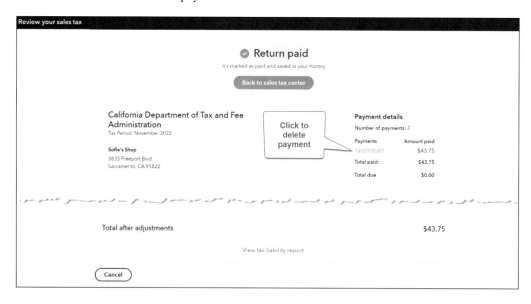

Click the payment date.

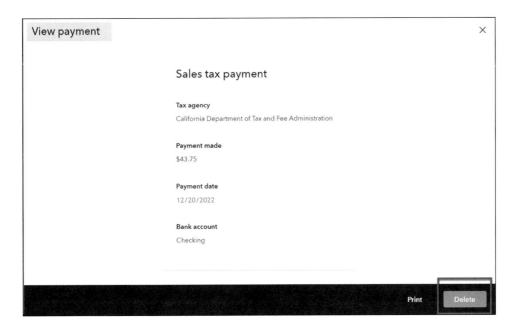

Figure 8.23
Sales tax payment
screen

Click **Delete**.

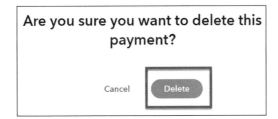

Figure 8.24
Deletion confirmation
screen

Click **Delete** in the **Are you sure you want to delete this payment?** dialog box that appears next.

QBO automatically reopens the sales tax review screen (Figure 8.13) so that the tax remittance can be reprocessed.

Sales Tax Payment transactions can also be deleted by drilling down (clicking) on the transaction in journal reports to open the **View payment** screen (Figure 8.23).

ENTERING CASH RECEIPTS FROM NON-CUSTOMERS

In companies, most cash receipts come from customers. (At least we hope they do!) There are other sources of cash though:

- Borrowings
- Sales of company stock
- Sales of property or equipment
- Etc.

In previous chapters, all cash receipts were entered through one of the following forms:

- Sales Receipts
  - Used for cash or credit card sales to customers
- Payments
  - Used for cash or credit card payments by customers on account receivable balances

LO 8-3 Describe and demonstrate the process for recording miscellaneous cash receipts in QBO

eLecture

As you know, the default debit account in the underlying entry for both **sales receipt** and **payment** transactions in your homework company is **Undeposited Funds**, an asset account. Receipts are later transferred from **Undeposited Funds** to the appropriate **Bank** account through the **Deposit** form.

When cash is received from **non-customers**, the amounts are entered **directly** into the **Deposit** form.

The **Deposit** form is opened by clicking ⊕ New on the navigation bar and selecting **Bank Deposit**.

If there are pending undeposited funds, the **Bank Deposit** screen will look like Figure 8.25.

Figure 8.25

Example of deposit form with undeposited funds from customer receipts

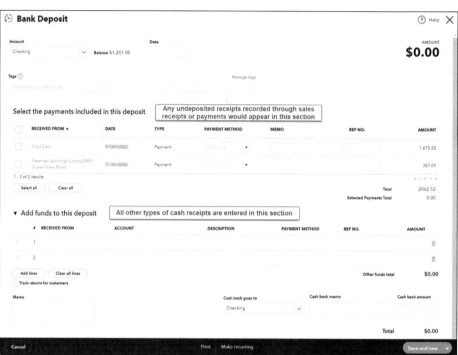

Users can add non-customer cash receipts to the **Add funds to this deposit** section. The only required fields are **ACCOUNT** and **AMOUNT** although most users would also identify the source of the cash (**RECEIVED FROM**), the payment method, and any reference number.

If there are no undeposited funds, the **Bank Deposit** screen will look like Figure 8.26.

Figure 8.26

Example of deposit form with no pending deposits

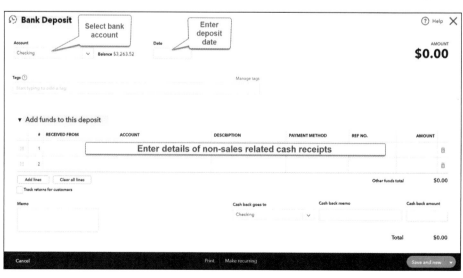

Non-customer receipts would be added in the **Add funds to this deposit** section of the form.

 HINT: Deposits should be grouped to correspond to the actual bank deposits. If a non-customer receipt is being deposited with customer receipts, both types should be recorded in the same deposit form.

Record a non-customer cash receipt for Craig's Design and Landscaping.
(Craig's Design received a $100 rebate check from one of its vendors (Norton Lumber). Craig's deposited it along with a few checks from customers.)

PRACTICE
EXERCISE
8.2

1. Click **+ New** on the navigation bar.

2. Click **Bank Deposit**.

3. Select **Checking** as the **Account**.

4. Enter the current date in the **Date** field.

5. Check the boxes next to the two payments listed in the **Select the payments included in the deposit** section.

   a. **Make a note** of the customer names appearing in the **RECEIVED FROM** column.

6. In the **Add funds to this deposit** section:

   a. Select **Norton Lumber and Building Materials** in the **RECEIVED FROM** column (first line).

   b. Select **Decks and Patios** as the **ACCOUNT**. (Select the **Decks and Patios** account that's in the **Job Expenses** group.)

   c. Enter "Rebate" as the **DESCRIPTION**.

   d. Select **Check** as the **PAYMENT METHOD**.

   e. Enter "1007" as the **REF NO.**

   f. Enter "100" as the **AMOUNT**.

7. The **Total** should be $2,162.52.

8. Click **Save and close**.

RECORDING BANK TRANSFERS

Many companies maintain more than one bank account. Other than the general checking account, a company will frequently have a separate checking account for payroll. They might also open a savings or a money market account to earn some interest on funds not needed for immediate operations.

LO 8-4 Describe the process for recording bank transfers in QBO

If the accounts are with the same bank, transfers between accounts can generally be made either electronically (through the bank's website) or by phone.

In QBO, electronic or phone transfers are recorded using the **Transfer** form. The **Transfer** form is accessed by clicking **+ New** on the navigation bar and selecting **Transfer** in the **Other** column.

Figure 8.27

Transfer form

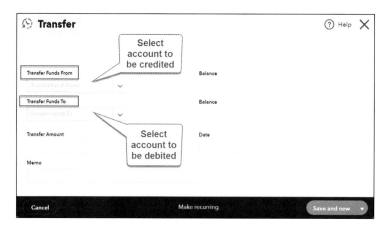

The account selected in the Transfer Funds From field represents the account to be credited. The account selected in the Transfer Funds To field represents the account to be debited. QBO will display the current balances in each account once they are selected.

The amount to be transferred is recorded in the Transfer Amount field. The date must also be entered.

PRACTICE EXERCISE 8.3

Transfer funds between accounts for Craig's Design and Landscaping.

(Craig's Design decides to open a money market account with a $500 transfer from checking.)

1. Click **+ New** on the navigation bar.

2. Click Transfer.

3. Select Checking in the Transfer Funds From dropdown menu.

    a. **Make a note** of how many accounts in the dropdown menu have the account type Bank.

4. Select + Add new in the Transfer Funds To dropdown menu.

    a. Select Banks.

        i. **TIP:** You may not see the financial statement classification menu option on your screen.

    b. Select Bank Accounts as the Account Type (Save account under field).

    c. Select Money Market as the Detail Type (Tax form section field).

    d. Leave the Name as Money Market.

    e. Click Save and Close. You should be back in the Transfer form.

5. Enter "500" as the Transfer Amount.

6. Enter the current date in the Date field.

7. In the Memo field, enter "Opened new money market account."

8. Click Save and close.

UPLOADING CREDIT CARD TRANSACTIONS INTO QBO

LO 8-5 Understand and demonstrate the QBO process for uploading credit card transactions

 HINT: There is no Practice Exercise for this section. (Transactions cannot be uploaded to the practice company because of frequent date changes.) The steps outlined can be used when completing your homework assignment.

Companies that provide credit cards to employees need to make sure that all transactions are properly recorded in QBO. In most cases, the credit card holders supply a report (with credit card receipts attached) to the accounting department. The transactions can then be entered from that report.

Companies can also download transactions into QBO from the credit card company. There are two ways to do that:

- Download transactions directly from the credit card company.
  - To do that, the user must add (link) the credit card account to QBO. Direct downloading is covered in Appendix 8A of this chapter.

- Download transactions from the credit card company into a CSV file and then upload them into QBO.

To ensure that all transactions are recorded and to simplify the reconciliation process, credit card transactions can be entered manually AND uploaded into the company file. This does not result in duplicate entries. Instead, the transactions are matched, and any necessary changes are added to the company file. This is what you'll be doing in your homework company.

Click **Banking** in the navigation bar and open the **Banking drawer** (tab). You should see your credit card company. If not, see **HINT** below.

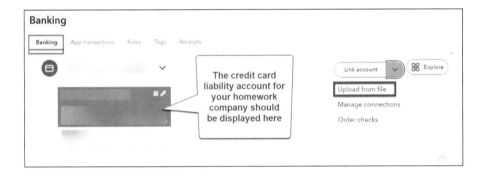

Figure 8.28

Banking screen

Select **Upload from file** in the **Link account** dropdown menu.

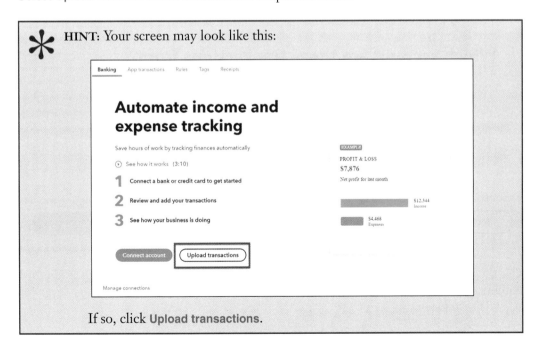

Figure 8.29

Upload selection screen

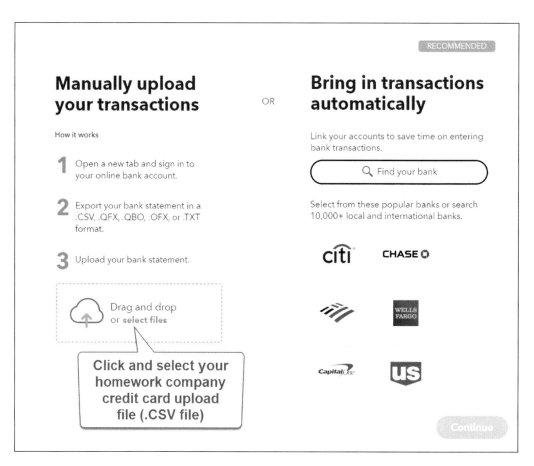

Browse to select the CSV file of downloaded transactions. (If you are using myBusinessCourse, the CSV file for your homework company can be downloaded from Student Ancillaries. If you're not using myBusinessCourse, the file will be provided to you by your instructor.)

Click Continue.

Figure 8.30

Selection of credit card account

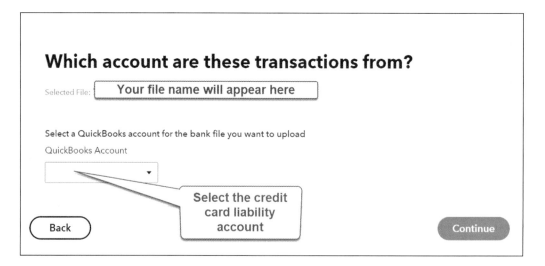

Use the dropdown menu under QuickBooks Account and select the appropriate credit card liability account.

Click Continue.

Figure 8.31
Mapping options

In the next screen, the fields in the uploaded spreadsheet are mapped to QBO. Complete the Map columns window as follows:

Step 1

● Is the first row in your file a header? **Yes**

● How many columns show amounts? **Two columns**

● What's the date format used in your file? **MM/dd/yyyy**

Step 2

● Date: **Column 1: Date**

● Description: **Column 2: Description**

● Amount:

  ▪ Money Received: **Column 3: Debit**

  ▪ Money Spent: **Column 4: Credit**

BEHIND THE SCENES Both credit card charges and payments are uploaded into QBO. Credit card charges (Money Spent) are credited to the credit card liability account. Credit card payments (Money received) are debited to the credit card liability account. The columns in those fields indicate the appropriate column in the worksheet.

Click Continue.

Figure 8.32

Transaction selection
for import screen

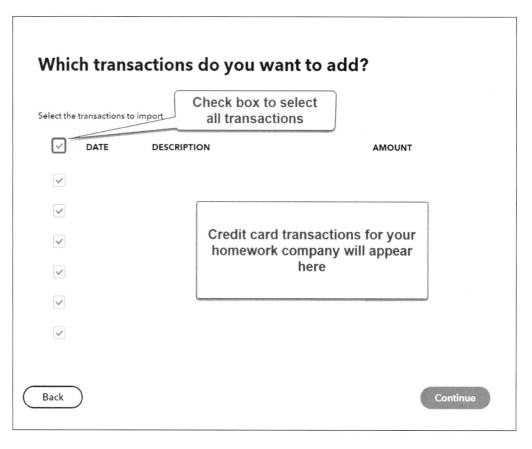

Select transactions to be imported into QBO.
　　Click **Continue**.

Figure 8.33

Acceptance of
transactions for import
screen

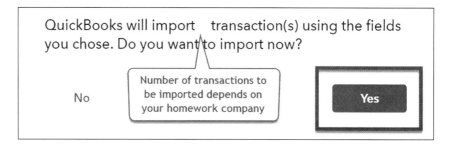

Click **Yes**.

Figure 8.34

Final acceptance
screen

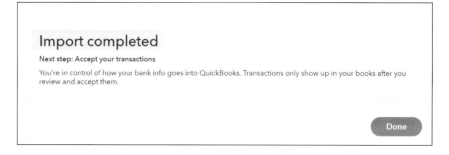

Once the import has been completed, you will need to match the uploaded transactions to the **Expense** transactions in QBO. Click **Done** to start the process. (Figure 8.35 is from the test drive company.)

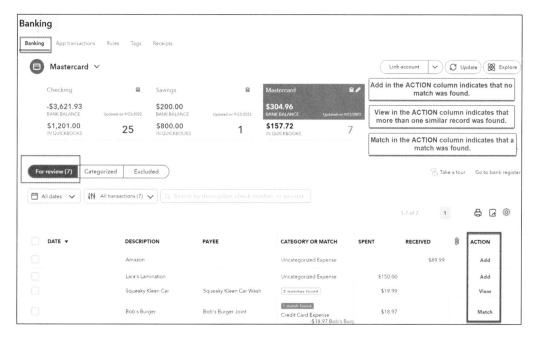

Figure 8.35

Imported transaction review screen

Although transactions can't be uploaded to the test drive company by users, there are some example uploaded transactions included in the test drive company file. To see them click **Banking** on the navigation bar and open the **Banking drawer** (tab). The transactions for the Mastercard account are shown in Figure 8.35.

There are three tabs on the screen.

- **For review**—This is where all the transactions go when initially uploaded. How to review them is explained below.

- **Categorized**—Transactions that have been reviewed by the user and then either **matched** or **added** on the **For review** tab automatically move to the **Categorized** tab.

- **Excluded**—Transactions that have been reviewed but can't be matched and shouldn't be added to QBO can be selected for exclusion by the user on the **For review** tab. Those transactions are automatically moved to the **Excluded** tab. Transactions that were downloaded to the wrong account and duplicate entries are two of the more common reasons for excluding transactions.

All transactions listed in the **For review** tab must be evaluated. QBO suggests actions in the **ACTION** column.

If **Match** appears in the **ACTION** column, QBO has matched that transaction to one previously recorded in QBO. Click **Match** to move the transaction to the **Categorized** tab.

 HINT: Matched transactions in the **For Review** tab can be edited (date or account changed) by clicking anywhere in the transaction row.

If **View** appears in the **ACTION** column on the **For review** tab, QBO has found more than one record that is similar to the uploaded transaction. Click **View** to open an edit screen.

If **Add** appears in the **ACTION** column, QBO has not found a matching transaction. Click anywhere in the transaction row (other than **Add**) to open the edit screen.

The options for recording a transaction depend on whether it represents money received (a debit to the account) or money spent (a credit to the account).

Options available on the edit screen for credits to the account (money spent) are shown in Figure 8.36.

Figure 8.36

Money spent
transaction edit screen

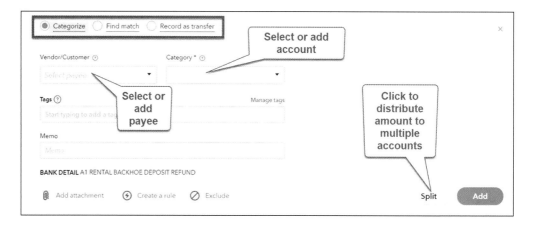

There are four options for recording credits to the account:

- **Find match**
    - QBO will search for and display similar transactions. Any of those matches can be selected.

- **Record as transfer**
    - A field for selecting the transfer account will be displayed.

- **Record as credit card payment**
    - Fields for selecting the credit card account and the payee will be displayed

- **Categorize**
    - Fields for selecting the appropriate account will be displayed. (**Categorize** was selected in Figure 8.36.)
    - If an amount should be distributed to multiple accounts (categories), click **Split** and enter distribution accounts and amounts. The **Split transaction** screen is shown in Figure 8.37.

Figure 8.37

Split screen

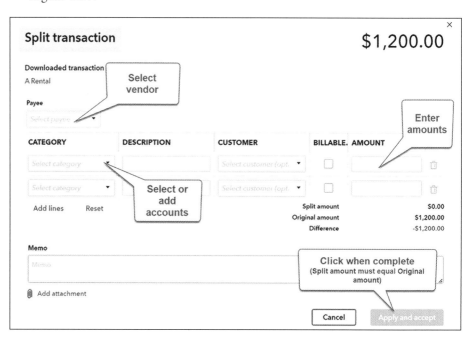

Click **Apply and accept** when complete.

There are three options for recording debits (money received) to the account: **Find match**, **Record as transfer**, and **Categorize**. The screens for each option are similar to those described above for recording credits (money spent) transactions.

Once the edit screens have been completed, click **Add** to record the transaction in QBO. **Added** transactions are moved to the **Categorized** tab.

> **BEHIND THE SCENES** You may see an account listed in the **CATEGORY** field of unmatched transactions. QBO uses natural language processing (a cognitive technology) to "guess" the appropriate classifications of uploaded transactions based on any text included in the CSV file. Cognitive technologies in QBO are covered in Chapter 13.

> **HINT:** If there is an error in the upload, a transaction can be moved to the **Excluded** tab by checking the box in the left column of the incorrect transaction and clicking **Exclude** in the popup menu bar that automatically appears above the list of transactions. If a transaction was excluded in error, clicking **Undo** returns the transaction to the **For Review** tab. Transactions on the **Excluded** tab can be permanently deleted.

Once the review has been completed, all transactions will have been **matched**, **added** or **excluded**. No transactions would appear on the **For review** tab.

When the credit card is later reconciled, all transactions listed on the **Categorized** tab will be automatically marked as cleared.

> **BEHIND THE SCENES** The general process outlined above can be used with banking transactions as well as credit card transactions. The process for downloading transactions directly from financial institutions covered in Appendix 8A.

INACTIVATING AND MERGING GENERAL LEDGER ACCOUNTS

LO 8-6 Understand how to inactivate or merge general ledger accounts in QBO

Companies generally set up their initial chart of accounts based on expected activities and informational needs. As companies grow and change, the chart of accounts usually expands. Often it expands substantially! An effective chart of accounts, though, contains only those accounts that provide useful detail for owners and managers.

Periodically, a company should take a look at the structure of its chart of accounts to make sure it still meets the needs of the company. We already know how to group accounts. Accounts can be moved from one group to another (within the same **account type**) and parent accounts can be added or deleted. But what do we do with accounts that are no longer needed or useful?

Accounts cannot be permanently deleted, but QBO does provide two tools for managing unused accounts:

- Inactivating accounts
- Merging accounts

Inactivating an Account

Inactivating an account is an option when a company needs to maintain detail about past transactions. Let's use an example. Let's say five years ago, a barbershop sold shampoo in addition to cutting hair. It has since discontinued selling products because of the high cost of maintaining inventory. The barbershop no longer needs the inventory account or the cost of goods sold account. It might, however, need that information in the future. That might be the case if it is ever audited or if it decides to reconsider merchandise sales.

Once an account is inactivated, it will not be available for searching, for filtering, or for use in future transactions. Inactivated accounts **will**, however, appear on reports if the accounts had balances in the report period. The phrase "(deleted)" will appear after the account name.

Inactivating an Account with a Zero Balance

Inactivating an account with a zero balance is a relatively simple process.

To inactivate the account in QBO, click the ⚙ on the icon bar and select **Chart of Accounts**.

Figure 8.38

Tool for inactivating account

Chart of Accounts
‹ All Lists

	NAME	TYPE	DETAIL TYPE	QUICKBOOKS BALANCE	BANK BALANCE	ACTION
	Prepaid Expenses	Other Current Assets	Prepaid Expenses	0.00		View register ▼

Batch actions ▼   Filter by name   All ▼   ✏ 🖶 ⚙

Edit
Make inactive (won't reduce usage)
Run report

Run Report   New ▼

In the **ACTION** column of the account you want to inactivate, select **Make inactive**. QBO will ask you to confirm your decision. Once an account has been made inactive, it is no longer visible on the default **Chart of Accounts** screen.

Reactivating Accounts

Accounts can be reactivated. The first step is to make the account visible in the chart of accounts. The simplest process is to click the ⚙ icon just above the **ACTION** column in the **Chart of Accounts**.

Figure 8.39

Tool to display inactive accounts in chart of accounts screen

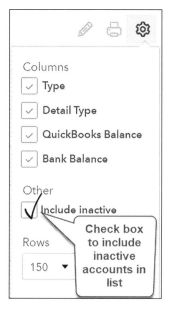

✏ 🖶 ⚙

Columns
☑ Type
☑ Detail Type
☑ QuickBooks Balance
☑ Bank Balance

Other
☑ Include inactive

Check box to include inactive accounts in list

Rows
150 ▼

Check the **Include inactive** box and refresh the screen.

Figure 8.40

Tool for reactivating an inactive account

Click **Make active** in the **ACTION** column. The account will now be available to use in transactions, filters, or searches.

Inactivating an Account with a Non-zero Balance

QBO allows users to inactivate accounts with balances. This would not normally be something done by an accountant, but sometimes accounts are inactivated in error, and it's important to understand what happens to those account balances.

If the account being inactivated is a permanent (balance sheet) account, QBO will display the following message:

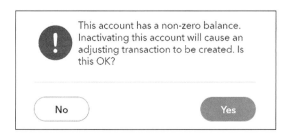

Figure 8.41

Error message when inactivating an account

If **Yes** is selected, QBO will automatically make a journal entry to clear the account (bring it to zero). The offset account used is **Opening Balance Equity** (an **equity account type**). For example, if a user **inactivated** Prepaid Insurance and that account had a $200 debit balance, QBO would make the following entry:

		200	
Opening Balance Equity		200	
Prepaid Insurance			200

If the account to be inactivated is a temporary (revenue or expense) account, no journal entry will be made. The account (identified as a deleted account) would still appear on applicable profit and loss reports with the balance at the point it was inactivated. For example, if Rent Expense with a balance of $500 was deleted, it would continue to appear on profit and loss reports as Rent Expense (deleted) through the end of the year.

If accounts with balances at the time of inactivation are reactivated, the transaction detail prior to the inactivation will be visible. The entry made by QBO to zero out **permanent** accounts, however, will NOT be reversed. The reactivated account will show a zero balance and a journal entry would need to be made.

Merging Accounts

Merging an account would be the best option when an account does not (and maybe never did) provide useful detail. Let's use another example. Let's say the accountant for a barbershop set up separate general ledger accounts for every **service** item. There was an account for shampoos, another for haircuts, another for beard trims, etc. Those accounts were unnecessary because the revenue detail is already available in **Sales by Item** reports. It would make sense, then, to merge some or all of those accounts.

Merging an account really means transferring activity out of the account you no longer wish to use INTO an appropriate existing account. There needs to be two accounts: the "transferor account" (the account you want to eliminate) and the "transferee account" (the account that you intend to keep). The **account types** and **detail types** of the two accounts must be the same.

To merge an account, the Chart of Accounts list must be open. In the **ACTION** column of the "transferor account" (the account you want to eliminate), select **Edit**.

Change the **Account name** to the name of the "transferee account" (the account you intend to keep). The name must be **identical** or you'll create a new account.

Figure 8.42

Message displayed when accounts are merged

> **BEHIND THE SCENES** The identical accounts will be highlighted in the **EDIT ACCOUNT PREVIEW** screen as you make the change.

When you click **Save**, QBO will give you two options.

Clicking **Yes, merge accounts** will inactivate the transferor account. All transactions posted to the account will now appear in the transaction detail of the remaining account.

> **!** **WARNING:** Although you can reactivate a merged account, the transactions will remain in the transferee account.

PRACTICE
EXERCISE
8.4

MBC
Homework

Manage the chart of accounts in Craig's Design and Landscaping.

(The Promotional expense account is inactivated, and the Bookkeeper and Accounting expense accounts are merged.)

1. Click the on the icon bar.

2. Click **Chart of Accounts**.

3. Click **See your Chart of Accounts**, if necessary.

4. Inactivate an account.

    a. In the **ACTION** column for **Promotional** expense, click the arrow next to **Run Report** and select **Make inactive**.

    b. Click **Yes**.

5. Merge an account.

    a. In the **ACTION** column for **Bookkeeper** (an **expense** account), click **Run Report**.

        i. **TIP:** If no transactions appear in the report, change the **Report period** to **All Dates**.

    b. **Make a note** of the amount of the check to **Books by Bessie**.

        i. If no transactions appear in the report, change the **Report period** to **All Dates**.

(continued)

(continued from previous page)

       c. Click **Back to chart of accounts** (top left corner under **Account QuickReport**).

       d. In the **ACTION** column for **Bookkeeper** expense, click the arrow next to **Run Report** and select **Edit**.

       e Change the **Account name** to "Accounting."

           i. Make sure you enter the name exactly as noted. If you have any differences, QBO will not merge the accounts. You should see both accounts highlighted in the **EDIT ACCOUNT PREVIEW** section.

       f. Click **Save**.

       g. Click **Yes, merge accounts** at the prompt to merge.

           i. **TIP:** If this prompt doesn't appear, you most likely made a spelling error when you entered the account name. Log out of the test-drive. Open the test-drive again and go back to Step 5a.

       h. Click **Save** again.

       i. Verify that the **Bookkeeper** account is no longer listed in the **Chart of Accounts** list. **TIP: Bookkeeper** was a sub-account of **Legal & Professional Fees**.

       j. In the **ACTION** column for **Accounting** expense, click **Run Report**.

       k. Select **All Dates** in the **Report period** dropdown menu.

       l. Verify that the check to **Books by Bessie** identified in Step 5b of this Practice Exercise is included in the account balance.

       m. **Make a note** of the balance in the account.

    6. Click **Dashboard** to exit out of the **Chart of Accounts** window.

ADDING NOTES TO REPORTS

LO 8-7 Describe how to add commentary to QBO reports

At the end of an accounting period, after all adjustments have been made, the accountant should be comfortable with the balances in each of the accounts on the financial statements. For many accounts, there are subsidiary ledgers or worksheets that provide documentation. For example, agings (by customer or by vendor) support accounts receivable and accounts payable account balances. Bank reconciliations support cash balances. **Sales by Item** reports provide support for revenue and cost of goods sold amounts.

For other accounts (such as prepaid or unearned revenue accounts), there may not be any standard, formal documentation. For control purposes (and in case of memory lapses!), the accountant would want to document the balances in those accounts as well.

There is a feature in QBO reports that allows the user to add notes to reports. This feature can be very useful to accountants as part of the end-of-period process. For example, instead of preparing an offline worksheet detailing the components of Prepaid Expenses, the accountant can simply include that detail in the balance sheet report for the period by adding a note.

Other uses of this feature might include:

- Adding a note to an **inventory valuation summary** report, reminding the reader that a particular item is nearing obsolescence.

- Adding a note to an **open purchase order** report, reminding the reader to contact the vendor and determine the status of a backorder.

A report must be open before notes can be added.

Figure 8.43

Tool to open note box in report

Clicking **Add notes** on the report menu bar adds a new field at the bottom of the report.

Figure 8.44

Example of note box in report

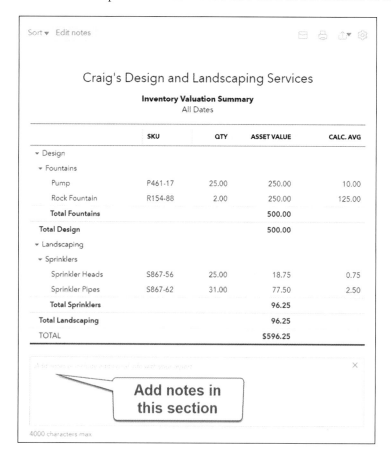

Note boxes can include up to 4,000 characters.

Reports that contain notes can be printed, emailed, or saved as a PDF file. The notes will appear at the bottom of the page.

Reports with notes can also be saved for future reference by clicking **Save customization** at the top of the report window.

Figure 8.45

Options when saving reports

A unique name should be given to the saved report. Customized reports can be saved in groups and can also be restricted to certain users.

For example, an **inventory valuation summary** report might be saved in a group of inventory reports accessible to all users. Customization would look something like this:

Figure 8.46

Example of options selected on saved report with notes

Saved reports are accessed by clicking **Reports** on the navigation bar and selecting the **Custom Reports** tab.

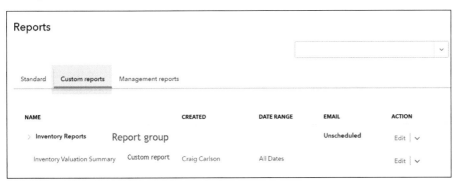

Figure 8.47

Access to saved, customized reports

All saved reports will be displayed by group on the **Custom Reports** tab.

Saved reports can be edited and modified.

Add a comment to a report.

(Craig's Design adds a note to the balance sheet related to the cost of its truck.)

1. Click Reports on the navigation bar.

2. Click Balance Sheet in the Favorites section.

3. **Make a note** of the balance in Accounts Payable (A/P).

4. Click Add notes.

5. In the notes field, type "Cost to refit the truck is not yet included in the Truck account balance."

6. Click Save customization.

7. Enter "Balance Sheet with Notes" as the Custom report name.

8. Click Add new group.

9. Enter "Month End Reports" as the New group name.

10. Click Add.

11. Click Save.

12. Click the printer icon to open a preview of the customized report.

13. **Make a note** of where, in the report, the comment appears.

14. Click Close.

15. Click Dashboard to exit out of reports.

CHAPTER SHORTCUTS

Adjust inventory quantities

1. Click **+ New** on the navigation bar.
2. Click Inventory Qty Adjustment.

Record payment of sales tax

1. Click Sales tax on the navigation bar.
2. Click View tax return in the appropriate row.

Record non-customer cash receipt

1. Click **+ New** on the navigation bar.
2. Click Bank Deposit.

Record bank transfer

1. Click **+ New** on the navigation bar.
2. Click Transfer.

Inactivate an account

1. Click ⚙ on the icon bar.
2. Click Chart of Accounts.
3. Select Make inactive in the ACTION column of the account to be inactivated.

Merge two accounts

1. Click ⚙ on the icon bar.
2. Click Chart of Accounts.
3. Select Edit in the ACTION column of the account to be merged.
4. Change the name of the account to match (exactly) the name of the account to be retained.

CHAPTER REVIEW

Matching
Match the term or phrase (as used in QuickBooks Online) to its definition.

1. quantity on hand
2. inventory quantity adjustment
3. custom report
4. transfer
5. merging
6. add funds to this deposit
7. inactive account
8. sales tax liability report

Assignments with the MBC are available in myBusinessCourse.

_____ number of inventory items available

_____ transaction type used to record the movement of money between bank accounts

_____ section of the bank deposit form used to record non-customer cash receipts

_____ tool used to transfer all activity from one account into another account

_____ transaction type used to record quantity corrections to inventory items

_____ account that is unavailable for posting or searching

_____ saved report that may include manually entered user comments

_____ report of taxable sales revenue and related tax amount by jurisdiction

Multiple Choice

1. Adjustments to inventory can be made in QBO:
   a. to the current quantity of inventory on hand only.
   b. to the current value of inventory on hand only.
   c. to both the current value and current quantity of inventory on hand.

2. When sales tax is charged to a customer, the amount is credited to _____.
   a. an accounts payable account type
   b. an income account type
   c. an other current liability account type
   d. a sales tax payable account type

3. It is possible, in QBO, to:
   a. delete an account by merging the account with another.
   b. permanently delete an account that has been used in a transaction.
   c. inactivate a permanent account with a balance without creating an adjusting entry.
   d. separate two accounts that have been merged.

4. An inactive account in QBO:
   a. can be used in new transactions.
   b. can be used to filter reports.
   c. can be used in the search function.
   d. None of the above statements are true.

5. Recording proceeds from a bank loan could be done:
   a. only through a general journal entry.
   b. only by entering a deposit.
   c. either by creating a general journal entry or by entering the transaction as a deposit.

BEYOND THE CLICKS—THINKING LIKE A MANAGER

Accounting: Physically counting inventory is normally done at least annually in retail companies. The physical count is then compared to the quantity on hand in the accounting system (QBO, for example). List two events that would make the physical count of a specific item less than the quantity reported in the accounting system. List two events that would make the physical count greater than the reported quantity.

Information Systems: Part A: How would you use (filter) the Audit Log if you needed to look at all cash transactions recorded by a specific employee? The Audit Log tool in QBO was introduced in the introduction to Section Three. Part B: Find and View an Edited event in Craig's Landscaping and Design. How many times has the transaction been changed? What changes were made to the transaction? **TIP:** You may have to scroll down quite a ways to find an edited transaction.

ASSIGNMENTS

Assignment 8A

Math Revealed!

2/29/24

✓   You call Martin at home and tell him that the bank balance is quite low. He meets with his banker at City Bank of Sacramento and explains the situation. The bank agrees to provide a $4,000 loan at 6% based on Martin's personal credit. The loan is set up to be repaid over a 12-month period ($344.27 per month including interest). You record the deposit of $4,000 into the company's checking account. **TIP:** You're going to need to set up a new account for this loan. Think carefully when choosing the **account type**.

✓   Your friend, Samantha Levin, agrees to come in to help Martin count the inventory on hand.

●   She counts the inventory at the end of the day and gives you this list:

Taken by Samantha Levin	Inventory Count Sheet—2/29	Unit of Measure	Quantity on Hand
Books and Tools			
	Dry erase boards	Units	14
	Kit	Units	12
	Notebooks	Packages of 5	4
	Puzzles	Units	3
	Ready	Units	19
	Sports	Units	17
	Statistics	Units	10
Math Games			
	Console	Units	5
	Equations	Units	5
	Fractions	Units	5
	Ratios	Units	5

✓   You do a few rechecks to make sure the count is correct, which it is.

●   You talk to Martin about the shortages. He believes that some of the items were probably used by the tutors during the Mathmagic Clinic. You decide to charge the inventory adjustment to the Tutoring supplies expense account.

●   You adjust the inventory quantities in QBO to agree to the count using 2/29 as the transaction date. **TIP:** You can either add all products to the **inventory adjustment** window and change only those items that differ from the count, or you can compare the count sheet provided above to the **Product/Service List** in QBO first and then add only those items that need adjustment to the window.

●   You use FebInvAdj as the **reference no.**

- ● **TIP:** To check your accuracy, click **Save**. Click **More** and select **Transaction journal**. The total adjustment should be $41.

✓ Because Samantha is willing to stay a bit longer, you ask her to count the supplies on hand. She tells you that there is only $9 worth of tutoring supplies on hand. You adjust the accounts appropriately and leave a note for Martin about the need to purchase more supplies. You use Feb24.1 as the **Journal no.**

✓ It took Samantha only two hours to count the inventory and supplies. You write her a check (#1123) for $50 ($25 per hour) and charge the amount to the Contract labor account.

✓ You get ready to pay your sales tax liability.

- ● You review your **Sales Tax Liability** report. The total tax liability for February sales is $32.82. (Most of your product sales were made to the Center for Academic Excellence, a reseller of the products.)

- ● You remit your taxes.

  - ■ **TIP: If you're completing your assignment in March 2024 or later**, open the Sales Tax Center (Figure 8.11) and click **View Tax Return** to record the tax remittance. (Don't worry about entering a check number.) **If you're completing your assignment prior to March 1, 2024**, you will not be able to use the normal process as outlined in the chapter. Instead, create a check (#1124) to CDTFA (California Dept of Tax and Fee Admin) and charge the California Department of Tax and Fee Administration Payable account for the $32.82.

After month end:

✓ You receive the February bank statement. You see that the bank charged a $20 processing fee for the NSF check from Kim Kowalski. You enter the charge when you reconcile the statement to your records using 2/29 (the reconciliation date) as the transaction date.

CITY BANK OF SACRAMENTO
51 Capital Avenue
Sacramento, CA 95822 (916) 585-2120

Student Name Math Revealed!
3835 Freeport Blvd
Sacramento, CA 95822
Account # 1616479　　　　　　　　　　　　　　　　**February 29, 2024**

	CREDITS	CHARGES	BALANCE
Beginning Balance, February 1			$7,498.18
2/1, Check 1107, 24 Hour Quick Stitch Clinic		$180.00	7,318.18
2/2, Check 1109, Frank's Furniture		1,690.00	5,628.18
2/2, Check 1110, Martin Smith		2,500.00	3,128.18
2/3, Check 1108, Parent's Survival Weekly		112.00	3,016.18
2/5, Check 1113, Pro Spaces		850.00	2166.18
2/5, Check 1114, Richard Smith		12.50	2153.68
2/6, Check 1111, Student		300.00	1,853.68
2/7, Deposit	$403.95		2,257.63
2/7, Deposit	1,105.00		3,362.63
2/9, Deposit	679.00		4,041.63
2/15, Check 1115, Prime Visa Company		1,680.02	2,361.61
2/16, Chargeback for NSF check		105.00	2,256.61
2/16, Processing fee, NSF check		20.00	2,236.61
2/16, Deposit	127.40		2,364.01
2/20, Deposit	1,396.94		3,760.95
2/22, Check 1112, Isla Parker		16.31	3,744.64
2/24, Check 1118, Samantha Levin		125.00	3,619.64
2/26, Deposit	675.00		4,294.64
2/27, Check 1117, Books Galore		190.00	4,104.64
2/27, Check 1119, Martin Smith		1,000.00	3,104.64
2/29, Loan proceeds	4,000.00		7,104.64
Ending Balance, February 29			**$7,104.64**

✓ Martin has downloaded the credit card transactions for you from the credit card company's website. He gives you the file so that you can upload these transactions into QBO. You have been entering all of the receipts Martin has given you but you want to be sure all the transactions match and that he didn't miss a receipt.

- You upload the credit card transactions using the CSV file. **TIP:** If you are using myBusinessCourse, download the *7e Math Revealed Credit Card Upload for Chapter 8* from Student Ancillaries. If you're not using myBusinessCourse, the file will be provided to you by your instructor. To upload the file to QBO, click Banking on the navigation bar and open the Banking tab. You should see the Prime Visa Payable account. Select Upload from file in the Link account dropdown menu. If you don't see the account, click Upload transactions.

- You select (or drag and drop) the CSV file into the Manually upload your transactions section. You select 220 Prime Visa Payable as the QuickBooks Account to use for the upload.

- In the Let's set up your file in QuickBooks screen, you complete the two steps.

  Step 1
  - Is the first row in your file a header? **Yes**
  - How many columns show amounts? **Two columns**
  - What's the date format used in your file? **MM/dd/yyyy**

  Step 2
  - Date: **Column 1: Date**
  - Description: **Column 2: Description**
  - Amount:
    - Money Received: **Column 3: Debit**
    - Money Spent: **Column 4: Credit**

- You import all six transactions and accept transactions.

- For all items with Match in the ACTION column on the review tab, you click Match.

- You see one transaction that QBO was unable to match. **TIP:** Add appears in the ACTION column for unmatched transactions.

  - You ask Martin about this. He searches through his desk and finds the receipt for 2/21. He purchased gas at Cardinal Gas & Snacks. You verify the Payee and update the category to the appropriate account, if necessary. You add the transaction.

❊ **HINT:** If you have more than one unmatched transaction, you may have missed entering a transaction in an earlier chapter or you may have entered multiple transactions with the same vendor on a single Expense form. If you missed a transaction, verify the vendor (payee) name, select the appropriate account, and click Add. If you incorrectly entered multiple transactions with the same vendor, you can Add the charges here but then you'll need to delete the earlier entries.

If none of your transactions match, you most likely imported the file incorrectly. Go to Student Ancillaries for tips on how to correct this.

✓ You receive the credit card statement in the mail and prepare the credit card reconciliation. When you finish the reconciliation, you set up the balance for payment later. You use FebCC as the Bill no.

PRIME VISA COMPANY
55 Wall Street
New York, NY 10005

Student Name Math Revealed!
3835 Freeport Blvd
Sacramento, CA 95822
Account # 212456770439

	PAYMENTS	CHARGES	February 29, 2024 BALANCE
Beginning Balance, February 1			$1,680.02
2/5-LA Gasoline Stop		$ 45.00	1,725.02
2/5-Good Sleep Inn		280.00	2,005.02
2/5-Good Sleep Inn		125.00	2,130.02
2/10-Prime Visa	$1,680.02		450.00
2/21-Cardinal Gas & Snacks		26.80	476.80
2/24-Dick's Diner		22.60	499.40
Ending Balance, February 29			**$499.40**

Minimum Payment Due: $10.00   **Payment Due Date: March 15**

✓ You realize you forgot to pay yourself for work done in February. You create an account called "Accrued Expenses" (Account #221) and record the $300 due you for your accounting work. You use Feb24.2 as the entry number. **TIP:** Use other current liabilities as the detail type (Tax form section field).

✓ You review the account balances and make additional adjusting journal entries for February (dated 2/29) as needed, carefully considering the following:

- Your last loan payment to Martin's father was made on 2/27 and covered interest for the month of February.

- Martin borrowed the $4,000 from the bank on 2/29. Interest will start accruing on 3/1.

- You review your revenue and unearned revenue accounts to make sure all earned revenue (and only earned revenue) is recognized.

  ■ All the income billed in February was earned in February so you don't need to defer any revenue.

  ■ For Unearned revenue, you review the entries made in January. The unearned revenue for Annie Wang at the end of January was for sessions held in February. The unearned revenue for Teacher's College was for a workshop held in February. You make the appropriate entry to properly recognize any February revenue.

- You record depreciation for the shelving placed in service on 2/1. The cost was $820. You think the shelving will have a $100 salvage value. You depreciate it over the lease term (24 months). **TIP:** Don't forget to depreciate all the fixed assets purchased in prior months. The depreciation amount for those items will be the same as the entry in January.

- You make other adjusting journal entries, dated 2/29, as needed.

  ■ **TIP:** Look at all the current asset and liability accounts on the balance sheet. Should any of them be adjusted? Look at the profit and loss statement. Are there expenses recorded that shouldn't be recognized in February? Are there expenses that should have been recorded but haven't been? It's often very helpful to be able to compare months when doing month-end work. Consider customizing the profit and loss report by changing the dates to 1/1 to 2/29 and selecting Months in the Display columns by dropdown menu.

✓ You review your chart of accounts.

- You aren't using the Inventory Shrinkage account (a Cost of Goods Sold account) so you make it inactive.

- You decide to make a journal entry to move the $875 paid to Les & Schmidt for the marketing study out of Accounting and consulting fees and into a new Marketing expenses account. You use account #642. **TIP:** Consider whether it should be a sub-account. You can use Other Business Expenses as the detail type (Tax form section field).

Check numbers 2/29

Checking account balance:. . . . . $ 4,035.98

Total assets: $21,556.98

Total liabilities: . . . . $ 9,636.73

Net income for the two months ending 2/29:. . . . $ 8,641.25

Suggested reports for Chapter 8:

All reports should be in portrait orientation.

- Journal (2/29 entries only)

- Balance Sheet as of 2/29

- Profit and Loss for February (with year to date column included)

- Inventory Valuation Summary as of 2/29

- Bank Reconciliation Summary 2/29

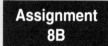

Salish Software Solutions

2/29/24

✓ Sally meets with her banker at Sacramento City Bank. She wants to have easy access to funds in case a good opportunity comes along. The banker explains that with a line of credit, Sally can borrow as much as she needs up to the credit line maximum. Only interest (on any unpaid balance) will be due on a monthly basis although Sally can make principal payments at any time. The bank agrees to provide Sally with a $5,000 line. Interest will be set at 6%. Interest payments will be due on the last day of the month. The line will have a term of one year. Sally doesn't borrow on the line today but you set up the account so it's ready for the future. **TIP:** Think carefully when choosing the **account type**.

✓ Oscar Torres agrees to come in to count the inventory on hand.

- He counts the inventory at the end of the day and gives you this list:

Taken by Oscar Torres	Inventory Count Sheet—2/29	Unit of Measure	Quantity on Hand
Accounting Products			
	Contractor	Units	3
	Easy1	Units	12
	Retailer	Units	3
Management Products			
	Engineering	Units	2
	Legal	Units	2
	Medical	Units	2
	Organizer	Units	16
	Tracker	Units	20

- You do a few rechecks to make sure the count is correct, which it is.

- You're a little surprised that so many **Organizers** are missing. You discuss it with Sally but neither of you can come up with an explanation. You decide to keep a closer eye on the storage cabinet in the future.

- You make an adjustment for the inventory count, charging the differences to a new **cost of goods sold type** account called Inventory Adjustments (#509). You use detail type: **Supplies & Materials—COGS** and use FebInvAdj as the **reference no.** You use 2/29 (the last day of the month) as the transaction date. **TIP:** You can either add all products to the **inventory adjustment** window and change only those items that differ from the count or you can compare the count sheet provided above to the Product/Service List in QBO first and then add only those items that need adjustment to the window.

- **TIP:** To check your accuracy, click **Save**. Click **More** and select **Transaction journal**. The total adjustment should be $105.

✓ It took Oscar an hour to count the inventory. You write him a check (#1123) for $20 and charge the amount to a new Contract labor expense account (#675). You use **Cost of Labor** as the **detail type** (**Tax form section** field). You set it up as a sub-account of 670 Labor Costs (**Save account under** field).

✓ You go ahead and look at the amount of office supplies there are on hand. You estimate the cost at $225. You make the adjustment using Feb24.1 as the entry number and 2/29 as the date.

✓ You get ready to pay your sales tax liability.

   ● You review your **Sales Tax Liability** report. The total tax liability for February sales is $70.00.

   ● You remit your taxes.

      ■ **TIP: If you're completing your assignment in March 2024 or later**, open the Sales Tax Center (Figure 8.11) and click **View Tax Return** to record the tax remittance for February. (Don't worry about entering a check number.) **If you're completing your assignment prior to March 1, 2024**, you will not be able to use the normal process as outlined in the chapter. Instead, create a check (#1124) to CDTFA (California Dept of Tax and Fee Admin) and charge the California Department of Tax and Fee Administration Payable account for the $70.

After month end:

✓ Sally has downloaded the credit card transactions for you from the credit card company's website. She gives you the file so that you can upload these transactions into QBO. You know you have been entering all of the receipts Sally has given you but you want to be sure all the transactions match and that she didn't miss a receipt.

   ● You upload the credit card transactions to QBO using the CSV file. **TIP:** If you are using myBusinessCourse, download the *7e Salish Software Credit Card Upload for Chapter 8* from Student Ancillaries. If you're not using myBusinessCourse, the file will be provided to you by your instructor. To upload the file, click **Banking** on the navigation bar and open the **Banking** tab. You should see the Capital Three Visa Payable Account. Select **Upload from file** in the **Link account** dropdown menu. If you don't see the account, click **Upload transactions**.

   ● You select (or drag and drop) the CSV file into the **Manually upload your transactions** section. You select 220 Capital Three Visa Payable as the **QuickBooks Account** to use for the upload.

   ● In the **Let's set up your file in QuickBooks** screen, you complete the two steps.

      Step 1
      ● Is the first row in your file a header? **Yes**
      ● How many columns show amounts? **Two columns**
      ● What's the date format used in your file? **MM/dd/yyyy**

      Step 2
      ● Date: **Column 1: Date**
      ● Description: **Column 2: Description**
      ● Amount:
         ■ Money Received: **Column 3: Debit**
         ■ Money Spent: **Column 4: Credit**

   ● You import all seven transactions and accept transactions.

   ● For all items with **Match** in the **ACTION** column on the review tab, you click **Match**.

   ● You see one transaction that QBO was unable to match. **TIP: Add** appears in the **ACTION** column for unmatched transactions.

      ■ You ask Sally about this. She searches through her desk and finds the receipt for 2/16. She had taken a couple of people from Butter and Beans out to lunch at Screamin' Bean. (Good client relations!) You enter the **Payee** and update the **category** to the appropriate account, if necessary. You **add** the transaction.

HINT: If you have more than one unmatched transaction, you may have made an error with the upload settings for the file or missed entering a transaction in an earlier chapter or you may have entered multiple transactions with the same vendor on a single **Expense** form. If you missed a transaction, verify the vendor (payee) name, select the appropriate account, and click **Add**. If you incorrectly entered multiple transactions with the same vendor, you can **Add** the charges here but then you'll need to delete the earlier entries.

   If none of your transactions match, you most likely imported the file incorrectly. Go to Student Ancillaries for tips on how to correct this.

✓ You receive the credit card statement in the mail and prepare the credit card reconciliation.

CAPITAL THREE
55 Wall Street
New York, NY 10005

Student Name Salish Software Solutions
3835 Freeport Blvd
Sacramento, CA 95822
Account # 646630813344

February 29, 2024

	PAYMENTS	CHARGES	BALANCE
Beginning Balance			$1,139.00
2/2, AAASP		$195.00	1,334.00
2/4, Top Of The Hill		53.77	1,387.77
2/4, Bell Gas		35.00	1,422.77
2/4, The Franciscan		227.15	1,649.92
2/9, Payment	$1,139.00		510.92
2/16, Screamin' Beans		21.85	532.77
2/26, Roscoe's		28.50	561.27
Ending Balance, 2/29			**$ 561.27**
Minimum Payment Due: $10.00		**Payment Due Date: March 15**	

✓ You finish the reconciliation and set up the balance for payment later. You use FebCC as the **Bill no.**

✓ You receive the February bank statement. You see that the bank charged a $20 processing fee for the NSF check from Dew Drop Inn. You enter the charge when you reconcile the statement to your records, using 2/29 as the transaction date.

SACRAMENTO CITY BANK
1822 Capital Avenue
Sacramento, CA 95822 (916) 585-2120

Student Name Salish Software Solutions
3835 Freeport Blvd
Sacramento, CA 95822
Account # 855922

February 29, 2024

		CREDITS	CHARGES	BALANCE
Beginning Balance, February 1				**$12,385.00**
2/1	Check 1109, Oscar Torres		$ 100.00	12,285.00
2/2	Check 1107, Hacker Spaces		200.00	12,085.00
2/3	Check 1100, Marie Elle		75.00	12,010.00
2/3	Check 1111, Student name		300.00	11,710.00
2/4	Check 1112, Alki Property Management		650.00	11,060.00
2/6	Check 1115, Dell Finance		150.00	10,910.00
2/6	Check 1110, Sally Hanson		2,000.00	8,910.00
2/7	Deposit	$ 852.60		9,762.60
2/7	Deposit	3,500.00		13,262.60
2/9	Deposit	350.00		13,612.60

(continued)

(continued from previous page)

SACRAMENTO CITY BANK
1822 Capital Avenue
Sacramento, CA 95822 (916) 585-2120

Student Name Salish Software Solutions
3835 Freeport Blvd
Sacramento, CA 95822
Account # 855922   **February 29, 2024**

		CREDITS	CHARGES	BALANCE
2/11	Check 1114, Western Phone Company		95.00	13,517.60
2/14	Check 1113, Sacramento Light & Power		103.95	13,416.65
2/16	Check returned for insufficient funds		350.00	13,063.65
2/16	Fee for NSF check		20.00	13,043.65
2/19	Deposit	362.60		13,406.25
2/20	Check 1116, Capital Three		1,139.00	12,267.25
2/21	Deposit	4,050.00		16,317.25
2/26	Deposit	610.00		16,927.25
Ending Balance - February 29				**$16,927.25**

✓ You realize you forgot to pay yourself for work done in February. You create an account called "Accrued Expenses" (Account # 221) and record the $300 due you for your accounting work. You create Feb24.2 as the entry number. **TIP:** Use Other current liabilities as the detail type (Tax form section field).

✓ You review your revenue and unearned revenue accounts to make sure all earned revenue (and only earned revenue) is recognized.

● For the revenue accounts, you check with Sally to make sure that all the hours and fees billed in February were completed in February. All the income billed in February was earned in February so you don't need to defer any of that revenue.

● For Unearned revenue, you review the entries made in January. The unearned revenue for Butter and Beans at the end of January was for the remaining 20 hours of work billed on INV-1009. Sally lets you know that all that work has now been completed. The unearned revenue for Albus Software was for a workshop held in February. You make the appropriate entry to properly recognize February revenue.

✓ You record depreciation for the month of February for all fixed assets, including depreciation on the $1,500 cabinets placed in service on February 1st. You depreciate the cabinets over 5 years. Sally doesn't think there will be any resale value at the end of the service life.

✓ You made the last payment to Dell Finance on 2/1. The next payment is not due until March. The $150 payment on February 1 covered January interest ($12.50) and reduced the loan balance by $137.50. **TIP:** The annual interest rate is 5%.

✓ You make other adjusting journal entries, dated 2/29 as needed.

● **TIP:** Look at all the current asset and liability accounts on the balance sheet. Should any of them be adjusted? Look at the profit and loss statement. Are there expenses recorded that shouldn't be recognized in February? Are there any expenses that weren't recorded that should be? It's often very helpful to be able to compare months when doing month-end work. Consider customizing the profit and loss report by changing the dates to 1/1 to 2/29 and selecting Months in the Display columns by dropdown menu.

✓ You review your chart of accounts.

● You see that QBO has created a new Cost of Goods Sold account (Inventory Shrinkage). You realize this was created by default when you made your inventory adjustment entry. You decide to use the default account set up by QBO so you merge 509 Inventory Adjustments into the Inventory Shrinkage account. You want to keep the account number.

■ **TIP:** You will need to edit the Inventory Adjustment account by changing the name to Inventory Shrinkage and removing the account number. Then you can go back in and change the name and account number.

Check numbers 2/29

Checking account balance: $10,891.50
Net income for the two months ending 2/29: $11,613.80
Total assets: $32,477.50
Total liabilities: . . . .$ 7,205.70

Suggested reports for Chapter 8:

- Journal (2/29 entries only)
- Balance Sheet as of 2/29
- Profit and Loss for February (with year to date column included)
- Inventory Valuation Summary as of 2/29
- Bank Reconciliation Report 2/29
- Credit Card Reconciliation Report 2/29

APPENDIX 8A CONNECTING QBO TO BANK ACCOUNTS

LO 8-8 Understand how transactions directly downloaded from bank are processed in QBO

Downloading Transactions from Bank Accounts

One of the most time-saving features of QBO is the ability to download banking and credit card transactions directly into the company file.

Although you will not be able to use the direct download feature in the homework file, you can get a feel for the process in the test drive company.

There are three fictitious accounts connected to the test drive company (Mastercard, Checking, and Savings).

Click **Banking** on the navigation bar. The screen will look something like this:

Figure 8A.1

Banking screen

Transactions are automatically downloaded nightly from most financial institutions although some institutions limit the number of downloads.

Click **Checking**. There are three tabs: **For Review, Categorized**, and **Excluded**.

Figure 8A.2

For Review tab of Banking screen

For each connected account, downloaded transactions first appear on the **For Review** tab. Users can click anywhere in a downloaded transaction other than in the **ACTION** column to expand the details.

For each downloaded transaction, there will be one of three options available in the **ACTION** column.

- **Match**
  - QBO has found a match for the transaction in the company file. QBO uses the following logic for determining matches:
    - ◆ Transaction downloaded from the bank matches a transaction manually entered in QBO.
    - ◆ Downloaded transaction matches an open balance on an **invoice/bill**.

Figure 8A.3

Expanded Match transaction

  - User can
    - ◆ accept QBO's categorization by clicking **Match** in the **ACTION** column.
    - ◆ click anywhere in the transaction line to manually change the **category**.
- **View**
  - QBO found multiple possible matches for the transaction.
  - User can see the possible matching records by clicking **View** in the **ACTION** column.

Figure 8A.4

Expanded View transaction

  - ◆ If one of the possible matching records is acceptable, user would click **Match**.
  - ◆ If none of the possible matching records is acceptable, user could click **Categorize** to manually select the **category** (account).
  - ◆ If the transaction represents a transfer, user would click **Record transfer** and identify the offset account.
- **Add**
  - QBO was unable to find a match for the transaction.

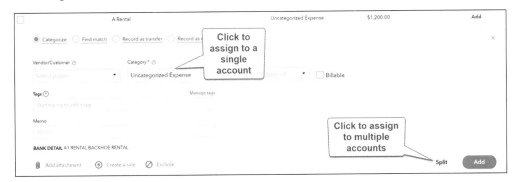

Figure 8A.5

Expanded Add transaction

        ◆   **Uncategorized income** is displayed in the **CATEGORY** field if the transaction represents a cash receipt; **Uncategorized expense** is displayed in the **CATEGORY** field if the transaction represents a cash disbursement.

    ■ Users would click **Add** after manually selecting the appropriate **category** (account).

> **!** **WARNING:** Sometimes the **Vendor/Payee** field is not completed when a transaction is downloaded. (The payee name may, instead, be listed in the **Memo** field.) Although not required, it's best practice to select (or add) the payee's name. Only transactions with a vendor name in the **Vendor/Payee** field will be included in the Vendor Center and accessible in searches by **Payee** or **Vendor**.

Users can change a transaction to a **Transfer** (movement of cash from one account to another) in any of the expanded transaction screens.

    Users are able to distribute a transaction to multiple accounts by clicking **Split** in the **Add** screen.

Figure 8A.6

Split transaction screen

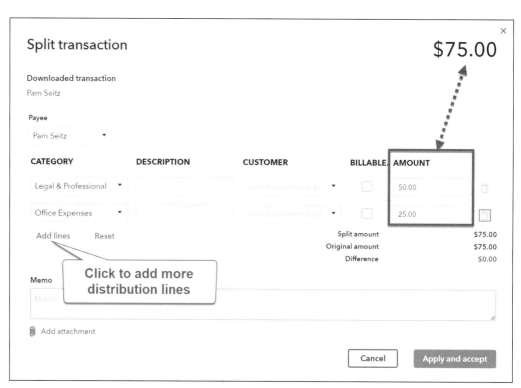

Fields available on the **Split transaction** screen depend on the type of transaction being edited.

    Once the user reviews the transaction and selects either **Match** or **Add**, the transaction will be recorded and moved to the **Categorized** tab.

Figure 8A.7

Option to undo banking transaction added to QBO

If a user incorrectly added or matched a transaction, clicking **Undo** on the **Categorized** tab will return the transaction to the **For Review** tab.

Reviewed transactions can also be added to QBO in batches.

Figure 8A.8

Batch processing options

A check is placed in each reviewed row, and **Accept** is selected. Transactions can also be excluded in batches.

Occasionally, duplicate transactions will be downloaded into QBO. Using the **Exclude Selected** batch option will move the transactions to the **Excluded** tab. **Excluded** transactions can be deleted.

> **BEHIND THE SCENES** QBO downloads account withdrawals from bank accounts (checks, automatic withdrawals) using the **Expense transaction type**. The same transaction type (Expense) is used for downloads of credit card charges.

Setting Banking Rules

Users can set **rules** to guide QBO in managing downloaded transactions. To set rules, click **Banking** on the navigation bar and select the **Rules** tab.

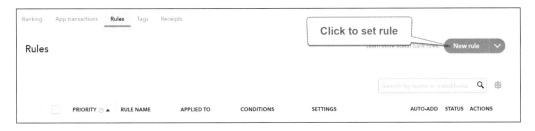

Figure 8A.9

Bank rules tab

Click **New rule**.

Figure 8A.10

Setup of bank rules

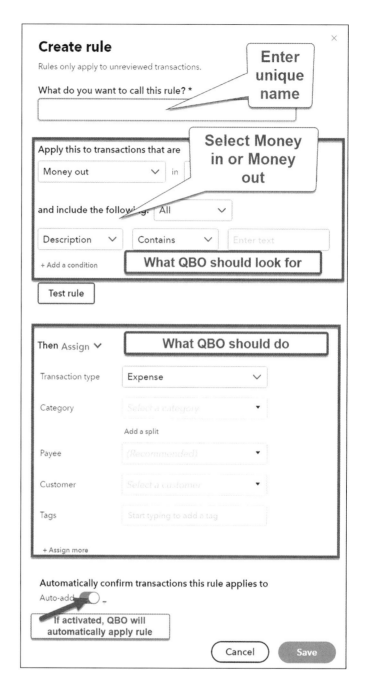

Rules can be created for bank deposit transactions (**Money in**) and bank withdrawal transactions (**Money out**).

Each rule can have up to five conditions. The user defines whether a single transaction must meet all of the conditions or if only one condition must be met. Each condition relates to either **bank text**, **description**, or **amount**. The filtering options depend on which of the three conditions are selected. For example, if **amount** is selected, the user can choose between **Equals**, **Is greater than**, **Is less than**, or **Doesn't equal**.

The treatment for any transaction meeting the conditions is defined in the **Then Assign** section. The dropdown menu options available will change depending on whether the rule applies to **Money in** transactions or **Money out** transactions but **transaction type**, **payee** (name), and **category** (account) are always the primary fields.

For each downloaded transaction, only one rule will be applied. The order in which the rules are listed in the **Rules** list determines the priority of application.

QuickBooks

Beyond the Basics

So far, we've covered how basic transactions in the sales, purchase, and end-of-period cycles of service and merchandising companies are recorded and managed in QuickBooks Online.

Although recording transactions is a very important part of accounting, reporting accounting activity in a way that is useful to management is just as important. In this section, a number of tools and features that can be very useful in managing a business will be introduced.

We'll also look at more detailed ways of tracking revenues and costs in QBO. Construction companies, law firms, accounting firms, architectural firms, and custom shops are just a few examples of the types of companies that normally need the ability to track worker time by client and direct costs (costs specific to a client). The information is useful in managing the business and, in many cases, is needed for billing purposes. We'll look at features in QBO that allow users to track projects and to identify time and costs as billable.

Chapter 9 covers segment reporting (using classes and locations) and budgeting, two important management tools in QBO. Managing recurring entries and creating reversing entries will also be covered

Chapter 10 covers project costing and billing for time and expenses.

Chapter 11 covers a variety of other tools in QBO including creating custom fields, customizing forms, managing attachments, and exporting reports to Excel.

Management Tools

Road Map

In your first financial accounting course, you might have heard or read a definition of accounting that went something like this:

Accounting is a system in which an organization's economic events are identified, recorded, summarized, analyzed, and reported. From this system comes financial information that can be used by management, creditors, and investors to plan and evaluate.

In this course, we focus on **recording and reporting** transactions in an electronic environment but it's also important to look at ways accounting software might be helpful in the planning and evaluation functions of an organization.

In this chapter, we're going to cover a few of the tools in QBO that can be used to provide useful information to management.

- Tracking operating results by class and by location

- Preparing budgets

We're also going to cover a few time-saving tools (recurring and reversing transactions). Tagging (a new reporting tool first introduced in early 2020) will be covered in Appendix 9A.

TRACKING AND REPORTING BY BUSINESS SEGMENT

LO 9-1 Develop and use segment reporting tools in QBO

eLecture

Segment A subdivision of an entity for which supplemental financial information is disclosed.

One of the main advantages of computerized accounting systems is the incredible amount of detail that can effectively AND efficiently be maintained. The use of inventory items in QBO is a good example of that. A company can easily track revenues and costs for every model of every product sold by a company and still have a one-page income statement!

Class and location are additional tools in QBO available for tracking detail. Both are used to represent specific reporting **segments**. Examples of business segments include:

- Departments

- Divisions

- Sales regions

- Product lines

- Service types

- Stores

> **BEHIND THE SCENES** Classes and locations are not linked in any way to general ledger accounts. They are simply tools for identifying the segment of the business that a particular transaction is related to.

Users can activate class tracking or location tracking or both. Using class or location tracking is not mandatory in QBO. It is a preference.

Users can have up to five levels of tracking for classes and locations in QBO Plus. Levels 2–5 are known as sub-classes or sub-locations.

Although the two features are similar, there is one important distinction between the two. If class tracking is used, a preference can be set allowing users to link each line item within a transaction (a form) to a specific class. If location tracking is used, the entire transaction is linked to one specific location on all forms other than timesheets and journal entries. (On timesheets and journal entries, it is possible to assign location by line item.)

Because of that difference, it generally makes the most sense to use **location** tracking for business units like stores or departments or divisions and to use **class** tracking for focus areas, like product lines or service types that cross a number of business units.

Both types are available for filtering in reports. For example, if you had a Consulting Services **class**, you could filter a sales report or a profit and loss report so that only transactions classified as Consulting Services would be included in your report. If you had a Portland **location**, you could filter a report of expenses so that only Portland expenses would be included. If you were using both **classes** and **locations**, you could filter a report so that only Consulting Services transactions in the Portland office were included.

Segment tracking requires additional work so it should only be used if an organization CAN be separated into segments AND there are meaningful differences between the segments that make them worth tracking.

As an example, let's look at three retail companies selling jewelry. Company A has one store and one manager and only sells diamond rings. Company B has five stores and five managers and only sells diamond rings. Company C has three stores and three managers and sells diamond rings and also provides cleaning and repair services related to diamond rings.

Company A **could** set up a **class** for every type of diamond ring sold but that information is already available in **product** reports. The company could also set up a **class** for every day of the week but that probably wouldn't give management much meaningful information and would require a LOT of allocation! Company A has only one store so **location** tracking is unnecessary. Company A doesn't appear to have any meaningful segments.

Company B, on the other hand, might use **locations** to track sales and costs for each of their five stores. Management could then use that information to evaluate product mix at the various stores, to evaluate the performance of store managers or in planning for new stores. Because the only product is diamond rings, it would be unlikely that using **classes** would be helpful.

Company C, like Company B, might use **locations** to track operations for the three stores. **Classes** might be used to track information about sales from rings separate from information about the cleaning and repair services they provide.

Here are two tips for using segment tracking:

- Set up **classes** or **locations** for the segments that provide the most useful information.
  - Segment information is useful if it can help a company evaluate or plan or if segment detail is necessary for reporting to regulatory authorities.

- Make sure all transactions are assigned to a segment.
  - Most companies set up a separate **class** and **location** to be used to track activities that don't fit in one of the other identified business segments. If, for example, a company sets up a **class** for each product line, owners' salaries or corporate legal fees might be examples of transactions that would be assigned to an "Other" or "Administration" **class**.

 HINT: Intuit introduced a new tracking tool, called **tagging**, in early 2020. **Tags**, like **classes** and **locations**, can be used to report on various activities. Appendix A of this chapter provides additional information.

Turning on Class Tracking

Setting up **class** tracking is done in **Account and Settings**. (Use the ⚙ on the icon bar to open **Account and Settings**.)

Open the **Advanced** tab.

Figure 9.1

Access to class and location tracking

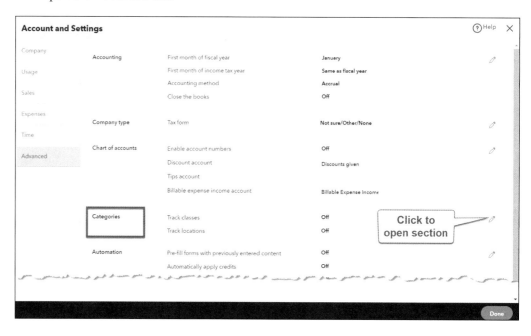

Click the **pencil** icon in the **Categories** section.

Figure 9.2

Class tracking setting and options

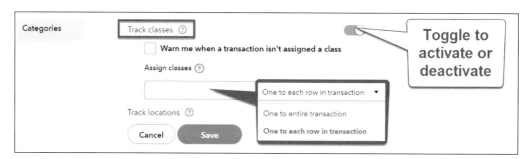

Toggle the **Track classes** button to activate the tool.

Using the **Warn me when a transaction isn't assigned a class** feature is an optional (but very useful!) tool.

There are two options available under **Assign classes**.

Selecting **One to each row in transaction** provides more flexibility because it allows you to easily enter transactions that include activities for more than one **class**. Selecting **One to entire transaction** would save time in companies that would not have multiple **class** activities in the same transaction.

Once **class** tracking is turned on, fields will be available on most forms for designating the appropriate classification. Figure 9.3 is an example of a **check** form after **class** tracking is activated with assignment by row.

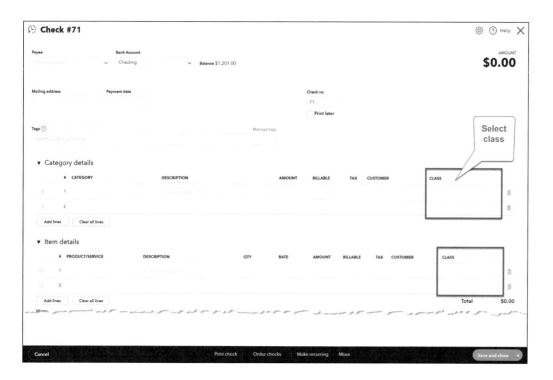

Figure 9.3

Class field on invoice form

If **class** tracking had been activated with assignment by transaction, a **Class** field would appear to the right of the **Check no.** field.

> **BEHIND THE SCENES:** **Payment** and **bill payment** forms do not include fields for tracking **location** or **class** because the segments would already have been identified on the associated **invoice** and **bill** forms. **Class** and **location** fields would also not be included on **transfer** forms.

Turning on Location Tracking

Setting up **location** tracking is also done on the **Advanced** tab of **Account and Settings**. Click the **pencil** icon in the **Categories** section to turn **location** tracking on.

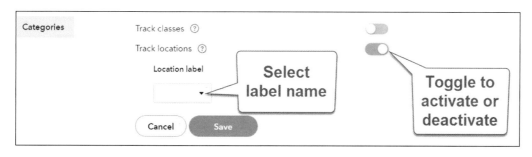

Figure 9.4

Location tracking setting

QBO uses "location" as the default title for this type of segment, but users can change the title to any one of the following:

Label options for
location tracking

> ✳ **HINT:** It sometimes takes a few minutes for a switch in **location** title to take
> effect. Try refreshing your browser if you don't see the change right away.

Once **location** tracking is turned on, fields will be available on most forms for designating the appropriate classification. Figure 9.6 is an example of a **bill** form after **location**
tracking was activated and **Store** was selected as the **location label**.

Location field on bill
form

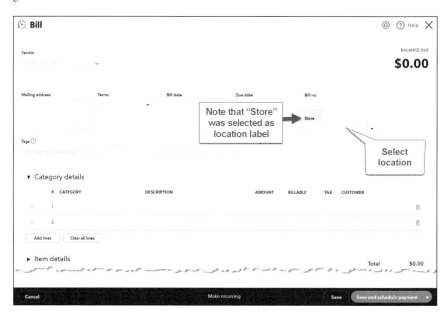

> ❗ **WARNING:** The settings changed in this practice exercise will be used in
> Practice Exercises 9.2 through 9.4. You'll save yourself some time if you
> continue through to the end.

Turn on class tracking for Craig's Design and Landscaping.
(Craig's Design decides to track revenues and costs related to their primary sources of
revenue.)

1. Click the ⚙ on the icon bar.

2. Click **Account and Settings**.

(continued)

(continued from previous page)

3. Open the Advanced tab.

4. Click the pencil icon in the Categories section.

5. Toggle the button next to Track Classes to activate the feature. Check the box next to Warn me when a transaction isn't assigned a class.

6. Select one to each row in transaction in the Assign classes dropdown menu.

7. Toggle the button next to Track Locations to activate the feature.
   a. **Make a note** of the label options available in the dropdown menu.

8. Select Territory in the Location label dropdown menu.

9. Click Save.

10. Click Done.

Setting Up Classes and Locations

Once you've activated segment reporting in QBO and identified the segments you want to track, creating specific **classes** and **locations** is a simple process.

Click the ⚙ on the icon bar.

Figure 9.7

Access to Class and Location lists

Click All Lists under the Lists column.

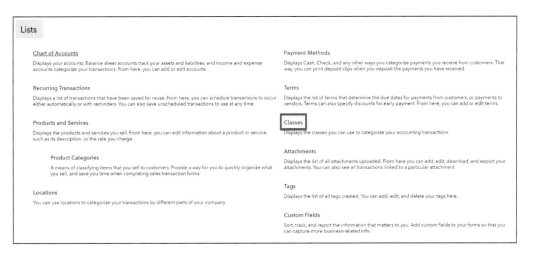

Figure 9.8

Access to Class lists

Click **Classes**.

Click **New**.

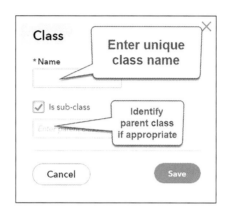

Enter a **Name** for the **class**. Check **Is sub-class** and select the appropriate **parent class** if multiple **class** levels are used.

 HINT: You can't rearrange the order of the **classes** on the **Class List**. The order listed is the order that will be displayed on reports. If it's important to have the **classes** in a particular order, companies might consider using numbers as part of the **class** names. The names could then be edited later to change the order. Reports can also be downloaded into Excel and reordered there. (Exporting to Excel is covered in Chapter 11.)

Clicking **Save** completes the setup of a new **class**.

The process for setting up **locations** is similar to the process for **class** setup.

Click the ⚙ on the icon bar and select **All Lists** to open the following window.

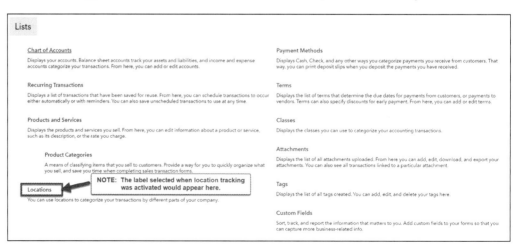

Click **Locations**.

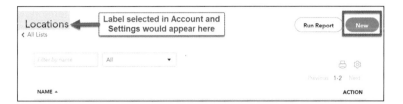

Figure 9.12

Access to new location setup

Click **New**.

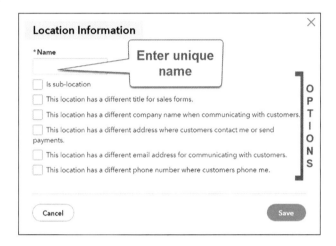

Figure 9.13

New location service record

There are a variety of options available when setting up **locations**. If **Is sub-location** is checked, a field for selecting a parent location would be displayed.

In the remaining options, QBO allows users to customize titles of forms and contact information for various locations. For example, if a user wanted to use a different company name and phone number for each store on **invoices**, **sales receipts**, and other forms sent to customers, a setup might look something like Figure 9.14.

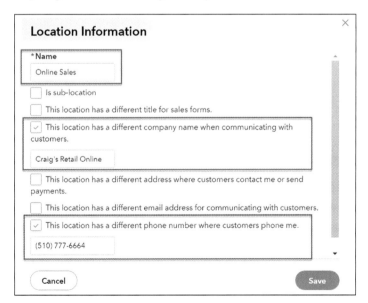

Figure 9.14

Location options

Clicking **Save** completes the setup of a new **location**.

Classes and **locations** can be edited or inactivated by selecting **Edit** or **Make inactive** on the dropdown menu in the **ACTION** column of the appropriate list.

PRACTICE
EXERCISE
9.2

MBC

Set up classes and locations for Craig's Design and Landscaping.

(Craig's Design has decided to track operations by type of service and by territory. One class, labeled Design and Installation, will be used to report on landscape design services. A class labeled Gardening will be used to track all gardening services. A class labeled General will be used for all shared costs. Two territories will be used (Midtown and Uptown).)

1. If you have logged out since the last practice exercise, you'll need to activate class and location tracking by following the instructions in Practice Exercise 9.1.

2. Click the on the icon bar.

3. Click All Lists.

4. Click Classes.

   a. Click New.

   b. Enter "Design and Installation" as the Name.

   c. Click Save.

   d. Click New to add a second class.

   e. Enter "Gardening" as the Name.

   f. Click Save.

   g. Click New to add the class for tracking general costs.

   h. Enter "General" as the Name.

   i. Click Save.

5. Click the ⚙ on the icon bar.

6. Click All Lists.

7. Click Territories.

   a. Click New.

   b. Enter "Midtown" as the Name.

   c. Leave the other boxes unchecked.

   d. Click Save.

   e. Click New to add another territory.

   f. Enter "Uptown" as the Name.

   g. Leave the other boxes unchecked.

   h. Click Save.

8. Click Dashboard to exit out of the window.

> **! WARNING:** Practice Exercises 9.3 and 9.4 use the classes set up in this exercise. You'll save yourself some time if you continue through to the end.

Adding Class to Item Records

To minimize data entry and standardize reporting, **classes** can be directly linked to **products** and **services** in the item record if you selected the option to assign classes to each row in a transaction. This option is not available if you selected the option to assign a class to the entire transaction. (**Locations** cannot be linked to other records.)

Click ⚙ on the icon bar and select **Products and services**.

Select **New** to create a new item or **Edit** to revise an existing item.

Figure 9.15

Class field in service item record

Select the appropriate segment in the **Class** field.

Once a **class** is linked to a **product** or **service**, **class** fields on sales or purchase transactions that include those items will be automatically updated. **Class** can be changed on specific transactions if necessary.

Assign classes to products.

(Craig's Design decides to link some services to the Gardening class.)

1. If you have logged out since the last practice exercise, you'll need to redo Practice Exercises 9.1 and 9.2 before moving forward.

2. Open the **Products and services** list.

   a. Click the on the icon bar.

   b. Click **Products and Services**.

3. Link two **Services** to the **Gardening class**.

   a. Click **Edit** in the **ACTION** column of the **Trimming** row.

   b. Select **Gardening** in the **Class** dropdown menu.

   c. Click **Save and Close**.

   d. Click **Edit** in the **ACTION** column of the **Pest Control** row.

   e. Select **Gardening** in the **Class** dropdown menu.

   f. Click **Save and Close**.

4. Click **Dashboard** to exit **Products and Services**.

PRACTICE EXERCISE 9.3

MBC

 WARNING: The next practice exercise uses the work just completed. You'll save yourself some time if you continue without logging or timing out.

Adding Class and Location to Transactions

Assigning classes and locations is done within forms (invoices, bills, journal entries, timesheets, etc.). The assignment can be changed at any time by simply editing the form.

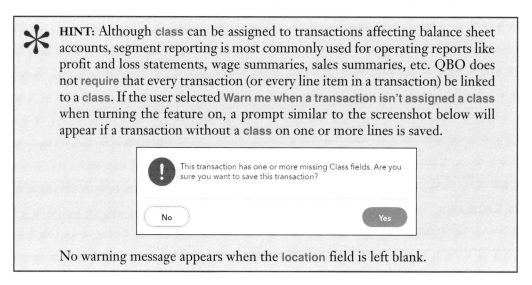

> **HINT:** Although class can be assigned to transactions affecting balance sheet accounts, segment reporting is most commonly used for operating reports like profit and loss statements, wage summaries, sales summaries, etc. QBO does not require that every transaction (or every line item in a transaction) be linked to a class. If the user selected Warn me when a transaction isn't assigned a class when turning the feature on, a prompt similar to the screenshot below will appear if a transaction without a class on one or more lines is saved.
>
> > ! This transaction has one or more missing Class fields. Are you sure you want to save this transaction?
> >
> > No   Yes
>
> No warning message appears when the location field is left blank.

Since only one location can be assigned to a single form in most cases, the location field is usually located in the top right section of the form.

If the preference for adding class to row items is selected, fields for entering class are normally entered in one of the final columns for each row. If the preference is set to one class per transaction, the class field is normally displayed directly below the location field. Placement of the fields on a bill form is shown in Figure 9.16.

Figure 9.16

Location and Class fields on a bill form

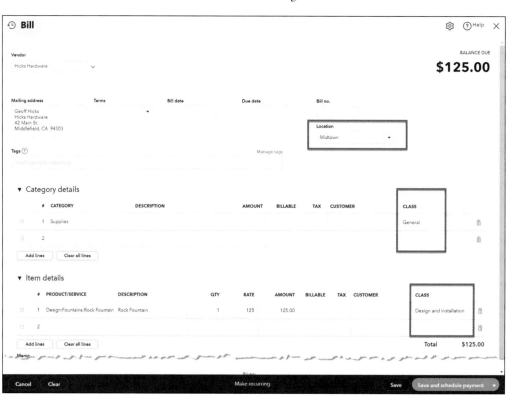

BEHIND THE SCENES If you take a minute to think about it, you'll realize that there's quite a bit of information included in the bill shown in Figure 9.16. In this one form, the user would have:

- Increased inventory
- Expensed some supply costs
- Tracked costs by segment
- Set up a liability

PRACTICE
EXERCISE
9.4

Assign classes to a few transactions for Craig's Design and Landscaping.
(Craig's Design invoices Rondonuwu Fruit and Vegi for some gardening work and records a check for a consultation with an advertising agency about promoting the design services in the Uptown neighborhood.)

1. If you have logged out since the last practice exercise, you'll need to redo Practice Exercises 9.1 through 9.3.

2. Click **+ New** on the navigation bar.

3. Click Invoice.

   a. Select Rondonuwu Fruit and Vegi as the customer.

   b. Use the current date as the Invoice date.

   c. Select Midtown as the Territory.

   d. Select Trimming as the PRODUCT/SERVICE.

   e. Leave the QTY and RATE as is.

   f. Make sure the box in the TAX field is checked.

   g. The Class field should have auto-filled with Gardening.

   h. Select California (8%) in the select a sales tax rate dropdown menu.

   i. **Make a note** of the total amount due.

   j. Click Save and close.

4. Click **+ New** on the navigation bar.

5. Click Check.

   a. Select Lee Advertising as the vendor.

   b. Use the current date as the Payment date.

   c. Leave the check number as is.

   d. **Make a note** of the check number.

   e. Select Uptown as the Territory.

   f. Select Advertising as the CATEGORY.

   g. Enter "Consultation" as the DESCRIPTION.

   h. Enter "500" as the AMOUNT.

   i. Select Design and Installation as the Class.

   j. Click Save and close.

Reporting by Class or Location

There are several reports that are frequently used to report segment information, but most reports can be filtered by **class** or **location**.

The **Profit & Loss by Class** and **Profit & Loss by Location** reports are probably the ones most commonly used. Both reports can be accessed in the **Business Overview** section of **Reports**. Each **class** or **location** will be shown in a separate column. Any transactions that have NOT been classified will appear in a **Not Specified** column.

> ✳ **HINT:** Users can drill down on transactions appearing in the **Not Specified** column. The transactions can then be edited so that they are properly classified.

Figure 9.17

Example of Class report

Craig's Design and Landscaping Services

Profit and Loss by Class

Classes created and assigned by authors

	DESIGN AND INSTALLATION	GARDENING	GENERAL	TOTAL
▾ Income				
Landscaping Services	853.00	861.25		$1,714.25
Pest Control Services		140.00		$140.00
Total Income	**$853.00**	**$1,001.25**	**$0.00**	**$1,854.25**
GROSS PROFIT	**$853.00**	**$1,001.25**	**$0.00**	**$1,854.25**
▾ Expenses				
Automobile		54.55		$54.55
Job Expenses	247.17			$247.17
Legal & Professional Fees		300.00	305.00	$605.00
Utilities			142.94	$142.94
Total Expenses	**$247.17**	**$354.55**	**$447.94**	**$1,049.66**
NET OPERATING INCOME	**$605.83**	**$646.70**	**$ (447.94)**	**$804.59**
NET INCOME	**$605.83**	**$646.70**	**$ (447.94)**	**$804.59**

Figure 9.18

Example of Location report

Craig's Design and Landscaping Services

Profit and Loss by Location

Locations created and assigned by authors

	GENERAL	MIDTOWN	UPTOWN	TOTAL
▾ Income				
Landscaping Services		662.25	1,052.00	$1,714.25
Pest Control Services		70.00	70.00	$140.00
Total Income	**$0.00**	**$732.25**	**$1,122.00**	**$1,854.25**
GROSS PROFIT	**$0.00**	**$732.25**	**$1,122.00**	**$1,854.25**
▾ Expenses				
Automobile			54.55	$54.55
Job Expenses		158.08	89.09	$247.17
Legal & Professional Fees	355.00		250.00	$605.00
Utilities	142.94			$142.94
Total Expenses	**$497.94**	**$158.08**	**$393.64**	**$1,049.66**
NET OPERATING INCOME	**$ -497.94**	**$574.17**	**$728.36**	**$804.59**
NET INCOME	**$ -497.94**	**$574.17**	**$728.36**	**$804.59**

The **Sales and Customers** and **Expenses and Vendors** sections in **Reports** include a number of segmented reports preset by QBO.

CREATING AND USING BUDGETS

"The general who wins the battle makes many calculations in his temple before the battle is fought. The general who loses makes but few calculations beforehand."—Sun Tzu

LO 9-2 Explain and use the budgeting process in QBO

Managing a business is certainly not like going to war but having a plan and being able to evaluate actual results against that plan can definitely help a business succeed.

A financial plan for a business is commonly called a "budget." In a simple budget, revenues and costs are generally estimated by month. Estimates might be based on:

- Past experience
- Projections of sales growth (or contraction)
- Industry statistics
- Combinations of the above

There are a number of tools in QBO for creating and using profit and loss budgets.

Creating Budgets

Companies can create multiple budgets in QBO.

Profit and loss budgets can be prepared for a company overall, by **Customer**, by **Class**, or by **Location**. In this course, we'll cover creating a budget for a company overall.

All of the planning tools in QBO are accessed by first clicking the ⚙ on the icon bar.

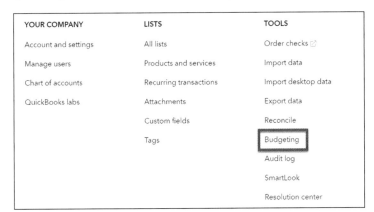

Figure 9.19

Access to budgeting feature

Select **Budgeting** in the **Tools** column.

Figure 9.20

Link to budget screen

Click **Add budget**.

Figure 9.21

Initial budget setup
screen

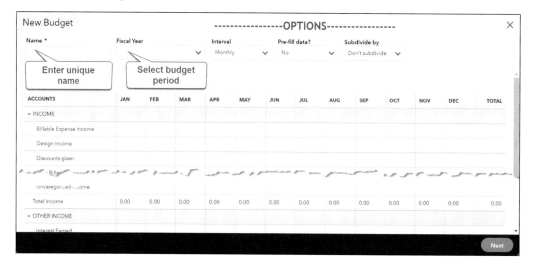

A unique name should be entered in the **Name** field. The appropriate **Fiscal Year** should also be selected.

Users can create monthly, quarterly, or yearly budgets. (The choice is selected in the **Interval** field.) For the most flexibility in reporting, most companies would create monthly budgets.

Users have two choices for entering data in a budget. Their choice is selected in the **Pre-fill data?** dropdown menu.

Figure 9.22

Options for setting
budget amounts

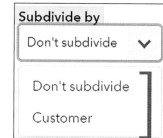

- Budgets can be started from scratch. (**No** selected in the **Pre-fill data?** dropdown menu shown in Figure 9.22.)

- Budgets can be filled with actual data from one of the two prior fiscal years. (The appropriate year selected in **Pre-fill data?** field.)
    - Edits can be made to budgets created using prior period data.

All budgets must be set up by account and by period (month, quarter, or year). You can expand the budget by adding **location**, **class**, or **customer**. This is called **subdividing** in QBO.

Figure 9.23

Options for budget
detail level

Subdivide by
Don't subdivide

Don't subdivide
Customer

A company could have an overall budget, budgets for each **class**, budgets for each **location**, AND budgets for each **customer** (project). Each one would be created separately and each would include amounts by account and by period.

Click **Next** in the bottom right corner of the budget screen (Figure 9.21) after all options are selected. The next step is to enter the budget amounts.

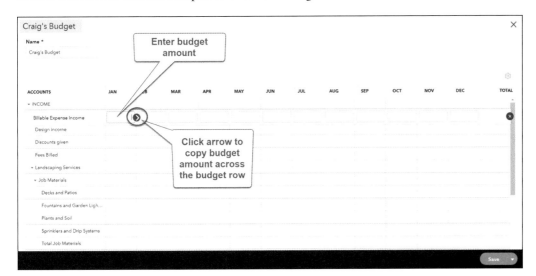

Figure 9.24

Budget screen

Enter the budget amounts in the appropriate month fields. It is not necessary to enter an amount for every month or for every account. There are some income and expense accounts that may have activity only in the first half of the year or only in every other month. Companies may not want to budget amounts for insignificant accounts used infrequently. Budget amounts should represent the best estimates of the expected activity.

If it's expected that an account will have the same activity in successive periods, enter the amount in the first month and click the right arrow next to the amount to copy across the row. You can copy across from any field in the budget form by clicking the blue arrow that appears to the right of the field.

Click **Save and close** when all budget amounts have been entered.

! WARNING: Practice Exercise 9.6 is based on the work you will perform in this Practice Exercise. To save yourself time, complete Practice Exercises 9.5 and 9.6 **before** you log out.

PRACTICE
EXERCISE
9.5

Set up a budget for Craig's Design and Landscaping.
(Craig's Design decides to create a simple budget for 2024.)

1. Click the on the icon bar.

2. Click **Budgeting** in the **Tools** column.

3. Click **Add budget**.

4. Enter "Craig's Budget" as the **Name**.

5. Select **FY2024(Jan 2024–Dec 2024)**.

(continued)

(continued from previous page)

6. Select Monthly as the Interval.

7. Select No in Pre-fill data?.

8. Select Don't subdivide in Subdivide by.

9. Click Next.

10. In the INCOME section,
    a. Click in the Jan field of Design income.
       i. Enter "2,000" and click the right arrow. **TIP:** Verify that 2,000 has been added in the February through December design income fields.
    b. Click in the Jan field of Fountains and Garden Lighting.
       i. Enter "500" and click the right arrow.
    c. Click in the Jan field of Installation.
       i. Enter "4,000" and click the right arrow.

11. In the COST OF GOODS SOLD section,
    a. Click in the Jan field of Cost of Goods Sold.
       i. Enter "200" and click the right arrow.

12. In the EXPENSES section,
    a. Click in the Jan field of Advertising.
       i. Enter "200" and click the right arrow.
    b. Click in the Mar field of Equipment Repairs.
       i. Enter "300" in the Mar, Jun, Sep, and Dec fields.
    c. Click in the Jan field of Job Materials.
       i. Enter "400" and click the right arrow.
    d. Click in the Jan field of Rent or Lease.
       i. Enter "1,200" and click the right arrow.
    e. Click in the Jan field of Office Expenses.
       i. Enter "300" and click the right arrow.
    f. Click in the Mar field of Taxes and Licenses.
       i. Enter "50" in the Mar and Oct fields.

13. Click Save and close.

14. Click Dashboard to exit out of the budget window.

15. **Complete the next practice exercise before logging out.**

Creating Budget Reports

There are a variety of budget reports in QBO. All of them can be accessed in the Business overview section of Reports.

● The Budget Overview report presents budget figures only.

NOTE: These are not the numbers from Practice Exercise 9.5

Craig's Design and Landscaping Services
Budget Overview: Craig's Budget - FY24 P&L
January - December 2024

	JAN 2024	FEB 2024	MAR 2024	APR 2024	MAY 2024	JUN 2024	JUL 2024	AUG 2024	SEP 2024	OCT 2024	NOV 2024	DEC 2024	TOTAL
▼ Income													
Design income	1,200.00	1,200.00	1,200.00	1,200.00	1,200.00	1,200.00	1,200.00	1,200.00	1,200.00	1,200.00	1,200.00	1,200.00	$14,400.00
Landscaping Services	5,000.00	5,000.00	5,000.00	5,000.00	5,000.00	5,000.00	5,000.00	5,000.00	5,000.00	5,000.00	5,000.00	5,000.00	$60,000.00
Total Income	**$6,200.00**	**$6,200.00**	**$6,200.00**	**$6,200.00**	**$6,200.00**	**$6,200.00**	**$6,200.00**	**$6,200.00**	**$6,200.00**	**$6,200.00**	**$6,200.00**	**$6,200.00**	**$74,400.00**
▼ Cost of Goods Sold													
Cost of Goods Sold	2,000.00	2,000.00	2,000.00	2,000.00	2,000.00	2,000.00	2,000.00	2,000.00	2,000.00	2,000.00	2,000.00	2,000.00	$24,000.00
Total Cost of Goods Sold	**$2,000.00**	**$2,000.00**	**$2,000.00**	**$2,000.00**	**$2,000.00**	**$2,000.00**	**$2,000.00**	**$2,000.00**	**$2,000.00**	**$2,000.00**	**$2,000.00**	**$2,000.00**	**$24,000.00**
GROSS PROFIT	**$4,200.00**	**$4,200.00**	**$4,200.00**	**$4,200.00**	**$4,200.00**	**$4,200.00**	**$4,200.00**	**$4,200.00**	**$4,200.00**	**$4,200.00**	**$4,200.00**	**$4,200.00**	**$50,400.00**
▼ Expenses													
Advertising	100.00	100.00	100.00	100.00	100.00	100.00	100.00	100.00	100.00	100.00	100.00	100.00	$1,200.00
													$0.00
▼ Maintenance and Repair													
Equipment Repairs	0.00	0.00	300.00	0.00	0.00	300.00	0.00	0.00	300.00	0.00	0.00	300.00	$1,200.00
Total Maintenance and Repair	**0.00**	**0.00**	**300.00**	**0.00**	**0.00**	**300.00**	**0.00**	**0.00**	**300.00**	**0.00**	**0.00**	**300.00**	**$1,200.00**
Office Expenses	300.00	300.00	300.00	300.00	300.00	300.00	300.00	300.00	300.00	300.00	300.00	300.00	$3,690.00
Rent or Lease	1,200.00	1,200.00	1,200.00	1,200.00	1,200.00	1,200.00	1,200.00	1,200.00	1,200.00	1,200.00	1,200.00	1,200.00	$14,400.00
▼ Utilities													$0.00
Telephone	200.00	200.00	200.00	200.00	200.00	200.00	200.00	200.00	200.00	200.00	200.00	200.00	$2,400.00
Total Utilities	**200.00**	**200.00**	**200.00**	**200.00**	**200.00**	**200.00**	**200.00**	**200.00**	**200.00**	**200.00**	**200.00**	**200.00**	**$2,400.00**
Total Expenses	**$1,800.00**	**$1,800.00**	**$2,100.00**	**$1,800.00**	**$1,800.00**	**$2,100.00**	**$1,800.00**	**$1,800.00**	**$2,100.00**	**$1,800.00**	**$1,800.00**	**$2,100.00**	**$22,800.00**
NET OPERATING INCOME	$2,400.00	$2,400.00	$2,100.00	$2,400.00	$2,400.00	$2,100.00	$2,400.00	$2,400.00	$2,100.00	$2,400.00	$2,400.00	$2,100.00	$27,600.00
NET INCOME	$2,400.00	$2,400.00	$2,100.00	$2,400.00	$2,400.00	$2,100.00	$2,400.00	$2,400.00	$2,100.00	$2,400.00	$2,400.00	$2,100.00	$27,600.00

Figure 9.25

Budget Overview report

- The default **Budget vs. Actuals** report presents actual and budget figures by month. The dollar difference (actual less budget) and the percentage relationship of actual to budget (actual divided by budget) are also displayed for each account.

 HINT: There are many options for customizing the **Budgets vs Actuals** report in the **Rows/Columns** section of the **Customize report** sidebar.

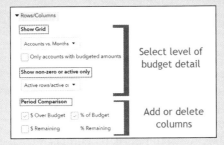

In the **Show Grid** section, the level of detail can be changed. Budgets can be condensed to show only quarterly or annual amounts or to show only active accounts or accounts with budgeted amounts.

Columns can be added or deleted in the **Period Comparison** section. The **$ Remaining** and **% Remaining** columns can be particularly helpful to include in reports given to managers during the budget period.

NOTE: The **Budget vs Actuals** report customization tools may have been updated. If possible, click **Old layout** or **Switch to classic view**. If that's not possible, check the Student Ancillaries page in myBusinessCourse for updated information or check with your instructor.

Prepare budget report for Craig's Design and Landscaping.
(Craig's Design wants to review the budget just created.)

1. If you logged or timed out after the last practice exercise, go back and set up the budget again using the directions in Practice Exercise 9.5.

2. Click **Reports** on the navigation bar.

3. Open the **Standard** tab.

PRACTICE
EXERCISE
9.6

Homework
MBC

(continued)

(continued from previous page)

    4. Click **Budget Overview** in the **Business overview** section.

    5. Make a note of the budgeted **GROSS PROFIT** for 2024.

    6. Make a note of the budgeted **NET INCOME** for 2024.

    7. Click **Dashboard** to close the window.

REVERSING ENTRIES

LO 9-3 Explain the purpose of and demonstrate the use of reversing entries in QBO

We're sure it's clear by now that accountants typically make a lot of adjusting journal entries when financial statements are prepared.

Many (if not most) of the adjusting entries are made to properly recognize (or defer) revenues or expenses for the reporting period. These adjusting entries must be made because physical transactions (sending out invoices to customers, receiving bills from vendors, preparing paychecks for employees, etc.) don't always occur in the month that the related activities should be recognized in the financial statements.

> **BEHIND THE SCENES** This book is written assuming the accrual method of accounting is used. (The accrual method is required under GAAP.) Companies that use the cash method of accounting recognize revenue when collected and expenses when paid. Entries to defer revenues or expenses would not be required.

For example, many companies receive bills from vendors in the month **after** costs are incurred. A bill received from the company's attorney for work performed in January might be received (and dated) in February. Since the work was performed in January, the expense should be recognized in January.

If the accountant enters the **bill** using the bill date, the expense will be recognized (reported on the income statement) in February. January's legal expense will be understated (too low) and February's legal expense will be overstated (too high). The accountant **could** enter the **bill** using a January date so that January's income statement is correct, but then the accounts payable subsidiary ledger wouldn't be accurate.

Most accountants solve the problem by entering an adjusting journal entry in January to recognize the expense. The **bill** received from the vendor in February is entered using the bill date. The expense and the liability, of course, now appear in TWO months; in January through the adjusting journal entry and in February through the **bill**. To correct for this, the accountant makes an adjusting journal entry in February to offset the duplicate charge.

Reversing entries in QBO are a tool for minimizing the possibility of duplicate transactions not being cleared. When an adjusting entry is dated the month **before** the standard entry (form) is recorded, the accountant can flag the journal entry as a **reversing entry**. QBO will then automatically create a new entry (dated the first day of the subsequent month) to completely reverse the original entry. That way, when the appropriate form is created, it will **not** result in a double recognition of the same transaction. **Reversing entries** are very easy to create.

As an example, let's say a company hired an attorney to look over some employment contracts. The attorney estimated the fee would be about $1,000. The attorney did the work in November and sent a bill, dated December 15, to the company for the $1,000. The expense needs to be recognized in November (since the work was performed in November) so the company would make an adjusting entry dated November 30.

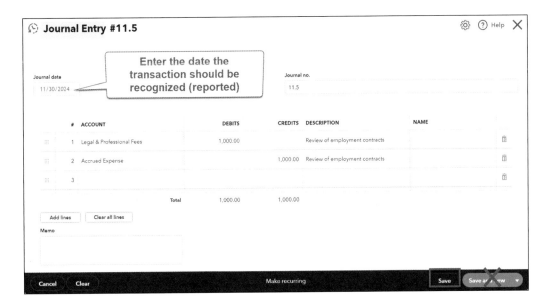

Figure 9.26
Journal entry example

> **BEHIND THE SCENES** When accruing expenses, a separate liability account (accrued expenses in Figure 9.26) is normally used. This avoids multiple entries to the vendor subsidiary ledger. Similarly, a separate asset account is used when income is accrued (when income has been earned but has not yet been invoiced to the customer).

Once the entry is saved (click **Save**, not **Save and new**), the option to reverse the entry becomes available.

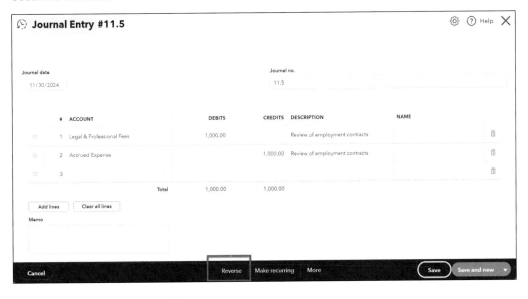

Figure 9.27
Access to reversing entry feature

Clicking **Reverse** automatically creates a new entry.

Figure 9.28

Reversing entry

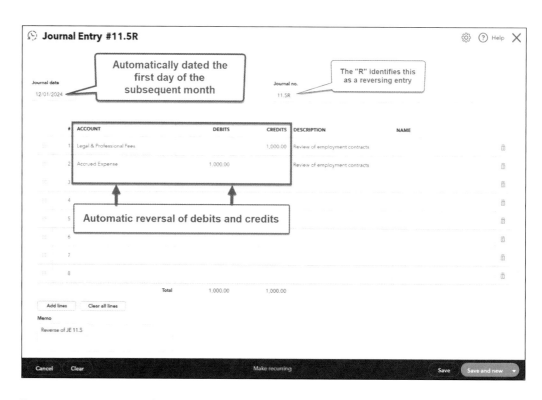

Reversing entries are **always** automatically dated the first day of the subsequent month. The date can be changed later if appropriate.

When the attorney's bill is received in December, it would be entered as a **bill** using December 15 as the **bill date**. The debit to Legal & Professional Fees will be offset by the credit to Legal & Professional Fees from the reversing entry shown above. The expense is now properly reported in November's profit and loss statement and the **bill** will have the correct December 15 date.

The activity in the expense account would look like this:

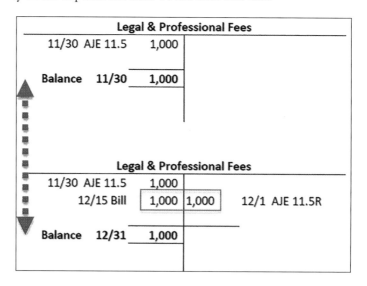

WARNING: Once created, reversing entries are not linked to the original entry. Deleting or modifying the original entry will not change the reversing entry. Changes to the reversing entry will not affect the original entry.

Prepare a reversing entry for Craig's Design and Landscaping.
(Craig's Design receives a $500 bill for legal services performed in the prior month. The bill is dated in the current month.)

1. Click on the navigation bar.

2. Select **Journal Entry**.

3. Enter the last day of **last** month in the Journal Date field.

4. In the first row, select Lawyer in the ACCOUNT field.

   a. **Make a note** of the parent account for Lawyer.

5. Enter "500" in the DEBITS column.

6. In the second row select **+ Add new** in the ACCOUNT column.

7. Select Other Current Liabilities as the account type (Save account under field).

8. Select Other Current Liabilities as the detail type (Tax form section field).

9. Enter "Accrued Expenses" in the Name field.

10. Click Save and close. You will be back on the journal entry form.

11. Enter "500" in the CREDITS field.

12. Click Save.

    a. Click Yes if you get a message about missing classes.

13. Click Reverse.

14. The reversing entry will be displayed.

    a. **Make a note** of the journal entry date for the reversing entry.

15. Click Save and close.

    a. Click Yes if you get a message about missing classes.

PRACTICE
EXERCISE
9.7

Homework
MBC

RECURRING TRANSACTIONS

Some companies have transactions that occur every month, in the same amount. For example, office cleaning service companies often bill customers a set fee for a particular monthly cleaning service. The entry for straight-line depreciation is another possible example.

LO 9-4 Understand the various types of recurring transactions in QBO

QBO allows users to set up these recurring transactions so that they are easily recreated on a set schedule.

To set up a **recurring transaction**, click the ⚙ on the icon bar.

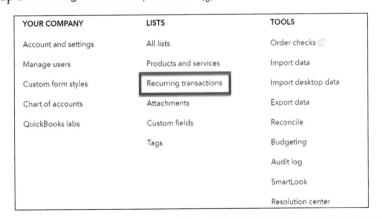

Figure 9.29

Access to recurring transaction center

 HINT: Recurring transactions can also be created within most forms.

Click **Recurring Transactions**.

Figure 9.30

Access to recurring
transaction form

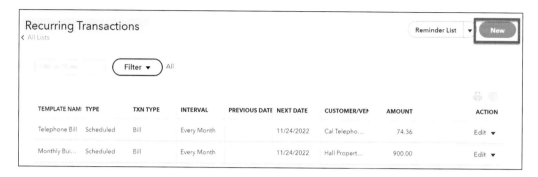

> **HINT:** The transactions you see in Figure 9.30 were automatically set up by
> Intuit in the test drive company.

Click **New** to enter a new transaction.

Figure 9.31

Options for recurring
transactions

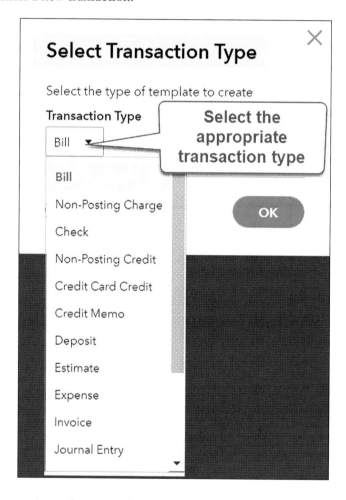

The type of transaction to be entered is selected first.

The options available in the **recurring transaction** setup form would depend on the type of transaction selected. For example, if **Invoice** was selected, the form would look something like Figure 9.32.

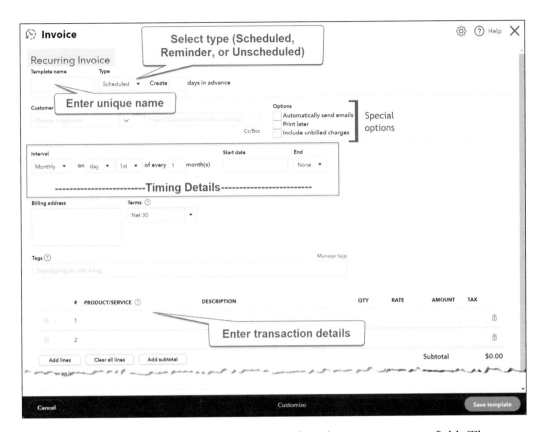

Figure 9.32

Setup form for a
recurring invoice

A name for the recurring entry must be entered in the **Template name** field. The name should clearly identify the purpose of the recurring entry. For example, "Weekly-Melton" would be a reasonable name for an entry to bill John Melton for weekly gardening services.

There are a number of options for recurring entries:

- In the **Type** field, transactions can be set as:

  - **Scheduled**
    - Transactions will be automatically created.

  - **Reminder**
    - Transactions will be added to a reminder list but will not be created until the user chooses to create them. (The user would then have the option of not recording the entry in a particular period.)

  - **Unscheduled**
    - Transaction is saved in the **Recurring Transactions** list but would not appear on the reminder list and would not be automatically created.
    - **Unscheduled** would be the **type** selected when users don't have all the necessary information for the transaction yet.
    - The **type** could also be used to set up a template for a complex transaction that the user wants to have available when needed.

If **scheduled** or **reminder** transaction templates are created:

- The frequency of the transaction would be set in the **Interval** fields.
- The date of the first entry would be identified in the **Start date** field.
- The user can specify how far into the future the transaction should be entered by entering a date or number of occurrences in the **End** field.

Special options available when **recurring invoices** are set up include automatically emailing invoices to customers, batching **invoices** to be printed later, and automatically adding any unbilled time or costs to the **invoice**. (Billable time and costs are covered in Chapter 10.)

A **recurring invoice** for Craig's Design and Landscaping might be set up something like Figure 9.33.

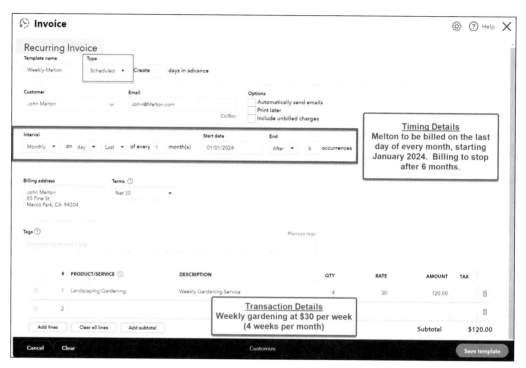

Figure 9.33

Example of recurring invoice setup form

Click **Save template** to complete the setup.

All **recurring** transactions can be accessed in the **Recurring Transactions** list (accessed by clicking the ⚙ on the icon bar and selecting **recurring transactions**).

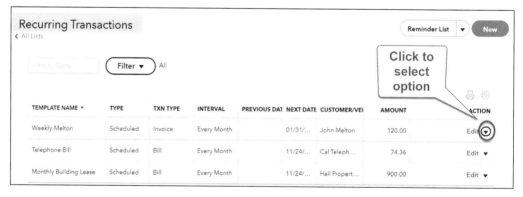

Figure 9.34

Recurring transaction list

The options available in the **ACTION** column depend on the type of **recurring transaction**. For the Weekly-Melton invoice, the options in addition to **Edit** would be:

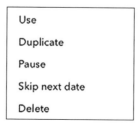

Figure 9.35

Options for editing recurring invoices

If **Use** is selected, a transaction would be created using the details from the **recurring** transaction. The form can be edited before saving.

If **Duplicate** is selected, an **invoice** would be created that includes the same terms, etc. This is a useful feature for a company that has a number of similar fixed monthly fee customers. Changes to customer name, etc. could be made on the duplicated form. A new **template name** would be entered to save the duplicated transaction.

The **Pause** and **Skip next date** options are used to delay recording **scheduled** transactions.

The **ACTION** options for recurring **journal entries** are the same as those for **invoices**. For **bills**, **ACTION** options include **Edit**, **Use**, **Duplicate**, and **Delete**.

The **recurring transaction** details are included on the **Reminder List** (identified on Figure 9.34).

> **WARNING: Recurring transactions** can be very useful but they must be monitored, especially if they are set up as automatic entries.

Prepare a recurring entry for Craig's Design and Landscaping.

(Craig's Design has decided to try placing a small ad ($20 per month) in a local magazine, Trees for Sacramento. The advertising fee will be charged to the company credit card. Craig decides to place the ad over the next six-month period.)

PRACTICE

EXERCISE 9.8

1. Click **+ New** on the navigation bar.

2. Select **Expense**.

3. Select **+ Add new** in the **Who did you pay?** field to open a new vendor record.

   a. Enter "Trees for Sacramento" in the **Company name** and **Vendor display name** fields (in the **Name and contact** section).

   b. Click **Save**.

4. Select **Visa** as the **Payment account**.

5. Enter the current date as the **Payment date**.

6. Select **Visa** as the **Payment method**.

7. **Make a note** of the number of methods (other than **Add new**) appearing in the **Payment method** dropdown menu.

8. In the first row of the **Category details** section, select **Advertising** in the **CATEGORY** field.

9. Enter "20" in the **AMOUNT** column.

10. Click **Make recurring** in the black bar at the bottom of the form.

11. Change the **Template name** to "Magazine ad."

12. Select **Scheduled** in the **Type** field.

13. Leave **Trees for Sacramento** as the **Payee**.

14. Select **Visa** as the **Account**.

15. Select **Monthly**, **last** and **Friday** in the **Interval** fields.

16. Enter the current date as the **Start date**.

(continued)

(continued from previous page)

17. Select After in the End field.
18. Enter "6" in the occurrences field.
19. Click Save template.
20. Click the ⚙ icon.
21. Select Recurring transactions in the Lists column.

CHAPTER SHORTCUTS

Set up class and location tracking
1. Click the ⚙ on the icon bar.
2. Click Account and Settings.
3. Click Advanced.
4. Click the pencil icon in Categories section.
5. Toggle the buttons next to Track classes and Track locations.

Set up classes or location
1. Click the ⚙ on the icon bar.
2. Click All Lists.
3. Click Classes or Locations.
4. Click New.

Create a budget
1. Click the ⚙ on the icon bar.
2. Click Budgeting.

Set up a recurring transaction
1. Click the ⚙ on the icon bar.
2. Click Recurring transactions.

Create reversing entry
1. Click **+ New** on the navigation bar.
2. Click Journal entry.
3. Enter details for initial entry.
4. Click Save.
5. Click Reverse.

CHAPTER REVIEW

Matching

Assignments with the 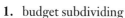 are available in myBusinessCourse.

Match the term or phrase (as used in QBO) to its definition.

1. budget subdividing
2. class tracking
3. budget vs. actuals report
4. reversing entry
5. budget
6. budget overview
7. location tracking
8. profit and loss by class report

_____ report that displays revenue and expenses by class for a specified period of time

_____ tool most likely to be used to classify revenues and expenses by product line

_____ report that shows variances between actual and budgeted results for a period of time

_____ tool most likely to be used to classify revenues and expenses by store

_____ estimate of future operating results

_____ tool used to add class, location, or customer when creating a budget

_____ an entry created by a user that is the exact opposite of an entry in a prior period

_____ report that shows budgeted account balances for a period of time

Multiple Choice

1. In QBO, a **class** might represent a specific _____.
   a. department in a company
   b. customer type
   c. product line
   d. any of the above could be used

2. Which of the following statements is true?
   a. **Class** tracking is done automatically by QBO.
   b. A **class** must be assigned to every entry in a transaction.
   c. Users can track by **class** or **location** but not both.
   d. Only one **location** can be set per vendor bill.

3. Budgets can be created for:
   a. the company overall.
   b. a specific customer (project).
   c. a specific **class**.
   d. a specific **location**.
   e. any of the above.

4. When creating a budget for a company with a 12/31 year end, you enter $300 in March for one of the rows and click the blue arrow next to the field. The amount that will appear as the **total** for that row will be:
   a. $3,000.
   b. $2,700.
   c. $600.
   d. $300.

5. If a recurring transaction is set as **unscheduled**, _____.
   a. you will receive a reminder to record the transaction after two weeks
   b. it will be entered once and only once
   c. it will be available for posting, but QBO will not automatically create the transaction
   d. None of the above answers are correct. There is no such thing as an unscheduled recurring transaction.

BEYOND THE CLICKS—THINKING LIKE A MANAGER

Accounting: Who should be responsible for creating budgets? Explain your answer. How might managers use budget information? (Think about department managers as well as corporate managers.)

Information Systems: Aki's Accounting provides bookkeeping services for multiple clients for a monthly fee of $500, billed in advance. Aki and his staff also provide other services periodically (tax return preparation, financial planning, etc.). Additional services are billed, in arrears, on an hourly basis. Aki asks you to set up **recurring invoices** for his clients. What type would you use? Which settings and options would you select? What concerns, if any, would you have with Aki's use of **recurring invoices**?

ASSIGNMENTS

✳ **HINT:** If you didn't turn off all automation in Chapter 2, you might want to consider doing that now. It's easy to get confused when QBO automatically adds accounts to your transactions. Click the ⚙ on the icon bar and select **Account and Settings**. In the **Automation** section of the **Advanced** tab, turn **Pre-fill forms with previously entered content** to **Off**.

3/1/24

✓ You talk to Martin today about the need for more management tools to help him run his business effectively. You both decide that using **class** tracking would be helpful.

✓ You turn on **class** tracking in the **Advanced** tab of **Account and Settings**.

- You want to be able to assign a class to individual rows in transaction forms.
- You also turn on the "warning" feature. You don't want to have to go back and fix issues later.

✓ You decide to set up four **classes**.

- Products
  - To be used for tracking revenues and costs related to sales of products and product training revenues.
- Workshops
  - To be used for tracking revenues and costs related to workshop presentations.
- Tutoring
  - To be used for tracking revenues and costs related to all tutoring services.
- Administrative
  - To be used for tracking general business costs.

✓ You realize that it will save you time in the long-run to go ahead and assign a **class** to each of the products and services that you sell. You open the **Products and Services** list and assign the **classes** as follows:

- You assign the Workshops **class** to the Educator Workshop service.
- You assign the Tutoring **class** to the Crisis, Mathmagic, Persistence and Refresher services.
- You assign the Products **class** to all the **Inventory type** products.
- You don't assign a **class** for items in the **Other** or **Other Charges categories**. You'll determine the **class** when you record transactions that include these items.
- **TIP:** If you want to make sure you've assigned the appropriate class, create a **Product/Service List** report. Customize the report by adding **Class** in the **Rows/Columns** section of the customization sidebar.

✓ You also decide you want to use the budgeting tool in QBO.

✓ You create a monthly profit and loss budget for 2024 from scratch (no subdividing). (You use "2024 Budget" for the name.) You use the following estimates:

- Tutoring ($3,500 for January to June; $5,000 per month for July through December)
- Workshops ($5,500 for February; $4,500 for March through December)
- Sales of Product Income ($1,500 for February; $2,500 from March through December)
- Cost of Goods Sold ($1,000 for February; $1,650 for March through December)
- Facility Costs
  - Rent ($850 every month)
  - Utilities ($150 in January; $250 for February through December)
- Labor costs
  - Professional development ($200 per month)

- Contract labor ($125 for January through March; $700 for April and May; $900 for September through December)
- Office and Tutoring Costs
  - Office supplies ($25 every month)
  - Tutoring supplies ($200 every month)
  - Depreciation ($150 every month)
- Marketing Costs
  - Advertising ($100 per month)
- Professional Services and Insurance
  - Accounting and consulting fees ($300 for January and February, $500 for March through December)
  - Insurance ($40 every month)
- Other Costs
  - Gasoline ($50 every month)
  - Bank service charges ($10 every month)
- Interest expense ($15 every month)

✓ You let Martin know that the budget shows $76,945 in profit for the year. **TIP:** You might need to click **Save** to see the totals.

3/4/24

✓ You write yourself a check (# 1125) for the work you did in **February**. **TIP:** Remember to use **Administrative** as the **class** if a cost isn't directly related to tutoring, workshops, or product sales.

✓ You look at the collections report and notice that you have quite a few past due bills. You make calls to Debbie Han, Paul Richard, and Annie Wang.
- Debbie and Annie apologize and agree to send their checks in a few days.
- Paul explains that he's been waiting to receive a credit for the two missed sessions in February. You tell him that you'll talk to Martin and get that credit memo to him as soon as possible.

✓ You ask Martin about Paul's missed sessions. He explains that he forgot to tell you about that. You create a credit memo for $100 (CM-1015) in QBO and send it off to Paul. You charge the $100 to the **Crisis** item since that was the package Paul had purchased. The amount is small so you decide to recognize the credit memo in March. **TIP:** Enter 0 as the **QTY** and $100 as the **AMOUNT**. You enter "Credit for missed sessions. Sorry for the delay!" in the **Message displayed on credit memo** box. **TIP:** The **CLASS** field should automatically fill with Tutoring. If it doesn't, go ahead and select it here and then go back to the **Products and Services List** and make sure you've assigned a **class** to each item.

✓ Martin lets you know that he will be putting on another **Educator Workshop** for Dynamic Teaching later this month. Based on the content and the expected attendance, Martin plans to charge $3,150. You decide **not** to create a **delayed charge**. You'll wait to create the **invoice** when you have all the details.

✓ You look at your unpaid bills and realize you forgot to pay Frank's Furniture. You call and apologize. You pay all bills due on or before 3/15, net of available credits. The total of the three checks is $1,399.40. The first check number is 1126.

3/5/24

✓ You receive two checks in the mail and record them in QBO:
- $420 from Annie Wang for INV-1009. Check #2895, dated 3/5.
- $1,000 from Debbie Han for INV-1016. Check #4555, dated 3/5.

✓ You deposit both checks in the bank. The total deposit is $1,420.

✓ You receive the remaining products ordered from Books Galore on PO-100 and PO-103. In addition to the books, Books Galore charged $336.27 for some supplies Martin had called them about. ($305.85 for tutoring supplies; $30.42 for office supplies) You charge the cost of the tutoring supplies to the Supplies on Hand account. You expense the office supplies. The total amount on the invoice (#2244) is $911.27. (The terms are Net 30.) **TIP:** Because the POs were created before class was added to inventory items, you will have to complete the class fields.

3/6/24

✓ Martin gets a call from Harold at Mad Math, a tutoring center for elementary school age children. He heard about the math games from the Center for High Academic Achievement (Elk Grove) and places an order for two consoles and one of each game (Equations, Fractions, and Ratios). Martin ships out the order and you prepare INV-1021 for $1,027.69 (after sales tax is added).

- Mad Math's address is 1388 Taller Drive, Sacramento, CA 95822. Terms are Net 30. The games will be used at the center so the sale is taxable.

✓ Martin calls the director at the Elk Grove location to thank her for the referral. He asks you to give Elk Grove a $100 credit on its next workshop. You prepare a delayed credit (DC-1001), charging the $100 to Educator Workshop. **TIP:** Delayed credits were introduced in Chapter 6. Enter 0 as the QTY and $100 as the AMOUNT.

✓ Martin had gotten so many requests from students and parents for more tutoring time, he decided to offer two Mathmagic clinics this month. The first one was last Saturday (3/2). 45 students showed up. They all paid cash ($1,125). You record the revenue on SR-111, dated 3/2.

3/8/24

✓ Martin gives you the detail for the tutoring sessions he had this week. He also sold a few products to these customers.

- You create invoices (starting with INV-1022 and dated 3/8) for:
  - Navi Patel—One week of Crisis starting 3/4 plus one Geometry in Sports Book (Sports) and one Geometry Kit (Kit). The total invoice after sales tax is $296.76 and terms are Net 15.
  - Debbie Han—Two weeks of Persistence starting 3/1 and one Getting Ready for Calculus (Ready) book. Net 15. The total invoice after sales tax is $242.63.

✓ Martin delivers another order to the Downtown location of the Center for High Academic Achievement. You prepare INV-1024 for $755.

- 10 Geometry in Sports (Sports)
- 10 Solving Puzzles: Fun with Algebra (Puzzles)
- 5 Getting Ready for Calculus (Ready)
- 5 Geometry Kits (Kit)

✓ There is a MathMagic clinic coming up soon and Martin wants you to make sure there are enough products on hand. You review the inventory and create two purchase orders.

- PO-105 ($220) is for 9 Puzzles and 5 Sports from Books Galore.
- PO-106 ($155) is for 5 Dry-Erase and 10 Notebooks from Math Shack.
- Kits are low in stock as well but 8 are on order (PO-104).

✓ Parent's Survival Weekly calls and asks if Martin wants to run another ad for his workshops. They are getting ready to print their next edition. You check with Martin and he decides to run a slightly larger ad for the Mathmagic clinic coming up later this month. You pay the $135 advertising fee with the VISA credit card. Since this is related to tutoring, you assign this to the Tutoring class.

✓ Martin gets a call from Books Galore. The company president has started a new program called "Thanks for being a great customer." Every month one customer receives a $50 credit against any outstanding invoices. This month Math Revealed! was the lucky recipient. Martin has decided to use it to offset the advertising fee from Parent's Survival Weekly so you record the credit (BG-101) and charge it to Advertising expense. You assign it to the Tutoring class.

3/12/24

✓ You receive two utility bills in the mail. Both are dated 3/12.

- Sacramento Utilities for March services, #01-88112, $202.47. The terms are Net 30.

- Horizon Phone for March service, #121-1000, $40.95. The terms are Net 30.
✓ You receive a check from the Center for High Academic Achievement for INV-1024. The check (#9759819) was for $755.

3/14/24

✓ Martin gives you the information on his tutoring sessions for the week. You record them using 3/14 as the sales date. Everyone wanted to pay with their Mastercard. Fortunately, Math Revealed is set up to accept both VISA and Mastercard. **TIP:** VISA and Mastercard receipts would need to be deposited separately.

- Alonso Luna—8 **Refresher** sessions $440 (SR-112)
- Marley Roberts—2 **Persistence** $210 (SR-113)

✓ You prepare deposits for the credit card receipts and for the cash and check received since 3/5. The total on the credit card deposit (after the 2% merchant fee) is $637. Since the credit cards were used to pay tutoring fees, you assign the merchant fee to the Tutoring **class**. The cash and check deposit totals $1,880.

✓ The **Educator Workshop** at Dynamic Teaching went well. More people attended than were expected so Martin was glad he increased the fee. You create an invoice (INV-1025) for $3,150. **TIP:** You can change the amount directly on the form. You do not need to change the default price in the item record.

✓ You pay all bills due on or before the 31st of March. You take all available credits. The first check # is 1129. **TIP:** The four bills paid total $1,487.33.

3/15/24

✓ You receive the following checks in the mail.

- $650 from Paul Richard for INV-1015. Check # 45777, dated 3/15. **TIP:** Go back and read the *Applying Credit Memos to Open Invoices When Customer Payments Are Recorded* section of Chapter 3 if you're having trouble applying the credit.
- $796.76 from Navi Patel for INV-1019 and INV-1021. Check #4555, dated 3/15.

✓ All the items ordered from Books Galore on PO-105 arrive. The shipment includes a bill (#2298) for $220. The payment terms are Net 30.

✓ The Elk Grove Location of the Center for High Academic Achievement asked Martin to come out Monday and do a one day **Educator Workshop** for a fee of $1,500. He asks you to prepare the invoice so he can take it with him. They also asked him to bring 5 each of the **Ready** and **Statistics** books. You prepare INV-1026 dated 3/15. The invoice totals $1,695 after the **delayed credit** is applied.

- **TIP:** When the delayed credit is applied, the quantity field in that row may show a negative 1. If it does, remove the quantity so that reports of units sold remain accurate. Make sure the **Amount** field in that row shows a negative $100 and the total is $1,695.

✓ The order from Math Shack (PO-106) arrives just in time for the Saturday clinic. A bill (#M61142) for $155 is included. The terms are Net 15.

- The **Kits** backordered from PO-104 are not included. You call Math Shack. They promise to look into the order.

3/18/24

✓ Mathmagic was almost standing room only on Saturday. 50 students attended. You record the sale (all cash) (SR-114 for $1,721.98).

- Total tutoring income collected was $1,250.
- Product sales (all taxable):
    - 5 **Notebooks**
    - 4 **Dry Erase**
    - 6 **Ready**
    - 3 **Sports**

✓ You deposit the checks received on the 15th with the cash from Saturday's Mathmagic clinic. The total is $3,168.74.

3/19/24

✓ Martin let you know that Samantha Levin had helped out for 8 hours at the two Mathmagic clinics this month. You write her a check (# 1133) for $200 ($25 per hour) and charge it to contract labor. You select the class based on the type of work Samantha helped with.

✓ You call Cartables and place an order for 3 of every Math Games product (including the consoles). PO-107 totals $1,140.

3/25/24

✓ Gus Ranting is back again! He's sure that his son is wasting his time at the Mathmagic Clinic. Martin lets him know that his son is a great kid who obviously believes the tutoring is helping him. He shows Gus his son's work and encourages him to follow up with the math teachers at the school. He gives Gus a partial refund of $15 (RR-102) but says this will be the last time for any refunds. You issue the refund from the Checking account, check #1134.

✓ Mad Math calls and lets Martin know that the math games are really helping the students. They order another console and one of each game (Fractions, Equations, and Ratios). Martin delivers the products and you prepare INV-1027 for $619.88.

✓ Martin hands you two gas receipts for March. One, dated 3/14 for $21 and one dated 3/22 for $20. He used the Visa card each time to pay for the gas he purchased at Cardinal Gas & Snacks. You enter the charges in QBO using the credit card receipt dates. You use the Administrative class.

3/28/24

✓ Math Shack calls and says there's a shipping delay with the Kits ordered on PO-104. The Kits should arrive in May. You check and see that only six geometry kits were sold in March and you still have some in stock so you're not concerned. You leave the purchase order open.

✓ You receive the following checks in the mail.
  - Dynamic Teaching $2,700 for INV-1018. (Check # 5235)
  - Eliot Williams $105 for INV-1020 (Check #8166)

✓ Martin gives you the information on his tutoring sessions for the last half of March. You record them using 3/28 as the sales date. This time everyone paid with cash. (Martin apologizes for forgetting to get the cash to you!) All sessions were completed by 3/31.
  - Annie Wang—2 Crisis $500 (SR-115)
  - Kim Kowalski—2 Crisis $500 (SR-116)

✓ You deposit the checks and cash in the bank. The deposit total is $3,805.

3/29/24

✓ You write Martin a dividend check for $3,000. (Check #1135) **TIP:** Use the Administrative class.

✓ You write Martin's father (Richard Smith) a check (#1136) for interest for the month of March plus a principal payment of $200. **TIP:** Calculate the interest on the unpaid balance of the note. The note has an annual rate of 6%.

✓ You know Les & Schmidt did some more marketing work for Martin in March but you haven't received an invoice from them. You ask Martin and he says the agreed-upon fee was $425. You go ahead and create a journal entry (Mar24.1), dated 3/31 to record the expense in the proper period. The marketing plan is related to growing the Workshop business. You create a reversing entry so that you can enter the bill when it's received without duplicating the expense. **TIP:** You need to click Save on entry Mar24.1 before you can create the reversing entry. Use Accrued Expenses as the liability account and 642 Marketing expense as the expense account.

✓ Parent's Survival Weekly calls and offers Martin a reduced price of $80 per ad if he agrees to run a monthly ad for a six month period. The ad would appear in the first issue each month.

The $80 will be automatically charged to the VISA card on the 1st of each month. Martin agrees but does not want to start this until May. Since this will automatically be charged to the VISA credit card you set up a new **scheduled Recurring Transaction**. You select **Expense** as the transaction type, use Parent's Ad as the **Template name**, and set the **interval** to be the 1st day of each month beginning on 5/1/24 and ending after 6 occurrences. You assign this to the tutoring **class**.

✓ You talk to Martin about your increasing workload. He is very appreciative of your work and agrees to pay you $500 (accounting fees) starting in March. You enter a **bill** (ACCT24, dated 3/31) for accounting fees with Net 10 terms. You decide to set this up as a **scheduled recurring transaction (bill)**. **TIP:** Click **Save** before you move forward.

- You click **Make recurring** on the black bar at the bottom of the form and complete the template. You enter Accounting as the **template name**. Future bills are scheduled for the **last** day of each month with 4/30/24 as the **Start date**. You don't identify an end date.

✓ You also ask Martin about any unearned revenue. He confirms that all billed revenue has been earned as of the end of March.

✓ There is no planned activity for the weekend, so you spend the rest of the day making the final adjustments for March. **TIP:** Remember, if an expense isn't directly related to sales of products, workshops, or tutoring, it should be charged to the **administrative class**.

✓ You don't have your bank statement yet but you go online and see that the balance is $11,559.99 at 3/29. You reconcile the books to the $11,559.99 balance using 3/31 as the reconciliation date. There were no service charges during March. All deposits for March have cleared. All checks written prior to 3/20/24 cleared the bank. **TIP:** Checks include **check**, **refund**, and **bill payment transaction types**.

✓ You also reconcile the Prime Visa credit card account. The online balance is $176. All March credit card transactions are included on the statement. You enter a bill for payment later. You use MarCC as the **bill no.** and 3/31 as the date. **TIP:** Use **Administrative** as the **class**.

✓ You compare the inventory on hand to the inventory report in QBO. All amounts agree.

✓ You make additional journal entries, dated 3/31, after considering the following:

- Tutoring supplies on hand equal $124.25.
- No new equipment was purchased in March.
  - You decide to track all facilities and equipment expenses in the **Administrative** class.
- The annual interest rate on both loans is 6%. No payments were made on the bank loan in March. **TIP:** Martin borrowed the money on 2/29.
- You look carefully at the profit and loss statement and make sure that all March expenses are properly recorded. (**TIP:** Include the **Prior Period** column on your profit and loss report. Compare the March expenses with the February expenses. Are there any of the common operating expenses missing? Do any of the expenses appear unusually high?)
- You look carefully at the balance sheet paying particular attention to Other Current Assets and Other Current Liabilities. Many of the common month-end adjustments affect accounts in those categories. **TIP:** Look at the journal entries you made dated 2/29. There will likely be similar entries for March.

Check numbers 3/31

Checking account balance:. . . . . . .$ 8,332.99
Other current assets: . . . .$ 2,614.25
Total assets: $25,179.94
Total liabilities: . . . .$ 9,027.63
Gross profit (March). $10,034.00
Net income for March:. . . . .$ 7,232.06

Suggested reports for Chapter 9:

All reports should be in portrait orientation.

- Balance Sheet as of 3/31
- Profit and Loss (March)
  - Include a year-to-date column in the report
- Profit and Loss by Class (March)
- A/R Aging Summary as of 3/31
- A/P Aging Summary as of 3/31
- Sales by Product/Service Summary (March)
- Inventory Valuation Summary (March 31)
- Recurring Template List
- Budget Overview Report 2024 (by Quarter)
  - To display quarters, click Customize, click Rows/Columns, select Accounts vs Qtrs on Show Grid dropdown menu.
  - **TIP:** QBO won't save reports that include a : (colon) in the report name. Modify the name before saving.
- Budget vs Actual report (January 1 through March 31)
  - Click Customize and click Rows/Columns. In the Show Grid dropdown menu, select Accounts vs Total.
  - **TIP:** QBO won't save reports that include a : (colon) in the report name. Modify the name before saving.
- Journal report (March)

Assignment 9B

Salish Software Solutions

✳ HINT: If you didn't turn off Automation in Chapter 2, you might want to consider doing that now. It's easy to get confused when QBO automatically adds accounts to your transactions. Click the ⚙ on the icon bar and select Account and Settings. In the Automation section of the Advanced tab, turn Pre-fill forms with previously entered content to Off.

3/1/24

✓ Business is going well for Sally. She has a number of different revenue streams and new opportunities keep coming her way. You talk to her about the need to understand how each segment of her company is doing. She's open to your suggestions.

✓ You turn on class tracking in the Advanced tab of Account and Settings.
- You want to be able to assign a class to individual rows in transaction forms.
- You also turn on the "warning" feature. You don't want to have to go back and fix issues later.

✓ You decide to set up four classes.
- Products
  - To be used for tracking revenues and costs related to sales of products.
- Workshops
  - To be used for tracking revenues and costs related to Workshop presentations.
- Consulting
  - To be used for tracking revenues and costs related to all software consulting services.

- ◆ e.g., Installation, Setup, Training
- Administrative
  - ▪ To be used for tracking general business costs.

✓ You realize that it will save you time in the long-run to go ahead and assign a **class** to each of the products and services that you sell. You open the **Products and Services** list and assign the **classes** as follows:

- You assign the Workshop **class** to both the Tips and Picks workshop services.
- You assign the Consulting **class** to the Fix, Select, Set Up and Train services.
- You assign the Products **class** to all the **Inventory** type products.
- You don't assign a **class** for items in the **Other category** or the **Other Charges category**. You'll determine the **class** when you record transactions that include these items.

  TIP: If you want to make sure you've assigned the appropriate class, create a **Product/Service List** report. Customize the report by adding **Class** in the **Rows/Columns** customization sidebar.

✓ You also decide you want to use the budgeting tool in QBO.

✓ You create a monthly profit and loss budget for 2024 from scratch (no subdividing). (You use "2024 Budget" for the name.) Sally gives you some projections that she put together when she was first starting out. You use her numbers as a starting place:

- Software Selection and Installation—$4,000 January through February; $5,000 March through December
- Troubleshooting Revenue—$450 every month
- Workshop Revenues—$2,000 January; $5,000 February through December
- Sales of Product Income—$3,000 February; $3,500 March to June; $4,000 July to December
- Cost of Goods Sold—$1,500 February; $2,000 March through June; $2,500 July through December
- Facility Costs
  - ▪ Rent—$650 every month
  - ▪ Telephone—$100 every month
  - ▪ Utilities—$100 every month
- Office Costs
  - ▪ Office supplies—$100 every month
  - ▪ Depreciation—$275 January; $300 February; $350 March through December
- Professional Fees and Insurance
  - ▪ Accounting and consulting—$300 January; $875 February; $300 March; $350 April through December
  - ▪ Insurance—$65 every month
- Professional Development Costs
  - ▪ Technical reading materials—$100 every month, starting in March
  - ▪ Software Seminar—$500 in February and June
- Marketing Costs
  - ▪ Advertising—$100 every month
  - ▪ Client relations—$100 every month
- Workshop Costs
  - ▪ Space rental $600 every other month starting in January
- Labor Costs
  - ▪ Contract Labor—$2,000 every month, starting in April

- Other Costs
  - Bank service charges—$20 every month
- Interest expense—$15 every month
- You let Sally know that the budget shows $89,600 in profit for the year. **TIP:** You might need to click **Save** to see the totals.

3/4/24

✓ You spent a lot of time working on the budget last Friday and got a bit behind on your work.

✓ You make the $150 monthly debt payment to Dell Finance. (Check #1125.) You use the **Administrative class** since this is not directly related to any product or service the company sells. **TIP:** You're paying interest through 2/29 plus some principal.

✓ You write yourself a check (Check #1126) for the work you did in **February**.

✓ Sally places an order for 4 copies of **Retailer** from Simply Accounting. You record the $1,200 order on PO-104.

✓ Sally brings you a VISA credit card receipt for her $1,200 purchase of an **annual** subscription to Advances in Software Design, a well-respected magazine. The magazine is published monthly. She received the March issue already. This is a professional development type of cost (technical reading materials). You use the **administrative class**.

✓ Metro Market calls and talks to Sally about scheduling an **Effective Troubleshooting (Tips)** workshop next week for some of the company's IT staff. It's short notice but Sally agrees to do it next Friday (the 8th). Sally quotes them a fee of $2,500. You decide not to create a **delayed charge**. You'll create the invoice when you know all the details.

3/5/24

✓ You receive three checks in the mail and record them in QBO. All were dated 3/5.
  - $510 from Fabulous Fifties for INV-1021. Check # 86910
  - $550 from Butter and Beans for INV-1020. Check # 9299
  - $330 from Reyelle Consulting for INV-1014. Check # 9759201

✓ You deposit the checks in the bank. The total deposit is $1,390.

✓ You receive 4 of the 5 **Easy1** products ordered from Abacus Shop on PO-103. In addition to the software, Abacus shipped one laptop Sally had ordered for use in the field. The total cost of the laptop was $1,320 (including tax). Because the laptop will be used for multiple purposes, you charge it to the **administrative class**. Sally thinks the laptop will be used for two years. The total amount on the invoice (#8944-50) is $1,720. **TIP:** Because the PO was created before **class** was added to **inventory** items, you will have to complete the **class** field.

✓ You write a $600 check to Hacker Spaces to pay for the rental space for the Metro Market workshop later this week. You record the payment (Check #1127). **TIP:** Assign this to a **class** that matches the type of service Sally is providing to Metro Market.

✓ You check the bills that need to be paid. You pay the one bill for $2,100 that is due on or before March 10. Use check # 1128.

3/6/24

✓ Sally decides to do some advertising of her new management products. She places an ad in the Sacramento Journal. The ad will run in the March online issue, out 3/11. She uses the credit card to pay the $250 fee. Since the ad promotes the company's products, you assign this expense to the **Products class**.

✓ The software ordered from Simply Accounting on PO-104 arrives, along with a bill for $1,200 (65501-9) dated 3/6. Simply Accounting's payment terms are 2% 10, Net 30.

3/8/24

✓ You receive two bills in the mail. Both are dated 3/8.

- Sacramento Light and Power's March bill (for heat and light) #01-94442—$90.18. The terms are Net 30.
- Western Phone March bill #9144-64 for $122.45. The terms are Net 30.

✓ You also receive 2 checks in the mail, both dated 3/8.

- Check #77066 from Alki Deli for $250, in payment of INV-1019.
- Check #989899 from Metro Market for $500, in payment of INV-1018.

✓ You deposit the checks in the bank. ($750 total).

3/11/24

✓ You pay all bills due on or before 3/21. There are three bills. The total amount paid is $3,076.27 after using the vendor credit available; the first check number is #1129.

✓ The Effective Troubleshooting (Tips) workshop for Metro Market was a success. Sally says she even got some leads on other companies that might be interested in her services. You record the invoice (INV-1023), dated 3/11, to Metro with terms of Net 15. The total amount billed is $2,500. **TIP:** The CLASS field should automatically fill with Workshops. If it doesn't, go back to the Product/Service List and make sure you've assigned a class to each item.

3/14/24

✓ Although it looks like there will be enough cash to pay bills, Sally decides to draw the full $5,000 on the line. She wants to have a bit of a cushion in case a really good deal comes along. You record the deposit into your account by Sacramento City Bank. **TIP:** You already have an account set up for the credit line.

✓ Sally can't believe the response she's getting from her ad in the *Sacramento Journal*. She has already gotten calls from 5 different companies. Two of them stopped by today to pick up the software. Both paid with a credit card (VISA). You make sure that the office address (3835 Freeport Blvd) shows in the Location of sale field so that the appropriate amount of tax is charged.

- Delightful Dental purchased Managing Your Medical Practice (Medical) for $543.75 (SR-108).
- Westside Engineers purchased Managing Your Engineering Firm (Engineering) for $543.75 (SR-109).

✓ Sally places an order with Abacus Shop. You record the order on PO-105. The total is $1,750.

- 2 Medical
- 2 Engineering
- 1 Legal

3/15/24

✓ You realize that the early payment discount on Simply Accounting's bill #65501-9 expires soon. You create a vendor credit for the purchase discount of $24 (2% of $1,200). You use DISC-SA as the ref no. and select Products as the class. You pay the bill with check #1132 for $1,176.

3/18/24

✓ You receive a check in the mail from Reyelle Consulting in full payment of INV-1017, dated 3/18. The check (9759301) is for $1,200.

✓ You deposit the credit card receipts received last week and the check received today. The credit card deposit totals $1,065.75 (after the 2% fee). The check deposit totals $1,200. You assign the credit card fee to the Administrative class.

3/19/24

✓ Reyelle Consulting calls and asks Sally to deliver more software. Sally delivers the software CDs to both Reyelle locations. You prepare separate invoices with terms of Net 30 for:

- Sacramento shipment
  - 6 each of the following software CDs:

- ◆ **Organizer**
  - ◆ **Tracker**
  - ▪ INV-1024 totals $660.
- ● Davis shipment
  - ▪ 4 each of the following software CDs:
    - ◆ **Organizer**
    - ◆ **Tracker**
  - ▪ INV-1025 totals $440.

✓ Sally lets you know that she needs to order 20 **Organizers** and 15 **Trackers** from Personal Software. You prepare PO-106. The purchase order total is $950.

3/20/24

✓ Sally continues to receive calls about the management products so she decides to put on a workshop in the office next week. She decides to charge $75 per attendee. She sends out an email to all the people who have contacted her for information.

✓ Cezar Software pays INV-1022 with a $2,000 check (#740062) dated 3/20.

✓ You deposit the check from Cezar into the bank. The deposit totals $2,000.

✓ Sally gives you the information on her client work through March 15th. You invoice the customers using 3/20 as the sales date.
- ● Fabulous Fifties—20 **Train** hours $1,000 (INV-1026). The terms are Net 15.
- ● mSquared Enterprises—16 **Set Up** hours $1,200 (INV-1027). The terms are Net 30.

✓ All products ordered from Abacus Shop (PO-105) are received today. You record the bill, dated 3/20, (#8944-55) for $1,750. Terms are Net 15.

✓ You notice that the 5th copy of **Easy1** you ordered from Abacus on PO-103 still hasn't arrived. Sally gives them a call. They explain that they're having trouble getting that product from their supplier. She decides to go ahead and cancel the PO for now. You change the PO status to **closed** in QBO. **TIP:** Consider using the search feature to find the purchase order. You can ignore the warning about the missing **class**.

3/22/24

✓ Reyelle Consulting (Davis) returned another **Organizer**. Sally asks you to create a credit memo. You create CM-1025 for $50 and mail it to Reyelle.

✓ Sally calls Personal Software to complain about the quality of the **Organizers**. They apologize and give you a credit for $25 when they stop by to pick up the **Organizer**. (4494CM)

✓ You receive a check for $2,500 from Metro Market in the mail. The check (#989950), dated 3/22, is payment in full for INV-1023.

✓ You pay the Dovalina & Diamond and Abacus Shop bills. The total is $2,325. The first check is #1133.

3/26/24

✓ Twenty-five people showed up for the demonstration on Monday. A few of the attendees also purchased software. Everyone wanted to pay with their Mastercard. Fortunately, Salish Software Solutions is set up to accept both VISA and Mastercard. **TIP:** VISA and Mastercard receipts would need to be deposited separately.
- ● You record the income using a **sales receipt** (SR-110 dated 3/25, the date of the demonstration), and Cash Customer as the **customer**. You use **Picks** as the **service** item.
- ● The total including the sale of one each of **Medical**, **Engineering**, and **Legal** was $3,506.25. **TIP:** Tax would only be charged on the product sales.

✓ Sally lets you know that Oscar Torres helped with the workshop. He worked for 2 hours. You write Oscar a check (Check #1135) dated 3/26 for $40 and charge it to the Workshop helper account.

✓ You deposit the Metro Market check from 3/22 and the credit card receipts from Monday into the bank. You use 3/26/24 as the date of the deposit.

- The check deposit totals $2,500.
- The credit card deposit , less the 2% fee, totals $3,436.12. You use **Administrative** as the **class** for the credit card fee.

✓ You receive a partial shipment of the software you ordered from Personal Software on PO-106. Three of the **organizers** were not included. The bill, dated 3/26 (#792114), totals $875. The terms are Net 30. You contact Personal Software. The customer service representative apologizes and lets you know the remaining items will be sent out next week.

3/28/24

✓ Sally gives you the information on her client work since March 15th. You record the invoices using 3/28 as the invoice date.

- Fabulous Fifties—4 **Train** hours and 10 **Fix** hours $800. INV-1028
- Lou's Barber Shop—8 **Fix** hours $480. INV-1029
- mSquared Enterprises—6 **Set Up** hours and 10 **Train** hours $950. INV-1030
- Champion Law—20 **Set Up** hours $1,500. INV-1031

✓ The Sacramento Journal calls and offers Sally a reduced price of $200 per ad if she agrees to run a monthly ad for a six month period. Sally agrees but does not want to start this until May. The $200 will be automatically charged to the VISA card on the 1st of each month, so you set up a new **scheduled Recurring Transaction**. You select **Expense** as the transaction type and you set the interval to be the 1st day of each month beginning on 5/1/24 and ending after 6 occurrences. You name the template Sacramento Ad and assign this to the Products **class**.

✓ You write a check (#1136) for $2,500 to Sally for March dividends.

✓ Before you leave for the day, you talk to Sally about the credit line. You have a healthy cash balance now and you suggest that Sally pay down the line a bit. She can always borrow again if needed. Sally agrees. You pay Sacramento City Bank $2,500 **plus** interest with check #1137. **TIP:** The simple annual interest rate charged by the bank is 6%. Sally borrowed $5,000 on 3/14. Use ½ month for the interest payment. Remember, interest should be calculated on the full amount borrowed, not the amount being paid back.

✓ You also talk to Sally about setting a fixed fee of $350 per month for your services starting in March. She is very happy with your work and agrees to the amount. You enter a **bill** (ACCT24) for accounting fees dated 3/31 with Net 10 terms. You decide to set this up as a **scheduled recurring transaction (bill)**. **TIP:** Click **Save** before you move forward.

- You click **Make recurring** on the black bar at the bottom of the form and complete the template. You enter Accounting as the **template name**. Future bills are scheduled for the last day of each month with 4/30/24 as the **Start date**. You don't identify an end date.

3/29/24

✓ There is no planned activity for the weekend, so you spend the day making the final adjustments for March.

✓ You don't have your bank statement yet but you go online and see that the balance is $20,831.10. You reconcile to the $20,831.10 balance using 3/31 as the reconciliation date. All deposits made in March cleared the bank. All checks written prior to 3/20 cleared the bank. There were no service charges. **TIP:** Checks include **check** and **bill payment transaction types**.

✓ You also reconcile the credit card account. The online balance is $1,450.00. All March credit card transactions are included on the statement. You enter a bill payment later. You use MarCC as the **bill no.** and 3/31 as the reconciliation and bill date.

✓ You remember that Dovalina & Diamond came in for a follow-up meeting with Sally. You haven't received their bill yet. Sally says that the bill will be for $150. You go ahead and create a journal entry (Mar24.1) to record the consulting fees expense in the proper period. You select **Administrative** as the **class**. You create a **reversing entry** dated 4/1 so that you can enter the bill when it's received without duplicating the expense. **TIP:** You need to click **Save** on entry

Mar24.1 before you can create the reversing entry. Use the Accrued Expenses account to record the liability.

✓ You compare the inventory on hand to the inventory report in QBO. All amounts agree.

✓ You make additional journal entries, dated 3/31, after considering the following:

- Supplies on hand equal $150.
- The last payment to Dell Finance was 3/4. **TIP:** The annual, simple interest rate on the loan is 5%. Round to two decimals.
- You purchased a laptop on 3/5 for $1,320. It was placed in service right away. You go ahead and take a full month's depreciation on the computer. Sally thinks it will last 2 years, with no salvage value. **TIP:** There's no change in the monthly depreciation expense for the assets purchased prior to March 1.
- You confirm with Sally that all sales to customers have been completed during the month.
- You look carefully at the profit and loss statement and make sure that all March expenses are properly recorded. (**TIP:** Include the Prior Period column on your profit and loss report. Compare the March expenses with the February expenses. Are there any of the common operating expenses missing? Do any of the expenses appear unusually high?)
- You look carefully at the balance sheet paying particular attention to Other Current Assets and Other Current Liabilities. Many of the common month-end adjustments affect accounts in those categories. **TIP:** Look at the journal entries you made dated February 29th. There will likely be similar entries for March.

Check numbers 3/31

> **Checking account balance:** $13,453.60
> **Other current assets:** $10,170.00
> **Total assets:** $39,871.10
> **Total liabilities:** . . . .$ 8,467.16
> **Gross profit (March):** $11,594.00
> **Net income for March:** . . . .$ 8,632.14

Suggested reports for Chapter 9:

All reports should be in portrait orientation.

- Balance Sheet as of March 31
- Profit and Loss (March)
  - Include a year-to-date column in the report
- Profit and Loss by Class (March)
- Accounts Receivable Aging Summary (March 31)
- Accounts Payable Aging Summary (March 31)
- Sales by Product/Service Summary (March)
- Inventory Valuation Summary (March 31)
- Recurring Template List
- Journal Report (March)
- Budget Overview Report 2024 (by Quarter)
  - To display quarters, click Customize, click Rows/Columns, select Accounts vs Qtrs on Show Grid dropdown menu.
  - **TIP:** QBO won't save reports that include a : (colon) in the report name. Modify the name before saving.
- Budget vs Actual report (January 1 through March 31)
  - Click Customize and click Rows/Columns. In the Show Grid dropdown menu, select Accounts vs Total.
  - **TIP:** QBO won't save reports that include a : (colon) in the report name. Modify the name before saving.

APPENDIX 9A CREATING AND MANAGING TAGS

Most of you are familiar with the idea of tagging from various web services (e.g., social networks and blogs). Tagging is simply a convenient way to organize and find information.

Tagging in QBO works in much the same way as it does in other web services. In QBO:

- A **tag** is a keyword or phrase.
- One or more **tags** can be added to most sales and purchase transactions.
  - **Tags** currently cannot be added to **journal entries** or **transfers**.
- **Tags** can be grouped.
  - You can create up to 40 **tag groups**.
- You can add an unlimited number of **tags** to a transaction, but each **tag** must come from a different group.

LO 9-5 Describe the use of transaction tags in QBO

Creating Tag Groups

To create a **tag group**, click ⚙ on the icon bar.

YOUR COMPANY	LISTS	TOOLS
Account and settings	All lists	Order checks ☐
Manage users	Products and services	Import data
Chart of accounts	Recurring transactions	Import desktop data
QuickBooks labs	Attachments	Export data
	Custom fields	Reconcile
	Tags	Budgeting
		Audit log
		SmartLook
		Resolution center

Figure 9A.1

Access to tag management

Click **Tags**.

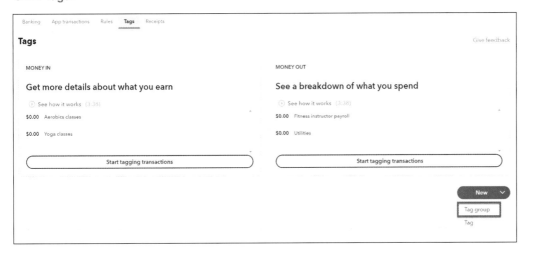

Figure 9A.2

Link to new tag group setup

> ✳ **HINT:** **Tags** can also be accessed by clicking **Banking** on the navigation bar and selecting the **Tags** tab.

Open the **Tags** tab and select **Tag group** in the **New** dropdown menu.

Figure 9A.3

Tag group setup screen

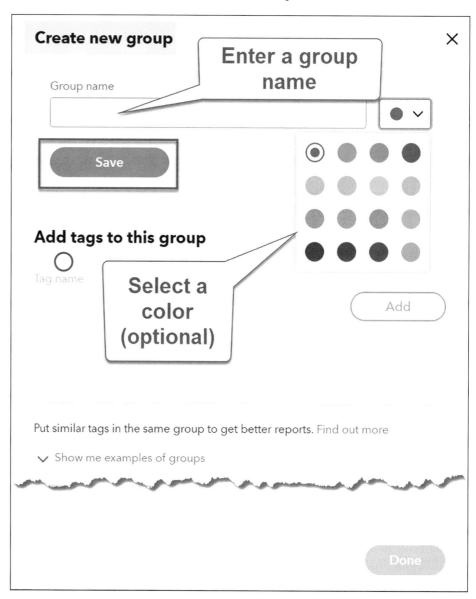

Enter the name for your **tag group**. You can also use a different color for each group as a highlighter.

Click **Save**.

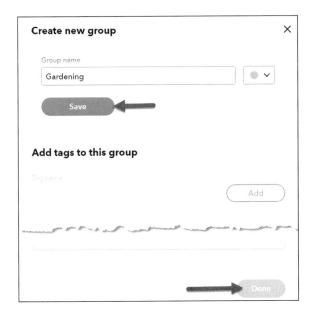

Figure 9A.4
Example of new tag group

Click **Done**.

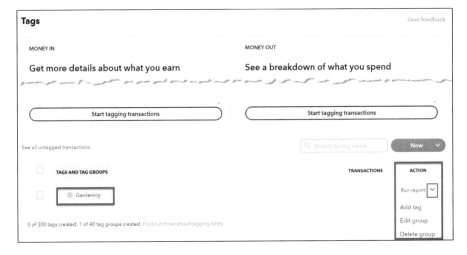

Figure 9A.5
Options for tag groups

In the Tags Center, **tag groups** can be edited (name and color) or deleted.

Creating Tags

Tags can be set up in the Tags Center or directly on a specific transaction form.

To set up a **tag** in the Tags Center, click ⚙ on the icon bar and select **Tags** or click **Banking** on the navigation bar and select the **Tags** tab.

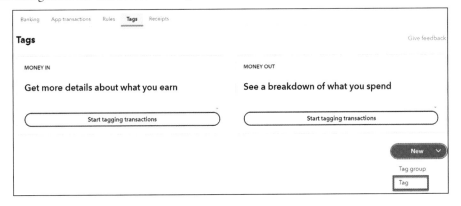

Figure 9A.6
Tags Center

Select **Tag** in the **New** dropdown menu.

Figure 9A.7

Tag setup screen

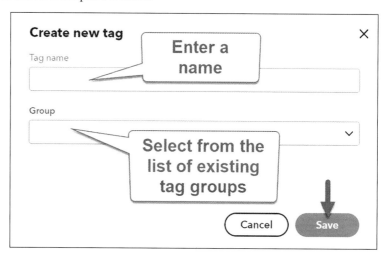

Enter a name and select a **Tag group** if appropriate.
Click **Save**.

Adding Tags to Transactions

Tags can be added to most transactions. The process is independent of the transaction form used.

As an example, when the **tag** feature is activated, the top half of a **bill** form would look something like Figure 9A.8.

Figure 9A.8

Tag field on form

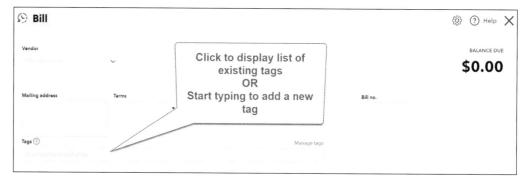

Click inside the **Tags** field.

Figure 9A.9

Example of tags available to add to form

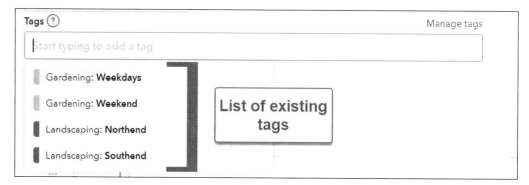

A list of existing **tags** will be displayed. Clicking one or more of the **tags** adds them to the form.

You can also create a new **tag** to add.

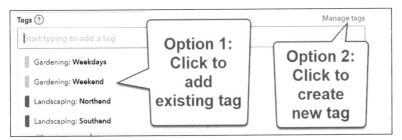

Figure 9A.10

Options for creating a new tag within a form

To create a new **tag**, you can type a new name in the field and click **+ Add**, or you can click **Manage tags** and select **Create new tag**. New **tags** can be linked to an existing **group** under either option. You cannot create a new **tag group** within a transaction form.

Reporting on Tagged Transactions

A summary of activity is available in the Tags Center.

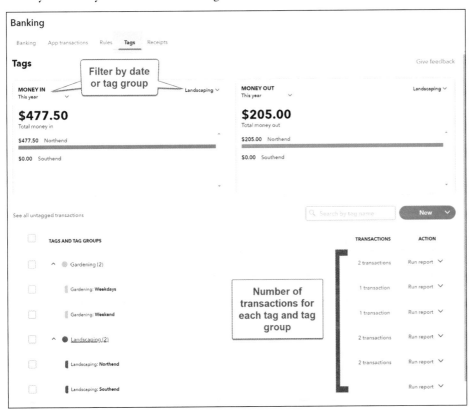

Figure 9A.11

Tags Center

The page can be filtered by date or by **tag group**. Additional reports will be available by clicking **Run report** in the **ACTION** column.

How Do Tags Differ from Classes and Locations?

In general, **tags** are a bit more flexible.

	TAGS	CLASSES	LOCATIONS
Number per transaction	Unlimited*	≤ the number of line items	1 (for most)
Number per specific line item	None	1	None (for most)

* Each tag must come from a different tag group

Project Tracking and Billing for Time and Expenses

In this chapter, we're going to cover billing for time and expenses.

Most of the time, companies don't need to track employee time by customer or by project. In a retail store, for example, management generally doesn't track how much profit the store makes on a specific customer during the month. Instead, management might track how much gross profit the store makes on sales of a specific product or how much profit it makes in a specific store. Management may need to track which store an employee works in but it doesn't generally need to track how much time a specific employee spent helping a specific customer. Restaurants, banks, manufacturing companies, and gas stations are examples of other companies that don't normally need to track time by customer. This chapter will not apply to those types of companies. (We covered tracking profit by department or location in Chapter 9.)

However, there are many companies that **do** need to track time by customer and/or project.

For example, let's look at two construction companies. One bills its customers under "time and materials" contracts. The other bills its customers under "fixed fee" contracts. The time and materials contractor is billing for labor and materials plus some kind of markup. Payroll records **must** include the hours for each customer, by project **and** by type of work if billing rates differ, because those hours will be used to invoice customers. If those hours are tracked in QBO (which they can be), the invoicing process is more efficient.

The fixed fee contractor generally bills a percentage of the agreed-upon price (the fixed fee) as the work progresses. The number of hours worked aren't needed to prepare the invoice. However, in order to evaluate project profitability, fixed fee contractors need to be able to compare the revenue earned on a specific project to the specific costs of that project. That information helps them evaluate the company's overall performance and the specific performance of project managers and improves their ability to bid on future projects.

Tracking revenues and costs by job is commonly known as project or job costing.

BEFORE WE BEGIN

Understanding a few basic concepts will help when working with projects in QBO:

- **Projects** are always linked to a **customer**.
  - **Projects** are identified in the **Customer** field of forms.

- Multiple projects can be tracked for a single customer.
  - Time and expenses can be charged to **customers** as well so be careful to identify the specific **project** when recording transactions.

- Multiple **projects** for a **customer** cannot be billed on the same invoice. A separate invoice is created for each project.

- Hours worked and any external costs incurred on a project must be defined as billable if you intend to later charge the customer for those hours or costs. A **billable** field is included on all appropriate forms (**timesheets, bills, checks,** etc.).
  - External costs that are charged to a **project** but not identified as **billable** will be included in project reports but will not be accessible when preparing **invoices** or **sales receipts**.

LO 10-1 Explain and use **projects** in QBO for job-costing.

WORKING WITH PROJECTS

Setting Up Projects

Project tracking is a preference in QBO. The default setting in most new company files is **On**. If **Projects** appears on the navigation bar, the feature has been activated.

If **Project** tracking has not been activated, click the ⚙ on the icon bar and select **Account and settings**.

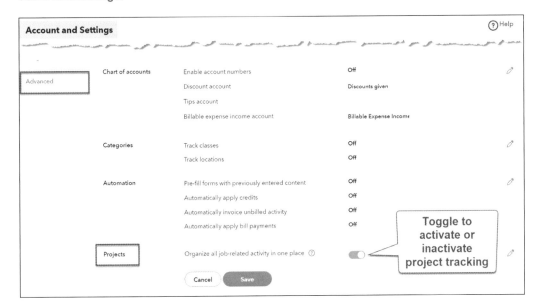

Figure 10.1

Project activation tool

On the **Advanced** tab, click the **pencil** icon in the **Projects** section.

The toggle switch next to **Organize all job-related activity in one place** is used to activate or inactivate the feature.

Click **Save** to activate **projects** and **Done** to exit the **Account and Settings** window.

Once **project** tracking is activated, a link will appear in the navigation bar.

Figure 10.2

Navigation bar with
Projects activated

To set up a project, click **Projects** on the navigation bar.

The first time you access **projects**, the screen will look something like Figure 10.3.

Figure 10.3

Initial project screen

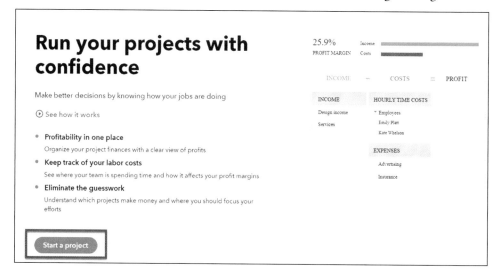

Click **Start a project** to open a sidebar.

Figure 10.4

Project setup screen

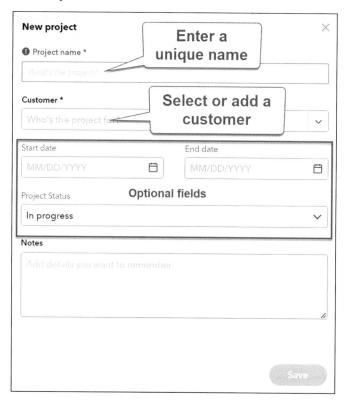

On the sidebar, enter a **project name** and select the **customer**. Entering project dates and status is optional. You can also enter notes. Some companies might want to add information about the scope of the project or the names of customer personnel in charge of the project. Click **Save**.

 HINT: It may take some time, usually less than five minutes, for a new **project** to be accessible in transaction forms. Try refreshing your browser. You may need to log out and log back into your homework company if it's been more than five minutes.

Add jobs for Craig's Design and Landscaping.

(Craig's Design has just gotten a request from Jeff's Jalopies for some landscaping work. Jeff has other projects in mind for the future so Craig's Design wants to set up a project for tracking hours spent on the landscaping job.)

1. Turn on project tracking. (If **Projects** appears in the navigation bar, it is already active. Skip to Step 2.)

   a. Click the ⚙ on the icon bar.

   b. Click **Account and Settings**.

   c. Click **Advanced**.

   d. Click **Projects**.

   e. Toggle **Organize all job-related activity in one place** to on.

   f. Click **Save** and **Done**.

2. Set up job.

   a. Click **Projects** on the navigation bar.

   b. Click **Start a project**.

   c. Enter **Jalopies' Landscaping** as the **project name**.

   d. Select **Jeff's Jalopies** as the **Customer**.

   e. **Make a note** of the options in the **Project Status** dropdown menu.

   f. Click **Save**.

   g. Click **Dashboard** to exit the Project Center.

Managing Projects

Click **Projects** on the navigation bar to access the Project Center. The Project Center will look like Figure 10.5 after completing Practice Exercise 10.1 and recording an **invoice** and a **bill** for the **project**.

Figure 10.5

Project Center

BEHIND THE SCENES For companies that don't want to link actual labor costs to **projects** in QBO, **cost rates** can be set up. These rates are used for project estimates **only**. There are no journal entries created.

Click **Employee hourly rate** in the top right corner of the Project Center (Figure 10.5). Click **Add** in the **COST RATE** column for Emily Platt.

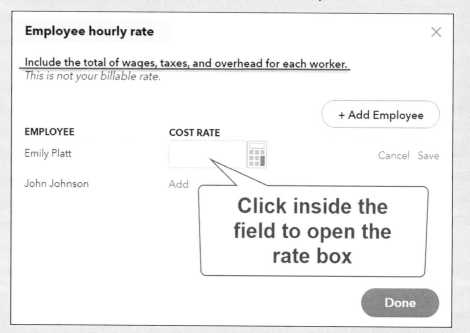

The rate entered might include wages, payroll taxes, and company overhead. These costs would be included in the summary profit amounts displayed in the Project Center. The costs would **not** be included in project profitability reports although they would be included in the calculation of **PROFIT MARGIN** displayed in the Project Center (Figure 10.5).

Summary information including **PROFIT MARGIN** is displayed on the main page for all **projects**.

BEHIND THE SCENES In QBO, the **PROFIT MARGIN** of a project is calculated as:

$$\frac{\text{Billed project revenues} - \text{All costs charged to the project}}{\text{Billed project revenues}}$$

Information displayed in the Project Center can be changed by clicking the small gear icon above the **ACTIONS** column and selecting or deselecting columns.

Using the **OPTIONS** dropdown menu in the **ACTIONS** column, **projects** can be marked as completed or canceled. Notes can be added to the **project**, and the **project** name can be changed by selecting **Edit this project**.

Click a specific **project** to see additional details.

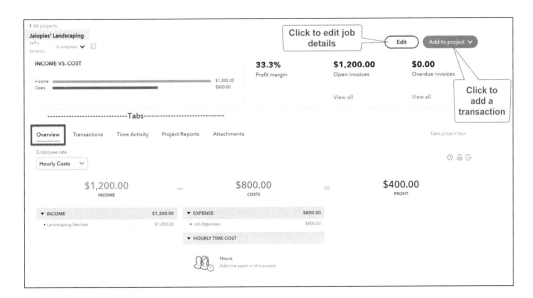

Figure 10.6

Project screen

There are five tabs on a **project** screen.

- **Overview**
  - Summary of profit to date is displayed.
  - Includes links to transaction forms (**invoices**, **bills**, **expenses**, or **timesheets**).

- **Transactions**
  - All recorded transactions related to project are displayed.
  - Clicking anywhere in a transaction row will open the form.

- **Time activity**
  - Hours by date and employee/vendor are displayed.
  - Includes link to **timesheet**.

- **Project reports**
  - Includes links to reports
    - **Project Profitability**
    - **Time cost by employee or vendor**
    - **Unbilled time and expenses**

- **Attachments**
  - Includes project documents or images previously uploaded to QBO
  - Includes link to upload additional materials

HINT: You can also access a specific project record by opening the **Customers drawer** on the **Sales** link in the navigation bar and clicking a customer name.

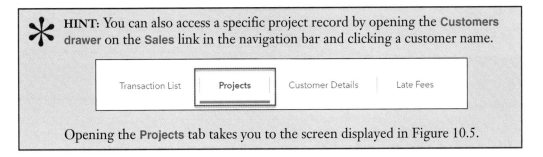

Opening the **Projects** tab takes you to the screen displayed in Figure 10.5.

LO 10-2 Understand how payments to independent contractors are tracked in QBO

Independent contractor Self-employed person or entity performing work for another entity as a nonemployee

SETTING UP INDEPENDENT CONTRACTORS

In Chapter 4, we covered setting up 1099 vendors (landlords, attorneys, independent contractors, etc.) in QBO. In this chapter, we're going to look specifically at independent contractors.

Independent contractors are often used by companies to work on projects. This works especially well when a company is growing. As new customers come in, there might be too much work for existing employees to manage but not quite enough new work to justify hiring another permanent employee.

> **BEHIND THE SCENES** The difference between an **independent contractor** and an employee is not clear-cut. In fact, there are 57 questions on the form the Internal Revenue Services uses (SS-8) in making the determination! In general, though, a person would be considered an independent contractor if they are in control of how the work is done, if they provide much of the equipment and supplies needed to complete the work, and if they provide similar services to others.

To set up an independent contractor, open the **Contractors** drawer of **Payroll** on the navigation bar.

Figure 10.7

Access to contractor setup screen

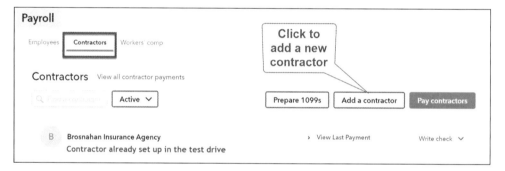

Click **Add a contractor**.

> ✳ **HINT:** Any vendors previously set up as 1099 vendors will appear on the screen shown in Figure 10.7. If there were no 1099 vendors in a company file, an **Add your first contractor** screen would be displayed.

Figure 10.8

Contractor setup screen

The contractor's name is entered here. If the user elects to have the contractor enter the tax information online, an email address must be entered as well.

Click **Add contractor** to continue.

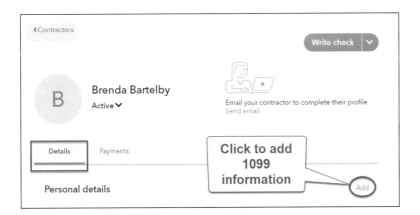

Figure 10.9

Link to vendor setup screens

If the user does not invite the contractor to enter personal information online, the user must click **Add** to complete the setup.

Figure 10.10

Options for contractor type

The contractor type (individual or business) is selected first.

If **Individual** is selected, the sidebar will expand to allow for entry of additional details.

Figure 10.11

Contractor setup screen

A tax ID number and name and address information are required. (The screen for **Business** has similar fields.)

Click **Save** to complete the setup.

The independent contractor is automatically added to the Vendor List. Similarly, independent contractors initially set up through the **Vendors** tab of **Expenses** (and identified as 1099 vendors) are automatically added to the **Contractor** list. Additional information about the vendor (terms, billing rates, phone number, etc.) can only be entered in the vendor's record.

 HINT: If independent contractors perform billable services, the account to be debited when the contractor bill for **services** is entered (or a check is created) is identified in the **service** item record.

Check the box next to **I purchase this product/service from a vendor** to open the **Purchasing information** section of the item record. Enter the description to be displayed on purchase forms and the account to be debited when entering contractor charges. A default cost and preferred vendor can also be identified.

PRACTICE
EXERCISE
10.2

Add an independent contractor for Craig's Design and Landscaping.

(Craig has a large installation project coming up soon and expects to need some additional help. One of Craig's employees has a friend (Sue Stevens) who has landscaping experience and is looking for work. Craig brings her on as an independent contractor.)

1. Set up Sue Stevens as a **Contractor**.

   a. Click **Payroll** on the navigation bar.

   b. Click **Contractors**.

(continued)

(continued from previous page)

    c. Click **Add a contractor**.

    d. Enter "Sue Stevens" as the **Name**.

    e. Remove the checkmark in the box next to **Email this contractor to complete their profile**.

    f. Click **Add contractor**.

    g. On the **Details** tab of the contractor record, click **Add** next to **Personal details**.

    h. Check **Individual**.

    i. Enter the following information:

       i. Sue Stevens

       ii. 444-54-4474 as the social security number.

       iii. 2111 Riversedge Drive
           Sacramento, CA 95822

       iv. **Make a note** of the fields in the contractor setup sidebar that are not required.

    j. Click **Save**.

2. Edit Sue's vendor record.

    a. Click **Expenses** on the navigation bar.

    b. Open **Vendors** tab.

    c. Click **Sue Stevens**.

    d. Click **Edit**.

    e. In the **Additional info** section, select **Due on receipt** as the **Terms**.

    f. Click **Save**.

    g. Click **Dashboard** to exit the vendor screen.

USING TIMESHEETS TO TRACK HOURS

The timesheet feature in QBO is available to track hours worked by both hourly and salaried employees in a company and by independent contractors. Timesheet data can be used to do one or more of the following:

LO 10-3 Describe and demonstrate how **timesheets** are used in QBO

eLecture

- If the user subscribes to a payroll plan in QBO, timesheets can be used to:
  - Track labor costs by project for all employees.
  - Track paid time off for all employees.
  - Create a paycheck based on hours worked for hourly employees.
- Users with or without payroll activation can use timesheets to:
  - Track billable hours for invoicing customers.
  - Track billable and non-billable hours for management purposes.

Payroll activity will be covered in Chapter 12. In this chapter, timesheets will only be used to track hours for billing purposes.

    The time tracking process in QBO changed significantly in 2021. The test drive company included some, but not all, of the new features as of April 2022. The next sections will describe the system in place in your homework company. There is no Practice Exercise for this section.

Setting Up Time Tracking

Certain QBO features must be activated to track hours by customer or project and identify billable hours. Time tracking is free in QBO, but you may need to search a bit before taking advantage of that option!

Click the ⚙ on the icon bar and select **Account and settings**.

Open the **Time** tab.

Figure 10.12

Initial link to activate time tracking

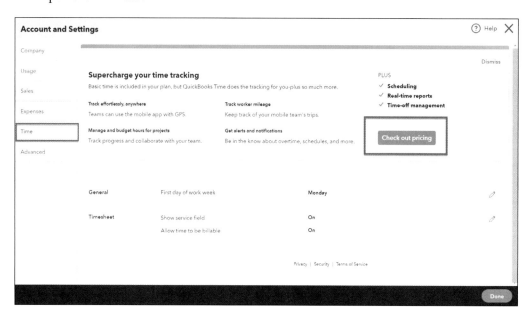

If you see the page shown in Figure 10.12, click **Check out pricing**.

Scroll down to the **bottom** of the page.

Figure 10.13

Option to activate manual time tracking

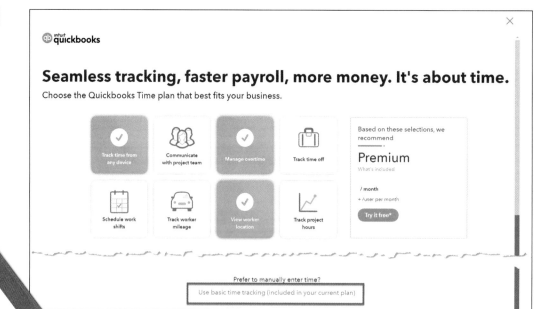

~~~lect **Use basic time tracking (included in your current plan)**. You will now be able to~~~mesheets.

~~using the **time entries** feature, you'll need to edit a few settings.~~

~~⚙ icon on the icon bar and select **Account and settings**.~~

~~**Time** tab.~~

Click the pencil icon in the General section to open it for editing.

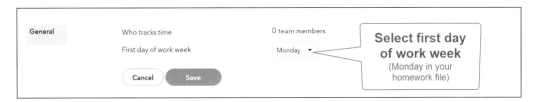

Select Monday in the First day of work week dropdown menu.

The General section may include an option to select time-tracking users. To check, click O team members.

If you see an option to Show contractors, toggle On.

Open the Timesheet section (Figure 10.16).

Toggle Show service field and Allow time to be billable to On.

Check the box next to Show billing rate to users entering time and click Save.

Click Done on the Account and Settings page.

Click Dashboard to close the Time Entries screen.

Entering Timesheet Data

Timesheets are accessed through the Time tab on the navigation bar.

Once you have an employee or contractor set up, there are several ways to access a timesheet:

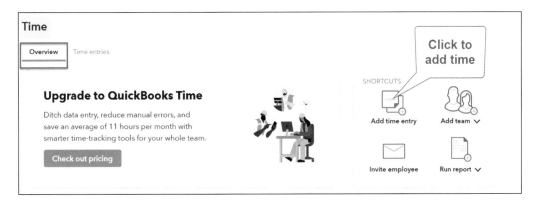

- You can click **Add time entry** in the **SHORTCUTS** section on the **Overview drawer** (tab) of the Time Center (Figure 10.17).

Figure 10.18

Access to timesheet

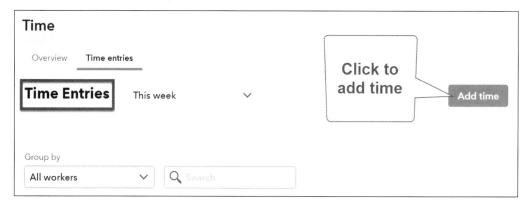

- You can click **Add time** on the **Time entries drawer** (tab) of the Time Center (Figure 10.18).
- Or you can click **Time entry** in the **MONEY OUT** section on the **Get things done** tab of the **Dashboard**.

Any of the above options will open a sidebar that lists all employees and contractors.

Figure 10.19

Name selection for time entry

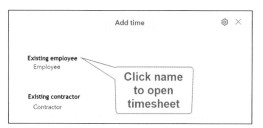

Select the appropriate individual to open a timesheet.

Figure 10.20

Timesheet

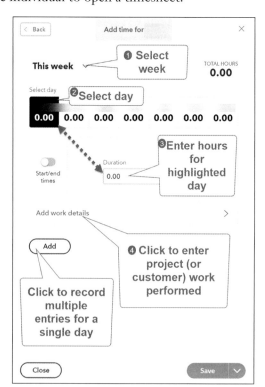

Select the week. (Click **Custom** to select a week other than the current or prior week.) Click the appropriate day. Enter hours worked in the **Duration** field. To add multiple entries for a single day, click **Add**. This would be necessary for companies whose employees work on multiple projects in a single day.

If the hours should be tracked or billed, click **Add work details**.

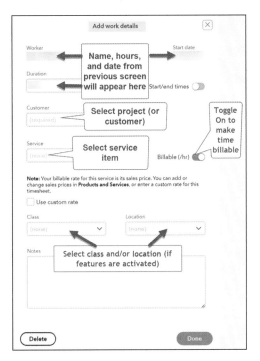

A customer (or project) must be selected if hours are being tracked. **Billable(/hr)** should be toggled on if the customer will be billed for the hours.

QBO automatically uses the rate associated with the item selected in the **Service** field for billing purposes. That rate can be changed by checking the **Use custom rate** box and entering a new rate **if** the company selected that option when time tracking was activated (Figure 10.16). **Class** and **location** fields will only appear if segment tracking was activated.

Click **Done**.

Hours are entered in the same fashion for each day of the week.

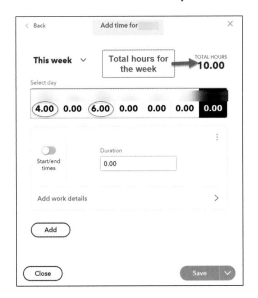

When all hours for the week have been entered, the total hours worked by the worker are displayed on the timesheet screen.

Click **Save**.

> **BEHIND THE SCENES** No journal entries are created when time is entered. Employee labor costs are recorded when **paychecks** are created. (Payroll is covered in Chapter 12.) The revenue associated with billable hours is recorded when the **invoice** is created. Invoicing customers for time is covered in the **BILLING FOR TIME AND COSTS** section of this chapter.

Editing Timesheets

Time data can be edited by opening the timesheet and selecting the item to be changed.

Click **Time** on the navigation bar and open the **Time entries drawer** (tab).

Figure 10.23

Access to completed timesheets

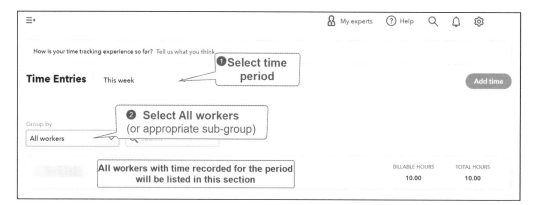

Select the time period.

> **HINT:** If you select **Custom** as the time period, you must select a start and end date on the displayed calendar.

Select **All Workers** in the **Group by** dropdown menu. (You can also select a sub-group like employees or contractors.)

Click the worker's name for whom you need to make the change.

Figure 10.24

Timesheet details

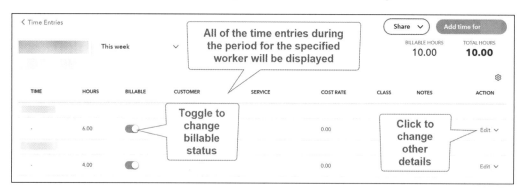

All entries for the specified worker during the identified time period will be displayed. The billable status can be changed on the initial screen (Figure 10.24). Click **Edit** to change the date, number of hours, customer/project, or service item.

Figure 10.25

Timesheet edit screen

 WARNING: If you edit a **timesheet after** the hours have been billed (have been added to an **invoice**), the **invoice** will **not** be automatically adjusted. The **invoice** would need to be manually adjusted. Billing for time is covered in the **BILLING FOR TIME AND COSTS** section of this chapter.

TRACKING COSTS OTHER THAN LABOR BY PROJECT

There are usually costs other than labor that a company incurs when working on customer jobs. If a company is going to get a clear picture of profits earned on a project, these costs (usually referred to as direct costs or direct expenses) need to be linked to the **project** in QBO.

In addition, many companies that work with projects (jobs) bill some or even all direct expenses to their customers. For example, construction companies would likely bill their customers for appliances purchased for their home. Law firms would likely bill their clients for work performed by outside investigators.

If certain features are turned on in QBO, users can flag purchases as billable to specific customers when **bills**, **checks**, and **expenses** are entered. Those charges are then available when **invoices** are created.

LO 10-4 Demonstrate how direct costs other than labor can be tracked by **project** in QBO

Turning on Features for Tracking and Billing Direct Expenses

Features needed to track and bill expenses are activated by clicking the ⚙ on the icon bar and selecting the **Expenses** tab in **Account and Settings**.

Figure 10.26

Access to settings for billing costs to customers

Click the **pencil** icon in the **Bills and expenses** section.

Figure 10.27

Options available for
tracking and billing
direct costs

Track expenses and items by customer

Make expenses and items billable

Check box
to activate
markup
feature

Settings for tracking
and billing direct costs

Track expenses and items by customer must be turned **On** if a company tracks project costs.
Make expenses and items billable must also be turned **On** if a company intends to bill customers for some or all direct costs.

There are two initial questions that must be answered if a company bills customers for
direct costs:

- Does the company expect to earn a profit on costs it incurs on behalf of customers?
- Are billable direct costs subject to sales tax?

Generating Profits on Direct Costs

The simplest way to generate a profit on a direct cost is to "mark up" the cost charged to
the customer. This is normally done using a percentage. For example, an accounting firm
might incur a cost of $500 on software purchased for a client's use. If the company decides
to mark up the cost by 10%, the client would be billed $550. (The $500 cost plus the 10%
($50) markup.) The firm's profit would be $50 (the $550 billed to the client less the $500
cost of the software).

To record markups in QBO, the box next to **Markup with a default rate of** must be checked
(Figure 10.27). If the company has a standard markup rate that is applied to direct costs,
the rate can be entered as a default. The rate can later be changed on specific transactions.
Entering billable costs is covered in the **Identifying Costs as Billable** section of this chapter.

Taxability of Direct Costs Billed to a Customer

Taxability of customer charges is dictated by state laws. However, in general, direct costs
(plus markup) billed to customers are subject to sales tax unless the company paid tax as
part of the original purchase or the direct cost isn't taxable.

If the box next to **Charge sales tax** is checked (Figure 10.27), QBO will, by default,
include direct costs when determining sales tax amounts. This can be changed on specific
sales transactions.

Companies would check the box if most billable costs were taxable.

> **BEHIND THE SCENES** If taxes are paid by the company on the original purchase,
> the full amount (tax included) should be billed to the customer. No additional tax
> would, of course, be added to that amount.

Accounting for Direct Costs Billed to Customers

When direct costs are billed to customers on an **invoice** or **sales receipt**, QBO creates a
journal entry for:

- the amount the customer owes
- the amount of any markup
- the amount of the direct expense

The amount the customer owes is debited to Accounts Receivable if the customer is billed on an **invoice** or Undeposited Funds (or Checking) if the customer is billed on a **sales receipt**.

The account credited for the markup amount, if any, must be identified in the **Chart of accounts** section of the **Advanced** tab of **Account and Settings**.

Figure 10.28

Account selection field for markup income

 HINT: The **Markup income account** field only appears if the markup feature has been activated on the **Expenses** tab of **Account and Settings**.

The account credited for the direct cost (the amount incurred on behalf of the customer, not the markup amount) is a little more complicated.

Let's go back to the **Expense** window in **Account and Settings** again.

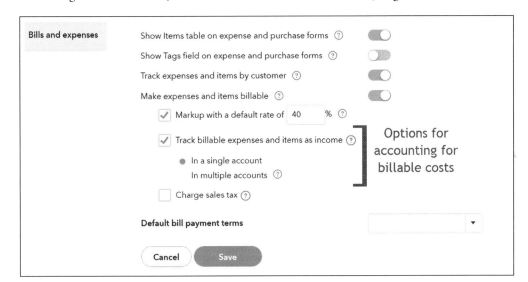

Figure 10.29

Options for accounting for billable costs

If **Track billable expenses and items as income** is NOT checked (Figure 10.29), then the amount charged to the customer for the direct cost will be credited to the account that was debited when the original cost was entered. For example, let's say a company incurred $320 in travel costs billable to a customer. When the bill for the travel costs is entered, the company might debit a Travel and Entertainment Expense account and flag the cost as billable. The journal entry underlying the **bill** would be:

	Travel and Entertainment Expense	320	
	Accounts Payable		320

The company adds a 10% markup to all direct costs. When the invoice is later created to bill the customer for the travel, QBO would automatically debit the $352 to Accounts receivable and credit $320 to the Travel and Entertainment Expense account and $32 to the markup account identified in the **Advanced** tab of **Account and Settings**. The journal entry underlying the **invoice** would be:

	Accounts receivable	352	
	Travel and Entertainment Expense		320
	Markup on billable direct costs		32

The balance in the Travel and Entertainment Expense account, related to this transaction, would be zero. The general ledger activity would look like this:

A/R (Asset)	A/P (Liability)	Markup on billable costs (Income)	Travel & Entertainment Expense
352	320	32	320 | 320
			0

If **Track billable expenses and items as income** IS checked (Figure 10.29), the company must decide whether to track the expenses in a single account or in multiple accounts. If the billable expenses are tracked in a single account, then the account to be credited must be identified in the **Advanced** tab of **Account and Settings**.

The **Chart of accounts** section on the **Advanced** tab would look something like Figure 10.30 if an income account called Reimbursed job costs was set up.

Figure 10.30

Account selection field for billable costs if treated as income-single account

Using the travel cost example again, the journal entry underlying the **invoice** would now look like this:

	Accounts receivable	352	
	Reimbursed job costs		320
	Markup on billable costs		32

The general ledger activity would look like this:

A/R (Asset)	A/P (Liability)	Markup on billable costs (Income)	Reimbursed Job costs (Income)	Travel & Entertainment Expense
352	320	32	320	320

If **Track billable expenses and items as income** is checked and **in multiple accounts** is also selected (Figure 10.29), any **expense** or **cost of goods sold** account that might include billable costs must be associated with an income account. As of April 2023, the field is not available when accounts are set up (or edited) using the new account setup screen covered in Chapter 1. The field is available when a new account is set up inside a form (i.e., when **+ Add new** is selected in the **Category** field). That field is shown in Figure 10.31.

Figure 10.31

Account selection field for billable costs if treated as income—multiple accounts

Account

Account Type	*Name
Expenses ▾	Travel
*Detail Type	Description
Travel ▾	

Use **Travel** to track travel costs.

For food you eat while traveling, use **Travel meals**, instead.

☐ Is sub-account

Enter parent account ▾

☑ Use for billable expenses
Income Account

Enter income account ▾

> Select account to be credited when customer is charged for a direct cost

Cancel   Save and Close ▾

Going back once more to the example we were using, let's say that in addition to travel costs, the company purchased $700 in job materials billable to the customer. If the **income** associated with Job Materials was Landscaping Services and the **income account** identified in the Travel account was Reimbursed job costs, the journal entry underlying the **invoice** would now look like this assuming no sales taxes were charged to customer:

Accounts receivable		1,122	
Landscaping Services			700
Reimbursed job costs			320
Markup on billable costs			102

The general ledger activity would look like this:

A/R (Asset)	A/P (Liability)	Markup on billable costs (Income)	Reimbursed Job costs (Income)	Landscaping Services (Income)	Travel & Entertainment Expense	Direct Job Costs (Expense)
1122	320	102	320	700	320	700
	700					
	1,020					

Turn on features for billing direct costs to customers.

(Craig's Design decides to bill customers a 5% markup on costs incurred specifically for the project. The markup amount will be tracked in an income account. Billable costs will not be tracked in income accounts.)

1. Click the ⚙ on the icon bar.

2. Click **Account and settings**.

3. Open the **Expenses** tab.
   a. Click the **pencil** icon in the **Bills and expenses** section.
   b. Make sure **Track expenses and items by customer** and **Make expenses and items billable** are both activated.
   c. Check the box next to **Markup with a default rate of**.

PRACTICE
EXERCISE
10.3

Homework
MBC

(continued)

(continued from previous page)

> > *d.* Enter "5" in the percent field.
> > *e.* Uncheck **Track billable expenses and items as income.**
> > *f.* Click **Save.**
>
> **4.** Open the **Advanced** tab.
> > *a.* Click the **pencil** icon in the **Chart of accounts** section.
> > *b.* Select **+ Add new** in the dropdown menu for **Markup income account.**
> > *c.* Select **Income** as the **account type** (**Save account under** field).
> > *d.* Select **Other Primary Income** as the **detail type** (**Tax form section** field).
> > *e.* Enter "Markup on billable direct costs" as the **Name.**
> > *f.* Click **Save and close.**
> > *g.* Click **Save.**
>
> **5.** Click **Done.**

Identifying Costs as Billable

Any costs (including costs of **products** and **services**) can be identified as **billable** to a specific customer/project on **Expense, Check,** or **Bill** forms. Although customers can be identified on **Purchase Orders,** costs cannot be marked as billable until the related **bill** is entered.

The necessary fields are automatically added to the forms when the option of tracking and billing customers for direct costs is turned on in **Account and Settings.** Tracking and billing options are explained in the **Turning on Features for Tracking and Billing Direct Expenses** section of this chapter.

For example, the form for entering a **Check** looks something like Figure 10.32 after the tracking feature is turned on.

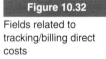
Figure 10.32

Fields related to tracking/billing direct costs

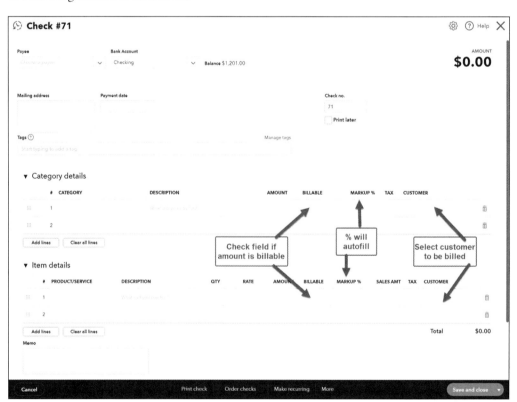

The **BILLABLE** field must be checked. The **CUSTOMER** must also be selected. This would be the **project** name if projects existed for the customer.

In the **Category details** section, the default markup % identified on the **Expenses** tab of **Account and Settings** will automatically display in the **MARKUP %** field if the line is marked as **billable**. The percent can be changed.

The **MARKUP %** field calculations are more complicated in the **Item details** section.

- If there is no default cost listed in the **product** or **service** item record, the default markup rate set in **Account and Settings** will display and will be used to determine the **SALES AMT**.

- If there is a default cost listed in the **product** or **service** item record, QBO autofills the **AMOUNT** and **SALES AMT** fields with the default **cost** and default **sales price/rate** amounts identified in the **product** or **service** item record when the item is initially selected in the **PRODUCT/SERVICE** field and the line is marked as billable. The **MARKUP %** field autofills with the percentage difference between the two fields. For example, let's say wheelbarrows were sold by Craig's. If the default **cost** is $31.25 and the default **sales price/rate** is $68.75, the **MARKUP %** would show as 120% ($68.75 – $31.25 = $37.50. $37.50/$31.25 = 1.2 (120%)).

> **BEHIND THE SCENES** Technically, QBO is using a gross margin calculation, not a markup calculation here. If markup was used, the sales amount for an item with a cost of $31.25 and a markup of 120% would be $37.50. ($31.25 × 1.2 = $37.50)

- If the **AMOUNT** field (the cost) is changed, the **SALES AMT** field will automatically change to provide the same margin. For example, let's say the **AMOUNT** field in our wheelbarrow example was changed from $31.25 to $50. The **SALES AMT** field would automatically change to $120 ($120 – $50 = $70; $70/$50 = 1.2 (120%)).
  - $120 would be the amount used when the cost was later billed to the customer on an **invoice**.
  - The item record defaults are not changed.
- If the **MARKUP %** field was changed, the **SALES AMT** would again automatically change. Back to that wheelbarrow: If the **AMOUNT** was $50 and the **MARKUP %** was changed from 120% to 90%, the **SALES AMT** would change to $95 ($95.00 – $50.00 = $45.00. $45.00/50.00 = .9 (90%)).

> **!** **WARNING:** When an independent contractor performs services for a company's clients and the company bills those hours at a marked up rate, the billable hours are normally entered through **timesheets**. Those hours are then available to add to the customer **invoice** using the rate set in the **service** item record. To avoid duplication, users must be careful not to mark those same hours as **billable** when the contractor's **bill** is recorded in QBO. For tracking purposes, only the **service** item and customer or project name should be identified on the **bill**.

Enter a billable cost for Craig's Design and Landscaping.
(Craig's Design staff work overtime on the Cool Cars job at the client's request. Craig stops at Bob's Burger Joint to pick up dinner for the crew and pays with a check. He decides to bill the client for the meal but not charge them a markup.)

PRACTICE
EXERCISE
10.4

(continued)

(continued from previous page)

1. Click **+ New** on the navigation bar.
2. Select **Check** in the **Vendors** column.
3. Select **Bob's Burger Joint** in the **Choose a payee** field.
   a.   Ignore any **Bills** displayed in the sidebar.
4. Leave **Checking** as the bank account.
5. **Make a note** of the **balance** (dollar balance) displayed next to Checking.
6. Use the current date as the **Payment date**.
7. Enter "83" as the **Check no.**
8. Select Meals and Entertainment as the **CATEGORY** in the **Category details** section.
9. Enter "43" as the **AMOUNT**.
10. Check the **BILLABLE** box.
11. Delete any **MARKUP %**. **TIP:** A markup field would only appear if you didn't log out after the last practice exercise.
12. Select **Cool Cars** as the **CUSTOMER**.
13. Click **Save and close**.

BILLING FOR TIME AND COSTS

LO 10-5 Describe and demonstrate how time and costs can be billed to customers in QBO

eLecture

If there are pending billable hours or costs for a specific customer, the details will appear in a sidebar when a customer is selected in an **invoice** form. At the time this book was written, billable hours and direct costs were not available when entering a **sales receipt**.

In the new **invoice** form, the sidebar will look something like Figure 10.33 for customers with billable hours and billable costs:

Figure 10.33

Example of sidebar of billable time and costs

The sidebar would look similar if you're using the **old layout** (**classic view**).

Billable charges can be added to the invoice by clicking **Add** in the sidebar for individual charges. If all hours and direct costs were added, the **invoice** would look something like Figure 10.34.

Figure 10.34

Example of invoice for billable hours and costs

Most fields (**RATES, QTY, DESCRIPTION**, etc.) can be changed before the form is saved.

> **BEHIND THE SCENES** The **rate** used on an **invoice** for labor hours will be the rate specified in the **service** item record, **not** the wage rate.

The markup is shown on a separate line for internal purposes only. This allows the user to change the tax status for either the item or the markup if necessary. In some states, markup amounts are subject to sales tax even if the cost itself is not.

The final invoice might look something like this:

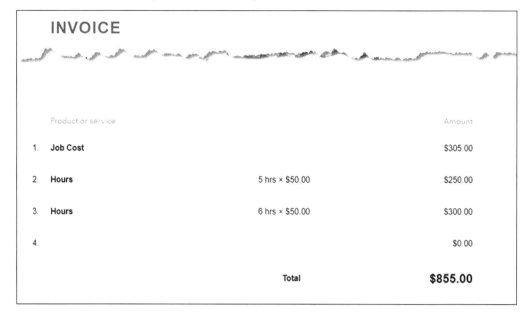

	Product or service		Amount
1.	Job Cost		$305.00
2.	Hours	5 hrs × $50.00	$250.00
3.	Hours	6 hrs × $50.00	$300.00
4.			$0.00
		Total	**$855.00**

BEHIND THE SCENES If an invoice is later deleted, the status of any included billable hours or costs automatically changes back to "billable."

PRACTICE
EXERCISE
10.5

Charge a Craig's Design and Landscaping client for time.
(Craig's Design decides to use project tracking. Direct costs are incurred on a patio job for Mark Cho. The time and costs are recorded and Mark Cho is invoiced.)

1. Change some settings for billable costs in Craig's Design.
   a. Click the ⚙ on the icon bar.
   b. Click Account and Settings.
   c. Open the Expenses tab and click the pencil icon in the Bills and expenses section. **TIP:** Track expenses and items by customer and Make expenses and items billable should be on. Track billable expenses and items as income should also be on. In a single account should be selected.
   d. Check the box next to Markup with a default rate of and enter 40 as the %.
   e. Click Save.
   f. Open the Advanced tab.
   g. Open the Chart of accounts section.
   h. Select Billable Expense Income as the Markup income account. (The same account will be used for both the cost and the markup.)
   i. Click Save.
   j. Click Done.

2. Change a service item setup to allow for recording work done by subcontractors.
   a. Click the ⚙ on the icon bar.

(continued)

(continued from previous page)

  b. Click **Products and services**.

  c. For **Installation**, select **Edit** in the **ACTION** column dropdown menu.

  d. Check the box next to **I purchase this product/service from a vendor**.

  e. Select **Cost of Labor** as the **Expense account**.

  f. Click **Save and close**.

3. Set up the new project using the default settings in Craig's Design.

  a. Click **Projects** on the navigation bar.

   i. If **Projects** does not appear in your navigation bar, you will need to activate that feature using the directions provided in Step 1 of Practice Exercise 10.1 before moving forward.

  b. Click **Start a project**.

  c. Enter "Cho Patio" as the project name.

  d. Select **Mark Cho** as the **Customer**.

  e. Click **Save**.

4. Enter a bill from Pam Seitz (a Craig's Design subcontractor) for the 36 hours she spent on the Cho project. **TIP:** Since time works differently in the test drive company, hours will be entered using the **bill** form.

  a. Click **+ New** on the navigation bar.

  b. Click **Bill**.

  c. Select **Pam Seitz** in the name field.

  d. Use the current date as the **Bill date** and **Net 30** as the **Terms**.

  e. Enter "PS-142" as the **Bill no.**

  f. Select **Installation** as the **Product/Service** in the first row of the **Item details** section.

  g. Enter "36" as the **QTY** and "40" as the **RATE**.

  h. Check the **BILLABLE** box.

  i. Leave the **MARKUP%** at 40.

   i. **Make a note** of the **SALES AMT**.

  j. Select Cho patio as the **CUSTOMER/PROJECT**.

  k. Click **Save and new**.

5. Enter a $250 billable charge for rental of equipment used on the Cho job.

  a. Select **Hicks Hardware** as the **Vendor**.

  b. Select **Net 30** as the **Terms**.

  c. Use the current date as the **Bill date**.

  d. Enter "1234" as the **Bill no.**

  e. Select **Equipment Rental** (a subaccount of **Job Expenses**) as the **CATEGORY** in the **Category details** section.

  f. Enter "$250" as the amount.

  g. Check the **Billable** box.

  h. Leave the **MARKUP%** at 40.

  i. Select Cho Patio as the **CUSTOMER/PROJECT**.

(continued)

(continued from previous page)

    j. Click **Save and close**.

6. Bill Mark Cho for time and costs.

    a. Click **+ New** on the navigation bar.

    b. Click **Invoice**.

    c. Select Cho Patio as the **Customer**. **TIP:** The project will be listed under **Mark Cho**.

    d. Select **Net 30** as the **Terms**.

    e. Use the current date as the **Invoice date**.

    f. On the sidebar, click **Add all**.

        i. **Make a note** of the **Balance due**.

    g. Click **Save and close**.

> **BEHIND THE SCENES** If a timesheet had been used to enter Pam Seitz's time, the billing rate used on the Mark Cho **invoice** would have been the rate identified in the **Installation** item record, not the billable amount calculated from the **bill** entered for Seitz's time.

7. Look at a Cho Patio profit report.

    a. Click **Projects** on the navigation bar.

    b. Click Cho Patio.

    c. Click the **Project Reports** tab.

    d. Click **Project Profitability**.

        i. **Make a note** of the profit on the Cho Patio job. **TIP:** QBO shows the profit as **NET INCOME**.

8. Click **Dashboard** on the navigation bar to exit the Project Center.

QuickCheck
10-1

> Employees at Davis Industries work for four hours on the Selma project. Their billing rate is $100 per hour. Their wage rate is $40 per hour. A special tool costing $35 was needed for the job. This cost of the tool plus a markup of 10% was charged to the client. How much profit did Davis make on the Selma project?

PREPARING PROJECT REPORTS

LO 10-6 Define and prepare **project** reports in QBO

There are a variety of reports that can be used to review and evaluate projects. Four of the most commonly used reports are:

- Profit and Loss by Customer
  - Shows revenues and direct costs for each **customer**, **project**, or **sub-customer**, by general ledger account, for a specified accounting period.
  - Accessed in the **Business Overview** section of **Reports**.

- Project Profitability
  - Shows revenues and direct costs for a specific **project**.
  - Accessed by clicking **Projects** on the navigation bar, clicking the **project** name, and opening the **Project Reports** tab.

- Unbilled Time and Expenses
  - Shows all unbilled direct costs and hours for a specific **project**.
  - Accessed by clicking **Projects** on the navigation bar, clicking the **project** name, and opening the **Project Reports** tab.

Prepare project reports for Craig's Design and Landscaping.

NOTE: Make sure you log out of QBO before beginning this Practice Exercise. Since no projects have been set up in the test-drive file, a report of profits on sub-customers is looked at in this Practice Exercise.

1. Click **Reports**.

2. Click **Profit and Loss by Customer** in the **Business Overview** section.
   a. In the **Report period** dropdown menu, select **All Dates**.
   b. In the **Display columns by** dropdown menu, select **Customers**.
   c. Click **Customize**.
   d. Open the **Filter** section.
   e. Check the **Customer** box.
   f. Select **0969 Ocean View Road** and **55 Twin Lane** in the dropdown menu for **Customer**. (Both are sub-customers of **Freeman Sporting Goods**. The same report could be used for **projects**.)
   g. Click **Run Report**.
   h. **Make a note** of the net income amount for each sub-customer.

3. Click **Dashboard** to close the report window.

PRACTICE EXERCISE 10.6

Davis earned a profit of $243.50. Total revenue related to hours was $400 (4 × $100 per hour). Total billed to Selma for the tool was $38.50 ($35 plus a 10% ($3.50) markup). Total cost to Davis was $160 for labor (4 × $40 per hour) and $35 for the tool.

ANSWER TO QuickCheck 10-1

CHAPTER SHORTCUTS

Add a project
1. Click **Projects** on the navigation bar.
2. Click **New project**.

Enter a timesheet
1. Click **Time** on the navigation bar.
2. Open the **Time entries** tab.
3. Click **Add time**.
4. Click the employee or contractor name.

Track or bill costs to customers.
1. On purchase form, enter **customer/project** name in the row.

2. Check **Billable** if amount will be billed to customer.
3. Accept or change any **MARKUP %**.

Charge customers for billable time and expenses
1. Click **+ New** on the navigation bar.
2. Click **Invoice**.
3. Choose the **customer** or **project**.
4. Add billable hours or costs appearing in the sidebar.

CHAPTER REVIEW

Matching

Match the term or phrase (as used in QuickBooks Online) to its definition.

1. project
2. unbilled charges report
3. account and settings
4. Project Profitability report
5. billable
6. add all
7. project customer
8. markup %

_____ customer associated with one or more separately tracked projects

_____ command included in the sidebar of an invoice form

_____ name of window used to select features and set preferences

_____ identifiable job tracked for a specific customer

_____ report that summarizes revenues and expenses by job

_____ status of hours or direct costs to be charged to customers

_____ list of all pending employee hours and direct costs identified as billable

_____ default rate used to increase direct cost billable to customer

Multiple Choice

1. An engineering company enters into "fixed fee" and "time and materials" contracts with its clients. The company _____.
   a. would have no reason for tracking labor hours for "fixed fee" jobs
   b. would have no reason for tracking labor hours for "time and materials" jobs
   c. would normally track labor hours for both "fixed fee" and "time and materials" jobs
   d. must track hours for "time and materials" jobs but should never track hours for "fixed fee" jobs

2. A **service** item must be selected for timesheet entries _____.
   a. only if time will be billed to a client
   b. only if the user tracks time by job but doesn't bill time to clients
   c. if the user tracks time by client (whether time is billed or not)
   d. None of the above. **Service** items must be identified for all timesheet entries.

3. The rates used to bill clients for employee or independent contractor hours are _____.
   a. found in the **service** item record
   b. found in the employee record
   c. always set when the **invoice** or **sales receipt** is created
   d. found in either the **service** item record or employee record, depending on preferences selected

4. Which of the following statements is not true?
   a. Both **expenses** and **product** or **service** items can be identified as **billable** as part of the entry of a vendor bill.
   b. Changes to billable hours and rates can be made in the **invoice** form.
   c. Changes to the **markup %** field can be made when billable items are entered on a **bill**.
   d. Changes to the **sales amt** field can be made when billable items are entered on a **bill**.

5. The **Profit and Loss by Customer** report is found in the _____ section of **Reports**.

    a. Sales and Customers

    b. Projects

    c. Business Overview

    d. For my accountant

BEYOND THE CLICKS—THINKING LIKE A MANAGER

Accounting: Home remodeling contractors typically enter into either fixed-fee or time-and-material contracts with clients. From a management point of view, what are the advantages and disadvantages of both types of contracts?

Information Systems: List five types of sensitive business or personal client information that might be stored on law firm networks. For each type of information, give an example of an outside party that might be interested in obtaining that information.

ASSIGNMENTS

4/1/24

Assignment 10A

Math Revealed!

Assignments with the
 MBC are available in <br> myBusinessCourse.

✓ Martin gets a phone call from Jan Sprint, Assistant Director of Instruction for Sacramento Public Schools. Many of Sacramento's middle schools have purchased the math games that Math Revealed! is selling. For the most part, the games have been great, but some of the students are struggling. Jan is hoping that Martin can provide some game training/tutoring assistance. Martin explains that he can't take on the tutoring work himself, but he'd be willing to find and supervise a tutor. The tutor would work with groups of 4-5 students for a fee of $50 per hour. Jan wants to give this a try at two of Sacramento's schools (American River and Capitol Hill).

✓ Martin talks with one of his former classmates (Kenny Chen). Kenny is interested in in the opportunity and agrees to start next Monday.

  ● Kenny will submit timesheets to you weekly.

  ● Martin agrees to pay him $35 per hour.

✓ Martin's not sure how much work he'll have for him and Kenny will continue to offer his services to other companies, so you plan to treat him as a **contractor** in QBO at least for the next couple of months. You set Kenny up through the **Contractors** tab in **Payroll**.

Name	Kenny Chen
Street address	259 Rosa Court
City, State	Sacramento, CA
Zip code	95822
SSN	999-88-7777
Terms	Net 15

TIP: After you set Kenny up as a **contractor**, you'll need to enter the **terms** in the vendor record.

✓ You turn on **Time tracking** in the **Time** tab of **Account and Settings**.

 HINT: To activate manual time tracking, you may need to click **Check out pricing**. Basic time tracking is selected at the bottom of the page. Return to the **Time** tab in **Account and Settings** to set your preferences.

  ● You set Monday as the **first day of work week**.

  ● You toggle **Show service field** and **Allow time to be billable** to On.

  ● You check the box next to **Show billing rate to users entering time**.

✓ You set up Sacramento Public Schools as a new customer.

- 2566 Central Avenue
  Sacramento, CA 95822
  Terms are Net 30.

✓ School administrators want information about the training hours by school so you decide to use the project feature in QBO. You add the two schools as projects. Both of them have Sacramento Public Schools as the Customer. These are ongoing projects so you don't add any dates. **TIP:** If Projects doesn't show up on the navigation bar, you'll need to activate the projects feature on the Advanced tab of Account and Settings.

- American River
- Capitol Hill

✓ You also set up a new service item. **TIP:** The service item is not taxable.

- Item name: Game tutoring
- Category: Tutoring
- Class: Tutoring
- Description: Tutoring with Math Games
- Sales price/rate: $50 (per hour)
- Income account: 400 Tutoring Revenue
- Cost: $35 **TIP:** To see the purchase section, check the I purchase this product/service from a vendor box.
- Expense account: 625 Contract labor
- Description: Tutoring with Math Games
- Preferred Vendor: Kenny Chen

✓ You write checks for the following:

- Rent $850 (Check 1137 to Pro Spaces)
- Monthly loan payment to the City Bank of Sacramento ($215.17—Check #1138) **TIP:** Some of that payment covers March interest accrued in Chapter 9.

4/2/24

✓ You pay the seven bills due on or before the 15th of April starting with check #1139. The total paid is $2,205.69 (six checks).

✓ Martin is putting on several workshops this month. For the first one at Teacher's College this Friday and Saturday, he needs to have a projector and screen. The College agrees to cover the cost.

- You turn on the features related to tracking and billing expenses and items by customer in the Expenses tab of Account and Settings.

  ▪ You make sure Track expenses and items by customer and Make expenses and items billable are both turned on.

  ▪ Martin has agreed on a markup of 5% with the Center. He thinks he'll use the same markup on other costs incurred for customers.

  ▪ You decide **not** to track the billable expenses and items as income.

  ▪ You do **not** check the Charge sales tax box.

  ▪ On the Advanced tab of Account and Settings, you click + Add new in the Markup income account field. You set up a new account (480 Markup Income) as the markup income account. You use Service/Fee Income as the detail type (Tax form section field).

✓ You decide to track reimbursable costs in a separate account. You set up a "Reimbursable costs" account as an Expense and an Other Miscellaneous Service Costs detail type. You make it a sub-account of 690 Other Costs and use "698" as the account number.

4/4/24

✓ Martin goes to Paper Bag Depot and picks up a projector and a screen. The total, including tax, is $482.45. He uses the VISA to make the purchase. You make it billable to Teacher's College. You enter "Projector and screen" in the description field. **TIP:** This is a non-taxable reimbursable cost for the Teacher's College workshop.

✓ You receive the $425 bill from Les & Schmidt for March's marketing services. The bill (#3358) is due in 30 days. **TIP:** This entry will offset the reversing entry you made to 642 Marketing expense in Chapter 9. The class was Workshops.

✓ Martin brings back some supplies he purchased from Paper Bag Depot. He bought them on account. (Invoice #8009, $139.25, Terms of Net 15) Tutoring supplies totaled $120.80. You charge those to the Supplies on Hand account. You expense the $18.45 in office supplies.

- You notice that the vendor changed the terms from Net 30 to Net 15. You use the Net 15 but intend to give them a call next week to follow up.

✓ Mad Math has developed a new online tutoring program using a video conferencing platform. The sales manager has decided to try selling some of the math games to their customers as part of the new online program, and he orders 5 consoles and 4 of each game (Fractions, Equations, and Ratios).

- You set up a new project for Mad Math (Online Program), so you can track this business separately.

- You decide to wait until you know the products have shipped before you create Mad Math's invoice.

✓ Since there is not enough inventory on hand to fill the order, Martin calls Cartables and asks them to ship the consoles and games (the entire order) directly to Mad Math. They agree and fax you a bill for $1,765 (#956224-53, dated 4/4). The terms are 2% 10, Net 30. You do **not** mark the items as billable. (You will be billing them using the regular sales price.) You do identify the project though. **TIP:** This bill is not related to PO-107.

4/5/24

✓ The Center for High Academic Achievement (Downtown) places an order for books. You ship them out and bill the Center for the following:

- 4 Statistics
- 10 Puzzles
- 10 Ready
- 5 Sports
- The invoice (INV-1028) totals $806. The terms are Net 30.

✓ You realize inventory is getting low on books so you create PO-108 to Books Galore for $790 for the following books:

- 15 Statistics
- 10 Puzzles
- 15 Ready
- 5 Sports

✓ All the products ordered from Cartables on PO-107 arrive this afternoon. Bill #956225-64, dated 4/5, for $1,140 is included. Terms are 2% 10, Net 30.

✓ Now that Martin knows the math games are being used in schools, he plans to contact some of the middle schools in neighboring towns. He also hopes to convince Sacramento Public Schools to order from Math Revealed. He'll wait before placing another order but he has great hopes for the products.

4/8/24

✓ Martin lets you know that the workshop for the Teacher's College was a success. You create an invoice (INV-1029) for the agreed-upon fee of $3,200 for the Educator Workshop plus the charge for the projector/screen setup and the related markup on the invoice. The workshop fee was a little higher than last time because Martin added some additional training sessions. The total invoice amount is $3,706.57. The terms are Net 30. "Projector and screen" should appear in the **DESCRIPTION** field for the $482.45 amount. If not, type it in.) **TIP:** Since Martin already paid sales tax on the projector and screen, tax is not charged to Teacher's College.

✓ You also hear that Cartables shipped the order to Mad Math so you prepare INV-1030 for the 5 **Consoles** and 12 games (4 of each of the three games). Since Mad Math is a reseller of these products, you uncheck the **TAX** box in each row. You'll wait until to see how much reselling Mad Math will do before you change the tax status in the customer record. The invoice totals $2,655. **TIP:** Make sure you select the **project** in the **Customer** field.

4/9/24

✓ You receive the following checks, all dated 4/9, in the mail:

- Dynamic Teaching—$3,150 in payment of INV-1025, check #743255
- Debbie Han—$242.63 in payment of INV-1023, check #4576
- Mad Math—$1,647.57 in payment of INV-1021 and INV-1027, check #88421

✓ You deposit the checks in the bank. The deposit totals $5,040.20.

✓ Kenny turns in his timesheet for the week.

Date	Day of the Week	Project	# of hours	Billable?
4/1	Monday	American River	5	Y
4/2	Tuesday	Capitol Hill	6	Y
4/3	Wednesday	Capitol Hill	5	Y
4/4	Thursday	American River	6	Y
4/5	Friday			
		Total Hours	22	

- You enter Kenny's timesheet data using **Game Tutoring** as the **service** item, the **project** as the **customer**, and **Tutoring** as the **class**. All hours are billable.
- You also enter a **bill** for the amount Martin owes Kenny ($770—KC409). You use **Game Tutoring** for the **service** item. Since you will be creating the invoice for Sacramento Public Schools using the timesheet hours, you don't make the charges billable here. **TIP:** Don't forget to charge the hours to the correct **project** though. Kenny spent 11 hours at Capitol Hill and 11 hours at American River.

✓ You create invoices for Kenny's work at Sacramento Public Schools. The invoices are dated 4/9 with terms of Net 30.

- American River (INV-1031) $550
- Capitol Hill (INV-1032) $550

✓ 40 students showed up at the Mathmagic clinic on Saturday (4/6). All paid cash. No products were sold this time. You create SR-117 to record the $1,000 in revenue.

4/10/24

✓ Martin created a new workshop he's calling "Making Math Come Alive." He's hosting the first workshop at Dynamic Teaching tomorrow.

- You set up the new **service** item (**Alive**). You use **Workshops** as the **category** and **Workshops** as the **class**. You select 405 Workshop Revenue as the **income account**. You leave the **salesprice/rate** blank. Workshops are not taxable.

✓ All items arrive for PO-108. The shipment from Books Galore includes invoice #2315, dated 4/10, for $790, with Net 30 terms.

✓ Martin needs some handheld calculators for his tutoring sessions. You purchase 5 of them at Math Shack for $24.75, using the credit card. Martin doesn't think these will last for more than a few months so you charge them to Supplies on Hand.

4/11/24

✓ Martin gave the Alive workshop at Dynamic Teaching today and he brought along a math instructor to help. Dynamic Teaching agreed to pay a fee of $1,400 for Martin's services and agrees to pay for the additional help including Martin's customary 5% markup. The instructor is charging $400.

- The instructor is:

  Olen Petrov
  > 2 Granite Way
  > Sacramento, CA 95822

- You set him up as a contractor. Olen is an individual so you enter his social security number (191-99-9911). His terms are Net 15.

✓ You enter Olen's bill for the $400 service (#04-13 with terms of Net 15) and make it billable to Dynamic Teaching. Since Dynamic Teaching had agreed to cover Olen's fee plus the 5% markup, you charge it to the Reimbursable costs account. You enter "Fee for Olen Petrov" in the DESCRIPTION field. The instructor's fee is not taxable.

✓ You create an invoice for Dynamic Teaching. (INV-1033) for $1,820. **TIP:** The Alive workshop fee was $1,400 before adding in Olen's fee plus the markup.

4/12/24

✓ You decide to pay all bills due on or before 4/30 plus the Cartables bill dated 4/5 (#956224-53). You create a vendor credit (DISC) to record the 2% early discount on the $1,765 bill from Cartables. This is a purchase discount. You assign Products as the class.

- There are four bills. Total amount paid is $3,038.95. The first check number is #1145.

✓ Martin gives you the information on his tutoring sessions for the first half of the month. He's been doing less individual tutoring lately. He's considering hiring some college students to grow that side of the business while he concentrates on workshops and product sales. All sessions were completed as of 4/15. You prepare invoices, dated 4/12, for the following.

- Alonso Luna—2 Persistence $210 (INV-1034, Net 15)
- Paul Richard—1 Crisis $250 (INV-1035, Net 15)
- Jon Savidge – 1 Crisis $250 (INV-1036, Net 15)

✓ You receive a $1,695 check (#97788212), dated 4/12, from the Center for High Academic Achievement in payment of INV-1026. You deposit the check and the cash from the Mathmagic clinic in the bank at the end of the day. The total deposit is $2,695.

✓ You receive two utilities bills in the mail. Both are dated 4/12.

- Sacramento Utilities for April services, #01-88991, $251.15. The terms are Net 30.
- Horizon Phone for April service, #121-1180, $46.22. The terms are Net 30.

4/15/24

✓ Martin gives you Kenny's timesheet for last week:

Date	Day of the Week	Project	# of hours	Billable?
4/8	Monday	American River	5	Y
4/9	Tuesday	American River	5	Y
4/10	Wednesday	Capitol Hill	6	Y
4/11	Thursday	Capitol Hill	5	Y
4/12	Friday			
		Total Hours	21	

- You enter Kenny's timesheet data using Game Tutoring as the service item, project as the customer, and Tutoring as the class for all billable hours.
- You also enter a bill, dated 4/15, for the amount Martin owes Kenny ($735—KC415). You use Game Tutoring for the service item. Since you will be creating the invoice for Sacramento Public Schools using the timesheet hours, you don't make the charges billable here. **TIP:** Don't forget to charge the hours to the correct project. Kenny worked 10 hours at American River and 11 hours at Capitol Hill.

✓ You create invoices for Kenny's work. The invoices are dated 4/15 with terms of Net 30.
- Capitol Hill (INV-1037) $550
- American River (INV-1038) $500

✓ You remember that the March sales taxes are due. You write a check (#1149) to remit sales taxes of $176.94. **TIP:** Use a check form if you can't pay the tax through the Sales Tax Center. The vendor is CDTFA (California Dept of Tax and Fee Admin). The class is Products.

✓ Martin brings you the receipt for lunch at Kathy's Coffee ($19.68) with Kenny. They met this morning to go over the school tutoring program. Kenny says it's going very well. The games are really helping the students and the teachers are pleased. He hopes to be able to expand the service to all Sacramento middle schools. Martin paid for their lunch with the VISA card. You consider this a staff relations cost and use the same class you use for Kenny's time.

✓ You want to give Martin a clear picture of operations so you make some adjusting journal entries, dated 4/15, related to activity in the first half of the month.
- You check the inventory. All counts agree to the quantities in QBO.
    - You notice some low stock items (Dry-Erase, Kit, and Notebooks). You're still waiting for the Kits to come in from PO-104. Martin says he'll put in an order before the next Mathmagic clinic for Notebooks and Dry-Erase.
- Tutoring supplies on Hand at 4/15 equal $144.30. There were no office supplies on hand. Martin is planning to restock tomorrow. You use Apr24.1 as the entry number.
- You adjust the following expense accounts so that they represent about one-half of April's expenses.
    - Rent expense should be $425
    - Utilities expense should be $150
    - Insurance expense should be $20
    - Depreciation expense should be $75
    - Interest expense should be $20
    - Accounting expense should be $250
    - **TIP:** In some of the above entries you'll be debiting expenses; in some you'll be crediting expenses. Consider using Other Prepaid Expenses and Accrued expenses in some of the adjustment entries.
- You ask Martin whether he has used the credit card to purchase gasoline in April. He says he hasn't needed to fill the tank.

Check numbers 4/15

Checking account balance:. . . . $ 9,581.44
Other current assets: . . . . $ 4,625.67
Total assets: $33,477.18
Total liabilities: $10,189.08
Net income for April 1–15:. . . . $ 7,135.79

Suggested reports for Chapter 10:
- Balance Sheet as of 4/15
- Profit and Loss (April 1–15)
    - Include a year-to-date column
- Profit and Loss by customer (4/1–4/15)
- Accounts Receivable Aging Summary as of 4/15
- Accounts Payable Aging Summary as of 4/15
- Inventory Valuation Summary as of 4/15
- Journal Report (4/1–4/15)
- Profit and Loss by Class (April 1–15)
- Sales by Product/Service Summary (April 1-15)

4/1/24

✓ Sally just got a call from Hiroshi Tanaka, the IT director at Delucca Deli, a Northern California deli chain. He had gotten Sally's name from the IT Director at Metro Market. They've decided to start expanding their operations and would like to hire Sally to make sure all their new stores are properly set up to use their in-house technology. They also want her to train all the new store managers. She is excited about the opportunity but explains that she wouldn't be able to do work herself. Hiroshi is fine with using assistants as long as Sally is available if needed. They agree on a rate of $75 per hour for the work.

✓ Sally gives Olivia Patel a call. Sally successfully worked with Olivia a few years ago on a large project and they've stayed in touch ever since. Olivia agrees to work with Sally on the Delucca project and will start this week.

 ● Sally agrees to pay Olivia $50 per hour.

 ● Olivia will submit timesheets to you weekly.

✓ Sally's not sure how much work she'll have for Olivia and Olivia will continue to offer her services to other companies, so you plan to treat her as a **contractor**. You set Olivia up in QBO through the **Contractors** tab in **Payroll** (on the navigation bar).

Name	Olivia Patel
Street address	3667 Admiral Avenue
City, State	Sacramento, CA
Zip code	95822
SSN	455-22-9874
Terms	Net 15

TIP: After you set up Olivia as a contractor, you will need to enter the **terms** in the vendor record.

✓ You turn on **Time tracking** in the **Time** tab of **Account and Settings**.

 HINT: To activate manual time tracking, you need to click **Check out pricing.** Basic time tracking is selected at the bottom of the page. Return to the **Time** tab in **Account and Settings** to set your preferences.

 ● You set Monday as the **first day of work week**.

 ● You toggle **Show service field** and **Allow time to be billable** to **On**.

 ● You check the box next to **Show billing rate to users entering time**.

✓ You set up Delucca Deli as a new customer.

 ● 3582 Expansion Drive
   Sacramento, CA 95822
   Terms are Net 15.

✓ Since the rates are higher for this type of work, you decide to set up a new nontaxable **service** item.

 ● Name: Group Train

 ● Category: Consulting and Installation

 ● Class: Consulting

 ● Description: Group software training at corporate location

 ● Sales price/rate: $75 (per hour)

 ● Income accounting: 400 Software Selection and Installation

 ● Cost: $50 **TIP:** To see the purchase section, check the **I purchase this product/service from a vendor** box.

 ● Description: Group software training at corporate location

- Expense account: 675 Contract labor
- Preferred vendor: Olivia Patel

✓ Although all **invoices** will be paid by Deli, management does want information about the hours by location so you decide to use the project feature in QBO. You add the first two locations as **projects**. All of them have Delucca Deli as the **customer**. These are ongoing projects so you don't add any dates. **TIP:** If you don't see **Projects** on the navigatino bar, you'll need to activate the **projects** feature on the **Advanced** tab of **Account and Settings**.

- Mendocino
- Sausalito

✓ You write checks for the following:

- Rent $650 (#1138) to Alki Property Management
- Monthly Dell Finance payment $150 (#1139) **TIP:** This includes March interest.

4/2/24

✓ Metro Market has asked Sally to put on another **Tips** workshop this month since some of its IT employees were unable to attend the one in March. Sally agrees to host the workshop at Hackers next Monday but this time she asks Metro Market to cover the rental space cost (plus a 10% markup). The company agrees and Sally finalizes arrangements with Hacker Spaces.

✓ You realize you're going to have to activate some features in QBO to handle billable costs.

- You decide to track reimbursable costs in a separate account. You set up a "Reimbursable costs" account as an **Expenses account type** and an **Other Miscellaneous Service Cost detail type** (**Tax form section** field). You make it a sub-account of **690 Other Costs** and use "698" as the account number.
- You turn on the features related to tracking and billing expenses and items by customer in the **Expenses** tab of **Account and Settings**. **TIP:** You may need to open **Make expenses and items billable** to see the options.
  - You decide **not** to track the billable expense as income.
  - You do **not** check the **Charge sales tax** box.
  - Sally will be charging a 10% markup on Metro Markets direct costs. She expects to use the same rate for other customers.
- You do want to track the markup amounts separately. On the **Advanced** tab of **Account and Settings**, you add a new account in the **Markup income account** dropdown menu (480 Markup Income). You use **Service/Fee income** as the **detail type** (**Tax form section** field).
- You write a check to Hacker Spaces for $600 (#1140) to pay for the rental space for the Metro Market workshop. You make it billable with a 10% markup. This will not be taxable. **TIP:** If you're going to bill the cost to Metro Market, it's a reimbursable expense.

✓ You receive a $1,000 check in the mail from Fabulous Fifties in payment of INV-1026. Check #87101 was dated 4/2.

✓ You deposit the check into the bank.

4/3/24

✓ Sally is putting on a workshop next week for Albus Software. It's a newly developed workshop she's calling "Getting to the Source of the Problem." You set up a new **service** item. You name it "Source." You leave the **Sales price** blank for now. Workshops aren't taxable. In case Sally asks Oscar or Olivia to help with the workshop, you select account 665 (Workshop helpers) as the **Expense** account. **TIP:** Choose the appropriate **category** and **class**.

✓ You pay all bills that are due before April 14th. You pay three bills, starting with check #1141, totaling $562.63.

4/4/24

✓ Both locations of Reyelle Consulting place an order for more **trackers** and for some of the management software products. They have quite a few professional services clients and they think they might be able to sell the product to them. They're going to start with a small order and see how it goes.

	Davis:	Sacramento:
Tracker	5	3
Engineering	1	0
Legal	0	1
Medical	1	0

- You create INV-1032 for the Davis location and INV-1033 for the Sacramento location. The invoice totals are $1,300 and $680 respectively. The terms are Net 30. Sally ships the order to Reyelle.

✓ Sally let you know that inventory of the management products is getting low and asks you to place the following orders:

- PO-107; Personal Software, 10 **Trackers**, Total $300
- PO-108; Abacus Shop; 3 each of **Engineering**, **Legal**, and **Medical**. Total $3,150

✓ You receive the following bills in the mail today. Both are dated 4/4.

- Sacramento Light and Power's April bill (for heat and light) #01-988811—$100.80. The terms are Net 30.
- Western Phone Company's April bill #9299-64 for $120.30. The terms are Net 30.

4/5/24

✓ mSquared Enterprises has referred a new customer to Sally. After talking with Sally, the new customer decides to hire Sally to do some work for them. You set up the new customer:

- Green Design
  254 Indiana St
  Sacramento, CA 95822
  Terms are Net 15.

✓ You realize that PO-106 (Personal Software) is still open. Since you just placed a new order yesterday, you call and tell Personal Software to cancel the remaining items on PO-106. You close the purchase order in QBO.

✓ You receive the $150 bill from Dovalina & Diamond for March's accounting services. The bill (#3425) is due in 30 days. **TIP:** This entry will offset the reversing entry you made to 631 Accounting and Consulting fees in Chapter 9.

✓ Olivia turns in her timesheet for the week.

Date	Day of the Week	Project	# of hours	Billable?
4/1	Monday			
4/2	Tuesday	Sausalito	4	Y
4/3	Wednesday	Mendocino	7	Y
4/4	Thursday	Mendocino	7	Y
4/5	Friday	Sausalito	6	Y
		Total Hours	24	

- You enter Olivia's timesheet data using **Group Train** as the **service** item, the **project** as the **customer**, and **Consulting** as the **class**. All hours are billable.
- You also enter a **bill** for the amount Sally owes Olivia ($1,200—OP405). You use **Group Train** for the **service** item. Since you will be creating the invoice for Delucca using the timesheet hours, you don't make the charges billable here. **TIP:** Don't forget to charge the hours to the correct **project** though. Olivia spent 10 hours at Sausalito and 14 hours at Mendocino.

✓ You create invoices for Olivia's work for Delucca Deli. The invoices are dated 4/7 with terms of Net 15.

- Sausalito $750 (INV-1034)
- Mendocino $1,050 (INV-1035)

4/8/24

✓ The **Tips** workshop for Metro Market was a success. You record the invoice (INV-1036) to Metro with terms of Net 15. The total amount billed (including the space rental cost and the $2,500 workshop fee) is $3,160.

✓ You receive the following checks in the mail:
- mSquared Enterprises—$1,200 in payment of INV-1027. Check # 8811
- Fabulous Fifties—$800 in payment of INV-1028. Check #88244

✓ You deposit the checks in the bank. The deposit totals $2,000.

✓ Sally called in very sick. She's got a terrible case of the flu and won't be able to be at the **Source** workshop. She has already called Olivia who is more than willing to help out.

4/10/24

✓ The **Source** workshop at Albus was a success. Olivia did a great job. She even was able to convince the company to purchase, for resale, some of Salish's accounting software products. You enter Olivia's bill for $500 (OP410), net 15. This is not a reimbursable cost so you charge it to the Workshop helper account. You identify Albus Software as the **customer** but you don't make the amount billable.

✓ Since Albus is reselling the products, you edit the customer record to identify them as tax exempt. The tax id number is SRY-789-4456-2.

✓ You also prepare the **invoice** for Albus (INV-1037). The total fee set by Sally was $2,500 for the **Source** workshop. The company also purchased two **Retailer** products.
- The invoice (INV-1037) totals $3,700. Terms are Net 30.

✓ You received the products ordered from Personal Software on PO-107 today. All the ordered items were included. The bill (#778922) totaled $300. Terms are Net 30.

✓ You pay all four bills due on or before 4/30.
- There are three checks, starting with check #1144. The amount paid totaled $4,000. (You take the $25 credit from Personal Software.)

✓ You remember that the sales taxes are due. You write a check (#1147) to remit sales taxes of $218.75 for March sales tax collected. **TIP:** Use a **check** form if you can't pay the tax through the Sales Tax Center. The vendor is CDTFA (California Dept of Tax and Fee Admin). The **class** is **Products**.

4/11/24

✓ You receive the following checks in the mail, all dated 4/11:
- Champion Law $1,500 in payment of INV-1031, Check #2045
- Lou's Barber Shop $480 in payment of INV-1029, Check #3811
- Reyelle Consulting $1,050 in payment of INV-1024 and INV-1025, Check #9759412. Reyelle takes the $50 available credit. **TIP:** Go back and read the *Applying Credit Memos To Open Invoices When Payments Are Recorded* section of Chapter 3 if you're having trouble applying the credit.

✓ Sally lets you know that she spent 4 hours on an urgent file repair for Leah Rasual. Leah paid the $240 with her VISA. You create a **Sales Receipt** (SR-111) for 4 hours of **File Repair (Fix)**.

✓ You deposit the checks received today into the bank account. The deposit totals $3,030.

✓ You record a second deposit for the credit card transaction less the 2% credit card fee. You assign the fee to the **Administrative class**. The deposit totals $235.20

4/12/24

✓ Sally emails you details of her client work for the last week. You prepare invoices, dated 4/12, for the following.

- Green Design 7 hours of **Set Up** ($525—INV-1038)
- mSquared Enterprises—5 hours of **Train** and 10 hours of **Fix** ($850—INV-1039)

✓ Sally gives you a receipt from Paper Bag Depot for $45.00. They were having a sale and she wanted to replenish a few of the office supplies to use over the next few months. She used the VISA card. You record the purchase and assign the transaction to the **Administrative class**.

✓ You received the products ordered from Abacus Shop on PO-108 today. All the ordered items were included. The bill (#8944-65) totaled $3,150.

✓ Sally meets with Olivia at The Blue Door to discuss progress on Delucca Deli. Olivia thinks everything's going well so far and is wondering if more projects will be coming later in the month. Sally agrees to check with Hiroshi at Delucca and will let her know. Sally uses the VISA to pay for the $105.82 lunch. She doesn't want to charge Delucca so you expense the amount to 678 Staff meetings expense. You don't charge the cost to any of the projects. You assign this to the **Administrative class**.

✓ Olivia turns in her timesheet for the second week of April. She completed the training for each Delucca location.

Date	Day of the Week	Project	# of hours	Billable?
4/8	Monday			
4/9	Tuesday	Sausalito	6	Y
4/10	Wednesday	Mendocino	4	Y
4/11	Thursday			
4/12	Friday			
		Total Hours	10	

- You enter Olivia's timesheet data using **Group Train** as the **service** item and the **project** as the **customer**. The **class** is **Consulting**. All hours are billable.
- You also enter a **bill** for the amount Sally owes Olivia for her work at Delucca ($500—OP412). You use **Group Train** for the **service** item. Since you will be creating the invoice for Delucca using the timesheet hours, you don't make the charges billable here. **TIP:** Don't forget to charge the hours to the correct **project** though.

✓ You create invoices for Olivia's work for Delucca Deli. The invoices are dated 4/12 with terms of Net 15.
- Sausalito $450 INV-1040
- Mendocino $300 INV-1041

✓ You suggest that Sally pay down the line of credit again. She agrees and you cut a check (#1148) for $1,500. **TIP:** Apply the full $1,500 to the loan balance. Sally will pay interest to the bank at the **end** of the month. You will accrue interest for the $1,500 (plus the unpaid balance on the line of credit) as part of your 4/15 journal entries.

4/15/24

✓ You and Sally are going to meet soon to go over the first 3 ½ months of the year. You want to give her a clear picture of operations so you make some adjusting journal entries related to activity in the first half of the month. You number the first entry Apr24.1.
- Supplies on Hand at 4/15 equal $150.
- You check the inventory. All counts agree to the quantities in QBO.
- You adjust the following expense accounts so that they represent approximately one-half of April's expenses.
  - Rent expense should be $325
  - Utilities expense should be $50.40
  - Telephone expense should be $60.15
  - Insurance expense should be $32.50
  - Depreciation expense should be $176.75
  - Interest expense should be $11.64
  - Accounting and consulting fee $175

- ■ Technical reading materials should be $50 (half month of the subscription to Advances in Software Design)
  - ● **TIP:** In some of the above entries you'll be debiting expenses; in some you'll be crediting expenses. Use Other Prepaid Expenses and Accrued Expenses as needed. Costs not attributable to a specific type of service or customer would be included in the **Administrative class**.

Check numbers 4/15

Checking account balance:	$12,037.42
Other current assets:	$12,075.05
Total assets:	$46,918.22
Total liabilities:	$ 8,244.34
Net income for April 1–15:	$ 7,269.94

Suggested reports for Chapter 10:

- ● Balance Sheet as of 4/15
- ● Profit and Loss (April 1–15)
  - ■ Include a year-to-date column
- ● Profit and Loss by Class (April 1–15)
- ● Profit and Loss by Customer (4/1–4/15)
- ● Accounts Receivable Aging Summary as of 4/15
- ● Accounts Payable Aging Summary as of 4/15
- ● Inventory Valuation Summary as of 4/15
- ● Journal Report (4/1–4/15)
- ● Sales by Product/Service Summary (April 1–15)

APPENDIX 10A WORKING WITH ESTIMATES

LO 10-7 Understand how **estimates** are created and managed in QBO

Construction contractors and other companies that enter into large, long-term contracts often provide up-front estimates of the total expected cost of the project to their clients. The estimates will normally list, in some detail, the various components of the job. As the work is performed, the company bills the client for the work completed.

An important benefit of estimates is that they define what is being included in the scope of the project. Clients that request changes to the original scope would be given an estimate related to the change. (These are often called "change orders.") In a time and materials job, well-constructed estimates help reduce misunderstandings between the client and the company.

Estimates can be used even when the company is charging a fixed fee for the job. In a fixed fee job, an estimate is used simply to define what work is included in the fee. The fixed fee amount would be changed only if the client requested additional work not specified in the original agreement.

Companies can create estimates in QBO and can use those estimates when billing for work performed.

If a company only invoices the client when the project is complete, an estimate is created and then used to prepare a single invoice. Quantities and prices can be changed when the invoice is prepared, but any changes are not saved to the original estimate.

If a company invoices the client as work is completed (the more typical arrangement), the progress invoicing feature must be activated.

Activating Progress Invoicing

Progress invoicing is activated on the **Sales** tab of **Account and Settings**.

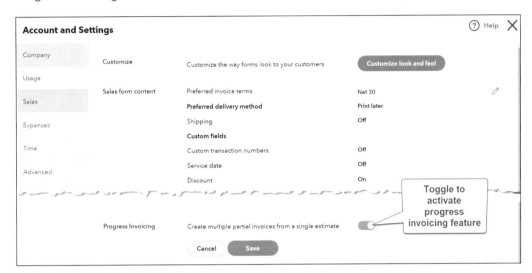

Figure 10A.1

Progress invoicing
activation window

Use the toggle button next to **Create multiple partial invoices from a single estimate** to turn the feature **On**.

 HINT: Progress invoicing requires a few changes to the invoice template. A popup request to update the template will need to be accepted before moving forward.

Creating Estimates

To create an **estimate**, click **+ New** on the navigation bar.

CUSTOMERS	VENDORS	EMPLOYEES	OTHER
Invoice	Expense	Single time activity	Bank deposit
Receive payment	Check	Weekly timesheet	Transfer
Estimate	Bill		Journal entry
Credit memo	Pay bills		Statement
Sales receipt	Purchase order		Inventory qty adjustment
Refund receipt	Vendor credit		Pay down credit card
Delayed credit	Credit card credit		
Delayed charge	Print checks		

Figure 10A.2

Access to estimate
form

Click **Estimate**.

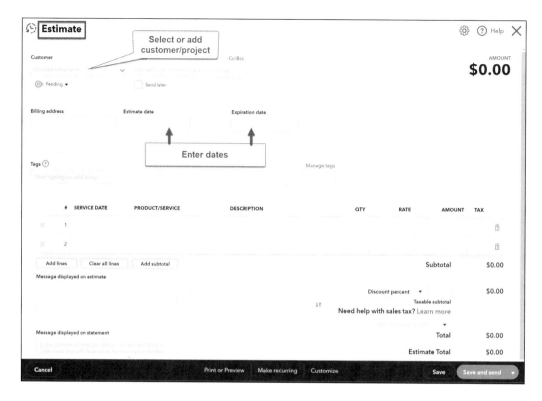

A client would normally be expected to either accept or reject an estimate in a reasonable period of time. If a client waits too long, costs to the company may have changed considerably. The date by which an estimate must be accepted is entered in the **Expiration date** field.

If the company set estimated dates for specific tasks, the **SERVICE DATE** column would be removed. Customizing forms is covered in Chapter 11.

A completed **estimate** might look something like Figure 10A.4.

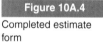

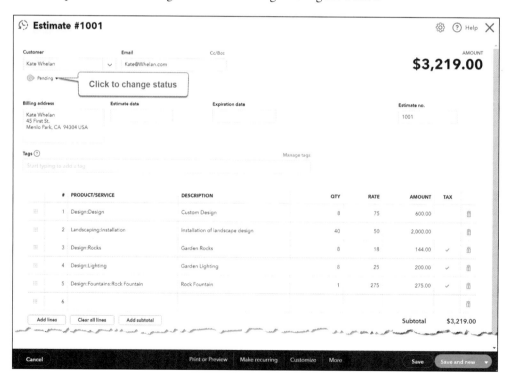

Once the client has reviewed and either accepted or rejected the estimate, the status can be changed by clicking the arrow next to **Pending**. The status options are:

Figure 10A.5
Estimate status options

Creating Invoices from Estimates

To bill for some or all of the **estimate**, click ➕ **New** on the navigation bar and click **Invoice**. (As of now, estimates cannot be billed through **sales receipts** in QBO.)

Select the client's name in the **Customer** field.

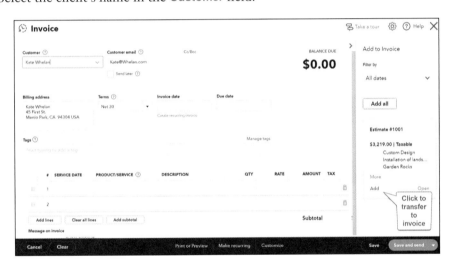

Figure 10A.6
Option to add estimate data to invoice

Click **Add** on the sidebar to transfer the information from the **estimate** to the **invoice**.

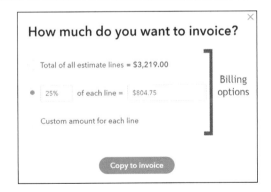

Figure 10A.7
Billing options in progress invoicing—first billing

When **progress billing** is activated, the next screen (Figure 10A.7) displays billing options.

- The estimate can be billed in full.

- A percentage of each line can be billed.

- An amount for each line can be billed.

If a percentage was selected, the initial invoice would look something like Figure 10A.8.

Figure 10A.8

First partial billing of estimate

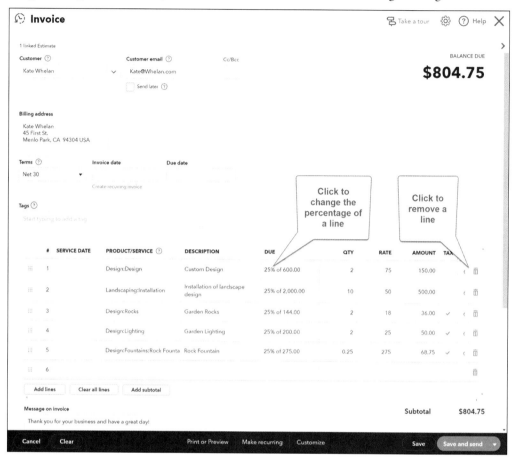

The process is repeated for all subsequent billings.

Figure 10A.9

Option to add remaining estimate data to invoice

The estimate is not changed to reflect prior billings so the sidebar will always show the original total.

Click Add to transfer the information from the estimate to the invoice.

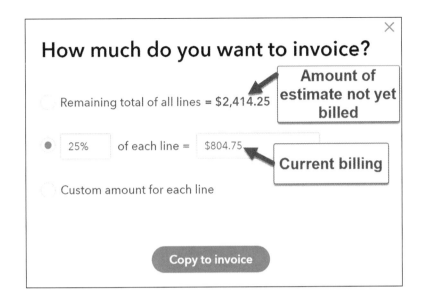

Figure 10A.10

Billing options in
progress invoicing—
second billing

The billing option screen will always show the balance remaining on the **estimate** (the
estimate total less amounts billed on any previous **invoices**). Users can choose to invoice
the balance, invoice a percentage of the **original** **estimate** (not a percentage of the current
balance), or invoice specific dollar amounts (by line item).

Summaries of billing activity will be displayed in the bottom right corner of each invoice form linked to the **estimate**. The summary on the final **invoice** might look something
like this:

Estimate #1001	$3,219.00
Invoice #1038	$804.75
This invoice (#1040)	$1,609.50
Invoice #1039	$804.75
Total invoiced	$3,219.00

Figure 10A.11

Summary of billing
activity added to
invoices linked to
estimates

Once all amounts have been billed, the **estimate** will be automatically marked as **closed**.

Creating Change Orders

Clients may request additional work during the project. To document those changes, a
change order is often created. In QBO, change orders can be created by using a copy of
the original estimate.

Figure 10A.12

Option to duplicate
estimate

Click **Copy** in the **More** menu of the original **estimate**.

Figure 10A.13

Estimate for a change
order

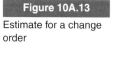

Creating Purchase Orders from Estimates

If **estimates** include **inventory** or **non-inventory** items that must be purchased specifically for the project, a company can create a purchase order directly from the **estimate** if the **purchase order** feature is activated.

HINT: **Purchase orders** must be created before the **estimate** is closed.

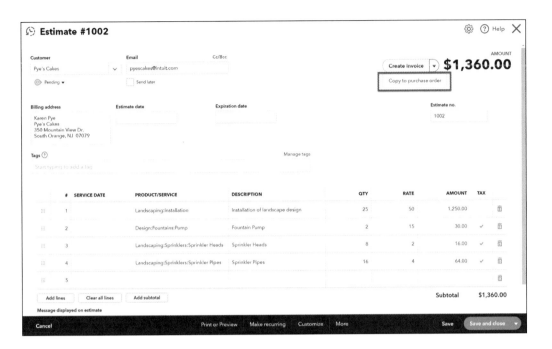

Figure 10A.14

Option to create
purchase order from
estimate

Click **Copy to purchase order** in the top right section of the estimate. (The **estimate** must be **saved** before the option to **Create invoice** or **Copy to purchase order** appear.)

The following message will appear:

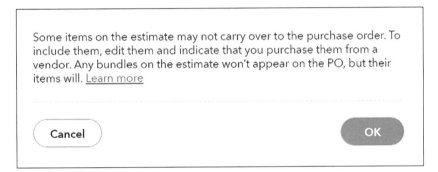

Figure 10A.15

Estimate warning
message

Click **OK**.

Only items with purchase information in the item record will be included on the **purchase order**. That would include **inventory** and **non-inventory** items and any **services** performed by subcontractors.

Figure 10A.16

Purchase order created from estimate

The **purchase order** is completed by adding a **vendor** and making any necessary changes. If the items included are purchased from multiple vendors, the **purchase order** would need to be copied.

Additional Tools

Road Map

	Learning Objective	Topic	Subtopic	Page	Practice Exercises	Videos
LO 11-1	Discuss and use tools available for customing reports in QBO [p. 11-2]	Saving customized reports		11-2	11.1	Saving customized reports
LO 11-2	Design a management report in QBO; interpret operating results for report period [p. 11-5]	Creating management report packages		11-5	11.2	Creating management report packages
LO 11-3	Explain how to create custom fields in QBO [p. 11-11]	Creating custom fields		11-11	11.3	
LO 11-4	Understand and demonstrate the process for creating customized sales forms in QBO [p. 11-13]	Customizing sales forms		11-13		Customizing forms
LO 11-5	Explain and demonstrate how to export reports from QBO to Excel [p. 11-17]	Exporting reports to Excel		11-17		
LO 11-6	Discuss the use of attachments in QBO [p. 11-19]	Uploading and managing attachments	Adding attachments to customer or vendor records	11-19		
			Adding attachments to transactions	11-20		
			Adding attachments directly to the Attachment lists	11-21		
LO 11-7	Understand and demonstrate the process for uploading receipts into QBO [p. 11-23]	Uploading receipts		11-23		

In this chapter, we will cover a few additional tools in QBO that can be very useful in practice.

SAVING CUSTOMIZED REPORTS

LO 11-1 Discuss and use tools available for customing reports in QBO

> **!** **WARNING:** In early 2023, Intuit started updating the customization tools on a few of the QBO reports. Directions for customizing the **Product/Service List** report were provided in APPENDIX 1A New Report Customization Tools. Other reports may have been updated after your textbook was printed. If you see a report that doesn't match the screenshot in your book, start by looking for an option to return to a previous version. In most cases, you'll see a link **Old layout** or **Switch to classic view**. If there is no link, check the Student Ancillaries page in myBusinessCourse for information about the updated form or ask your instructor.

The reports most commonly used by companies are automatically included in QBO. In addition, QBO makes it relatively easy to customize reports to meet the specific needs of a company.

For example, Craig's Design and Landscaping might create a Journal report in QBO that includes only sales transactions.

eLecture

Figure 11.1

Customized journal report

Craig's Design and Landscaping Services
Daily Sales Journal
November 8

DATE	NUM	CUSTOMER	ACCOUNT	DEBIT	CREDIT
11/08.	1001	Amy's Bird Sanctuary	Accounts Receivable (A/R)	$108.00	
		Amy's Bird Sanctuary	Landscaping Services		$100.00
		Amy's Bird Sanctuary	Board of Equalization Payable		$8.00
				$108.00	**$108.00**
11/08	1009	Travis Waldron	Accounts Receivable (A/R)	$103.55	
		Travis Waldron	Services		$103.55
				$103.55	**$103.55**
11/08,	1032	Travis Waldron	Accounts Receivable (A/R)	$414.72	
		Travis Waldron	Landscaping Services:Job Mater...		$300.00
		Travis Waldron	Landscaping Services:Job Mater...		$84.00
		Travis Waldron	Board of Equalization Payable		$30.72
				$414.72	**$414.72**
TOTAL				**$626.27**	**$626.27**

The above report was customized from the standard Journal report as follows:

- The date range was changed at the top of the screen.

- In the Customize sidebar:

  - Transaction types were filtered to include only invoices, sales receipts, and credit memos. (Filter section)

  - The NAME, TRANSACTION TYPE, and MEMO/DESCRIPTION columns were removed. The CUSTOMER column was added and moved to appear after the transaction number. (Rows/Columns section)

  - The title of the report was changed. (Header/Footer section)

Once the customized report is created, the report can be saved by clicking Save customization on the toolbar at the top of the report to open a final dialog box.

Figure 11.2
Setup fields for saving reports

In the dialog box, the user enters a name for the saved report. Users can also add it to a report group. In Share with, the creator of the report can select All, which allows all users to access the report, or None, which limits access exclusively to the creator.

 HINT: If **specific dates** are listed in the date range fields of a saved report, those dates will be retained when the report is later accessed. (That is, the report dates will not automatically update.) If a date range is selected in the Report period dropdown menu (This Month-to-date, Last year, etc.), the report will be updated appropriately.

Saved reports can be accessed by clicking Reports on the navigation bar and opening the Custom reports tab.

Figure 11.3
Custom reports list

All reports in a report group can be scheduled for delivery by email on a scheduled basis. Click Edit in the ACTION column of the report group to set up the email schedule:

Figure 11.4
Access to set up custom report email schedule

Turn Set email schedule to ON.

Figure 11.5

Custom report email options

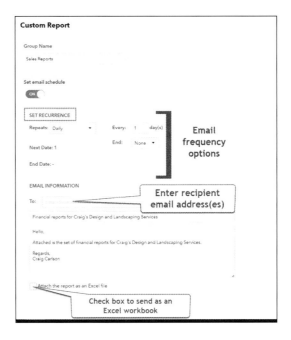

Users can set when reports are sent in the **SET RECURRENCE** section. Reports are sent as PDF files unless **Attach the report as an Excel file** is selected.

PRACTICE
EXERCISE
11.1

Customize and save a report for Craig's Design and Landscaping.
(Craig wants to review a monthly report of sales invoices.)

1. Click **Reports** in the navigation bar and open the **Standard** tab.

2. Click **Transaction List by Customer** in the **Sales and Customers** section.

   a. If you see **Switch to classic view** at the top of the screen, the report has been updated. Click **Switch to classic view** to complete this Practice Exercise.

3. Select **This Month-to-date** as the **Report period** and click **Run report**.

   a. If no data appears in the report, select **Last Month** as the **Report period** and click **Run report**.

4. Click **Customize**.

5. Open the **Rows/Columns** section.

   a. Select **None** in the **Group by** dropdown menu.

   b. Click **Change columns**.

   c. Uncheck **Posting**.

   d. Click the **keypad** icon next to **Num** and drag it to the top of the column.

   e. Close the **Rows/Columns** section.

      i. **TIP:** Sections are closed by clicking the triangle to the left of the section name.

6. Open the **Filter** section.

   a. Check the **Transaction type** box.

   b. Check **Invoice** in the dropdown menu.

   c. Close the **Filter** section.

(continued)

(continued from previous page)

7. Open the Header/Footer section.

   a. Enter "Monthly Invoices" in the Report title field.

8. Click Run report.

9. **Make a note** of the AMOUNT for Invoice #1037.

10. **Make a note** of the ACCOUNT for #1034.

11. Click Save Customization.

12. Leave Monthly Invoices as the Custom report name.

13. Click Add new group.

14. Enter "Sales Reports" as the New group name.

15. Click Add.

16. Select None in the Share with dropdown menu.

17. Click Save.

18. Click Back to report list (top left corner of the report page).

19. Open the Custom reports tab.

20. Verify that your new report and report group appear in the list.

CREATING MANAGEMENT REPORT PACKAGES

There are certain reports that are commonly shared with management every month. The financial statement group is one example. One method for sharing reports was described in the SAVING CUSTOMIZED REPORTS section of this chapter.

QBO has also set up a number of more formal management report packages that can be edited to fit the needs of the company.

To access management reports, click Reports on the navigation bar and select the Management reports tab.

LO 11-2 Design a management report in QBO; interpret operating results for report period

eLecture

Figure 11.6

Management report list

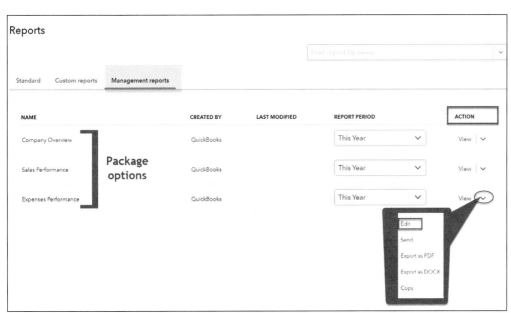

In most company files, you'll see the three management report options (packages) that appear in Figure 11.6. If you only see two options, review the **HINT** on this page.

- **Company Overview**
  - The default package includes a **Balance Sheet** and a **Profit and Loss** report.
- **Sales Performance**
  - The default package includes an **A/R Aging Detail**, a **Sales by Customer Summary**, and a **Profit and Loss** report.
- **Expenses Performance**
  - The default package includes an **A/P Aging Detail**, an **Expenses by Vendor Summary**, and a **Profit and Loss** report.

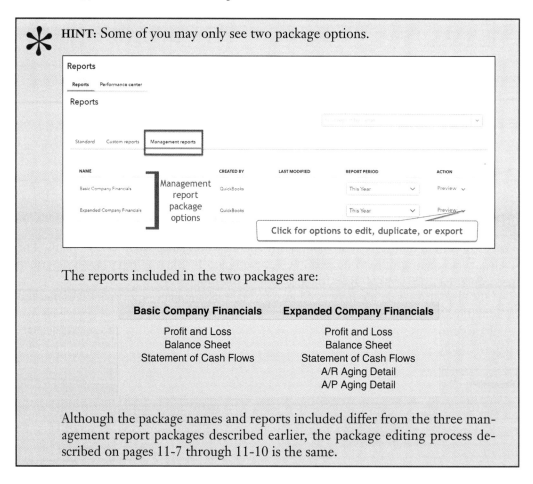

HINT: Some of you may only see two package options.

The reports included in the two packages are:

Basic Company Financials	Expanded Company Financials
Profit and Loss	Profit and Loss
Balance Sheet	Balance Sheet
Statement of Cash Flows	Statement of Cash Flows
	A/R Aging Detail
	A/P Aging Detail

Although the package names and reports included differ from the three management report packages described earlier, the package editing process described on pages 11-7 through 11-10 is the same.

Each report package includes a title page, table of contents, two pages for adding commentary, and the default group of reports. The reports included and other features can be edited by selecting **Edit** in the **ACTION** column dropdown menu highlighted on Figure 11.6.

If the **Company Overview** management report was selected for edit, the initial screen would look something like Figure 11.7.

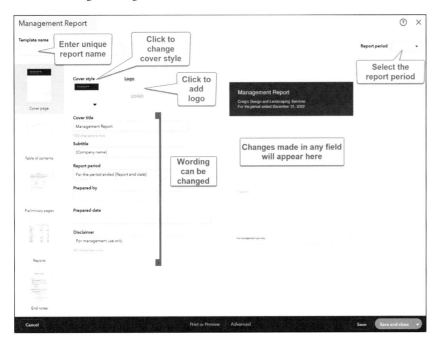

Figure 11.7

Cover page screen for Company Overview management report

Changes to the **cover page** of the report are made on the first screen. (The **template name** can also be changed here.) The **Report period** is selected in this screen, and users can select from a number of different **cover styles**. The company logo can also be added to the cover. (Logos are uploaded to QBO in the **Company name** section on the **Company** tab of **Account and Settings**.)

Open the **Table of contents** tab (left navigation bar).

Figure 11.8

Table of contents screen for Company Overview management report

Reports included in the package will be displayed on the **Table of Contents** screen. Default reports can be removed and other reports added on the **Reports** tab. To remove the **Table of Contents**, uncheck the box in the top left corner of the screen.

Open the **Preliminary pages** tab.

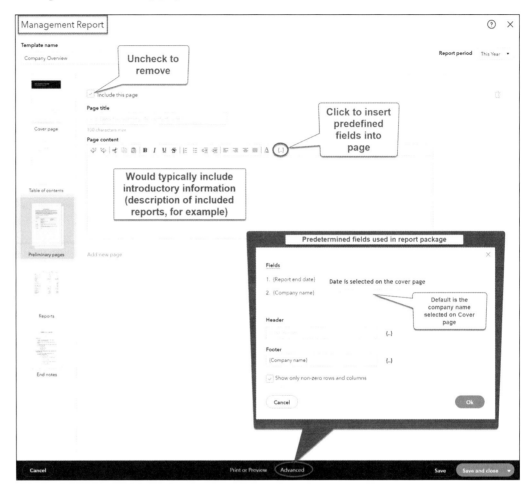

The purpose of **preliminary pages** is to give users a place to add introductory or explanatory information. There is certain information (predetermined fields) that can be automatically inserted into the page by clicking the **{..}** link on the toolbar. The predetermined fields can be accessed through the **Advanced** link in the black bar at the bottom of the screen. They include the company name and the report date. **Preliminary pages** do not need to be included in the management report.

Open the **Reports** tab.

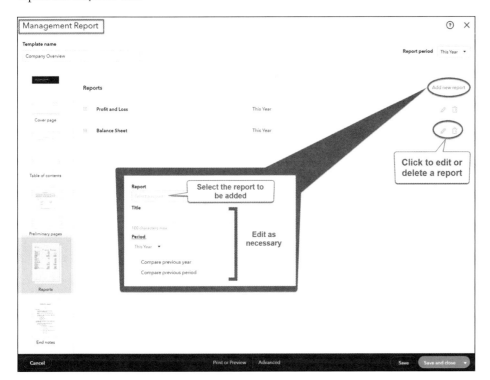

Figure 11.10
Report selection screen for Company Overview management report

Financial reports to be included are identified on the **Reports** tab. Reports (standard or customized) can be added or deleted. In addition, basic editing can be done on some of the reports by clicking the **pencil** icon. For example, on the Profit and Loss and Balance Sheet report, the title and period covered can be edited. Comparative information (previous year or previous period) can also be added.

Open the **End notes** tab.

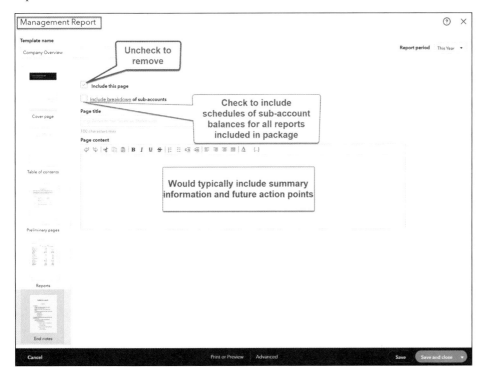

Figure 11.11
End notes screen for Company Overview management report

End notes, like preliminary pages, are optional. Final conclusions about financial operations or information about future plans could be included here.

Management report packages typically include condensed reports (parent accounts/categories only). If the box next to Include breakdown of sub-accounts is checked, separate schedules of all sub-accounts related to included reports will be added to the package.

If changes have been made to the defaults provided by QBO, a field for entering a new report name would appear after clicking Save and close.

> **✳ HINT:** Reports can be immediately emailed to other users after edits are made by clicking Send on the Save and close dropdown menu. They can also be emailed later by selecting Send in the ACTION column dropdown menu in the Report Center (Management Reports tab).

PRACTICE EXERCISE 11.2

Create a management report for Craig's Design and Landscaping.
(Craig wants a full sales management report.)

1. Click Reports in the navigation bar.

2. Open the Management reports tab.

3. Select Edit in the ACTION column dropdown menu of the Sales Performance row. **TIP:** If you don't have a Sales Performance package, edit the Expanded Company Financials package.

4. On the Cover page tab, enter "Sales and Customer Reports" as the Template name.

   a. Select This Quarter in the Report period dropdown menu (top right corner of screen).

   b. Select a different Cover style.

      i. **Make a note** of the number of available styles.

   c. Enter "Sales Report" as the Cover title.

   d. Enter your name in the Prepared by field.

   e. Enter the current date in the Prepared date field.

5. Open the Table of contents tab.

   a. Make sure Include Table of Contents is checked.

6. Open the Preliminary pages tab.

   a. Enter "Summary" as the Page title.

   b. Enter "Package includes sales data for the current month. Questions should be forwarded to Accounting." in the Page content box.

7. Open the Reports tab.

   a. Click the trash icon next to all reports other than the A/R Aging Detail report.

   b. Click Add new report.

      i. Select the Sales by Customer Summary report.

      ii. Leave the Title and Period as is.

   c. Click Add new report again.

      i. Select Collections Report.

      ii. Leave the Title and Period as is.

(continued)

(continued from previous page)

8. Open the End notes tab.

    a. Enter "Action Plan" as the Page title.

    b. Enter "A/R clerk will follow up, by phone, on all past due accounts by Monday" in the Page content box.

9. Click Save and close.

10. Your new report should now appear on the Management Report screen. If it doesn't, try refreshing your browser.

11. Click View in the ACTION column.

    a. **Make a note** of the amount owed by Mark Cho on Invoice #1035. **TIP:** This invoice will show up on the A/R Aging Detail report.

12. Click Close.

CREATING CUSTOM FIELDS

Although QBO provides many fields for tracking information, companies may need additional fields not currently built in to QBO.

LO 11-3 Explain how to create custom fields in QBO

For example, a Sales representative field on sales forms would be very useful for companies that pay commissions to their sales staff. A purchasing agent field on purchase orders might be useful for companies that want to track purchases made by various employees.

QBO allows users to add up to three custom fields that can be used in most sales transactions and up to three custom fields for use in purchase orders.

Custom fields are included in All Lists (accessed through the ⚙ on the icon bar).

Figure 11.12

Access to custom fields

Lists

Chart of Accounts
Displays your accounts. Balance sheet accounts track your assets and liabilities, and income and expense accounts categorize your transactions. From here, you can add or edit accounts.

Recurring Transactions
Displays a list of transactions that have been saved for reuse. From here, you can schedule transactions to occur either automatically or with reminders. You can also save unscheduled transactions to use at any time.

Products and Services
Displays the products and services you sell. From here, you can edit information about a product or service, such as its description, or the rate you charge.

Product Categories
A means of classifying items that you sell to customers. Provide a way for you to quickly organize what you sell, and save you time when completing sales transaction forms.

Custom Form Styles
Customize your sales form designs, set defaults, and manage multiple templates.

Payment Methods
Displays Cash, Check, and any other ways you categorize payments you receive from customers. That way, you can print deposit slips when you deposit the payments you have received.

Terms
Displays the list of terms that determine the due dates for payments from customers, or payments to vendors. Terms can also specify discounts for early payment. From here, you can add or edit terms.

Attachments
Displays the list of all attachments uploaded. From here you can add, edit, download, and export your attachments. You can also see all transactions linked to a particular attachment.

Tags
Displays the list of all tags created. You can add, edit, and delete your tags here.

Custom Fields
Sort, track, and report the information that matters to you. Add custom fields to your forms so that you can capture more business-related info.

Click **Custom Fields**.

Click **Add custom field**.

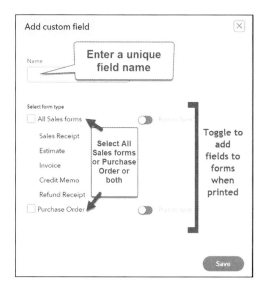

The label for the new field is entered in the **Name** field. Users then select whether the field
applies to sales forms or purchase orders or both.

If the user checks the **All Sales forms** box, the new field will appear on all sales transactions other than **delayed credits** and **delayed charges**. Currently, the only purchase form
that can include custom fields is the **purchase order**.

Custom fields are only visible to internal users (individuals creating transactions in
QBO) unless **Print on form** is toggled on. Click **Save** to add the new field to QBO.

The custom field list for a company that has created three fields (two for sales forms
and one for purchase orders) is shown in Figure 11.15.

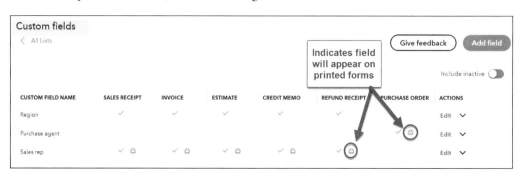

The **Purchase agent** and **Sales rep** fields will appear on printed forms. The **Region field** will only be visible to internal users.

PRACTICE
EXERCISE
11.3

Add some custom fields for Craig's Design and Landscaping.
(Craig wants to include the project manager initials as a custom field on invoices and the project manager and the purchasing agent initials as a custom field on purchase orders.)

1. Click the ⚙ in the icon bar.

2. Click **All Lists**.

3. Click **Custom Fields**.

4. Click **Add a custom field**.

5. Enter "Project Manager" as the **Name**.

6. Check **All Sales Forms**.

7. Toggle **Print on form** on.

8. Click **Save**.

9. Use your mouse to hover over the printer icon that appears in the **INVOICE** column.
   Make a note of the message displayed.

CUSTOMIZING SALES FORMS

QBO has designed the basic sales forms needed in a business (**invoices**, **sales receipts**, and **estimates**). Most likely, however, a company will want to customize these forms by adding the company logo, changing descriptions, or adding or deleting information included in the form.

Basic customization of the new **invoice** form, first released in early 2023, was covered in the **Recording Sales on Account** section of Chapter 3.

Sales receipt and **estimate** forms can also be customized.

LO 11-4 Understand and demonstrate the process for creating customized sales forms in QBO

> **!** **WARNING:** If Intuit has released new **sales receipt** and **estimate** forms by the time you're reading this book, revised instructions for customizing forms will be posted in Student Ancillaries (accessible to you if you're using my-BusinessCourse). If you're not using myBusinessCourse, your instructor will provide those directions to you. The instructions below assume no changes to those forms.

A **sales receipt** will be used to demonstrate the customization process.

Open the form by clicking **+ New** on the navigation bar and selecting **Sales receipt**.

Figure 11.16

New form style access

Click **Customize** in the menu bar at the bottom of the form.
Select **New style**.

Figure 11.17

Design tab of custom form window

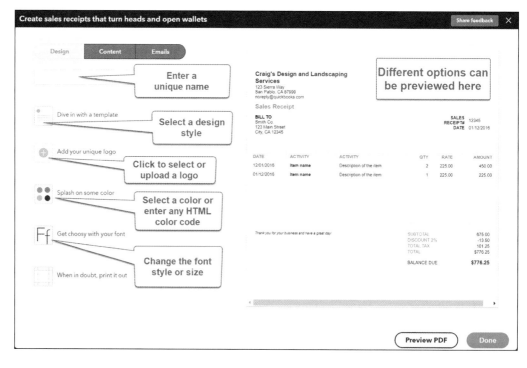

On the **Design** tab, the style of the form is set up. Clicking **Dive in with a template** displays six different invoice styles. The style differences include colors, font, and basic layout.

Users can further change colors and fonts on the selected style by clicking **Splash on some color** and **Get choosy with your font**. A company logo can also be added to the form.

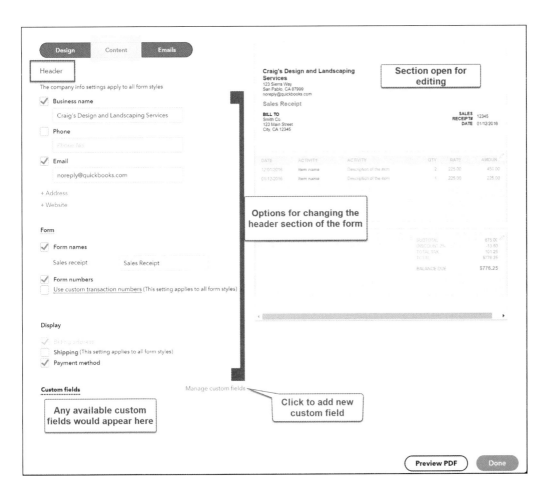

Figure 11.18

Content tab of custom form window (header section open for editing)

The **Content** tab includes options for adding or removing header and footer information and options for including various columns in the body of the form. Clicking the **pencil** icon in a section of the form opens it for editing. The options displayed on the left side of the screen depend on the section open for editing. The **Header** section of the form is open for editing in Figure 11.18. Fields displayed (including custom fields) can be added or removed.

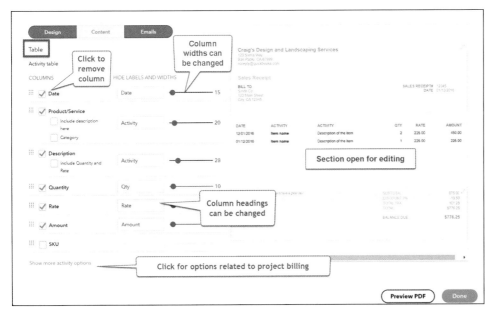

Figure 11.19

Content tab of custom form window (body section open for editing)

The body of the form is open for editing in Figure 11.19. (**EDIT LABELS AND WIDTHS** was clicked to show options.) Columns can be added or removed. Label and column widths can be changed as well.

Figure 11.20

Content tab of custom form window (footer section open for editing)

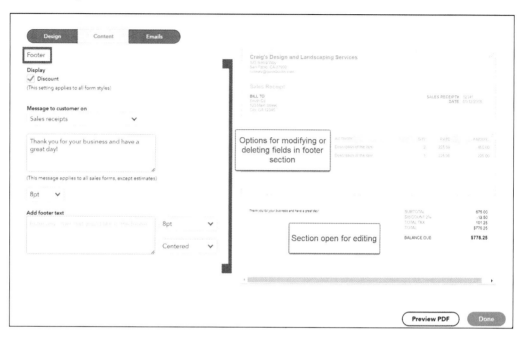

The **Footer** section of the form is open for editing in Figure 11.20. Text can be added or edited on customer messages. Users can also select whether to display discounts or deposits.

Figure 11.21

Emails tab of custom form window

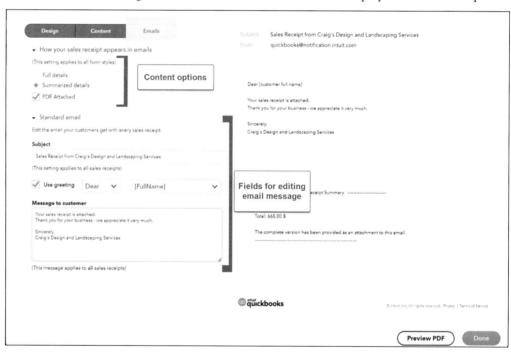

Users can create a custom email message on the **Emails** tab.

Using Customized Forms

Once a custom form has been created, it can be reused for future transactions.

Figure 11.22

Custom form center

Open the **Customize** dropdown menu in the black bar at the bottom of the form, and select the customized report name.

There is no practice exercise for this section. You will be creating a custom form as part of the Chapter 11 assignment, so use the directions above to help you.

EXPORTING REPORTS TO EXCEL

There are a number of reasons that a user might want to export a QBO report to Excel:

LO 11-5 Explain and demonstrate how to export reports from QBO to Excel

- The report format cannot be modified sufficiently in QBO to meet the needs of the users.

- A user might want to create a report that combines QBO data with data maintained elsewhere.

- A user might want to use Excel analysis tools on QBO data.

To export a report, the report window must be open.

Figure 11.23

Tool for exporting report to Excel

On the dropdown menu next to the **export** icon, click **Export to Excel**. A balance sheet exported to Excel for Craig's Design and Landscaping Services is displayed in Figure 11.24.

Figure 11.24

Example of report
exported to Excel

	A	B
1	**Craig's Design and Landscaping Services**	
2	**Balance Sheet**	
4		
5		Total
6	ASSETS	
7	Current Assets	
8	Bank Accounts	
9	Checking	1,201.00
10	Savings	800.00
11	Total Bank Accounts	$ 2,001.00
12	Accounts Receivable	
13	Accounts Receivable (A/R)	5,281.52
14	Total Accounts Receivable	$ 5,281.52
15	Other Current Assets	
16	Inventory Asset	596.25
17	Undeposited Funds	2,062.52
18	Total Other Current Assets	$ 2,658.77
19	Total Current Assets	$ 9,941.29
20	Fixed Assets	
21	Truck	
22	Original Cost	13,495.00
23	Total Truck	$ 13,495.00
24	Total Fixed Assets	$ 13,495.00
25	TOTAL ASSETS	$ 23,436.29

Formatting in Excel will be consistent with the formatting in QBO. Formulas for subtotals and totals will be retained in Excel, as can be seen in Figure 11.25:

Figure 11.25

Formulas in report
exported to Excel

	A	B
1	**Craig's Design and Landscaping Services**	
2	**Balance Sheet**	
3		
4		Total
5	ASSETS	
6	Current Assets	
7	Bank Accounts	
8	Checking	=1201
9	Savings	=800
10	Total Bank Accounts	=(B8)+(B9)
11	Accounts Receivable	
12	Accounts Receivable (A/R)	=5281.52
13	Total Accounts Receivable	=B12
14	Other Current Assets	
15	Inventory Asset	=596.25
16	Undeposited Funds	=2062.52
17	Total Other Current Assets	=(B15)+(B16)
18	Total Current Assets	=((B10)+(B13))+(B17)
19	Fixed Assets	
20	Truck	=13495
21	Total Fixed Assets	=B20
22	TOTAL ASSETS	=(B18)+(B21)

There is no practice exercise for this section. You may be exporting a report to Excel as part of your Chapter 11 assignment. If so, use the directions above to help you.

UPLOADING AND MANAGING ATTACHMENTS

Companies generally have a variety of documents specific to their customers and vendors. Examples include:

LO 11-6 Discuss the use of attachments in QBO

- Contracts with customers or vendors
- Sales orders from customers
- Lease agreements related to equipment or facilities
- Correspondence with customers or vendors

These documents can be uploaded to QBO and linked to customer or vendor records or to specific transactions. Having ready access to those documents and being able to attach them to customer/vendor records in QBO or to QBO forms can save a significant amount of time for users.

Documents can be uploaded in a variety of file formats (PDF, DOC, XLSX, JPG, etc.). There is no limit to the number of attachments that can be uploaded to a company file, but there is a 20MB file size limit to a single attachment.

Adding Attachments to Customer or Vendor Records

Customer- or vendor-specific documents would generally be added to the appropriate vendor record. For example, a completed 1099 Form for an independent contractor could be added to the contractor's vendor record.

Click **Expenses** on the navigation bar.

Click the **Vendors** tab and click the appropriate vendor name to open the vendor record.

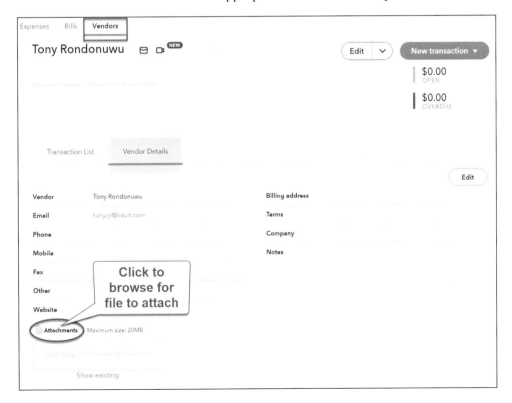

Figure 11.26

Attachments section of vendor record

On the **Vendor Details** tab, click the **paperclip** icon and locate and click the document to be added to the record or drag and drop the document into the **Attachments** box.

Figure 11.27

Example of file uploaded to vendor record as an attachment

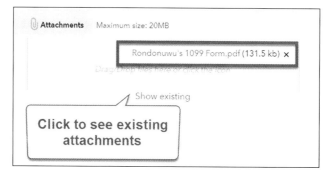

> ❗ **WARNING:** Clicking the X next to the attachment will permanently delete it. Users should make sure another version of the document is retained outside of QBO.

Adding Attachments to Transactions

Documents can also be added to any QBO transaction form. For example, a landscaping contractor (like Craig's) could add a picture of a completed project to a customer **invoice**.
    Click **+ New** on the navigation bar and select **Invoice**.

Figure 11.28

Attachments section of an invoice form

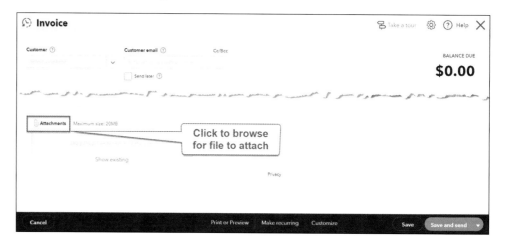

In the **Attachments** box, click the **paperclip** icon to locate the document to be added to the form or drag and drop the document into the box.

Figure 11.29

Example of file uploaded to invoice as an attachment

If the **Attach to email** box is checked, the file will be emailed to the customer with the invoice.

Adding Attachments Directly to the Attachment Lists

All attachments are maintained in the **Attachments** list in QBO.

    The list can be accessed by clicking the ⚙ on the icon bar.

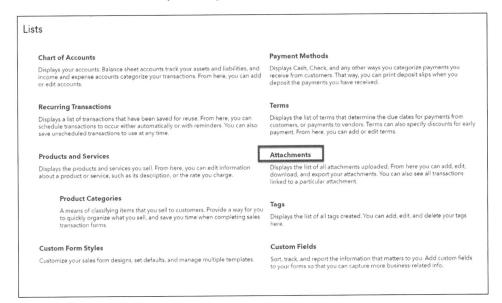

Figure 11.30

Access to Attachments list

Click **Attachments** in the **LISTS** column.

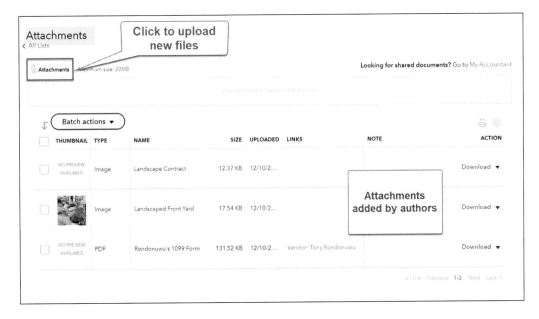

Figure 11.31

Attachments list

Attachments can be uploaded directly into the **Attachments** list by clicking the **paperclip** icon (upper-left corner of the screen displayed in Figure 11.31) to browse for the document to be added to the list or by dragging and dropping the document into the **Attachments** box.

    All documents in the list are available for attachment to customer or vendor records or to a transaction form.

    For example, a company might upload a standard contract terms document to a customer's record in QBO.

Figure 11.32

Access to available attachments

Click **Show existing** on the **Customer Details** tab.

Figure 11.33

Available attachments screen

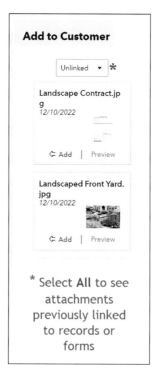

A sidebar opens that displays **attachments**. To see all **attachments**, select **All** on the drop-down menu under **Add to Customer**. To display only those attachments not linked to other customers, vendors, or transaction forms, select **Unlinked**.

Click **Add** to attach the file to the record.

There is no practice exercise for this section.

UPLOADING RECEIPTS

It's not unusual for companies to provide credit cards to employees. Having a company credit card allows employees to make purchases on the company's behalf, for travel, client entertainment, parking fees, etc., without using personal credit cards or cash. Employee credit cards are assigned to specific employees but are tied to the primary business card account. Most company cards carry the company's name as well as the name of the employee.

For control purposes and for determining the appropriate distribution of credit card charges, companies will usually require employees to submit original receipts. Unfortunately, paper credit card receipts are easily lost. And sometimes, employees fail to organize and hand in the receipts on a timely basis. Uploading credit card receipts to QBO minimizes these issues. The process would work something like this:

LO 11-7 Understand and demonstrate the process for uploading receipts into QBO

● The employee makes a purchase and obtains a receipt.

    ▪ Notes can be made on the receipt to help accounting determine the appropriate account distribution.

● The employee takes a picture of the receipt or scans the receipt to create a PDF file.

● The employee emails the image (jpeg, jpg, gif, or png) or PDF to accounting.

● The files are then uploaded into the system and added to the company file as **expense** transactions.

✳ **HINT:** A company can set up a special email address (name@qbodocs) for this purpose by clicking **Forward from email** on the **Receipts** tab in **Banking**. Only employees with access to the file (**Standard** users) can forward receipts using the email. (Users are covered in SECTION THREE of this book.)

Click **Banking** on the navigation bar and click **Receipts**.

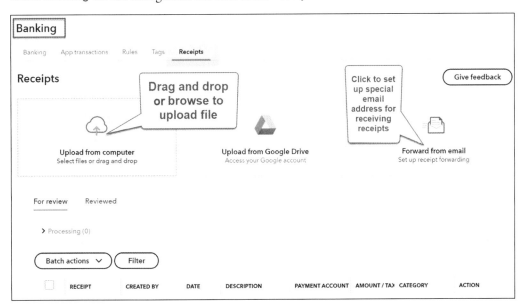

Figure 11.34

Receipt upload screen

Browse for the file or drag and drop the file into the **Receipts** box.

Figure 11.35

Uploaded receipt
before review

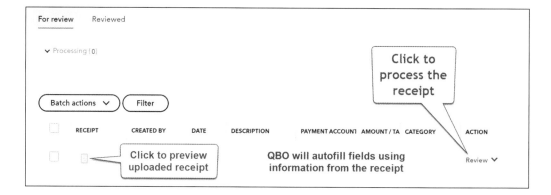

QBO will autofill all of the fields in the **For review** tab based on information included in the uploaded file.

> ✳ **HINT:** Extraction of the information from the image may take some time. Try refreshing your browser after a few minutes if you don't see the uploaded file in QBO in the **For review** section of the screen.

Once you see the transaction in the **For review** tab, click **Review** in the **ACTION** column.

Figure 11.36

Screen for verifying and adding details of uploaded receipt

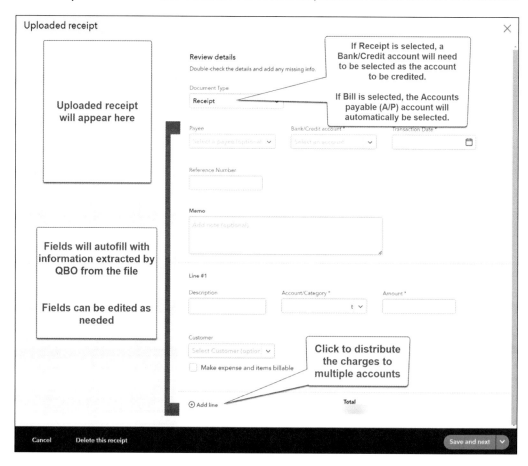

For uploaded credit card receipts, **Receipt** should be selected as the **Document Type**.

Most of the fields, other than the **Bank/Credit account**, will be autofilled by QBO. For uploaded credit card receipts, the **Bank/Credit account** would normally be a credit card liability account.

The accuracy of the other fields should be verified. The fields can be changed if necessary.

Click **Save and next.**

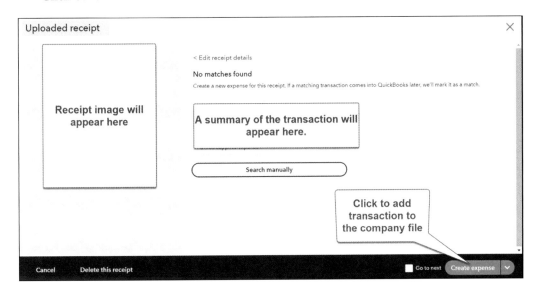

QBO will look for an existing transaction that matches the receipt details. If none is found (the normal case for uploaded receipts), clicking **Create expense** adds the transaction to the company file. The transaction is recorded as an **expense transaction type** and will be available on the credit card account reconciliation screen.

All uploaded receipts will be available in the **Attachments** list accessible through the ⚙ menu.

> **BEHIND THE SCENES** Receipts can also be emailed directly to the company file. Images will appear automatically in the **For review** tab. Emailing receipts is not covered in this course.

Credit card receipts are not the only charges that can be uploaded directly into QBO. Users can also upload vendor invoices. The process is the same except that users must select **Bill** in the **Document type** field on the **Receipt details** screen (Figure 11.36). **Bill document types** are entered as **bill** transactions in QBO with a corresponding credit to the accounts payable account. Uploaded vendor invoices are then available to pay through the **pay bills** form.

Receipt uploading is not available in the test drive company, so there is no practice exercise for this section. You will be uploading a receipt (in PDF format) as part of the Chapter 11 assignment.

CHAPTER SHORTCUTS

Save a customized report
1. Click Reports on the navigation bar.
2. Open the report to be customized.
3. Customize the report.
4. Click Save customization.

Create a management report package
1. Click Reports on the navigation bar.
2. Click Management Reports.
3. Click Edit on the ACTION dropdown menu for the report to be adjusted.

Create a custom field
1. Click the ⚙ on the icon bar.
2. Click All lists.
3. Click Custom Fields.
4. Click Add custom field.

Customize a form
1. Open the form.
2. Open the Customize menu in the black bar at the bottom of the form.

3. Select New style.

Export a report to Excel
1. Click Reports on the navigation bar.
2. Select report to be exported.
3. Click Export to Excel on the dropdown menu next to the export icon.

Upload a receipt
1. Click Banking.
2. Open the Receipts tab.
3. Upload the receipt.

Upload attachments
1. Click the ⚙ on the icon bar.
2. Click Attachments.
3. Drag and drop the document into the Attachments box OR click the paperclip icon above the Attachments box to search for the document.

CHAPTER REVIEW

**Assignments with the
🅜 are available in
myBusinessCourse.**

Matching

Match the term or phrase (as used in QuickBooks Online) to its definition.

1. custom field
2. management report
3. paperclip icon
4. design

5. form template
6. custom reports
7. attachment
8. end notes

_____   a specific form style for customization

_____   tab in the Reports screen to locate reports that have been modified and saved for future use

_____   document that has been uploaded to QBO

_____   page in a management report that includes user comments

_____   name of tab in custom form template window

_____   link to browse for documents to upload as attachments

_____   a formal set of reports included in QBO

_____   a user-created field on sales and purchase order forms

Multiple Choice

1. If a receipt is uploaded with a **document type receipt**, the transaction
   a. will be recorded as an **Expense**.
   b. will be recorded as a **Bill**.
   c. will be recorded as a **Check**.
   d. will be recorded as a **Receipt**.

2. On November 15, you customize and save a profit and loss report. The specified dates in the report are September 1 to October 31. On December 15, you run the saved report. The report will show profitability for:
   a. the period September 1 to December 15.
   b. the period September 1 to November 30.
   c. the period September 1 to October 31.
   d. the period December 1 to December 15.

3. Up to _____ **custom fields** can be created for use in sales transactions.
   a. two
   b. three
   c. six
   d. ten

4. A user-created customized form can be created for all the following except _____.
   a. **Invoice**
   b. **Estimate**
   c. **Sales Receipt**
   d. **Purchase Order**

5. The list of saved customized reports is found on the _____.
   a. **Custom reports** tab of the **Reports** screen
   b. **Standard** tab of the **Reports** screen
   c. **Management reports** tab of the **Reports** screen
   d. navigation bar

BEYOND THE CLICKS—THINKING LIKE A MANAGER

Accounting: Prepare a Management Report for the company Sales Manager at Craig's Design and Landscaping. Include two comments on either the Preliminary page or in End notes. Both comments should highlight a significant sales-related balance, transaction, or trend that you believe would be of interest to the sales manager. Which QBO reports did you include in the packet? Explain your two comments.

Information systems: Design three sales transaction custom fields for your homework company. Explain why the information in the fields would be useful to company management. Would the fields be visible on forms provided to customers? Why or why not?

ASSIGNMENTS

4/18/24

✓ You're meeting with Martin next week to go over the company's operating results. You decide to create a management report for him.

✓ You upload the image you want to use for the company logo to the **Company** tab of **Account and Settings**. **TIP:** When you search for appropriate images, make sure you're looking for non-commercial licenses.

✓ You customize (and save) the following reports to include in the package:

> **!** **WARNING:** If the report customization tools have been updated in your homework company file, you may not be able to make all of these changes. Create your management report using the standard reports updated for date.

- Balance Sheet as of 3/31
    - negative numbers in parentheses
    - non-zero rows and columns only
- Profit and Loss 1/1–3/31
    - by month with a total column
    - negative numbers in parentheses
    - non-zero rows and columns only
- Profit and Loss 4/1–4/15
    - negative numbers in parentheses
    - non-zero rows and columns only
    - no YTD column
- Budget vs Actual report 1/1–3/31
    - total only (not by month)
    - columns for dollar difference (**$ over budget**) and percentage of budget column
    - negative numbers in parentheses
    - non-zero rows and columns only
    - **TIP:** QBO won't save reports that include a : (colon) in the report name. Modify the name before saving.

✓ You decide to use the **Company Overview** management report package. **TIP:** If you don't have a **Company Overview** package, use the **Basic Company Financials** package.

- You add the logo to the **cover page** and make one other style change.
    - **TIP:** You'll need to find or create a logo and upload it in the **Company name** section on the **Company** tab of **Account and Settings** first.
- You include a **Table of Contents**.
- On **Preliminary pages**, you include comments about the first quarter operating results.
    - **TIP:** You'll need to review the reports before you can add the comments. You can create the management report, view it, and then go back in and edit the report to add your comments. You can include comments about differences between months, trends, or overall results.
- You add the customized reports you created earlier to the **Reports** tab.
    - **TIP:** Make sure you're uploading the customized reports. You may need to delete reports automatically included by QBO. The **Budget vs Actual** report may not be accessible. You can still complete the assignment without it.

- You leave out the **End notes** page.
- You save the report so you can use it again next quarter.

✓ You're a little surprised at QBO's formatting of the balance sheet. You download the customized 3/31 balance sheet report you created for the **management report** to Excel and change the formatting to better comply with what you learned in your financial accounting course. **TIP:** There are normally far fewer subtotals and dollar signs in standard financial statements! Go ahead and leave the accounts in account number order.

  - **TIP:** When reports are exported, formulas for subtotals and totals are included. You might need to review those as you're editing.

4/22/24

✓ You review the report with Martin. He finds the information and your comments very helpful. You decide to make quarterly reviews a regular practice.

5/1/24

✓ Martin is considering hiring some college students to provide tutoring services to Sacramento Public Schools. He is also considering adding some new salespeople to sell the math games line. He wants to be able to identify the person responsible for the revenue on sales forms. You create a custom field for that purpose and call it "Representative." You want the name to show on the forms sent to customers.

✓ Martin asks if you can change the **sales receipt** form a bit. He'd like to see the following:

  - The logo added to the form.
  - The representative's name on the form.
  - A different design style.

✓ You use the new form on a **sales receipt** (SR-130) for Alonso Luna for 3 **Persistence** sessions dated 5/1. He paid the $315 with check number 5843.

  - Martin was Alonso's representative.

✓ Martin has provided you a copy of a receipt for the purchase of supplies from Paper Bag Depot using the VISA card. You want to test the **Receipt** feature in QBO to see how it works and to be able to link supporting documents with transactions.

  - **TIP:** If you are using myBusinessCourse, download the *7e Math Revealed Receipt Upload for Chapter 11 PDF* from Student Ancillaries. If you're not using myBusinessCourse, the file will be provided to you by your instructor.
  - You click **Banking** on the navigation bar and select the **Receipt** tab.
  - You upload the receipt to the file area. **TIP:** You may have to refresh your browser or change tabs and then return to the **Receipt** tab before you see your uploaded file.
  - You select **Review** from the **ACTION** column and enter the **Receipt details**. The supplies will be used over the next few months for tutoring. **TIP:** Martin used the VISA card.
  - You finish by selecting **Create expense** in the final screen.

5/3/24

✓ You deposit the $315 check from Alonso Luna.

Suggested reports for Chapter 11:

- Management Report as described above.
- Balance Sheet as of 3/31 in Excel with formatting changes described in the assignment.
- Sales receipt for Alonso Luna dated 5/1 using your customized form.
  - **TIP:** To save the form as a PDF, click **Print or Preview** at the bottom of the form. Click **Print or Preview** again. Click **download** and save the file.
- **Journal** report for May activity.

Assignment 11B

Salish Software Solutions

4/18/24

✓ You and Sally agree to meet later this week to go over the first quarter's results. You decide you want to put together a management report for her.

✓ You upload the image you want to use for the company logo to the Company tab of Account and Settings. **TIP:** When you search for appropriate images, make sure you're looking for non-commercial licenses.

✓ You customize (and save) the following reports to include in the package:

> **! WARNING:** If the report customization tools have been updated in your homework company file, you may not be able to make all of these changes. Create your management report using the standard reports updated for date.

- Balance Sheet as of 3/31
  - negative numbers in parentheses
  - non-zero rows and columns only
- Profit and Loss 1/1–3/31
  - by month (include a total column)
  - negative numbers in parentheses
  - non-zero rows and columns only
- Profit and Loss 4/1–4/15
  - negative numbers in parentheses
  - non-zero rows and columns only
  - no YTD column
- Budget vs Actual report 1/1–3/31
  - total only (not by month)
  - columns for dollar difference ($ over budget) and percentage of budget column
  - negative numbers in parentheses
  - non-zero rows and columns only
  - **TIP:** QBO won't save reports that include a : (colon) in the report name. Modify the name before saving.

✓ You decide to use the Company Overview management report package. **TIP:** If you don't have a Company Overview package, use the Basic Company Financials package.

- You add the logo to the cover page and make one other style change.
  - **TIP:** You'll need to find or create a logo and upload it in the Company name section on the Company tab of Account and Settings first.
- You include a Table of Contents.
- On Preliminary pages, you include comments about the first quarter operating results.
  - **TIP:** You'll need to review the reports before you can add the comments. You can create the management report, view it, and then go back in and edit the report to add your comments. You can include comments about differences between months, trends, or your overall results.
- You add the customized reports you created earlier to the Reports tab.
  - **TIP:** Make sure you're uploading the customized reports. You may need to delete reports automatically included by QBO. The Budget vs Actual report may not be accessible. You can still complete the assignment without it.
- You leave out the End notes page.

- You save the report so you can use it again next quarter.

✓ You're a little surprised at QBO's formatting of the balance sheet. You download the customized 3/31 balance sheet report you created for the **management report** to Excel and change the formatting to better comply with what you learned in your financial accounting course. **TIP:** There are normally far fewer subtotals and dollar signs! Go ahead and leave the accounts in account number order.

  - **TIP:** When reports are exported, formulas for subtotals and totals are included. You might need to review those as you're editing.

4/22/24

✓ You review the management report with Sally. She thanks you for putting together a professional package and you discuss future plans for the company.

5/1/24

✓ Sally is in negotiation with several regional companies to offer setup and training services. She knows she's going to need to hire some help. She wants to be able to identify the person responsible for specific projects on sales forms. You create a custom field (called Representative). You want the name to show on the forms sent to customers.

✓ Sally asks if you can change the **sales receipt** form a bit. She'd like to see the following:

- The logo you chose for the management report added to the form.
- The sales representative's name on the form.
- A different design style.

✓ You use the new form on a **sales receipt** (SR-125) for mSquared Enterprises for 15 hours of **Train** time and 1 **Organizer** dated 5/1. They paid the $804.38 with check #21442.

  - Sally was the sales representative.

✓ Sally has provided you a copy of a receipt for the purchase of supplies from Paper Bag Depot. You want to test the **Receipt** feature in QBO to see how it works and to be able to link supporting documents with transactions.

  - **TIP:** If you are using myBusinessCourse, download the *7e Salish Software Receipt Upload for Chapter 11 PDF* from Student Ancillaries. If you're not using myBusinessCourse, the file will be provided to you by your instructor.
  - You click **Banking** on the navigation bar and select the **Receipt** tab.
  - You upload the receipt to the file area. **TIP:** You may have to refresh your browser or change tabs and then return to the **Receipt** tab before you see your uploaded file.
  - You select **Review** from the **ACTION** column and enter the **Receipt** details. The general office supplies will be used over the next few months. **TIP:** Sally used the VISA card.
  - You finish by selecting **Create expense** in the final screen.

5/3/24

- You deposit the $804.38 check from mSquared Enterprises.

Suggested reports for Chapter 11:

- Management Report as described above

- Balance Sheet as of 3/31 in Excel
  - With formatting changes described in the assignment

- Sales receipt for mSquared Enterprises dated 5/1 using customized form.
  - **TIP:** To save the form as a PDF, click **Print or Preview** at the bottom of the form. Click **Print or Preview** again. Click **Download** and save the file.

- **Journal** report for May activity.

QuickBooks

SECTION FIVE

Paying Employees

Employee-related functions (hiring, managing, paying, evaluating, terminating, etc.) are some of the most complex functions in business. They are also some of the most important. There aren't many businesses that can be successful over the long term if they don't have a strong employee base.

In accounting for payroll, the primary focus is on:

- Calculating, processing, and recording employee compensation.
- Recording, reporting, and remitting payroll taxes and employee benefits.

Those two processes may look straightforward but, as anyone who has worked in payroll could tell you, they can be very complex.

BEFORE WE MOVE FORWARD

The payroll system in QBO is highly automated. Employer and employee payroll taxes are all directly calculated by QBO based on the federal, state, and local laws applicable to the company. Payroll tax reporting and tax remittances are automatically processed by QBO.

The high level of automation makes it impossible for payroll to be active in the test-drive company. Intuit does give users the option to try the payroll system on a 30-day free trial. You will be setting up a new company file and activating the payroll system in Chapter 12.

12 Payroll Activity

Road Map

LO	Learning Objective	Topic	Subtopic	Page	Videos
LO 12-1	Understand basic payroll concepts and terms [p. 12-5]	Payroll primer	Becoming an employer	12-5	
			Hiring employees	12-5	
			Compensation	12-7	
			Payroll taxes—reporting and remitting	12-7	
			Other payroll deductions and costs	12-9	
LO 12-2	Demonstrate an understanding of the payroll system in QBO [p. 12-9]	Payroll system walkthrough	Set up a new company file	12-9	
			Activate payroll	12-16	Activate payroll
			Add employees	12-18	Add employees
			Finish the payroll setup	12-30	Finish the payroll setup
			Process payroll	12-38	Process payroll
			Remit payroll taxes	12-41	Remit payroll taxes
			Access payroll reports	12-44	
			Edit employees when necessary	12-45	

WHAT IS THE PAYROLL CYCLE?

- Hire employees and obtain their tax information.
- Track employee time if appropriate.
- Calculate compensation and withholdings for each employee for the pay period.
- Distribute paychecks to employees with information about current and year-to-date payroll information.
- Calculate employer taxes.
- Remit employee withholdings and employer taxes.
- File required tax reports with federal and state taxing authorities.

In a manual system, managing employees and processing payroll are very labor intensive. If any employees are paid on an hourly basis, employees must submit timesheets used in calculating compensation. Withholdings and deductions must be determined for each employee before paychecks can be prepared. Employer taxes must be calculated and tax forms must be completed. And, of course, payroll transactions must be journalized and entered into the general ledger. These functions are done in all types of companies (service, merchandising, and manufacturing).

PROCESSING PAYROLL IN QBO

Payroll is not a standard feature in QBO (i.e., not automatically available in all QBO products). To record payroll transactions, users can choose to:

- Activate a QBO payroll service.
    - All payroll transactions are completed in QBO.
    - Employee information and tax reports are maintained in QBO.
- Add a payroll app from an external payroll provider to QBO.
    - Payroll transactions are directly downloaded to QBO.
    - Employee information and tax reports are maintained in the payroll provider's system.

 HINT: Apps from several well-known payroll providers (ADP and Paychex, for example) are available in QBO.

- Manually enter payroll transactions into QBO using journal entry or check transaction types and maintain employee information and tax reports outside of QBO.
    - Payroll management would either be done internally (by company employees) or through an external payroll provider not directly linked to QBO.

Federal and state payroll tax rates and wage thresholds change fairly regularly, and labor laws can be complicated. Unless a company has a strong human resources department, it can be challenging for company staff to stay current. Most small to medium-sized companies use an external payroll service provider (QBO, for example).

PAYROLL PLANS AVAILABLE IN QBO

For an additional monthly fee, users can subscribe to one of QBO's payroll plans.

- Core
  - Withholding taxes and other deductions are automatically calculated as part of creating employee paychecks.
  - Federal and state payroll taxes are calculated, reported to tax agencies, and paid automatically. (This includes year-end filings.)
    - QBO does not automatically report and remit local payroll taxes.
  - Next-day direct deposit is available for employees.
  - Users can track paid time off, contributions to retirement plans, and other types of employee deductions.
- **Premium** includes all features of **Core**. In addition:
  - Same-day direct deposit is available.
  - Employees can report time on any device. Hours can be reviewed, edited, and approved in QBO.

CHAPTER 12 STRUCTURE

Because payroll is not available in the test-drive or homework company files, the structure of Chapter 12 will be unique. There are two main parts.

Payroll Primer	Payroll System Walkthrough
The **PAYROLL PRIMER** section includes: • A review of payroll basics (compensation, payroll taxes, etc.) • General information about payroll in QBO's **Premier** payroll plan	In the **PAYROLL SYSTEM WALKTHROUGH** section you will be: • Creating a new QBO company file • Editing payroll settings • Adding employees • Processing payroll Completion of the steps in this section constitutes the homework for Chapter 12.

PAYROLL PRIMER

Becoming an Employer

LO 12-1 Understand basic payroll concepts and terms

Before a company can hire or pay employees, it must obtain a federal identification number (EIN number) and a state employer identification number. In some states, separate numbers related to state unemployment taxes and workers' compensation must be obtained. Federal and state identification numbers are entered as part of the payroll activation process in QBO. They can also be added or edited by clicking the ⚙ in the icon bar and selecting **Payroll settings**.

Employers are responsible for complying with all federal and state labor laws. Labor laws prescribe standards for wages, hours, working conditions, etc. Detailed information can be found at the U.S. Department of Labor's website (https://www.dol.gov/). Links to state labor departments can be found on https://www.dol.gov/agencies/whd/state.

Hiring Employees

An employee must complete the following documents before he or she starts working:

- Federal I-9 (Federal Eligibility Verification) form
  - Employee must identify a reason for employment eligibility (citizen, lawful permanent resident, etc.) and sign form.
  - Employer reviews documents supporting employment eligibility and signs form.

- Federal W-4 (Employee's Withholding Certificate) form
  - Employee must identify his/her address, social security number, and filing status and sign form.
  - Used to determine amount for federal income tax to withhold on employee paychecks.
  - Input into QBO as part of the employee setup.
- State withholding form (in states with personal income taxes)
  - Same purpose as the Federal W-4.

BEHIND THE SCENES

Form **W-4**	**Employee's Withholding Certificate**	OMB No. 1545-0074
Department of the Treasury Internal Revenue Service	Complete Form W-4 so that your employer can withhold the correct federal income tax from your pay. Give Form W-4 to your employer. Your withholding is subject to review by the IRS.	2023

Step 1: Enter Personal Information

(a) First name and middle initial / Last name / (b) Social security number

Address

Does your name match the name on your social security card? If not, to ensure you get credit for your earnings, contact SSA at 800-772-1213 or go to *www.ssa.gov*.

City or town, state, and ZIP code

(c) ☐ Single or **Married filing separately**
☐ **Married filing jointly** or **Qualifying surviving spouse**
☐ **Head of household** (Check only if you're unmarried and pay more than half the costs of keeping up a home for yourself and a qualifying individual.)

Complete Steps 2–4 ONLY if they apply to you; otherwise, skip to Step 5. See page 2 for more information on each step, who can claim exemption from withholding, other details, and privacy.

Step 2: Multiple Jobs or Spouse Works

Complete this step if you (1) hold more than one job at a time, or (2) are married filing jointly and your spouse also works. The correct amount of withholding depends on income earned from all of these jobs.

Do **only one** of the following.

(a) Reserved for future use.

(b) Use the Multiple Jobs Worksheet on page 3 and enter the result in Step 4(c) below; **or**

(c) If there are only two jobs total, you may check this box. Do the same on Form W-4 for the other job. This option is generally more accurate than (b) if pay at the lower paying job is more than half of the pay at the higher paying job. Otherwise, (b) is more accurate . . . . ☐

TIP: If you have self-employment income, see page 2.

Complete Steps 3–4(b) on Form W-4 for only ONE of these jobs. Leave those steps blank for the other jobs. (Your withholding will be most accurate if you complete Steps 3–4(b) on the Form W-4 for the highest paying job.)

Step 3: Claim Dependent and Other Credits

If your total income will be $200,000 or less ($400,000 or less if married filing jointly):

Multiply the number of qualifying children under age 17 by $2,000 $ _____

Multiply the number of other dependents by $500 . . . . . $ _____

Add the amounts above for qualifying children and other dependents. You may add to this the amount of any other credits. Enter the total here . . . . | 3 | $

Step 4 (optional): Other Adjustments

(a) **Other income (not from jobs).** If you want tax withheld for other income you expect this year that won't have withholding, enter the amount of other income here. This may include interest, dividends, and retirement income . . . . | 4(a) | $

(b) **Deductions.** If you expect to claim deductions other than the standard deduction and want to reduce your withholding, use the Deductions Worksheet on page 3 and enter the result here . . . . | 4(b) | $

(c) **Extra withholding.** Enter any additional tax you want withheld each **pay period** . . | 4(c) | $

Step 5: Sign Here

Under penalties of perjury, I declare that this certificate, to the best of my knowledge and belief, is true, correct, and complete.

Employee's signature (This form is not valid unless you sign it.) / **Date**

Employers Only

Employer's name and address / First date of employment / Employer identification number (EIN)

For Privacy Act and Paperwork Reduction Act Notice, see page 3. / Cat. No. 10220Q / Form **W-4** (2023)

Withholding amounts are based on the following:

- For employees without dependents, with only one job, and without additional withholding requirements, the amount of federal income taxes withheld is calculated based on their federal filing status (Step 1c on Form W-4).

(continued)

(continued from previous page)

- If an individual's filing status is Married, Filing Jointly, and their spouse works, they would be considered to have more than one job.
- Directions for determining tax withholdings for employees with multiple jobs are available on Form W-4. (See Step 2 on the W-4.)

- For employees with dependents or with additional withholding requirements, the amount of federal income taxes withheld is based on their federal filing status PLUS information included in Steps 3 and 4 of Form W-4.
  - The adjustment for dependents is calculated in Step 3. This only applies to taxpayers making less than $200,000 (or less than $400,000 if married, filing jointly).
  - Other adjustments (increases or decreases) are reported in Step 4. Directions for determining those amounts are included on Form W-4 available at irs.gov.

Compensation

Employees are normally paid in the form of a salary (usually stated as an annual or monthly amount) or an hourly wage. In addition, they might be paid:

- Bonuses
  - Bonus (additional) pay is often given to salaried or hourly employees as a reward for the achievement of a specific, individual goal.
  - Sometimes bonuses are paid to employees when the company itself meets certain financial goals.

- Commissions
  - Commission pay is typically based on sales volume (units or dollars). For example, a salesperson might be paid 5% of each sales dollar generated from their customer.

- Overtime premiums
  - When certain employees work more than a prescribed number of hours in a day or in a week, most states require employers to pay them a premium for those hours. State laws mandate the standard hour limits and the type of employees eligible for overtime pay.

- Paid time off (also known as sick pay and vacation pay)
  - Most employers allow their employees to be paid for a certain number of hours at their standard rate, even when absent due to illness or vacation.

The total amount earned by an employee during a pay period is called the employee's **gross pay**. The amount of the paycheck (gross pay less taxes and other withholdings) is called the employee's **net pay**.

Gross pay The amount an employee earns before any withholdings or deductions.

In QBO Payroll, compensation options are known as **pay types**. Each employee must be set up initially as an **Hourly**, **Salary**, or **Commission Only** employee. Additional **pay types** (e.g., **overtime, paid time off, bonus,** or **commission**) can be added to hourly or salaried employees.

Net pay The amount of an employee's paycheck, after subtracting withheld amounts.

Payroll Taxes—Reporting and Remitting

There are federal, state, and local payroll taxes. Some are the responsibility of the employer, some are the responsibility of the employee, and some are a shared responsibility of both employer and employee. Payroll taxes that are the responsibility of the employee are automatically withheld from employee paychecks in QBO Payroll.

Most payroll taxes are calculated as a percentage of a base amount. The percentage and the base will depend on the specific payroll tax. Tax rates and base amounts can (and do!) change periodically.

Federal payroll taxes include:

- Federal income (FIT)—Employee only tax
  - The base amount of FIT withheld is determined by the employee's filing status. See the BEHIND THE SCENES insert on page 12-6 for more information.

- FICA (Social Security and Medicare)—Shared tax
  - Both employer and employee pay a social security tax of 6.2% of wages up to a maximum wage threshold.
    - Maximum wage thresholds change. $160,200 was the threshold in 2023.
  - Both employer and employee pay a Medicare tax of 1.45% of ALL wages. Employees pay an **additional** 0.9% of wages over a threshold based on their filing status. The threshold for a single individual was $200,000 in 2023.

- Federal unemployment (FUTA)—Employer only tax
  - Employers pay a 6% FUTA tax on wages up to a threshold of $7,000 for each employee. Employers are eligible for a credit of up to 5.4% of wages for any state unemployment taxes paid.
    - The tax rate, threshold amount, and credit rate have not changed since 1983.

State payroll taxes may include personal income tax, unemployment taxes, disability insurance, and others. In California, the state payroll taxes include:

- Personal income (PIT)—Employee only tax

- State unemployment (UI)—Employer tax

- Employment training (ETT)—Employer tax

- State disability (SDI)—Employee tax

> **BEHIND THE SCENES** Employers are also required to maintain workers' compensation insurance in most states. Workers' compensation provides benefits for workers who are injured or contract an illness due to their work. In some states, employers pay into a state government program. Other states allow employers to purchase the coverage from private insurance carriers or self-fund their workers' compensation plan.

In QBO Payroll, all payroll taxes are automatically calculated based on the employer's location(s) and information provided by employees and federal and state taxing authorities.

Schedules for reporting and remitting federal payroll taxes (employer and employee shares) depend on the size of a company's payroll.

- Federal income tax and FICA taxes are reported quarterly on Form 941. Remittance timing varies based on the size of the payroll tax liability.
  - Small companies (generally those with payroll tax liabilities of less than $2,500 per quarter) can deposit 941 taxes with the quarterly return.
  - Companies with payroll tax liabilities greater than $50,000 during the 12 months ending June 30 of the **prior** year must deposit 941 taxes semi-weekly. (For 2023,

the prior year would end June 30, 2022.) Deposits must be remitted electronically.

- ▪ All other companies must deposit 941 taxes monthly. Deposits must be remitted electronically.

- Federal unemployment taxes are reported on Form 940. Remittance timing varies based on the size of the payroll tax liability.
  - ▪ The FUTA tax deposit requirement is based on the company's FUTA tax liability **year-to-date**. A deposit is due once the year-to-date tax liability exceeds $500 (calculated quarterly).

Schedules for reporting and remitting state and local payroll taxes (employee and employer shares) are set by the various tax authorities. Some states adopt the federal remittance and filing schedules.

Other Payroll Deductions and Costs

Employers often provide benefits to employees. These might include:

- Medical insurance
  - ▪ Can be fully or partially paid by the employer

- Retirement plans
  - ▪ Can be fully or partially paid by the employer

Employee and employer contributions related to health or retirement plans are set up as part of the employee record in QBO. Employee contributions are automatically withheld from employee paychecks.

Employers may also withhold funds from employee paychecks related to garnishments (child support, tax levies, etc.), union dues, repayment of cash advances, etc. These deductions are also set up in the employee record in QBO.

PAYROLL SYSTEM WALKTHROUGH

The Chapter 12 homework assignment for either *Math Revealed!* or *Salish Software Solutions* consists of following the steps outlined in this section. When you have completed the steps, you will have worked through the full QBO Payroll process for two employees.

In Step 1, you'll start by setting up a new company file and activating the 30-day payroll trial option. Follow the instructions for this step carefully.

LO 12-2 Demonstrate an understanding of the payroll system in QBO

STEP 1—Set Up a New Company File

The process for setting up your payroll company file is similar to the one you followed in Chapter 2. This time, however, you'll only be importing your chart of accounts.

Your instructor will send you an invitation for the new file.

Figure 12.1

New company setup

Figure 12.1

New company setup

Accept the invitation and sign in using your homework company email address and password.

 HINT: Registering with the same email address allows you to access multiple companies using the same login. When you log in at qbo.intuit.com, all companies associated with the same email address/password are displayed.

Figure 12.2

Welcome screen

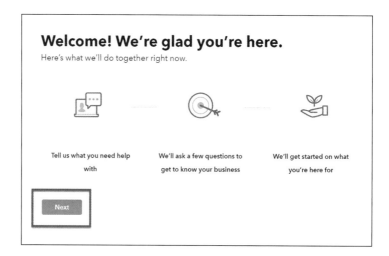

Click **Next** in the Welcome screen to start the setup process.

Once you've signed in to the new file, use the following table to help you with the company setup. Remember, QBO changes fairly often! The wording or the order of the setup questions might differ. Some of the questions in Table 12.1 may not appear as part of your setup. New questions may be added. Use your best judgment. If you don't know how to answer a question, reach out to your instructor.

Table 12.1

Company setup
questions

Screen Heading	Answers
What's your business name? or What do you call your business?	Enter a name that's distinct from your homework company name. For example, you could use your homework company name followed by the word "Payroll." Do **not** check the box next to **I'm moving from QuickBooks Desktop and want to bring in my data** if that option appears.
How do you manage your business finances today?	**Spreadsheets or pen & paper.**
How long has your company been in business?	**Under a year.**
What kind of business is this?	Click **No** if asked if the company is an LLC. Click **C Corp** or **Corporation.**
What's your industry?	Enter "Professional services" in the field. Select **All other professional, scientific, and technical services** from the displayed options.
How does your business make money?	Click **We provide services** and **We sell products.**
Do you track projects?	**Never.**
What's your main role?	Click the option that includes the word **Accountant.**
Is the company your main source of income?	**No.** Select **I do freelance/contract work.**
Who works at this business?	Click **Employees.** Select **2-5** as the **Number of employees.** **TIP:** After selecting **Employees,** you may see a screen that includes the question **Want to add QuickBooks Online Payroll Premium?.** If so, select **Yes** and click **Next.**
Does an expert help with your books?	**Yes. TIP:** You're the expert!
What apps do you use for your business?	Click **I don't use any apps** or **Skip for now.**
Link your accounts and see everything in place	Click **Skip for now.**
What do you want to do in QuickBooks?	Click all options **other than** those related to accepting payments, tracking mileage, tracking time, creating estimates, or purchasing insurance.
What should we do first?	**Get ready to invoice.**

Once you finish answering the setup questions, you may see a series of invitations.

Figure 12.3

Invoice setup invitation

Click **Next.**

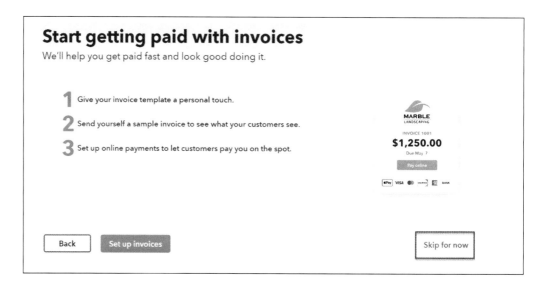

Click **Skip for now**.
Click **Let's go** in the final setup screen.
You should now be on the **Dashboard**.

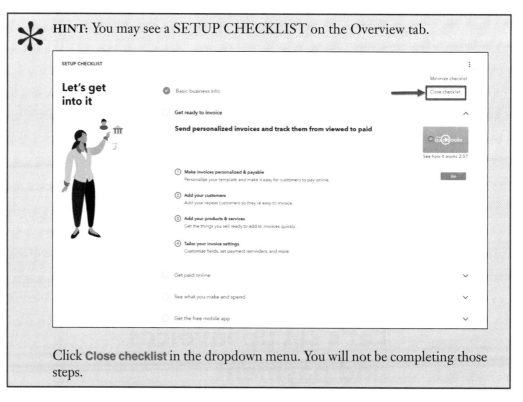

You will need to change a few settings before moving forward. Click the ⚙️ on the icon bar.

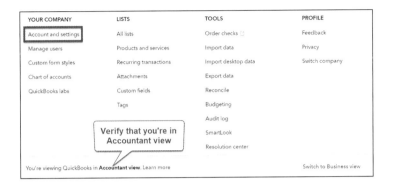

Figure 12.5

Link to file settings

Select **Account and Settings**.

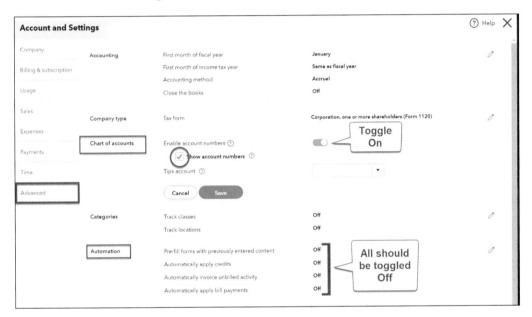

Figure 12.6

Advanced settings
selection screen

On the **Company** tab, enter the address (3835 Freeport Blvd, Sacramento, CA 95822) and click **Save**.

On the **Advanced** tab (Figure 12.6), turn **Enable account numbers** to **On** and check the box next to **Show account numbers**.

Toggle all **Automation** settings to **Off**. You may also want to extend the time before QBO automatically logs you out to 3 hours in the **Other preferences** section of the **Advanced** tab in **Account and Settings**.

Click **Save** in each modified section.

Click **Done** to exit **Account and Settings**.

You will now need to purge the default chart of accounts and import the same chart of accounts you used in your homework company file.

Change the URL address to read https://app.qbo.intuit.com/app/purgecompany. (Leave any C number that appears after https://.)

Press **Enter**.

Figure 12.7

Warning before file purge

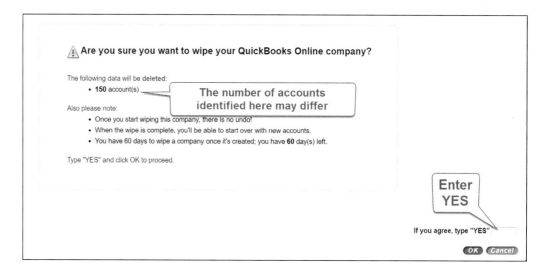

Enter **YES** in the box at the bottom right of the screen and click **OK**.

Figure 12.8

Options for account setup

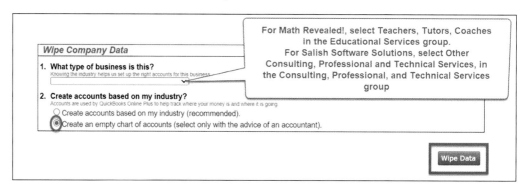

Complete the purge by answering the two questions on the screen using the instructions in Figure 12.8. Click **Wipe Data**.

Click the ⚙ on the icon bar.

Figure 12.9

Link to import file data

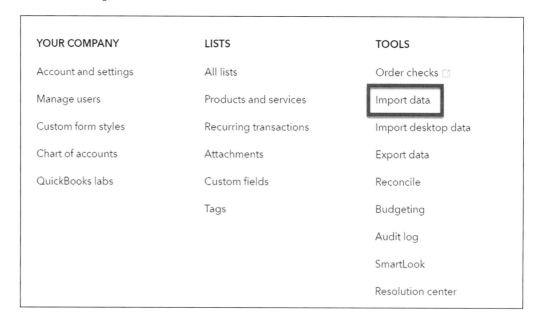

Click **Import Data**.

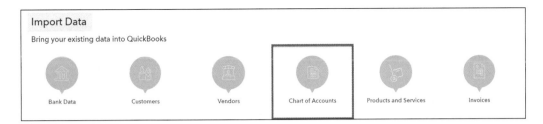

Figure 12.10

Selection of data to be imported

Select **Chart of Accounts**.

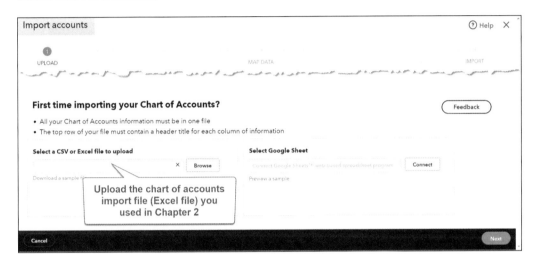

Figure 12.11

Selection of import file

Click **Browse** and select the Chart of Accounts Excel file that you used to set up your home-work company file in Chapter 2. You will be selecting **one** of the following:

● 7e Math Revealed Chart of Accounts for Importing.xlsx

● 7e Salish Software Chart of Accounts for Importing.xlsx

Click **Next**.

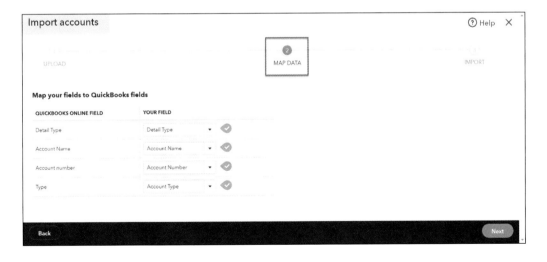

Figure 12.12

Mapped fields for account import

Verify that the fields in the Excel file match the QBO fields. If they don't, click **Back**. You'll need to make sure you're using the correct Excel file.

Select **Next** when all fields are properly mapped.

Figure 12.13

Accounts to be
imported

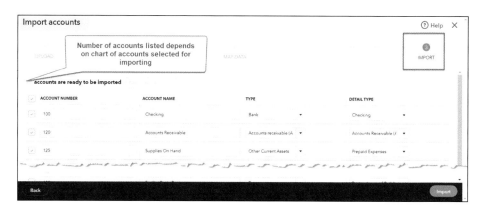

Review the accounts in the list and correct any errors.

Click Import.

STEP 2—Activate Payroll

Before activating payroll, increase the cash balance to cover the payroll transactions you will be recording. (You wouldn't want to bounce a payroll check!) You can record a **deposit**, or you can create the following **journal entry**. The transaction date (either method) should be the first day of the **current** month (the month in which you're doing the assignment).

Account #	Account Name	Debit	Credit
100	Checking	10,000	
300	Common Stock		10,000

If you use a **deposit** form, you can leave the **RECEIVED FROM** and **PAYMENT METHOD** fields blank. **Common Stock** should be selected in the **ACCOUNT** field.

To activate payroll, click **Payroll** on the navigation bar.

Figure 12.14

Link to payroll
activation

Click **Get started** on the **Overview** tab.

> **HINT:** Payroll is a QBO feature that changes regularly. The order of payroll setup questions may change and you may see additional questions or different screens. Use your best judgment when confronted with slight differences. If the differences are significant, check for updates posted in Student Ancillaries or check with your instructor.

Figure 12.15
Question about prior payroll in calendar year

Select **No** to answer the **Have you paid employees in 2023?** question. (If you're doing your homework in 2024, the question will ask about 2024!)

Click **Next**.

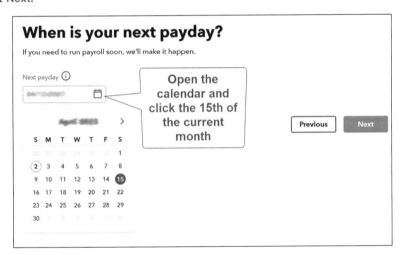

Figure 12.16
Identification of initial pay date

Select the 15th of the current month when asked **When is your next payday?**. (Use the 15th even if it falls on a weekend.)

Click **Next**.

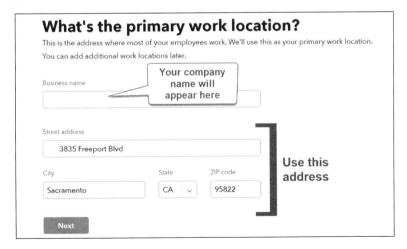

Figure 12.17
Identification of business location

Enter 3835 Freeport Blvd, Sacramento, CA, 95822 as the address for your payroll company.

Click **Next**.

The Email address field in the Who's your payroll contact? screen should be the one used to set up the company file. You can use any name but the Business phone will need to be a valid number. For security purposes, Intuit may ask you to enter a code sent to your phone when working in payroll.

Click Next.

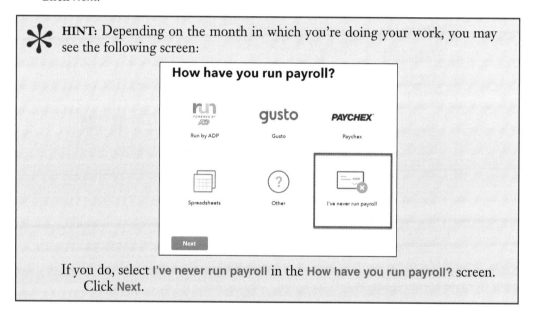

HINT: Depending on the month in which you're doing your work, you may see the following screen:

If you do, select I've never run payroll in the How have you run payroll? screen. Click Next.

STEP 3—Add Employees

You will be adding two employees: Shaniya Montero and Abe Martin.

Click Add employee.

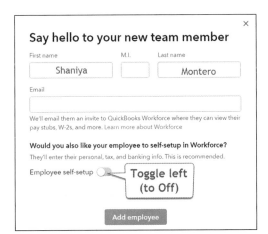

Figure 12.20

Employee name screen

Enter the name of your first employee (Shaniya Montero) and turn off the **Employee self-setup** option.

> **BEHIND THE SCENES** **Employee self-setup** is a tool allowing employees to enter personal, tax, and banking information directly into QBO. We will not be using that tool.

Click **Add employee**.

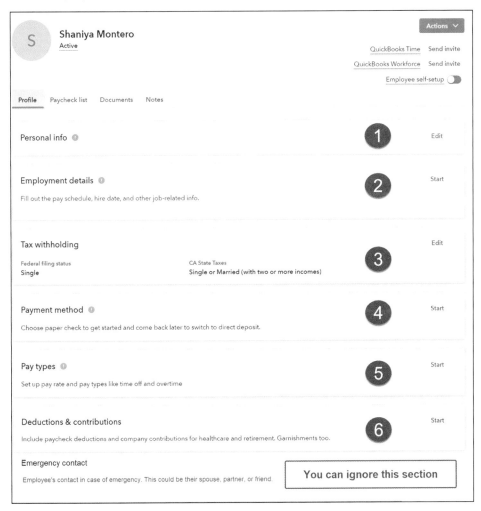

Figure 12.21

Employee profile tab

The **Profile** tab in Shaniya's employee record will open.

You will be entering information in six of the seven sections.

Section 1 Click **Edit** to complete the **Personal info** section.

Enter Shaniya's birth date, contact information, and social security number in the appropriate fields. You don't need to enter gender or phone numbers.

> ✳ **HINT:** In payroll, dates need to be entered using the following format: mm/dd/yyyy.

Click **Save** to return to the **Profile** tab (Figure 12.21).

Section 2 Click **Start** in the **Employment details** section.

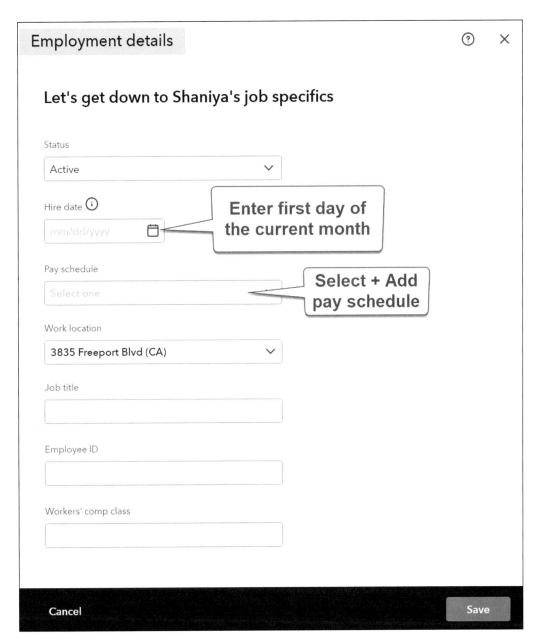

Figure 12.23
Pay schedule selection

Enter the first day of the current month as the **Hire date**. (The current month is the month you're completing the homework.) If you see an **Update tax withholding for Shaniya** message, click X to close the box. You don't need to update withholdings.

BEHIND THE SCENES QBO uses the hire date in determining whether a paycheck should be created for an employee during a particular payroll period.

Because Shaniya is the first employee, you'll need to create a company pay schedule first. Select **+ Add pay schedule** in the **Pay schedule** dropdown menu.

Figure 12.24

New pay schedule

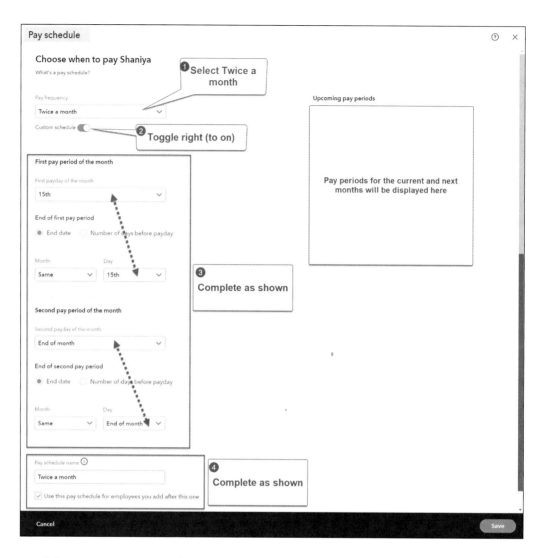

Select **Twice a Month** in the **Pay frequency** dropdown menu.

Toggle **Custom schedule** to on.

Select **15th** as the **First payday of the month** and **End of month** as the **Second payday** of the month. The **End dates** of the first and second pay periods are the **15th** and **End of month**, respectively.

Enter "Twice a Month" as the **Pay schedule name** and check the **Use this pay schedule for employees you add after this one** box.

> **BEHIND THE SCENES** Companies might pay groups of employees on different schedules (e.g., weekly for hourly employees, semi-monthly for salaried employees). Multiple pay schedules can be created in a QBO company file.

Click **Save** to return to the **Employment details** screen.

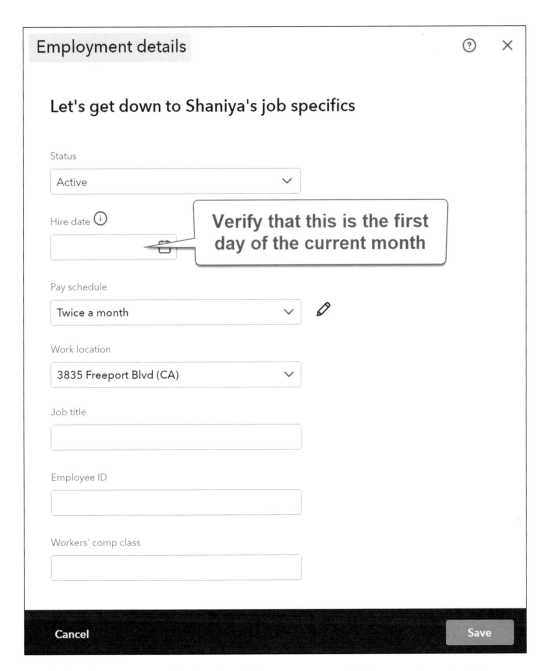

Verify that the **Hire date** is the first day of the **current** month (the month you're doing your homework) and that the **Pay schedule** is **Twice a month**.

Leave the company address as the **Work location**.

Click **Save** to return to **Profile** tab (Figure 12.21).

Section 3 Click **Start** in the **Tax Withholding** section.

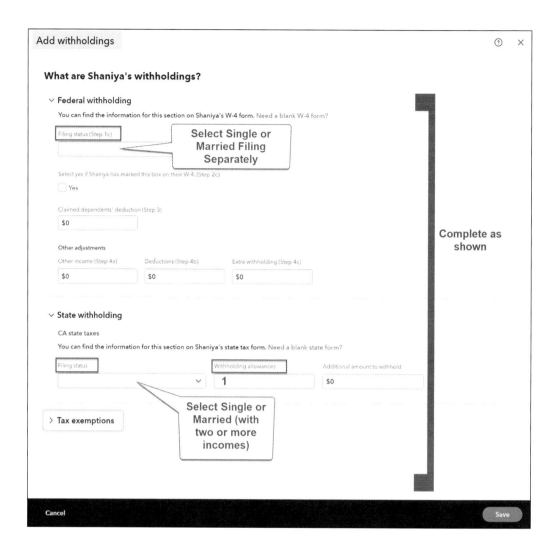

Shaniya's federal and state tax filing statuses are entered next. The information entered in the **What are Shaniya's withholdings?** screen is taken from the employee-completed W-4 form and, if applicable, the employee-completed state withholding form. Shaniya provided the following information:

- Federal filing status: **Single or Married Filing Separately**
    - Shaniya has no dependents and does not want any additional monies withheld.

- California filing status: **Single or Married (with two or more incomes)**, 1 allowance, no additional monies withheld

    Only the fields highlighted in Figure 12.26 need to be completed.
    Click **Save** to return to the **Profile** tab (Figure 12.21).

Section 4 Click **Start** in the **Payment method** section.

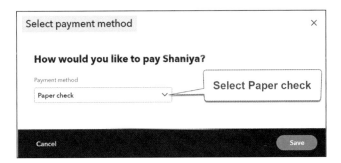

Figure 12.27

Payroll payment
method selection

Select **Paper check** in the dropdown menu.

> **BEHIND THE SCENES** QBO can be set up to handle direct deposit of employee
> checks. This would require the company to connect a bank account to its QBO file.

Click **Save** to return to **Profile** tab (Figure 12.21).

Section 5 Click **Start** in the **Pay Types** section.

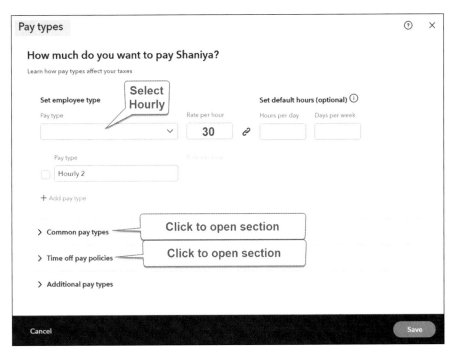

Figure 12.28

Compensation and
policies screen

Shaniya is paid $30 per hour, so select **Hourly** in the **Pay type** dropdown menu and enter
"30" in the **Rate per hour** box.

> **BEHIND THE SCENES** If an hourly employee normally works a set schedule
> (same hours and days per week), defaults can be entered in the employee record.
> Default hours will automatically be included in payroll processing. The hours can
> be changed before paychecks are created.

Open the **Common pay types** section.

Figure 12.29

Selection of overtime policies

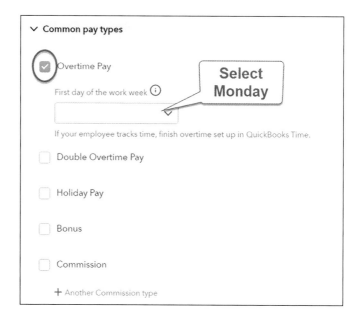

Check the Overtime Pay box. (QBO will automatically calculate overtime pay using 1.5 times the hourly rate.)

Select Monday as the First day of the work week.

Open the Time off pay policies section.

In the Paid time off dropdown menu, select Add new paid time off policy. A sidebar (panel) will open on the right.

Figure 12.30

Addition of time off policy

Companies typically accrue paid time off each pay period or at the beginning of the year. For Shaniya, select At beginning of year in the Hours are accrued dropdown menu and enter "80" in the Hours per year box. Enter "Annual paid leave" in the Description field.

BEHIND THE SCENES Instead of a paid-time off (PTO) policy, some companies may separate sick and vacation pay. Under any of those policies, companies may elect to accrue hours at the beginning of the year, per pay period, per hour worked, or on the employee's anniversary date (date of hire). Companies may have different leave policies for different employees. QBO will track available leave time based on the pay policy identified in the employee's record.

Click **Save** to close the sidebar.

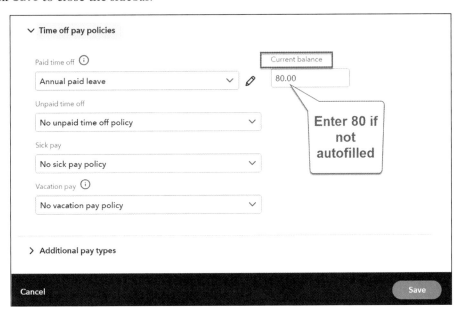

Figure 12.31

Time off policies

After verifying that "80" shows in the **Current balance** box (for paid time off), click **Save** to return to the **Profile** tab (Figure 12.21).

Section 6 Click **Start** in the **Deductions & contributions** section.

The only deductions (other than payroll taxes) in your payroll company will be a 401(k) plan administered by "Employee First" (the provider). Both the employee and the company contribute 3% of gross pay per pay period to the plan.

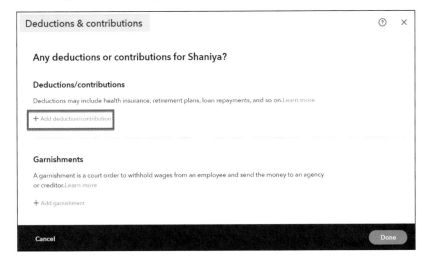

Figure 12.32

Deductions screen

Click **+ Add deduction/contributions**. A sidebar (panel) will open on the right. **NOTE:** New fields appear as you complete the form.

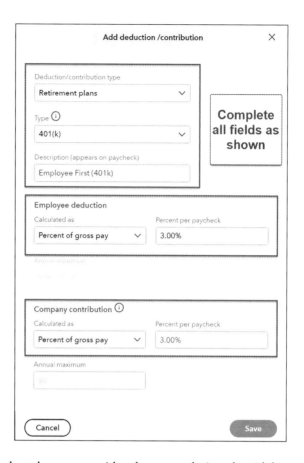

Use the screenshot above as a guide when completing the sidebar.

BEHIND THE SCENES 401(k) plans can be solely funded by employees, solely funded by employers, or jointly funded. Contributions may be calculated as a percentage of wages or as a fixed amount per pay period. Employer contribution amounts are often capped by the company at a certain annual amount. The maximum annual contribution amount for employees is set by law. In 2023, the maximum was set at $22,500. If you're doing your work in 2023, the 2024 maximum will be displayed.

Click **Save**.
Click **Done** to exit the **Deductions & contributions** screen.
All sections for Shaniya are now completed.

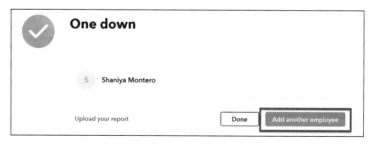

Click **Add another employee**.

 HINT: If you don't see Figure 12.34, click **Payroll** on the navigation bar, open the **Employees drawer** (tab), and click **Add an employee**.

You will now go through the same sections for Abe Martin. This time, however, you will be able to use certain options (like **pay schedules**) that you created in the setup for Shaniya.

Use the following information to complete the sections:

Personal info	The second employee's name is Abe Martin. You will not be using the Employee self-setup feature for Abe. Abe's birthdate is 07/23/1991. His address is 4560 Del Rio Rd, Sacramento, CA 95822. His social security number is 222-79-8765.
Employment details	Abe was hired on the first day of the current month. (The month in which you're doing your homework.) He's on the same Twice a month **pay schedule** as Shaniya and has the same **work location**.
Tax withholding	His federal filing status is **Single or Married Filing Separately**. Abe has no dependents. His California filing status is **Single or Married (with two or more incomes)**. California allowances are: 1 No additional monies are to be withheld for federal or state income taxes.
Payment method	Abe will be paid with a paper check.
Pay types	Abe is paid a salary of $55,000 per year. You can leave the default hours/days. He is not eligible for overtime. He is eligible for the same Annual paid leave plan as Shaniya. Verify that 80 shows in the **Current balance** field.
Deductions and contributions	Abe has one deduction: Employee First (401k). His 3% contribution is matched by a 3% employer contribution.

When all sections are complete, click **Done**.
In the **Payday coming up?** screen, click **Continue setup**.

 HINT: If you don't see the **Payday coming up?** screen, click **Payroll** on the navigation bar and open the **Overview drawer** (tab).

Figure 12.35
Workers' comp offer

This is an advertisement for a workers' compensation policy offered by an Intuit partner.
Click **I'm already covered**.

> **BEHIND THE SCENES** California requires most employers to either have a Workers' Compensation insurance policy or be self-insured to cover cash benefits and/or the cost of medical care for employees who are injured or become ill as a direct result of the work they perform.

You should now be back on the Overview tab of the Payroll Center.

> **HINT:** If you were moved directly to the Overview tab of the Payroll Center and didn't see Figure 12.35, click Start next to Add a worker's comp policy and click I'm already covered.

You will be finishing the payroll setup in STEP 4.

eLecture

STEP 4—Finish the Payroll Setup

Entering federal and state payroll tax information and identifying the accounts to be debited and credited in payroll transactions are done next.

Figure 12.36

Overview tab of Payroll Center

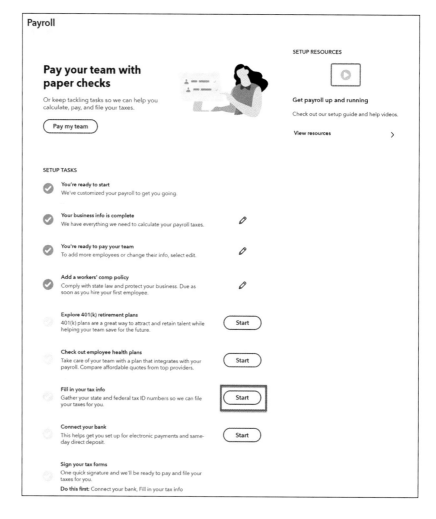

HINT: We will not be reviewing specific 401(k) plans in this course. If you're interested in reading about 401(k) plans, click **Start** next to **Explore 401(k) plans**. Otherwise, ignore the invitation.

Click **Start** next to **Fill in your tax info.**
There are three tabs in the tax setup window.

Figure 12.37

General tab of payroll taxes setup screen

The company name and address fields on the **General** tab will autofill. **Other** should be selected as the **Company type.** (Your company is not a sole proprietorship or nonprofit corporation, the only other options in the dropdown menu.)
Click **Next.**

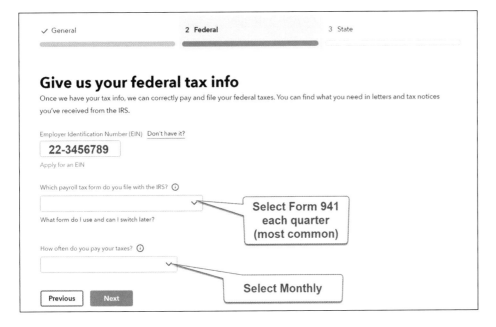

Figure 12.38

Federal tab of payroll taxes setup screen

Federal payroll tax information is entered next. Your company's employer identification number is 22-3456789. (You do not need to enter the hyphen when entering the identification number. Formatting of tax numbers is automatic in QBO.)

You file Form 941 quarterly. Payroll taxes are deposited monthly.

Click **Next** to enter state payroll tax information.

Figure 12.39

State tab of payroll taxes setup screen

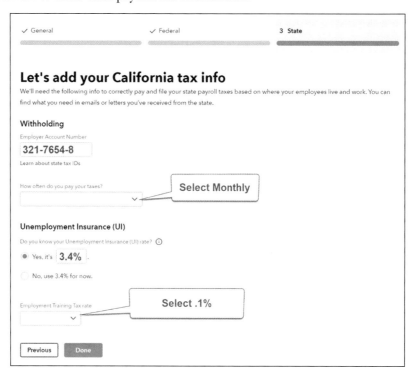

Your state employer number is 321-7654-8. (You do not need to enter the hyphen when entering the identification number. Formatting of tax numbers is automatic in QBO.) You deposit payroll taxes monthly. In California, employers pay for unemployment insurance. Your company's UI rate is 3.4%. The Employment Training Tax rate is 0.1%.

Click **Done**.

The final setup steps, including identifying the accounts to be debited and credited in payroll transactions, are done in **Payroll Settings**.

Click the ⚙ on the icon bar.

Figure 12.40

Link to payroll settings screen

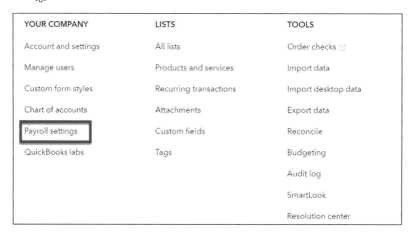

Click **Payroll Settings**.

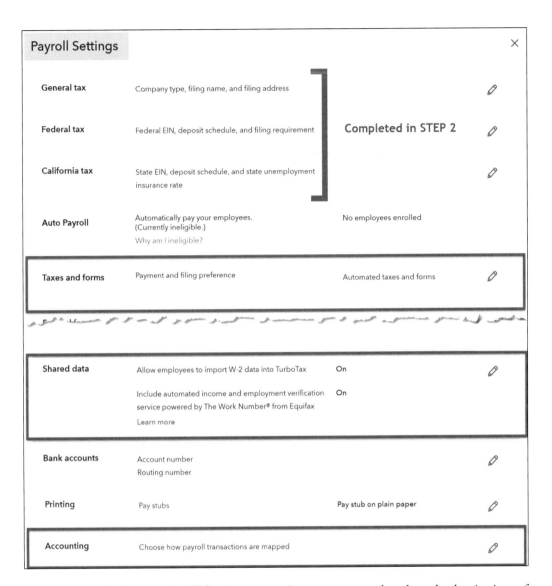

Figure 12.41

Payroll Settings screen

The general, federal, and California tax sections were completed at the beginning of STEP 4. You will only need to make changes in the sections highlighted in Figure 12.41

Open the **Taxes and forms** section to turn off automation in QBO payroll processing.

Figure 12.42

Payroll automation option

Uncheck the box next to **Automate taxes and forms**.

Under **How do you plan to handle taxes**, toggle **I'll initiate payments and filings using QuickBooks**. Users can still get reminders and access to forms in QBO without automating the process.

Click **Save**.

Click **Yes** in prompt about turning off automation.

Open the **Shared data** section (Figure 12.41).

Toggle both options to **Off**.

Open the **Accounting** section of **Payroll settings** (Figure 12.41) to set accounting preferences.

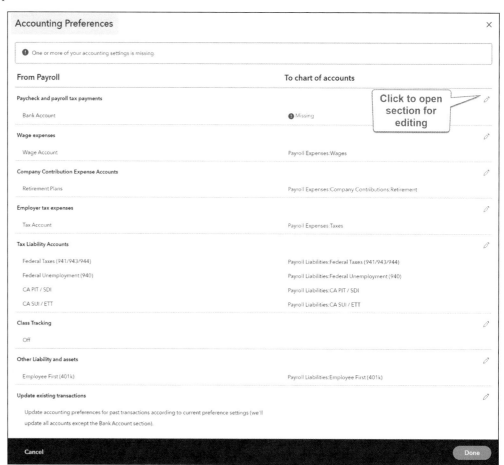

Click the pencil icon in the **Paycheck and payroll tax payments** section.

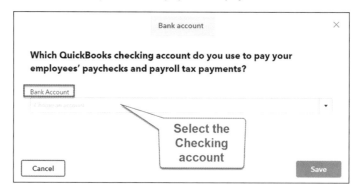

Select the checking account in the **Bank account** dropdown menu. This is the account that will be credited when employee paychecks and payroll tax remittance checks are recorded.

In the remaining sections, you will be identifying the general ledger accounts that should be debited or credited in payroll transactions. For payroll expenses (wages, employer payroll taxes, and employer-paid benefits), users have the option of setting up separate accounts for individual employees, for different types of labor, different groups of taxes, etc. In your homework, you will be posting all payroll-related expenses to one of three accounts: Salaries & wages expense, Payroll tax expense, or Employee benefits expense.

Click the pencil icon in the Wage expenses section.

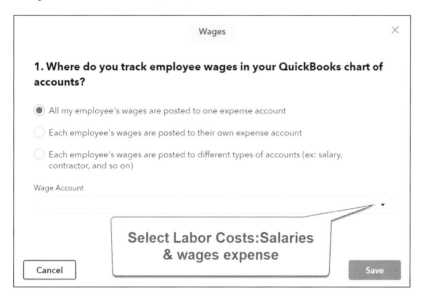

Figure 12.45
Wage distribution account

Select Salaries & wages expense (a subaccount of Labor Costs) as the account to be debited for compensation.

Click Save.

Click the pencil icon in the Company contribution expenses section.

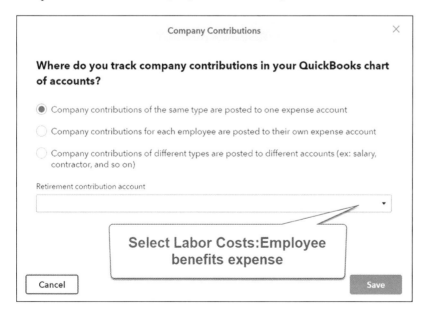

Figure 12.46
Employer-paid benefits distribution account

Select Employee benefits expense (a subaccount of Labor Costs) as the account to be debited for the company's 401(k) contributions.

Click Save.

Click the pencil icon in the Employer tax expenses section.

Figure 12.47

Employer payroll tax
distribution accounts

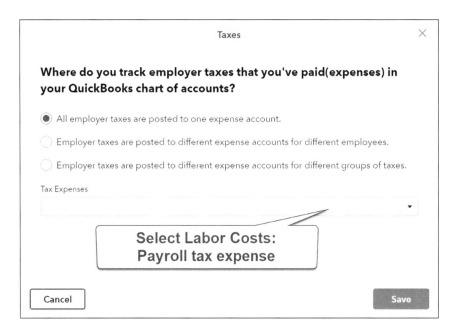

Select the **Payroll tax expense** account (a subaccount of **Labor Costs**).
   Click **Save**.
   Click the pencil icon in the **Tax Liability Accounts** section.

Figure 12.48

Tax liability distribution
accounts

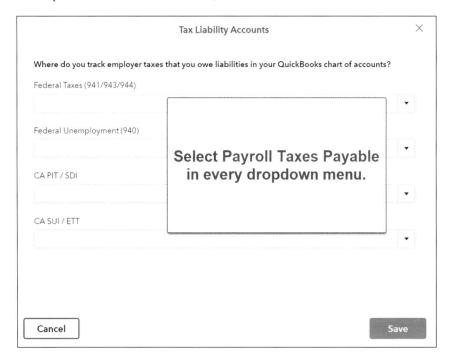

Select the **Payroll Taxes Payable** account for all tax liability accounts.
Click **Save**.
Click the pencil icon in the **Other liability and assets** section.

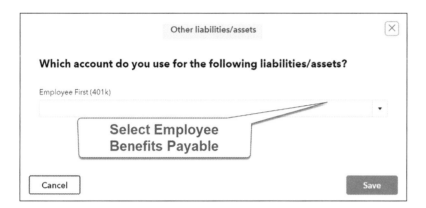

Figure 12.49

Other payroll-related
distribution accounts

Select **Employee Benefits Payable** as the account to be credited for employee and employer
retirement contribution liabilities.

Click **Save**.

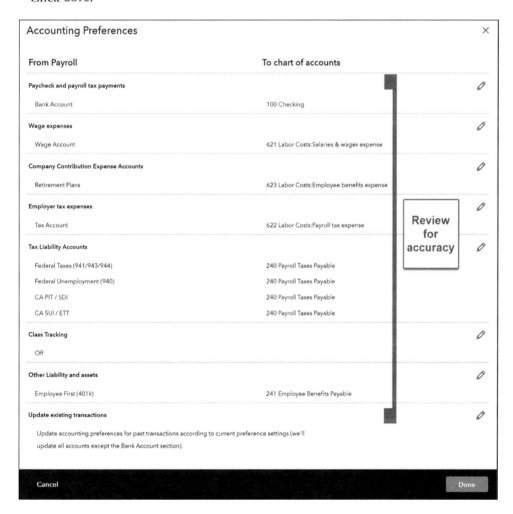

Figure 12.50

Completed accounting
preferences

Make sure your accounts match those in Figure 12.50. Edit if necessary.

Click **Done**.

Click **Done** again or click **Dashboard** on the navigation bar to exit the **Payroll Settings**
window.

eLecture

STEP 5—Process Payroll

Click **Payroll** on the navigation bar and open the **Employees drawer** (tab).

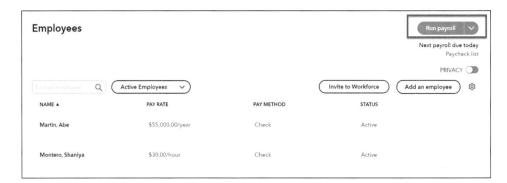

Click **Run payroll**.

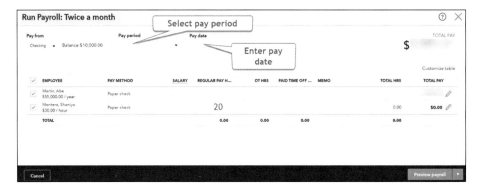

Select the first through the 15th of the **current** month in the **Pay period** field.

If you are completing your assignment before the 15th of the month, enter the 15th in the **Pay date** field. If you are completing your assignment after the 15th, enter the current date as the **Pay date**. (QBO will not allow you to use a paycheck date earlier than the current date. The pay period covered is not affected by a difference in the pay date.)

Enter 20 in the **REGULAR PAY HRS** box for Shaniya. (Abe's salary will autofill.)

Click **Preview payroll**.

A summary of the payroll (wages, payroll taxes, and other deductions) will appear on the next screen.

Paychecks can be edited. To edit a **paycheck** (before it's processed), click the pencil icon in the **NET PAY** column. You will not be editing any **paychecks**.

Click **Submit payroll**.

Figure 12.54

Identification of payroll check numbers

The final step is to enter the numbers of the paper checks. Use 2001 for Abe Martin and 2002 for Shaniya Montero.

Click **Finish payroll**.

To process payroll for the second half of the month, click **Payroll** on the navigation bar and select the **Employees** tab.

 HINT: You may see a message about finishing payroll setup on the **Overview** tab. You can ignore the message. All settings needed for payroll processing have been completed.

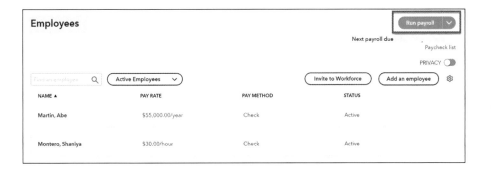

Figure 12.55

Link to run payroll through Employee Center

Click **Run payroll** and repeat the process used in recording payroll for the first half of the month.

 HINT: You may see a message about setting up direct deposit for an employee even if you selected **Paper check** for both Shaniya and Abe. You can ignore the message.

In the first screen, select the second half of the current month in the **Pay period** drop-down menu and enter the last day of the current month in the **Pay date** field.

 HINT: You may see a request to finish setting up direct deposit (even if you selected **paper check**) for both employees. Click **Remind me later**.

Enter 32 regular hours and 2 overtime hours for Shaniya. Abe's salary will autofill.

Click **Preview payroll**.

Verify that total hours for Shaniya are 34 and click **Submit payroll**.

In the final screen, use 2003 as the paycheck number for Abe and 2004 as the paycheck number for Shaniya.

Click Finish payroll.

BEHIND THE SCENES Certain fields in **paychecks** can be edited if the checks have been recorded in QBO but not delivered to the employee or if the employee has returned the undeposited check.

Click the employee name in the Employee Center.

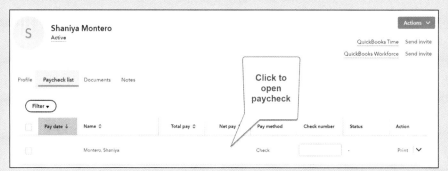

Open the **Paycheck list** tab and click the check to be edited.

Click **Edit** in the **Make adjustment** dropdown.

Click the arrow to the left of each section to see the fields that can be edited. In most cases, those fields include:

● Hours and hourly rate (for hourly employees)

● Overtime hours for salaried employees

● Federal and state income tax amounts

● Employee and employee 401(k) contribution amounts

If more significant changes need to be made, the **paycheck** should be deleted by selecting **Delete** or **Void** in the **Make adjustment** dropdown menu and then reissued. Again, this would only be done if either the check had not been delivered to the employee or the employee returned the check.

eLecture

STEP 6—Remit Payroll Taxes

Users who activate payroll in QBO are automatically set up to auto-file most federal and state payroll taxes for the **first** payroll month even if automation was turned off. This cannot be changed until the first day of the following month. Since you are doing the assignment during that first month, you will only record tax remittances in your homework company file for certain California employer taxes.

Click **Taxes** on the navigation bar and open the **Payroll Tax drawer** (tab).

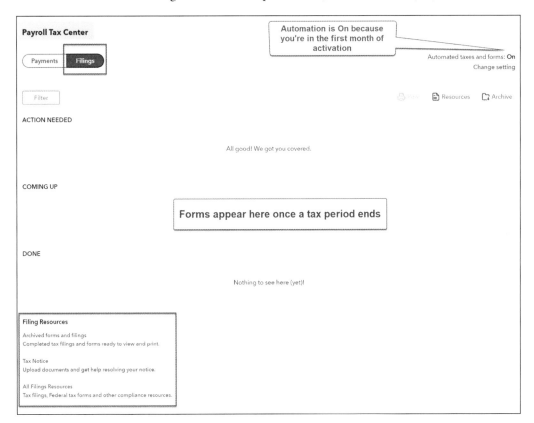

Figure 12.56

Payroll tax center

The Payroll Tax Center includes two tabs: **Filings** and **Payments**.

On the **Filings** tab, there are links to a variety of resources, including information about filing requirements and COVID-19 payroll programs. There are also links to standard employee and employer federal and state compliance forms and links to completed, ready-for-filing tax forms.

Because you are processing payroll in the current month, you should not see any tax forms listed in the **Upcoming filings** section. Forms appear once a payroll period is completed and payroll taxes are due.

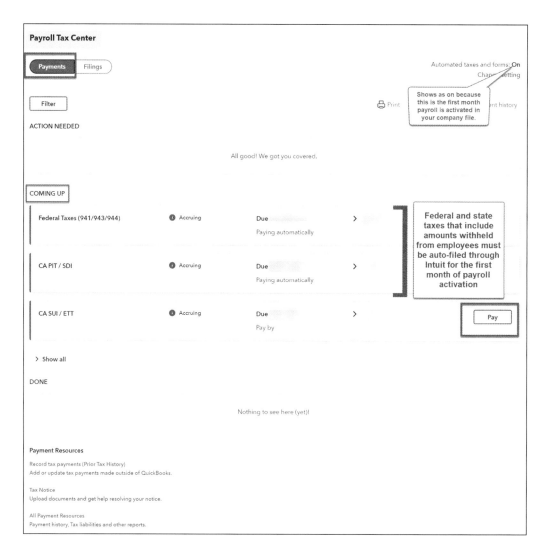

Figure 12.57

Payments tab in Payroll
Tax Center

On the Payments tab, liabilities to date and future payment dates are displayed. QBO **does** allow users to pay accrued payroll taxes in advance. However, since this is the first month payroll has been processed in your homework company, you will only be able to pay some of the state employer payroll taxes. (Starting with the second month, all federal and state taxes can be paid before the end of the payroll period.)

Click Pay in the CA SUI/ETT row.

You will receive a message warning you against paying payroll taxes before the tax period has ended. Click Yes, continue.

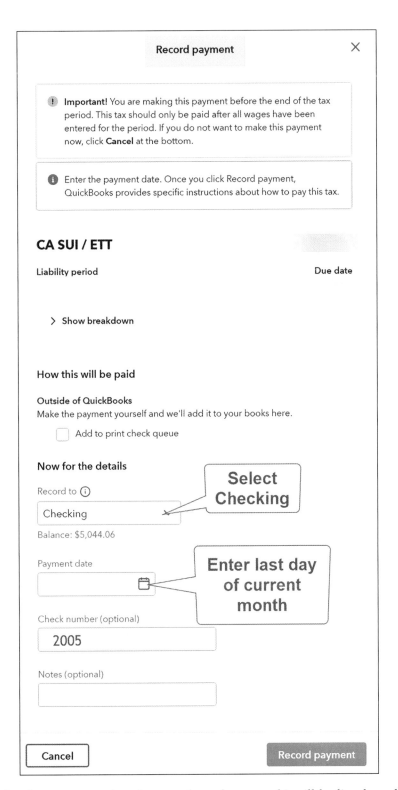

Figure 12.58

Payroll tax payment
screen

The calculated tax amounts (employer and employee totals) will be listed on the Record Payment screen.

Select Checking in the Record to dropdown menu. Enter the last day of the current month in the date field. Enter 2005 as the Check Number.

Click Record payment.

Figure 12.59

Payroll tax payment
confirmation

Payment details are included on the confirmation screen. Users can also print a form from this screen that can be used when submitting electronic payments to the taxing authority.

Figure 12.60

Summary of California
payroll tax remittance

A completed form suitable for mailing would be provided here if the taxing authority did not accept electronic payments. You do not need to print out the worksheet.

STEP 7—Access Payroll Reports

To view available payroll reports, click **Reports** on the navigation bar.

Payroll reports are included in the **Payroll** section on the **Standard** reports tab.

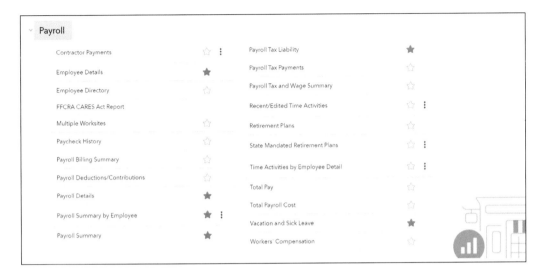

Figure 12.61

Payroll section of reports menu

Commonly used payroll reports are starred in Figure 12.61.

 HINT: On some payroll reports, the options to print or save to PDF are included in the **Share** dropdown menu in the top right corner of the report.

STEP 8—Edit Employees When Necessary

 HINT: You should not need to complete this step in your homework company. You should, however, review the section so that you are familiar with the process of editing employees in QBO.

Employees are managed on the **Employees** tab of the Payroll Center.

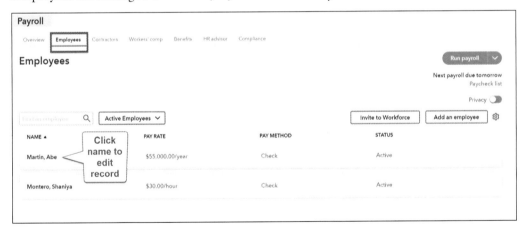

Figure 12.62

Employee Center

To edit an employee, click his/her name in the **Employees** tab of the Payroll Center.

You will be returned to the employee record screen shown in Figure 12.21. Edits can be made in any of the sections.

CHAPTER SHORTCUTS

Add an employee
1. Click **Payroll**
2. Open **Employees** tab
3. Click **Add an employee**

Edit an employee
1. Click **Payroll**
2. Open **Employees** tab
3. Click the name of employee to change
4. Click the pencil icon in the section to be edited

Pay an employee
1. Click **Payroll**
2. Open **Employees** tab
3. Click **Run payroll**

Edit a paycheck
1. Click **Payroll**
2. Open the **Employees** tab
3. Click employee name to open employee record
4. Open **Paycheck list** tab
5. Click paycheck to be changed
6. Select **Edit** in the **Make adjustment** dropdown menu

CHAPTER REVIEW

Assignments with the are available in myBusinessCourse.

Matching

Match the term or phrase (as used in QuickBooks Online) to its definition.

1. employee status
2. payroll settings
3. pay type
4. pay frequency
5. paycheck
6. pay policies
7. pay schedule
8. personal info

_____ a category of compensation

_____ transaction type used to record wage payments to employees

_____ tool available to pay employees in specific cycles

_____ how often employee wages are paid

_____ section in employee record where contact information and birth date are recorded

_____ place where general ledger accounts used in recording payroll accounts are identified

_____ indicator of employee's current standing as an employee

_____ includes information about available paid time off benefits offered by a company

Multiple Choice

1. W-4 information for new employees is entered in which section of the new employee setup?
   a. Does employee have any deductions?
   b. What are the employee's withholdings?
   c. What are the employee's personal details?
   d. Personal info.

2. Which of the following statements is true?
   a. Employees are limited to one **pay type**.
   b. An employee must be identified as either a salaried, hourly, or commission only employee.

   c. Salaried employees would never be eligible for overtime pay.

   d. Hourly employees can be assigned only one hourly pay rate.

3. Which of the following taxes are paid by both the employee and the employer?

   a. Federal withholding

   b. Federal unemployment

   c. FICA

   d. State withholding (if applicable)

4. Taxes withheld from employees are:

   a. remitted on or before the tax report due date, depending on the size of the employer.

   b. always remitted monthly.

   c. always remitted within three days of issuing paychecks.

   d. always remitted with the tax report.

5. Which of the following is not an expense of the employer?

   a. State unemployment

   b. Federal unemployment

   c. FICA

   d. All of the above are expenses of the employer.

BEYOND THE CLICKS—THINKING LIKE A MANAGER

Accounting: The sales manager is deciding between two possible compensation structures for sales staff. Under one plan, salespeople would receive a base compensation of $80,000 per year plus a 1% commission on all sales to their customers. Under the other plan, the base compensation would drop to $40,000 per year, but the commission rate would increase to 5%. What are the advantages and disadvantages, to the **company**, of both plans? As the accounting manager, would you have a preference? Why or why not?

Information Systems: Payroll functions in QBO include: adding and editing employee information (pay rates, leave policies, etc.), processing payroll, and managing payroll settings. Currently, users either have full access or no access to payroll functions. Name two ways an employee with full access to the payroll functions could commit fraud. What could a company do to prevent or detect the fraud examples you identified? (Assume you can't reprogram QBO!)

ASSIGNMENT

The **PAYROLL SYSTEM WALKTHROUGH** section of the chapter was the assignment for Chapter 12.

Suggested reports for Chapter 12

TIP: Click **Share** in the top right corner of the report and select **Export to Excel** or **Print or save PDF** to save or print your report.

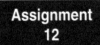

- Payroll Details (customized to remove **Other pay**, **Pay period**, and **Pay method** columns)
    - For the pay period ending on the 15th
    - For the pay period ending on the last day of the month
- Employee Details
- Payroll Tax Liability
    - For the 1st through the last day of the payroll month
- Payroll Summary by Employee
    - For the 1st through the last day of the payroll month

QuickBooks

SECTION SIX

Artificial Intelligence, Data Analysis, and QBO

Ever since humans first started engaging in trade and barter activities that involved shipping goods or selling/purchasing on account, some sort of recordkeeping has been required. Archaeologists have found evidence of trading records, dating back thousands of years, in Egyptian and Mesopotamian civilizations. Once there were records, the data from those records started to be used to highlight operating results and financial positions.

As commerce grew and transactions became more complex, accounting systems became more sophisticated. The first accounting "textbook," written by Luca Pacioli and published in 1494, explained the double-entry bookkeeping system you learned in your introductory financial accounting course. Pacioli didn't just give the rules, though; he also explained the purpose of the system. He wrote, "If you are in business and do not know all about it, your money will go like flies, that is, you will lose it." Sage advice! Fast-forward 525+ years. If Pacioli were alive today, he might be overwhelmed by how much company owners can "know" about their business.

This section looks at new types and sources of information and new tools for analyzing that information.

Chapter 13 covers the growth in data available for analysis, new technologies, and how Intuit uses these technologies in QBO to increase automation and provide additional management tools.

Chapter 14 covers various types and tools of data analysis and when they might be used. Best practices for communicating insights to management are also covered.

Big Data, Artificial Intelligence, and QBO

Road Map

WHAT IS BIG DATA?

LO 13-1 Understand the meaning of the term "big data"; explain types, sources, and methods for processing data

Merriam-Webster defines data as:

1. *Factual information . . . used as a basis for reasoning, discussion or calculation.*
2. *Information in digital form that can be transmitted or processed.*
3. *Information output by a sensing device or organ that includes both useful and irrelevant or redundant information and must be processed to be meaningful.*

Data can be quantitative (numerical) or qualitative (non-numerical). Quantitative information is used to measure or count. Qualitative data is used to classify or categorize.

There is no standard, agreed-upon definition of **Big Data**. However, big data is generally understood to mean a set of high-volume, high-variety, and high-velocity information. Gartner, a leading research and advisory company, defined big data as "data that contains great variety, arriving in increasing volumes, with ever-higher velocity." Some data scientists and researchers add "unknown veracity" as another characteristic of big data.

In big data, **volume** refers to the amount of data. According to **IDC** (a global provider of research and advisory information),[1] an estimated 96 zettabytes of data were created or replicated in 2022. In the future, data generation is expected to increase 21.2% per year. At that rate, data generation would exceed 200 zettabytes in 2025. (Just so you know, there are 21 zeros in one zettabyte.) Massive amounts of data cannot be managed on a single machine. They must be stored in clusters over multiple physical or virtual machines.

Variety refers to the type and source of data. Data can include numbers, symbols, words, sounds, or video—any information that can be stored in digital form. Data might be generated from business software applications, posts on social media, phone calls, smartwatches, industrial machines, employee suggestion boxes, and so on. Big data would typically include different types of data coming from a number of different sources.

Velocity refers to the speed at which the data is being produced. The amount of data is not only growing; it's growing exponentially as more people gain internet access, and more technology is created that connects humans to machines and machines to machines. Collecting and processing data is complicated by the speed at which that data is generated.

Veracity refers to the quality (accuracy) of the data. Data quality can be negatively affected by untrustworthy data sources, inconsistent or missing data, statistical biases, and human error.

In summary, a collection of data, a dataset, would be considered "big data" if:

- The dataset is too large to be managed by traditional methods.
- The dataset includes a variety of data types from a variety of sources.
- The amount of data in the dataset is expanding rapidly.
- The accuracy and reliability of the data may be uncertain.

BEHIND THE SCENES If you want a better sense of how much data is being generated, you might want to view the *Data Never Sleeps 10.0* infographic released by Domo, Inc. at the end of 2022. (Domo is a cloud-based business intelligence tool, similar to Tableau and Power BI.) According to their research, in every minute of every day, on average:

- 5.9M searches are conducted on Google.
- People send 16M texts.
- 66K photos are shared on Instagram.

You can see the full infographic at domo.com/data-never-sleeps

---

[1] Burgener, Rydning, *High Data Growth and Modern Applications Drive New Storage Requirements in Digitally Transformed Enterprises*, IDC, July 2022

Types and Sources of Big Data

There are three basic types of data:

- Structured data
    - Highly organized, resides in a tabular format (rows and columns)
    - Easy to search, sort, or combine
    - Only about 10–20% of all data is structured.
- Unstructured data
    - No predefined structure
    - Difficult to search, sort, or combine
- Semi-structured data
    - Doesn't reside in a tabular format but contains tags or markers that can be used in search functions
    - Moderately difficult to search, sort, or combine

Examples of Data Types		
Structured	**Unstructured**	**Semi-structured**
Relational databases	Images	Email messages
Spreadsheets	Text	Log files
Web forms	Videos	Streaming data
E-commerce transactions	Audio files	

Certain types of information can be structured, unstructured, or semi-structured, depending on how the data is captured and stored. Examples include data from IoT devices, social media posts, satellite imagery, and GPS data.

According to multiple industry analysts, 80–90% of worldwide data is unstructured or semi-structured. Although big data can include all three types of data, unstructured data is the most high-volume, high-variety, and high-velocity.

Data can be:

- derived from a company's IT systems (accounting, human resources, production, etc.).
- streamed from smart devices (medical devices, industrial equipment, wearables, etc.).
- obtained from customers through their activities in web applications.
    - Spotify, Amazon, and Uber are examples of companies that use data from customer search and purchase activity.
- obtained from other companies through application programming interfaces (APIs). APIs act as intermediaries between two companies (the company application or server requesting specific information and the company application or server providing the requested information).
    - QBO has an API that is used by third parties to develop and manage software that can be integrated with QBO.
- accessed through open data sources like the US government's data.gov.
    - There are over 250,000 datasets on Data.gov (https://www.data.gov/). One dataset includes information from consumer complaints made to the Federal Communications Commission (FCC) since 2014. About half of the complaints are related to unwanted calls (telemarketing, solicitation, etc.)!

> **BEHIND THE SCENES** Analysts and industry leaders are currently questioning the value of focusing so heavily on "big data" in data analysis and artificial intelligence. One concern is that the relevance of historical data can be quickly compromised by sudden economic, demographic, or political shifts. (Case in point: For many businesses, pre-2020 financial data became obsolete within weeks of the first case of COVID-19.) Processing big data also takes considerable time and resources. As the economy moves forward and technology advances, decision-makers need quick access to data from a wide variety of sources.
>
> The technology advisory firm Gartner predicts that by 2025, 70% of organizations will shift their focus from big data to "small" and "wide" data. "Small data" simply means a dataset that is easily accessible (often coming from within the organization itself) and workable. Small data analytics focus on identifying short-term, actionable insights. "Wide data" would include structured and unstructured data from a wide variety of sources. Wide data analytic techniques focus on identifying links between heterogeneous datasets. Wide datasets, which can be large but don't have to be, are often used in machine learning.

Processing Data (Extracting, Transforming, and Loading)

Combining and then organizing structured, semi-structured, and unstructured data results in a powerful source of information for organizations.

There are many different data processing tools and systems. Regardless of the tool or system, the process generally involves three steps:

- Data is copied or exported from the various data sources.
    - Sources could include accounting software systems, documents, images, sensors from factory equipment, survey data, etc.
    - Known as **extracting** data

- Inconsistent, inaccurate, or duplicated data is corrected or removed. If necessary, data is reformatted to better fit the needs of users.
    - Known as **transforming** data

- Data is stored in a centralized repository.
    - Known as **loading** data

The first step is to **extract** useable data from the data source(s). Structured data is already in a row/column format, but unstructured or semi-structured data is not. The extraction process for non-structured data requires some translation work.

Let's say a company wants to look at customer satisfaction data for its various products or services. Customer comments posted to its website might be a great source of information. Artificial intelligence algorithms (discussed in the next section) could be used to analyze the words in the comments and translate the text into one of three categories (satisfied, unsatisfied, neutral). The extracted data might now show comment identification numbers in rows; product, date, location, and satisfaction levels in columns. (Company employees could also read all the comments and manually create a dataset, but that might take a lot of time!)

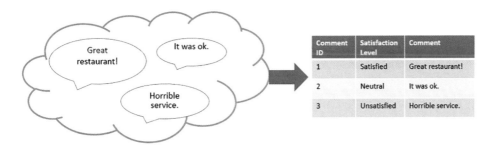

In many data processing systems, **transforming** the data is the second step. An essential part of the data transformation process is **data cleaning** (removing duplicates and empty (null) rows and columns and identifying and correcting inconsistencies). Changes to the data itself might also be necessary. Single columns might be split into multiple columns, or data values might be reformatted.

Single column split into multiple columns

Data		Month	Day	Year
5/10/2025		5	10	2025
5/18/2025		5	18	2025
5/20/2025		5	20	2025
6/3/2025		6	3	2025
6/8/2025		6	8	2025

For example, a field defining sales regions using a numeric code might be changed to a text field using the region name. Mapping data from multiple sources might also be part of the transformation process.

If the extracting and transforming steps are done first, the data is typically loaded into a **data warehouse**. This approach is known as ETL (extract, transform, load). Various users within the organization can access the data warehouse to create smaller databases for internal use.

Some companies reverse the order of the last two steps. Data is loaded **before** it's transformed (ELT instead of ETL), and the extracted data is often loaded into a **data lake** instead of a data warehouse. Data lakes can hold both structured and unstructured data, so with ELT, much of the translation of unstructured data is done as part of the transformation process.

Data warehouse Large repository of processed data collected from different sources.

Data lake Large repository of raw data collected from different sources.

> **BEHIND THE SCENES** A **data mart** includes processed data specific to a single business unit (or business line). It's often a subset of a data warehouse but can be a standalone system. Since data marts contain far less data than data warehouses, processing is quicker, and security is more robust.

IBM, **Microsoft**, and **Oracle** are three companies that offer data processing platforms.

To make sense of the data, companies often use business analytics solutions like Tableau or Power BI. Excel can also be used. These software applications allow companies to turn datasets into interactive visualizations (in graphic and pictorial formats) that can be shared across organizations. Visualizations are discussed in Chapter 14.

WHAT IS ARTIFICIAL INTELLIGENCE AND HOW IS IT USED?

Artificial Intelligence

Artificial intelligence (AI) is the simulated capacity for abstract, creative, and deductive thought (human capabilities) in computer systems (machines). Although there are researchers

LO 13-2 Differentiate between types of artificial systems (AI) and have a basic understanding of tools used to develop those systems

involved in developing computers that can do **any** task a human can do, most data science progress is still in the area of artificial narrow intelligence (ANI), sometimes referred to as weak AI. In ANI, the focus is on developing computer systems that can carry out specific tasks (drive a car, take an order, classify a transaction, etc.) that humans would typically do.

> **BEHIND THE SCENES** Other types of artificial intelligence include:
> - Artificial general intelligence (AGI), sometimes referred to as strong AI
>   - Systems capable of performing **any** intellectual task that a human could do, including reasoning, learning, and problem-solving
>   - Would be able to adapt to new situations
> - Artificial Superintelligence (ASI)
>   - Systems that are more intelligent than any human in every possible way
>   - Would be capable of solving problems that are currently beyond human understanding
>
> Some consider generative AI a distinct type of AI or even the first example of AGI. However, it's usually considered to be a subfield of ANI. Generative AI systems can create new data or content, such as text, images, or text given user prompts. ChatGPT, Bard, and DALL-E are examples of generative AI. There are currently no examples of ASI.

Types of Artificial Intelligence Systems

Artificial intelligence systems are computer systems designed to perform tasks that typically require human-like intelligence (for example, reasoning, perception, and decision-making). AI systems are powered by computer models that are trained by algorithms using datasets. Some AI systems use big data in the training process; others are trained on smaller, targeted datasets.

> **BEHIND THE SCENES** In computer science, an algorithm is a set of rules (instructions) used to perform computations or automate processes. **Rules-based algorithms** are written by humans (programmers) and can only be modified by humans.
> **Machine learning algorithms** start with a framework and some parameters developed by humans and are then trained on large datasets. In the training process, parameters automatically adjust to improve performance. (Parameters can also be adjusted by humans.) The algorithms can then be used to make predictions or decisions about data that has not been encountered before.

AI systems can be classified into different types based on how the technology is used. Commonly used systems include:

- Natural language processing (NLP)
  - A type of AI that focuses on enabling machines to understand and interpret human language.
  - Machine learning and rules-based algorithms are used to analyze text and speech.
  - Used in chatbots, voice assistants like Siri and Alexa, translation software, etc.
- Computer vision
  - A type of AI that focuses on enabling machines to see and interpret the visual world.

- Machine learning and rules-based algorithms are used to analyze images, recognize objects, and identify patterns.
- Used in self-driving cars, surveillance, and medical imaging, etc.
- Speech recognition
  - A type of AI that focuses on enabling machines to recognize and interpret spoken language.
  - Machine learning and rules-based algorithms are used to convert audio signals to text that a machine can understand.
  - Used in voice-controlled devices and voice assistants like Siri.
- Robotic process automation (RPA)
  - Refers to the use of software robots to automate routine, repetitive tasks.
  - Rules-based algorithms are used to program the software robot to perform a specific series of tasks in a specific order.
  - Used in data entry, order monitoring, customer support, etc.

Machine Learning Models

Machine learning models, used to make predictions or simulate scenarios, are a fundamental component of AI systems. Examples of machine learning models include:

- Linear regression—a model used to predict a numerical value based on one or more input variables

- Decision tree—a model used to categorize or make predictions based on answers to previous questions

- Random forest—a model that combines multiple decision trees to improve accuracy

- Neural network—a model that consists of multiple layers of interconnected nodes that work together to predict output values

> **BEHIND THE SCENES**   With deep learning, considered a subset of machine learning, many layers of neural networks are used to create models. The neural network looks for increasingly complex patterns as data passes through each layer. More patterns result in more accurate predictions for decisions. Very large datasets are needed for deep learning models.

Models are trained using algorithms and datasets. There are many different training techniques. Three of the most common are supervised, unsupervised, and reinforced learning.

Supervised learning

In supervised learning, the algorithm is trained on a labeled dataset. Labeled datesets have predefined inputs (such as images or texts) and outputs (such as labels or categories). The algorithm learns to predict the output from the input by finding patterns in the training data. Self-driving vehicle applications use supervised learning to identify pedestrians or other vehicles. Quality control applications use supervised learning to identify damaged merchandise on an assembly line.

Unsupervised learning

Datasets with no predefined outputs are used in unsupervised learning. Instead of learning to map inputs to defined outputs, the algorithm looks for patterns and groupings in the datasets. Unsupervised learning has been used in creating medical imaging devices for radiologists and pathologists and in developing customer profiles for retailers.

Reinforcement learning

In reinforcement learning, the algorithms are provided with a set of actions, various parameters, and desired results. The algorithms explore different options and learn to take actions that maximize the desired results. Reinforcement learning is used to develop fraud detection systems and automated stock-trading algorithms. It's also used in the development of computer games.

AI models are used in the following ways:

- In software applications that run on local computers or servers
- In the cloud, where they can be accessed remotely by software applications or services
- On edge devices such as smartphones or cameras.

> ✳ **HINT:** The term "edge" in this context refers to proximity to end users or sensors. The edge of a network is where data is being generated or consumed.

ARTIFICIAL INTELLIGENCE IN QBO

 LO 13-3 Recognize uses of AI in QBO

Intuit continues to develop QBO, and artificial intelligence plays a significant part in that development.

You have already worked with a variety of QBO processes that are powered by AI.

- Banking transaction uploads (Chapter 8) and downloads (Appendix 8A)
  - QBO first looks to match the downloaded transaction to an existing transaction.
    - ○ rules-based and machine learning algorithms are used
  - If no matching transaction is found, QBO "guesses" an appropriate general account.
    - ○ rules-based and machine learning algorithms are used
- Scheduled recurring transactions (Chapter 9)
  - The rules are initially set by the user (frequency, account distributions, etc.). QBO automatically creates the transaction.
  - rules-based algorithms are used
- Receipt and bill capture (Chapter 11)
  - QBO first looks to match the receipt to an existing transaction.
    - ○ Extracted text is analyzed using NLP algorithms to identify inportant information.
    - ○ Rules-based and machine learning algorithms are then used to match the receipt to existing transactions.
  - If no matching transaction is found, QBO identifies an appropriate general account based on the similarities in text or amounts to historical transactions.
    - ○ rules-based and machine learning algorithms are used

QBO's cash flow planning tool (not covered in this book) uses AI systems to predict future cash inflows and outflows. In QBO Accountant and QBO Advanced, AI-powered reporting features are used to generate graphs and charts.

PRIVACY AND ETHICAL ISSUES WITH BIG DATA AND ARTIFICIAL INTELLIGENCE

LO 13-4 Identify and explain ethical issues with big data

Big data and artificial intelligence are exciting topics, but with new technologies come new issues.

Privacy (or lack of privacy) is of paramount concern. Think of the amount of information you're likely giving to an online retailer. Once you sign up, the company can track your purchases, use of coupons, returns, calls to customer support, address changes, when and how many times you visited the website, and what you looked at when you were on the site. Assumptions about your age, marital status, income, and whether or not you have children can be inferred from your purchasing history. You may or may not be aware of the information the retailer has collected. Even if you are aware, you may not realize how that information is being used or whom it's being shared with.

And that's just information provided to online retailers. The information many of us regularly post on social media sites can reveal more about our personal lives than we realize. If in the wrong hands, that information can even be dangerous.

Companies have privacy concerns, as well. According to a survey by IBM and Ponemon,[2] the average global cost of a **data breach** in 2022 was $4.35 million. Of the survey respondents, 83% reported that they had experienced more than one data breach and 60% reported that the breaches led to increased prices to customers. The industry with the highest average cost ($10.10 million) was healthcare. The country with the highest average cost ($9.44 million) was the United States. (The study was geographically limited. For example, it did not include data from China, Russia, or African countries other than South Africa.) The study found that the most **common** way attackers gained access to computer systems was through the use of **compromised credentials**. The second most common method and the most costly were the result of **phishing attacks**.

There was one positive trend highlighted in the study. Organizations with high levels of security automation (cognitive technologies that augment or replace human security controls) experienced financial losses 57% lower than organizations with no security automation.

Breaches of company computer systems aren't the only privacy concern for businesses. Information intentionally or unintentionally leaked by employees or bad reviews posted by customers on social media or company websites can negatively affect future business.

There are also ethical concerns with AI.

For example, some deep learning models are designed to **automatically** (without human intervention) adapt their structure during training in response to the data being processed. These modifications can have a significant impact on the performance of the model. Explainable AI (XAI), a relatively new field, refers to the development of AI models and systems that can provide clear explanations of their outputs or decisions to humans. Increased transparency should help increase our confidence in a system's output and decisions.

Built-in bias is another concern. Human beings create the algorithms, and AI systems "learn" from the datasets used in the training process. If the algorithms used or the datasets reflect assumptions or preferences, the applications powered by that AI may result in suboptimal or discriminatory practices. That's of particular concern in applications used in recruiting, credit scoring, and judicial sentencing. In 2015, Amazon learned that its new recruiting software was not promoting women applicants. Why? It turns out that the dataset used to train the system consisted of resumes submitted to the company over the prior 20-year period. The vast majority of applicants during that period were men. Amazon's system had "learned" from the data that male candidates were preferable and proceeded to penalize resumes that included the word "women's" or were from candidates who attended all-women's colleges.

Accountability for failures of AI will also need to be determined. If a patient dies after being misdiagnosed by medical software powered by AI, who is responsible? The doctor, the hospital, the data scientist? Or what if a self-driving car doesn't stop at a red light and

Data breach Release of confidential, sensitive, or protected information to unauthorized entities.

Compromised credentials Lost or stolen usernames, passwords, or other identifying information.

Phishing attacks Counterfeit communications (usually emails) sent to employees/owners in attempts to obtain sensitive information (passwords, login information) or to install malware.

---

[2] IBM Security and Ponemon Institute LLC, *Cost of a Data Breach Report 2022*, July 2022.

damages another vehicle? Who should pay for that damage? The driver, the insurance company, the data scientist?

Finally, companies should consider the impact on employees as they automate more tasks using AI and terminate the employees who formerly did those tasks. Retraining is a possibility considered by many companies. Severance pay, job search assistance, and extended health benefits are other possible solutions.

FINAL NOTE

LO 13-5 Describe ways that accounting systems may change with growth of AI systems

As artificial intelligence continues to grow, the way accounting systems operate will also undergo significant changes. AI-powered accounting systems will enable faster and more accurate data processing, analysis, and reporting. Using machine learning algorithms, these systems will learn from patterns and trends in financial data to predict future outcomes, identify anomalies, and provide real-time insights to businesses. The more you understand these new technologies and how they can be used, the better prepared you will be.

CHAPTER REVIEW

Matching

Assignments with the MBC **are available in myBusinessCourse.**

Match the term or phrase (as used in this chapter) to its definition.

1. volume
2. structured data
3. variety
4. extract

5. algorithm
6. veracity
7. load
8. data breach

_____   amount of data

_____   sources and types of data

_____   move data to a data warehouse

_____   set of rules or instructions

_____   accuracy of data

_____   copy or export data

_____   clearly formatted data

_____   unauthorized release of information

Multiple Choice

1. Which of the following might include both structured and unstructured data?
   a. Chart of accounts
   b. Email
   c. Report of sales by region
   d. Balance sheet

2. Which of the following is not considered a characteristic of big data?
   a. High-Volume
   b. High-Velocity
   c. High-Variety
   d. High-Cost
   e. All of the above are characteristics of big data.

3. Removing duplicates in a dataset is often done as part of the _____ step.
   a. extract
   b. transform
   c. load
   d. Duplicates would never be included in a dataset.

4. In supervised learning,
   a. datasets include inputs and outputs
   b. datasets include inputs but no predefined outputs
   c. no datasets are needed
   d. a set of actions, various parameters, and desired results must be provided

5. Which of the following might result in a data breach?
   a. An employee checks their personal email on a company computer and opens an attachment.
   b. An external party hacks into a company computer using a stolen password.
   c. An employee sends a transaction file to the wrong person.
   d. Any of the above might result in a data breach.

BEYOND THE CLICKS—THINKING LIKE A MANAGER

Accounting: Your company has just announced its decision to significantly increase the number of AI-based technology tools used in the business next year. Your accounts receivable, accounts payable, and payroll clerks have expressed deep concerns to you about losing their jobs. What could the company do to alleviate their fears? Should they?

Information systems: Your company has just announced its decision to significantly increase the number of AI-based technology tools used in the business next year. You were not included in the group that made that decision, but the company president has asked you to take over from here and manage the transition. What is the first thing you might do?

ASSIGNMENTS

The assignments have been created for students who are familiar with Excel. If you are new to Excel, check with your instructor.

Help with the assignment steps is available in the eLecture in the Chapter 13 module in myBusinessCourse.

It's 2025, and Math Revealed! is now selling its inventory products through a 3rd party e-commerce site. While the e-commerce site is excellent at some things, it is not integrated with QBO, so you have to import all the sales made from the e-commerce site into QBO. **TIP:** You will be going through the extract, transform, and load process (ETL) discussed on pages 13-6 and 13-7 of this chapter.

Assignment 13A

Math Revealed!

STEP 1: Extract the data

✓ You have already downloaded all of the e-commerce sales transaction data for 2025 to an Excel workbook. **TIP:** If you're using myBusinessCourse, the workbook (7e QBO MR Ch13 Sales Data) can be downloaded from Student Ancillaries in myBusinesCourse. If you're not using myBusinessCourse, your instructor will provide the workbook to you.

STEP 2: Transform the data

✓ Since this is only the second time you've imported invoices (the first time is when you initially set up your company file), you want to make sure the file is ready to import into QBO. You decide to start by reviewing the invoice import process. You open the import guide and **make a note** of:

- The required file format
- The required data fields
- The maximum number of rows that can be imported at one time

    TIP: To access the import guide, click ⚙ on the icon bar and select Import Data. Click Invoices and Download import guide. You will not need to add any columns to the workbook.

✓ You open the downloaded Excel workbook and review the fields and transactions. Right away, you notice that the **Customer** column fields include both the customer name and address. **TIP:** Often, when data is extracted from a system, multiple fields are put together in one column of data. The field in your workbook contains a delimiter that allows you to separate the data easily. Dictionary.com defines a delimiter as "a blank space, comma, or other character or symbol that indicates the beginning or end of a character string, word, or data item."

- You remove all unnecessary data in the **Customer** column so that only the customer name remains. **TIP:** You do not need to separate the first and last names of customers.

✓ You use Excel to check for and remove duplicate transactions. **TIP:** For purposes of this assignment, each invoice only has one line item (one row). In real-world scenarios, you could have one invoice with multiple lines.

- **Make a note** of how many duplicate rows were removed.

> **HINT:** Think about where possible duplicates might be and what is okay to be duplicated. For example, is it okay to have customers repeated? Is it okay to have an item repeated? Is it okay to have an invoice number repeated?

✓ You review the fields in the **Item(Product/Service)** column and correct any that are formatted incorrectly. **TIP:** All products and services are assigned to categories in your company file. Every product or service should be listed as: *Category name:Product/Service name (e.g., Math Games:Equations)*. If necessary, refer back to your QBO company file to determine the correct category for a specific product.

- **Make a note** of the number of items (products) formatted incorrectly.

✓ You know that all the data fields in the dataset should contain content (text, numbers, or dates). You use Excel to locate any fields with missing data. Using the clues from other lines of data, you complete the missing fields. **TIP:** If a **Term** is missing, use the **InvoiceDate** and **DueDate** fields to determine the appropriate term.

- **Make a note** of the number of fields with missing data.

✓ You save the file using the proper file type. **TIP:** The correct file type was listed in the import guide.

STEP 3: Load the data into QBO

✓ You import the invoices into QBO. **TIP:** The invoice import process was covered in Chapter 2 (STEP 9.)

> **WARNING:** When this book was published, the invoice import process would not work if the sales tax feature was active in a QBO company file. Sales tax was activated in your company file in Chapter 6, so if you have completed that chapter, you will not be able to import the invoices. Continue on to STEP 4.

STEP 4: Summarize the e-commerce sales for 2025

✓ You use Excel functions to determine the following using the data in the cleaned (transformed) Excel workbook:

- Total e-commerce revenue for 2025

- Average unit price in 2025

- Number of unique customers **TIP:** Count the parent customer and each sub-customer as unique.

- Customer with highest sales revenue in 2025

- **Parts of a Whole (Fractions)** games sold in 2025

It's 2025, and Salish Software Solutions is now selling its inventory products through a 3rd party e-commerce site. While the e-commerce site is excellent at some things, it is not integrated with QBO, so you have to import all the sales made from the e-commerce site into QBO. **TIP:** You will be going through the extract, transform, and load process (ETL) discussed on pages 13-6 and 13-7 of this chapter.

Assignment 13B

Salish Software Solutions

STEP 1—Extract the data

✓ You have already downloaded all of the e-commerce sales transaction data for 2025 to an Excel workbook. **TIP:** If you're using myBusinessCourse, the workbook (7e QBO SS Ch13 Sales Data) can be downloaded from Student Ancillaries in myBusinesCourse. If you're not using myBusinessCourse, your instructor will provide the workbook to you.

STEP 2—Transform the data

✓ Since this is only the second time you've imported invoices (the first time is when you initially set up your company file), you want to make sure the file is ready to import into QBO. You decide to start by reviewing the invoice import process. You open the **import guide** and **make a note** of:

- The required file format
- The required data fields
- The maximum number of rows that can be imported at one time
  TIP: To access the **import guide**, click ⚙ on the icon bar and select **Import Data**. Click **Invoices** and **Download import guide**. You will not need to add any columns to the workbook.

✓ You go back to the Excel workbook and review the fields and transactions. Right away, you notice that the **Customer** column fields include both the customer name and address. **TIP:** Often, when data is extracted from a system, multiple fields are put together in one column of data. The field in your workbook contains a delimiter that allows you to separate the data easily. Dictionary.com defines a delimiter as "a blank space, comma, or other character or symbol that indicates the beginning or end of a character string, word, or data item."

- You remove all unnecessary data in the **Customer** column so that only the customer name remains. **TIP:** You do not need to separate the first and last names of customers.

✓ You use Excel to check for and remove duplicate transactions. **TIP:** For purposes of this assignment, each invoice only has one line item (one row). In real-world scenarios, you could have one invoice with multiple lines.

- **Make a note** of how many duplicate rows were removed.

 HINT: Think about where possible duplicates might be and what is okay to be duplicated. For example, is it okay to have customers repeated? Is it okay to have an item repeated? Is it okay to have an invoice number repeated?

✓ You review the fields in the **Item(Product/Service)** column and correct any that are formatted incorrectly. **TIP:** All products and services are assigned to categories in your company file. Every product or service should be listed as: *Category name:Product/Service name (e.g., Management Products:Legal)*. If necessary, refer back to your QBO company file to determine the correct category for a specific product.

- **Make a note** of the number of items (products) formatted incorrectly.

✓ You know that all the data fields in the dataset should contain content (text, numbers, or dates). You use Excel to locate any fields with missing data. Using the clues from other lines of data, you complete the missing fields. **TIP:** If a **Term** is missing, use the **InvoiceDate** and **DueDate** fields to determine which Term applies.

- **Make a note** of the number of fields with missing data.

✓ You save the file using the proper file type. **TIP:** The correct file type was listed in the import guide.

STEP 3—Load the data into QBO

✓ You import the invoices into QBO. **TIP:** The invoice import process was covered in Chapter 2 (STEP 9.)

 WARNING: When this book was published, the invoice import process would not work if the sales tax feature was active in a QBO company file. Sales tax was activated in your company file in Chapter 6, so if you have completed that chapter, you will not be able to import the invoices. Continue on to STEP 4.

STEP 4—Summarize the e-commerce sales for 2025

✓ You use Excel functions to determine the following using the data in the cleaned (transformed) Excel workbook:

- Total e-commerce revenue for 2025
- Average unit price in 2025
- Number of unique customers **TIP:** Count the parent customer and each sub-customer as unique.
- Customer with highest sales revenue in 2025
- Number of Easy Does It (Easy1) accounting software packages sold in 2025

14

Data Analytics and Data Visualization

Road Map

LO	Learning Objective	Topic	Subtopic	Page	Videos
LO 14-1	Define and recognize various types of data analytics [p. 14-2]	What is data analytics?	Descriptive analytics	14-2	
			Diagnostic analytics	14-2	
			Predictive analytics	14-3	
			Prescriptive analytics	14-3	
LO 14-2	Identify data analysis tools in QBO and data visualization software; identify and use data analysis tools in Excel [p. 14-3]	Tools for data analysis	Analysis tools in QBO	14-3	
			Analysis tools in spreadsheet programs	14-4	
			Analysis tools in data visualization software	14-15	
LO 14-3	Discuss best practices in data visualization [p. 14-17]	Best practices in data visualization	Select an appropriate chart type	14-18	Assignment Help
			Use color to highlight the data	14-18	
			Add text to explain and add context	14-19	
			Remove unnecessary elements	14-19	
			Make sure the visualizations are objective and balanced	14-19	
LO 14-4	Understand the need for technology skills in accounting [p. 14-20]	Beyond the numbers and into the future		14-20	

Data analysis went on long before anyone had heard of "big data" and long before artificial intelligence existed anywhere outside of science fiction. For example, Henry Ford used analytics in measuring the speed of automobile assembly lines in the early 1900s.

The first data analysis projects, of course, were done manually (with pencil and paper!) using an organization's data and data found in books and periodicals. Once productivity software like Excel became available, accountants could key in financial information from the internal accounting records and from outside sources and then quickly categorize and summarize that data.

New technologies like those discussed in Chapter 13 now make it possible for us to include financial and non-financial data from various sources in the analysis process.

WHAT IS DATA ANALYTICS?

LO 14-1 Define and recognize various types of data analytics

Data analytics involves examining data to draw conclusions and insights from that data. There are four primary types of data analytics.

Figure 14.1

Four types of data analytics

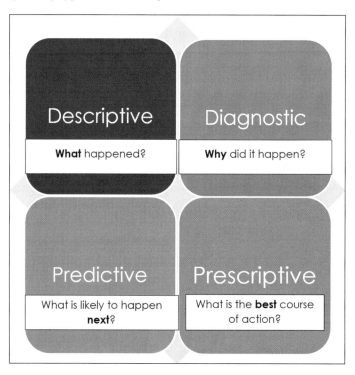

Descriptive Analytics

Descriptive analytics addresses what, how many, where, and when type questions. Historical accounting reports are the basis for much of the descriptive analytics in a business. In QBO, you're using descriptive analytics when you:

- prepare a profit and loss report
- prepare an inventory valuation detail report

Diagnostic Analytics

Diagnostic analytics involves drilling down on information to determine **why** something occurred. In QBO, a budget variance report can be used to identify why the company's net income was lower than expected. Maybe a particular revenue source was down, or a specific expense category was up. In Excel, PivotTables can be used for this purpose. For example, suppose a dataset included information about sales dollars by location and the location store manager's years of experience. A PivotTable might illustrate that sales dollars are lower at locations where the store manager is new. Similar analytic tools are available in other types of software.

Predictive Analytics

Predictive analytics is all about identifying trends and relationships. Predictive analytics often uses statistical modeling techniques. For example, suppose a dataset included information from the past two years about sales dollars by product, month, and store. Statistical modeling techniques could be used to determine how closely the month and the store location correlates to (tracks with) sales of specific products. If a strong correlation exists, the store manager could use that information to estimate revenues for the next quarter. The **cash flow planner** in QBO (not covered in this book) is a predictive analysis tool.

Prescriptive Analytics

Prescriptive analytics uses information from descriptive, diagnostic, and predictive analytics to suggest the best course of action in a specific scenario. For example, a retail company could use prescriptive analytics to determine the most appropriate product mix to place on the shelves at each of their stores using data from sales records, current vendor pricing, competitor pricing, population changes, etc. Onboard computer systems in electric vehicles can use data about weather conditions, traffic patterns, and even the driving habits of the vehicle's owner to optimize battery usage, ensuring efficient energy use.

TOOLS FOR DATA ANALYSIS

Analysis Tools in QBO

As noted in **WHAT IS DATA ANALYTICS?**, there are many reports in QBO Plus that can be used for descriptive and diagnostic analytics. Examples include:

LO 14-2 Identify data analysis tools in QBO and data visualization software; identify and use data analysis tools in Excel

- Budget vs Actuals

- Profit and Loss as % of total income

- Profit and Loss Comparison

- Project Profitability Summary

- Sales by Customer

- Sales by Product/Service

Some data visualization tools are available on the **Business overview** tab on the **Dashboard**.

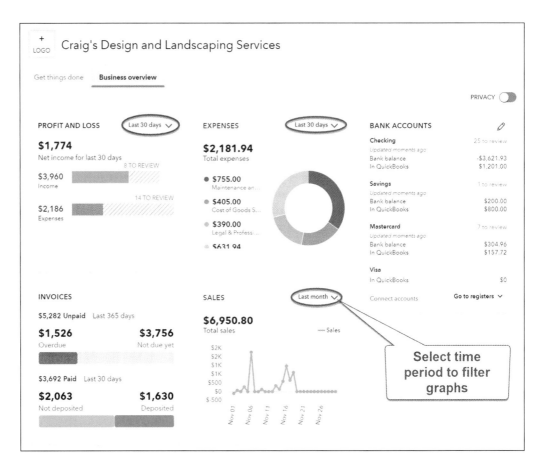

Currently, users can view graphs for sales and expenses over the time period selected in the dropdown menus.

The **Cash flow planner** tool allows users to create forecasts of cash activity using the following:

- Historical transactions from bank accounts connected to QBO

- Projected cash receipts and disbursements using due dates on **invoices** and **bills**

- Planned cash receipts and disbursements entered by the user
    - One-time or repeating

The projection period can be for the current month, the next three months, the next six months, and so on, up to 24 months.

Analysis Tools in Spreadsheet Programs

There are many different analysis tools in spreadsheet programs like Microsoft Excel and Google Sheets. In this section, we'll be looking at a **few** Excel tools available in Microsoft 365. Many of these are also available in older versions of Excel. Similar tools would be available in other spreadsheet programs.

PivotTables

Many of you are already familiar with **PivotTables**. PivotTables are interactive summaries of data found in a spreadsheet. Using PivotTable tools, data can be grouped, filtered, and rearranged in nearly endless ways.

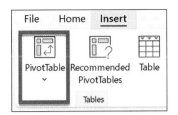

Figure 14.3

PivotTable tool

To create a PivotTable, highlight (select) the data to be analyzed on the spreadsheet. (You can also click on a cell anywhere within the dataset.) Open the **Insert** tab on the **Ribbon** (main menu bar in Excel) and select **PivotTable** in the **Tables** group.

A simple PivotTable for a company with multiple locations and sales representatives might look something like this:

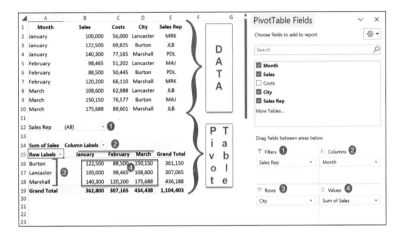

Figure 14.4

Example of a
PivotTable in Excel

PivotTables are most useful in answering "what" and "why" type questions (descriptive and diagnostic analytics). For example, in Figure 14.4, company management can quickly answer questions about why sales totaled over $1 million. They can see that the Marshall location had the most sales overall, that sales dropped in all cities in February, and that sales almost doubled in Burton between February and March. The filter field could be used to see the sales by month and city for individual sales reps. The PivotTable could also be modified to show cities in columns with month and sales reps in rows.

Charts (known as **PivotCharts**) can be directly created from **PivotTables**.

To create a **PivotChart**, click on a cell within the **PivotTable**. Open the **PivotTable Analyze** tab and click **PivotChart** in the **Tools** group. Select the chart type. A **PivotChart** for the data in Figure 14.4 might look something like this:

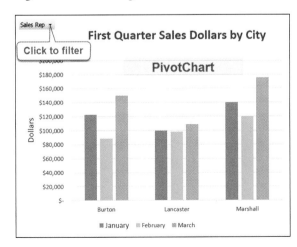

Figure 14.5

Clustered column
PivotChart

Filters added to the PivotTable will appear automatically on the PivotChart. Changes in the original dataset will automatically update related PivotTables and PivotCharts.

Correlation and Regression Functions

Two commonly used predictive analytics tools in Excel are **correlation** and **regression**.

Correlation In statistics, correlation is the degree to which two variables move in coordination with each other.

Regression analysis Regression analysis measures the relationship, if any, between a dependent variable and one or more independent variables.

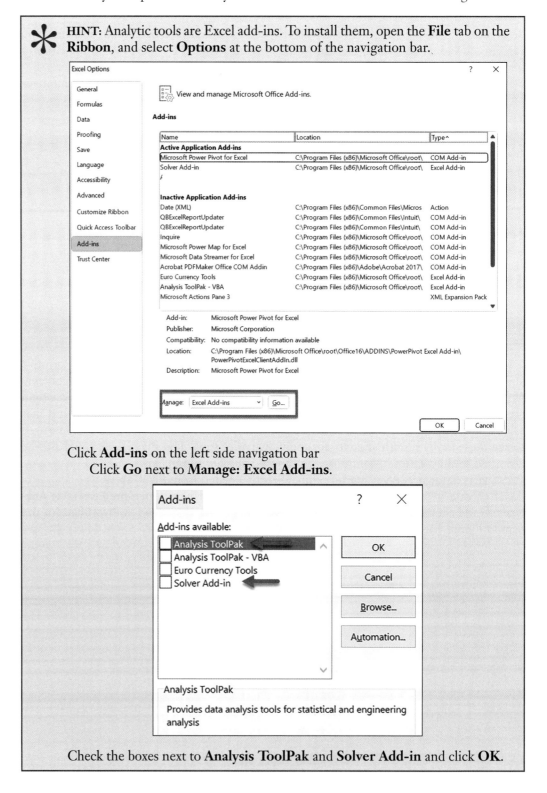

HINT: Analytic tools are Excel add-ins. To install them, open the **File** tab on the **Ribbon**, and select **Options** at the bottom of the navigation bar.

Click **Add-ins** on the left side navigation bar
Click **Go** next to **Manage: Excel Add-ins**.

Check the boxes next to **Analysis ToolPak** and **Solver Add-in** and click **OK**.

Figure 14.6

Access to data analysis functions

Open the **Data** tab on the **Ribbon**. Both **Correlation** and **Regression** are found in the **Data Analysis** dropdown menu in the **Analyze** group.

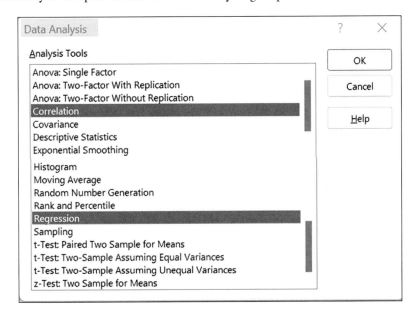

Figure 14.7

Data Analysis menu

The **Correlation** function (**CORREL**) determines if two measurements vary together (increase or decrease in a similar pattern) and can be used in predictive analytics. Excel will calculate the correlation percentage for every two-variable combination in a dataset. The correlation data is displayed in a table on the worksheet.

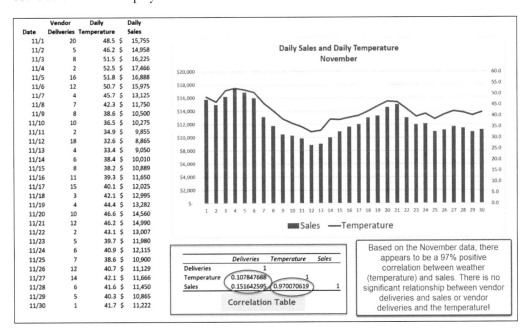

Figure 14.8

Correlation example

Correlation data can be a useful planning tool. Let's say a company used the **Correlation** function to look at three sets of data over a one-month period: daily temperature, daily sales in dollars, and number of product deliveries each day. If sales revenue is found to increase when temperatures rise and decrease when temperatures fall (see Figure 14.8), a retail manager could predict changes in sales volume by paying close attention to weather forecasts! Forecasts wouldn't help much at all when predicting vendor deliveries.

The **Regression** function (**LINEST**) is also used to determine relationships. However, the end product of regression analysis is an equation that can be used to estimate a result. In accounting, regression analysis is often used to estimate total costs given changes in volume.

Figure 14.9

Regression example

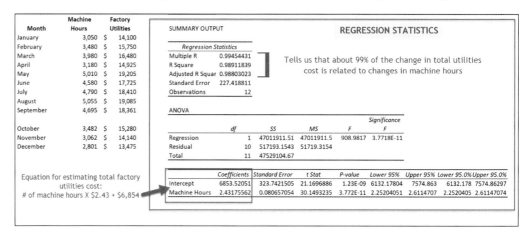

In Figure 14.9, regression analysis was used to estimate total monthly factory utilities costs given estimated machine-hours. The analysis found that there is a base monthly utility cost of approximately $6,854. (The base cost represents the minimum cost just to maintain services. The base cost is identified as the **Intercept** in Figure 14.9.) The total cost of utilities is expected to increase by roughly $2.43 for every machine-hour.

> **BEHIND THE SCENES** Reviewing all the different regression statistics displayed in Figure 14.9 is beyond the scope of this book. For more information about regression analysis, you might want to check out https://openstax.org/details/books/introductory-statistics, a free textbook published through OpenStax.

Forecasting Tool

Forecasting, another form of predictive analytics, can also be done in Excel. Forecasting uses historical data to estimate future results. In accounting, that data might be sales volume, sales dollars, profit, salaries, etc.

Forecasting can be done in Excel by adding **Trendlines** to line charts or by using the **Forecast Sheet** tool.

Figure 14.10

Chart menu

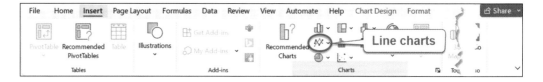

To add **trendlines** to line charts, highlight the historical data in the worksheet. Open the **Insert** tab on the **Ribbon** and click the line chart icon in the **Charts** group. Excel will automatically create a chart showing the historical data.

Figure 14.11

Trendline chart element

A **trendline** is added by checking the **Trendline** box on the **Chart Elements** menu. The number of forecasted periods is entered, and the type of trendline (linear, exponential, polynomial, etc.) is selected.

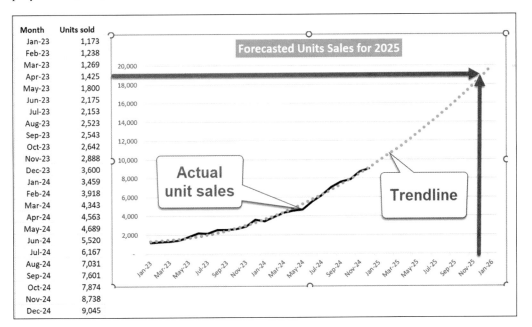

Figure 14.12

Example of a forecast using Trendline

In Figure 14.12, a polynomial trendline was added to a chart created using monthly unit sales data from two prior years. The chart shows a sales forecast for December 2025 of approximately 19,000 units.

> **BEHIND THE SCENES** When a **trendline** is added to a chart, Excel automatically defaults to a linear trend/regression type. If your data values increase or decrease at a steady rate, a linear line will likely produce the most accurate trendline. If your data is more complex, you may want to use a different type of trendline. Click anywhere on the trendline to open the **Format Trendline** sidebar.

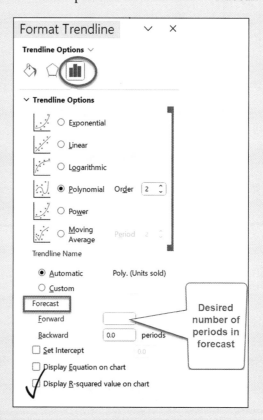

Open the columnar icon tab and select the trendline type.

The following trendline types are often used with financial data:

- Logarithmic: Often used when data values quickly increase (or decrease) and then level out.

- Polynomial: Often used when data values fluctuate. The order of the polynomial trendline depends on the number of fluctuations in the data. The more fluctuations there are, the higher the order number.

- Exponential: Often used when data values rise or fall at increasingly higher rates.

The type of trendline that best reflects the data can be determined by looking at the R-Squared value. (Check the **Display R-Squared value on chart** box and the value will be displayed on the chart.) The R-Squared value is a regression statistic. The closer the value is to 1, the better the fit.

The second forecasting tool, the **Forecast Sheet**, is accessed by opening the **Data** tab on the **Ribbon** and clicking **Forecast Sheet** in the **Forecast** group.

Figure 14.13

Link to Forecast Sheet tool

Forecast sheets present a range of forecasted results in chart form.

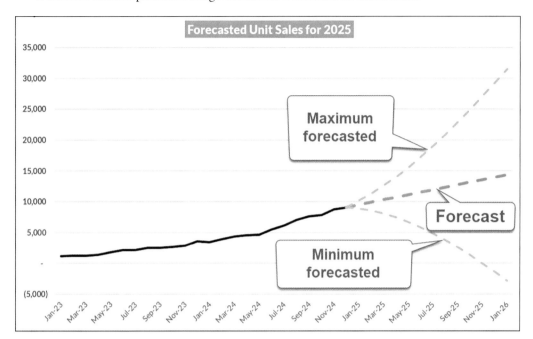

Figure 14.14

Example of a forecast using Forecast Sheet

The data used to create the chart in Figure 14.12 was also used in Figure 14.14. It is not possible to change the type of trend line (linear, exponential, polynomial, etc.) in forecast sheets.

> **BEHIND THE SCENES** Both forecasts and budgets are tools used by management in planning for the future. Although they are often used together, there are distinct differences. A budget represents a plan for the future based on estimates of prices, costs, and volumes. A forecast represents likely results given past performance. Budgets are goals; forecasts are predictions.

Solver Tool

The **Solver** function is a prescriptive analytics tool in Excel. It's used to determine the best course of action given an objective and one or more constraints.

Figure 14.15

Access to Solver tool

Solver is accessed in the **Analyze** group on the **Data** tab in Excel.

Let's say a hardware store sells a number of different products. The physical size and the per-unit profit differ between products. (Details about demand, unit profit, and size for each of the hardware store's products are shown in Figure 14.16.) The manager knows that it would take 44,343,925 cubic inches to store enough products to meet the monthly demand. Unfortunately, there's only 40,000,000 cubic inches of shelf space available! **Solver** can be used to determine the mix of products that maximizes profits.

Figure 14.16

Example of Solver

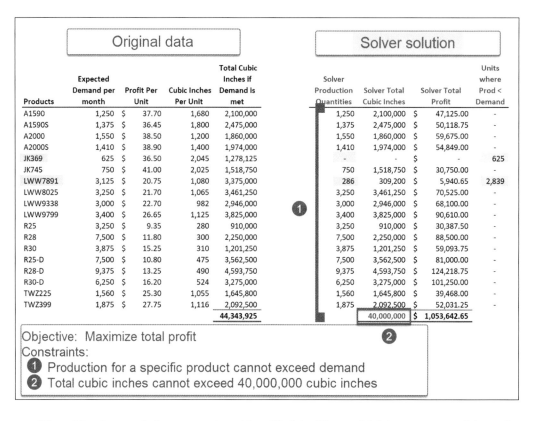

Objective: Maximize total profit
Constraints:
① Production for a specific product cannot exceed demand
② Total cubic inches cannot exceed 40,000,000 cubic inches

The objectives and the constraints identified in Figure 14.16 were entered into the **Solver** dialog box (Figure 14.17).

Figure 14.17

Solver Parameters

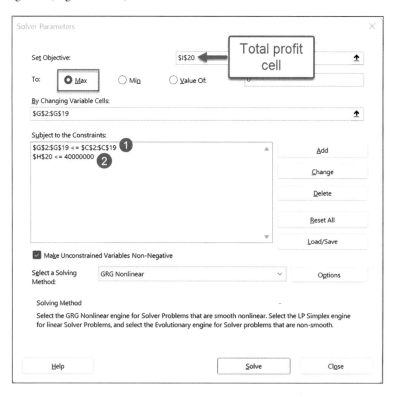

Excel's solution is displayed in Figure 14.16. To maximize profit, Excel suggests eliminating Product JK369 and only carrying 286 LWW7891 units in stock.

HINT: A store would not normally need to maintain a full month of stock on the shelf at any one point in time and would likely carry more than eighteen products! We've ignored reality a bit to provide you with a simple illustration of the **Solver** tool.

Analyze Data Tool

Excel added a new analytics tool a few years ago.

Figure 14.18

Analyze Data tool

Click anywhere in a set of data and click **Analyze Data** in the **Analysis** group on the **Home** tab. (It might also be called IDEAS or Data Analysis.)

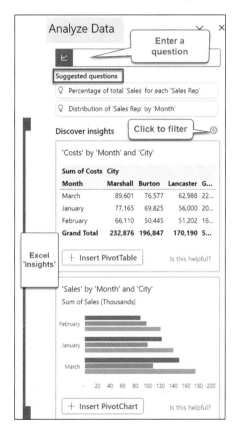

Figure 14.19

Analyze Data dialog box

Type a question into the search field or click on one of Excel's suggested questions. Excel uses artificial intelligence (specifically natural language processing) to answer the question using charts and tables; no formulas are required! Excel will also create snapshots of charts and tables and offer short "insights" even if you don't enter a question! For example, on a suggested PivotChart of sales quantities by product for a retail shoe store, an insight might read: Women's Sneakers and Children's Sandals have noticeably higher "Qty". Clicking the small gear icon allows you to limit the number of fields used in the suggested tables and charts.

Sometimes the charts and tables created automatically will highlight a relationship or trend you hadn't thought of; sometimes the suggested tables or graphs are less useful.

BEHIND THE SCENES Datasets must often be edited or reformatted before the data is analyzed. This can be done using the **Get & Transform Data** tool in Excel. (**Get & Transform** is also known as **Power Query**.)

Data can be imported (extracted) from a variety of sources.

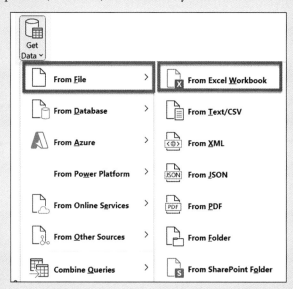

Possible data sources include Excel, text, or PDF files, various databases, data from Azure (Microsoft's cloud platform), etc.

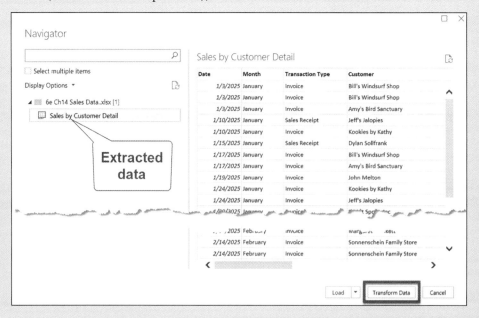

Once the data is extracted, data cleaning can be done by clicking **Transform Data**. The data is transformed in a dedicated window (**Power Query Editor**).

(continued)

(continued from previous page)

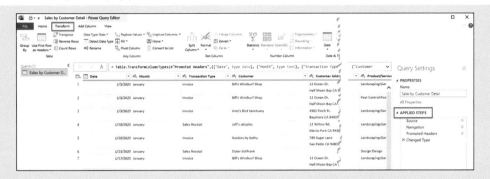

Using the **Power Query Editor**:

- data types can be changed

- columns can be added, split, or reformatted

- null rows can be deleted

- etc.

Each step is displayed in the **APPLIED STEPS** box.

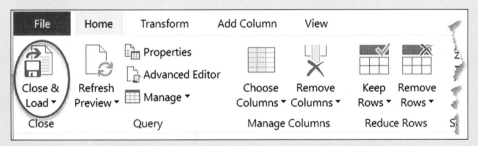

Once the data transformation is complete, Power Query takes a picture of the data set and loads it into a new or existing Excel workbook for further analysis (creating PivotTables, using analysis functions, etc.).

Analysis Tools in Data Visualization Software

When it comes to data analysis, data visualization software is an excellent tool for interacting with and communicating data. It is not a replacement for spreadsheet software. Excel is a better tool for data cleaning and data creation using multi-layered calculations.

What data visualization software systems do very well is allow users to explore data interactively. That interaction can increase users' understanding of the data and result in insights that can be used in managing an organization.

A **visualization** is a visual representation of data. That might be a graph, a table, a chart, or even a map. Although visualizations can be created in spreadsheets, the process is faster and easier using data visualization software like Tableau, Qlik, or Microsoft's Power BI. (Figure 14.20 and Figure 14.21 are from Tableau.)

Visualization Graphical representation of data.

In the software:

- Large amounts of data from a variety of sources can be imported into files.

    - Data can come from Excel workbooks, PDFs, databases, websites, etc.

- Visualizations are created by dragging and dropping fields.

- Calculated fields can be created.

- Chart types and elements can be changed with a single click.
- Filters can be tied to single visualizations or multiple visualizations within the file.
- Multiple visualizations can be combined to create **dashboards**.
- Dashboards can be shared and used without affecting the underlying data.
- Security can be added to dashboards. For example, a store manager might be limited to data for a specific store; a regional manager might be limited to data for all stores in his or her region.
- Text can be added to a single visualization or a series of visualizations to create a data story.

Dashboard
Interactive set of related visualizations.

Figure 14.20

Visualization worksheet

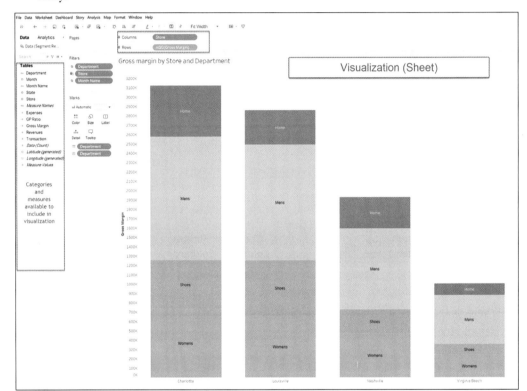

Using data visualization software is similar to creating a PivotTable in Excel and then turning it into a PivotChart.

- Fields are added to rows and columns.
- The chart type is selected.
  - Charts can be customized using labels, changing fonts and colors, etc.
- Filters can be selected.

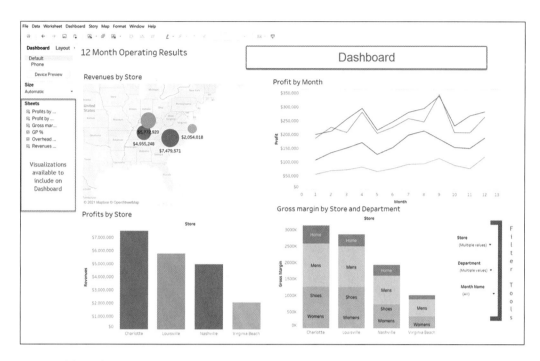

Figure 14.21

Example of a Tableau Dashboard

Dashboards consist of multiple visualizations. The **Business overview** tab on QBO's **Dashboard** page is a simple visualization dashboard.

BEST PRACTICES IN DATA VISUALIZATION

Data analysis is an exploratory process that often starts with specific questions. It requires curiosity, the desire to find answers, and a good level of tenacity because those answers aren't always easy to come by. Data visualization involves the visual representation of data, ranging from single charts to comprehensive dashboards. Effective visualizations significantly reduce the amount of time it takes for your audience to process information and access valuable insights.[1]

LO 14-3 Discuss best practices in data visualization

Data visualization is all about making data accessible and understandable. You're probably familiar with the saying, "A picture is worth a thousand words." We could probably modify that to "Data visualizations are worth a thousand words." Better yet—"Well-designed visualizations and dashboards are worth at least a thousand words."

There are two basic types of visualizations. **Explanatory visualizations** are created to educate and inform. They can be a single visualization or a series of visualizations (sometimes referred to as a **datastory**). **Exploratory visualizations** (usually combined in a dashboard) are tools for further analysis. Filtering tools are critical in exploratory visualizations.

When creating visualizations, it helps to start by asking yourself a few questions.

1. What is the purpose of the visualization? Will it be used to answer a question, explain a situation, or provide information that might generate new insights?

2. Who will be using the visualizations? Do they already have a solid understanding of the data that will be included? Will they need to be able to drill down on information? Should all users have access to all the data? Will the data need to be regularly updated?

---

[1] Murray, Eva, *What Is the Difference Between Data Analysis and Data Visualization?*, Forbes, March 29, 2019. (Eva Murray is one of thirty-four global Tableau Zen Masters.)

Once you have the answers to those questions, you should be able to determine:

● the data that will be needed

● where to find that data (sources)

● whether a single visualization will suffice or whether you need to create a dashboard

Select an Appropriate Chart Type

The next step is to select the appropriate visualizations. There are many different types of charts and graphs available in spreadsheet or data visualization software. The most common types are:

● Bar (horizontal) and column (vertical) charts
   ▪ Often used to compare categories of data
● Line charts
   ▪ Often used to show changes in data over time
● Pie charts
   ▪ Often used to show data elements
● Scatter plots and bubble charts
   ▪ Often used to show relationships between variables
● Map charts
   ▪ Often used to illustrate differences in data volumes between geographic locations

Use Color to Highlight the Data

Color choices can help in highlighting important data.

Figure 14.22

Color as highlighter

For example, in Figure 14.22, color is used to highlight the two months that did not meet the $25 million monthly sales goal.

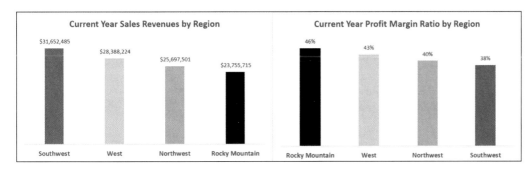

Figure 14.23

Color as unifier

In dashboards, using the same color scheme in related visualizations can reduce the amount of effort needed to identify trends and anomalies. The dashboard in Figure 14.23 uses the same color for each sales region. Although the Southwest region generated the most sales dollars, it's easy to see that it had the lowest profit margin ratio. The opposite is true for the Rocky Mountain region.

Add Text to Explain and Add Context

Text is often added to visualizations, especially explanatory visualizations. Text can help prevent misinterpretation by clearly describing what's happening with the data. It can also summarize or highlight critical points, which can save user time. In exploratory visualizations, text can add context to the numbers. Dynamic texts (text that changes with the data) are particularly useful. Dynamic text boxes can be created in Excel, Tableau, and Power BI.

Remove Unnecessary Elements

The purpose of data visualization is to bring order to chaos, to allow a user to quickly read and understand multiple attributes of a particular issue, topic or data point.[2]

In visualizations, "less is more." Remove gridlines, axes titles, and legends if the message is clear without them. Effects like **3D format**, **shadow**, and **glow** can be distracting and are generally discouraged.

Make Sure the Visualizations Are Objective and Balanced

Visualizations are powerful. They can provide clarity and stimulate discussion. They can also confuse or mislead, either intentionally or unintentionally.

Here are some examples of confusing or misleading visualizations:

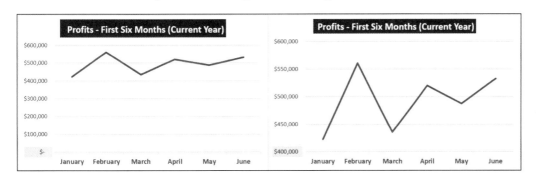

Figure 14.24

Effect of changing axis range

---

[2] Natoli, Joe, https://givegoodux.com/simplify-ui-data-visualizations-7-simple-steps/. (Joe Natoli is a UX (User experience) consultant, author, and speaker.)

In Figure 14.24, the vertical axis range in the chart on the right was shortened, starting at $400,000 instead of $0 (the vertical axis on the chart on the left). That design choice overemphasized the volatility of month-to-month profit results.

Figure 14.25

Misuse of pie chart type

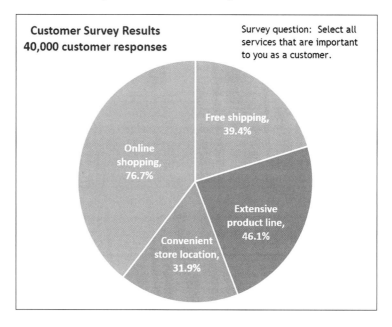

Pie charts can be an effective way to show relative elements of a whole. They can be less useful if the sum of the categories exceeds 100%! Figure 14.25 shows the results of a customer satisfaction survey. Forty thousand customers were asked to identify which customer services were important to them. They could choose more than one service. It's clear from the chart that over 75% of the respondents chose online shopping as a preferred service. It's not clear how many of those same respondents selected one or more other options, how many customers picked one option only, or whether there was a strong relationship between the size of the product line and either in-store or online shopping options.

BEYOND THE NUMBERS AND INTO THE FUTURE

LO 14-4 Understand the need for technology skills in accounting

By the time the school year is over (and even by the time this book is in print), technology will have changed and advanced even further. It is an exciting time as these advancements will open new opportunities for accounting students ready to merge their knowledge of accounting systems and processes with their understanding of technologies and innovations.

Newly developed software applications will bring more unstructured data into accounting systems, and businesses will be looking for accountants who can assist management with the analysis and interpretation of that data. Public accounting firms are increasing their use of analytics in their audits of financial statements and in the consulting services they provide and will need employees who are well versed in information technology.

In Robert Half's 2022 Accounting & Finance Salary Guide, the in-demand skills and certifications listed were cloud-based systems (#1), CPA license (#2), customer relationship management software (#3), data analysis and visualization (#4), enterprise resource planning systems (#5), advanced Excel (#6), industry-related experience (#7), and QuickBooks (#8). This should tell you something about the direction of the accounting profession! If possible, try to add some technology courses to your class schedule.

As you look forward to your future, think beyond the debits and credits. Start exploring the many new opportunities available to accountants and look for ways to develop and expand your technology skills.

CHAPTER REVIEW

Matching

Match the term or phrase (as used in this chapter) to its definition.

1. visualization
2. Business view tab
3. predictive analytics
4. diagnostic analytics

5. dashboard
6. descriptive analytics
7. PivotTable
8. prescriptive analytics

Assignments with the are available in myBusinessCourse.

_____ set of related visualizations in a single platform

_____ analysis focused on the identification of past trends

_____ analysis focused on determining the best course of action

_____ graphical representation of data

_____ analysis focused on forecasting results

_____ interactive summary of data

_____ analysis focused on identifying the reasons behind data results

_____ Simple visualization dashboard in QBO

Multiple Choice

1. The Correlation function in Excel _____.
    a. measures how closely one variable tracks another over time
    b. calculates the difference between two variables
    c. determines whether changes in one variable cause changes in another variable
    d. is used to forecast results in a future period

2. In QBO, a Budget vs Actuals report is an example of _____.
    a. Predictive analytics
    b. Prescriptive analytics
    c. Diagnostic analytics
    d. Descriptive analytics

3. Which type of chart would be the least useful in comparing sales revenue by product?
    a. Line chart
    b. Column chart
    c. Bar chart
    d. Pie chart

4. Your business is growing, and you want to apply for a bank loan for your growing business. What type of analytics would you most likely use to convince the lender that your company will be able to repay the loan?
    a. Descriptive
    b. Diagnostic
    c. Predictive
    d. Prescriptive

5. Which of the following cannot be done in the Transform function in Excel?
    a. Change the data type in a column
    b. Split data in a column
    c. Create a graph
    d. Remove columns or rows

BEYOND THE CLICKS—THINKING LIKE A MANAGER

Accounting: Clear Sights (an eyeglass manufacturer) has decided to develop a new commission structure for its sales representatives. What type(s) of data analytic(s) would be useful in this situation? What type of data would you need to include to perform that analysis?

Information Systems: Management has asked for a dashboard it can use to review and analyze operating results. You have information (by date and product) for units, revenues, and costs. Identify four visualizations that you think would be useful. What chart type would you choose for each?

ASSIGNMENT

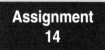

This assignment has been created for students who have a strong understanding of Excel. If you are new to Excel, check with your instructor.

Before you begin

You will need to download the 7e Ch14 Sales Data.xlsx file. If you're using myBusinessCourse, you can download the file from Student Ancillaries. If you're not using myBusinessCourse, your instructor will provide the file to you.

The file includes transactions from the test drive company (modified slightly) and additional transactions added for this assignment. **TIP:** Consider making a copy of the file before starting your assignment.

Background information

You are the accountant for Craig's Design and Landscaping. In May 2025, Craig lets you know that he is thinking about opening a new location as a way to expand his business, and you offer to put together some information for him.

Craig has been doing design work for customers outside of the San Francisco area where Craig's Design and Landscaping is located, so you decide to start by looking at sales by geographic location for the first four months of 2025. The file you downloaded is a modified version of the Sales by Customer Detail report, with customer addresses added.

Get the data ready to use

✓ You review the available data in the file and decide that the following will be the most useful elements in your analysis:

- Month
- State and Zip Code of Customers
- Sales amounts for each service and product sold

✓ You think you might be able to use transaction type, customer name, quantity, and sales price as well.

✓ You format the information in the dataset.

- You delete unnecessary rows. **TIP:** You'll need to keep a header row.
- You create a column for Month (spelled out) next to the Date column.

✓ You use Excel's **Get & Transform** tool to parse some of the columns.

- You only need the state and zip code for your analysis, so you parse the customer address field. **TIP:** State and zip code are in the eight digits on the far right of each cell.

  ▪ You put state and zip code in separate columns. To properly sort, you format zip codes as text (5 digit minimum). You add leading 0s to any zip code with less than 5 digits. **TIP:** Make sure you clear any white space in the new column fields.

- You also parse the Product/Service column so you can quickly sort information by product/service type. **TIP:** Names in the Product/Service column include parent names. You are only interested in the item itself. For example, Rock Fountain is the item name in the field name Design:Fountains:Rock Fountain.

✓ You **close and load** the data to a new workbook. **TIP:** You may want to **unlink** the data (**Table Design** tab) in your new workbook.

- You check to make sure your fields are formatted correctly in the new workbook before moving on.
  - Text in State and Zip code columns
  - Number in Qty, Sales Price, and Amount columns. You use two decimals for Sales price and Amount fields, no decimals in Qty fields.
  - Short Date in Date column.

✓ You check for errors and inconsistencies in cells in the State and Sale Price columns and make the necessary corrections.

- You assume blank State fields represent in-store sales. You use CA 94803 for those transactions. **TIP:** To avoid formatting issues in future steps, enter the zip code with a preceding apostrophe ('94803).

- You're not interested in discounts given to customers, so you remove any rows that include data related to those discounts in the Sales Price column. **TIP:** Percentages are used in determining discount amounts at Craig's (either 5% or 10%). When you used **Get & Transform** as a tool, the percentage cells in the original dataset were converted to decimals.

✓ You delete any unnecessary columns. **TIP:** You previously identified Date, Month, Transaction type, Customer, State, Zip Code, Product/Service, Qty, Sales Price, and Amount as potentially useful elements in your analysis.

✓ You review the column titles and formats and modify them as needed. You'll be using the titles in reports, so you want them to be descriptive.

✓ **TIP:** You may want to consider saving a copy of your workbook at this point.

Analysis—Part 1

✓ You start by looking at sales by type of services over the last four months. You want to be able to filter the data by state.

- You create a PivotTable using those fields and determine:
  - Month with the highest Sod revenue.
  - Total Gardening revenue in New Jersey during the four months.
  - Product or service that generated the most revenue in California during the four months.
  - Total Gardening revenues in Arizona during the four months.
  - Percentage of overall sales from Design services during the entire four months.

✓ You realize that the PivotTable you just created doesn't provide information about the geographic closeness of customers. Craig's Design and Landscaping offices are located near San Francisco. Craig could always open another location in the same general area, but you've already seen that Arizona may be a possibility. A location in Southern California may be an option as well.

- You create another PivotTable to look at sales by Product/Service and by Zip Code. You want to be able to filter the data by month.
- You use the PivotTable to determine:

- The zip code with the highest overall sale revenues.
- The zip code with the highest total Design revenues.
- The zip code with the highest sales of Rock Fountains in April, in dollars.
- The zip code with the lowest percentage of sales revenue.

✓ You think Craig might be looking for a location outside of the San Francisco area, so you decide to group all the zip codes into regions (Northern California, Southern California, Arizona, and New Jersey.) **TIP:** All zip codes starting with 93 are in Southern California, all zip codes starting with 94 are in Northern California, and all zip codes starting with 85 are in the Tucson area of Arizona.

- You create another PivotTable to determine:
  - The area with the highest Design revenue over the four months.
  - The percentage of Rock Fountain sales in Arizona during March.
  - Average Gardening revenue in Northern California in March.

BEHIND THE SCENES In Analysis—Part 1, you primarily used PivotTables as a starting point to look for trends and relationships. Craig can use that information as he considers the following:

1. Is there a location that could be eliminated from consideration based on the analysis?

2. Is Craig more interested in expanding his Design work or his Gardening services? If he has a preference, additional analysis should be done that focuses on specific services or products.

3. What about sales prices per service/product? Are those rates consistent between locations? Should additional analysis be done?

 WARNING: Analysis—Part 2 can only be done if you have access to Microsoft 365 (Windows or Mac). Check with your instructor if you have an older version of Excel.

Analysis—Part 2

✓ You open the sales data worksheet. **TIP:** This would be the worksheet that includes the data used to create each of your PivotTables.

✓ You decide to look at the tables and charts suggested by Excel's **Analyze Data** tool. You click **Analyze Data** on the **Home** tab.

✓ You take a look at the suggested tables and charts in the sidebar.
- **Make a note** of a table, chart, or insight that is an example of:
  - Descriptive analytics
  - Diagnostic analytics

✓ You decide to use the **Analyze Data** tool to look at specific elements.

✓ You click ⚙ next to **Discover insights** and deselect all but **Customer, State, Zip Code,** and **Amount.**

✓ In the **Summarize value by** dropdown menu next to **Amount,** you select **Average.** You click **Update. TIP:** A new set of suggested tables and charts should appear.
- Which state had the highest average amount of sales?

✓ You click ⚙ again and select all fields. You change the value of **Amount** back to **Sum** and click **Update**.

✓ You enter the following question in the **Ask a question about your data** field: Which customer has the highest total **Amount** during the period?

- What was the answer provided in the displayed report(s)?

APPENDIX

Is Computerized Accounting Really the Same as Manual Accounting?

Accounting equation An expression of the equivalency of the economic resources and the claims upon those resources of a business, often stated as Assets = Liabilities + Stockholders' Equity.

Before we compare the two, let's briefly review the basics of accounting.

Accounting is an information system. The primary purposes of the system are:

- To identify and record accounting transactions
- To analyze, summarize, and report information about business activities

We identify accounting transactions by considering the impact, if any, of an economic event on the **accounting equation** (Assets = Liabilities + Equity). If any of the elements in the equation (assets, liabilities, or equity) change as the result of the event, it's an accounting transaction and must be recorded.

> **BEHIND THE SCENES** Assets are resources with future benefit that the entity owns or has a right to. Liabilities are obligations of the entity payable with money, product, or service. Equity represents owner claims on the assets of the entity. Equity includes owner investments in the company plus any undistributed earnings. The components of earnings are revenues and expenses.

Journal entries An entry of accounting information into a journal.

Debits An entry on the left side (or in the debit column) of an account.

Credits An entry on the right side (or in the credit column) of an account.

We record accounting transactions using the double-entry bookkeeping system. Accounting transactions are expressed as **journal entries**. Each journal entry includes the date of the transaction, the names of the accounts to be debited and credited, and the amounts. Every journal entry must balance (the sum of the debit amounts must equal the sum of the credit amounts) so that the accounting equation stays in balance. **Debits** increase the left side of the equation; **credits** increase the right side of the equation. Debits decrease the right side of the equation; credits decrease the left side of the equation.

The entries are then recorded in (posted to) the appropriate accounts. All the accounts and all the activity in the accounts are collectively known as the general ledger. Accounts are often depicted like this (referred to as T-accounts):

A-1

Account Name

Debit	Credit

Accrual basis of accounting
Accounting method whereby sales revenue is recorded when earned and realized and expenses are recorded in the period in which they help to generate the sales revenue.

Cash basis of accounting
Accounting method whereby sales revenue is recorded when cash is received from operating activities and expenses are recorded when cash payments related to operating activities are made.

To understand when and how journal entries are made, you need to know the method of accounting being used by the entity. The two primary methods are the **accrual basis of accounting** and the **cash basis of accounting**.

There are a few basic accounting principles that are fundamental to understanding when to record revenue and expenses under the accrual method of accounting. These are part of the body of generally accepted accounting principles (GAAP) that guide accountants.

- **Revenue recognition principle**—Revenue should be recognized when the earnings process is complete and collectibility of the revenue is reasonably certain.

- **Expense recognition (matching) principle**—Expenses should be recognized in the same period as the related revenue. In other words, expenses incurred to generate revenue should be recognized with the revenue generated.

Under the cash basis of accounting, revenue is recognized when collected and expenses are recognized when paid. The cash basis of accounting is not allowed under GAAP but cash-based reports can provide useful information to management so some companies prepare both accrual and cash-based reports.

The primary way we summarize and report information about business activities is through the preparation of four basic financial statements. These statements are issued at the end of an accounting period (generally a month, quarter, or year).

- The balance sheet presents the financial condition of the entity at a point in time.
  - All asset, liability, and equity accounts appear on the balance sheet.
  - The balance sheet is also known as the statement of financial position.

- The income statement presents the operating results of the entity for a period of time.
  - All revenue and expense accounts appear on the income statement.
  - The income statement is also known as the profit and loss statement or statement of operations.

- The statement of stockholders' (or owner's) equity presents the changes in equity during a period of time.
  - The changes would include any additional investments from owners, any distributions to owners, and operating earnings (or losses) during the period.

- The statement of cash flows presents the cash inflows and outflows over a period of time.
  - The cash flows are grouped into three categories: operating activities, investing activities, and financing activities.

ACCRUAL AND CASH BASIS ACCOUNTING IN QUICKBOOKS ONLINE

Most companies use the accrual basis of accounting and that is the default basis in QBO.

You can choose, however, to use the cash basis for reporting transactions in QBO. This is done on the **Advanced** tab of **Account and Settings** (accessed by clicking the ⚙ on the icon bar).

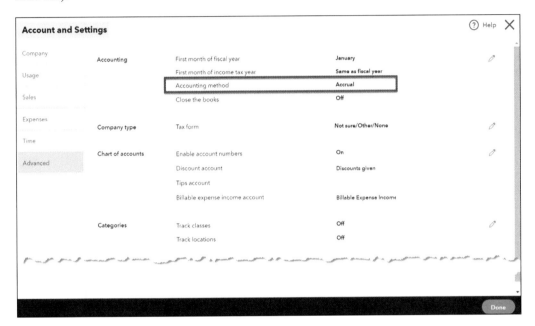

Figure AppA.1

Access to accounting method selection

Click **Accounting method.**

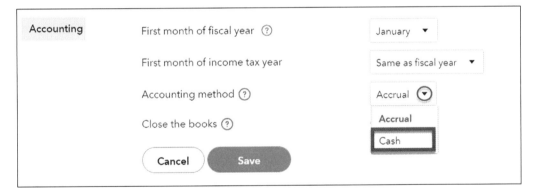

Figure AppA.2

Option to select accounting method

Select **Cash** in the dropdown menu next to **Accounting method.**

Click **Save** to complete the change of method.

Although most reports will now default to the cash basis, there are some reports that automatically default to the accrual method even when the user has selected cash as the preferred method. Taxable sales summary and detail reports are examples of reports that always default to the accrual method.

Users can also convert an accrual basis report to the cash basis by customizing the report. A condensed **Profit and Loss** report converted to the cash basis might look something like Figure AppA.3.

Figure AppA.3

Example of collapsed profit and loss report on Cash basis

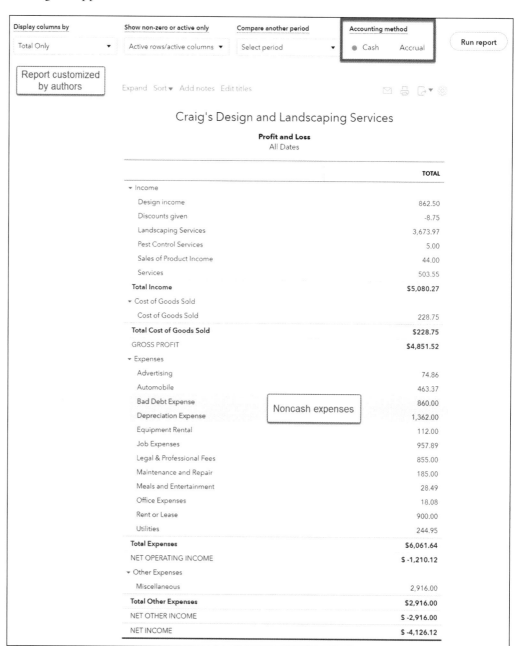

There are some issues with converting accrual reports to cash basis reports. As you can see in Figure AppA.3, certain noncash accounts like Depreciation and Bad Debt expense appear on the cash-basis **Profit and Loss** report. Also, if prepaid or accrued expenses had been recorded on the accrual basis, QBO would not adjust them in the conversion process. These issues result in inaccurate reports.

The best solution is to create the accrual basis reports in QBO, export them to Excel, and then make any additional adjustments necessary to fully convert from accrual to cash.

COMPARISON OF COMPUTERIZED AND MANUAL ACCOUNTING SYSTEMS

As stated in Chapter 1, a computerized accounting system is **fundamentally** the same as a manual accounting system. If that's true, we should be able to find the same journal entries, journals, general ledger accounts (T-accounts), and trial balances in QBO that you would find in a manual system, right? They might look a little different, but they should be there.

Journal Entries

As you've learned, QBO creates a journal entry for almost every *form* completed by the user. Let's take a look at the entry underlying Invoice #1036 to Freeman Sporting Goods:0969 Ocean View Road.

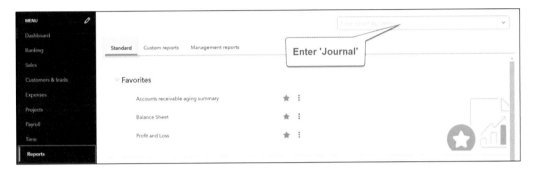

Figure AppA.4

Link to transaction journal

Click **Reports** on the navigation bar and open the **Standard** tab.
  Enter "Journal" in the search field.

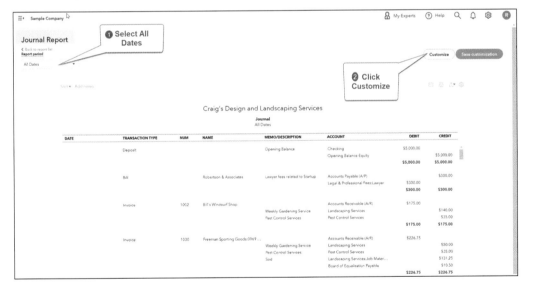

Figure AppA.5

Transaction journal

Select **All dates** in the **Report period** field.
  Click **Customize**.

Figure AppA.6

Report customization
panel

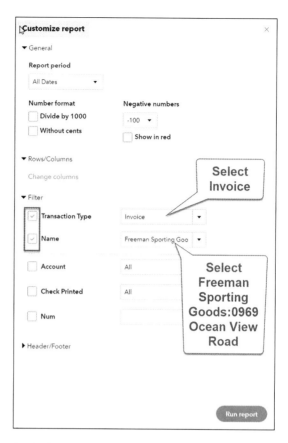

In the **Filter** section, check the box next to **Transaction Type** and select **Invoice** in the drop-down menu.

Check the box next to **Name** and select **Freeman Sporting Goods:0969 Ocean View Road** in the dropdown menu.

Click **Run report**.

Figure AppA.7

Example of journal
entry underlying a
sales transaction

This is the journal entry that was created when Invoice #1036 was entered.

Journals

In manual systems, separate journals (sometimes called special journals) are maintained for different types of transactions (sales, purchases, etc.). This simply makes it easier for the user when entering transactions. Special journals are used so that transactions for the period (usually a month) can be posted in summary (instead of in detail) to the general ledger. In QBO, each transaction (in detail) is automatically posted to the general ledger so special journals aren't needed to simplify posting.

As an example, the Sales Journal might look something like this in a manual system:

Date	Customer	Invoice #	A/R (DR)	Design income (CR)	Landscaping Services (CR)	Job Materials (CR)	Sales Tax Payable (CR)
	John Melton	1007	750.00	750.00			
	Amy's Bird Sanctuary	1021	459.00			425.00	34.00
	Jeff's Jalopies	1022	81.00		75.00		6.00
	TOTALS		1,290.00	750.00	75.00	425.00	40.00

Each transaction is recorded, in full, on a separate line instead of in journal entry form. In journal entry form, the first line (Invoice #1007) would be:

Accounts receivable		750.00	
Design Income			750.00

At the end of the period, the columns are totaled and all the sales transactions are recorded in one single journal entry as follows:

Accounts Receivable		1,290.00	
Design Income			750.00
Landscaping Services			75.00
Job Materials			425.00
Sales Tax Payable			34.00

Although QBO doesn't automatically create special journal reports, a user can create a similar report fairly easily. These reports can be saved so they can be easily accessed every month. (Saving customized reports is covered in Chapter 11.)

A **Transaction Detail By Account** report customized to show specific **Invoice** transactions for a period of time and with Debit and Credit columns added would look something like Figure AppA.8.

Figure AppA.8

Transaction detail report customized to show invoice transactions only

Customized by authors

Craig's Design and Landscaping Services

Sales Journal

DATE	TRANSACTION TYPE	NUM	NAME	DEBIT	CREDIT
▾ Accounts Receivable (A/R)					
04/08/2022	Invoice	1002	Bill's Windsurf Shop	$175.00	
04/08/2022	Invoice	1030	Freeman Sporting Goods:0969 …	$226.75	
05/09/2022	Invoice	1031	Freeman Sporting Goods:0969 …	$387.00	
Total for Accounts Receivable (A/R)				**$788.75**	
▾ Board of Equalization Payable					
04/08/2022	Invoice	1030	Freeman Sporting Goods:0969 …		$10.50
05/09/2022	Invoice	1031	Freeman Sporting Goods:0969 …		$22.00
Total for Board of Equalization Payable					**$32.50**
▾ Landscaping Services					
04/08/2022	Invoice	1002	Bill's Windsurf Shop		$140.00
04/08/2022	Invoice	1030	Freeman Sporting Goods:0969 …		$50.00
05/09/2022	Invoice	1031	Freeman Sporting Goods:0969 …		$90.00
Total for Landscaping Services					**$280.00**
▾ Job Materials					
05/09/2022	Invoice	1031	Freeman Sporting Goods:0969 …		$275.00
04/08/2022	Invoice	1030	Freeman Sporting Goods:0969 …		$131.25
Total for Job Materials					**$406.25**
▾ Pest Control Services					
04/08/2022	Invoice	1002	Bill's Windsurf Shop		$35.00
04/08/2022	Invoice	1030	Freeman Sporting Goods:0969 …		$35.00
Total for Pest Control Services					**$70.00**

The accounts are listed in rows instead of columns in the QBO Sales Journal, but the basic information is the same.

General Ledger and T-Accounts

There is, of course, a general ledger in QBO. You can easily create a report to see the individual activity in a specific account in QBO. It doesn't look exactly like a T-account, but it is close.

Click Reports on the navigation bar.

Click General Ledger in the For my accountant section. A report customized to show the Checking account for a period of time and to include Debit and Credit columns (other columns removed) would look something like Figure AppA.9.

Figure AppA.9

General ledger report customized to show activity in a single account

Customized by authors		Craig's Design and Landscaping Services					
			General Ledger				
DATE	**TRANSACTION TYPE**	**NUM**	**NAME**		**DEBIT**	**CREDIT**	**BALANCE**
▾ Checking							
Beginning Balance							4,490.76
	Payment		Amy's Bird Sanctuary		$105.00		4,595.76
	Bill Payment (Check)	7	Hicks Hardware			$250.00	4,345.76
	Expense	8	Hicks Hardware			$24.36	4,321.40
	Check		Tony Rondonuwu			$100.00	4,221.40
	Cash Expense		Bob's Burger Joint			$5.66	4,215.74
	Cash Expense		Squeaky Kleen Car Wash			$19.99	4,195.75
	Cash Expense		Chin's Gas and Oil			$52.14	4,143.61
	Check	70	Chin's Gas and Oil			$185.00	3,958.61
	Payment	1886	Cool Cars		$694.00		4,652.61
	Bill Payment (Check)	11	Hall Properties			$900.00	3,752.61
	Check	2	Mahoney Mugs			$18.08	3,734.53
	Expense	13	Hicks Hardware			$215.66	3,518.87
	Sales Receipt	1003	Dylan Sollfrank		$337.50		3,856.37
	Cash Expense		Bob's Burger Joint			$3.86	3,852.51
	Bill Payment (Check)	1	Brosnahan Insurance Agency			$2,000.00	1,852.51
Total for Checking					**$1,136.50**	**$3,774.75**	

As you can see in Figure AppA.9, account balances are shown in a separate column in QBO instead of at the bottom of each T-account. That might be a slightly different format than the T-accounts you're familiar with from your financial accounting courses, but the information is the same.

Trial Balances

A trial balance is a report listing all the accounts and their balances at a point in time. In a manual system, trial balances are prepared for two primary reasons:

● To make sure the debits equal the credits in the general ledger.

● To use as a worksheet for preparing the financial statements.

In a computerized system like QBO, users don't need a trial balance for those reasons. Why? First, the program will not allow the user to create an unbalanced entry. (Unless, of course, the system malfunctions!) Second, QBO prepares the financial statements automatically.

Trial balance reports are available in QBO, however, and can be useful for other reasons.

Trial Balance reports are accessed in the **For my accountant** section of **Reports**. The report looks something like Figure AppA.10.

Figure AppA.10

Example of a trial balance report

Customized by authors	Craig's Design and Landscaping Services		
	Trial Balance		
		DEBIT	**CREDIT**
Checking		4,625.00	
Accounts Receivable (A/R)		543.00	
Undeposited Funds		226.75	
Accounts Payable (A/P)			0.00
Mastercard			158.08
Board of Equalization Payable			32.50
Opening Balance Equity			5,000.00
Landscaping Services			280.00
Landscaping Services:Job Materials:Fountains and Ga…			323.00
Landscaping Services:Job Materials:Plants and Soil			131.25
Landscaping Services:Job Materials:Sprinklers and Dri…			108.00
Pest Control Services			70.00
Job Expenses:Job Materials:Plants and Soil		158.08	
Legal & Professional Fees:Accounting		250.00	
Legal & Professional Fees:Lawyer		300.00	
TOTAL		**$6,102.83**	**$6,102.83**

BEHIND THE SCENES It's really only the ending date that determines the amounts on a trial balance report. If you entered 12/31/24 to 12/31/24, you would get the same amounts as you got entering 6/30/24 to 12/31/24. Remember, a trial balance shows us the account balances at a point in time (not period of time). However, entering a specific period does give you the option of clicking on an amount and seeing the transactions that occurred during the identified period.

APPENDIX

Account Types and Common Transaction Types Used in QBO

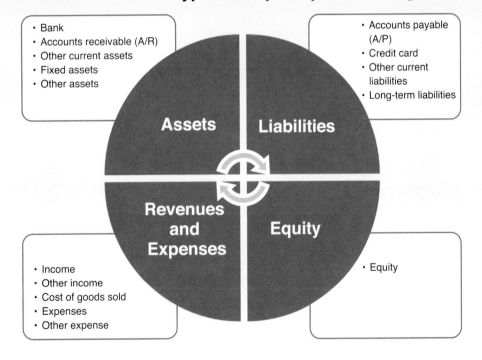

QuickBooks Account Types Grouped by Accounting Element

- Bank
- Accounts receivable (A/R)
- Other current assets
- Fixed assets
- Other assets

- Accounts payable (A/P)
- Credit card
- Other current liabilities
- Long-term liabilities

Assets

Liabilities

Revenues and Expenses

Equity

- Income
- Other income
- Cost of goods sold
- Expenses
- Other expense

- Equity

Common Transaction Types	Description
Bill	Bill received from vendor for purchase on account
Bill payment	Payment on vendor balance by cash/check/credit card
Charge	Pending customer charge
Check	Direct payment (not including payroll checks, payments on vendor balances, payments of payroll or sales taxes)
Credit	Pending customer credit
Credit card credit	Credit from vendor on credit card purchase
Credit memo	Credit given to customer (cash or credit sales)
Deposit	Bank deposit
Estimate	Estimate of fees
Expense	Direct payment generally made using a credit card
Inventory qty adjust	Adjustment to inventory quantity
Invoice	Sale on account
Journal entry	General journal entry
Liability payment	Payment of payroll liability
Paycheck	Employee payroll check
Payment	Customer payment on account balance
Purchase order	Order to vendor
Refund	Refund to customer
Sales receipt	Cash sale
Sales tax payment	Remittance of state sales taxes
Statement	Direct charge to customer account balance
Transfer	Transfers between cash accounts
Vendor credit	Credit received from vendor

Note: There are a few other transaction types in QBO that are not listed here.

Common Options Available on Various Forms

⟲—Allows you to view recent transactions of the same type

✖—Allows you to exit out of the form

Audit history (on **More** dropdown menu)—Allows you to view the history of the transaction (date entered/modified, user name, etc.)

Cancel—Allows you to "erase" all the data entered on the form. This would only be used in the initial creation of the form.

Copy (on **More** dropdown menu)—Allows you to make a duplicate of the form

Delete (on **More** dropdown menu)—Allows you to delete the transaction

Make recurring—Allows you to memorize the form for later use

Mark as paid—Allows you to access a **bill payment** form directly from a saved **bill** form

New style (on **Customize** dropdown menu of certain forms)—Allows you to create a custom form.

Print or Preview—Allows you to print or view the form (Available on all sales forms. Print option is available on Purchase order and Check forms.)

Reverse—Allows you to create a journal entry dated the first day of the subsequent month that cancels the effect of a saved journal entry. This is only available after you save the original entry.

Revert—Allows you to return to the original saved form. This is only available when you open a saved form, make changes, and want to undo those changes. This would not be available if you had already saved the new version.

Save—Allows you to save the current form without exiting

Save and close—Allows you to save the current form and exit

Save and new—Allows you to save the current form and open a new form of the same type

Save and schedule payment—Allows you to schedule a payment date for **bills**. Only available for users with a bank connection set up in QBO

Save and send—Allows you to save the current form and forward it to the customer via email (Also available on Purchase order forms.)

Schedule payment—Allows you to schedule payment of a specific **bill** using an online bill payment system. Available on the **Expenses drawer** (tab)

Schedule payments online—Allows you to schedule payment of bills through a bill pay system. This is only available on **Pay bills** screen.

Transaction journal (on **More** dropdown menu)—Allows you to view the journal entry underlying the form

Void (on **More** dropdown menu)—Allows you to erase the amounts on the form but keep the remaining data

Index

my BusinessCourse

Interactive content that runs on any device.

Built for PCs, MACs, iPads, Laptops, Tablets, Smartphones

my BusinessCourse is an online learning and assessment program intended to complement your textbook and faculty instruction. **Access to** my BusinessCourse **is included with the purchase of a new textbook**, but access can be purchased separately.

Tools that Facilitate Student Success

◆ **eLectures** cover each chapter's learning objectives and concepts. Consistent with the text and created b the authors, these videos are ideal for remediation and online instruction.

◆ **Guided Examples** are narrated video demonstrations created by the authors that show students how to solve select problems from the textbook.

◆ Immediate feedback with **auto-graded homework** (available only when instructors elect to use online homework in the course).

In five recent surveys of nearly 4,200 students who used MBC, **95.5%** responded that MBC helped them learn accounting.

www.mybusinesscourse.com

Cambridge
BUSINESS PUBLISHERS

www.cambridgepub.com

ISBN 978-1-61853-574-0